EFFICIENT READING

EFFICIENT READING

SEVENTH EDITION

JAMES I. BROWN
UNIVERSITY OF MINNESOTA, EMERITUS

VIVIAN V. FISHCO
COCONINO COUNTY COMMUNITY COLLEGE

D. C. HEATH AND COMPANY
LEXINGTON, MASSACHUSETTS TORONTO

Address editorial correspondence to:

D. C. Heath
125 Spring Street
Lexington, MA 02173

Acquisitions Editor: Paul A. Smith
Developmental Editor: Linda M. Bieze
Production Editor: Bryan Woodhouse
Designer: Jan Shapiro
Production Coordinator: Charles Dutton
Text Permissions Editor: Margaret Roll

Photo Credits
Front cover: Ted Hansen/Slide Graphics, Watertown, MA
Back cover: *top*—Richard III; *bottom*—Photo by Rob Carr ©1992
For permission to use copyrighted material, grateful acknowledgment is made to the copyright holders listed on pages v-viii, which are hereby considered an extension of this copyright page.

Published simultaneously in Canada.

Printed in the United States of America.

International Standard Book Number: 0-669-29758-5

Library of Congress Catalog Number: 92-71418

10 9 8 7 6 5 4 3 2 1

TEXT CREDITS

Dorrine Anderson "Business Body Language—Understanding the Signals" by Dorrine Anderson from *Passages* (Northwest *Inflight* Magazine, Vol. 7, #10) pp. 10–13.

James Ansara "The Educated Man," by James Ansara, reprinted with permission from *The Atlantic Monthly,* November 1937.

Ewart A. Autry "We Quit Talking—and Now the Cupboard Is Bare" by Ewart A. Autry. Reprinted from *Minutes,* Magazine of Nationwide Insurance, Fall 1970.

Virgil Baker "The 30,000 Words a Day We Talk" by Virgil Baker, reprinted with permission of *Science Digest,* September 1955. © The Hearst Corporation.

Smiley Blanton "The Bible's Timeless—and Timely—Insights." Reprinted with permission from the August 1966 *Reader's Digest.* Copyright © 1966 by The Reader's Digest Assn., Inc.

J. Samuel Bois "Language As a Tool," from *Explorations in Awareness,* by J. Samuel Bois, Harper & Brothers, 1957. Reprinted by permission of the Estate of J. Samuel Bois.

Malcolm Boyd "How to Really Talk to Another Person" by Malcolm Boyd from *Parade* Magazine, February 1989. Reprinted by permission of the author.

Stewart Brent "Starting to Read" by Stuart Brent from the *University of Chicago Magazine,* Winter 1975, p. 37.

Heywood Broun Permission granted by Bill Cooper Associates Agency, Inc. for "The Fifty-First Dragon," by Heywood Broun as adapted from *The Collected Edition of Heywood Broun.* Copyright 1921, 1941 by Heywood Hale Broun.

James I. Brown Exercises on pp. 300, 304, 308, 312, 316, 320, 324, 328, 332, 336, 340, and 444 from *Guide to Effective Reading,* D. C. Heath and Co., copyright © 1966.

James I. Brown "Handling the Knowledge Explosion" adapted from "The *Look* 20-Day Course in Quick Reading," by James I. Brown, *Look Magazine* (January 27, 1970) © 1970 Cowles Broadcasting, Inc.

James I. Brown "Super-Speeds for the Knowledge Explosion" adapted from "The *Look* 20-Day Course in Quick Reading," by James I. Brown, *Look Magazine* (January 27, 1970) © 1970 Cowles Broadcasting, Inc.

James I. Brown "What Has Listening Done for Us?" Adapted from "Listening—Ubiquitous Yet Obscure" by James I. Brown, *Journal of the International Listening Assoc.,* Vol. 1, Number 1, Spring 1987. Reprinted by permission.

James I. Brown "A Master-Word Approach to Vocabulary" by James I. Brown. Reprinted by permission from the May 1949 issue of *Word Study* © 1949 by Merriam-Webster, Inc., Publishers of the Merriam-Webster ® Dictionaries.

Gelett Burgess "Conversation Is More Than Talk" by Gelett Burgess. Reprinted by permission of the author from *Your Life,* December 1947.

David Campbell From *If you Don't Know Where You're Going, You'll Probably End Up Somewhere Else* by David Campbell, Ph.D. © 1974 Tabor Publishing, a division of DLM, Inc., Allen, TX 75002. Exercise on pp. 476–477 is also from this source.

Joseph Campbell "How to Read a Dollar Bill" from *The Power of Myth,* by Joseph Campbell & Bill Moyers. Copyright © 1988 by Apostrophe S Productions, Inc., and Bill Moyers and Alfred Van der Marck Editions, Inc., for itself and the estate of Joseph Campbell. Used by permission of Doubleday, a division of Bantam, Doubleday, Dell Publishing Group, Inc.

Nardi Reeder Campion "Ask, Don't Tell" by Nardi Reeder Campion. Reprinted with permission from the August 1966 *Reader's Digest.* Copyright © 1966 by The Reader's Digest Association, Inc.

Lesley Conger "Owed to the Public Library" by Lesley Conger from *The Writer's Handbook,* edited by Sylvia K. Burack. Reprinted by permission from *The Writer,* Copyright © 1982 by The Writer, Inc., Boston, MA.

Farnsworth Crowder "America's Penniless Millionaire" by Farnsworth Crowder. Reprinted by permission of the *Christian Herald Magazine,* July 1938. Copyright 1938 by Christian Herald Association, Inc.

George Cuomo "How Fast Should a Person Read?" by George Cuomo. Copyright © 1962 Saturday Review Magazine Co. Reprinted by permission of the publisher and author.

Edgar Dale "How to Improve Your Vocabulary" by Edgar Dale. Reprinted by permission from the March, 1958, issue of *Good Housekeeping Magazine.* © 1958 by the Hearst Corporation.

Alma Denny "How to Write Letters" by Alma Denny From *The Rotarian,* March 1989. Reprinted with permission from The Rotarian.

Joan Didion "Why I Write" by Joan Didion, Copyright © 1976 by Joan Didion. Originally published in *The New York Times* Book Review. Reprinted by permission of Joan Didion.

Troy Duster "Understanding Self-segregation on the Campus" by Troy Duster from *The Chronicle of Higher Education,* September 25, 1991. Reprinted with the permission of the author.

Don Fabun "The Dynamics of Change" © 1967 by Kaiser Aluminum & Chemical Corp. Reprinted by permission.

Paul Gallico "The Feel" by Paul Gallico, from *Farewell to Sport.* Reprinted by permission of Harold Ober Associates Incorporated. Copyright 1937, 1938 by Paul Gallico. Copyright Renewed 1964, 1968 by Paul Gallico.

George Gallup "You Can't Get Ahead Today Unless You Read" by George Gallup. From the *Ladies' Home Journal,* August 1960. Reprinted by permission of the author.

John E. Gibson "Your Voice Gives You Away" by John E. Gibson. Reprinted with permission of *Science Digest* (March 1952). © The Hearst Corporation.

Susan Goodman "Presumed Innocents" by Susan Goodman from *Modern Maturity,* December 1991–January 1992. Reprinted with the permission of the author.

Arthur Gordon "Two Words to Avoid, Two to Remember" by Arthur Gordon. Copyright © 1968 by Arthur Gordon. Reprinted with permission from the January 1968 *Reader's Digest* and by permission of the author.

Albert Gore, Jr. "Information Superhighways," by Albert Gore, Jr. Reprinted with permission from *The Futurist,* published by the World Future Society, 4916 Saint Elmo Avenue, Bethesda, Maryland 20814.

Michael E. Gorman "The Hustle (How to Get Good Grades and Still Enjoy College)" by Michael E. Gorman from *The College Review Board,* No. 120, Summer 1981. Used with permission.

Henry F. Graff From *America The Glorious Republic* by Graff, et al. Copyright © 1990 by Houghton Mifflin Company. Reprinted by permission of Houghton Mifflin Company.

Alex Haley "Why Reading Matters" by Alex Haley from *Parade* Magazine, September 2, 1990. Reprinted with permission from *Parade,* Copyright © 1990.

Marlys J. Harris Excerpted from *Money* Magazine, August 1982. Reprinted by permission of the author, Marlys J. Harris.

S. I. Hayakawa "Your Words Make You What You Are." Field Enterprises, Inc. Article by S. I. Hayakawa, reprinted with permission.

Nancy Henderson "Tactics That Win Good Part-time Jobs" by Nancy Henderson. Reprinted by permission from the May 1990 issue of *Changing Times* Magazine. Copyright © 1990 The Kiplinger Washington Editors, Inc.

E. D. Hirsch, Jr. From *Cultural Literacy* by E. D. Hirsch, Jr. Copyright © 1987 by Houghton Mifflin Company. Reprinted by permission of Houghton Mifflin Company. All rights reserved.

Morton L. Janklow "You CAN Be Persuasive" by Morton L. Janklow from *Parade* Magazine, December 29, 1985. Reprinted with permission from *Parade,* Copyright © 1985.

Frank G. Jennings "Warming Up To Words" and "Why Do We Read?" from *This is Reading* by Frank G. Jennings, published by Teachers College Press, 1965; republished by Plenum Publishing Corp., 1982. Reprinted by permission.

Kaiser Aluminum "Creativity (A Matter of Definition)" *Kaiser Aluminum News,* Volume 25, No. 3, *You and Creativity,* Kaiser Aluminum & Chemical Corp. Reprinted with permission.

Kiplinger Washington Editors, Inc. "Ten Tips to Help You Write Better." Reprinted by permission from the June 1980 issue of *Changing Times* Magazine. Copyright © 1980 The Kiplinger Washington Editors, Inc.

Kiplinger Washington Editors, Inc. "Write a Resumé That Gets the Job." Reprinted by permission from the July 1975 issue of *Changing Times* Magazine. Copyright © 1975 The Kiplinger Washington Editors, Inc.

Harold Kushner "Was There Something I Was Supposed to Do with My Life?" by Harold Kushner from *When All You Ever Wanted Isn't Enough.* Copyright © 1986 by Kushner Enterprises, Inc. Reprinted by permission of Summit Books, division of Simon & Schuster, Inc.

Michael Lemonick "Disposing of the Nuclear Age" from *Time,* October 21, 1991. Copyright 1991 the Time Inc. Magazine Company. Reprinted by permission.

Madeleine L'Engle "The Road to Success in Writing" from *A Circle of Quiet* by Madeleine L'Engle. Copyright © 1972 by Madeleine L'Engle Franklin. Reprinted by permission of HarperCollins Publishers.

Norman Lewis Exercises on pp. 346–347 and 350–351 from *Coronet* magazine, February 1946. Copyright 1946 by Esquire, Inc. Exercises on pp. 380 and 382 from *Coronet* magazine, November 1946. Reprinted with the permission of the author.

Malcolm X From *The Autobiography of Malcolm X* by Malcolm X with Alex Haley. Copyright © 1964 by Alex Haley and Malcolm X. Copyright © 1965 by Alex Haley and Betty Shabazz. Reprinted by permission of Random House, Inc.

William Mathews From *Investigating The Earth* by William Mathews, et al. Copyright © 1987 by Houghton Mifflin Company. Reprinted by permission of Houghton Mifflin Company.

W. Somerset Maugham "The Verger," extracted from *The Complete Short Stories of W. Somerset Maugham,* Vol. 2,

Doubleday, 1952. Reprinted by permission of A. P. Watt Ltd. on behalf of The Royal Literary Fund.

Robert McCrum, et al From *The Story of English* by Robert McCrum, William Cran, and Robert MacNeil. Copyright © 1986 by Robert McCrum, William Cran, and Robert MacNeil. Used by permission of Viking Penguin, a division of Penguin Books USA, Inc.

Cyra McFadden "In Defense of Gender" by Cyra McFadden. © 1981 by The New York Times Company. Reprinted by permission.

Elisabeth McPherson and Gregory Cowan "Reading for A's" from *Background for Writing* by Elisabeth McPherson and Gregory Cowan Copyright © 1967 by Elisabeth McPherson and Gregory Cowan. Reprinted by permission of McGraw-Hill, Inc.

Margaret Mead and Rhoda Metraux "Too Many Divorces, Too Soon" by Margaret Mead and Rhoda Metraux from *Redbook,* February 1974. Reprinted by permission of the Institute for Intercultural Studies and Rhoda Metraux.

Hugh Mearns "It's Not What You Say—But How You Say It" by Hugh Mearns from *The Rotarian,* June 1944, pp. 26–27.

Marlys Millhiser "The First Word" by Marlys Millhiser, reprinted with permission from *The Writer.* Copyright © 1982 by The Writer, Inc., Boston, MA, Publishers.

Robert Montgomery "How to Remember: Some Basic Principles" Reprinted, by permission of the publisher, from *Memory Made Easy* by Robert Montgomery, pages 11–15. © 1979 by AMACOM, a division of American Management Association. All rights reserved; "Basic Building Blocks for Total Listening" by Robert L. Montgomery. Reprinted by permission of the publisher from *Listening Made Easy* by Robert L. Montgomery, © 1981 AMACOM, a division of American Management Association. All rights reserved.

William Morris "Test Your Vocabulary" by William Morris. Reprinted by permission from the November 1954 issue of *Changing Times* Magazine. Copyright © 1954 The Kiplinger Washington Editors, Inc.

Bruce E. Moses "The 11 Toughest Job Interview Questions . . . and How to Answer Them" by Bruce E. Moses. This article has been reprinted through the courtesy of Halsey Publishing Co., publishers of *Delta Sky* magazine and by permission of the author.

Ralph G. Nichols "Listening Is a 10-Part Skill" by Ralph G. Nichols. Reprinted by permission, from *Nation's Business,* July 1957. Copyright 1957, U. S. Chamber of Commerce.

George Orwell Excerpt from *The Road to Wigan Pier* by George Orwell, reprinted by permission of Harcourt Brace Jovanovich, Inc.

Patricia O'Toole "Around the World in 80 Nanoseconds." First appeared in *Lear's,* January 1991.

B. W. Overstreet "After This Manner, Therefore, Listen" by B. W. Overstreet. Reprinted by permission of author and publisher from the April 1946 issue of the *Wilson Library Bulletin.* Copyright © 1946 by the H. W. Wilson Company.

Marvin Perry From *History Of the World* by Marvin Perry, et al. Copyright © 1990 by Houghton Mifflin Company. Reprinted by permission of Houghton Mifflin Company.

Richard Rodriguez "None of This Is Fair" by Richard Rodriguez. Reprinted by permission of Georges Borchardt, Inc. for the author. Copyright © 1977 by Richard Rodriguez. First appeared in *Politicks and Other Human Interests.*

Henry Schindall "The Most Unforgettable Character I've Met" From *The Reader's Digest,* October 1949. Reprinted by permission of the author.

Martin Seligman From *Learned Optimism* by Martin E. P. Seligman. Copyright © 1991 by Martin E. P. Seligman. Reprinted by permission of Alfred A. Knopf.

Lydel Sims "Mark Twain's Speechmaking Strategy" by Lydel Sims. Reprinted from *TWA Ambassador* Magazine with permission of the author and publisher. Copyright 1976 by Trans World Airlines, Inc.

Nancy Spiller "The Future Shock's Doc" by Nancy Spiller from *American Way,* Sept. 1, 1988. Reprinted by permission of the author, a Los Angeles–based writer.

Lyman Steil "On Listening and Not Listening" by Dr. Lyman K. Steil, President, Communication Development, Inc., 25 Robb Farm Road, St. Paul, Minnesota 55110. Reprinted by permission.

Gloria Steinem "The Great Paradigm Shift" from *Revolution From Within* by Gloria Steinem. Copyright © 1992 by Gloria Steinem. By permission of Little, Brown and Company.

Frank J. Taylor "The Three Lives of David Starr Jordan" by Frank J. Taylor from May 1963 issue of *The Reader's Digest,* pp. 113–117.

Kurt Vonnegut "How to Write with Style" by Kurt Vonnegut from International Paper's *Power of the Printed Word* series. Reprinted by permission of International Paper.

Ken Wibecan "A Family Festival—Kawanzaa: An African-American Original." Reprinted with permission from Ken Wibecan and *Modern Maturity,* Copyright 1991, American Association of Retired Persons.

Morton Winthrop "Do You Know How Words Can Make You Rich?" by Morton Winthrop. From *This Week* Magazine, October 30, 1960. Reprinted by permission of the author.

Hank Wittemore "The Most Precious Gift" by Hank Wittemore, *Parade* Magazine, Dec. 22, 1991. Reprinted by permission of the author and the author's agents, Scott Meredith Literary Agency, Inc. 845 Third Avenue, New York, New York 10022.

Text Credits

Paul Witty "Vocabulary First-Aid" by Paul Witty from *How to Become a Better Reader,* Copyright 1953. Reprinted by permission of Science Research Associates, a Division of the Macmillan/McGraw-Hill School Publishing Company, a New York general partnership.

Florence I. Wolff et al. Excerpts from *Perceptive Listening* by Florence I. Wolff, Nadine C. Marsnik, William S. Tacey, and Ralph G. Nichols, Copyright © 1983 by Holt, Rinehart and Winston, Inc., reprinted by permission of the publisher.

Eugene Wright "Do You Need a Time Stretcher?" *Journal of Communication.* Vol. 1, No. 2: pp. 25–29, November 1951. Reprinted by permission of the International Communication Association and the author.

TO THE INSTRUCTOR

The seventh edition of *Efficient Reading* is designed to:

- Generate heightened interest in reading, vocabulary development, and communication
- Provide a practical classroom-tested format to facilitate maximum reading and vocabulary improvement
- Uncover individual needs in reading and vocabulary development in order to facilitate improvement
- Fit reading into a broad communication framework to promote growth in all four areas of communication
- Provide useful connections and interrelationships among reading, writing, speaking, and listening in order to further overall competency in communication

As with earlier editions, this seventh edition is for use in college and adult reading programs, reading laboratories and clinics, and college English classes. This text has grown out of firsthand teaching experience with more than 6,000 students of reading at the University of Minnesota.

In organization, the seventh edition follows the plan of the earlier editions, a format that both teachers and students felt was effective. This edition retains 46 of the selections from the sixth edition—those of most interest as indicated by users and reviewers of the earlier edition. This edition contains a total of 87 selections, four more than the earlier edition, permitting a somewhat greater choice for classroom use.

As in the previous edition, pacing sheets are included. They permit you to pace students at any of six speeds in a class situation, using the oral commands "Begin," "Next," and "Stop." It also permits students to tape the commands on a cassette and pace themselves. This eliminates the need for costly individual reading accelerators while retaining a technique that students feel is most helpful for improving reading efficiency.

As in earlier editions, we have included selections rated from Easy to Difficult on the Flesch Reading Ease Scale, in order to parallel the wide range of reading ability found among college students and adults. For example, incoming freshmen at the University of Minnesota typically range from the sixth grade to beyond the college senior level in reading ability. In each of the seven sections, selections are arranged in order, from easiest to most difficult. Difficulty levels can easily be checked, using either the index on pages 481–482 or the alphabetical index on pages 483–484, a new feature in this edition.

This book also lends itself to use in freshman composition classes, with the added benefit of self-help improvement in reading. As Lambuth said in his *Golden Book on Writing,* the vocabulary, usage, and idiom so essential to good writing can be acquired "only by wide and intelligent reading. And in no other way whatsoever." Dr. Ramon Veal, professor of language, put it this way: "A student who cannot read with true comprehension will never learn to write well." This text provides the ideal connection needed for a writing-reading approach.

In general, the broad communication approach provides a model pattern for overall development. After all, communication pervades every aspect of living. Its study is, in a sense, the study of society. Such an approach provides a perfect foundation for maximum improvement in reading, as well as in the companion areas of writing, speaking, and listening.

NEW FEATURES

Thanks to teacher suggestions, this seventh edition has some important new features. Although standardized tests of reading provide the only truly accurate and valid measures of performance, additional informal diagnoses still fill an important need. You will find for the first time an exercise subject index beginning on page 239. This provides exercise information to help both teacher and student with a variety of specific problems. This heuristic, self-discovery source gives students immediate access to help.

Another new feature is found in Section VII. Eleven of the exercises have a reading-test format—a short passage, followed by both detail and thought questions. Passages drawn from nationwide tryouts for the *Nelson-Denny Reading Test* make up most of these exercises. They permit exact comparisons of a kind not normally found in any textbook. With these exercises, students may, therefore, compare their performance exactly with nationwide normative data, to achieve important diagnostic insights. (These passages were selected from unused material for the final forms, G and H, of the widely used *Nelson-Denny Test,* published by The Riverside Publishing Company, 1993.)

Some teachers find the following nine-step course pattern useful, as found in James I. Brown's *Guide to Effective Reading* (D. C. Heath, 1966):

1. Proper orientation and diagnosis of reading strengths and weaknesses
2. Careful observation and analysis of performance
3. Proper management of the learning process
4. Skimming and scanning activities
5. Establishing helpful word-grouping habits
6. Dealing with paragraph structure
7. Dealing with organization
8. Developing productive attitudes and interests
9. Coping with examinations

Another possible pattern is that found in a taped series of television lectures intended for use with the *Efficient Reading* text. This series, produced by Telstar Division, 10 North 10th Avenue, Hopkins, Minnesota 55343, incorporates a twelve-step sequence for teaching reading. Each lecture focuses on a different way to achieve reading efficiency:

1. The Know Thyself Road
2. The Visualizing Road
3. The Vocabulary Road
4. The Easy Learning Road
5. The Pacing Road
6. The Formula Road
7. The Skimming-Scanning Road
8. The Main Idea Road
9. The Word Grouping Road
10. The Paragraph Reading Road
11. The Writer's Plan Road
12. The Dynamic Communication Road

Finally, no matter what approach you use, no matter what combination of classroom activities you select, remember Emerson's insightful dictum: "'Tis the good reader that makes the good book." Now rephrase that to place yourself in the picture and to highlight the challenges and satisfactions of teaching reading: "'Tis the good teacher that makes the good reader."

ACKNOWLEDGMENTS

We wish to thank our colleagues at the University of Minnesota for their guidance and help over the years, especially Dr. Eugene S. Wright, who worked most closely with James I. Brown during his teaching years there. And for much of the material on listening, special thanks must go to Dr. Ralph G. Nichols, the pioneer in that field.

Thanks must also be given to the following individuals whose reviews were so helpful in preparing this seventh edition: David R. Carlson, Springfield College; Kathryn M. Gardner, West Valley College; Verna M. Hopper, Texas College; Mary L. Lott, St. Louis Community College at Forest Park; and Peter A. Peroni, Bucks County Community College. We also wish to thank our editors at D. C. Heath—Senior Acquisitions Editor Paul A. Smith, Developmental Editor Linda Bieze, Senior Production Editor Bryan Woodhouse, and Editorial Assistant Shira Eisenman—for their guidance through all the stages of this revision. Especially we wish to thank Ruth Brown, who went over every page of the manuscript, making valuable suggestions and perceptive criticism during its preparation. Her training and experience as a certified tutor and teacher of reading provided invaluable insights.

James I. Brown
Vivian V. Fishco

To the Student

In our print-filled world, academic success depends in large part on how well you read. This book will help you develop the reading efficiency so important in college and for the rest of your life.

Take a look at some particulars. Suppose you spend two hours of preparation for every hour spent in class. For a normal class load, that means reading an average of thirty hours a week. Let's say also that you read textbooks at about 200 words a minute with average comprehension.

How important is increasing your reading efficiency? Suppose you make a 100-word-a-minute improvement in reading rate without any loss in comprehension—a 50 percent gain. You can now do one hour's reading in only forty minutes' time. That saves you 10 hours a week, 100 hours a quarter, and 300 hours a year. In four years of college that adds up to a grand total of 1200 hours saved—the equivalent of 250 eight-hour days. And you can learn to do it in one quarter or semester!

But that's only the beginning. Think of the much bigger problem you face—keeping up in the business and professional world for the rest of your life. In short, by taking the time *now* to improve your reading efficiency, you literally *make* the time needed later on for more reading as well as for any other activities—social, professional, or recreational. Obviously, getting full value from the printed page with a minimum of time and effort deserves your top priority.

That brings us to another point. No matter how poorly or how well you now read, you are probably reading below your maximum potential. For example, that hypothetical 50 percent increase just mentioned should be relatively easy to attain. As a matter of fact, reports from reading centers and programs around the country usually mention much greater gains.

Excellent improvement can come either from classroom instruction or from individual programs of study. For example, the first fifty students who completed the University of Minnesota's correspondence course in efficient reading improved, on average, from 281 to 885 words per minute—an improvement of more than 200 percent—and with improved comprehension as well. The Independent Study Division of the National University Extension Association awarded its prestigious Certificate of Merit to the University of Minnesota for this outstanding independent-study course.

Furthermore, average and above-average readers seem to have as much room for improvement as others. A group of top executives, after only ten class sessions, improved from an above-average initial rate of 318 to 834 words per minute, with 8 percent more comprehension, using an earlier edition of this book. Evidence of this kind suggests that no matter how well you now read, you still have ample room for improvement.

But your progress in reading, if it is to be rapid and lasting, must be based on a solid foundation of communication. Reading, writing, speaking, and listening are all so closely interrelated that improvement in any one facilitates improvement in all the others—*provided* you capitalize on those interrelationships instead of on isolated skills.

The whole communication complex deserves special attention for still another reason. Ask yourself what knowledge is most worth having. Is it not the knowledge that is most useful? Research findings reveal that you spend 70 percent of your waking time in doing one thing—communicating! You are either listening, speaking, reading, or writing most of the day. This makes communication a matter of major importance—knowledge most worth acquiring. This book capitalizes to the fullest extent on a broad communication approach.

Notice the two-part organization used to emphasize these interrelationships. Take full advantage of this organization to speed your progress in reading more efficiently.

The first section of Part One, "Background," contains eighteen selections, chosen to bring you a comprehensive overview of the complex communication process. You'll find selections to sharpen your awareness of the role played in effective communication by interest, attitude, habits, imagination, observation, and cultural literacy. Other selections deal with the mushrooming growth and importance of communication and with the place of change and creativity. Still other selections bring you useful principles of memory improvement, suggest ways of organizing your time and activities to best advantage, and emphasize language as the tool of communication.

The next five sections build on this firm foundation with readings that speed your mastery of all communication skills. Section II provides in-depth coverage of reading—the central focus of activity. Sections III and IV concentrate on writing and speaking, pointing up relationships that further the growth of your communication ability. Section V, on listening, treats listening as the companion skill to reading—the two channels you depend on for intellectual growth and development. Section VI treats the one element underlying almost all communication—words. In a sense, adding one new word to your vocabulary makes you not only a better reader but a better speaker, listener, and writer as well. Developing added word power pays major dividends!

The last section, Section VII, shifts the emphasis from *how* to communicate to *what* to communicate—a reminder that communication is usually a means to an end rather than an end in itself. As one educator put it: "In a very real sense the destiny of our society and of each of us individually will be determined by our ability to communicate with one another and with citizens of other nations about contemporary problems."

Part Two of this book lets you personalize your efforts. For each selection there is an in-depth check of comprehension, a vocabulary test, timing and pacing aids, and exercises to help you master a variety of specific communication problems.

Your first step in using this book will be to get better acquainted with your strengths and weaknesses as a reader, writer, speaker, and listener. For instance, do you write better than you read? One student, a poor reader, scored consistently low on objective tests where rapid, accurate reading was required. In one course in which both objective and subjective tests were given, his grades on the objective type ranged from C down to F. On the subjective tests in the same course, he never scored below a B. He told of spending twenty hours preparing for a botany quiz, which, because it was objective, brought him only a C. Yet, whenever he demonstrated his grasp of a subject in writing, he performed well. For him, inefficient reading was a major handicap.

Your first move, then, will be to use this book to find out exactly how fast you read and how much you comprehend. See at what difficulty levels you read with adequate understanding. You'll find indexes of difficulty on pages 481–484. Determine whether you comprehend better when reading or when listening. Also check up on yourself as a writer and speaker. How do you rate yourself on sentence and paragraph structure and on your ability to organize effectively? What's your vocabulary level? Is it adequate for your communication needs?

This book is designed to make such explorations easy. For example, you'll find ten questions on each selection to check comprehension. The first five always cover details, the last five center on how well you interpret, evaluate, draw inferences, or get the central idea—skills that come under the general heading of reflective, or critical, reading. These Comprehension Check Questions are equally useful in exploring your listening ability. Get someone to read one of the selections aloud to you. Then use the ten-item comprehension test to see how well you listen.

In addition, work through the five vocabulary questions for each selection. Identify the words you need to add to your vocabulary. And use these same questions to develop added skill in using contextual clues to arrive at word meanings.

Check your answers with the Answer Key. Whenever you disagree with an answer, go over the selection again carefully to find concrete evidence for both your answer and the keyed answer. Discuss questionable items with someone else. Try to uncover all relevant data. Such analysis and discussion will do much to sharpen your awareness of emphasis, clarify organization, and fit details into the larger picture. This helps you in writing and speaking as well as in reading and listening.

Use the word counts and timing aids to explore rate and comprehension relationships. For example, take a three-dimensional look at yourself as a (1) relaxed normal reader, (2) serious student, and (3) hurried reader. First, read a selection no faster or slower than you would if you were to pick up a magazine at home and read an article. Just relax and read normally. Check rate and comprehension. Now take another selection and read it as you would an important assignment; for top comprehension, you need a score of 90 to 100. Again check rate and comprehension. In this situation, some readers actually comprehend less; they concentrate so intently on each detail that they actually become confused. Finally, try a third selection, reading it at your absolute top reading speed. What is your top speed and what comprehension results?

You can call the difference between your slowest and fastest rate in those explorations your "index of flexibility"—the range of rates presently at your command. Your comprehension scores will suggest the level of skill accompanying each rate.

The following figures from three community-college reading-improvement classes will give you a clearer picture of yourself. Most of the students were below-average readers.

N Normal	230 wpm	58% comprehension
C for Comprehension	215 wpm	67% comprehension
S for Speed	334 wpm	57% comprehension

Compare those averages with the following figures for the first 100 students (above-average readers) to complete a twelve-week efficient-reading course over educational TV.

Initial Scores	*End-of-course scores*
N 293 wpm 64% comp.	*N* 614 wpm 78% comp.
C 197 wpm 73% comp.	*C* 489 wpm 77% comp.
S 359 wpm 64% comp.	*S* 903 wpm 66% comp.

Now compare your scores with these. The better you know yourself, the better your progress. Such comparisons will identify which areas need major attention.

Although all selections are arranged for self-timing, you should consider what specific purposes or what kinds of materials lend themselves most appropriately to rapid reading. When you are reading strictly for information, what rate for you is most appropriate? Does slow reading tend to overaccent details and obscure main ideas? How rapidly should you read for enjoyment? Would seeing a full-length movie in slow motion increase or lessen your enjoyment? Keep these questions in mind as you make your preliminary explorations.

After you have a clear picture of yourself as a communicator, you're ready for the final step—intelligently planned practice. Actually, if you take the first step carefully you ensure the success of the second. Only when you know exactly what your problems are can you give them proper attention. For help, refer to the subject index of exercises, beginning on page 239. Work through the four exercises under "Diagnosis" before going on.

Suppose, for example, that your problem is comprehension. You have already completed Exercise 19, pages 282–283, which focuses on factors affecting comprehension. For further help, look over the exercises listed under the heading "Comprehension," selecting those that seem most pertinent.

Is lack of concentration a concern? If so, increasing your reading rate should help. Check your top-speed comprehension. Compare it with your normal score for further evidence. Comprehension question 6 always checks the main idea. Do you tend to miss that question? If so, look at the Special Index of Reading-Related Exercises under the subheading "Of the Main Idea" for specific help.

Or suppose you find that you are a "one-speed" reader. Again, the Special Index will let you know exactly what to do. Those exercises listed under "Rate Flexibility" will encourage you to to cultivate a wider range of rates. Check similarly in other areas of the Special Index to uncover other specific needs. You can then direct your practice efforts to best advantage.

Finally, as you work to improve your reading ability, savor the satisfaction of knowing that you are acquiring skills basic to the highest educational endeavor. As Carlyle said: "If we but think of it, all that a university or final highest school can do for us is still but what the first school began doing—teach us to *read*."

James I. Brown
Vivian V. Fishco

CONTENTS

PART ONE
READING SELECTIONS

SECTION I
BACKGROUND
3

SECTION II
ON READING
51

Efficient Reading

Part One

Reading Selections

SECTION I

BACKGROUND

Future Shock's Doc

Nancy Spiller

Knowledge! That's the very heart of communication. That's what you must have to survive. The following article—and this entire book—will help you develop enviable skill in coping with the overwhelming avalanche of knowledge coming your way—in school and out.

"The biggest sin of the new age is to be boring," says Canadian futurist Frank Ogden from amid a high-tech circus on his Vancouver houseboat. Video screens, VCRs, computers and shortwave radios compete for attention with primitive Polynesian tools and carvings. Lurking near his feet is Nabu, the guard robot. Outside on the dock, two satellite dishes are his umbilical cord to the world.

No one ever has accused Ogden, a.k.a. "Dr. Tomorrow," of being boring. Outrageous—yes. When he has told teachers their methods are obsolete, labor unions they're dinosaurs and big business it's asleep at the wheel, there have been those, he says proudly, who've thrown chairs and cups of coffee and walked out in a huff. When he predicts that robots will replace human spouses by the year 2010 and suggest China buy Australia as a site for its population overflow, many skeptics question his seriousness. His favorite reply is: "All ideas are serious when their times come."

But a growing number of businesses—including the British Columbia Medical Association, Century 21 Real Estate of Canada, Canada's Waste Management Ltd. and the British Columbia Utilities Commission—private investors and even countries (which prefer to remain anonymous) are looking to Ogden as a prime source for information on the latest global trends.

In an age in which Ogden claims knowledge is doubling every 20 months, he has kept tabs on the flow for the past 10 years. Working from his peanut-shaped boat (a converted grain-storage shed), Ogden tirelessly tracks some 200 international television stations and regularly taps into 3,700 databases in search of the latest high-tech developments. He spreads the word as lecturer, consultant, syndicated columnist, television producer and host (his *Hi-Tech, Hi-Touch Japan* airs on the Discover Channel), and head of his own electronic clipping service: 21st Century Communications.

"Shock value," Frank Klassen says of Ogden's appeal. Klassen publishes Ogden's column in the *Sunday News*, a biweekly Vancouver tabloid with a circulation of 400,000. "He's one of the few columnists in the country who's on the leading edge of what might happen. He keeps people on their toes." In so doing, Klassen adds, Ogden has developed an "almost cult following."

"Frank is plugged into all that's happening in the free world," says Peter Thomas, president of Century 21 Real Estate of Canada. Thomas uses Ogden as a lecturer and futurist consultant. "He keeps me in touch with concepts and ideas which I otherwise might miss."

"North Americans don't know what's going on," Ogden says of his mission. In wire-framed glasses and well-worn flannel and wool, the 69-year-old self-styled visionary looks more like a retired professor than a purveyor of futuristic facts. A lopsided grin tilts a dimpled mustache, and jug ears protrude impishly from his egg-shaped head.

"I show what's happening in the world that we're not even aware of," he says. Typical ignorance was encountered at a recent gathering for the North American Food Manufacturers and Processors Association, he says. "The presidents of the two biggest tomato companies were there, and they were not aware that the Japanese were growing 15,000 tomatoes from a single seed—*inside and in the shade.* They were just shocked."

Ogden claims to have 40,000 such revelations on file and features about 100 of them in this talks. The collection of gosh-gollies runs the gamut from apple trees that look like flagpoles to robot nurses and grocery clerks. He barely can let a minute go by without introducing something new.

"You know about the Forum Phone?" he asks, plucking one from a desk-side pile of gadgets and launching into the virtues of the British-made phone. It fits in the palm of the hand, is as thin as a pocket calculator, costs one-tenth the price of a cellular phone and works from public tele-points in airports, subway stations and convenience stores.

Then there's the Norwegian Gamma-knife, a gamma-ray device that excises brain tumors. Other items include airplanes with computer, fax, and phone centers at each seat; a Japanese ceramic house that's fire- and earthquake-proof and takes just 2 1/2 hours to build; and French robots that make the highest grade of Camembert cheese.

And though some of those news items sound like "Buck Rogers meets the *National Enquirer*" (one column on cloning is headlined "Amazon Women Created"), he assures that everything in his lectures is backed up "with videotape, slides or the actual product." Like the clip of musical robots that play Simon and Garfunkel tunes. "If 10 percent of the audience has heard 10 percent of what I say, there's no charge." So far, he says, he has had no requests for refunds of his $3,000-minimum lecture fee.

Much of his information comes from Japan. "It's where all the action is," he says. A Tokyo contact mails weekly cassettes of the evening news, which is simulcast in English and Japanese. "Our news is emotionally and politically oriented. Theirs is technologically and economically oriented."

In the same way the British have ruled the age of empire and the United States has led the industrial age, Ogden is convinced the Japanese are leading the age of communications.

"Information means more to the Japanese than it does to us," he says. "They know it's the new ore of the future. We get some information: we say that's no good. They know it's good if they can find out how to use it."

Their appetite is insatiable, he says. "The Japanese are translating 700 documents from English to Japanese for every one we translate from Japanese to English. Every tourist here is a spy—not deliberately; they just absorb information." And, Ogden says with a shrug, "they're smarter than us."

The fact that the Japanese have been able to turn their collective vision toward the future while the West lingers in the industrial age has tremendously helped them get ahead. "They were a nation of ancestor-worshippers," he says. "They were always looking backwards. They've decided to go forward. Almost overnight, they're now looking through the windshield instead of in the rear-view mirror."

A similar decision led Ogden to an interest in futurism. After a World War II tour of duty with the Royal Canadian Air Force, he enrolled in college—then promptly quit. "Everyone was looking backward," he says. "It was damaging my brain. Even then, what they were teaching didn't match reality. I just started looking forward.

"If schools were factories," he continues, repeating a line he often delivers to teachers' groups, "we would have closed them 10 years ago because they're not producing a salable product. Kids can't get jobs because they don't know what's happening." The Japanese, he says, send their teachers to summer school to keep up with the changing information in their fields.

"You've got to live with uncertainty, be comfortable with it," he says. To survive the future, we'll have to "learn to walk on quicksand and dance with electrons." Those who can't will be left behind. "You're gonna have the growth of the techno-peasant—incapable of doing anything other than what they know from the industrial age."

If the scenario sounds anarchic, don't be alarmed. "Chaos is coming," he says, ever the optimist, "but chaos is the most creative environment. I can't wait."

With that, he fires another barrage of entertaining predictions. High-rise office towers are the "ghost towns of the future. You don't need the hierarchy that you had in the industrial age, and you don't need the storage space." With optical crystals, the history of the United States can fit in a shoe box. Secretaries will be replaced by "voicewriters" that turn dictation into electronic mail. Cars will be equipped with microwave ovens. Knowledge will flow into homes with the push of a button, like water from the tap.

What happens when the sink backs up? The phrase "information overload" doesn't exist in Ogden's vocabulary. "I don't believe there is such a thing. We're only using 1 percent of our brain." You may think you're reached your limit, he says, but "there is no limit. We're in a time not only revolutionary," Ogden pronounces, "but evolutionary."

Catching the weary look of a visitor who's seen one too many video clips on dancing robots, Ogden can't help but chide, "No one ever told you evolution was going to be easy."

Number of words 1380
See page 241 for questions
Reading time in seconds _______
See page 495 for conversion table

The Dynamics of Change

Don Fabun

Change! That's what this book focuses on. Use it to change your reading habits, skills, and interests. Use it to sharpen your awareness of the total communication picture—writing, speaking, listening, and reading. Use it to help you walk with increased confidence in this world of ever-accelerating change.

At exactly 5:13 A.M., the 18th of April, 1906, a cow was standing somewhere between the main barn and the milking shed on the old Shafter Ranch in California, minding her own business. Suddenly, the earth shook, the skies trembled, and when it was all over, there was nothing showing of the cow above ground but a bit of her tail sticking up.

For the student of change, the Shafter cow is a sort of symbol of our times. She stood quietly enough, thinking such gentle thoughts as cows are likely to have, while huge forces outside her ken built up all around her and—within a minute—discharged it all at once in a great movement that changed the configuration of the earth, and destroyed a city, and swallowed her up. And that's what we are going to talk about now: how, if we do not learn to understand and guide the great forces of change at work on our world today, we may find ourselves like the Shafter cow, swallowed up by vast upheavals in our way of life—quite early some morning.

One foot inextricably trapped in the clockwork mechanism of 19th Century science, and the other planted fearfully in the newly radiant soil of the 20th Century, Henry Adams, then 60 years old—and a student of change for forty of those—stood in the Gallery of Machines at the Great Paris Exposition of 1900 and saw—more clearly than most men of his time, or of now—one of the great fracture points in human history.

It was to be another sixty years and two World Wars later before the dimensions of the change he saw had become the common currency of popular journalism and awareness of change an accepted tool for survival.

For most of his life, Adams had been trying to make some sense out of history. It had not been an easy quest, for history appears to be what we want to make of it, and Adams found he could not make much of it.

In his *Education*, Adams said, "Satisfied that the sequence of men led to nothing and that the sequence of society could lead no further, while the mere sequence of time was artificial and the sequence of thought was chaos, he turned at last to the sequence of force, and thus it happened, after ten years pursuit, he found himsel flying in the Gallery of Machines . . . his historical neck broken by the irruption of forces totally new."

What Adams had seen was that change is observed motion, and motion is the product of applied force. Man had begun by acquiring fire—and that was a force—and then sometime later the use of wind and water, and then he put water and fire together and turned the steam engine loose on the world. The period of time between each new acquisition and application of power was successively shorter. It was only a little after steam that he began applying electrical force and even more shortly after that he discovered and put to work nuclear force.

By 1900, the power of the electrical age was best symbolized in the dynamo, a force that Adams found parallel to the force of the Christian Cross in the affairs of men. And, in the discoveries of Roentgen and Curie, in the hidden rays of the suprasensual, the dimensions of a vast new world powered in its course by the dance of electrons, were—at the turn of the century—already visible to those few pairs of eyes curious enough to see them.

It was possible to plot the progress of these new forces in graphs, and when this was done, and the different graphs compared, it was seen that—in almost any application of force you wanted to measure—there was a constant acceleration; the changes became larger and they occurred more frequently as we moved forward in time.

Several years ago, *Scientific American* plotted Adams' "Law of Acceleration." Graphs were made up of such processes as the discovery of natural forces, and the time lag between each successive discovery; tables were made that plotted the isolation of natural elements, the accumulation of human experience, the speed that transportation has achieved from the pace of a man walking to space satellites, and the number of electronic circuits that could be put into a cubic foot of space. In every case, the rising curves on the graphs showed almost identical shapes, starting their rise slowly, then sharper and sharper until, in our times, nearly every trend line of force is embarked on a vertical course.

Some of the idea of the dimensions of change in our times, and the acceleration of it, can be found in the fact that, "Half of all the energy consumed by man in the past two thousand years has been consumed within the last one hundred." Kenneth Boulding, the economist and writer, finds that, "For many statistical series of quantities of metal or other materials extracted, the dividing line is about 1910. That is, man took about as much out of mines before 1910 as he did after 1910."

The picture of our world that emerges is as if all the rockets at Cape Kennedy were to go off at once, in some grand Fourth of July, and their skyward-soaring trails were the trend lines of our exploding technology.

Writing on "The Era of Radical Change," in *Fortune* magazine, Max Ways has said, "Within a decade or two it will be generally understood that the main challenge to U.S. society will turn not around the production of goods but around the difficulties and opportunities involved in a world of accelerating change and ever-widening choices. Change has always been a part of the human condition. What is different now is the pace of change, and the prospect that it will come faster and faster, affecting every part of life, including personal values, morality, and religions, which seem most remote from technology.

"So swift is the acceleration that trying to 'make sense' of change will come to be our basic industry. Aesthetic and ethical values will be evolving along with the choices to which they will be applied. The question about progress will be 'how good?' rather than 'how much?' "

He goes on to point out that, "The break between the period of rapid change and that of radical change is not sharp; 1950 is an arbitrary starting date. More aspects of life change faster until it is no longer appropriate to think of society as mainly fixed, or changing slowly, while the tide flows around it. So many patterns of life are being modified that it is no longer useful to organize discussion or debate mainly around the relation of the new to the old.

"The movement is so swift, so wide and the prospect of acceleration so great that an imaginative leap into the future cannot find a point of rest, a still picture of social order."

We are told that 25 per cent of all the people who ever lived are alive today; that 90 per cent of all the scientists who ever lived are living now; the amount of technical information available doubles every ten years; throughout the world, about 100,000 journals are published in more than 60 languages, and the number doubles every 15 years.

We are told these things, but we do not always act as if we believed them. "The fact is," says Alvin Toffler, "—and simple observation of one's own friends and associates will confirm it—that even the most educated people today operate on the assumption that society is relatively static. At best they attempt to plan by making simple straight-line projections of present trends. The result is unreadiness to meet the future when it arrives. In short, 'future shock.'

"Society has many built-in time spanners that help link the present generation with the past. Our sense of the past is developed by contact with the older generation, by our knowledge of history, by the accumulated heritage of art, music, literature and science passed down to us through the years. It is enhanced by immediate contact with the objects that surround us, each of which has a point of origin with the past, each of which provides us with a trace of identification with the past.

"No such time spanners enhance our sense of the future. We have no objects, no friends, no relatives, no works of art, no music or literature that originate in the future. We have, as it were, no heritage of the future."

And so, not having one, and needing it, we will have to develop one. This can be done, perhaps, by examining the forces of change around us and by trying to understand how they originated, where they are likely to be going, and how we can to some extent, by guiding them, cushion ourselves against "future shock."

We might begin by seeing ourselves in a somewhat different relationship to time than we are accustomed to. We can agree that there is not much we can do to affect the past, and that the present is so fleeting, as we experience it, that it is transformed into the past as we touch it. It is only the future that is amenable to our plans and actions. Knowing this, we can draw a broad general outline of the kind of future world we feel we would be most happy in. And because we have now arrived at a stage in our development, or shortly will arrive there, where our most pressing problems are not technological, but political and social—we can achieve the world that we want by working together to get it.

The forces of change *are* amenable to our guidance. If we seem to be hurried into the future by a runaway engine, it may be that the main reason it is running away is that we have not bothered yet to learn how it works, nor to steer it in the direction we want it to go.

Number of words 1680
See page 245 for questions
Reading time in seconds _______
See page 495 for conversion table

SELECTION 3

Is There a World Language?

Robert McCrum, William Cran, and Robert MacNeil

Exactly what do you communicate with most of the time? With language, of course. Probably the English language! For that reason, doesn't it make sense to give that language a closer inspection? Shouldn't you understand more about its history, its present status and usefulness? Here's your chance.

On 5 September 1977, the American spacecraft Voyager One blasted-off on its historic mission to Jupiter and beyond. On board, the scientists, who knew that Voyager would one day spin through distant star systems, had installed a recorded greeting from the people of the planet Earth. Preceding a brief message in fifty-five different languages for the people of outer space, the gold-plated disc plays a statement, from the Secretary-General of the United Nations, an Austrian named Kurt Waldheim, speaking on behalf of 147 member states—in English.

The rise of English is a remarkable success story. When Julius Caesar landed in Britain nearly two thousand years ago, English did not exist. Five hundred years later, *Englisc*, incomprehensible to modern ears, was probably spoken by about as few people as currently speak Cherokee—and with about as little influence. Nearly a thousand years later, at the end of the sixteenth century, when William Shakespeare was in his prime, English was the native speech of between five and seven million Englishmen and it was, in the words of a contemporary, "of small reatch, it stretcheth no further than this iland of ours, naie not there over all."

Four hundred years later, the contrast is extraordinary. Between 1600 and the present, in armies, navies, companies and expeditions, the speakers of English—including Scots, Irish, Welsh, Americans and many more—traveled into every corner of the globe, carrying their language and culture with them. Today, English is used by at least 750 million people, and barely half of those speak it as a mother tongue. Some estimates have put that figure closer to one billion. Whatever the total, English at the end of the twentieth century is more widely scattered, more widely spoken and written, than any other language has ever been. It has become *the* language of the planet, the first truly global language.

The statistics of English are astonishing. Of all the world's languages (which now number some 2700), it is arguably the richest in vocabulary. The compendious *Oxford English Dictionary* lists about 500,000 words; and a further half-million technical and scientific terms remain uncataloged. According to traditional estimates, neighboring German has a vocabulary of about 185,000 words and French fewer than 100,000, including such Franglais as *le snacque-barre* and *le hit-parade.* About 350 million people use the English vocabulary as a mother tongue: about one-tenth of the world's population, scattered across every continent and surpassed, in numbers, though not in distribution, only by the speakers of the many varieties of Chinese. Three-quarters of the world's mail, and its telexes and cables, are in English. So are more than half the world's technical and scientific periodicals: it is the language of technology from Silicon Valley to Shanghai. English is the medium for 80 per cent of the information stored in the world's computers. Nearly half of all business deals in Europe are conducted in English. It is the language of sports and glamour: the official language of the Olympics and the Miss Universe competition. English is the official voice of the air, of the sea, and of Christianity: it is the ecumenical language of the World Council of Churches. Five of the largest broadcasting companies in the world (CBS, NBC, ABC, BBC, CBC) transmit in English to audiences that regularly exceed one hundred million.

English has a few rivals, but no equals. Neither Spanish nor Arabic, both international languages, have this global sway. Another rival, Russian, has the political and economic under-pinning of a world language, but far from spreading its influence outside the Soviet empire, it, too, is becoming mildly colonized by new words known as *Russlish*, for example *seksapil* (sex appeal) and *noh-khau* (know-how). Germany and Japan have, in matching the commercial and industrial vigor of the United States, achieved the commercial precondition of language-power, but their languages have also been invaded by English, in the shape of *Deutchlish* and *Japlish*.

The remarkable story of how English spread within predominantly English-speaking societies like the United States, Canada, Australia and New Zealand is not, with the benefit of hindsight, unique. It is a process in language that is as old as Greek, or Chinese. The truly significant development, which has occurred only in the last one hundred years or so, is the use of English, taking the most conservative estimates, by three or four hundred million people for whom it is not a native language. English has become a *second* language in countries like India, Nigeria or Singapore where it is used for administration, broadcasting and education. In these countries, English is a vital alternative language, often unifying huge territories and diverse populations. When Rajiv Gandhi appealed for an end to the violence that broke out after the assassination of his mother, Mrs. Indira Gandhi, he went on television and spoke to his people in English. In anglophone Africa, seizures of power are announced in English. Then there is English as a *foreign* language, used in countries (like Holland or Yugoslavia) where it is backed up by a tradition of English teaching, or where it has been more recently adopted, Senegal for instance. Here it is used to have contact with people in other countries, usually to promote trade and scientific progress, but to the benefit of international communication generally. A Dutch poet is read by a few thousands. Translated into English, he can be read by hundreds of thousands.

The emergence of English as a global phenomenon—as either a first, second or foreign language—has recently inspired the idea (undermining the claims we have just made) that we should talk not of English, but of many Englishes, especially in Third World countries where the use of English is no longer part of the colonial legacy, but the result of decisions made since independence. But what kind of English is it? This is a new and hotly contested debate. The future, of course, is unpredictable, but one thing is certain: the present flux of English—multi-national standard or international Babel?—is part of a process that goes back to Shakespeare and beyond.

Number of words 1010
See page 247 for questions
Reading time in seconds _______
See page 495 for conversion table

Selection 4

Language as a Tool

J. Samuel Bois

You communicate with language. But has language another use? Certainly so. A very important use—as a tool to increase your brain power! Read the following article to get the details. And remember: this entire text focuses on sharpening that extremely important tool—on making you a much smarter communicator.

There are many things you can do with a hammer: you may drive nails and pull them, split a board, break stones, bang someone on the head, and so forth. But there are things that you cannot do with a hammer: you cannot saw a piece of wood, drive a screw, or bore a hole.

A tool has a function, a range of uses. The limits of that range are not always very sharp; a skillful worker may achieve wonders with the most primitive tools. But there is a point where he has to stop because the tool is totally inadequate to do what has to be done. With a stethoscope and a thermometer a good physician can diagnose many ailments, but he will need a microscope to examine a sample of tissue that he suspects of being cancerous.

The tool is not independent of the tool-user, and the tool-user is not independent of his tool. Taken together, they form an operating unit that works as a whole. Tools can be considered as extensions of man's sense organs, and of his arms, hands, and legs. The automobile gives us the seven-league boots of fairy tales, the airplane gives us wings, the hydraulic press gives us the muscular strength of a Titan.

What of our brain? Have we any tools that have increased its power, its speed, and efficiency? Yes, we have. A child in the elementary grades of school can now perform long multiplications and divisions that were considered as the exclusive achievements of experts in the Middle Ages. The tool that he is using is the positional notation of numbers, or the device of giving a number ten times its original value when we write it in the first column to the left, one hundred times its value when we write it in the second column, and so forth. This was a great invention which came from India through Arab scholars. History shows that it was resisted very strongly for generations, just as the first labor-saving devices were not welcomed by manual laborers in the early days of machinery. To appreciate the difference between this mathematical tool and those that were used before, divide CVIII by IX, using exclusively the Roman numeral notation, and see how long it will take you to get the answer.

Like physical tools, the brain tools have their limitations. They are very useful within a certain range of operation, but they cannot cope with problems outside that range. For instance, the metric system, based on the decimal notation, passes much more easily from volume to weight than does the cumbersome English system of feet and pounds. But if you try to express *exactly* in decimals the one-third of a meter, you cannot. To profit by the advantages of the metric system, you must forego the measurements that are inconsistent with it. No tool can do everything; no system is an all-purpose system. If your brain adopts a tool, it increases its capacity and limits it at the same time. We choose our tools according to what we have to do; we have to become better acquainted with our brain tools and change them freely when we have to.

We are coming now to a most important notion. Unless we agree about it, we are bound to misunderstand each other. So, please take time to ponder over the statement emphasized a few lines further down. You may find it obvious, baffling, mysterious, exaggerated, or what not—I don't know. To me, it is a key statement. If you don't accept it, please do not go beyond it,—or proceed at your own risk. Here it is:

Our Everyday Language Can Be Viewed As A Brain Tool

Language as a tool. What does this mean in the light of what has been said before? It means this:

1. Language is the tool we use to do most of our thinking. In other words, thinking could be described as *talking to ourselves.*

2. The better the tool, the better the job. A rich and flexible language makes thinking rich and flexible.

3. The language and the thinker (the tool and the tool-user) form a working unit, in which each element helps and limits the activities of the other.

4. Language is organized into a system by virtue of its rules of syntax, and it throws out of our thinking unit—that is, out of our functioning brain—all statements that are inconsistent with its system, just as the metric system forces us to ignore the exact third of a meter.

5. If we become aware of the limitations of our language, we may recognize what limitations it imposes upon our brain.

6. By pushing outward the limitations of our language (by improving the tool range and the functioning of the tool) we may increase the capacity of the human brain, as the mathematicians did when they removed the shackles of the Roman numerals and introduced the positional notation.

Are we going to compare languages, say French and English, Russian and German, Nootka and Cree, and decide which is the "best" thinking tool? No. I am not a linguist, and I don't think anyone has both the competence and the authority to promote such a change.

Are we going to insist on those "increase-your-vocabulary" exercises and tests that appear in the *Reader's Digest* and similar publications? No. A larger and more precise vocabulary is surely a good thing, but while it increases the *elements* of our language, it does not affect its *structure*; it does not bring it to a higher dimension.

Are we to advocate a new language, either simplified from a current one, like Basic English, or derived from a whole family of related idioms, like Esperanto, Volapük, or Interlingua? Not at all.

Are we going to become purists, people who dabble in etymology, Greek roots, and word history, for the purpose of restoring the *pure, original* meaning of words? Nothing is further from our purpose.

These questions, and similar ones, are all going in directions where countless pathways have been trodden down by pioneers and their eager followers. If you expect a new version of any of these schemes, or a combination of some or all of them, you will be disappointed.

Our explorations will take us in other directions and into other dimensions. Our starting point is that language can be viewed as a tool that combines with our brain to form one thinking unit. You have noticed it when you attempted to learn French, Spanish, or any other language. For a while you kept *thinking in English* while clothing your thoughts with the terms of the new language. Eventually, the new thinking tool became "homogenized" with your brain, and you discovered that you could think either in English or in the new language. Translation meant "rethinking" the experience or the stream of thoughts in a different language.

The tool and the tool-user form a complex unit. We may separate them "mentally," but in practice they work as a whole.

Number of words 1180
See page 249 for questions
Reading time in seconds _______
See page 495 for conversion table

The Last Class

Alphonse Daudet

Can you separate yourself from your language? And can you separate your own language from your own culture? The following story points up the trauma of such a separation. As you will see, you must think of communication as something done within a tight cultural framework. Let that awareness make you a better communicator.

I was very late for school that morning, and I was terribly afraid of being scolded, especially as Monsieur Hamel had told us that he should examine us on participles, and I did not know the first thing about them. For a moment I thought of staying away from school and wandering about the fields. It was such a warm, lovely day. I could hear the blackbirds whistling on the edge of the wood, and in the Rippert field, behind the sawmill, the Prussians going through their drill. All that was much more tempting to me than the rules concerning participles; but I had the strength to resist, and I ran as fast as I could to school.

As I passed the mayor's office, I saw that there were people gathered about the little board on which notices were posted. For two years all our bad news had come from that board—battles lost, conscriptions, orders from headquarters; and I thought without stopping:

"What can it be now?"

Then, as I ran across the square, Wachter the blacksmith, who stood there with his apprentice, reading the placard, called out to me:

"Don't hurry so, my boy; you'll get to your school soon enough!"

I thought that he was making fun of me, and I ran into Monsieur Hamel's little yard all out of breath.

Usually, at the beginning of school, there was a great uproar which could be heard in the street, desks opening and closing, lessons repeated aloud in unison, with our ears stuffed in order to learn quicker, and the teacher's stout ruler beating on the desk:

"A little more quiet!"

I counted on all this noise to reach my bench unnoticed; but as it happened, that day everything was quiet, like a Sunday morning. Through the open window I saw my comrades already in their places, and Monsieur Hamel walking back and forth with the terrible iron ruler under his arm. I had to open the door and enter, in the midst of that perfect silence. You can imagine whether I blushed and whether I was afraid!

But no! Monsieur Hamel looked at me with no sign of anger and said very gently:

"Go at once to your seat, my little Frantz; we were going to begin without you."

I stepped over the bench and sat down at once at my desk. Not until then, when I had partly recovered from my fright, did I notice that our teacher had on his handsome blue coat, his plaited ruff, and the black silk embroidered breeches, which he wore only on days of inspection or of distribution of prizes. Moreover, there was something extraordinary, something solemn about the whole class. But what surprised me most was to see at the back of the room, on the benches which were usually empty, some people from the village sitting, as silent as we were: old Hauser with his three-cornered hat, the ex-mayor, the ex-postman, and others besides. They all seemed depressed; and Hauser had brought an old spelling-book with gnawed edges, which he held wide-open on his knee, with his great spectacles askew.

While I was wondering at all this, Monsieur Hamel had mounted his platform, and in the same gentle and serious voice with which he had welcomed me, he said to us:

"My children, this is the last time that I shall teach you. Orders have come from Berlin to teach nothing but German in the schools of Alsace and Lorraine. The new teacher arrives to-morrow. This is the last class in French, so I beg you to be very attentive."

Those few words overwhelmed me. Ah! The villains! that was what they had posted at the mayor's office.

My last class in French!

And I barely knew how to write! So I should never learn! I must stop short where I was! How angry I was with myself because of the time I had wasted, the lessons I had missed, running about after nests, or sliding on the Saar! My books, which only a moment before I thought so tiresome, so heavy to carry—my grammar, my sacred history—seemed to me now like old friends, from whom I should be terribly grieved to part. And it was the same about Monsieur Hamel. The thought that he was going away, that I should never see him again, made me forget the punishments, the blows with the ruler.

Poor man! It was in honor of that last lesson that he had put on his fine Sunday clothes; and I understood now why those old fellows from the village were sitting at the end of the room. It seemed to mean that they regretted not having come oftener to the school. It was also a way of thanking our teacher for his forty years of faithful service, and of paying their respects to the fatherland which was vanishing.

I was at that point in my reflections, when I heard my name called. It was my turn to recite. What would I not have given to be able to say from beginning to end that famous rule about participles, in a loud, distinct voice, without a slip! But I got mixed up at the first words, and I stood there swaying against my bench, with a full heart, afraid to raise my head. I heard Monsieur Hamel speaking to me:

"I will not scold you, my little Frantz; you must be punished enough; that is the way it goes; every day we say to ourselves; 'Pshaw! I have time enough. I will learn to-morrow.' And then you see what happens. Ah! it has been the great misfortune of our Alsace always to postpone its lessons until to-morrow. Now those people are entitled to say to us: 'What! You claim to be French, and you can neither speak nor write your language!' In all this, my poor Frantz, you are not the guiltiest one. We all have our fair share of reproaches to address to ourselves.

"Your parents have not been careful enough to see that you were educated. They preferred to send you to work in the fields or in the factories, in order to have a few more sous. And have I nothing to reproach myself for? Have I not often made you water my garden instead of studying? And when I wanted to go fishing for trout, have I ever hesitated to dismiss you?"

Then, passing from one thing to another, Monsieur Hamel began to talk to us about the French language, saying that it was the most beautiful language in the world, the most clear, the most substantial; that we must always retain it among ourselves, and never forget it, because when a people falls into servitude, "so long as it clings to its language, it is as if it held the key to its prison." Then he took the grammar and read us our lesson. I was amazed to see how readily I understood. Everything that he said seemed so easy to me, so easy. I believed, too, that I had never listened so closely, and that he, for his part, had never been so patient with his explanations. One would have said that, before going away, the poor man desired to give us all his knowledge, to force it all into our heads at a single blow.

When the lesson was at an end, we passed to writing. For that day Monsieur Hamel had prepared some entirely new examples, on which was written in a fine, round hand: "France, Alsace, France, Alsace." They were like little flags, waving all about the class, hanging from the rods of our desks. You should have seen how hard we all worked and how silent it was! Nothing could be heard save the grinding of the pens over the paper. At one time some cockchafers flew in; but no one paid any attention to them, not even the little fellows, who were struggling with their straight lines, with a will and conscientious application, as if even the lines were French. On the roof of the schoolhouse, pigeons cooed in low tones, and I said to myself as I listened to them:

"I wonder if they are going to compel them to sing in German too!"

From time to time, when I raised by eyes from my paper, I saw Monsieur Hamel sitting motionless in his chair and staring at the objects about him as if he wished to carry away in his glance the whole of his little schoolhouse. Think of it! For forty years he had been there in the same place, with his yard in front of him and his class just as it was! But the benches and desks were polished and rubbed by use; the walnuts in the yard had grown, and the hop-vine which he himself had planted now festooned the windows even to the roof. What a heartrending thing it must have been for that poor man to leave all those things, and to hear his sister walking back and forth in the room overhead, packing their trunks! For they were to go away the next day—to leave the province forever.

However, he had the courage to keep the class to the end. After the writing, we had the lesson in history; then the little ones sang all together the *ba, be, bi, bo, bu.* Yonder, at the back of the room, old Hauser had put on his spectacles, and, holding his spelling-book in both hands, he spelled out the letters with them. I could see that he too was applying himself. His voice shook with emotion, and it was so funny to hear him, that we all longed to laugh and to cry. Ah! I shall remember that last class.

Suddenly the church clock struck twelve, then the Angelus rang. At the same moment, the bugles of the Prussians returning from drill blared under our windows. Monsieur Hamel rose, pale as death, from his chair. Never had he seemed to me so tall.

"My friends," he said, "my friends, I—I—"

But something suffocated him. He could not finish the sentence.

Thereupon he turned to the blackboard, took a piece of chalk, and, bearing on with all his might, he wrote in the largest letters he could: "VIVE LA FRANCE!"

Then he stood there, with his head resting against the wall, and without speaking, he motioned to us with his hand:

"That is all; go."

Number of word 1750
See page 251 for questions
Reading time in seconds ______
See page 495 for conversion table

SELECTION 6

Two Ways of Looking at Life

Martin E. P. Seligman

Your communication strongly reflects your outlook on life. Take a closer look at that connection. Are you a pessimist—or an optimist? Can you see how your way of looking at life actually does color your communication? And remember: change your outlook and you change your communication.

The father is looking down into the crib at his sleeping newborn daughter, just home from the hospital. His heart is overflowing with awe and gratitude for the beauty of her, the perfection.

The baby opens her eyes and stares straight up.

The father calls her name, expecting that she will turn her head and look at him. Her eyes don't move.

He picks up a furry little toy attached to the rail of the bassinet and shakes it, ringing the bell it contains. The baby's eyes don't move.

His heart has begun to beat rapidly. He finds his wife in their bedroom and tells her what just happened. "She doesn't seem to respond to noise at all," he says. "It's as if she can't hear."

"I'm sure she's all right," the wife says, pulling her dressing gown around her. Together they go into the nursery.

She calls the baby's name, jingles the bell, claps her hands. Then she picks up the baby, who immediately perks up, wiggling and cooing.

"My God," the father says. "She's deaf."

"No she's not," the mother says. "I mean, it's too soon to say a thing like that. Look, she's brand-new. Her eyes don't even focus yet."

"But there wasn't the slightest movement, even when you clapped as hard as you could."

The mother takes a book from the shelf. "Let's read what's in the baby book," she says. She looks up "hearing" and reads out loud: " 'Don't be alarmed if your newborn fails to startle at loud noises or fails to orient toward sound. The startle reflex and attention to sound often take some time to develop. Your pediatrician can test your child's hearing neurologically.' "

"There," the mother says. "Doesn't that make you feel better?"

"Not much," the father says. "It doesn't even mention the other possibility, that the baby is deaf. And all I know is that my baby doesn't hear a thing. I've got the worst feeling about this. Maybe it's because my grandfather was deaf. If that beautiful baby is deaf and it's my fault, I'll never forgive myself."

"Hey, wait a minute," says the wife. "You're

going off the deep end. We'll call the pediatrician first thing Monday. In the meantime, cheer up. Here hold the baby while I fix her blanket. It's all pulled out."

The father takes the baby but gives her back to his wife as soon as he can. All weekend he finds himself unable to open his briefcase and prepare for next week's work. He follows his wife around the house, ruminating about the baby's hearing and about the way deafness would ruin her life. He imagines only the worst: no hearing, no development of language, his beautiful child cut off from the social world, locked in soundless isolation. By Sunday night he has sunk into despair.

The mother leaves a message with the pediatrician's answering service asking for an early appointment Monday. She spends the weekend doing her exercises, reading, and trying to calm her husband.

The pediatrician's tests are reassuring, but the father's spirits remain low. Not until a week later, when the baby shows her first startle, to the backfire of a passing truck, does he begin to recover and enjoy his new daughter again.

This father and mother have two different ways of looking at the world. Whenever something bad happens to him—a tax audit, a marital squabble, even a frown from his employer—he imagines the worst: bankruptcy and jail, divorce, dismissal. He is prone to depression; he has long bouts of listlessness; his health suffers. She, on the other hand, sees bad events in their least threatening light. To her, they are temporary and surmountable, challenges to be overcome. After a reversal, she comes back quickly, soon regaining her energy. Her health is excellent.

The optimists and the pessimists: I have been studying them for the past twenty-five years. The defining characteristic of pessimists is that they tend to believe bad events will last a long time, will undermine everything they do, and are their own fault. The optimists, who are confronted with the same hard knocks of this world, think about misfortune in the opposite way. They tend to believe defeat is just a temporary setback, that its causes are confined to this one case. The optimists believe defeat is not their fault: Circumstances, bad luck, or other people brought it about. Such people are unfazed by defeat. Confronted by a bad situation, they perceive it as a challenge and try harder.

These two habits of thinking about causes have consequences. Literally hundreds of studies show that pessimists give up more easily and get depressed more often. These experiments also show that optimists do much better in school and college, at work and on the playing field. They regularly exceed the predictions of aptitude tests. When optimists run for office, they are more apt to be elected than pessimists are. Their health is unusually good. They age well, much freer than most of us from the usual physical ills of middle age. Evidence suggests they may even live longer.

I have seen that, in tests of hundreds of thousands of people, a surprisingly large number will be found to be deep-dyed pessimists and another large portion will have serious, debilitating tendencies toward pessimism. I have learned that it is not always easy to know if you are a pessimist, and that far more people than realize it are living in this shadow. Tests reveal traces of pessimism in the speech of people who would never think of themselves as pessimists; they also show that these traces are sensed by others, who react negatively to the speakers.

A pessimistic attitude may seem so deeply rooted as to be permanent. I have found, however, that pessimism is escapable. Pessimists can in fact learn to be optimists, and not through mindless devices like whistling a happy tune or mouthing platitudes ("Every day, in every way, I'm getting better and better"), but by learning a new set of cognitive skills. Far from being the creations of boosters or of the popular media, these skills were discovered in the laboratories and clinics of leading psychologists and psychiatrists and then rigorously validated. . . .

Twenty-five years of study has convinced me that if we *habitually* believe, as does the pessimist, that misfortune is our fault, is enduring, and will undermine everything we do, more of it will befall us than if we believe otherwise. I am also convinced that if we are in the grip of this view, we will get depressed easily, we will accomplish less than our potential, and we will even get physically sick more often. Pessimistic prophecies are self-fulfilling.

Number of words 1120
See page 253 for questions
Reading time in seconds _______
See page 495 for conversion table

How to Remember: Some Basic Principles

Robert L. Montgomery

How do you communicate something you've forgotten? You can't! Now's the time to fit memory into the communication picture. Don't be content with a 10 percent level of remembering. Tap the following three basic laws and triple that figure. After all, improved memory means improved communication.

THE PREREQUISITES

Most of us, psychologists say, don't use more than 10 percent of our native ability to remember. That's comparable to running a car on one or two cylinders and just poking along.

Why don't we use more of our inherent memory power? There are several answers. First, because we haven't been trained to. Nowhere in our schooling were we taught how to use our powers of memory. And second, because we often just don't *care*. And that leads me to the three things that I feel are essential to a more powerful memory.

First, you must have a burning *desire* to improve your memory. *You must care about it.* Most people struggle along with poor memories, enduring endless frustrations and embarrassments in their daily lives, because they just don't want to be bothered remembering the constant barrage of names, numbers, facts, and information. What you have to do is remind yourself of the many benefits of a good memory: the increased confidence I promised you, the popularity, the peace of mind. Aren't those three alone enough to stir a desire in you to improve?

The second prerequisite is the ability to *concentrate.* You will be effective in remembering to the degree that you care enough to concentrate. A short period of intense concentration will often enable you to accomplish more than years of dreaming.

The third prerequisite was revealed to me by former Postmaster-General James Farley of New York City. Mr. Farley was cited by associates for having the most remarkable memory in this century. I asked him his secret.

"There's no real secret," he said. "You simply must *love people.* If you do, you won't have any trouble remembering their names, and a lot more about them than that."

And that's the third essential: You must *care about people.* It wasn't long after I talked to Mr. Farley that I came across an interesting line from Alexander Pope. "How vast a memory has love," he wrote. Certainly a deeper interest in people, and in your work as well, should make your desire to remember and your concentration much easier.

THE BASIC LAWS

Visualize. Now you're ready to learn the basic techniques for developing your memory. The first essential is to *visualize.* Picture what you want to remember. Since 85 percent of all you learn and remember in life reaches you through your eyes, it is absolutely vital that you visualize the things you want to recall later. To do that, you must above all become *aware.* And awareness involves becoming both a keen observer and an active listener. You have to see clearly and hear accurately in order to picture vividly what you want to remember. Too many people go through life only partly awake, only partly aware. They don't forget names; they never hear them clearly in the first place. The art of *retention* is the art of *attention.*

Become curious, observant, and sensitive to everything around you. See the roof detail on that old building. Notice the difference between the tree greens of April and of August. Hear the difference between the sirens of an ambulance, a fire truck, a police car. Sharpen your senses of sight and hearing—they're the most important. Together, those two senses account for 95 percent of our memory power. Two ancient sayings highlight the importance of visualizing. "One time seeing is worth a thousand times hearing." And "A picture is worth ten thousand words."

Repeat. If school didn't bother to teach us formal memory work, it did teach us the need for *repeating*. We were taught to memorize by repeating a poem, a date, or the alphabet over and over again. Radio and television commercials rely heavily on repetition to remind listeners to buy, buy, buy.

Is there an American who doesn't recognize "Try it, you'll like it" or "I can't believe I ate the whole thing"? Burger King's famous "Have it your way" moved McDonald's, who got busy and created the line, "You, you're the one." When slogans like these are set to music, people don't just remember them—they even sing them. And there you have the secret of success: repetition.

Associate. Before we get into actual demonstrations of the kinds of memory and the application of techniques, there's one more key to memory, and it's the most important. The one indispensable fundamental is the requirement that you *associate* anything you want to recall later. Association is the natural as well as the easy way to assure instant recall. Your brain is more remarkable than even the most amazing computer in the world. And the principle on which it works is association. The brain is, in fact, an associating machine. To recall a name, date, or fact, what the brain needs is a cue, a clue.

Let's step back into history for a moment. Over 2,000 years ago Aristotle defined what he called the Primary Laws of Association. There is the Law of Resemblance or Similarity, where one impression tends to being to mind another impression which resembles it in some way. There is the Law of Contrast or Opposites, which says that where there are two or more opposing impressions, the presence of one will tend to recall the others. And finally there is the Law of Contiguity or Togetherness. If two or more impressions occur at the same time, or follow close on one another in either time or space, thinking of one will recall the other.

There are secondary Laws of Association as well, and these are known as Recency, Frequency, and Vividness. *Recency* means we tend to recall associations made recently much better than those made months or years ago. *Frequency* implies that the more often you repeat an association, the easier it will be to recall. And *vividness* means that the more graphic or striking the association is, the quicker you'll be able to recall it.

In summary, the requirements for improving your memory are concentration, a desire to remember, and a love for people.

And the techniques for mastering the art of memory are visualizing, repeating, and associating.

One final note, this time on how to study: Memorizing anything is easier and faster when you practice for a half hour or so, and then go off and forget it for a while. Work again later for another half hour, then take another break. Tests have proved time and again that we learn better and faster when we alternate work and rest in a sort of wave pattern. The rest period actually reinforces the learning.

Now then, can you remember all that?

Number of words 1100
See page 255 for questions
Reading time in seconds ______
See page 495 for conversion table

Creativity

Kaiser Aluminum News

Effective communication demands creativity. If what you say or write is the same old thing, who wants to hear it—or read it? Pull creativity into the picture. Use it to breathe life and interest into anything and everything you communicate. Read on. Find out what creativity is and what it does.

We don't know, of course, just where you happen to be at this moment, but chances are that you are in a manufactured environment; your office, your home, a school room, library, or public vehicle where you have time to read. Glance about and you will see that almost everything surrounding you has been invented and designed by someone else; some person at some time engaged in a creative act, and the sum total of those acts makes up the world you live in. This applies not only to your physical environment, but your mental one as well—your mind is filled almost entirely by symbols originally formed by creative persons.

Consider what these creative products are made from. Very simple things; things that existed in nature, now combined into new patterns. The chair you sit in did not exist in the tree from which the material came, but in the mind of a creative person who conceived of it and designed it. And so with the desk and table, the rug on the floor, the drapery at the windows, the very floor and walls and ceiling that surround you. All are patterns formed by creative persons who found new combinations for quite simple and ordinary things.

The essence of the creative act is to see the familiar as strange, to ask yourself, "What if?" It is the unquestioning acceptance of the already existing that keeps people from being creative; it is an attitude of mind, rather than the lack of innate ability to create.

The wind had been blowing dust around for millions of years, but it was not until 1901 that H. C. Booth thought of using wind in reverse, and thus created the vacuum cleaner to pick up dust.

We inherit, not through our genes, but through our childhood training, the feeling that what is, is "right." Even the idea of discussing creativity as a human act did not enter the mainstream of human consciousness until the 18th Century. Up until then, it was almost universally held that everything there was, or ever would be, had been formed in one grand act of Creation, and the role of poor mortals was limited to discovering what was already there. We think we know better now; that all of life is a creative process; that the world is constantly new, and that the efforts of human beings to respond to it endlessly create new patterns that shape the environment as it is experienced.

Thus the important question is not, why do some people appear to be creative? But, rather, why is it that some people do not appear to use the creative ability with which they are endowed? Humanity stands at the wave front of a phase of an ongoing process, the constant and creative modification of environment, that has been going on since living things first moved upon the earth. Alone of all these creatures, we are aware that we *are* part of a process, and thus can consciously direct it.

First, we should make clear what we mean by creativity. There are many definitions, but there really is not much difference between them. All agree that the creative act results in a product that is "new" or "original" or "different" from the one that preceded it.

"Not much, but still a little more, Than was in the world before."

Creativity pervades nature; living things are constantly engaged in the process of combining inorganic elements into new patterns that become cells of blood or bone; new combinations and patterns of inert, primordial things. Through imprinted genetic messages, these originally creative acts tend to become repetitive, and thus are no longer creative. The mollusk can only form shell from calcium; the plant can only make cells from the radiation, air, water and minerals of its environment. Humanity has similar, built-in, genetic imprints, too, but in addition people have something else, an ability to form new or original patterns of things. What is built-in, in people, is not the response, but the ability to respond in various ways.

Our definition of creativity, then, is that it is "the process by which original patterns are formed and expressed."

We feel that this process is basically the same whether the pattern be expressed as an invention, a change in technique, a work of art or mathematics, a piece of music or a scientific theory.

We also are saying that the pattern need not be "new" in the sense that no one ever thought of it before, but only that it be original with the person himself or herself. History is full of instances of simultaneous invention. It is also full of instances of inventions that have been made in one era, lost for long periods of time, and re-invented later on. By our definition, all these acts were equally creative, whether the products were "useful" or not.

We can never establish "newness" because our knowledge of history is so incomplete. We *can* establish originality because it relates to the personal transaction between the person and the environment.

Newton, like everyone else, had seen apples fall before, and had seen the moon many times, but for the first time, he saw that "both were falling," and thus created a theory of gravitation. The idea was original for him.

At this point, we should make some distinction between discovery and invention; both of which are creative acts. Columbus discovered America, he did not invent it. Hero invented the steam engine; it had not existed before him.

In invention, the creative process *forms* an original pattern; in discovery, the creative process *reveals* one. Discovery constantly adds to the number of things from which new patterns can be made; new patterns, particularly in technology, enable new discoveries to be made. The two—discovery and invention—are phases in the creative process that are in resonance, each reinforcing the other.

Creativity is a state of mind, and it is most widely expressed by very young children, because their confrontation with their environment is constantly made up of original discoveries and inventions. In time, through social pressures to conform and the repetition of experience, most of them lose this sense of wonder and become less and less creative, trapped in a concrete mold not of their own making.

It has been said that the creative person is essentially "a perpetual child." The tragedy is that most of us grow up.

Number of words 1070
See page 257 for questions
Reading time in seconds_______
See page 495 for conversion table

SELECTION 9

The Importance of Being Interested

H. Addington Bruce

Emerson once said: "Beware of what you want—for you will get it." Was that true with Franklin, Darwin, and Mozart? Perhaps it's want-to, *not* I. Q., *that's most important. If so, how much do* you *want to improve as a communicator? Strengthen that interest; then watch it pay off.*

Many years ago there lived in the city of Boston a small boy whose days were spent in a singularly wearisome way. At the age of ten, when most boys are dividing their time between school and play, he was busy all day boiling soap, cutting wicks for tallow candles, filling candle molds, and otherwise drudging as assistant to his father in the soap and candle business. It was a business in which the father took an honest pride, and in thus apprenticing his youngest son to it, he did so with the expectation of giving him full charge and ownership in later years.

As it happened, the son's mind was filled with thoughts of other things than soap and candles. He worked faithfully enough at the kettles and wicks and molds; but he worked with such scant enthusiasm and such little skill that his father soon perceived that he would never become an expert candle-maker. Bitterly disappointed, he nevertheless appreciated the folly of compelling his son to persist in an occupation manifestly uncongenial to him. To another and much older son he one day said:

"Will you take Ben into your printing shop? He will never be a successful chandler, but he may make a fair printer. At any rate, I wish you would give him a chance."

Into the printing ship, accordingly, young Ben went, somewhat against his will, for the handling of inky type seemed to him only a trifle less unpleasant than dealing with greasy molds. But he presently made the important discovery that through typesetting he was in a position both to gain knowledge for himself and to make knowledge available for other people by putting it into print. Forthwith he became interested in printing as he had never been in candle-making; also, he became fired with a desire to learn all he could about as many subjects as possible, and he developed, besides, an ambition to turn author and see his own thoughts take form on the printed page.

Behold him, then, sometimes sitting up the whole night long over Plutarch's *Lives*, *The Spectator*, Locke's *Essays*, and kindred works of information and literary power. Behold him in the fervor of his zeal turning vegetarian at the age of sixteen, because the greater cheapness of his meals would allow him more money for books. Behold him scribbling and rescribbling in the effort to give clear expression to the ideas forming in his mind as a result of his wide reading and hard thinking. Finally, behold him timidly slipping under the door of his brother's newspaper office an unsigned essay written in a disguised hand—an essay so good that, on publication, its authorship was variously ascribed to leading writers of the day.

Thereafter he toiled more industriously than ever—printing, reading, thinking, writing. Ere he was thirty he was widely known, and long before his death he was acclaimed on two continents as one of the wisest of men. We of to-day, looking back from the vantage-point of more than a century later, feel that the praise of his contemporaries was not misplaced. For the whilom candle-maker who thus rose to eminence was none other than Benjamin Franklin, philosopher, scientist, diplomat, and apostle of America's freedom.

Take, similarly, the history of an English lad born some twenty years after Franklin died. More happily circumstanced, being the son of a successful physician, this boy was given all the advantages of good schooling. But he did not seem to draw much profit from his lessons. In fact, as he himself has told us, both his father and his teachers were inclined to regard him as "rather below the common standard in intellect." To make matters worse from the father's point of view, he showed a marked distaste for the tasks of the schoolroom, and an equally marked fondness for vagabondage.

Gun in hand, he would roam for hours through verdant lanes or across the open country. "You care for nothing but shooting, dogs, and rat-catching, and you will be a disgrace to yourself and all your family," his father once predicted, mournfully. As the boy grew older, his propensity for idling seemed only to increase. In spite of this, hoping against hope that he would settle down to serious things, his father entered him at the University of Glasgow, with the idea of fitting him for the practice of medicine. "It is no use," the boy frankly avowed after a few months at Glasgow. "I hate the work here, and I cannot possibly be a physician." So earnest were his protests that he was transferred to Cambridge University, on the understanding that he would study to be a clergyman.

At Cambridge, as good fortune would have it, he entered the natural history class of an eminent and enlightened scholar, Professor Henslow, who sent him into the woods and fields to make collections of plants and insects. Free again to roam under the clear blue skies, but this time with a lofty purpose set before his mind, a passion for achievement took possession of him. The boy whom other teachers had found dull and lazy proved himself, under Professor Henslow's inspiring guidance, a marvel of industry and mental vigor. There was no longer any thought of the "last resort" plan of putting him into the ministry. He would, he assured his now delighted father, devote his whole life to the study of nature's laws.

Thus it came about that, when his college days were over, he eagerly accepted an opportunity to accompany a Government exploring expedition. During that long voyage in southern seas he accumulated a remarkable collection of specimens. What was far more important, he brought back with him to England, after a five years' absence filled with hardships, a mass of new ideas regarding fundamental principles in natural science—ideas which, being masterfully scrutinized and sifted, were afterwards to make him world-famous as Charles Darwin, originator of the doctrine of evolution.

Again, there was born in the [Austrian] city of Salzburg, about the middle of the eighteenth century, a bright-eyed boy, the son of a Court musician. As was inevitable by reason of his father's vocation, this child, from the hour he first opened his eyes and ears to the world about him, daily heard melody from violin, clavier, and harpsichord. Before he was three years old it was noticed that he not only seemed to take great delight in listening to music, but also that he often attempted with his little fingers to strike harmonious intervals on the clavier. His father, amused but impressed, offered to give him lessons; joyfully the child accepted, and at once a start was made.

Thenceforth music dominated his waking thoughts. The toys of childhood were cast aside, and in their stead he played with the keyed and stringed instruments to which his father gave him ready access. From the first he astonished all around him by his wonderful skill. By the time he was four he could play several minuets on the harp and he was busily composing themes, and in his sixth year he was able to play the violin so well that he once assisted his father and a celebrated violinist in rehearsing trios which the latter had recently composed. Modest, unassuming, bending his every effort to progress in the art which had so fascinated him, the youngster passed in quick succession from one notable feat to another. On all sides the prediction was heard: "If this boy keeps on as he has begun, he will be one of the world-masters of music." Those who are familiar with Mozart's marvelous compositions for church, opera-house, and concert-room know well that the prediction was amply fulfilled.

Now, I have recalled these beginnings of the careers of Franklin, Darwin and Mozart because they strikingly illustrate a profound psychological truth the significance of which can scarcely be overestimated. It is a truth, to be sure, that has long been partially recognized. But its full meaning has not been—and could not be—appreciated until quite recently. Only within the past few years has scientific research effected sundry discoveries which make its complete recognition possible and of supreme importance—of such importance that practical application of the principles involved would make for an immediate and stupendous increase in human happiness, efficiency, and welfare.

Stated briefly, the truth in question is that success in life, meaning thereby the accomplishment of results of real value to the individual and to society, depends chiefly on sustained endeavor springing out of a deep and ardent interest in the tasks of one's chosen occupation. It is not enough merely to be a "hard worker." The world is full of people who slave faithfully at their respective duties, perhaps earn a handsome living, but know in their hearts that they have failed to achieve their possibilities. Yet the trouble with them simply is that they are not really interested in what they are doing. They are "misfits," as Franklin was in his father's candle-shop and Darwin at the University of Glasgow. Unlike Franklin and Darwin, they have not been so fortunate as to stumble eventually upon a vocation capable of inciting in them a passionate enthusiasm; unlike Mozart, they have not had a father wise enough to perceive their natural inclinations and brave enough to safeguard the development of these by an early education. Had they been thus circumstanced, who knows but that they might have attained results fairly comparable with the results attained by Franklin and Darwin and Mozart—all through the dynamic power of interest.

Indeed, evidence is accumulating that it is in this, rather than in any exceptional structure of the brain, that we have the true explanation of the wonderful achievements of so-called "men of genius." Looked at superficially, the mental processes of the man of genius undoubtedly seem to differ greatly from those of the ordinary man. In the case of the former, great ideal, marvelous "inspirations," often spring into consciousness seemingly of their own accord. Napoleon used to say that his battles frequently were won by tactics devised by him on the spur of the moment. "The decisive moment approached, the spark burst forth, and one was victorious." Goethe has testified that not a few of his themes, and sometimes whole poems, came to him from he knew not where. On Schiller's own testimony, when he was consciously at work, creating and constructing, his imagination did not serve him "with the same freedom as it had done when nobody was looking over its shoulder." Likewise we have Mozart's statement that his compositions "came involuntarily, like dreams."

All this, I say, seems very different from the workings of the mind of the ordinary man. Yet, after all, exactly the same sort of thing occurs to the latter. He, too, has his "happy thoughts," his occasional "flashings" of wise decisions, correct solutions of baffling problems, etc. Noticeably, however, his happy thoughts and flashings are always connected with matters to which he has devoted much conscious attention, matters which have been of great interest to him. It is as though, by thinking of them earnestly, he has set in motion some hidden mechanism that has enabled him, smoothly and easily, and all unknown to himself, to arrive at definite conclusions *beneath the threshold of consciousness.*

Precisely thus with the man of genius. A

Napoleon's inspirations are not concerned with nature's laws; those of a Darwin have nothing to do with military conquest, those of a Mozart relate neither to problems of science nor problems of war. No, the inspirations of every man of genius are concerned solely with the subject in which, perhaps from earliest childhood, he has taken the greatest interest, and to which he has devoted the greatest thought. Napoleon, it is known, was so absorbed in military matters that, even at the opera, his mind would be incessantly occupied with some such problem as: "I have ten thousand men at Strasbourg, fifteen thousand at Magdeburg, twenty thousand at Würzburg. By what stages must they march so as to reach Ratisbon on three successive days?" The flowering of Darwin's great discovery was not the work of a moment, but was preceded by years of patient, arduous observation.

Mozart, beginning the study of music at the age of three, remained a zealous student all his days.

"Nobody," runs his own account, "takes as much pains in the study of composition as I. You could not easily name a famous master in music whom I have not industriously studied, often going through his works several times." Walking, or at the theater, or even while engaged in social amusements, he lived in a self-created atmosphere of music. "In Prague," Otto Jahn has recorded, "it once happened that Mozart, while he was playing billiards, was humming a motif, and from time to time would look into a book he had with him. Afterward he confessed he had been at work upon the first quintette of the 'Zauberflöte'!" And we have his wife's testimony: "In truth, his head was working all the time, his mind was ever moving, he composed almost unceasingly." As with Napoleon, Darwin, and Mozart, so with all men of genius of whose lives we have any detailed record.

It may, then, be stated as a well-established fact that intense interest plus persistent effort is the prime essential to the highest success in any sphere of human activity. . . .

Number of words 2250
See page 259 for questions
Reading time in seconds _______
See page 495 for conversion table

Selection 10

The Fifty-First Dragon

Heywood Broun

Your attitude affects your communication. As William James said, "Believe that life is worth living and your belief will help create the fact." Belief! Was that the essential difference between the fiftieth and fifty-first dragon in the following story? Apply the power of positive thinking. It's an important facet of communication.

Of all the pupils at the knight school Gawaine le Cœur-Hardy was among the least promising. He was tall and sturdy, but his instructors soon discovered that he lacked spirit. He would hide in the woods when the jousting class was called, although his companions and members of the faculty sought to appeal to his better nature by shouting to him to come out and break his neck like a man. Even when they told him that the lances were padded, the horses no more than ponies and the field unusually soft for late autumn, Gawaine refused to grow enthusiastic. The Headmaster and the Assistant Professor of Pleasaunce were discussing the case one spring afternoon and the Assistant Professor could see no remedy but expulsion.

"No," said the Headmaster, as he looked out at the purple hills which ringed the school, "I think I'll train him to slay dragons."

"He might be killed," objected the Assistant Professor.

"So he might," replied the Headmaster brightly, but he added, more soberly, "we must consider the greater good. We are responsible for the formation of this lad's character."

"Are the dragons particularly bad this year?"

interrupted the Assistant Professor. This was characteristic. He always seemed restive when the head of the school began to talk ethics and the ideals of the institution.

"I've never known them worse," replied the Headmaster. "Up in the hills to the south last week they killed a number of peasants, two cows and a prize pig. And if this dry spell holds there's no telling when they may start a forest fire simply by breathing around indiscriminately."

"Would any refund on the tuition fee be necessary in case of an accident to young Cœur-Hardy?"

"No," the principal answered, judicially, "that's all covered in the contract. But as a matter of fact he won't be killed. Before I send him up in the hills I'm going to give him a magic word."

"That's a good idea," said the Professor. "Sometimes they work wonders."

From that day on Gawaine specialized in dragons. His course included both theory and practice. In the morning there were long lectures on the history, anatomy, manners and customs of dragons. Gawaine did not distinguish himself in these studies. He had a marvelously versatile gift for forgetting things. In the afternoon he showed to better advantage, for then he would go down to the South Meadow and practice with a battle-ax. In this exercise he was truly impressive, for he had enormous strength as well as speed and grace. He even developed a deceptive display of ferocity. Old alumni say that it was a thrilling sight to see Gawaine charging across the field toward the dummy paper dragon which had been set up for his practice. As he ran he would brandish his ax and shout "A murrain on thee!" or some other vivid bit of campus slang. It never took him more than one stroke to behead the dummy dragon.

Gradually his task was made more difficult. Paper gave way to papier-mâché and finally to wood, but even the toughest of these dummy dragons had no terrors for Gawaine. One sweep of the ax always did the business. There were those who said that when the practice was protracted until dusk and the dragons threw long, fantastic shadows across the meadow Gawaine did not charge so impetuously nor shout so loudly. It is possible there was malice in this charge. At any rate, the Headmaster decided by the end of June that it was time for the test. Only the night before a dragon had come close to the school grounds and had eaten some of the lettuce from the garden. The faculty decided that Gawaine was ready. They gave him a diploma and a new battle-ax and the Headmaster summoned him to a private conference.

"Sit down," said the Headmaster. "Have a cigarette."

Gawaine hesitated.

"Oh, I know it's against the rules," said the Headmaster. "But after all, you have received your preliminary degree. You are no longer a boy. You are a man. To-morrow you will go out into the world, the great world of achievement."

Gawaine took a cigarette. The Headmaster offered him a match, but he produced one of his own and began to puff away with a dexterity which quite amazed the principal.

"Here you have learned the theories of life," continued the Headmaster, resuming the thread of his discourse, "but after all, life is not a matter of theories. Life is a matter of facts. It calls on the young and the old alike to face these facts, even though they are hard and sometimes unpleasant. Your problem, for example, is to slay dragons."

"They say that those dragons down in the south wood are five hundred feet long," ventured Gawaine, timorously.

"Stuff and nonsense!" said the Headmaster. "The curate saw one last week from the top of Arthur's Hill. The dragon was sunning himself down in the valley. The curate didn't have an opportunity to look at him very long because he felt it was his duty to hurry back to make a report to me. He said the monster, or shall I say, the big lizard?—wasn't an inch over two hundred feet. But the size has nothing at all to do with it. You'll find the big ones even easier than the little ones. They're far slower on their feet and less aggressive, I'm told. Besides, before you go I'm going to equip you in such fashion that you need have no fear of all the dragons in the world."

"I'd like an enchanted cap," said Gawaine.

"What's that?" answered the Headmaster, testily.

"A cap to make me disappear," explained Gawaine.

The Headmaster laughed indulgently. "You mustn't believe all those old wives' stories," he said. "There isn't any such thing. A cap to make you disappear, indeed! What would you do with it? You haven't even appeared yet. Why, my boy, you could walk from here to London, and nobody would so much as look at you. You're nobody. You couldn't be more invisible than that."

Gawaine seemed dangerously close to a relapse into his old habit of whimpering. The Headmaster reassured him: "Don't worry; I'll give you something much better than an enchanted cap. I'm going to give you a magic word. All you have to do is to repeat this magic charm once and no dragon can possibly harm a hair of your head. You can cut off his head at your leisure."

He took a heavy book from the shelf behind his desk and began to run through it. "Sometimes," he said, "the charm is a whole phrase or even a sentence. I might, for instance, give you 'To make the'—No, that might not do. I think a single word would be best for dragons."

"A short word," suggested Gawaine.

"It can't be too short or it wouldn't be potent. There isn't so much hurry as all that. Here's a splendid magic word: 'Rumplesnitz.' Do you think you can learn that?"

Gawaine tried and in an hour or so he seemed to have the word well in hand. Again and again he interrupted the lesson to inquire, "And if I say 'Rumplesnitz' the dragon can't possibly hurt me?" And always the Headmaster replied, "If you only say 'Rumplesnitz,' you are perfectly safe."

Toward morning Gawaine seemed resigned to his career. At daybreak the Headmaster saw him to the edge of the forest and pointed him to the direction in which he should proceed. About a mile away to the southwest a cloud of steam hovered over an open meadow in the woods and the Headmaster assured Gawaine that under the steam he would find a dragon. Gawaine went forward slowly. He wondered whether it would be best to approach the dragon on the run as he did in his practice in the South Meadow or to walk slowly toward him, shouting "Rumplesnitz" all the way.

The problem was decided for him. No sooner had he come to the fringe of the meadow than the dragon spied him and began to charge. It was a large dragon and yet it seemed decidedly aggressive in spite of the Headmaster's statement to the contrary. As the dragon charged it released huge clouds of hissing steam through its nostrils. It was almost as if a gigantic teapot had gone mad. The dragon came forward so fast and Gawaine was so frightened that he had time to say "Rumplesnitz" only once. As he said it, he swung his battle-ax and off popped the head of the dragon. Gawaine had to admit that it was even easier to kill a real dragon than a wooden one if only you said "Rumplesnitz."

Gawaine brought the ears home and a small section of the tail. His school mates and the faculty made much of him, but the Headmaster wisely kept him from being spoiled by insisting that he go on with his work. Every clear day Gawaine rose at dawn and went out to kill dragons. The Headmaster kept him at home when it rained, because he said the woods were damp and unhealthy at such times and that he didn't want the boy to run needless risks. Few good days passed in which Gawaine failed to get a dragon. On one particularly fortunate day he killed three, a husband and wife and a visiting relative. Gradually he developed a technique. Pupils who sometimes watched him from the hill-tops a long way off said that he often allowed the dragon to come within a few feet before he said "Rumplesnitz." He came to say it with a mocking sneer. Occasionally he did stunts. Once when an excursion party from London was watching him he went into action with his right hand tied behind his back. The dragon's head came off just as easily.

As Gawaine's record of killings mounted higher the Headmaster found it impossible to keep him completely in hand. He fell into the habit of stealing out at night and engaging in long drinking bouts at the village tavern. It was after such a debauch that he rose a little before dawn one fine August morning and started out after his fiftieth dragon. His head was heavy and his mind sluggish. He was heavy in other respects as well, for he had adopted the somewhat vulgar practice of wearing his medals, ribbons and all, when he went out dragon hunting. The decorations began on his chest and ran all the way down to his abdomen. They must have weighed at least eight pounds.

Gawaine found a dragon in the same meadow where he had killed the first one. It was a fair-sized dragon, but evidently an old one. Its face was wrinkled and Gawaine thought he had never seen so hideous a countenance. Much to the lad's disgust, the monster refused to charge and Gawaine was obliged to walk toward him. He whistled as he went. The dragon regarded him hopelessly, but craftily. Of course it had heard of Gawaine. Even when the lad raised his battle-ax the dragon made no move. It knew that there was no salvation in the quickest thrust of the head, for it had been informed that this hunter was protected by an enchantment. It merely waited, hoping something would turn up. Gawaine raised the battle-ax and suddenly lowered it again. He had grown very pale and he trembled violently. The dragon suspected a trick. "What's the matter?" it asked, with false solicitude.

"I've forgotten the magic word," stammered Gawaine.

"What a pity," said the dragon. "So that was the secret. It doesn't seem quite sporting to me, all this magic stuff, you know. Not cricket, as we used to say when I was a little dragon; but after all, that's a matter of opinion."

Gawaine was so helpless with terror that the dragon's confidence rose immeasurably and it could not resist the temptation to show off a bit.

"Could I possibly be of any assistance?" it asked. "What's the first letter of the magic word?"

"It begins with an 'r,' said Gawaine weakly.

"Let's see," mused the dragon, "that doesn't tell us much, does it? What sort of a word is this? Is it an epithet, do you think?"

Gawaine could do no more than nod.

"Why, of course," exclaimed the dragon, "reactionary Republican."

Gawaine shook his head.

"Well, then," said the dragon, "we'd better get down to business. Will you surrender?"

With the suggestion of a compromise Gawaine mustered up enough courage to speak.

"What will you do if I surrender?" he asked.

"Why, I'll eat you," said the dragon.

"And if I don't surrender?"

"I'll eat you just the same."

"Then it doesn't make any difference, does it?" moaned Gawaine.

"It does to me," said the dragon with a smile. "I'd rather you didn't surrender. You'd taste much better if you didn't."

The dragon waited for a long time for Gawaine to ask "Why?" but the boy was too frightened to speak. At last the dragon had to give the explanation without his cue line. "You see," he said, "if you don't surrender you'll taste better because you'll die game."

This was an old and ancient trick of the dragon's. By means of some such quip he was accustomed to paralyze his victims with laughter and then to destroy them. Gawaine was sufficiently paralyzed as it was, but laughter had no part in his helplessness. With the last word of the joke the dragon drew back his head and struck. In that second there flashed into the mind of Gawaine the magic word "Rumplesnitz," but there was no time to say it. There was time only to strike and, without a word, Gawaine met the onrush of the dragon with a full swing. He put all his back and shoulders into it. The impact was terrific and the head of the dragon flew away almost a hundred yards and landed in a thicket.

Gawaine did not remain frightened very long after the death of the dragon. His mood was one of wonder. He was enormously puzzled. He cut off the ears of the monster almost in a trance. Again and again he thought to himself, "I didn't say 'Rumplesnitz'!" He was sure of that and yet there was no question that he had killed the dragon. In fact, he had never killed one so utterly. Never before had he driven a head for anything like the same distance. Twenty-five yards was perhaps his best previous record. All the way back to the knight school he kept rumbling about in his mind seeking an explanation for what had occurred. He went to the Headmaster immediately and after closing the door told him what had happened. "I didn't say 'Rumplesnitz,'" he explained with great earnestness.

The Headmaster laughed. "I'm glad you've found out," he said. "It makes you ever so much more of a hero. Don't you see that? Now you know that it was you who killed all these dragons and not that foolish little word 'Rumplesnitz.'"

Gawaine frowned. "Then it wasn't a magic word after all?" he asked.

"Of course not," said the Headmaster, "you ought to be too old for such foolishness. There isn't any such thing as a magic word."

"But you told me it was magic," protested Gawaine. "You said it was magic and now you say it isn't."

"It wasn't magic in a literal sense," answered the Headmaster, "but it was much more wonderful than that. The word gave you confidence. It took away your fears. If I hadn't told you that you might have been killed the very first time. It was your battle-ax did the trick."

Gawaine surprised the Headmaster by his attitude. He was obviously distressed by the explanation. He interrupted a long philosophic and ethical discourse by the Headmaster with, "If I hadn't of hit 'em all mighty hard and fast any one of 'em might have crushed me like a, like a —" He fumbled for a word.

"Egg shell," suggested the Headmaster.

"Like a egg shell," assented Gawaine, and he said it many times. All through the evening meal people who sat near him heard him muttering, "Like a egg shell, like a egg shell."

The next day was clear, but Gawaine did not get up at dawn. Indeed, it was almost noon when the Headmaster found him cowering in bed, with the clothes pulled over his head. The principal called the Assistant Professor of Pleasaunce, and together they dragged the boy toward the forest.

"He'll be all right as soon as he gets a couple more dragons under his belt," explained the Headmaster.

The Assistant Professor of Pleasaunce agreed. "It would be a shame to stop such a fine run," he said. "Why, counting that one yesterday, he's killed fifty dragons."

They pushed the boy into a thicket above which hung a meager cloud of steam. It was obviously quite a small dragon. But Gawaine did not come back that night or the next. In fact, he never came back. Some weeks afterward brave spirits from the school explored the thicket, but they could find nothing to remind them of Gawaine except the metal parts of his medals. Even the ribbons had been devoured.

The Headmaster and the Assistant Professor of Pleasaunce agreed that it would be just as well not to tell the school how Gawaine had achieved his record and still less how he came to die. They held that it might have a bad effect on school spirit. Accordingly, Gawaine has lived in the memory of the school as its greatest hero. No visitor succeeds in leaving the building to-day without seeing a great shield which hangs on the wall of the dining hall. Fifty pairs of dragons' ears are mounted upon the shield and underneath in gilt letters is "Gawaine le Cœur-Hardy," followed by the simple inscription, "He killed fifty dragons." The record has never been equaled.

Number of words 3000
See page 261 for questions
Reading time in seconds _______
See page 495 for conversion table

Selection 11

The Educated Man

James Ansara

How are communication and education related? Do you educate yourself to communicate? Do you communicate to educate yourself? Lin Yutang once said, "The wise man reads both books and life itself." Does the following dramatic story say much the same thing? How differently can ideas be communicated?

My father was a man steeped in the aphorisms and parables of his race, with which he spiced even his everyday conversation. Best of all I liked the stories he often resorted to to illustrate truisms. I remember the first time he told the one about the education of Sheikh Yusif's son. I had finished college, and my problem was whether to continue my intellectual pursuits or to launch myself into the practical activities of the world. One evening I sought to discuss the matter with him, but instead of giving me his advice he offered to tell me a story that his father had once told him. It was after dinner and we were having black coffee flavored with the essence of roses. Between long, satisfying sips, this was the story he told: —

Once there was a sheikh, Yusif al-Hamadi, who was determined that some day his only son, Ali, should become a learned man.

When Ali completed his elementary studies under his tutors, the Sheikh called together his advisers and asked them where his son could acquire the best possible education. With one voice, they answered, "The University of El-Azhar, in Cairo."

So at El-Azhar, then the most renowned university in the whole world, the son of Sheikh Yusif studied with great energy and soon proved himself a true scholar. After eight years of study, the Ulama of the university pronounced Ali an educated man, and the son wrote that he was returning home.

As a scholar, Ali scorned the vanities of life and departed from Cairo riding a jackass and wearing the coarse raiment of an ascetic. Jogging along with his books behind him and his diploma fastened to his side, Ali lost himself in meditating upon the writings of the poets and philosophers.

When he was only a day's journey from his home, the young scholar entered a village mosque to rest for a while. It was Friday and the place was full of worshippers. A Khatib was preaching on the miraculous deeds of the Prophet.

Now Ali, as a result of his profound study of the

teachings of the Prophet, had become an uncompromising puritan of the Faith. Therefore, when the Khatib told his credulous congregation that Mohammed caused springs to flow in the desert, moved mountains, and flew on his horse to heaven, Ali was outraged.

"Stop!" cried Ali. "Believe not this false man. All that he has told you are lies, not the true faith. Our teacher, Mohammed, was not a supernatural being, but a man who saw the light, the truth —"

The Khatib interrupted to ask the young man upon what authority he contradicted him. Ali proudly informed him that he was a scholar, a graduate of the great University of El-Azhar. The preacher, with a sneer on his face, turned toward his congregation.

"This man, who calls himself a scholar, is a heretic, an atheist who dares come among you, the Faithful, and throw doubt upon the greatness of our Prophet Mohammed, blessed be his name. Cast him out of the mosque; he contaminates its sanctity."

The people seized Ali and dragged him to the street, beating and kicking him and tearing his clothes. Outside, his books and diploma were destroyed, and the unconscious Ali was tied to his jackass backward and stoned out of the village.

When word came of the approach of Ali, Sheikh Yusif and the neighboring sheikhs, whom the proud father had invited to join him to receive and honor his scholarly son, rode forth to meet the learned graduate of El-Azhar. But lo, the scholar was dangling from the back of a jackass, his learned head bouncing against its haunches. Bruised, half naked, he was muttering like an idiot.

Not for several days was Ali well enough to tell his father what had befallen him. When he finished, Sheikh Yusif sighed deeply and said, "Ali, you have come back to me only half educated. You must return to Cairo." The young man protested that there was nothing more the university could teach him, and Sheikh Yusif agreed. The rest of his education was to be outside of El-Azhar.

Back in Cairo, Ali was to discover a new world. According to his father's instructions, he spent the first six months in the shop of a merchant, bartering and wrangling in the busiest bazaar of Cairo. Following that, the chief of police took him in hand and introduced him to the life of the city in all its varied aspects. For a time he was a beggar outside one of the great mosques, a disciple of a magician, a waiter in a low café. Ali also came to know the life of a sailor, a wandering trader, and a laborer.

At the end of the fifth year, Ali informed his father that his education was completed and he was again returning home.

This time, the son of Sheikh Yusif left Cairo riding a spirited Arabian, dressed in silks and satins, and attended by a train of servants. His stops during the journey were brief, until he reached the village of the Khatib. It was again Friday and the same Khatib was declaiming the same miracles to the credulous peasants. Ali joined the congregation and listened to the words of the preacher with a rapture equal to that of his neighbors. His "Ah" and "Great is our Prophet" were even more fervent than those about him.

When the Khatib concluded his sermon, Ali humbly begged to be heard.

"In spite of my youth," said Ali, "I have studied much and traveled wide, seeking the truth and wisdom of our great Prophet, blessed be his name. But never have I heard or read a sermon equal in truth and piety to that of your reverend Khatib. Not only is he a learned man, but a holy one, for his knowledge of the life of the Prophet comes only from the deepest source of faith and piety, a knowledge denied to ordinary men. Fortunate are you in having such a saint. Fortunate am I too, for here ends my search for the holiest man of our age.

"O holy Khatib, fit companion of Caliphs, I beg of you a boon!"

The bewildered Khatib could only ask the nature of that boon.

"It is written in the Holy Koran that a relic from a saint brings endless blessings to the Faithful. A hair from thy beard, O Saintly One!"

Still perplexed, the Khatib could not, before his whole congregation, deny such a pious request. The young man with bowed head slowly mounted the *mumbar* and, in sight of all the people, with two extended fingers pulled a hair from the outthrust, flowing beard. Ali kissed it with deep reverence, folded it meticulously in a white silk kerchief, and placed it inside his shirt next to his heart.

A murmur arose from the congregation—their Khatib was a holy man! Even before Ali left the *mumbar*, the stampede toward the preacher had begun. By the time the son of Sheikh Yusif had forced his way through the mad crowd to the street, not a hair was left on the Khatib's face or head, not a shred of clothing on his body, and he lay behind the *mumbar* writhing and gasping like a plucked rooster.

That evening, Ali arrived home and there was great rejoicing in his father's house. His wit and dignity, his profound store of knowledge, his tact and manners, charmed all the guests and swelled the heart of his father with pride.

When at last the guests departed and Ali was alone with his father, he recounted to him his second visit to the village of the Khatib. The old Sheikh nodded his head approvingly and said: —

"Now, my son, I can die in peace. You have tempered book learning with worldly wisdom and returned a truly educated man."

Number of words 1320
See page 263 for questions
Reading time in seconds _______
See page 495 for conversion table

SELECTION 12

Getting Organized

Marlys Harris

According to research, you spend 70 percent of your waking time in doing one thing—communicating. You're either reading, writing, speaking, or listening—in short, communicating. How do you organize that big slice of your life? Read on. Help is at hand.

Deceptively, the principles of good organization—"First things first," "One thing at a time," "A place for everything and everything in its place," and "When in doubt, throw it out"— come right off Great-grandma Nettie's embroidered samplers. They're that obvious. So are the tactics: make lists, plan ahead, avoid distractions, clear away clutter. Getting organized is relatively easy. Staying that way is a lifetime project. You must hew to your goals with the ardor of a 12th-century monastic and avoid gossip sessions, unnecessary phone calls and long boozy lunches with the restraint of, well, a 12th-century monastic.

Despite all the professional and personal rewards it could provide, you've probably resisted getting yourself together. Yet to be organized, you don't have to arrange paper clips in symmetrical piles, eat your luncheon salad vegetables in alphabetical order or force your kids to make appointments to see you. You merely have to develop and use a system that helps you get things done. Says Margaret Cadman, a New York City management consultant who helps people and companies get organized: "There's no platonic ideal. Any system will work as long as it's a system."

But where to begin? Some people are wise to start with a cleanup because their mess has become so overwhelming. However, most consultants who help clients get organized believe that you should kick off your program by tackling the most difficult problem — time management. There always seems to be too much to do and not enough time to do it.

First, you should unjam your schedule by taking on less. Have the nerve to say no to those requests to head the Chip-and-Dip Committee for the company picnic or to write a memo on the Misuse of Company Stationery. Cutting down on the extras often helps you concentrate on what's important to you. Judy Lipton, 31, of Bellevue, Wash., focuses intently on her roles as wife, mother of four, full-time psychiatrist and civic activist. She rarely goes to parties, indulges in few social lunches, never watches TV and doesn't bother with theater or concerts. As she explains, "I eliminate unpleasant, unproductive or minimally useful activities."

Then there are the tasks that you can delegate to others. Tom Drucker, 36, a Los Angeles career consultant, and his wife, journalist Marcia Seligman, 45, took the extreme measure of hiring a 22-year-old man to be their "wife." He does the shopping, picks up the cleaning and performs the other household chores, which allows the couple to keep to a busy schedule of work and social activities. Of course, it comes as no surprise that you can pass the buck to subordinates and others whom you hire. However, you can also delegate work back to your boss. When she passes you in the hall, for example, you might remark, "Hi, Mrs. Bunbuster. I've been meaning to tell you that we've got a big problem with the spring curriculum plans and we'll need policy guidance." She will then have to look into the issue herself. That puts the mess on her desk. Naturally, if you are the boss, you must pass the hot potato back at once by replying, "Let me have your ideas by noon on Friday."

No matter how much or how little you want to accomplish, getting it all done usually requires following the standard practice of making a list. Writing it just before you leave work helps get you off to a fast start the next day. Stephanie Winston, author of *Getting Organized* (1978), suggests that you keep *two* lists. The first details all the foreseeable tasks you want to accomplish. Each day you pick 10 items from it to put on your daily list. "That's all anybody can reasonably do in a day," asserts Winston.

Lists work especially well in keeping complicated lives in hand. As senior partner of Rogers & Cowan, a big Hollywood public relations firm, Paul Bloch, 42, has his hands full catering to the needs of such film-star clients as James Caan, Dudley Moore and Elliot Gould. His workday, which starts at 7 A.M. so he can begin phoning clients in Paris, London and New York, consists of booking appearances, talking to newspaper columnists, arranging tours, negotiating deals and signing up new clients.

Twenty years ago Bloch got into the habit of writing a list before turning in for the night. Ritualistically, he uses yellow paper to set it apart from other paperwork and types his list in triplicate in red capital letters. Because he may list up to 50 tasks each weekday, including personal items such as buying a bottle of wine or asking a women for a date, Bloch puts an asterisk next to high-priority items to make sure he gets them done that day. When he completes a job, he crosses it out with a black pen. Bloch carries one copy with him, leaves another with his secretary for safekeeping and brings the third along in his Mercedes as an aide-mémoire.

Unfortunately, lists don't work well for everyone. Says Larry Baker, co-owner of the Time Management Center, a St. Louis, Mo. training firm: "Lists can defeat you before you start." People tend to make out a long daily list without reference to the length of time any task will take. "You wind up transferring most of Monday's 'to-dos' to Tuesday."

His solution is a combination time-management and behavior-modification program. First you keep a time log, writing down everything you do for two weeks to get a sense of the amount of time tasks typically take you. Then you set long-range goals for whatever phases of your life you deem important—career, family, hobbies, finances and spiritual development—and list activities that might help you accomplish them. For each goal, you pick one step toward it that you could reasonably take in a year.

Suppose you are a chemist who aims to become vice president in charge of new-product development. You might decide to research and write a report on the feasibility of manufacturing a line of low-calorie food for dieters, say, coq au vin, lemonade and pizza. You divide the project into smaller activities and give yourself deadlines for each. Perhaps you set a two-month deadline for finishing an exhaustive survey of market-research reports on foods that dieters crave but should not eat. Each week you list what you will have to do to meet your deadline—perhaps read and analyze two reports. You then list that task and all of the other tasks that you have to complete that week along with estimates of the time needed for each. Then you whip out your calendar and schedule all your projects, including perhaps an hour a day for product development. Larry Baker pleads that you set aside long periods of uninterrupted time for a complex, brain-busting task such as blending the elements of the pizza sauce. These are best scheduled during "peak time"—the hours of the day when you have the most energy.

In a recent time-management lecture, Baker told his audience of 40 executives that he was sure no more than half of them would ever attempt to do long-range goal setting. Nonetheless, there are ways to plan ahead effectively without getting stuck on your reason for living.

A number of books can help you tailor an organizational system to your own needs. Among the best: *Getting Organized* (Warner Books) by Stephanie Winston, a paperback for the housewife (or househusband) covering everything from financial records to chaotic closets; *How to Get Control of Your Time and Your Life* (Signet) by Alan Lakein, a guide to setting your lifetime goals; *Manage Your Time, Manage Your Work, Manage Yourself* (Amacom) by Merrill and Donna Douglass, an organizing manual for corporate executives; *Getting Things Done* (Bantam Books) by Edwin Bliss, an easy-to-read treatment of the most essential organizational principles; and *Working Smart* (Warner Books) by Michael LeBoeuf, a time-management guide aimed specifically at the workaholic.

Number of words 1320
See page 265 for questions
Reading time in seconds _______
See page 495 for conversion table

SELECTION 13

Cultural Literacy—What Is It?

E. D. Hirsch, Jr.

How do you communicate with the printed page? Easy! You just have to understand what's there. Wrong. You also have to understand what's not *there. That's the point of cultural literacy. Obviously, to communicate well, you should know what cultural literacy is all about. Here's your chance.*

The standard of literacy required by modern society has been rising throughout the developed world, but American literacy rates have not risen to meet this standard. What seemed an acceptable level in the 1950s is no longer acceptable in the late 1980s, when only highly literate societies can prosper economically. Much of Japan's industrial efficiency has been credited to its almost universally high level of literacy. But in the United States, only two thirds of our citizens are literate, and even among those the average level is too low and should be raised. The remaining third of our citizens need to be brought as close to true literacy as possible. Ultimately our aim should be to attain universal literacy at a very high level, to achieve not only greater economic prosperity but also greater social justice and more effective democracy. We Americans have long accepted literacy as a paramount aim of schooling, but only recently have some of us who have done research in the field begun to realize that literacy is far more than a skill and that it requires large amounts of specific information. The new insight is central. . . .

Professor Chall is one of several reading specialists who have observed that "world knowledge" is essential to the development of reading and writing skills. What she calls world knowledge I call cultural literacy, namely, the network of information that all competent readers possess. It is the background information, stored in their minds, that enables them to take up a newspaper and read it with an adequate level of comprehension, getting the point, grasping the implications, relating what they read to the unstated context which alone give meaning to what they read. In describing the contents of this neglected domain of background information, I try to direct attention to a new opening that can help our schools make the significant improvement in education that has so far eluded us. The achievement of high universal literacy is the key to all other fundamental improvements in American education.

Why is literacy so important in the modern world? Some of the reasons, like the need to fill out forms or get a good job, are so obvious that they needn't be discussed. But the chief reason is broader. The complex undertakings of modern life depend on the cooperation of many people with different specialties in different places. Where communications fail, so do the undertakings. (That is the moral of the story of the Tower of Babel.) The function of national literacy is to foster effective nationwide communications. Our chief instrument of communication over time and space is the standard national language, which is sustained by national literacy. Mature literacy alone enables the tower to be built, the business to be well managed, and the airplane to fly without crashing. All nationwide communications, whether by telephone, radio, TV, or writing are fundamentally dependent upon literacy, for the essence of literacy is not simply reading and writing but also the effective use of the standard literate language. In Spain and most of Latin America the literate language is standard written Spanish. In Japan it is standard written Japanese. In our country it is standard written English.

Linguists have use the term "standard written English" to describe both our written and spoken language, because they want to remind us that standard spoken English is based upon forms that have been fixed in dictionaries and grammars and are adhered to in books, magazines, and newspapers. Although standard written English has no intrinsic superiority to other languages and dialects, its stable written forms have now standardized the oral forms of the language spoken by educated Americans. The chief function of literacy is to make us masters of this standard instrument of knowledge and communication, thereby enabling us to give and receive complex information orally and in writing over time and space. Advancing technology, with its constant need for fast and complex communications, has made literacy ever more essential to commerce and domestic life. The literate language is more, not less, central in our society now than it was in the days before television and the silicon chip.

The recently rediscovered insight that literacy is more than a skill is based upon knowledge that all of us unconsciously have about language. We know instinctively that to understand what somebody is saying, we must understand more than the surface meanings of words; we have to understand the context as well. The need for background information applies all the more to reading and writing. To grasp the words on a page we have to know a lot of information that isn't set down on the page.

Consider the implications of the following experiment described in an article in *Scientific American*. A researcher goes to Harvard Square in Cambridge, Massachusetts, with a tape recorder hidden in his coat pocket. Putting a copy of the *Boston Globe* under his arm, he pretends to be a native. He says to passers-by, "How do you get to Central Square?" The passers-by thinking they are addressing a fellow Bostonian, don't even break their stride when they give their replies, which consist of a few words like "First stop on the subway."

The next day the researcher goes to the same spot, but this time he presents himself as a tourist, obviously unfamiliar with the city. "I'm from out of town," he says. "Can you tell me how to get to Central Square?" This time the tapes show that people's answers are much longer and more rudimentary. A typical one goes, "Yes, well you go down on the subway. You can see the entrance over there, and when you get downstairs you buy a token, put it in the slot, and you go over to the side that says Quincy. You take the train headed for Quincy, but you get off very soon, just the first stop is Central Square, and be sure you get off there. You'll know it because there's a big sign on the wall. It says Central Square." And so on.

Passers-by were intuitively aware that communication between strangers requires an estimate of how much relevant information can be taken for granted in the other person. If they can take a lot for granted, their communications can be short and efficient, subtle and complex. But if strangers share very little knowledge, their communications must be long and relatively rudimentary.

In order to put in perspective the importance of background knowledge in language, I want to connect the lack of it with our recent lack of success in teaching mature literacy to all students. The most broadly based evidence about our teaching of literacy comes from the National Assessment of Educational Progress (NAEP). This nationwide measurement, mandated by Congress, shows that between 1970 and 1980 seventeen-year-olds declined in their ability to understand written materials, and the decline was especially striking in the top group, those able to read at an "advanced" level. Although these scores have now begun to rise, they remain alarmingly low. Still more precise quantitative data have come from the scores of the verbal Scholastic Aptitude Test (SAT). According to John B. Carroll, a distinguished psychometrician, the verbal SAT is essentially a test of "advanced vocabulary knowledge," which makes it a fairly sensitive instrument for measuring levels of literacy. It is well known that verbal SAT scores have declined dramatically in the past fifteen years, and though recent reports have shown them rising again, it is from a very low base. Moreover, performance on the verbal SAT has been slipping steadily *at the top*. Ever fewer numbers of our best and brightest students are making high scores on the test.

Before the College Board disclosed the full statistics in 1984, antialarmists could argue that the fall in average verbal scores could be explained by the rise in the number of disadvantaged students taking the SATs. That argument can no longer be made. It's now clear that not only our disadvantaged but also our best educated and most talented young people are showing diminished verbal skills. To be precise, out of a constant pool of about a million test takers each year, 56 percent more students scored above 600 in 1972 than did so in 1984. More startling yet, the percentage drop was even greater for those scoring above 650—73 percent.

In the mid 1980s American business leaders have

become alarmed by the lack of communication skills in the young people they employ. Recently, top executives of some large U.S. companies, including CBS and Exxon, met to discuss the fact that their younger middle-level executives could no longer communicate their ideas effectively in speech or writing. This group of companies has made a grant to the American Academy of Arts and Sciences to analyze the causes of this growing problem. They want to know why, despite breathtaking advances in the technology of communication, the effectiveness of business communication has been slipping, to the detriment of our competitiveness in the world. The figures from NAEP surveys and the scores on the verbal SAT are solid evidence that literacy has been declining in this country just when our need for effective literacy has been sharply rising.

I now want to juxtapose some evidence for another kind of educational decline, one that is related to the drop in literacy. During the period 1970–1985, the amount of shared knowledge that we have been able to take for granted in communicating with our fellow citizens has also been declining. More and more of our young people don't know things we used to assume they knew.

A side effect of the diminution in shared information has been a noticeable increase in the number of articles in such publications as *Newsweek* and the *Wall Street Journal* about the surprising ignorance of the young. My son John, who recently taught Latin in high school and eighth grade, often told me of experiences which indicate that these articles are not exaggerated. In one of his classes he mentioned to his students that Latin, the language they were studying, is a dead language that is no longer spoken. After his pupils had struggled for several weeks with Latin grammar and vocabulary, this news was hard for some of them to accept. One girl raised her hand to challenge my son's claim. "What do they speak in Latin America?" she demanded.

At least she had heard of Latin America. Another day my son asked his Latin class if they knew the name of an epic poem by Homer. One pupil shot up his hand and eagerly said, "The Alamo!" Was it just a slip for *The Iliad*? No, he didn't know what the Alamo was, either. To judge from other stories about information gaps in the young, many American schoolchildren are less well informed than this pupil.

My son assures me that his pupils are not ignorant. They know a great deal. Like every other human group they share a tremendous amount of knowledge among themselves, much of it learned in school. The trouble is that, from the standpoint of their literacy and their ability to communicate with others in our culture, what they know is ephemeral and narrowly confined to their own generation. Many young people strikingly lack the information that writers of American books and newspapers have traditionally taken for granted among their readers from all generations. Our children's lack of intergenerational information is a serious problem for the nation. The decline of literacy and the decline of shared knowledge are closely related, interdependent facts.

Number of words 1930
See page 267 for questions
Reading time in seconds _______
See page 495 for conversion table

Selection 14

Habit: Make It Your Friend, Not Your Enemy

William James

In this world, what is strongest? Ovid, born in 43 B.C., thought he knew. He put it this way: "Nothing is stronger than habit." How can you put habit to work to maximize your efforts to improve reading and communication? William James has some suggestions.

"Habit a second nature! Habit is ten times natures," the Duke of Wellington is said to have exclaimed; and the degree to which this is true no one probably can appreciate as well as one who is a veteran soldier himself. The daily drill and the years of discipline end by fashioning a man completely over again, as to most of the possibilities of his conduct.

"There is a story," says Professor Huxley, "which is credible enough, though it may not be true, of a practical joker who, seeing a discharged veteran carrying home his dinner, suddenly called out, 'Attention!' whereupon the man instantly brought his hands down, and lost his mutton and potatoes in the gutter. The drill had been thorough, and its effects had become embodied in the man's nervous structure."

Riderless cavalry-horses, at many a battle, have been seen to come together and go through their customary evolutions at the sound of the bugle-call. Most domestic beasts seem machines almost pure and simple, undoubtingly, unhesitatingly doing from minute to minute the duties they have been taught, and giving no sign that the possibility of an alternative ever suggests itself to their mind. Men grown old in prison have asked to be readmitted after being once set free. In a railroad accident a menagerie-tiger, whose cage had broken open, is said to have emerged, but presently crept back again, as if too much bewildered by his new responsibilities, so that he was without difficulty secured.

Habit is thus the enormous fly-wheel of society, its most precious conservative agent. It alone is what keeps us all within the bounds of ordinance, and saves the children of fortune from the envious uprising of the poor. It alone prevents the hardest and most repulsive walks of life from being deserted by those brought up to tread therein. It keeps the fisherman and the deckhand at sea through the winter; it holds the miner in his darkness, and nails the countryman to his log-cabin and his lonely farm through all the months of snow; it protects us from invasion by the natives of the desert and the frozen zone. It dooms us all to fight out the battle of life upon the lines of our nurture or our early choice, and to make the best of a pursuit that disagrees, because there is no other for which we are fitted, and it is too late to begin again. It keeps different social strata from mixing. Already at the age of twenty-five you see the professional mannerism settling down on the young commercial traveler, on the young doctor, on the young minister, on the young counselor-at-law. You see the little lines of cleavage running through the character, the tricks of thought, the prejudices, the ways of the "shop," in a word, from which the man can by-and-by no more escape than his coat-sleeve can suddenly fall into a new set of folds. On the whole, it is best he should not escape. It is well for the world that in most of us, by the age of thirty, the character has set like plaster, and will never soften again.

If the period between twenty and thirty is the critical one in the formation of intellectual and professional habits, the period below twenty is more important still for the fixing of *personal* habits, properly so called, such as vocalization and pronunciation, gesture, motion, and address. Hardly ever is a language learned after twenty spoken without a foreign accent; hardly ever can a youth transferred to the society of his betters unlearn the nasality and other vices of speech bred in him by the associations of his growing years. Hardly ever, indeed, no matter how much money there be in his pocket, can he even learn to *dress* like a gentleman-born. The merchants offer their wares as eagerly to him as to the veriest "swell," but he simply *cannot* buy the right things. An invisible law, as strong as gravitation, keeps him within his orbit, arrayed this year as he was the last; and how his better-clad acquaintances contrive to get the things they wear will be for him a mystery till his dying day.

The great thing, then, in all education, is to *make our nervous system our ally instead of our enemy.* It is to fund and capitalize our acquisitions, and live at ease upon the interest of the fund. *For this we must make automatic and habitual, as early as possible, as many useful actions as we can,* and guard against the growing into ways that are likely to be disadvantageous to us, as we should guard against the plague. The more of the details of our daily life we can hand over to the effortless custody of automatism, the more our higher powers of mind will be set free for their own proper work. There is no more miserable human being than one in whom nothing is habitual but indecision, and for whom the lighting of every cigar, the drinking of every cup, the time of rising and going to bed every day, and the beginning of every bit of work, are subjects of express volitional deliberation. Full half the time of such a man goes to the deciding, or regretting, of matters which ought to be so ingrained in him as practically not to exist for his consciousness at all. If there be such daily duties not yet ingrained in any one of my readers, let him begin this very hour to set the matter right.

In Professor Bain's chapter on "The Moral Habits" there are some admirable practical remarks laid down. Two great maxims emerge from his treatment. The first is that in the acquisition of a new habit, or the leaving off of an old one, we must take care to *launch ourselves with as strong and decided an initiative as possible.* Accumulate all the possible circumstances which shall reenforce the right motives; put yourself assiduously in conditions that encourage the new way; make engagements incompatible with the old; take a public pledge, if the case allows; in short, envelop your resolution with every aid you know. This will give your new beginning such a momentum that the temptation to break down will not occur as soon as it otherwise might; and every day during which a breakdown is postponed adds to the chances of its not occurring at all.

The second maxim is: *Never suffer an exception to occur till the new habit is securely rooted in your life.* Each lapse is like the letting fall of a ball of string which one is carefully winding up; a single slip undoes more than a great many turns will wind again. *Continuity* of training is the great means of making the nervous system act infallibly right. As Professor Bain says:

"The peculiarity of the moral habits, contradistinguishing them from the intellectual acquisitions, is the presence of two hostile powers, one to be gradually raised into the ascendant over the other. It is necessary, above all things, in such a situation, never to lose a battle. Every gain on the wrong side undoes the effect of many conquests on the right. The essential precaution, therefore, is so to regulate the two opposing powers that the one may have a series of uninterrupted successes, until repetition has fortified it to such a degree as to enable it to cope with the opposition, under any circumstances. This is the theoretically best career of mental progress."

The need of securing success at the *outset* is imperative. Failure at first is apt to damp the energy of all future attempts, whereas past experiences of success nerve one to future vigor. Goethe says to a man who consulted him about an enterprise but mistrusted his own powers: "Ach! you need only blow on your hands!" And the remark illustrates the effect on Goethe's spirits of his own habitually successful career.

The question of "tapering off," in abandoning such habits as drink and opium-indulgence comes in here, and is a question about which experts differ within certain limits, and in regard to what may be best for an individual case. In the main, however, all expert opinion would agree that abrupt acquisition of the new habit is the best way, *if there be a real possibility of carrying it out.* We must be careful not to give the will so stiff a task as to insure its defeat at the very outset; but, *provided one can stand it,* a sharp period of suffering, and then a free time, is the best thing to aim at, whether in giving up a habit like that of opium, or in simply changing one's hours of rising or of work. It is surprising how soon a desire will die of inanition if it be *never* fed.

"One must first learn, unmoved, looking neither to the right nor left, to walk firmly on the strait and narrow path, before one can begin 'to make one's self over again.' He who every day makes a fresh resolve is like one who, arriving at the edge of the ditch he is to leap, forever stops and returns for a fresh run. Without *unbroken* advance there is no such thing as *accumulation* of the ethical forces possible, and to make this possible, and to exercise us and habituate us in it, is the sovereign blessing of regular work."

A third maxim may be added to the preceding pair: *Seize the very first possible opportunity to act on every resolution you make, and on every emotional prompting you may experience in the direction of the habits you aspire to gain.* It is not in the moment of their forming, but in the moment of their producing *motor effects*, that resolves and aspirations communicate the new "set" to the brain. As the author last quoted remarks: "The actual presence of the practical opportunity alone furnishes the fulcrum upon which the lever can rest, by means of which the moral will may multiply its strength, and raise itself aloft. He who has no solid ground to press against will never get beyond the stage of empty gesture-making. . . ."

As a final practical maxim, relative to these habits of the will, we may, then, offer something like this: *Keep the faculty of effort alive in you by a little gratuitous exercise every day.* That is, be systematically ascetic or heroic in little unnecessary points, do every day or two something for no other reason than that you would rather not do it, so that when the hour of dire need draws nigh, it may find you not unnerved and untrained to stand the test. Asceticism of this sort is like the insurance which a man pays on his house and goods. The tax does him no good at the time, and possibly may never bring him a return. But if the fire *does* come, his having paid it will be his salvation from ruin. So with the man who has daily inured himself to habits of concentrated attention, energetic volition, and self-denial in unnecessary things. He will stand like a tower when everything rocks around him, and when his softer fellow-mortals are winnowed like chaff in the blast.

The physiological study of mental conditions is thus the most powerful ally of hortatory ethics. The hell to be endured hereafter, of which theology tells, is no worse than the hell we make for ourselves in this world by habitually fashioning our characters in the wrong way. Could the young but realize how soon they will become mere walking bundles of habits, they would give more heed to their conduct while in the plastic state. We are spinning our own fates, good or evil, and never to be undone. Every smallest stroke of virtue or of vice leaves its never so little scar. The drunken Rip Van Winkle, in Jefferson's play, excuses himself for every fresh dereliction by saying, "I won't count this time!" Well! he may not count it, and a kind Heaven may not count it; but it is being counted none the less. Down among his nerve-cells and fibers the molecules are counting it, registering and storing it up to be used against him when the next temptation comes. Nothing we ever do is, in strict scientific literalness, wiped out. Of course this has its good side as well as its bad one. As we become permanent drunkards by so many separate drinks, so we become saints in the moral, and authorities and experts in the practical and scientific spheres, by so many separate acts and hours of work. Let no youth have any anxiety about the upshot of his education, whatever the line of it may be. If he keep faithfully busy each hour of the working day, he may safely leave the final result to itself. He can with perfect certainty count on waking up some fine morning, to find himself one of the competent ones of his generation, in whatever pursuit he may have singled out. Silently, between all the details of his business, the *power of judging* in all that class of matter will have built itself up within him as a possession that will never pass away. Young people should know this truth in advance. The ignorance of it has probably engendered more discouragement and faint-heartedness in youths embarking on arduous careers than all other causes put together.

Number of words 2245
See page 271 for questions
Reading time in seconds _______
See page 495 for conversion table

Your Words Make You What You Are

S. I. Hayakawa

So you want to communicate more effectively? Then look more closely at the vocabulary and language habits of those around you as well as at your own. According to Wendell Johnson, your sanity and well-being depend on it. That means communicating with yourself—most important. Let Hayakawa explain.

Do you—well, let's not make it personal—do your friends talk too much? Are there some among them who are never happy unless they are hogging the conversation?

Do you know people who are so wound up inside that they seem to continue talking whether they want to or not, raising one difficult question after another, yet never listening to the answers offered so that they end up still asking the same questions? (That's "oververbalization.")

Do you have friends who have only one or two topics of conversation and become bored the moment you start talking about anything else? (That's "content rigidity.")

Do you often have to listen to pointless stories that go on and on in endless circumstantial detail? (That's "dead level abstracting.")

Do you also know people whose talk consists entirely of predictable formulae—whether pompous academic clichés or slang phrases? (That's "formal rigidity.")

Do you have friends who are so afraid of making mistakes that they cannot open their mouths? (That's "underverbalization.")

And have you ever noticed that, in spite of the vast difference in output, the oververbalized often don't get any more said than the underverbalized?

In short, what are the language habits of the people around you—and also, what are your own? For many of these people are in messes, always quarreling, or always overexcited, or always suffering from feelings of inadequacy, or always being victimized by their own prejudices. They are people in quandaries. Is there any connection between their quandaries and their language habits? Are they, as Wendell Johnson says, merely the froth on the beer or an important ingredient of the beer itself?

It is Wendell Johnson's contention that one's language habits are a part of one's emotional and intellectual difficulties, as well as a part of one's sanity and well-being. Like other semanticists, he rejects the common notion that "peoples' words don't matter, it's what they think and feel and do that counts." The common notion ignores the reverse possibility, namely, that people may think and feel and act as they do because of the words and the patterns of words in terms of which they have been taught to describe themselves, the world about them, and their problems.

You cannot get an intelligent answer to a stupidly formulated question. Most of what we call "thinking" is simply a matter of talking to oneself silently. What kind of questions, then, do you ask yourself—and is it any wonder that you get dopey answers—or no answers at all? And since action is the result of what we have "thought," is not language the central instrument of our adjustment—or maladjustment? And by language Professor Johnson means not only one's vocabulary and syntax, but one's unconscious assumptions about the relationship between words and things. If you believe that "thirteen" is an "unlucky number" or that "spit is a nasty word," what kind of a theory of language have you got? And does not that theory of language affect deeply your evaluation of reality, and, therefore, your behavior?

For people in quandaries, then, Professor Johnson suggests not merely the usual inquires into physical health, the influences of childhood environment, present emotional conflicts, etc., but also into language habits—(1) the ways in which people verbally formulate their problems, (2) the ways in which they react to what other people say, and (3) the ways in which they react to their own formulations.

Of the three, all of them important, perhaps the most important is the last, since, as he says in one of his frequent penetrating observations, "Every speaker is usually his most interested and most affected listener." We are all like the Red Queen in "Alice." What we say three times is true. And, no matter how nonsensical the statement, it becomes even truer with each further repetition. Moreover, since the uttering of nonsense is rarely systematically discouraged, but is on the contrary actively promoted by a significant portion of our educators, our press, the radio, the advertising profession and the pulpit, it is hardly to be wondered at that we find ourselves, in our times, to be not only people in quandaries, but also labor unions in quandaries, employers in quandaries, political parties in quandaries, and nations in quandaries.

For years, as director of the psychological and speech clinic at the State University of Iowa, Professor Johnson has been "company to misery, holding the damp, trembling hand of frustration." Coming to him with "speech difficulties" to be straightened out, his students (and their parents) reveal one neurotic quandary after another lying at the root of their troubles. The similarity of the patterns of frustration and despair shown by innumerable patients early led Professor Johnson to the conclusion that "conditions peculiar to our general culture" rather than individualized aberrations, are responsible for most of the difficulties. Starting as a psychological speech clinician, therefore, he soon found it necessary to become both a cultural anthropologist and a social critic.

In selecting our language habits as the most general and most pervasive of the cultural conditions that contribute to frustration and neurosis, Professor Johnson follows the trail marked out by Alfred Korzybski's *Science and Sanity* (1933), which is by far the most suggestive work in the study of the relations between language and life. (It is significant that Korzybski originally referred to his work as "general anthropology.") Language, as Korzybski and Johnson agree, is the principal instrument by means of which human cultures are created and transmitted.

Culture, indeed, might be defined as the patterns of reaction by means of which groups respond to socially transmitted sets of signs, symbols, and sign-situations; and even our responses to nonverbal signs (traffic lights, religious symbols, the alignment of players on a football field, etc.) are instilled in us mainly through accompanying verbal instructions. But throughout our culture, we have inherited patterns of reaction to signs and symbols (including especially verbal signs and symbols) that are essentially prescientific and primitive.

An example of this primitivism is the kind of person who, unconsciously believing that, because there is such a word as "success," there is such a thing, keeps trying to attain it—without ever having attempted to formulate what he means by "success." In spite of good positions or comfortable incomes, such persons manage to keep themselves miserable, because the goal they set up for themselves is so vaguely defined that *they can't ever tell whether they have reached it or not.* Hence a lifelong uneasiness, with hypertension or gastric ulcers to boot. (If the reader asks at this point, "But what is success?" he needs Johnson's book very badly.)

Maladjusted people, he points out, keep asking incredibly silly questions, "Why did this have to happen to me?" "Is it right to make a lot of money?" "How can I be popular?" "What is the unpardonable sin?" "What is the meaning of life?" "People in quandaries," he says, "are peculiar not only because they persist in asking themselves such vague and unanswerable questions, but also because they don't realize that their questions are unanswerable. In fact, they don't seem to realize that their maladjustment is in any way related to their persistence in asking, and in trying to answer, such questions. They seem quite puzzled by the suggestion that their questions need rewording. They don't want to reword them. They want answers, absolute, now-and-forever, correct answers. And so they remain maladjusted, pursuing verbal will-o'-the-wisps with ever increasing tension and despair."

In other words, people in quandaries have no conception of language as an instrument or technique for the exploration of the realities concerning themselves and the external world. It is as if, just because they happened to find near them a pair of nail-clippers when they wanted to open a can of sardines, they were to keep on indefinitely trying to get at the sardines with the nail-clippers. In the discussion of personal problems, political and social issues, international war and peace, few of us do any better; we use any linguistic instrument that happens to be handy (left lying around by Dorothy Dix or Gabriel Heatter or your late lamented Aunt Harriet). The result is that, in our attempts at solving personal and social problems, we spend most of our time throwing verbal tools around without ever reaching the subverbal sardines—the world of not-words, where the facts, both of inner needs and of external reality, lie.

If the reader expects, on the basis of a cocktail

party acquaintance with semantics, that what he has to do in order to be saved is to learn some extremely complex discipline having to do with "the correct meanings of words," he will be disappointed. The general semantics of Korzybski, upon which Professor Johnson relies heavily, is based on modern sociology, anthropology, psychoanalysis, biology and mathematical physics. Out of these and other modern disciplines, general semantics distills certain "rules for orientation." It seeks to train people to check their language with the facts, to have adequate flexibility in their approach to problems, to be constantly on the lookout for factors that may have been omitted from one's calculations, to understand and evaluate in the light of the great sociological and cultural fact of human interdependence, and to be wary of those unanswerable questions which scientists have been trained to leave alone, but which, when discussed, split people into warring factions.

It seeks, in short, to train people in the application of scientific method to all of life, instead of to just a part of it. "The fundamental thesis of this book," as the author says, "is simply that science, clearly understood, can be used from moment to moment in everyday life, and that it provides a sound basis for warmly human and efficient living."

In large part the method of science "consists in (a) asking clear, answerable questions in order to direct one's (b) observations . . . which are then (c) reported as accurately as possible . . . after which (d) any pertinent beliefs or assumptions that were held before the observations were made are revised in the light of observations made." As the reader can see (although scientists themselves often don't), such a method of inquiry can be applied to personal and social problems no less than to the action of hydrocarbons.

But the opposite habits of (a) asking unanswerable questions, (b) making no observations, but relying on the magic of snarlwords, (c) reporting as facts inferences based on fears and prejudices and (d) refusing to revise one's beliefs despite hell and high water, are systematically instilled into us by our cultural environment. The problem, therefore, is the restoration of the mother wit with which we were originally endowed.

Professor Johnson says that learning general semantics is like learning to float, both extremely easy and extremely difficult: "You don't do anything in order to float. What you have to learn is to do nothing that would keep you from floating." Similarly, general semantics is largely a matter of learning to do nothing that would prevent you from using your natural intelligence—a fantastically difficult task for anyone living within earshot of modern propaganda.

Reading Professor Johnson's account of how to achieve the relaxed, alert and healthy orientations of modern science and general semantics is, like all liberating experiences, exciting and exhilarating. He has a genuine knack for explanation and a happy way of summing up a whole series of sober observations in a vivid epigram. (On scientific agreement: "If a doctor, two interns and a nurse all agree that there are no grasshoppers on your suit jacket, you might as well quit trying to brush them off.")

The reader will have to do some serious thinking in the course of the book, but because every theoretical consideration is illumined by sharp and often amusing examples drawn from politics, folklore, business, parenthood, literature, race relations and everyday life, he will derive the sense of understanding that comes from knowing not only what the author thinks, but how it feels to think that way.

Finally, in addition to giving at the close many suggestions for further amateur and professional research in semantics so that the reader may check the truth of what he says, Professor Johnson applies general semantics to the specific problem of stuttering. Both the theoretical formulations in his book and the results he has obtained in his speech clinic at the University of Iowa show that, by following up the leads suggested by general semantics, he has apparently solved the problem. *People in Quandaries,* therefore, offers both the pudding of semantics and a major proof. I can't imagine what more a reader could ask.

Number of words 2108
See page 273 for questions
Reading time in seconds _______
See page 495 for conversion table

Around the World in 80 Nanoseconds

Patricia O'Toole

Get our your crystal ball. You know what communications was *like. You know what it* is *like. Now imagine what it* will be *like off in the future. After all, the person who looks ahead, gets ahead, right? Here's your chance to see what's coming—but only an 80 nanosecond look!*

Risky business, surveying the universe and announcing what the future will look like. Easy to muff, and there's enough hubris in the act to make critics reach for their switchblades. Alvin Toffler, who has filed reports from the future for 20 years, has been derided for practicing "schlock sociology," upbraided for superficiality, and dismissed as a collector of "the fuzz that grows on the inside of think tanks." He survived, consoled no doubt by the international celebrity and bestsellerdom of his books, *Future Shock* (1970) and *The Third Wave* (1980).

Toffler knows better than to mention it, but how delectable it must be to see the scoffers proved wrong. Farfetched as it once seemed, communism did fall apart, computers are common household appliances, millions of Americans do work at home, and U.S. industry no longer rules the world economy.

Now Toffler is back, with *Powershift*, his vision of the changes likely to come about from the clashes of a most unholy trinity: knowledge, wealth, and violence. He predicts that power will shift increasingly to those best at "information judo"—people who can capitalize on technology, new discoveries, databases, competitors' secrets, and other kinds of knowledge. Because information "can be grasped by the weak and the poor" as well as the strong and the rich, Toffler believes the change is "truly revolutionary." Information is permanently subversive, "a continuing threat to the powerful."

In this brave new world the facts of life are two: struggle and instability. The freer the flow of information, the harder it is to hold on to power; and the harder it is to hold on to power, the greater the desire to control the flow of information. Once a computer network becomes the central nervous system of an office or factory, for example, workers cannot function without access to information—lots of it. But when workers know as much as their superiors do, they're likely to challenge authority. Bad news becomes more difficult to conceal. Equivocators are easily unmasked.

Conflicts over information are so widespread in the business world that they have given rise to a new breed, the chief information officer (CIO). Aside from buying new computers and orchestrating data, CIOs regulate employee access to information (which typically means excluding as many people as possible) and referee the brawls that tend to break out when executives try to decide whose assumptions will be built into the company's software. CIOs, Toffler says are the "executive thought police."

Toffler sees information judo as the martial art of the future, but *Powershift* suggests that business already has earned its black belt. As soon as a high tech company scores with a new computer chip, rivals worldwide take it apart to figure out how to copy it, a process known as "reverse engineering." No need to spend years and millions on research and development if someone else will do the work and spending for you. Industrial espionage, now traveling under the dignified alias of "competitive intelligence," is ubiquitous. Toffler reports that at General Mills even the janitors are expected to ask their vendors what janitors elsewhere are buying.

As citizens, Americans don't begin to hold their own on the information judo mat, Toffler believes. When I phoned him to talk about *Powershift* he despaired of the national reverence for statistics and our unskeptical acceptance of utterances from political quarters. Whenever government speaks, he said, "we need to ask, *Cui bono*? Whose interests are being served? And who massaged this information before it got to me?" Even the lowliest underdog has the power of disbelief (as Elizabeth Janeway noted in *Powers of the*

Weak), but Americans exercise it less often than many of their fellow humans. Toffler ascribes our credulousness to good fortune. Guaranteed a relatively free flow of information by the First Amendment, we enjoy thinking ourselves exempt from the censorship and prevarication typical of the world's kakistocracies.

If the damming up, doctoring, and denaturing of information ill serve a democracy, Toffler also thinks that an unrestricted flow of information might not be so good either. What would become of the confidentiality of medical records? The right to other kinds of privacy? What would happen to technological innovations? A pharmaceutical house, for instance, would hardly be encouraged to create new drugs if those drugs could be bootlegged before the company earned back its research expenses.

Yet the enforcement of such property rights is already impossible in some spheres. The high cost of college texts is driving students to make their own "books" at copying machines. Professors do the same thing, then sell the "books" more cheaply than the bookstore can. Consumers make knockoffs, too. Who at this point doesn't own audiocassettes, videotapes, or software programs copied from someone else's? The ease of duplicating information is making spies and pirates of us all.

Powershift is a deliberately dispassionate book, intended to make readers think rather than make them mad. My hunch is that Toffler hopes the have-nots will be able to use information to shift a little weight to their end of the teeter-totter, but he is no utopian. While some like to think that communications satellites and global media networks will bathe the planet in mutual understanding and peace, Toffler sees them as mere tools—amoral, and just as available to terrorists who hijack cruise ships as to the heroes of the struggle against apartheid.

The book's most nightmarish example of potential media terrorism involves a chilling parallel between today's European environmental extremists and the return-to-purity rhetoric that preceded Hitler's rise to power. Toffler asks the reader to picture an ecological catastrophe on the order of Bhopal but in Western Europe or the United States. Add economic distress and "fundamentalist cries that the disaster was inflicted by God as punishment for 'permissiveness' and immorality. . . . Imagine an attractive, articulate 'Eco-Adolf' who promises not just to solve the immediate crisis but to purify the society materially, morally, and politically—if only he is given extraconstitutional powers." Television cameras might be there to record the drama, but they could not stop it, any more than they stopped the bloodshed in Tiananmen Square.

Not all the news in Toffler's letter from the future is bad. Information, by virtue of its sheer abundance, already has begun to shift power away from the privileged few. When Britain banned the book *Spycatcher*, claiming that is compromised national security, media from other countries instantly broadcast *Spycatcher*'s "secrets" around the globe. The ban was lifted. And when a doctor diagnoses a disease, an inquisitive patient can dial up a medical database and retrieve the latest journal articles on the subject. "In short," Toffler writes, "the knowledge monopoly of the medical profession has been thoroughly smashed." Toffler does not cite this example, but the popularity of consumer guides rating automobile performance has spurred automakers to pay more attention to quality. There is no profit in making a lousy car when one is easily found out.

Despite his low regard for American education, Toffler is optimistic about the nation's chances for success in a world where knowledge is paramount. He takes heart from the country's steady stream of innovation, the world's hunger for American culture, and the evidence that for all the learning that doesn't happen in schools, a great deal goes on elsewhere. In our conversation he pointed out that 15 years ago few Americans knew their way around a computer. (Only a decade ago a reviewer of *The Third Wave* expressed amazement that Toffler had actually researched and written it using a computer.) Today there are some 18 million PCs in home use across the country, and most people didn't go to school to learn how to use them. Some hired consultants, others took workshops at computer stores, but most learned from friends.

In the global economy, Toffler sees a shift in manufacturing from countries with cheap labor to those with the brainiest factories. With refinements in technology and information, he writes, labor costs "become a smaller fraction of total costs of production," yielding "savings far beyond any that can be squeezed out of hourly workers." It may prove more efficient to "run an advanced facility in Japan or the United States, with a handful of highly educated, highly paid employees, than a backward factory in China or Brazil that depends on masses of badly educated, low-wage workers."

In addition to sketching the upheavals likely to come from the knowledge revolution, Toffler strides, seven leagues at a pace, through the vast territories of wealth and violence. He foresees an escalation of racial and sexual strife as more groups insist upon recognition of their distinctiveness, the continuation of the menacing arms buildup in the Third World, the spread of private spy networks, turbulence in Europe, and the possibility that members of one religion or another could create a radically different world order by banding together in a supranational alliance.

What will all these changes do to the human spirit? What kind of people are we likely to become if Alvin Toffler is right? Will life be better or worse? Toffler doesn't say. But he makes a reader wonder.

Number of words 1520
See page 275 for questions
Reading time in seconds _______
See page 495 for conversion table

Selection 17

Information Superhighways

Albert Gore, Jr.

Revolutions! History is full of them. Your present concern? The startling information revolution. Your first step—to understand exactly what it is. The next step—to develop ways of dealing with it. You know how to travel the highways; now head for the superhighways.

The United States could benefit greatly—in research, in education, in economic development, and in scores of other areas—by efficiently processing and dealing with information that is available but unused. What we need is a nationwide network of "information superhighways," linking scientists, business people, educators, and students by fiber-optic cable. This network would encourage a second information revolution.

In 1979, I proposed a network of information superhighways, and the only person I could find who was really enthusiastic about it was a gentleman from Corning Glass. Executives in the communications industry were at first reluctant to endorse this idea. Indeed, hostile would actually be a more accurate description.

Today, the idea has really taken hold in all of the industries related to communications, computing, and information. The president's science adviser, Allan Bromley, recently said that such a network is the single most cost-effective step America could take to become more competitive in the world economy. It is also the single most important step the United States could take to improve its proficiency in science and technology and research.

We're now drowning in information. We have automated the process of collecting information, but we have not successfully mastered the task of organizing and distilling the information for our productive use. Years ago, I created a new word called "ex-formation," information that exists outside the conscious awareness of any living being but that exists in such enormous quantities that it sloshes around and changes the context and the weight of any problem one addresses. The problem is to convert "ex-formation" into information and then to convert the information into knowledge and eventually to distill the knowledge into wisdom, the hardest process of all.

For example, the Mission to Planet Earth satellite program will soon send down to the Earth's surface from orbit every day a quantity of information equal to all the bits of data in the entire Library of Congress. We can't even handle the information we now have about Planet Earth.

Some have argued we already have all the information we need to decipher the operations of the climate system and the changes we're making to that system. NASA is proposing to send up a new generation of data-collecting satellites and spend 17 years compiling a lot more information. And yet, just one satellite system, Landsat, in orbit for the past 18 years, can photograph the entire Earth's surface every two weeks. More than 95% of Landsat's pictures are stored in digital form and have never fired a single neuron in a single human brain. Teams of researchers, using the most complicated models now available, cannot communicate with each other and work together productively to solve problems, because in order to communicate they have to find a way to download their models and their results onto magnetic tapes, take the tapes to another lab, and read the tapes so other researchers can review and talk about them.

As we face this critical problem, there is really no excuse for not enabling teams of researchers to link up with each other in real time with information flows appropriate to the tasks we have assigned them. A National Research and Education Network would make that possible.

Excess of Data, Hunger for Knowledge

Current U.S. information policy offers disturbing parallels to U.S. agricultural policy. Vast silos of grain are rotting in storage while millions starve to death. Worldwide, some 40,000 children under the age of 5 die of starvation and related maladies such as diarrhea every single day, and the nation allows these vast bins of food to rot. Likewise, storage bins of data coexist with ignorance and a hunger for the information needed to solve the problems this world confronts.

Global climate change is only one such problem. Major U.S. corporations spend millions of dollars seeking answers to questions about how to plan for the future and how to gain a competitive edge. In almost every case, all of the information they need to answer those questions is already available. But they have no idea how to find the needle in the haystack, how to sift through the "ex-formation" to get the information, to distill it, to get the knowledge and make the judgments required to guide those corporations.

Some argue we're now on the seventh generation of advanced computers while barely out of the first generation of computer network technology. What's going to happen when an advanced computer that costs $20 million today sells for $250,000? And what will happen when the competitors of American companies in a unified Europe and in the Pacific Rim have these computers readily available, communicating with their parts suppliers, with their marketers, with every important function in the corporation? U.S. companies will have them, too, but their value to the nation and to our global civilization will never be fully tapped until they can be linked together to allow the synergy, the mutually reinforcing advantage, to work for our benefit.

Of course, today scientists and engineers and a few million computer hobbyists know the power of computer networking, and they take the convenience of networking for granted. But imagine that the network could transmit not just text but video and voice. It is easy to imagine uses for such a system because prototypes are already available. But the prototypes are limited because they link only a few computers. Imagine what it would be like if everyone could log on. Already there's electronic mail, electronic banking, electronic shopping, electronic tax returns, electronic newspapers, but these applications are limited severely by the speed and size of our networks.

The really exciting services are yet to come. Researchers are already developing and demonstrating them. Today they are using supercomputers to build virtual realities that let users explore artificial worlds existing only in the computer's electronic circuitry. In a few years, that same technology could be used to develop interactive digital television programs brought into every home by optic fiber. The interactive features made possible in a network will revolutionize the nature of television yet again. The education potential and the entertainment potential, of course, are unlimited.

Similarly, the software being developed to allow massively parallel supercomputers to sort through these silos of data will be used to provide network users with access to digital libraries containing all the information in the Library of Congress and much more. Children could come home from school, sit down with a device no more complicated than a Nintendo machine, and with that device gain access to digital libraries and information that can expand their knowledge and awareness of the world around them and help them gain more control over their own lives.

But the most exciting uses are not even on the drawing boards yet because they are beyond our imaginations. Remember that electronic mail didn't exist until ARPANET (the U.S. Department of Defense's Advanced Research Projects Agency network) 20 years ago, and today electronic mail is a billion-dollar-a-year business and growing very rapidly. ARPANET wasn't built to carry e-mail. Nobody had even conceived of such a thing, but, as the potential expanded, our imagination expanded and new uses appeared.

The Fiber-Optics Revolution

Right now, fiber optics is starting an unpredictable and dramatic technological revolution in both computing and communications. The National Academy of Engineering lists fiber-optic communication as one of the most important scientific engineering achievements of the last 25 years. Clearly, it is every bit as revolutionary as was the transistor. A single cable can carry hundreds of thousands of times the number of channels carried by the largest copper television cable. That simple fact means that fiber will provide opportunities unimaginable with copper and make possible the digitization of America, including digital television, which will make HDTV as outdated as 78 rpm records. It will make it easy to shift billions of bits of data from one coast to the other in seconds. In many fundamental ways, fiber optics will change the way we view our world, just as the Copernican Revolution did.

How the revolution proceeds depends a lot upon the Bush administration, the courts, and Congress. The federal government funds half of the $140 billion of research and development done in the United States every year. Federal communications policies can block or promote the use of new technologies. Unfortunately, the U.S. government is not particularly good at dealing with technological revolutions.

Congress has been described as 535 raging incrementalists. Each year the president sends up his budget, and we trim 1% here and we add 1% there. That's not good enough anymore. The world is brand new. In 1945, on the eve of the Marshall Plan and NATO and free trade, General Omar Bradley said, "It is time we steered by the stars and not by the lights of each passing ship." This again is such a time. In the closing days of the 101st congressional session, the National High-Performance Computing Act of 1990, which would accelerate the appearance of the National Research and Education Network, was passed by the Senate, but not by the House of Representatives. The bill will be reintroduced in early 1991.

When one is in the middle of a technological revolution, one has two choices: to follow yesterday's nap or quickly chart a new course and grab the opportunities that we find. As a great philosopher once said, "What we have here is an insurmountable opportunity." A nationwide network of information superhighways has been an insurmountable opportunity, but we are now nearing the crest of the hill. We can see the vistas opening up on the other side. It is once again time to steer by the stars.

Number of words 1610
See page 277 for questions
Reading time in seconds ________
See page 495 for conversion table

SELECTION 18

The Feel

Paul Gallico

How does curiosity—the feel of things around you—relate to your ability to communicate? As you read on, you may wish to substitute names of sports heroes more current than the ones mentioned. No matter. The point of the article remains the same.

A child wandering through a department store with its mother is admonished over and over again not to touch things. Mother is convinced that the child only does it to annoy or because it is a child, and usually hasn't the vaguest inkling of the fact that Junior is "touching" because he is a little blotter soaking up information and knowledge, and "feel" is an important adjunct to seeing. Adults are exactly the same, in a measure, as you may ascertain when some new gadget or article is produced for inspection. The average person says: "Here, let me see that," and holds out his hand. He doesn't mean "see," because he is already seeing it. What he means is that he wants to get it into his hands and feel it so as to become better acquainted.

I do not insist that a curiosity and capacity for feeling sports is necessary to be a successful writer, but it is fairly obvious that a man who has been tapped on the chin with five fingers wrapped up in a leather boxing glove and propelled by the arm of an expert knows more about that particular sensation than one who has not, always provided he has the gift of expressing himself. I once inquired of a heavyweight prize-fighter by the name of King Levinsky, in a radio interview, what it felt like to be hit on the chin by Joe Louis, the King having just acquired that experience with rather disastrous results. Levinsky considered the matter for a moment and then reported: "It don't feel like nuttin'," but added that for a long while afterwards he felt as though he were "in a transom."

I was always a child who touched things and I have always had a tremendous curiosity with regard to sensation. If I knew what playing a game felt like, particularly against or in the company of experts, I was better equipped to write about the playing of it and the problems of the men and women who took part in it. And so, at one time or another, I have tried them all, football, baseball, boxing, riding, shooting, swimming, squash, handball, fencing, driving, flying, both land and sea planes, rowing, canoeing, skiing, riding a bicycle, ice-skating, roller-skating, tennis, golf, archery, basketball, running, both the hundred-yard dash and the mile, the high jump and shot put, badminton, angling, deep-sea, stream- and surf-casting, billiards and bowling, motor-boating and wrestling, besides riding as a passenger with the fastest men on land and water and in the air, to see what it felt like. Most of them I dabbled in as a youngster going through school and college, and others, like piloting a plane, squash, fencing, and skiing, I took up after I was old enough to know better, purely to get the feeling of what they were like.

None of these things can I do well, but I never cared about becoming an expert, and besides, there wasn't time. But there is only one way to find out accurately human sensations in a ship two or three thousand feet up when the motor quits, and that is actually to experience that gone feeling at the pit of the stomach and the sharp tingling of the skin from head to foot, followed by a sudden amazing sharpness of vision, clear-sightedness, and coolness that you never knew you possessed as you find the question of life or death completely in your own hands. It is not the "you" that you know, but somebody else, a stranger, who noses the ship down, circles, fastens upon the one best spot to sit down, pushes or pulls buttons to try to get her started again, and finally drops her in, safe and sound. And it is only by such experience that you learn likewise of the sudden weakness that hits you right at the back of the knees after you have climbed out and started to walk around her and that comes close to knocking you flat as for the first time since the engine quit its soothing drone you think of destruction and sudden death.

Often my courage has failed me and I have funked completely, such as the time I went up to the top of the thirty-foot Olympic diving-tower at Jones Beach, Long Island, during the competitions, to see what it was like to dive from that height, and wound up crawling away from the edge on hands and knees, dizzy, scared, and a little sick, but with a wholesome respect for the boys and girls who hurled themselves through the air and down through the tough skin of the water from that awful height. At other times sheer ignorance of what I was getting into has led me into tight spots such as the time I came down the Olympic ski run from the top of the Kreuzeck, six thousand feet above Garmisch-Partenkirchen, after having been on skis but once before in snow and for the rest had no more than a dozen lessons on an indoor artificial slide in a New York department store. At one point my legs, untrained, got so tired that I couldn't stem (brake) any more, and I lost control and went full tilt and all out, down a three-foot twisting path cut out of the side of the mountain, with a two-thousand-foot abyss on the left and the mountain itself on the right. That was probably the most scared I have ever been, and I scare fast and often. I remember giving myself up for lost and wondering how long it would take them to retrieve my body and whether I should be still alive. In the meantime the speed of the descent was increasing. Somehow I was keeping my feet and negotiating turns, how I will never know, until suddenly the narrow patch opened out into a wide, steep stretch of slope with a rise at the other end, and *that* part of the journey was over.

By some miracle I got to the bottom of the run uninjured, having made most of the trip down the icy, perpendicular slopes on the flat of my back. It was the thrill and scare of a lifetime, and to date no one has been able to persuade me to try a jump. I know when to stop. After all, I am entitled to rely upon my imagination for something. But when it was all over and I found myself still whole, it was also distinctly worthwhile to have learned what is required of a ski runner in the breakneck *Abfahrt* or downhill race, or the difficult *slalom*. Five days later, when I climbed laboriously (still on skis) halfway up that Alp and watched the Olympic downhill racers hurtling down the perilous, ice-covered, and nearly perpendicular *Steilhang*, I knew that I was looking at a great group of athletes who, for one thing, did not know the meaning of the word "fear." The slope was studded with small pine trees and rocks, but half of the field gained precious seconds by hitting that slope all out, with complete contempt for disaster rushing up at them at a speed often better than sixty miles an hour. And when an unfortunate Czech skidded off the course at the bottom of the slope and into a pile of rope and got himself snarled up as helpless as a fly in a spider's web, it was a story that I could write from the heart. I had spent ten minutes getting myself untangled after a fall, *without* any rope to add to the difficulties. It seems that I couldn't find where my left leg ended and one more ski than I originally donned seemed to be involved somehow. Only a person who has been on those fiendish runners knows the sensation.

It all began back in 1922 when I was a cub sportswriter and consumed with more curiosity than was good for my health. I had seen my first professional prizefights and wondered at the curious behavior of men under the stress of blows, the sudden checking and the beginning of a little fall forward after a hard punch, the glazing of the eyes and the loss of locomotor control, the strange actions of men on the canvas after a knockdown as they struggled to regain their senses and arise on legs that seemed to have turned into rubber. I had never been in any bad fist fights as a youngster, though I had taken a little physical punishment in football, but it was not enough to complete the picture. Could one think under those conditions?

I had been assigned to my first training-camp coverage, Dempsey's at Saratoga Springs, where he was preparing for his famous fight with Luis Firpo. For days I watched him sag a spar boy with what seemed to be no more than a light cuff on the neck, or pat his face with what looked like no more than a caressing stroke of his arm, and the fellow would come all apart at the seams and collapse in a useless heap, grinning vacuously or twitching strangely. My burning curiosity got the better of prudence and a certain reluctance to expose myself to physical pain. I asked Dempsey to permit me to box a round with him. I had never boxed before, but I was in good physical shape, having just completed a four-year stretch as a galley slave in the Columbia eight-oared shell.

When it was over and I escaped through the ropes, shaking, bleeding a little from the mouth, with rosin dust on my pants and a vicious throbbing in my head, I knew all that there was to know about being hit in the prize-ring. It seems that I had gone to an expert for tuition. I knew the sensation of being stalked and pursued by a relentless, truculent professional destroyer whose trade and business it was to injure men. I saw the quick flash of the brown forearm that precedes the stunning shock as a bony, leather-bound fist lands on cheek or mouth. I learned more (partly from photographs of the lesson, viewed afterwards, one of which shows me ducked under a vicious left hook, an act of which I never had the slightest recollection) about instinctive ducking and blocking than I could have in ten years of looking at prizefights, and I learned, too, that as the soldier never hears the bullet that kills him, so does the fighter rarely, if ever, see the punch that tumbles blackness over him like a mantle, with a tearing rip as though the roof of his skull were exploding, and robs him of his senses.

There was just that—a ripping in my head and then sudden blackness, and the next thing I knew, I was sitting on the canvas covering of the ring floor with my legs collapsed under me, grinning idiotically. How often since have I seen that same silly, goofy look on the faces of dropped fighters—and understood it. I held onto the floor with both hands, because the ring and the audience outside were making a complete clockwise revolution, came to a stop, and then went back again counter-clockwise. When I struggled to my feet, Jack Kearns, Dempsey's manager, was counting over me, but I neither saw nor heard him and was only conscious that I was in a ridiculous position and that the thing to do was to get up and try to fight back. The floor swayed and rocked beneath me like a fishing dory in an off-shore swell, and it was a welcome respite when Dempsey rushed into a clinch, held me up, and whispered into my ear: "Wrestle around a bit, son, until your head clears." And then it was that I learned what those little love-taps to the back of the neck and the short digs to the ribs can mean to the groggy pugilist more than half knocked out. It is a murderous game, and the fighter who can escape after having been felled by a lethal blow has my admiration. And there, too, I learned that there can be no sweeter sound than the bell that calls a halt to hostilities.

From that afternoon on, also, dated my antipathy for the spectator at prizefights who yells: "Come on, you bum, get up and fight! Oh, you big quitter! Yah yellow, yah yellow!" Yellow, eh? It is all a man can do to get up after being stunned by a blow, much less fight back. But they do it. And how a man is able to muster any further interest in a combat after being floored with a blow to the pit of the stomach will always remain to me a miracle of what the human animal is capable of under stress.

Further experiments were less painful, but equally illuminating. A couple of sets of tennis with Vinnie Richards taught me more about what is required of a topflight tournament tennis-player than I could have got out of a dozen books or years of reporting tennis matches. It is one thing to sit in a press box and write caustically that Brown played uninspired tennis, or Black's court covering was faulty and that his frequent errors cost him the set. It is quite another to stand across the net at the back of a service court and try to get your racket on a service that is so fast that the ear can hardly detect the interval between the sound of the server's bat hitting the ball and the ball striking the court. Tournament tennis is a different game from week-end tennis. For one thing, in average tennis, after the first hard service has gone into the net or out, you breathe a sigh of relief, move up closer and wait for the cripple to come floating over. In big-time tennis second service is practically as hard as the first, with an additional twist on the ball.

It is impossible to judge or know anything about the speed of a forehand drive hit by a champion until you have had one fired at you, or, rather, away from you, and you have made an attempt to return it. It is then that you first realize that tennis is played more with the head than with the arms and the legs. The fastest player in the world cannot get to a drive to return it if he hasn't though correctly, guessed its direction, and anticipated it by a fraction of a second.

There was golf with Bob Jones and Gene Sarazen and Tommy Armour, little Cruickshank and Johnny Farrell, and Diegel and other professionals; and experiments at trying to keep up in the water with Johnny Weissmuller, Helene Madison, and Eleanor Holm, attempts to catch football passes thrown by Benny Friedman. Nobody actually plays golf until he was acquired the technical perfection to be able to hit the ball accurately, high, low, hooked or faded and placed. And nobody knows what real golf is like until he has played a round with a professional and seen him play, not the ball, but the course, the roll of the land, the hazards, the wind, and the texture of the greens and the fairways. It looks like showmanship when a top-flight golfer plucks a handful of grass and lets it flutter in the air, or abandons his drive to march two hundred yards down to the green and look over the situation. It isn't. It's golf. The average player never knows or cares whether he is putting with or across the grain of a green. The professional *always* knows. The same average player standing on the tee is concentrated on getting the ball somewhere on the fairway, two hundred yards out. The professional when preparing to drive is actually to all intents and purposes playing his *second* shot. He means to place his drive so as to open up the green for his approach. But you don't find that out until you have played a round with them when they are relaxed and not competing, and listen to them talk and plan attacks on holes.

Major-league baseball is one of the most difficult and precise of all games, but you would never know it unless you went down on the field and got close to it and tried it yourself. For instance, the distance between pitcher and catcher is a matter of twenty paces, but it doesn't seem like enough when you don a catcher's mitt and try to hold a pitcher with the speed of Dizzy Dean or Dazzy Vance. Not even the sponge that catchers wear in the palm of the hand when working with fast-ball pitchers, and the bulky mitt are sufficient to rob the ball of shock and sting that lames your hand unless you know how to ride with the throw and kill some of its speed. The pitcher, standing on his little elevated mound, looms up enormously over you at that short distance, and when he ties himself into a coiled spring preparatory to letting fly, it requires all your self-control not to break and run for safety. And as for the things they can do with a baseball, those major-league pitchers . . . ! One way of finding out is to wander down on the field an hour or so before game-time when there is no pressure on them, pull on the catcher's glove, and try to hold them.

I still remember my complete surprise the first time I tried catching for a real curve-ball pitcher. He was a slim, spidery left-hander of the New York Yankees, many years ago, by the name of Herb Pennock. He called that he was going to throw a fast breaking curve and warned me to expect the ball at least two feet outside the plate. Then he wound up and let it go, and that ball came whistling right down the groove for the center of the plate. A novice, I chose to believe what I saw and not what I heard, and prepared to catch it where it was headed for, a spot which of course it never reached, because just in front of the rubber, it swerved sharply to the right and passed nearly a yard from my glove. I never had a chance to catch it. That way, you learn about the mysterious drop, the ball that sails down the alley chest high but which you must be prepared to catch around your ankles because of the sudden dip it takes at the end of its passage as though someone were pulling it down with a string. Also you find out about the queer fade-away, the slow curve, the fast in- and out-shoots that seem to be timed almost as delicately as shrapnel, to burst, or rather break, just when they will do the most harm—namely, at the moment when the batter is swinging.

Facing a big-league pitcher with a bat on your shoulder and trying to hit his delivery is another vital experience in gaining an understanding of the game about which you are trying to write vividly. It is one thing to sit in the stands and scream at the batsman: "Oh, you bum!" for striking out in a pinch, and another to stand twenty yards from that big pitcher and try to make up your mind in a hundredth of a second whether to hit at the offering or not, where to swing and when, not to mention worrying about protecting yourself from the consequences of being struck by the ball that seems to be heading straight for your skull at an appalling rate of speed. Because, if you are a big-league player, you cannot very well afford to be gun-shy and duck away in panic from a ball that swerves in the last moment and breaks perfectly over the plate, while the umpire calls: "Strike!" and the fans jeer. Nor can you afford to take a crack on the temple from the ball. Men have died from that. It calls for undreamed-of niceties of nerve and judgment, but you don't find that out until you have stepped to the plate cold a few times during batting practice or in training quarters, with nothing at stake but the acquisition of experience, and see what a fine case of the jumping jitters you get. Later on, when you are writing your story, your imagination, backed by the experience, will be able to supply a picture of what the batter is going through as he stands at the plate in the closing innings of an important game, with two or three men on base, two out, and his team behind in the scoring, and fifty thousand people screaming at him.

The catching and holding of a forward pass for a winning touchdown on a cold, wet day always make a good yarn, but you might get an even better one out of it if you happen to know from experience about the elusive qualities of a hard, soggy, mud-slimed football rifled through the air, as well as something about the exquisite timing, speed, and courage it takes to catch it on a dead run, with two or three 190-pound men reaching for it at the same time or waiting to crash you as soon as your fingers touch it.

Any football coach during a light practice will let you go down the field and try to catch punts, the long, fifty-yard spirals, and the tricky, tumbling end-over-enders. Unless you have had some previous experience, you won't hang on to one out of ten, besides knocking your fingers out of joint. But if you have any imagination, thereafter you will know that it calls for more than negligible nerve to judge and hold that ball and even plan to run with it, when there are two husky ends bearing down at full speed, preparing for a head-on tackle.

In 1932 I covered my first set of National Air Races, in Cleveland, and immediately decided that I had to learn how to fly to find out what that felt like. Riding as a passenger isn't flying. Being up there all alone at the controls of a ship is. And at the same time began a series of investigations into the "feel" of the mechanized sports to see what they were all about and the qualities of mentality, nerve, and physique they called for from their participants. These included a ride with Gar Wood in his latest and fastest speedboat, *Miss America X*, in which for the first time he pulled the throttle wide open on the Detroit River straightaway; a trip with the Indianapolis Speedway driver Cliff Bergere, around the famous brick raceway; and a flip with Lieutenant Al Williams, one time U.S. Schneider Cup race pilot.

I was scared with Wood, who drove me at 127 miles an hour, jounced, shaken, vibrated, choked with fumes from the exhausts, behind which I sat hanging on desperately to the throttle bar, which after a while got too hot to hold. I was on a plank between Wood and his mechanic, Johnson, and thought that my last moment had come. I was still more scared when Cliff Bergere hit 126 on the Indianapolis straightaways in the tiny racing car in which I was hopelessly wedged, and after the first couple of rounds quite resigned to die and convinced that I should. But I think the most scared I have ever been while moving fast was during a ride I took in the cab of a locomotive on the straight, level stretch between Fort Wayne, Indiana, and Chicago, where for a time we hit 90 miles per hour, which of course is no speed at all. But nobody who rides in the comfortable Pullman coaches has any idea of the didoes cut up by a locomotive in a hurry, or the thrill of pelting through a small town, all out and wide open, including the crossing of some thirty or forty frogs and switches, all of which must be set right. But that wasn't sport. That was just plain excitement.

I have never regretted these researches. Now that they are over, there isn't enough money to make me do them again. But they paid me dividends, I figured. During the great Thompson Speed Trophy race for land planes at Cleveland in 1935, Captain Roscoe Turner was some eight or nine miles in the lead in his big golden, low-wing speed monoplane. Suddenly, coming into the straightaway in front of the grandstands, buzzing along at 280 miles an hour like an angry hornet, a streamer of thick, black smoke burst from the engine cowling and trailed back behind the ship. Turner pulled up immediately, using his forward speed to gain all the altitude possible, turned and got back to the edge of the field, still pouring out that evil black smoke. Then he cut his switch, dipped her nose down, landed with a bounce and a bump, and rolled up to the line in a perfect stop. The crowd gave him a great cheer as he climbed out of the oil-spattered machine, but it was a cheer of sympathy because he had lost the race after having been so far in the lead that had he continued he could not possibly have been overtaken.

There was that story, but there was a better one too. Only the pilots on the field, all of them white around the lips and wiping from their faces a sweat not due to the oppressive summer heat, knew that they were looking at a man who from that time on, to use their own expression, was living on borrowed time. It isn't often when a Thompson Trophy racer with a landing speed of around eighty to ninety miles an hour goes haywire in the air, that the pilot is able to climb out of the cockpit and walk away from his machine. From the time of that first burst of smoke until the wheels touched the ground and stayed there, he was a hundred-to-one shot to live. To the initiated, those dreadful moments were laden with suspense and horror. Inside that contraption was a human being who any moment might be burned to a horrible, twisted cinder, or smashed into the ground beyond all recognition, a human being who was cool, gallant, and fighting desperately. Every man and woman on the field who had ever been in trouble in the air was living those awful seconds with him in terror and suspense. I, too, was able to experience it. That is what makes getting the "feel" of things distinctly worth while.

Number of words 4470
See page 279 for questions
Reading time in seconds _______
See page 495 for conversion table

Section II

On Reading

Selection 19

Starting to Read

Stuart Brent

Starting to read! What a life-changing step! With the start on life described here, no wonder the following author made a name for himself—as a Chicago television pioneer, as an author of children's books, and as the manager of the well-known Chicago bookstore bearing his name. Reading keeps the door to life wide open.

My father's hands were a miracle of perfection. He could build a house singlehanded. He could give you a haircut and butcher a cow. He could fix shoes and make tools and dies. He could farm and irrigate and build the prettiest doll houses in the world. He could make chairs, tables, cabinets; and even as I write this, I am staring at a pipe rack he made for me of hard wood set in a marble base. But it was not his genius as a craftsman which he passed on to me; it was his infatuation with reading.

My father immigrated from Russia in 1901 and through his manual skill became an assistant to the chief tool and die maker at the American Car and Foundry Company in Chicago. Ten years later, he became the chief tool and die maker himself. He was a man of activity, using his physical being all day long. But at night, after supper, he would retire to his favorite chair and open a book and smoke his pipe. Often in the morning he would arise from bed an hour earlier than necessary to finish reading what he had started the night before, so he could go to work "satisfied." It was a solitary addiction. He could not even discuss his reading with his near neighbors. Cohen, who lived on one side of us, couldn't put two words of English together. Rosenberg, our neighbor on the opposite side, couldn't care less. His only interests were pinochle and drinking tea (with lemon).

When I was a child, he often allowed me to go with him in the evening to the new public library that had just been opened on Homan Avenue, a distance of nearly three miles. The streets of Chicago's West Side were poorly lighted in those days, but it was possible to walk them without fear. My father would check out five books and depart with the books in one hand and my small hand in the other. Usually we walked in total silence until we got to Kobrick's grocery and delicatessen. As we approached the lighted window with its display of candies, bagels and honey cakes, and the salamis hanging from the ceiling, my heart would almost stop. Would father, this night, decide to buy some pipe tobacco, then, looking down from his towering height, ask if I would like a sucker or a bag of polly seeds?

In time, we became co-conspirators in the love of reading. Books might not make me a better wage earner, he said, but they could prevent boredom. The experience of reading a good book was like getting unstuck and reaching out toward something entirely new, even though you still wore the same tie and shirt and met the same people.

But the great beauty of the thing, he said, was that when you are reading, you are never alone. For my father, to be *aleyn* (the Yiddish for loneliness) was one of the tragic elements in man's experience.

His favorite writer was Tolstoy. "When you read Dostoevsky," he would say, "you descend into a coal mine without a ladder for climbing out. When you read Tolstoy, it's like the sun after living in an icebox."

Anatole France's *Penguin Island* and the criticisms of Walter Pater were favorites of his. He liked Scott and Dickens. No one understood Dickens until he had read *Our Mutual Friend*, he said. It would be a grave mistake to die without having read that book. You may be sure I read Dickens until I couldn't see straight.

I became a teen-ager imbued with the desire to read everything, to know everything, to be everything. With the advent of the depression, the fulfillment of these modest ambitions required considerable ingenuity. The entire atmosphere of our household was altered. First, my sister and her husband and two children moved in. Her husband had lost his job after eighteen years as a pants cutter at Hart, Schaffner and Marx. Then, my brother who was a salesman for the wholesale division of Marshall Field lost his job, so he and his wife and three children joined our crowded household. Now the only place to read was either in the bathroom or the public library.

Even during these difficult and sometimes tragic years, there were evenings filled with affection and fun. Everyone crowded into the big kitchen and then, between tea and sweet cakes and perhaps a drop or two, or even three, of sweet home-made wine, they would talk and tell deprecatory tales of human stupidity and laugh and cry at the same time. The warmth and marvel of those days have never left me.

I was seldom without a book. I read walking along the street; I read standing up, sitting down, I read and read and read. Before the depression and the great influx of family members, the very best time to read was on Saturday mornings. Normally my mother baked on Friday, and she had a genius for failing to remember that something was in the oven. So if I was lucky, there would be plenty of cookies or cake or strudel left, slightly burned, that nobody else would touch. But I loved it. Then, too, the house was strangely still on Saturday mornings. No one was home and I could turn up the volume of the phonograph as loud as I wished and sit and listen and read and eat cake. It was wonderful.

When reading became out of the question at home, I simply went to one of the two public libraries within walking distance. I liked best the one identified as the Douglas Park branch. It was newer, the seats more comfortable, the selection of books better.

While my remarkable father was responsible for my early love of books, Jesse Feldman, my teacher in senior high school literature, served to transform that love into an enduring and ever more passionate affair. His enthusiasm supported my own, and at the same time held the key to the wealth of possibilities that literature offers.

Through Jesse I learned the difference between a good book and a bad book. A good book is, very simply, a revealing book. A bad book is bad because it is dull. Its author is obviously lying, not necessarily by purveying misinformation, but because he lards his work with any information that falls to hand—a sort of narrative treatment of the encyclopedia. A good book stirs your soul. You find yourself lost, not in a world of fantasy, but in a world where everything is understood.

Nobody can get along without an interior life. The soul must be fed, or something ugly and anti-human fills the void. Spiritual nourishment is not a frill, apart from everyday necessity. The everyday and the ultimate expression of man do not exist apart. Synge remarked: "When men lose their poetic feeling for ordinary life and cannot write poetry of ordinary things, their exalted poetry is likely to lose its strength of exaltation, in the way men cease to build beautiful churches when they have lost happiness in building shops."

So many years have passed since my father started me in reading as a way of life—marking a passage in a letter from Melville to Hawthorne, his workman's hands caressing the page: "My development," Melville wrote, "has been all within a few years past. Until I was twenty-five I had no development at all. From my twenty-fifth year I date my life. Three weeks have scarcely passed, at any time between then and now, that I have not unfolded within myself." How proud I was to have got an earlier start!

I think of those days when my hair was long and I wore the only pair of pants I had until they were in shreds. I used to sit in the classroom with my overcoat on so that the patches on my behind would not show, or stay in the library until closing time was called. Then I'd go out into the solitary night, walking thoughtfully home. I didn't want money or success or recognition. I didn't want a single thing from anybody. I wanted only to be alone, to read; to think; to unfold.

Number of words 1375
See page 281 for questions
Reading time in seconds _______
See page 495 for conversion table

Selection 20

Handling the Knowledge Explosion

James I. Brown

Back in Biblical times, Solomon wrote, "Of making many books there is no end." Today that's truer than ever. Scientific and technical literature rolls off the presses at a staggering rate of 60 million pages a year. How can you cope with such an avalanche of print? Here's one possibility.

The knowledge explosion! We can't eliminate it. We can't disregard it. It's a fact of life. We can, however, learn to cope with it much more effectively. That's another fact of life.

What's the greatest problem with the knowledge explosion? Finding the time to deal with it—finding time to read! First, start by finding and investing only fifteen to thirty minutes a day. That slim sliver of time, managed properly as will be described, can make you up to twenty-one additional hours of time a week.

Here's how it works. Suppose you now read at 250 wpm. And suppose you read on the average one hour a day. In a sense, doubling your rate means making yourself seven extra hours of reading time a week. You can then do fourteen hours of reading in only seven hours' time. Put it another way. You have stretched your customary seven hours of reading a week into fourteen. In a year you have made yourself an extra 365 hours. Furthermore, why not work toward tripling or even quadrupling your rate? It can be done. In short, invest fifteen to thirty minutes a day. Make up to twenty-one extra hours a week.

Reading improvement should, in fact, serve you in three ways, not one. It should be your time-stretcher, your problem-solver, and your experience-extender. Carlyle catches this broad perspective so well when he says, "All that mankind has done, thought, gained, or been; it is lying as in magic preservation in the pages of books."

Now—exactly how do you invest that daily sliver of time? By taking off the brakes! You wouldn't think of driving your car with both foot and hand brake on. Yet, as a reader, several brakes probably slow you down.

Regressing

One common brake is regressing—looking back every now and than at something you just read. That's like moving backward every few steps as you walk—hardly the way to get ahead in a hurry. Regression may be pure habit—the way you've always read. It may be a vocabulary deficiency, the need to look again at a strange word. Or it may be the actual missing of a word or phrase, requiring a look back. See what it does to a complex sentence like this: Does this seem this seem even more tangled than more tangled than usual as the eyes the eyes frequently regress regress. Obviously this all-too-common habit plays havoc with reading speed, comprehension and efficiency.

Eye-movement photographs of some 12,000 college students show that they regress an average of 15 times in reading only 100 words. To be sure, they perform better than the average ninth grader, who regresses 20 times. In short, regressions can take one-sixth or more of your precious reading time. That makes them a major retarding factor. So—release the regressing brake. Enjoy an immediate spurt in reading speed—a gain of perhaps over 100 wpm. Class results show that awareness of the problem, which you now have, plus application of the suggestions to follow, should bring an 80% decrease in regressions.

Vocalizing

A second brake is vocalizing—pronouncing words to yourself as you read. We all did that as beginners. We were taught to sound out words, syllables, and even letters. No wonder traces of that habit persist. No wonder it still interferes with general reading efficiency.

wonder it still interferes with general reading efficiency. See how vocalizing slows you up. Read these words s l o w l y, s o u n d i n g t h e s y l - l a - b l e s a n d l - e - t - t - e - r - s.

At the lip level, vocalizing pulls your reading speed toward the speed of speech, probably less than 200 wpm. To diagnose, put a finger over your lips as you read silently. Do you feel any movement? To get rid of that habit, keep a memory-jogging finger on your lips as you read—a constant reminder.

Vocalizing at the voice box level is far more common. Less obvious, too! If your top reading speed is under 300 wpm, suspect that kind of vocalizing. Check further. Place your thumb and forefinger lightly on the side of your voice-box. If, as you read silently, you feel faint movements, you know your problem. Again, knowing the problem takes you a giant step toward its solution.

Word-by-Word Reading

The third troublesome brake is word-by-word reading. Suppose you have to move 200 books. Would you make 200 trips, one book at a time? Of course, not. Ten trips, twenty books a trip, would be more likely. As a reader, keep that same principle in mind.

Eye movement photographs reveal that in reading your eyes move jerkily along a line of print. Each short stop permits you to read a portion of the print. Without special training, research indicates that even college students are word-by-word readers. They take in only 1.1 words per fixation or look. Obviously one way to double or triple your rate is by learning to take in two or three words at a glance. Don't be satisfied with the usual one.

There they are—the three major causes of reading inefficiency, the three brakes that hold your reading to a snail's pace. Release them. Enjoy immediate returns. Fortunately, one single key principle, properly applied, will do the job.

The Solution

Successful reading improvement relies heavily on the key principle of faster-than-comfortable reading. That's true whether you're working on your own or taking a course. Here's why. This principle automatically eliminates regressions. You're pushing ahead so fast you haven't time to look back. Furthermore, your vocalizing is stopped—for the same reason. Finally, that added speed forces you to start dealing with word groups, not single words. One principle does it all.

Put this key principle to immediate use. Practice faster-than-comfortable reading with the selections in this book. To be sure, comprehension may suffer a bit at first. You're developing the added experience and skill needed to get it back. Practice will soon pay off, giving you better comprehension than ever.

Keep accurate rate and comprehension figures for each selection. Enter them in the back of the book. This lets you see progress.

Follow these suggestions faithfully. Start making up to twenty-one extra hours a week for yourself. You're developing habits that will serve you well the rest of your life.

One word sums up our age better than any other—*change*. But hasn't change always been present? True, but never before at such a breakneck pace. Today, the word *change* is not enough. It's *unprecedented* change, revealed largely through the explosion of print. At such a time, reading provides the best tool you have for keeping up and for avoiding future shock in a world continually being remade.

Number of words 1100
See page 285 for questions
Reading time in seconds ______
See page 496 for conversion table

Selection 21

Super-Speeds for the Knowledge Explosion

James I. Brown

Samuel Johnson once wrote, "The joy of life is variety." Paraphrase that to read, "The joy of reading is variety"—variety in things read and variety in specialized techniques used, as will be described below. Savor the added flexibility and versatility these techniques bring.

Think of the overwhelming magnitude of the knowledge explosion. Doubling or tripling your reading rate means almost nothing. You need super-speeds. Here's how to make quantum-like leaps to cover twenty or thirty times more print than ever before. And you do that *without increasing your rate*! In short, you'll read faster—without reading faster. To understand that paradox, tap the full potential of three special techniques—surveying, skimming, and scanning. They put you, not where the action is, but where the essence is.

Surveying

Surveying is the first amazing shortcut. It gives you the best possible overview in the shortest possible time. In short—you get the most for the least. With it, you make a giant leap in coverage. You can survey twenty to thirty articles in the time you normally take to read one. It works because it's firmly based on common characteristics of writing.

Take a closer look. With most articles or reports, the title usually gives you the best concise indication of what is to follow. Right? The first paragraph, then, goes on to orient you and get your interest. From that point on, major subdivisions are likely to be marked with headings. Other important parts may use italics, heavy type, graphs or tables for emphasis. Finally, more often than not, the final paragraph summarizes what's been said, points up the main idea or suggests action.

To survey, just translate those characteristics into action. This will focus on the essentials. Start by reading the title and the first paragraph. Then go into super-speed. Race on through, reading only headings, words in heavy type or italics, tables and graphs. Finally, slow down for the last paragraph. That's to be read. You should now have the very essence of the article in neat capsule form.

And remember, the more you use surveying, the more adept you'll become. As with any tool, the more experience, the greater the mastery. Never again should you have to plow through an entire article to find out if it has what you want. Surveying twenty or thirty in the same time will work much better.

Skimming

Now add the second super-speed technique to your repertoire—skimming. But don't think of skimming as fast, careless reading. It's careful reading—careful reading of key parts. As surveying, it also depends on certain basic features of written expression.

Skimming is built around common characteristics of paragraph structure. For example, the bulk of our reading, an estimated 55 to 85%, is of *expository paragraphs*, where the main idea is usually expressed in a topic sentence. In 60 to 90% of such paragraphs, the *topic sentence* comes first, with the next most likely spot last. When the topic sentence leads off, the *last* sentence usually reiterates or *summarizes* the topic idea. In addition, certain *key words* through the paragraph *supply* further *detail* and support the idea being developed. In short, as in this paragraph, reading one-fourth of the words still gives you the substance. *Skimming capitalizes on awareness of structure.*

Skimming combines the familiar surveying pattern with paragraph treatment. Start as if to survey until you're through with the first paragraph. Now for the difference. Don't race on, looking only for headings, italics and the like. Start skimming *all* paragraphs up to the last. Use the following pattern. Read the first sentence in each paragraph. Then shift into high gear, noting only the key words in the middle. Finally, read the last sentence in the paragraph. The preceding paragraph illustrates what you do. Italics point up the words to read as you skim. Notice how clearly the essentials stand out. End by reading the last paragraph, as with surveying.

You'll probably skim three to five times faster than you read. Style and paragraph length will, of course, make a difference. Often a skilled skimmer gets better comprehension than an average reader, despite the speed difference. Skimming tends to bring out heightened alertness and concentration. That may explain the better results. Increase your skill by daily practice. Skimming one article or book chapter a day will do wonders.

To stop here, however, would be to miss a second important role of skimming—as reading accelerator. Assume you're working to improve reading speed and comprehension. Perhaps you actually practice rapid reading 30 minutes a day. But you may read slowly several hours a day. How can you make progress? You're practicing slow reading more than fast. It might look equally impossible for a 200-pound father to teeter-totter with his 20-pound son. But that's no problem. The father merely sits closer to the fulcrum until he finds a perfect balance. In the same way, use skimming to counteract and balance the slowing drag of normal reading.

Try this suggestion. Don't read an important 3,000-word article at 200 wpm—a fifteen-minute task. Instead skim it at 1,500 wpm—an easy task. Then read it at 250 wpm. That skimming-reading combination actually takes you less time than the one slow reading. Furthermore you should have better comprehension—and a distinct gain toward higher normal reading speeds.

Scanning

Here's your third super-speed—scanning. It also serves two functions. It lets you quickly recheck certain desired facts as well as accelerate your reading rate.

You use scanning to find a specific bit of information within a large body of print—the proverbial needle in the haystack. This is the highest gear of all. Here you start with a specific question. Who won the game? What year was that? Where was the coup?

In my university reading classes, students scan initially at about 1,300 wpm. That's without special training or practice. One intensive scanning session is enough to raise the average to about 14,000 wpm, with equal accuracy. A few even pass the 25,000 mark. Here are the practice tips we use.

Visualize the detail. Everyone has noticed how, in looking at a page of print, your own name tends to jump into sight. This psychological fact suggests one way to insure accuracy. When you scan for a date, for example, visualize exactly how it will look on the page. Put a strong mind-set to work.

For another example, look at the figures in the accompanying illustration. How many are identical?

The word *figures* was intended to establish the wrong mind-set, one to hinder you from seeing the word you were looking at. Now let that new mind-set make the word (*tie*) pop out.

Use all available clues. If you scan for a proper name, focus on capital letters as a help. Synonyms, hyphens, italics or quotes are other possible clues.

Use structural tips. If you are scanning for the word "rubles," the word Russia should be a useful tip. If you want a detail about stock performance, let the phrase, "Dow Jones average" pull you up short at the right spot.

Use systematic scanning patterns. What's the best way to cover a printed page or column? Zigzag down the middle. Notice that if you look directly at the first and last words in a line of print, you leave untapped your full perceptual span. Look as far in as the second or third word at each end of the line. You can still see the words that come before and after. With a very narrow column, just run your eyes straight down the middle. That works well with newspaper columns.

Scanning is particularly useful after reading an article or textbook chapter when you want to fix pertinent details firmly in mind. Sharpen your scanning skill by doing two or three scanning problems a day. You want accuracy at a 15,000 to 20,000 wpm rate.

From now on put these three super-speed techniques to daily use. Let them extend your facility with print and accelerate your progress in getting comprehension. When fully developed and exploited, this hybrid combination should help you handle the knowledge explosion with enviable facility.

With exponential change the very essence of life today, a company can prosper one day and face ruin the next. That means that the individual who concentrates only on the present, actually jeopardizes his or her future. Balancing today's demands with tomorrow's needs. What a key problem to face. Reading can help bring signal success.

Number of words 1370
See page 289 for questions
Reading time in seconds _______
See page 496 for conversion table

SELECTION 22

Reading for Meaning

James I. Brown

You read for a multitude of reasons—for escape, for entertainment, for needed information, for therapy. But for all *kinds of reading and* all *purposes, getting the meaning holds top priority. Certainly that deserves careful close scrutiny. That also explains why this book has comprehension checks.*

Comprehension, when you think of it, has a top side and an under side, just as an ocean. The view from above, sun sparkling on the waves, is totally different from the view from below, with schools of fish darting about the weeds and rocks. Yet—it's the same ocean. So it is with comprehension.

Reading for details or facts focuses on the top side of comprehension—what's on the surface. That's the easier part. *Reading for meaning* opens up a fascinating new in-depth side of comprehension. Here you plunge into a whole world of previously hidden or partially hidden meaning.

The Detail-Meaning Relationship

One side is not enough. You need both. After all, you build meaning by fitting details together. At this point, reading and thinking become inseparable. Adler, in his book *How to Read a Book,* writes that complete comprehension is always present in one situation. When people "are in love and are reading a love letter, they read for all they are worth . . . they read between the lines and in the margins; they read the whole in terms of the parts, and each part in terms of the whole; they grow sensitive to context and ambiguity, to insinuation and implication. . . . Then, if never before or after, they read." Neither side of comprehension is neglected.

Let's examine more closely the detail-meaning relationship. Two are speaking. One says, "It's ten o'clock." What does she mean? Well, that's easy, you say. She means it's ten o'clock. It's just a pure statement of fact—a detail.

Let's dive in for a below-surface look at some possibilities. You know exactly what she *said.* But what did she *mean*?

Well, she could mean, "Let's go for our usual ten o'clock coffee break." To be sure, that's not what she said; it's what she meant, though. Her friend understood perfectly and replied, "Right! Let's go. What are we waiting for?"

Again, those same words could be an accusation. She might mean, "You said you'd be here at nine. You're a whole hour late!" Or she might be expressing surprise. "How come you're so early? You weren't supposed to arrive until ten-thirty." Again, she might mean, "Your watch is slow." Obviously, what's *said* and what's *meant* can be quite different. Beneath the world of surface detail, you can glimpse a truly fascinating new world opening up.

Getting Main Ideas

In the world of meaning, what's most important? It's getting the main or central idea of a book, chapter, paragraph, or example. Some readers can't see the forest for the trees. They get all the details accurately, but don't see how they add up. When they hear a story, they're likely to miss the point. Yes, getting the main idea deserves top priority.

How do you manage that? Just ask the right question. Ask yourself—"What's the point?" That question will start you along the road to the answer. For example, think back to the bit about "It's ten o'clock." Now raise the question: What's the point of that discussion? A variety of different meanings were advanced. But they all pointed up the need to consider both sides of comprehension—detail *and* underlying meaning, with special emphasis on meaning.

Drawing Inferences

Such words as *infer* and *imply* suggest still other areas in the world of meaning. To infer means to reason something out from given evidence. If someone *says* he's pleased, you *know* it. If he smiles, you have to *infer* it. That's the difference.

Try your hand at inferring with this story. A foreman hustled over to the construction site. "How long have you been working here?" he asked one person. The worker replied, "Ever since you arrived."

What inferential leap can you make? Well, you could infer that the worker was both lazy and stupid. True, he didn't actually say so. You'd have to infer it. An inference is that kind of thing—a leap from the known into the unknown.

Reaching Conclusions

As a mature reader, you'll also want to become proficient in building a chain of reasoning, the last step of which brings you to a logical finish—a conclusion. Someone yawns, his head nods, and his eyes close. Conclusion? He's sleepy.

Take another illustration. A Texan built three swimming pools in his spacious back yard. One he filled with warm water, another with cool. The third was empty. When asked about that, he explained. "The empty one is for two of my friends who can't swim." Conclusion? The Texan was *more* than rich. He was "filthy rich."

Here, as with the main idea, just ask the right question: What conclusion can I make? With that question in mind, read on. She: "Handsome men are always conceited." He: "Not always. I'm not." What's your conclusion about him? And why?

Determining Importance

Can you think of still another important area of meaning? Well, a really good reader should certainly know what points are most or least important.

How can you tell? Fortunately, writers rely heavily on three devices. First, they come right out and tell you what's most or least important. Usually, however, they're more subtle. You're likely to remember best the first or last point in a series. Writers know that and tend to put their most important points in those positions. Again, if you talk more about one thing than another, you suggest which you consider most important. Again, writers do the same. Lean on those three clues: (1) statement, (2) position, and (3) amount. They really help.

Fortunately, you've already taken the two best steps to improve reading for meaning. You know some specifics. You know what questions to raise. After all, a problem well identified is a problem half solved. You're aware of getting the main ideas, drawing inferences, reaching conclusions, and evaluating importance. Add such other areas as making generalizations, classifying, and determining purpose. They're also part of reading for meaning. It all adds up to more enjoyment with that fascinating in-depth side of comprehension.

Number of words 1000
See page 291 for questions
Reading time in seconds _______
See page 496 for conversion table

Selection 23

The Bible's Timeless—and Timely—Insights

Smiley Blanton, M.D.

A well-known psychiatrist demonstrates the extraordinary wisdom of the Bible in dealing with problems that have haunted the human race from the beginning—and are more than ever with us today. Apparently reading can do more than inform. It can be bibliotherapy, bringing curative and restorative power.

The other day a new patient noticed a Bible lying on my desk. "Do you—a psychiatrist—read the Bible?" he asked.

"I not only read it," I told him, "I study it. It's the greatest textbook on human behavior ever put together. If people would just absorb its message, a lot of us psychiatrists could close our offices and go fishing."

"You're talking about the Ten Commandments and the Golden Rule?"

"Certainly—but more, too," I said. "There are dozens of other insights that have profound psychiatric value. Take your own case. For the past hour you've been telling me how you've done this, tried that, all to no avail. It's pretty obvious that you're worrying yourself into a state of acute anxiety, isn't it?"

"That," he said dryly, "is why I'm here."

I picked up the Bible. "Here's some advice that St. Paul gives to the Ephesians. Just four words: *Having done all, stand.* Now, what does that mean? Exactly what it says. You've done your best, what more can you do? Keep running in circles? Plow up the same ground? What you really need—far more than a solution to this particular problem—is peace of mind. And there's the formula: relax, stand quietly, stop trying to lick this thing with your conscious mind. Let the creative power in your unconscious mind take over. It may solve the whole thing for you, if you'll just get out of your own way!"

My patient looked thoughtful. "Maybe I should do a little Bible reading on my own," he said.

It does seem foolish not to make use of the distilled wisdom of 3000 years. Centuries before psychiatry, the Bible knew that "the kingdom of God is within you." We psychiatrists call it the unconscious mind—but only the words are new, not the concept. From beginning to end the Bible teaches that the human soul is a battleground where good struggles with evil. We talk about the forces of hostility and aggression contending with the love-impulses in human nature. It's the same thing.

What psychiatry has done is to bring scientific terminology to the truths that the Bible presents in poetry, allegory and parable. What, in essence, did Freud and the other pioneers discover? That the human mind functions on the conscious *and* the unconscious level. That the thing we call conscience does, too, and that many emotional pressures and dislocations are caused by its hidden action.

It is tremendously exciting to read the Bible with even this much knowledge of psychiatry. Here are a few of my favorite passages, words so full of insight that I think they might well be memorized and repeated periodically by anyone who values his mental health.

- *Underneath are the everlasting arms.* For hundreds of years, troubled people have found comfort in these words from the Book of Deuteronomy. This is not surprising. One of the few fears we are born with is the fear of falling, so the idea of a pair of loving arms, sustaining and eternal, is an answer to the yearning in all of us to feel safe, to find security. Furthermore, one of the deepest forms of communication is *touch.* And so this Biblical image brings a great sense of peace. If you suffer from tension and insomnia, try repeating these words to yourself at bedtime. You may find them more effective than any sleeping pill.

- *Love they neighbor as thyself.* Many people think this noble concept comes from the New Testament. Actually you can also find it in Leviticus. The remarkable thing, to a psychiatrist, is its recognition that in an emotionally healthy person there must be self-love as well as love of others.

Lack of self-esteem is probably the most common emotional ailment I am called upon to treat. Often pressure from the unconscious mind is causing this sense of unworthiness. Suppose a woman comes to me, weighted down with guilt. I can't undo the things she has done. But perhaps I can help her understand why she did them, and how the mechanism of her conscience, functioning below the conscious level, is paralyzing her. And I can urge her to read and reread the story of the Prodigal Son. How can anyone feel permanently condemned or rejected in a world where this magnificent promise comes ringing down the centuries, the promise that love is stronger than any mistake, any error?

- *Take no thought for the morrow.* A modern rephrasing might well be, "Stop worrying about the future." Worry causes tension. Tension blocks the flow of creative energy from the unconscious mind. And when creative energy wanes, problems multiply.

Most of us know perfectly well that worry is a futile process. Yet many people constantly borrow trouble. "Sufficient unto the day," says the Bible, "is the evil thereof." There are plenty of problems in the here-and-now to tackle and solve. The only moment when you're really alive is the present one, so make the most of it. Have faith that the Power that brought you here will help you through any future crisis, whatever it may be. "They that wait upon the Lord," sang Isaiah, "shall renew their strength; they shall mount up with wings as eagles." Why? Because their faith makes them non-worriers.

- *As he thinketh in his heart, so is he.* This penetrating phrase from Proverbs implies that what you *think* you think is less important than what you really think. Every day in my office I see illustrations of this. Last week I was talking to a woman who had married during the Korean war. Her husband, a reserve officer, had volunteered for war duty and gone overseas, leaving her pregnant. He had been killed; she was left to bring up their son alone. Eventually she remarried, but now she was having difficulty with the 15-year-old boy.

It was apparent that she treated her son with unusual harshness and severity. "Why are you so strict with him?" I asked.

"Because I don't want him to grow up spoiled," she said instantly.

"Did it ever occur to you," I asked, "that when this boy's father went away voluntarily, leaving you, and got himself killed, something in you was enraged, something in you hated him? And isn't it just possible that some of this unadmitted hate has been displaced onto the child he left you with, although your conscious mind doesn't want to admit that either? Look into your heart and search for the truth there, below the rationalizations of your mind. Until you do, we're not going to get anywhere with this problem."

- *Where your treasure is, there will your heart be also.* Of course! *What* we shall love is the key problem of human existence, because we tend to become the reflection of what we love. Do you love money? Then your values will be materialistic. Do you love power? Then the aggressive instincts in you will slowly become dominant. Do you love God and your neighbor? Then you are not likely to need a psychiatrist!

We psychiatrists warn against sustained anger and hostility; we know that unresolved conflicts in the unconscious mind can make you physically ill. How does the Bible put it? *Let not the sun go down upon your wrath.* And: *A merry heart doeth good like a medicine.* Exactly so. These flashing sparks of truth from the pages of the Bible are endless!

If I were asked to choose one Bible passage above all others it would be this: *And ye shall know the truth, and the truth shall make you free.* In one tremendous sentence these words encompass the whole theory and method of psychotherapy. Nine times out of ten, when people come to me tormented by guilt, racked by anxiety, exhausted by unresolved hate, it is because they don't know the truth about themselves. It is the role of the psychiatrist to remove the camouflage, the self-deception, the rationalizations. It is his job to bring the unconscious conflicts into the conscious mind where reason can deal with them. As Freud said, "Reason is a small voice, but it is persistent." Once insight is gained, the cure can begin—because the truth *does* make you free.

We shall never have all the truth. Great questions of life and death, good and evil, remain unanswered—and must so remain, as the book of Job eloquently tells us. But this much seems plain to me: locked in the unconscious of each of us are the same elemental forces of love and hate that have haunted and inspired the human race from the beginning. With this hidden area of the human spirit psychiatry concerns itself—sometimes helpfully, sometimes not. But there is also an ancient book that deals with it, that understands it profoundly and intuitively, a book that for 3000 years has been a help in time of trouble to any person wise enough to use it.

Number of words 1490
See page 295 for questions
Reading time in seconds _______
See page 496 for conversion table

Selection 24

Feeding the Mind

Lewis Carroll

Someone said, "Tell me what you eat, and I will tell you what you are." In the following article Lewis Carroll seems to argue, "Not so. It's what you read *that makes you what you are." Does he make a convincing case?*

Breakfast, dinner, tea; in extreme cases, breakfast, luncheon, dinner, tea, supper, and a glass of something hot at bedtime. What care we take about feeding the lucky body! Which of us does as much for his mind? And what causes the difference? Is the body so much the more important of the two?

By no means; but life depends on the body being fed, whereas we can continue to exist as animals (scarcely as men) though the mind be utterly starved and neglected. Therefore Nature provides that, in case of serious neglect of the body, such terrible consequences of discomfort and pain shall ensue as will soon bring us back to a sense of our duty; and some of the functions necessary to life she does for us altogether, leaving us no choice in the matter. It would fare but ill with many of us if we were left to superintend our own digestion and circulation. "Bless me!" one would cry, "I forgot to wind up my heart this morning! To think that it has been standing still for the last three hours!" "I can't walk with you this afternoon," a friend would say, "as I have no less than eleven dinners to digest. I had to let them stand over from last week, being so busy—and my doctor says he will not answer for the consequences if I wait any longer!"

Well it is, I say, for us, that the consequences of neglecting the body can be clearly seen and felt; and it might be well for some if the mind were equally visible and tangible—if we could take it, say, to the doctor and have its pulse felt.

"Why, what have you been doing with this mind lately? How have you fed it? It looks pale, and the pulse is very slow."

"Well, doctor, it has not had much regular food lately. I gave it a lot of sugar-plums yesterday."

"Sugar-plums! What kind?"

"Well, they were a parcel of conundrums, sir."

"Ah! I though so. Now just mind this: if you go on playing tricks like that, you'll spoil all its teeth, and get laid up with mental indigestion. You must have nothing but the plainest reading for the next few days. Take care now! No novels on any account!"

Considering the amount of painful experience many of us have had in feeding and dosing the body, it would, I think, be quite worth our while to try and translate some of the rules into corresponding ones for the mind.

First, then, we should set ourselves to provide for our mind its *proper kind* of food; we very soon learn what will, and what will not, agree with the body, and find little difficulty in refusing a piece of the tempting pudding or pie which is associated in our memory with that terrible attack of indigestion, and whose very name irresistibly recalls rhubarb and magnesia; but it takes a great many lessons to convince us how indigestible some of our favorite lines of reading are, and again and again we make a meal of the unwholesome novel, sure to be followed by its usual train of low spirits, unwillingness to work, weariness of existence—in fact by mental nightmare.

Then we should be careful to provide this wholesome food in *proper amount.* Mental gluttony, or overreading, is a dangerous propensity, tending to weakness of digestive power, and in some cases to loss of appetite; we know that bread is a good and wholesome food, but who would like to try the experiment of eating two or three loaves at a sitting?

I have heard of a physician telling his patient—whose complaint was merely gluttony and want of exercise—that "the earliest symptom of hypernutrition is a deposition of adipose tissue," and no doubt the fine long words greatly consoled the poor man under his increasing load of fat.

I wonder if there is such a thing in nature as a *fat* mind? I really think I have met with one or two minds which could not keep up with the slowest trot in conversation, could not jump over a logical fence to save their lives, always got stuck fast in a narrow argument, and, in short, were fit for nothing but to waddle helplessly through the world.

Then, again, though the food be wholesome and in proper amount, we know that we must not consume *too many kinds at once.* Take the thirsty haymaker a quart of beer, or a quart of cider, or even a quart of cold tea, and he will probably thank you (though not so heartily in the last case!). But what think you his feelings would be if you offered him a tray containing a little mug of beer, a little mug of cider, another of cold tea, one of hot tea, one of coffee, one of cocoa, and corresponding vessels of milk, water, brandy-and-water, and buttermilk? The sum total might be a quart, but would it be the same thing to the haymaker?

Having settled the proper kind, amount, and variety of our mental food, it remains that we should be careful to allow *proper intervals* between meal and meal, and not swallow the food hastily without mastication, so that it may be thoroughly digested; both which rules for the body are also applicable at once to the mind.

First as to the intervals: these are as really necessary as they are for the body, with this difference only, that while the body requires three or four hours' rest before it is ready for another meal, the mind will in many cases do with three or four minutes. I believe that the interval required is much shorter than is generally supposed, and from personal experience I would recommend any one who has to devote several hours together to one subject of thought to try the effect of such a break, say once an hour—leaving off for five minutes only, each time, but taking care to throw the mind absolutely "out of gear" for those five minutes, and to turn it entirely to other subjects. It is astonishing what an amount of impetus and elasticity the mind recovers during those short periods of rest.

And then as to the mastication of the food: the mental process answering to this is simply *thinking over* what we read. This is a very much greater exertion of mind than the mere passive taking in the contents of our author—so much greater an exertion is it, that, as Coleridge says, the mind often "angrily refuses" to put itself to such trouble—so much greater, that we are far too apt to neglect it altogether, and go on pouring in fresh food on the top of the undigested masses already lying there, till the unfortunate mind is fairly swamped under the flood. But the greater the exertion, the more valuable, we may be sure, is the effect; one hour of steady thinking over a subject (a solitary walk is as good an opportunity for the process as any other) is worth two or three of reading only.

And just consider another effect of this thorough digestion of the books we read; I mean the arranging and "ticketing," so to speak, of the subjects in our minds, so that we can readily refer to them when we want them. Sam Slick tells us that he has learned several languages in his life, but somehow "couldn't keep the parcels sorted" in his mind; and many a mind that hurries through book after book, without waiting to digest or arrange anything, gets into that sort of condition, and the unfortunate owner finds himself far from fit really to support the character all his friends give him.

"A thoroughly well-read man. Just you try him in any subject, now. You can't puzzle him!"

You turn to the thoroughly well-read man: you ask him a question, say, in English history (he is understood to have just finished reading Macaulay); he smiles good-naturedly, tries to look as if he knew all about it, and proceeds to dive into his mind for the answer. Up comes a handful of very promising facts, but on examination they turn out to belong to the wrong century, and are pitched in again; a second haul brings up a fact much more like the real thing, but unfortunately along with it comes a tangle of other things—a fact in political economy, a rule in arithmetic, the ages of his brother's children, and a stanza of Gray's *Elegy*; and among all these the fact he wants has got hopelessly twisted up and entangled. Meanwhile every one is waiting for his reply, and as the silence is getting more and more awkward, our well-read friend has to stammer out some half-answer at last, not nearly so clear or so satisfactory as an ordinary schoolboy would have given. And all this for want of making up his knowledge into proper bundles and ticketing them!

Do you know the unfortunate victim of ill-judged

mental feeding when you see him? Can you doubt him? Look at him drearily wandering round a reading-room tasting dish after dish—we beg his pardon, book after book—keeping to none. First a mouthful of novel—but no, faugh! he has had nothing but that to eat for the last week, and is quite tired of the taste; then a slice of science, but you know at once what the result of that will be—ah, of course, much too tough for *his* teeth. And so on through the old weary round, which he tried (and failed in) yesterday, and will probably try, and fail in, tomorrow.

Mr. Oliver Wendell Holmes, in his very amusing book *The Professor at the Breakfast-table*, gives the following rule for knowing whether a human being is young or old. "The crucial experiment is this. Offer a bulky bun to the suspected individual just ten minutes before dinner. If this is easily accepted and devoured, the fact of youth is established." He tells us that a human being, "if young, will eat anything at any hour of the day or night."

To ascertain the healthiness of the *mental* appetite of a human animal, place in its hands a short, well-written, but not exciting treatise on some popular subject—a mental *bun*, in fact. If it is read with eager interest and perfect attention, *and if the reader can answer questions on the subject afterwards*, the mind is in first-rate working order; if it be politely laid down again, or perhaps lounged over for a few minutes, and then, "I can't read this stupid book! Would you hand me the second volume of *The Mysterious Murder?*" you may be equally sure that there is something wrong in the mental digestion.

If this paper has given you any useful hints on the important subject of reading, and made you see that it is one's duty no less than one's interest to "read, mark, learn, and inwardly digest" the good books that fall in your way, its purpose will be fulfilled.

Number of words 1866
See page 297 for questions
Reading time in seconds _______
See page 496 for conversion table

SELECTION 25

Owed to the Public Library

Lesley Conger

Norman Cousins said it well: "A library is the delivery room for the birth of ideas, a place where history comes to life." He might have added, "Knowing your way to the library is about all you need to know." If you really wish to learn, head for the library—you owe it to yourself!

Yesterday I fell in love with the public library all over again.

It was a mild, sweet day, not bright, not gloomy; faintly misty, but not wet. A perfect day, really. And because I had had an errand elsewhere, I approached the library from a direction I don't ordinarily use. It was like seeing a familiar, beloved face in a new and enchanting light. WALK, the traffic signal commanded me, but I stood bemused on the curb, just looking, until I found myself disobeying WAIT and loping across as the red turned green.

It's a middle-aged building, our library, rose brick and gray stone, built in a style that reminds me of some children's blocks I must have had when I was small, the kind that came with doors and windows and chimneys and arches. Georgian, Colonial? I don't know enough about architecture to tell you. But it's a lovely building, with tall windows arched at their tops, and broad stone steps leading up to the doors.

I usually take those steps two at a time. But yesterday I hesitated, and then I walked around the block. There are large elms lining the street, and on the inner edge of the sidewalk, a low concrete balustrade with a rail of the perfect width for young wall-walkers. Between the balustrade and the building grow rhododendron and other greenery, but along the walk concrete benches are set at intervals, each with a name chiseled upon its backrest: Henry Fielding, George

Eliot, William Makepeace Thackeray. . . . On Henry Fielding an old man dozes, knobby hands resting on top of his knobby cane. Behind George Eliot, inside the balustrade, a young man sits on the grass reading. Charles Dickens, Charlotte Brontë, Victor Hugo. . . . There is a girl in a long patchwork skirt sitting on Victor Hugo; she looks at me through great, round, violet sunglasses, which she doesn't really need. Edgar Allan Poe, Mark Twain, Bret Harte. . . . I wonder, do people always notice whose lap they are occupying? Is the girl with the violet glasses waiting for someone, and did she say she'd meet him at the Victor Hugo bench? Oliver Wendell Holmes, Robert Louis Stevenson. . . . Can you remain utterly indifferent to Charlotte Brontë once you've sat leaning against her, eating an apple, feeling the spring sunshine?

Dumas, Hawthorne, Irving. Trollope, Sterne, Austen. . . . There are over twenty benches—twenty-two, I think. Sir Walter Scott, Charles Kingsley, James Fenimore Cooper. And if you approach from the southwest corner, the first two benches you see are Charles Reade and George Borrow. . . . Reade and Borrow, borrow and read. Yes, of course, that's what I'm here for!—and I stop to tie my shoe on Borrow's knee.

On the building itself there are more names, clusters of names, engraved large and clear high up on the gray blocks of the frieze. Not only writers, there, but inventors, musicians, explorers, scientists, painters, religious leaders. Palestrina, Aeschylus, Zoroaster, Copernicus, Raphael. I am dizzy, but less from looking up than from thinking of them: all of them, inside the library, waiting for me—all mine, all just for the asking!

Someone once wrote me to comment on my knowledge of literature. *Enviously*. But there is nothing to envy. The truth is that I never studied literature, certainly not in college, where for some mysterious reason I spent half my time grubbing about in exotic languages, most of which I haven't used since. My college education stands me in no good stead when it comes to writing this chapter—or anything else, for that matter.

Let me confess something—though, indeed, it's not a confession if confessing means admitting to something I'd rather conceal. When I write about books and writers, I am a great deal of the time writing about books and writers I have myself just that moment encountered, and the greatest part of my enthusiasm is the joy of recent discovery.

For finding out is the most delightful part of knowing. And fresh knowledge, even be it concerning things old to others, is my favorite commodity.

Not long ago I pointed out that writing is an occupation with free entry. You need no diploma, no union card, no previous experience. It doesn't matter who you are; everyone's eligible.

Well, unlike most colleges and universities, the public library doesn't care who you are either. Victor Hugo doesn't care. Jane Austin doesn't care. Euripides doesn't care, and he is waiting there for you as much as he waits for me. To those who have asked me what kind of education a writer should have, and to those who have bemoaned their lack of an education, let me say that the best of *my* education has come from the public library—and still does, week after week. My tuition fee is bus fare and once in a while, five cents a day for an overdue book.

But despite the engraved names and despite the emotions they inspire in me, the library is not a pantheon, not some kind of temple dedicated to these gods of intellect and achievement, not a sterile memorial or a musty tomb. It holds not dry bones but still viable thoughts that can leap from a mind long dead to yours, through the agency of the printed page. And more—because of course it isn't Euripides that I seek out every time, or Thackeray, or Brontë or Poe. Last week it turned out to be Barbara Pym, Russell Baker, and John Updike; next week, who knows? Henry James, Jean Auel, and Shirley MacLaine? Or how about *The Cloister and the Hearth* (that's Reade) and *The Romany Rye* (that's Borrow)?

I rounded the block. Oh, it's a beautiful building, warm and mellow in the sunshine. For the sun is out now, and the girl with the violet glasses needs them after all. I look up at the frieze once more—Molière, Voltaire!—and I take the steps by twos and push my way through the heavy doors.

You don't need to know very much at all to start with, if you know the way to the public library.

Number of words 1030
See page 299 in questions
Reading time in seconds _______
See page 496 for conversion table

The Verger

Somerset Maugham

Oscar Wilde once said, "The difference between literature and journalism is that journalism is unreadable and literature is not read." Perhaps that explains why the verger looks on reading as he does. You'll want to know more about this interesting character. But remember, this is literature.

There had been a christening that afternoon at St. Peter's, Neville Square, and Albert Edward Foreman still wore his verger's gown. He kept his new one, its folds as full and stiff as though it were made not of alpaca but of perennial bronze, for funerals and weddings (St. Peter's, Neville Square, was a church much favoured by the fashionable for these ceremonies) and now he wore only his second-best. He wore it with complacence, for it was the dignified symbol of his office, and without it (when he took it off to go home) he had the disconcerting sensation of being somewhat insufficiently clad. He took pains with it; he pressed it and ironed it himself. During the sixteen years he had been verger of this church he had had a succession of such gowns, but he had never been able to throw them away when they were worn out and the complete series, neatly wrapped up in brown paper, lay in the bottom drawers of the wardrobe in his bedroom.

The verger busied himself quietly, replacing the painted wooden cover on the marble font, taking away a chair that had been brought for an infirm old lady, and waited for the vicar to have finished in the vestry so that he could tidy up in there and go home. Presently he saw him walk across the chancel, genuflect in front of the high altar and come down the aisle; but he still wore his cassock.

"What's he 'anging about for?" the verger said to himself. "Don't 'e know I want my tea?"

The vicar had been but recently appointed, a red-faced energetic man in the early forties, and Albert Edward still regretted his predecessor, a clergyman of the old school who preached leisurely sermons in a silvery voice and dined out a great deal with his more aristocratic parishioners. He liked things in church to be just so, but he never fussed; he was not like this new man who wanted to have his finger in every pie. But Albert Edward was tolerant. St. Peter's was in a very good neighbourhood and the parishioners were a very nice class of people. The new vicar had come from the East End and he couldn't be expected to fall in all at once with the discreet ways of his fashionable congregation.

"All this 'ustle," said Albert Edward. "But give 'im time, he'll learn."

When the vicar had walked down the aisle so far that he could address the verger without raising his voice more than was becoming in a place of worship he stopped.

"Foreman, will you come into the vestry for a minute. I have something to say to you."

"Very good, sir."

The vicar waited for him to come up and they walked up the church together.

"A very nice christening, I thought, sir. Funny 'ow the baby stopped cryin' the moment you took him."

"I've noticed they very often do," said the vicar, with a little smile. "After all I've had a good deal of practice with them."

It was a source of subdued pride to him that he could nearly always quiet a whimpering infant by the manner in which he held it and he was not unconscious of the amused admiration with which mothers and nurses watched him settle the baby in the crook of his surpliced arm. The verger knew that it pleased him to be complimented on his talent.

The vicar preceded Albert Edward into the vestry. Albert Edward was a trifle surprised to find the two churchwardens there. He had not seen them come in. They gave him pleasant nods.

"Good-afternoon, my lord. Good-afternoon, sir," he said to one after the other.

They were elderly men, both of them, and they had been churchwardens almost as long as Albert

Edward had been verger. They were sitting now at a handsome refectory table that the old vicar had brought many years before from Italy and the vicar sat down in the vacant chair between them. Albert Edward faced them, the table between him and them, and wondered with slight uneasiness what was the matter. He remembered still the occasion on which the organist had got into trouble and the bother they had all had to hush things up. In a church like St. Peter's, Neville Square, they couldn't afford a scandal. On the vicar's red face was a look of resolute benignity, but the others bore an expression that was slightly troubled.

"He's been naggin' them, he 'as," said the verger to himself. "He's jockeyed them into doin' something, but they don't 'alf like it. That's what it is, you mark my words."

But his thoughts did not appear on Albert Edward's cleancut and distinguished features. He stood in a respectful but not obsequious attitude. He had been in service before he was appointed to his ecclesiastical office, but only in very good houses, and his deportment was irreproachable. Starting as a page-boy in the household of a merchant-prince, he had risen by due degrees from the position of fourth to first footman, for a year he had been single-handed butler to a widowed peeress and, till the vacancy occurred at St. Peter's, butler with two men under him in the house of a retired ambassador. He was tall, spare, grave and dignified. He looked, if not like a duke, at least like an actor of the old school who specialised in dukes' parts. He had tact, firmness and self-assurance. His character was unimpeachable.

The vicar began briskly.

"Foreman, we've got something rather unpleasant to say to you. You've been here a great many years and I think his lordship and the general agree with me that you've fulfilled the duties of your office to the satisfaction of everybody concerned."

The two churchwardens nodded.

"But a most extraordinary circumstance came to my knowledge the other day and I felt it my duty to impart it to the churchwardens. I discovered to my astonishment that you could neither read nor write."

The verger's face betrayed no sign of embarrassment.

"The last vicar knew that, sir," he replied. "He said it didn't make no difference. He always said there was a great deal too much education in the world for 'is taste."

"It's the most amazing thing I ever heard," cried the general. "Do you mean to say that you've been verger of this church for sixteen years and never learned to read or write?"

"I went into service when I was twelve, sir. The cook in the first place tried to teach me once, but I didn't seem to 'ave the knack for it, and then what with one thing and another I never seemed to 'ave the time. I've never really found the want of it. I think a lot of these young fellows waste a rare lot of time readin' when they might be doin' something useful."

"But don't you want to know the news?" said the other churchwarden. "Don't you ever want to write a letter?"

"No, me lord, I seem to manage very well without. And of late years now they've all these pictures in the papers I get to know what's goin' on pretty well. Me wife's quite a scholar and if I want to write a letter she writes it for me. It's not as if I was a bettin' man."

The two churchwardens gave the vicar a troubled glance and then looked down at the table.

"Well, Foreman, I've talked the matter over with these gentlemen and they quite agree with me that the situation is impossible. At a church like St. Peter's, Neville Square, we cannot have a verger who can neither read nor write."

Albert Edward's thin, sallow face reddened and he moved uneasily on his feet, but he made no reply.

"Understand me, Foreman, I have no complaint to make against you. You do your work quite satisfactorily; I have the highest opinion both of your character and of your capacity; but we haven't the right to take the risk of some accident that might happen owing to your lamentable ignorance. It's a matter of prudence as well as of principle."

"But couldn't you learn, Foreman?" asked the general.

"No, sir, I'm afraid I couldn't, not now. You see, I'm not as young as I was and if I couldn't seem able to get the letters in me 'ead when I was a nipper I don't think there's much chance of it now."

"We don't want to be harsh with you, Foreman," said the vicar. "But the churchwardens and I have quite made up our minds. We'll give you three months and if at the end of that time you cannot read and write I'm afraid you'll have to go."

Albert Edward had never liked the new vicar. He'd said from the beginning that they'd make a mistake when they gave him St. Peter's. He wasn't the type of man they wanted with a classy congregation like that. And now he straightened himself a little. He knew his value and he wasn't going to allow himself to be put upon.

"I'm very sorry, sir, I'm afraid it's no good. I'm too old a dog to learn new tricks. I've lived a good many years without knowin' 'ow to read and write, and without wishin' to praise myself, self-praise is no recommendation, I don't mind sayin' I've done my duty in that state of life in which it 'as pleased a merciful providence to place me, and if I *could* learn now I don't know as I'd want to."

"In that case, Foreman, I'm afraid you must go."

"Yes, sir, I quite understand. I shall be 'appy to 'and in my resignation as soon as you've found somebody to take my place."

But when Albert Edward with his usual politeness had closed the church door behind the vicar and the two churchwardens he could not sustain the air of unruffled dignity with which he had borne the blow inflicted upon him and his lips quivered. He walked slowly back to the vestry and hung up on its proper peg his verger's gown. He sighed as he thought of all the grand funerals and smart weddings it had seen. He tidied everything up, put on his coat, and hat in hand walked down the aisle. He locked the church door behind him. He strolled across the square, but deep in his sad thoughts he did not take the street that led him home, where a nice strong cup of tea awaited him; he took the wrong turning. He walked slowly along. His heart was heavy. He did not know what he should do with himself. He did not fancy the notion of going back to domestic service; after being his own master for so many years, for the vicar and churchwardens could say what they liked, it was he that had run St. Peter's, Neville Square, he could scarcely demean himself by accepting a situation. He had saved a tidy sum, but not enough to live on without doing something, and life seemed to cost more every year. He had never thought to be troubled with such questions. The vergers of St. Peter's, like the popes of Rome, were there for life. He had often thought of the pleasant reference the vicar would make in his sermon at evensong the first Sunday after his death to the long and faithful service, and the exemplary character of their late verger, Albert Edward Foreman. He sighed deeply. Albert Edward was a non-smoker and a total abstainer, but with a certain latitude; that is to say he liked a glass of beer with his dinner and when he was tired he enjoyed a cigarette. It occurred to him now that one would comfort him and since he did not carry them he looked about him for a shop where he could buy a packet of Gold Flakes. He did not at once see one and walked on a little. It was a long street, with all sorts of shops in it, but there was not a single one where you could buy cigarettes.

"That's strange," said Albert Edward.

To make sure he walked right up the street again. No, there was no doubt about it. He stopped and looked reflectively up and down.

"I can't be the only man as walks along this street and wants a fag," he said. "I shouldn't wonder but what a fellow might do very well with a little shop here. Tobacco and sweets, you know."

He gave a sudden start.

"That's an idea," he said. "Strange 'ow things come to you when you least expect it."

He turned, walked home, and had his tea.

"You're very silent this afternoon, Albert," his wife remarked.

"I'm thinkin'," he said.

He considered the matter from every point of view and next day he went along the street and by good luck found a little shop to let that looked as though it would exactly suit him. Twenty-four hours later he had taken it and when a month after that he left St. Peter's, Neville Square, forever, Albert Edward Foreman set up in business as a tobacconist and newsagent. His wife said it was a dreadful come-down after being verger of St. Peter's, but he answered that you had to move with the times, the church wasn't what it was, and 'enceforward he was going to render unto Caesar what was Caesar's. Albert Edward did very well. He did so well that in a year or so it struck him that he might take a second shop and put a manager in. He looked for another long street that hadn't got a tobacconist in it and when he found it, and a shop to let, took it and stocked it. This was a success too. Then it occurred to him that if he could run two he could run half a dozen, so he began walking about London, and whenever he found a long street that had no tobacconist and a shop to let he took it. In the course of ten years he had acquired no less than ten shops and he was making money hand over fist. He went round to all of them himself every Monday, collected the week's takings and took them to the bank.

One morning when he was there paying in bundle of notes and a heavy bag of silver the cashier told him that the manager would like to see him. He was shown into an office and the manager shook hands with him.

"Mr. Foreman, I wanted to have a talk to you about the money you've got on deposit with us. D'you know exactly how much it is?"

"Not within a pound or two, sir; but I've got a pretty rough idea."

"Apart from what you paid in this morning it's a little over thirty thousand pounds. That's a very large sum to have on deposit and I should have thought you'd do better to invest it."

"I wouldn't want to take no risk, sir. I know it's safe in the bank."

"You needn't have the least anxiety. We'll make you out a list of absolutely gilt-edged securities. They'll bring you in a better rate of interest than we can possibly afford to give you."

A troubled look settled on Mr. Foreman's distinguished face. "I've never 'ad anything to do with stocks and shares and I'd 'ave to leave it all in your 'ands," he said.

The manager smiled. "We'll do everything. All you'll have to do next time you come in is just to sign the transfers."

"I could do that all right," said Albert uncertainly. "But 'ow should I know what I was signin'?"

"I suppose you can read," said the manager a trifle sharply.

Mr. Foreman gave him a disarming smile.

"Well, sir, that's just it. I can't. I know it sounds funny-like, but there it is, I can't read or write, only me name, an' I only learnt to do that when I went into business."

The manager was so surprised that he jumped up from his chair.

"That's the most extraordinary thing I ever heard."

"You see, it's like this, sir, I never 'ad the opportunity until it was too late and then some'ow I wouldn't. I got obstinate-like."

The manager stared at him as though he were a prehistoric monster.

"And do you mean to say that you've built up this important business and amassed a fortune of thirty thousand pounds without being able to read or write? Good God, man, what would you be now if you had been able to?"

"I can tell you that, sir," said Mr. Foreman, a little smile on his still aristocratic features. "I'd be verger of St. Peter's, Neville Square."

Number of words 2820
See page 303 for questions
Reading time in seconds _______
See page 496 for conversion table

SELECTION 27

How to Read a Dollar Bill

Joseph Campbell with Bill Moyers

Reading involves much more than print. You have to read faces. You have to read minds. And, as this selection makes clear, you also have to read symbols—a much different kind of reading. Don't get out your dollar bill until you've finished the article. Then get it out and reread each symbol carefully.

CAMPBELL: We need myths that will identify the individual not with his local group but with the planet. A model for that is the United States. Here were thirteen different little colony nations that decided to act in the mutual interest, without disregarding the individual interests of any one of them.

MOYERS: There is something about that on the Great Seal of the United States.

CAMPBELL: That's what the Great Seal is all about. I carry a copy of the Great Seal in my pocket in the form of a dollar bill. Here is the statement of the ideals that brought about the formation of the United States. Look at this dollar bill. Now here is the Great Seal of the United States. Look at the pyramid on the left. A pyramid has four sides. These are the four points of the compass. There is somebody at this point, there's somebody at that point, and there's somebody at this point. When you're down on the lower levels of this pyramid, you will be either on one side or on the other. But when you get up to the top, the points all come together, and there the eye of God opens.

MOYERS: And to them it was the god of reason.

CAMPBELL: Yes. This is the first nation in the world that was ever established on the basis of reason instead of simply warfare. These were eighteenth-century deists, these gentlemen. Over here we read, "In God We Trust." But that is not the god of the Bible. These men did not believe in a Fall. They did not think the mind of man was cut off from God. The mind of man, cleansed of secondary and merely temporal concerns, beholds with the radiance of a cleansed mirror a reflection of the rational mind of God. Reason puts you in touch with God. Consequently, for these men, there is no special revelation anywhere, and none is needed, because the mind of man cleared of its fallibilities is sufficiently capable of the knowledge of God. All people in the world are thus capable because all people in the world are capable of reason.

All men are capable of reason. That is the fundamental principle of democracy. Because everybody's mind is capable of true knowledge, you don't have to have a special authority, or a special revelation telling you that this is the way things should be.

MOYERS: And yet these symbols come from mythology.

CAMPBELL: Yes, but they come from a certain quality of mythology. It's not the mythology of a special revelation. The Hindus, for example, don't believe in special revelation. They speak of a state in which the ears have opened to the song of the universe. Here the eye has opened to the radiance of the mind of God. And that's a fundamental deist idea. Once you reject the idea of the Fall in the Garden, man is not cut off from his source.

Now back to the Great Seal. When you count the number of ranges on this pyramid, you find there are thirteen. And when you come to the bottom, there is an inscription in Roman numerals. It is, of course, 1776. Then, when you add one and seven and seven and six, you get twenty-one, which is the age of reason, is it not? It was in 1776 that the thirteen states declared independence. The number thirteen is the number of transformation and rebirth. At the Last Supper there were twelve apostles and one Christ, who was going to die and be reborn. Thirteen is the number of getting out of the field of the bounds of twelve into the transcendent. You have the twelve signs of the zodiac and the sun. These men were very conscious of the number thirteen as the number of resurrection and rebirth and new life, and they played it up here all the way through.

MOYERS: But, as a practical matter, there *were* thirteen states.

CAMPBELL: Yes, but wasn't that symbolic? This is not simply coincidental. This is the thirteen states as themselves symbolic of what they were.

MOYERS: That would explain the other inscription down there, *"Novus Ordo Seclorum."*

CAMPBELL: "A new order of the world." This is a new order of the world. And the saying above, *"Annuit Coeptis,"* means "He has smiled on our accomplishments" or "our activities."

MOYERS: He—

CAMPBELL: He, the eye, what is represented by the eye. Reason. In Latin you wouldn't have to say "he," it could be "it" or "she" or "he." But the divine power has smiled on our doings. And so this new world has been built in the sense of God's original creation, and the reflection of God's original creation, through reason, has brought this about.

If you look behind that pyramid, you see a desert. If you look before it, you see plants growing. The desert, the tumult in Europe, wars and wars and wars—we have pulled ourselves out of it and created a state in the name of reason, not in the name of power, and out of that will come the flowerings of the new life. That's the sense of that part of the pyramid.

Now look at the right side of the dollar bill. Here's the eagle, the bird of Zeus. The eagle is the downcoming of the god into the field of time. The bird is the incarnation principle of the deity. This is the bald eagle, the American eagle. This is the American counterpart of the eagle of the highest god, Zeus.

He comes down, descending into the world of the pairs of opposites, the field of action. One mode of action is war and the other is peace. So in one of his feet the eagle holds thirteen arrows—that's the principle of war. In the other he holds a laurel leaf with thirteen leaves—that is the principle of peaceful conversation. The eagle is looking in the direction of the laurel. That is the way these idealists who founded our country would wish us to be looking—diplomatic relationships and so forth. But thank God he's got the arrows in the other foot, in case this doesn't work.

Now, what does the eagle represent? He represents what is indicated in this radiant sign above his head. I was lecturing once at the Foreign Service Institute in Washington on Hindu mythology, sociology, and politics. There's a saying in the Hindu book of politics that the ruler must hold in one hand the weapon of war, the big stick, and in the other the peaceful sound of the song of cooperative action. And there I was, standing with my two hands like this, and everybody in the room laughed. I couldn't understand. And then they began pointing. I looked back, and here was this picture of the eagle hanging on the wall behind my head in just the same posture that I was in. But when I looked, I also noticed this sign above his head, and that there were nine feathers in his tail. Nine is the number of the descent of the divine power into the world. When the Angelus rings, it rings nine times.

Now, over on the eagle's head are thirteen stars arranged in the form of a Star of David.

MOYERS: This used to be Solomon's Seal.

CAMPBELL: Yes. Do you know why it's called Solomon's Seal?

MOYERS: No.

CAMPBELL: Solomon used to seal monsters and giants and things into jars. You remember in the *Arabian Nights* when they'd open the jar and out would come the genie? I noticed the Solomon's Seal here, composed of thirteen stars and then I saw that each of the triangles was a Pythagorean tetrakys.

MOYERS: The tetrakys being?

CAMPBELL: This is a triangle composed of ten points, one point in the middle and four points to each side, adding up to nine: one, two, three, four/five, six, seven/eight, nine. This is the primary symbol of Pythagorean philosophy, susceptible of a number of interrelated mythological, cosmological, psychological, and sociological interpretations, one of which is the dot at the apex as representing the creative center out of which the universe and all things have come.

MOYERS: The center of energy, then?

CAMPBELL: Yes. The initial sound (a Christian might say, the creative Word), out of which the whole world was precipitated, the big bang, the pouring of the transcendent energy into and expanding through the field of time. As soon as it enters the field of time, it breaks into pairs of opposites, the one becomes two. Now, when you have two, there are just three ways in which they can relate to one another: one way is of this one dominant over that; another way is of that one dominant over this; and a third way is of the two in balanced accord. It is then, finally, out of these three manners of relationship that all things within the four quarters of space derive.

There is a verse in Lao-tzu's *Tao-te Ching* which states that out of the Tao, out of the transcendent, comes the One. Out of the One come Two; out of the Two come Three; and out of the Three come all things.

So what I suddenly realized when I recognized that in the Great Seal of the United States there were two of these symbolic triangles interlocked was that we now had thirteen points, for our thirteen original states, and that there were now, furthermore, no less than six apexes, one above, one below, and four (so to say) to the four quarters. The sense of this, it seemed to me, might be that from above or below, or from any point of the compass, the creative Word might be heard, which is the great thesis of democracy. Democracy assumes that anybody from any quarter can speak, and speak truth, because his mind is not cut off from the truth. All he has to do is clear out his passions and then speak.

So what you have here on the dollar bill is the eagle representing this wonderful image of the way in which the transcendent manifests itself in the world. That's what the United States is founded on. If you're going to govern properly, you've got to govern from the apex of the triangle, in the sense of the world eye at the top.

Number of words 1740
See page 307 for questions
Reading time in seconds________
See page 496 for conversion table

Selection 28

Business Body Language—Understanding the Signals

Dorrine Anderson

Don't overlook another important reading ability—reading body language. Once you learn to read it, you can then "write" it. In making a job application, you should "write" your body language as carefully as you write your resumé. Now find out exactly how it's done.

It's one of those drab, overcast Mondays when you would rather be anywhere else. Walking down the street on your way to work, your thoughts are heavy. Your son's grades in school have slipped drastically. Your wife informed you over an uninteresting breakfast that your rent is going up. You have to fire a fine executive in your company today because his personal problems have made him ineffective on the job.

As you pass a shop window, your eye catches your own reflection. Startled, you look again, harder this time. This is the most depressing of all. Reflected in the glass is an older man, shoulders hunched, head down, feet dragging. "My gosh," you think, "what's happening to me?"

If you are already aware of the new speechless mode of communicating which involves body movements, you know what to do: Take a deep breath; straighten your back; adjust your shoulders back and down into a relaxed position; raise your chin a little higher than you normally do; pull your arms out from your body, elbows slightly bent; turn your toes out a little and take long, generous strides. You look and feel like a new person! The world seems brighter, and the problems you were brooding about shrink to their proper perspective. Like Liza Doolittle in "My Fair Lady," you have gained a new confidence by *doing.*

You may not know it, but you are using Silent Communication. Behavioral scientists believe that by changing the way he moves and gestures (kinesics) a person can actually change his attitude and even his personality.

Remember last Thursday? During the trip on the plane, you gave the finishing touches to a great presentation. As you looked it over, you thought of how much this merger could mean to your company. You'd done your homework well, and if you could convince Mr. Stern, the Executive V.P. in charge of Marketing with the power to make the final decision, you could end up in a V.P.'s office yourself. Waiting for his secretary to announce you, you ran your fingers lightly over your hair and glanced approvingly at the carefully chosen and immaculately pressed suit. "Yes," you reflected, "the board meeting went very well. There is no reason why Mr. Stern shouldn't put his signature on the contract." His secretary returned and escorted you into the decision-making office.

"How was the trip?" asked Mr. Stern, as he put his hand over the phone's mouthpiece and nodded you to a chair.

"Beautiful! Couldn't have been better," you replied with your most engaging smile. As he returned to his call, you opened your case and began setting up your presentation. The art department had out-done themselves for this one. They knew, too, that this joining of forces could put your organization in the Big League.

Stern finally hung up—only to answer two more waiting calls. Your enthusiasm began to dim a little, and as the smile on your face started to freeze, you changed it to a merely pleasant look.

"I'm terribly sorry," Mr. Stern told you from behind his impressive, oversized desk. "I'll have my secretary hold any more calls. I know your time is valuable."

"Oh, I understand perfectly," you assured him as you resurrected The Smile again. "Now, as you know. . . ."

"Just a minute. Before we begin, let's have coffee. How do you like yours?"

"Black," you answered in a subdued voice. The instructions for coffee completed, Stern leaned back in his high-backed swivel chair and began to studiously fill his pipe, puff it into life, and then to slowly digest its fine aroma. "Now, as you were saying . . . ."

"Mr. Stern, we at our company believe that we

have the answer to your complete marketing system." The pipe now burning sufficiently well, your prospect folded his arms and crossed his legs. The telephone was still, his eyes were on you—and then the pipe went out. Disgustedly knocking and scraping the ashes out, Mr. Stern began looking you over carefully; then his eyes wandered to the lamp behind you, finally settling on a pattern in the draperies. Your now unsteady voice announced the *pièce de résistance*—the art department's masterpiece. Stern's foot began jiggling; his fingers resisted a pile of notes as they drummed on the desk.

"Sounds great," he told you in a far-away voice. "We'll have to study your figures. When does your plane leave?"

You assured him that your reservation could be canceled if he needed more time. He assured you that he would, indeed, need at least a month or two to take the proposal through several additional channels. Your mouth felt flannelly. You knew you had flubbed the biggest opportunity in your business career. Where did you go wrong?

For whatever comfort it might be, the man was sending you negative signals from the first moment you entered the office. The phone calls were obviously a rude opener, particularly for a guest who had flown in especially for the meeting. But the real put-down to you and status-builder for him was the ego-building desk placed in the center of the room and his invitation to sit in a low chair on the far side of it. The only answer to such a situation would be to remain standing and possibly walk around a bit to maintain your position level, the logical explanation being a need to stretch out after the trip.

"Every move we make reveals our origins, our attitudes, the state of our psychological balance and even our health," says Mortimer R. Feinberg, Professor of Psychology at Baruch College, City University of New York. Beware whenever someone listens to you with folded arms. He is saying, "So you say. Prove it! I'm not buying." Mr. Stern's crossed legs completed the disinterested pose. An eager, responsive attitude would include: leaning forward with both feet on the floor placed a space apart, arms away from the body and forward, perhaps with a pencil ready to take notes. What did the jiggling foot and drumming fingers testify to? Mr. Stern obviously had his mind elsewhere and was nervously bearing with you out of courtesy only. When confronted by such a situation, it takes an alert mind to do a quick reversal of plans of presentation and shift the approach to one that will startle the adversary out of his preoccupation and make him eager to hear your next words.

Nonverbal communication is the loudest of all. The eye travels faster than the ear, and the signals we see are often more telling than the carefully formed phrases we hear. In fact, the verbal message we receive may actually be *contrary* to what the speaker feels or would like to say.

The Gestalt School of Psychology, based largely on Silent Communication, maintains that an individual's personality can be changed by adopting new body movements—not as simple as it sounds since these movements are largely involuntary. However, if one adheres to the school of thought that physical movements and attitudes are indicators of our mental state, knowing what signals to pay attention to gives the wherewithal to attempt a psychological change.

A few basic signals to watch for are:

• *The tilt of the head.* In a group, it's generally tilted toward the person you prefer. In a one-to-one situation, a forward tilt indicates open-minded listening.

• *The height of the chin.* The higher it's held, the stronger the ego. Hitler, Mussolini and Churchill were easily-read studies in body language. All three showed extreme aggressiveness, with out-thrust chins and penguinlike struts. Short men tend to hold themselves as tall as possible, perhaps to compensate for their lack of height, and often thrust their chin up and out, as through they're looking over the edge of a table for goodies. Think of Jimmy Durante and James Cagney, for example.

• *Shoulder position.* Shoulders that are held up indicate tenseness; shoulders held down and back show a relaxed attitude. Uneven shoulders suggest a controversy in the mind.

• *Leg attitude.* Legs tell legends. The more space allowed between them, the more open the mind generally is and the more open the mind generally is and the more extroverted the personality. Crossing and uncrossing the legs shows uneasiness and often a desire to mislead. When a person is truly attentive, he is usually almost immobile.

• *The stance.* Feet with toes turned in indicate a lack of self confidence, while feet close together and toes pointed straight ahead, tell of an overly conscientious and perhaps prissy character. If you observe turned-out toes, you'll recognize a blown-up ego to the degree of the out-turn. Remember Ma Kettle's famous stance? Marjorie Main used to portray this domineering, back-country woman with arms folded, her weight on the back foot with the heel of the forward foot touching the ground and the toe pointed up. The foot placement indicated a negative outlook, and her folded arms emphasized it.

• *Arm placement.* Coincides with leg and foot placement as to feelings of self worth. Notice if the arms hug the body or are freely out.

• *Gait.* A person's walk, including attitudes, smoothness, weight placement and speed, tells more about him than anything. Bounce a little as you place each step down and you'll gather a feeling of elation; it's a "top of the world" attitude. Watch a cool, self-possessed person and you'll see a smooth, almost gliding walk, while jerkiness indicates that the walker is suffering from frustration over problems. His thoughts are probably as disconnected as his movements are.

Shirley MacLaine's study of French prostitutes for her part as Irma La Douce involved months of observing the easy, loose, but carefully synchronized movements designed to lure men to their dens. Jimmy Stewart's awkward, ambling walk endears women to its boyishness. Models, clerics and military personnel are difficult to read, due to their intense training in prescribed body movements and walks. Observing carefully, you'll find that no two people walk exactly alike because the entire personality goes into it.

Charlton Heston, David Niven, Rex Harrison and Laurence Olivier are examples of people who have learned the lessons of Silent Communication. They have developed body attitudes that, together with voice and timing, immediately captivate any audience. In their business this mastery is referred to as "stage presence." However, anyone can develop it and learn to captivate even a preoccupied or negative audience.

If you'd like to test the validity of Silent Communication on yourself, observe your own body movements the next time you become very angry. Look at your hands. They'll be clenched tightly at your sides or clutching the arms of your chair or even your thighs. Now . . . concentrate on changing your attitude by slowly opening those fists and loosening the fingers until they are limp. The anger will be gone!

Try another test. Let's say you are applying for a position or making a presentation—in either case, you are selling something. What body language rules will help you to accomplish your objective? There is no set pattern, just as there is no written script for a given situation. You and your potential buyer are playing a new but age-old game. But you have the advantage of understanding and applying the proper physical movements. Should Mr. Smith come on too aggressively, you might want to play it cool. Sit back in your chair and present a relaxed attitude—arms placed easily away from your body on the arms of the chair, taking care not to appear overly confident or, worse yet, slouchy. Your movements should be easy, limited and smooth.

If you feel that you are being carefully sized up, convey a self-possessed, middle-of-the-road attitude by sitting midway in the chair and leaning forward slightly. A resistant or too passive reaction on his part will signal you to present a more alert, enthusiastic picture by easing yourself forward and using a little more animation in your gestures and responses. In any situation, the essential impression and feeling of calm control can be maintained by avoiding any movements that might indicate aggressiveness or tenseness. As any good actor knows, gestures should be used sparingly and only when there's a reason. You'll find this awareness of your body actions will, rather than supersede your thoughts and words, actually help you to be more alert to every aspect of the game.

Silent Communication can give you a new outlook on life and the people you encounter. Be aware of it. Observe the signals in others for better understanding, and manipulate your own attitudes. Applying your knowledge of kinesics means mastering one more technique that can give you a decided advantage in business. You'll discover your own "down" days becoming almost nonexistent if you control yourself to sit, stand and walk positively with your chin high, shoulders back and down, arms away from the body with the elbows slightly bent, legs slightly apart and toes turned out a little as they walk in a brisk stride. And you'll find others responding in kind to the signals you send through Silent Communication.

Number of words 2170
See page 311 for questions
Reading time in seconds _______
See page 496 for conversion table

SELECTION 29

Reading for A's

Elisabeth McPherson and Gregory Cowan

Sometimes you read for sheer pleasure, sometimes for inspiration, sometimes for specific problem-solving help. And, as explained in this selection, sometimes you read for better grades. Do you know how to manage that to your best advantage? If not, read on.

Where and when and what you study are all important. But the neatest desk and the best desk light, the world's most regular schedule, the best leather-covered notebook and the most expensive textbooks you can buy will do you no good unless you know how to study. And how to study, if you don't already have some clue, is probably the hardest thing you will have to learn in college. Some students can master the entire system of imaginary numbers more easily than other students can discover how to study the first chapter in the algebra book. Methods of studying vary; what works well for some students doesn't work at all for others. The only thing you can do is experiment until you find a system that does work for you. But two things are sure: nobody else can do your studying for you, and unless you do find a system that works, you won't get through college.

Meantime, there are a few rules that work for everybody. The first is *don't get behind.* The problem of studying, hard enough to start with, becomes almost impossible when you are trying to do three weeks' work in one weekend. Even the fastest readers have trouble doing that. And if you are behind in written work that must be turned in, the teacher who accepts it that late will probably not give you full credit. Perhaps he may not accept it at all.

Getting behind in one class because you are spending so much time on another is really no excuse. Feeling pretty virtuous about the seven hours you spend on chemistry won't help one bit if the history teacher pops a quiz. And many freshmen do get into trouble by spending too much time on one class at the expense of the others, either because they like one class much better or because they find it so much harder that they think they should devote all their time to it. Whatever the reason, going whole hog for one class and neglecting the rest of them is a mistake. If you face this temptation, begin with the shortest and easiest assignments. Get them out of the way and then go on to the more difficult, time-consuming work. Unless you do the easy work first, you are likely to spend so much time on the long, hard work that when midnight comes, you'll say to yourself, "Oh, that English assignment was so easy, I can do it any time," and go on to bed. The English assignment, easy as it was, won't get done.

If everything seems equally easy (or equally hard), leave whatever you like best until the end. There will be more incentive at half past eleven to read a political science article that sounded really interesting than to begin memorizing French irregular verbs, a necessary task that strikes you as pretty dull.

In spite of the noblest efforts, however, everybody does get a little behind in something some time. When this happens to you, catch up. Don't skip the parts you missed and try to go ahead with the rest of the class while there is still a big gap showing. What you missed may make it impossible, or at least difficult, to understand what the rest of the class is doing now. If you are behind, lengthen your study periods for a few days until you catch up. Skip the movie you meant to see or the nap you planned to take. Stay up a little later, if you have to. But catch up.

If you are behind not just in one class but in all of them, the problem is a little different. Maybe you have had a bad bout of mumps or an attack of the general confusion common to students in their first quarter of school. Whatever your ailment was, if it has put you two weeks behind in everything, probably you cannot hope to catch up. Your best bet, in these circumstances, is to face the situation and drop a class. With one less course to worry about, you can spend both the class hours and the study time reserved for that class in catching up with your remaining classes. It's too bad to drop a course in the middle of a term, but it's a lot better to finish your first quarter with twelve hours of C than with seventeen hours of D or F.

The second rule that works for everybody is *don't be afraid to mark in textbooks.* A good student's books don't finish the term looking as fresh and clean as the day they were purchased: they look used, well used. Some sections are underlined. Notes are written down the margins. Answers to some of the questions are sketched in. In fact, the books look at though somebody had studied them.

If you are the well-brought-up product of a public school, this method of studying books may horrify you. Perhaps in kindergarten you learned that it was naughty to scribble in your books with your crayon. In grade school it was made clear that anyone who wrote in a book was headed for juvenile court. In high school you discovered that even the student who wrote on bathroom walls was more respectable than the evil character that marked in his books. And up to now there were good reasons for these restrictions. It does seem senseless and wasteful to let a child ruin a book with crayon scribbles or to let an idle student deface a book with aimless doodles or caricatures of his homeroom teacher's long nose. Besides, the school district didn't want you to produce all the answers for the student who would use the book next year.

In college your books belong to you. Even so, you are still dogged by the same advice, this time from the college bookstore: don't write in the book if you want to sell it. Of course, some students do sell their books. These students figure that books cost a lot of money, that the courses are dull anyway, and when these students finish the term, they think they never want to see those books again. These students count themselves fortunate if the manager of the bookstore offers anything at all for their books. These pseudo-students are more interested in saving a dollar or so next year than in learning much right now. On the other hand, the student who wants to make the most of his textbooks will not worry about selling them; he'll worry about keeping them and using them to the best advantage.

Let's assume that *you* plan to keep your book. First, put your name in it, in large, clear writing so that when you leave it in the coffee shop, some honest student can return it to you. Then start marking it up. We are not suggesting, of course, that you dig up your old crayons or draw cartoons of your teachers in the margins. But some kinds of marking are both useful and economically sound. To get your money's worth from your text, you must do more with it than just read it.

To begin with, when you first get a new textbook, look at the table of contents to see what material the book covers. Flip through the pages to see what study aids the author has provided: subheadings, summaries, charts, pictures, review questions at the end of each chapter. After you have found what the whole book covers, you will be better prepared to begin studying the chapter you have been asked to read.

Before you begin reading the chapter, give it the same sort of treatment. Skim through the first and last paragraphs; look with more care at the subheadings; if there are questions at the end of the chapter, read them first so you will know what points to watch for as you read. After you are thus forewarned, settle down to the actual business of reading. Read the chapter all the way through, as fast as you comfortably can. Don't mark anything this first time through except the words that are new to you. Circle them. When you have finished the chapter, find out what these unknown words mean, and write the definitions in the margin opposite the word.

Then look again at the questions, seeing whether you have found the answers to all of them. Guided by the things the questions emphasize and your knowledge of what the whole chapter covered, go rapidly through the chapter again, underlining the most important points. If the chapter falls into three major divisions, underline the three sentences that come closest to summing up the idea of each division. Number these points in the margin: 1, 2, 3. For each major point you have numbered, underline two or three supporting points. In other words, underline the sections you think you might want to find in a hurry if you were reviewing the chapter.

What happens in class the next day, or whenever this assignment is discussed, will give you some check on whether you found the important points. If the teacher spends a lot of time on a part of the text you didn't mark at all, probably you guessed wrong. Get yourself a red pencil and mark the teacher's points. You can make these changes during the study time you have set aside for comparing class notes with the textbook.

One word of warning: don't underline everything you read. If you mark too much, the important material won't stand out, and you will be just as confused as if you had not marked anything at all.

The third rule useful to everybody is *don't let tests*

terrify you. If you have kept up in all your classes, if you have compared your class notes with your texts, if you have kept all your quizzes and gone over your errors, if you have underlined the important parts of each chapter intelligently, the chances are good that you can answer any questions the teacher will ask.

Being fairly sure that you can answer all the questions, however, is not the same thing as answering them. Nothing is more frustrating than freezing up during an important test, knowing all the answers but getting so excited at the sight of the test that half of what you actually know never gets written down.

Do you know the story of the lecturer who cured his stage fright by pretending that all the people listening to him were cabbages? A head of cabbage is no more capable of criticizing a lecture than cabbage soup would be. And who's afraid of a bowl of borsch? You might adapt this system to taking tests. Pretend that the test is only a game you are playing to use up an idle hour. Pretend that your test score is no more important than your score in canasta last night. But you tried to win at canasta; try for as high a test score as you can get without frightening yourself to death.

One way to insure a good score is to read the entire test before you answer any questions. Sometimes questions that come near the end will give clues to the answers on earlier questions. Even if you don't find any answers, you can avoid the error of putting everything you know into the first answer and then repeating yourself for the rest of the test.

Be careful, too, not to spend all your time on one question at the expense of the others. If you have sixty minutes to finish a test that contains ten questions, plan to spend five minutes on each question and save ten minutes at the end to read through what you have written, correcting silly mistakes and making sure you have not left out anything important. If some of the questions seem easier than others, answer the easiest first. There is no rule that says you must begin at the beginning and work straight through to the end. If you're going to leave something out, it might as well be the things you aren't sure of anyway.

Following these three suggestions, reading through the test, budgeting your time, doing the easy part first, will not guarantee A's on all your tests. To get A's on essay tests, you must be able to write well enough that your teacher is convinced you *do* understand. What following these suggestions *can* do, however, is help you make the most of what you know.

Number of words 2090
See page 315 for questions
Reading time in seconds _______
See page 496 conversion table

SELECTION 30

How Fast Should a Person Read?

George Cuomo

Some questions really can't be answered; some can and some must—or you're left forever in limbo. This author poses a must *question. After all, if you don't how fast you should read, how can you set a specific goal? What do you think of his answer?*

It's probably futile to hope to talk sensibly any more about so-called speed reading. The extremists have overrun the field and, as usual, preposterous statements and foolish misconceptions make good copy. Amidst the din, quieter voices go unheard.

The extremists of the left—using such effective platforms as the Jack Paar show—tell us that we should be reading at ten thousand words a minute, fifteen thousand, twenty thousand . . . .

Their right-wing counterparts thunder back with

equal irrelevance. George Steven's piece in the August 26, 1961, issue of this magazine, entitled "Faster, Faster!" is typical. Why not, he suggests, keep reading faster and faster until we can read all of Gibbon's *Decline and Fall* over a cup of instant coffee?

Why not, one could suggest in turn, carefully train ourselves to read slower and slower until it takes us a minute to read a single word? We could then blissfully spend something like 21,000 solid hours—or 2,625 eight-hour days—reading *Decline and Fall.*

To some, not knowing your reading rate is a source of pride. They don't want to know. One's reading rate is God-given, and to measure or question it or, heaven forbid, to try to improve it, is blasphemy. The assumption, of course, is that everybody's reading rate is just dandy as it is. Perhaps. But the facts scarcely encourage such blitheness of spirit.

At the other end of the scale, we have those whose pride springs from rates measured in rapidly multiplying tens of thousands. Bosh and foolishness, I say. Semantic humbug. Up in the rarified stratosphere of twenty or thirty thousand words a minute, a person is skimming, or surveying, or "getting the gist of the thing," but he isn't reading with anything resembling full or specific comprehension. With few exceptions, most people cannot read effectively at much better than two thousand words per minute.

Perhaps it would pay us to leave the extremes where they belong and look at the whole question realistically.

The average adult, for instance, reads about 250 words a minute. This is also the average I've found among college freshmen. But the variations in my classes run from 125 to 900. This means that some students were reading over *seven* times as fast as others. There's probably an even greater spread among the general public.

All right, one is tempted to reply, some people are simply faster readers than others, as they may also be taller, fatter, or better looking.

But speed itself does not tell the whole story, and no one except the figure-worshippers of the left and the figure-haters of the right is concerned with speed alone. What counts is a person's overall reading ability, agreed. But in this, speed plays an important and usually misunderstood part. Every reputable study has shown that reasonably fast readers perform not only as well as their slower equivalents, but often better.

Probably the most common and groundless misconception about reading is the one that equates even moderate speed with sloppiness. Actually, the slow readers are the sloppy ones. They read aimlessly and passively and have more trouble concentrating than do faster readers. In addition, they do not understand as much, do not evaluate as well, and do not remember as effectively. The person who says he always reads slowly because he is being careful is just fooling himself. He is neither as careful nor as diligent as he likes to think. He is simply inefficient. He's driving along a smooth, clear highway in the same low gear he uses to get his car out of the mud.

The fast reader is fast because he is alert and skilful. He has been trained—or has trained himself—to use his ability and his intelligence effectively. Thousands of persons, including President Kennedy, have proved that such training is both possible and practical.

The methods used cannot be fully explained in a brief article, but they are based on sound principles and have been approved by many respected and conservative educators. More important, they have consistently worked. A person is taught, for instance, to read several words, or a phrase, or perhaps a whole line, at a single eye-stop, instead of making such a stop for every word. A person with a rate of less than 250 words per minute almost always reads word by word. This method is so slow and inefficient that it actually hinders comprehension. In learning to read by meaningful word groups, a person enables his brain to function much closer to its capacity and almost invariably improves his comprehension.

There are of course additional ways of improving both speed *and* comprehension, all of them based on nothing more outrageous than a basic understanding of the reading process. For no matter how hard some people try to ignore the fact, reading—for all its ethereal possibilities—is a learned process, in which certain techniques operate more successfully than others. No one is born knowing how to read; he must be taught. He can be taught well or poorly. What most often happens, however—and this seems to be what the "slower, slower" people are fighting for—is that he is not taught at all. Left to his own devices, he typically develops a surprising number of bad reading habits, among which is the habit of reading too slowly for maximum comprehension or enjoyment.

Ironically, the strongest opposition to the teaching of effective reading techniques comes from those who base their arguments on "literary" considerations. Yet these are the same people who complain that the schools aren't spending enough time teaching students how to write well. Give them more spelling, they demand, more punctuation, grammar, sentence structure, paragraph development. A knowledge of fundamental writing techniques thus seems most desirable, but any attempt to teach comparable reading techniques is considered immoral. Obviously, technique alone will not make a person a good writer *or* a good reader, but if training and knowledge help in one discipline, might they not also help in the other?

The real issue here is not whether a person should or shouldn't read twenty thousand words a minute, or even whether he can or can't. The real issue is much more mundane than that, and much more important. It is whether the average person—now reading 250 words a minute—would not be a better reader in every way if he learned to read effectively at 600, 800, or a thousand words a minute. The evidence is quite convincing that he would.

A person whose rate is 250 words a minute is not only kept from reading well, but is often kept from reading at all. Let's take another look at *Decline and Fall.* At 250 words a minute, a person will take eighty-three hours to read it. How often does he, faced with such a task, simply decide he hasn't got time for it? Rightly or wrongly, this is often his decision, for he has only two alternatives: to spend eight-three hours on it, or no hours.

And this brings us to an important and generally neglected point. In actual fact, a person does not have a single reading rate. He has—or should have—many rates. He should be able to read as fast or as slow as he wants, or as the situation warrants.

But all people have what can be considered a "base" rate—the rate at which they normally read more or less average material. It is from this base rate that they should speed up or slow down in accordance with the demands of the material.

However, the reader with a low base rate—around 250—rarely does this. He reads Shakespeare and Spillane at essentially the same pace (which makes the "literary" arguments for slow reading that much more absurd). And even when he does try to shift gears, he isn't very successful. He can't get much faster because he's too unskilled, and he can't get much slower without coming to a dead halt.

The reader with a better base rate—say 800 words a minute—has a far broader range of potential variation. He can easily move up to a thousand words or better for casual reading, and can always slow down as much as he wants for studying, or for the reading of difficult or specialized material. The rapid reader is not a slave to speed; the slow reader *is* a slave to slowness.

Thus it's absurd to argue about "speed reading." The term is meaningless, because critics insist on interpreting it to mean that a person must read everything as fast as he possible can, must race headlong through Yeats and Milton and Donne and dash madly through *Moby Dick*. Quite the contrary. For if a person learns his lesson well, he will not be limited, if he wants to read a good-sized novel, to a choice of either no hours or ten hours. He can spend on it any number of hours in between. He can spend on it as much time and effort as he feels it deserves. More than that no writer, not Gibbon, nor Shakespeare, nor Spillane, can fairly ask of any reader.

Now, for the life of me I can't see why encouraging sensible reading techniques, and pointing out that most people read too slowly for satisfactory comprehension or appreciation, should be considered evil or anti-intellectual. Perhaps the explanation lies in the startling emotional investment most people have in their reading habits. Almost everyone who has worked in the field has noticed this. You can with impunity criticize a person's ignorance of arithmetic or spelling or sex or politics, but mention his reading techniques and immediately he's insulted. Good, bad, or indifferent, they're his and he loves them.

The whole question can really be put quite simply. If someone can prove to me that a reasonable increase in a person's reading rate causes resultant disadvantages—such a loss of comprehension, or a lessening of that person's appreciation or enjoyment—I'll happily throw the whole business over and learn all the chants of the "slower, slower" crowd.

By the same token, I'd like to see these people agree that if a person could read faster—without any such losses, and usually with appreciable gains—then the increase in speed would be a desirable good, and worth working for.

This doesn't seem too much to ask. But the radicals will probably howl anyway.

Number of words 1734
See page 319 for questions
Reading time in seconds ________
See page 496 for conversion table

Selection 31

The Most Precious Gift

Hank Whittemore

Imagine starting college at age 32—without ever having stepped into a classroom before! How could anyone succeed with such an unbelievable handicap? And how could such a situation arise in this country? Read on to answer those questions and more.

"Sometimes I do wonder where I came from," muses Robert Howard Allen of West Tennessee, who had never seen the inside of a classroom until, in 1981 at age 32, he entered college. No, he was not a late-blooming genius; but last May, after just a decade of school, he graduated from Vanderbilt University in Nashville with a master's degree and a Ph.D. in English. A gentle, unworldly spirit who plays the banjo and loves to make puns, he adds with an enigmatic grin, "Maybe I just fell out of the sky."

When Allen first appeared on the campus of Bethel College, a small Presbyterian school in McKenzie, 15 miles from his backwoods home, administrators were even more baffled. Here was a grown man who had never been to grammar school or high school, yet he had "blown the lid off" his college placement test. He stood 6 feet tall, with unkempt red hair, and his tattered sweater was held together by safety pins. There were holes in his shoes and his front teeth were gone. He had rarely set foot outside Carroll County, 120 miles west of Nashville, where he was born. He lived in a ramshackle farmhouse—one of three homes in the tiny hamlet of Rosser—without indoor plumbing. He had never ridden a bicycle or been inside a movie theater or out on a date.

With an aura of innocence, however, Allen's blue eyes sparkled from behind his steel-rimmed glasses as if he had a secret. And it turned out that he did—a secret that amounts to a triumph of faith.

From the age of 7, Robert Allen read books. Not just several books or even a few hundred, but thousands of every description—from Donald Duck comics to the Bible, from Homer to James Joyce—to the point where his head was filled with history and classical literature. The scope of his learning was far greater than that of any professor at Bethel, where he was invited to skip most of his freshman courses and enter as a sophomore. Yet, having spent his whole life in virtual isolation with elderly relatives, Allen himself had no idea how special he was.

He turned up at Bethel on a whim. "I'd started my own upholstery business in back of the house," he recalls, "but when the 1980 recession came on, there was no more work. So I thought I'd give education a whirl. I didn't think I could succeed at it, though. I just assumed that people in college knew more than I did."

In three years, he graduated summa cum laude.

Without realizing it, Robert Allen had proved the power of reading to transform an individual life. In circumstances that otherwise would have been unbearable, he had read as an unconscious act of sheer survival. "Books were my great comfort," he says simply. "They were my pastime and my playmates." Reading whatever he could get his hands on, he traveled freely across time and space, meeting the world's greatest philosophers and poets down through the ages.

"He's at home in mythological Babylon and in eight-century Judea," says Dr. William Ramsay, one of his Bethel advisers. "He became a citizen of the world without ever leaving Tennessee."

"Robert retains everything," says Prof. Vereen Bell, who teaches English at Vanderbilt, "so his head is just full of all this historical and mythological stuff that he has accumulated. In a sense, he missed the 20th century. He's in a kind of time warp, and I think he forever will be."

Allen's triumph had its seeds in suffering. His parents were divorced a few months before he was born. He yearned for his father but, to this day, has never seen him. His mother, Hazel, worked as a waitress and all but ignored him. "She was in the generation between the farmers and me," he says, "so I think she felt caught in that condition." When Robert was 6, his mother abandoned him, running off with a traveling shoe salesman. She left him to be raised by elderly relatives—his grandfather and three great-aunts and a great-uncle—living in the same household.

Even today, Allen can express his youthful pain only through his poetry, as when he writes that the mother "had no love for her stray mistake of a child" and that his grandmother "died just one spring later, too soon to fill my childhood with any love." It was Uncle Eddie Jones, his guardian, who decreed that school was "a waste of time" and blocked authorities from enrolling him.

"I never entirely understood it," Allen says, adding that he was also told that his father might return "to kidnap me, even though there was no evidence that he even knew I existed." In any event, he adds, "They kept me home. I really was pretty much isolated."

The county sent teachers for the homebound twice weekly for a year, but from age 7 the boy's formal education was over. In a house where at least one of his relatives was always sick or dying, growing up without friends, Allen listened to endless family stories; and Aunt Bevie Jones, Uncle Eddie's wife, began reading to him. "She had gone up to the eighth grade," he says, "but that was the only education in our family." Aunt Bevie taught him to read; his grandfather taught him to write; and the boy, in turn, read the King James Bible to his blind Aunt Ida, going through it twice from cover to cover.

Allen's male ancestors had been farmers, but since the '30s the men had become carpenters and house painters. The boy was destined to pick up these trades; but at age 12, while he was helping care for sick relatives at home, he began reading an old set of Shakespeare's works. "I opened it up and just about read it through at a sitting," he says, and today he'll quote long passages from *King Lear* and *The Tempest*—to name just two of his favorites—at a moment's notice.

Hungry for more, he began picking up books at yard sales for pennies apiece—works of mythology, history, poetry and anything else he could find. By his early 20s, Robert had some 2000 volumes and a goal: "I followed a vague, overall plan, which I more or less fulfilled," he recalls, "to study literature in the context of history from the earliest times to the present."

When he saw the Carroll County Library in nearby Huntingdon, it was like discovering gold. "Sometimes his Grandfather Jim and Aunt Bevie came with him," recalls Claudine Halpers, the staffer who eventually encouraged him to try for college. "They showed up every week or two, regular as clockwork. They were poor but not ashamed. Robert was his own person—unassuming, but very bright with a keen sense of humor."

On the shelves, Allen found the complete set of Will and Ariel Durant's *The Story of Civilization* and spent the next two years wading through its 10 massive volumes, simultaneously reading histories and classics for each time period. Out of pure enjoyment, he worked his way through the entire library, also teaching himself to read Greek and French to better absorb original versions. The works of Milton, Burns, Keats, Whitman, Wordsworth and other poets continued to feed his insatiable appetite for knowledge and what he now calls "language used to its highest potential."

At age 30, Robert Allen took a high school equivalency test and easily earned his diploma. Two years later, when Bethel College officials saw his placement scores, they eased his way with a work-study grant combining scholarship funds and a campus job.

By 1984, after three years as an amiable, older and unquestionably "different" figure on the Bethel campus, he topped his senior class with straight A's in all but typing. He scored 3.92 out of a possible 4.0 grade-point average. As graduation presents, the faculty bought him his first suit—which he accepted reluctantly, saying they should give it to "someone who really needs it"—and a set of new front teeth. Aunt Bevie, by now 77, attended the ceremonies where he received his diploma. The newspaper ran a story about him.

The publicity, however, led to a crushing blow. One Sunday, while attending the local Baptist church, Allen recalls in a soft tone of wonderment, "The pastor got up and preached a sermon on 'the sinfulness of these arrogant people who get their picture in the paper,' obviously meaning me. It was a very unpleasant experience."

Accepting a fellowship from Vanderbilt, with an eye toward ultimately teaching, Robert Allen packed up his belongings that fall and moved with Aunt Bevie to Nashville. It was his first venture beyond the green hills of West Tennessee and his entrance into the modern world of a "big city," where he took his first elevator ride.

While coping with noise and traffic, along with adjusting to university life, Allen decided it was finally time to reconcile with his mother, who had remarried and settled in Missouri. For three years, he had phoned her on Mother's Day, although she always seemed annoyed and even hostile. He told friends, "There's a new chance for us, because I can finally forgive. I just want to be a son to her." Near Christmas in 1984, he and Aunt Bevie drove to Missouri uninvited.

The incident is still hard for him to discuss. "We spent about an hour with her," he recalls, "and basically she was angry. She blamed everyone for not treating her well. I think she felt guilty. It was a tirade about how badly she had been raised." Allen left with Aunt Bevie while his mother was still shouting from the doorway. He cried all the way back to Tennessee.

The following summer, no longer able to take care of ailing Aunt Bevie, he was forced to put her into a nursing home in Huntingdon. He drove to visit her every other weekend until she died in 1988, leaving him to face the rest of his remarkable odyssey alone.

Aunt Bevie had lived long enough to see him earn his master's degree at Vanderbilt in 1986. Allen's thesis was a collection of his poetry, most of it autobiographical or based on the family tales he had heard as a child. For his doctoral dissertation, he began studying an early poem by William Butler Yeats, "The Wanderings of Oisin."

In 1990, on the verge of earning his Ph.D., he drove alone to Missouri to see his mother and try once more. He called from a nearby pay phone to announce his arrival, only to be told that she had died 10 days earlier. No one had notified him. He visited her grave, then drove back to Nashville.

During the first half of 1991, aside from attending graduation ceremonies at Vanderbilt, Robert Allen taught a semester of English at Bethel College. During the summer, he continued to live alone in McKenzie. There, he set aside a copy of *War and Peace* one afternoon to talk about the future. "I'd like to continue teaching and writing poetry," he told me. "In the past year I've been turning family history into a long series of poems, loosely linked together." What does the Ph.D. mean to him? "Well," he shrugged, "it means I can get a job." Any thoughts of eventually getting married? "No," he said with a smile—as if that were a possibility too far down the road to see.

"Robert is struggling with great courage to make himself more a part of the contemporary world," says Professor Bell, "so his story is going to go on and on."

At the doorway of his small, rented home, Robert Allen, age 42, stands with his Tolstoy edition in one hand, waving with the other. He smiles his enigmatic smile before turning and disappearing, at least for a while, into a distant time and place. Reading is what saved him; writing poetry about his family is both an exorcism of painful experiences and a bold journey of personal evolution. His secret seems to lie at some unfathomable depth, as if he were not only destined but determined, to finally solve the mystery for himself—to keep on falling out of the sky.

Number of words 2050
See page 323 for questions
Reading time in seconds _______
See page 496 for conversion table

SELECTION 32

Why Do We Read?

Frank G. Jennings

Keep purpose uppermost in all your plans and activities, and you'll soon taste the satisfaction of added achievement. Always ask, "Why?" That question puts purpose on a pedestal where you can't overlook it. Now—"Why read?"

We read to learn. We read to live another way. We read to quench some blind and shocking fire. We read to weigh the worth of what we have done or dare to do. We read to share our awful secrets with someone we know will not refuse us. We read our way into the presence of great wisdom, vast and safe suffering, or into the untidy corners of another kind of life we fear to lead. With the book we can sin at a safe distance. With Maugham's artist in *The Moon and Sixpence*, we can discommit ourselves of family responsibility and burn our substance and our talent in bright colors on a tropic isle. But this is no child's play. In this kind of reading there is profit and loss and to take the one and sustain the other our prior investments in psychological and intellectual securities must have been considerable and sound. Our maturity rating must be high enough to warrant the title *adult*.

Mature reading is more than and different from the mere application of the basic skills of "reading." It requires, of course, the cultivation of an ever growing vocabulary, in fact of several different though essentially related vocabularies. It requires some minimum level of physical well-being. It requires an ability to "shift gears," that is, to suit the way we read to what we read. Certainly a short story in a mass-circulation magazine neither requires nor deserves the attention we would give to one by Thomas Mann, Joseph Conrad, Sherwood Anderson or Katherine Mansfield. We would not study a sports column with the same intensity that we must bring to Albert Schweitzer's testament of faith. We don't read a cake recipe the way we read instructions on an income tax form. So, the adult must be able to read with discrimination as to the methods by which he reads. More especially he must be aware of the purposes for which he reads.

The same piece of writing may be read at many different levels, regardless of the author's obvious intent. If we choose to read for amusement, for recreation, for what is loosely now called escape, we should be able to do so, whether the writer be Plato or Mickey Spillane. This may shock some people's sensibilities, but it is hardly sensible to be so easily shocked. The book can be an instrument of widely different usage. It can be as fine and precise as a scalpel or as blunt and gross as a pole axe. Its service changes as we tell ourselves why we read.

Why ever we read, there are certain conditions that are present when we read as adults. We must be aware of all of them to some degree. For in the first place, an author is speaking to us. The child and the immature person is rarely aware that anyone is behind the book. We may avoid, if that is our purpose, any concern with the author's intent, even if he announces it loudly either in preface or in style. In the second place, even in the attitude of "escape," we work with our reading. We bring to bear upon the act of reading all that we are in terms of experience, all that we know, all that we are capable of feeling. Present at all times are clusters of attitudes, preconceptions, prejudices and preferences concerning the meanings of words and ideas. A white resident of Alabama cannot read Lillian Smith's *Strange Fruit* in quite the same way as a Philadelphia Quaker will read it. A labor leader won't read *The Legend of Henry Ford* by Keith Sward in quite the same way that a dedicated member of the Optimist Clubs might. A clergyman could not read Homer W. Smith's *Man and His Gods* with anything approaching the equanimity of a confirmed atheist.

A third condition that is present whenever we read as adults is really a corollary to the second. It is a kind of transaction between the writer and the reader. Although the author is done with his writing, he continues to work on the mind of each new or renewed reader. Marya Dmitrievna in *War and Peace* never enters twice in the same way the room at the Rostov's dinner party—but her vitality, her boisterous aliveness, is always there for any reader. The way a reader feels when he reads and the conditions under which he reads, physical as well as psychological, all contribute to how he reads. This is more apparent in poetry with its concentrated compass but it is present in all forms of writing to some degree. Tolstoy has made Marya available, it is the reader who makes her live, and she will be alive differently for different readers and even for the same reader at different times. What we are and what we are living through at a particular time reworks what we read and makes it a unique experience fraught with new meanings that we never suspected. In the fall of 1941, Matthew Arnold's lines from "Dover Beach" referred to something he could never have known: ". . . on the French coast the light/ Gleams and is gone; the cliffs of England stand,/ Glimmering and vast, out in the tranquil bay." They will always have a particular quality for those who lived through World War II. For others who came before or after, these lines will have different and perhaps less-potent meanings.

A fourth condition which is present in the reading of all but the most abstract of technical writing is that mature reading provides and even requires a *living through* an experience, not merely getting knowledge *about* a real or imagined happening. We actually come *with* Isak in Knut Hamsun's *Growth of the Soil*, into the strange and desolate new country and, depending on our abilities as readers, we sense some of his feelings and taste some of his unspoken hopes. This is more and different from the adolescent identification of a boy or girl who has been picked up by some powerfully written story in the delight of helpless suffering or joy, and carried to some seeming world-shattering conclusion. The mature reader is past most seduction but is not blasé. In working with the author he may be learning something new in the experience but he is also, in a measure, controlling the shape of that experience. He has to accept the fact of the fiction but he need not either love or hate what he sees. In some ways he participates in the growth of the characters he is reading about. He takes the hints and suggestions of the author and amalgamates them with the substance of his own actual and vicarious experiences giving a flesh-and-blood roundness to the creatures of the writer's fancy.

These conditions then, the reader's awareness of the presence of the author, the reader working with the author, the pressure of current experience and the reader's ability and necessity to *live through* the constructed characters and events, all combine to direct and to color the aspects of every particular act of reading.

But maturity in reading goes far beyond this. In fact these conditions, by themselves, do not add up to the total act of reading. For, whatever we read, be it a mail-order catalogue or a treatise on the gods, we integrate it with the continuing flow of experiences and dealings that is our life. This explains in part why, through the writings of others, past and contemporary, we are able to live so richly in so short a time.

Number of words 1270
See page 327 for questions
Reading time in seconds _______
See page 496 for conversion table

SELECTION 33

Do You Need a Time Stretcher?

Eugene S. Wright

Who hasn't said, "I don't have time"? According to Theophrastus, a philosopher and naturalist of ancient Greece, "Time is the most valuable thing one can spend." He could have added that, with time, we're all equally rich. Prince or pauper, we all have twenty-four hours a day. No one has more; no one has less. But can you really stretch time? Find out.

Something new has been added to our stereotype of the American executive. Besides being a rugged individualist—a competitive-spirited woman or a two-fisted self-made man—the modern industrial tycoon now boasts (almost without exception) a beautifully developed set of stomach ulcers. Heckled, harassed, and hurried by overlings, underlings, and a mass of details, the current overlord of the corporate millions just plain doesn't have time to do all the things that have to be done in order to keep peace with the board of directors at the office and the high command at home.

The problem was dramatized the other day in a letter received by the writer. "If you know where I can buy a 'time stretcher,'" the communicant writes, "I will give you a million dollars for it." And that's just what we must have, it seems, to restore our executive group to the fold of well-balanced, happy humanity. Nothing less than a "time stretcher" will enable overworked magnates to leave their bulging briefcases behind and return to the sanctuary of their homes without a mass of undigested reports standing in the way of a normal, relaxing home life.

Having for years proceeded on the assumption that time was an element which could not be tampered with, much less stretched, we felt that the plight of our business and industrial executives was quite hopeless indeed. But the offer of a million dollars often spurs men to extreme efforts and it is with such a reward in mind that the present observations are being made.

Granting, then, that some esoteric machine that is capable of stretching a minute into an hour or an hour into a day is quite beyond the realm of possibility even in this day of space travel, we are then faced with the necessity of finding a suitable substitute. And just such a substitute does exist. It is efficient reading.

"Now, just a minute," comes the clamor from the reading audience. "How can efficient reading be made to serve as a time stretcher?" The answer to that question is not difficult to explain, but some background is first required.

For years the general public has held to the notion that reading is a simple skill that, once mastered in about the third or fourth grade, will stick with you the rest of your life and will operate effectively in all types of reading situations. Not quite so, we now learn, as we realize that reading is a developmental process that begins early and continues along a path of ever-increasing complexity and refinement. Generally, however, the development stops when the pressures of the school are removed and the individual fails to meet and master material of increasing complexity. Of course, there are limits to this development placed upon each person by native ability, but seldom, if ever, does one encounter a reader who might be said to reach an optimum development in reading.

On the contrary, the author has encountered many college students and business people alike whose reading development was arrested at extremely low levels. Not uncommon are cases such as the graduate engineer who scored at the tenth grade level on a standardized reading test, or the M.D. who could not read college freshman material swiftly and meaningfully. Other notable instances where general ability and reading ability were far out of alignment have constantly cropped up in the twenty-one years that the author has worked with reading programs at the college and extension level at the University of Minnesota.

Even though there is extreme danger in making generalizations with respect to reading, most of the students encountered fortunately exhibit only simple reading disabilities; that is, they possess the necessary tools but just need them sharpened. Some few cases don't have the tools at all and need individual clinical help.

Out of these many individual experiences evolved the program of Efficient Reading at the University of Minnesota under the guiding hand of Dr. James I. Brown. Almost an immediate success when first offered under the General Extension Division, the course soon attracted lawyers, doctors, students, university staff members, social workers, clerks, mail carriers, bankers, business and industrial executives, and members of many other vocational groups. The training, naturally, seeks to improve the reading efficiency of the students—that is, to increase their speed of comprehension, to improve their reading vocabularies, to stimulate versatility and flexibility in reading, and to instill confidence in their ability to read rapidly and still comprehend well. In order to accomplish these objectives, the course provides for a large amount of guided practice in a multiplicity of reading situations, provides visual training, touches lightly on the psychology of reading, and gives frequent and large-sized doses of motivation. Among the devices employed are the tachistoscope, Controlled Reader, PDL perceptoscope, and the Master Word vocabulary building approach. Several complete sets of reading materials at various difficulty levels are also employed.

Observable results of the training seem to be manifold, ranging from testimonials from former students to the actual objective results computed in terms of rate and comprehension on material read. Naturally, most inquiries about the results of the training focus on the numerical evidences of gain, and in this department certain gratifying results can be reported. The average evening student, it may be concluded, after attending seventeen two-hour sessions over a period of one semester may expect to at least double his or her rate of reading in material of standard difficulty (measured by the Flesch formula) without affecting comprehension level.

It is easy to see now where the "time-stretching" feature of efficient reading comes in. Assume Ms. H. is an executive of a local industrial concern. In an effort to increase the effectiveness of her performance on the job she seeks to determine just how she is forced to occupy the time that she spends at her desk. She is startled to learn that approximately one-third of her 48-hour week is spent on various reading tasks—reading correspondence, reports, technical journals, general business publications, government directives, etc. Especially discouraging to Ms. H. is the fact that she feels the inefficiency of her reading skills and wishes she could read more rapidly, comprehend better, and retain more of what she reads. Motivated by an intense desire to do more with the time at her disposal, Ms. H. enrolls in the class in Efficient Reading. Shortly after the start of the first class she is further dismayed to find that she reads standard materials at the rate of only 200 words per minute and comprehends only 65 percent of what she reads. At the start she is reluctant to part with reading habits of lifelong duration and therefore does rather poorly for the first couple of weeks of the course. Finally, in desperation, and with a "cost-nothing-to-try" attitude, she forcibly breaks with her old techniques and searches for new and better methods. For another short period she is completely "at sea" in reading, with not even her old inefficient habits as consolation. Finally she arrives at a new point of integration, and from there on improves rapidly.

At the end of the course of training she is reading comfortably at 300 words per minute and comprehending better than ever before. By forcing herself slightly she is able to achieve a rate of 400 words per minute with at least as good comprehension as at the start of the program.

Now let's total up these gains in terms of "time stretching." Because she is able to read twice as fast as before, the 16 hours per week which Ms. H. formerly spent in reading are now cut to 8 hours, leaving her a full working day per week to utilize in further reading or in more productive activities. This, it would seem, amounts to "time stretching" just as surely as if we had employed the hypothetical machine mentioned above to do the job.

Then there are those who like to see results of this type preceded by the dollar sign. Converting these time gains to monetary gains seems to impart a more dramatic quality to the results reported. Assume again that Ms. H. is an $80,000 a year executive. If she is able to provide services equivalent to an additional day per week because of her training in efficient reading, the company will be in line for a $13,344.00 annual saving on Ms. H.'s time.

Besides savings in time and money Ms. H. will realize other intangible gains. Apart from being able to read more work-type reading in a given time, Ms. H. will find that her leisure reading skills have increased by an even greater percentage. Wider leisure reading will in turn impart greater understanding of social, political, and economic problems, allowing her to operate more knowingly in the areas of human relations and management. And in terms of personal development, few activities hold out such great potential as does wide reading.

Perhaps by now you have detected some personal references or interesting similarities to your present situation. Perhaps you have asked yourself, "Just what are the implications of these facts for me? How much of my working day could I save by doubling my reading rate? What would these savings amount to in terms of cash? What would my company be able to save by providing its complete executive force with training in efficient reading? What would doubled reading efficiency mean to me in terms of personal development?"

Throughout the country these questions have been asked and many industrial or professional groups have decided that this area holds forth great opportunities for corporate and personal benefits. Professional journals, trade journals, and house organs have reported results of these experimental programs. Without exception, these reports have been enthusiastically in favor of continued and improved courses of training in efficient reading.

From a seat at ringside it is easy to see that the future will bring a tremendous increase in training programs of this type. Business, professional, and industrial organizations have all expressed an interest in the training and have, on numerous occasions, requested that a demonstration of the activities of the course be presented at their meetings. As the result of one such demonstration a large St. Paul manufacturing company conducted a survey which turned up the astounding fact that a million dollar savings in management's time could be realized by training 200 of the company's top-level executives in efficient reading. Instances where such savings have already been effected are becoming more numerous in industrial management literature. Further expansion seems a certainty.

Considering the facts that no business or industrial area has a monopoly on reading and that our "time-stretching" device is not patentable, it might be well to investigate this matter of reading efficiency and attempt to determine just how much it could be made to serve the causes of personal and organizational development in a specific situation. And if a need is uncovered, the opportune time to start formulating a training program in this vital aspect of communication would seem to be now.

Most state universities at the present time have reading laboratories or reading clinics that serve the general public as well as the college population. In addition, various private "communication consultant" services offer training of the type described here. Such professional assistance in setting up a program appears to be a necessity if an adequate and sound program is to be developed. But whatever the source of the training, employ efficient reading as your "time stretcher" and help yourself to wider personal development and your company to greater job efficiency.

Number of words 1930
See page 331 for questions
Reading time in seconds _______
See page 496 for conversion table

SELECTION 34

Why Reading Matters

Alex Haley

"The degree of literacy in the United States hasn't kept pace with the demands of today's jobs." So says a recent news magazine, adding that about 21 million U.S. adults are functionally illiterate. For these men and women, performing adequately in a growingly complex workplace does pose a problem. Look at one case out of the millions!

While shopping in a Knoxville supermarket recently, I was startled when a smiling, personable clerk came up and grasped my hand. "My tutor just assigned me an article about you that's in my study book," he exclaimed. "Sir, I'm studying to learn to read."

The young man, who identified himself as Joseph Rivera, said he'd bluffed his way through high school until he finally dropped out to work full-time because he saw no pressing need for reading or writing.

The coincidence struck me as remarkable, since [I had just been asked] to write an article about the critical nationwide need for a higher level of literacy and reading. The obviously capable Mr. Rivera was an immediate and forceful symbol of what can happen when a young person fails to learn to read—and, fortunately, he also symbolizes how those in need can take themselves in hand and do something about it.

We talked a little more, then bade each other good-bye. I was fascinated by our conversation, and intrigued. There were a few more things I wanted to ask him.

Functional illiteracy is the inability of an individual to use reading, writing or math skills in everyday life. While no one knows precisely how many Americans cannot read, many major agencies and programs that focus on the problem have estimated the number at more than 27 million. Illiteracy connects to all sorts of problems, ranging from poverty to relations with spouses and children to the simple inability to fill out a request for a fishing license.

Several nonprofit organizations develop and establish programs to overcome illiteracy. They also train volunteers to tutor adults and young people. Two leading organizations are Literacy Volunteers of America and Laubach Literacy Action, both based in Syracuse, N.Y. And the First Lady heads The Barbara Bush Foundation for Family Literacy, which identifies successful programs, awards grants and supports training for teachers.

In addition, many newspapers across the country support literacy programs. In 1988, more than half the Fortune 500 companies offered literacy programs to their employees. The most important thing to recognize, as these programs teach us, is that the person we are talking about might very well be living right next door. And I believe that, by helping him or her, we help ourselves.

Much also is being done in public libraries across the country to awaken the joys of reading for individuals like Joseph Rivera.

In Harrisburg recently, I visited the "Propelling Reading" program developed by the Dauphin County, Pa., library system. This is clearly one of America's outstanding models of how first-graders are "propelled" into a love of books and reading.

Richard A. Bowra, director of the Dauphin County library system, noted that *every* first-grade classroom in the program contains a shelf of specially selected books, and that teachers, parents, older students and school library staffers read aloud to the first-graders every day.

"We've found that our vital link to our program's success is the immediate presence of the books in the classrooms," said Bowra. "Also we publish tips for parents about new books, and we have family-reading nights." The program has achieved such success, he said, that one of the nine branches has increased in use *seven* times since it was built in 1976.

"Mainly, it has worked so well because our program fits into an ordinary elementary school's curriculum and because it's fun for the kids, parents, teachers—especially because the kids feel their reading was *their* idea."

Another major success is in Fairfax County, Va., whose first library was a bookmobile that roamed the streets in 1939. That system today has 22 branches, a $19.7 million budget for 1991 and plans to build or expand 11 libraries. In some young people's departments, the libraries offer special attractions such as resident gerbils.

These unusual enticements evoke a warmth in me because they lead me to recall how my parents and grandparents came along with something different on the occasion of my fourth birthday in my dusty little cotton-farms hometown of Henning, Tenn. Sixty years later, I still remember vividly how they presented me with a foot-thick slice from a big California redwood tree. Small white markers were stuck in it at different places. With our family all solemnly gathered, my father used a pointer to illustrate how the tree's growth rings had come one each year, that each white marker represented some event, and the markers were situated at points corresponding to those years in the growth of the tree.

I was told that, if I'd read all I could, whenever I found something notably historic, then that could become another marker in my slice of tree. From then on, I read every book I could handle, along with my grandpa's newspapers for black people, which came by mail. Today, I absolutely believe that the reading inspired by the tree slice greatly influenced my becoming an author. It is also why I like most of all to write about historical subjects.

Those questions I had in mind about Joseph Rivera continued to tug at me, and finally I returned to the supermarket. I wanted to know more about how he had reached adulthood actually unable to read and what his life had been like as a result. We went to breakfast with his wife and baby daughter.

As I listened during our breakfast, Riviera told me the story of illiteracy far more vividly than all the statistics I'd read.

Joseph Rivera was born in New Orleans on Oct. 26, 1961, one of four sons of a Puerto Rican father who could neither read nor write English, "but he could repair any washing machine ever made," Rivera said, "and he could assemble an automobile's engine from its parts."

"My mind was on hustling for some spending money when I started school," Rivera said. "I'd stick a book up before my face or make pencil marks on a tablet to look like I was reading or writing, and when I got too big to be in that class, the teachers would pass me on."

"All the time, I was learning many ways to bluff it, so nobody would know I couldn't read or write. One good result was I learned to listen *very* closely to what other people said, because that fed me with clues to help me cover up if somebody asked me something. Maybe it might involve something printed on paper. Well, I'd glance at it real fast before I'd say, 'Yeah, right!' By this time, I'd learned I had to be real careful whom I'd let know I couldn't read, because plenty of people reacted as if you were afflicted with some catching disease."

"But by now I'd learned to fake. For example, if I took a date to a restaurant always I'd order for myself something I knew they had, like maybe the original New Orleans Po' Boy sandwich, which is fried oysters between French bread."

"Working in a warehouse, if somebody handed me an order list, well, at least I knew my ABCs enough that I could carefully compare the letters on the list and match them up with the letter on a box in the warehouse.

"I mean, I could do just about anything I wanted to do, except to *read.*"

It was around age 22 that he and Angela got married, Rivera said. She was from Knoxville, she worked for a music company, she could read like a whiz and she thought he was teasing when he told her he couldn't read.

"Then I took a job at the Schwegmann supermarket," he went on. "After a whole I rose to assistant floor supervisor. Then they next offered me a chance to train to be a store manager. Man, I could taste having that position, but I knew that every day a manager had to be reading all different kinds of stuff. My heart ached, I wanted that position so bad. But I told them I didn't feel I was ready yet."

"The company's officials knew something was wrong. Of course I could tell that, you know, from how they looked and acted when they happened to be anywhere around me. And that's about when I started coming home, real uptight and upset, and I'd holler at Angela."

"One evening, she hollered back, 'You can *do* something about it, if you really want to!'"

" 'Do *what*?' "

Finally, they ended up going to a teachers' supply house and got a cassette and a book.

Rivera had brought along that first lesson to show me. The book's first page contained a sketch of a bird and four words: "This is a bird."

"Do you want to believe I couldn't have read that to save my life?" Rivera flipped through subsequent pages of the book. "This is a dish . . . This is a girl . . . This is a hand."

He said, "All of this was about five years ago. And after this book, then, finally I did go to a reading tutor. That was the hardest thing I have ever done in my life—to go and admit to that woman, face-to-face, that I had a problem, I couldn't read, and I really had to do something about it."

Rivera paused. "At least that got me seriously started." He looked across the table at Angela, who was holding their daughter of 8 months, Maria.

"I'm going to tell you the truth. Over four years with tutors, I had come along a good way. But when Angela told me she was pregnant, when it meant that I was going to be the father of a baby, all of a sudden I knew what I had to do with the rest of my life. No more faking, no more bluffing my way. And from that day to this, I have been reading my head off. There is no way I'm not going to read at least an hour every day to that little one you're looking at! Just like reading, and just like her mother, this daddy's little girl has made a big difference in my life. I mean, they've all opened up for me a whole new world."

Joseph Rivera fell silent. His eyes had become moist with his emotion. I thought that it was maybe the ideal time to give him what I had brought. I withdrew from my bag a copy of *Roots*, which I opened on the table, and signed—writing rather slowly—with him and his wife watching: *"To Joseph, Angela and Maria Rivera, with Brotherly Love."*

Then I handed it to Rivera. Such were the messages we both felt to be conveyed, such were the significances—about the great meanings and values of literacy, and of reading—that he and I both quite openly had moist eyes.

Number of words 1800
See page 335 for questions
Reading time in seconds _______
See page 496 for conversion table

SELECTION 35

You Can't Get Ahead Today Unless You Read

George Gallup

"When I get a little money, I buy books; and if any is left, I buy food and clothes"—so said Erasmus. What an unusual priority! But—what an unusual man! Reading must have contributed its share, as it can still do today, according to George Gallup.

With knowledge in all fields expanding at a remarkable rate, and with competition growing keener for top positions in the business and professional world, the importance of reading must be carefully reassessed.

The cultural value of reading is well established. Likewise, the pleasures of reading have been widely extolled. These will not, therefore, be the chief concern of this article, but rather the very practical reasons why young and old should spend more time reading.

Fortunately, or unfortunately, competition starts at an early age in our highly competitive society. There was a time in America when the accepted formula for success was hard work. Today the formula calls for a college education. . . .

What has this to do with reading?

A well-established fact is that students who possess verbal facility tend to score the highest on college-entrance examinations. And verbal facility is gained almost entirely through extensive reading.

Many of the best professional colleges, whether they be law, medicine or engineering, now require students to have had two or more years of liberal-arts courses as a prerequisite for admittance. Some, indeed, are including courses in the humanities in their professional curricula. Verbal skills are essential if the student wishes to pass these courses.

Why is so much emphasis placed on verbal facility? One reason is that *words are the tools of thought.*

Abstract thinking is carried on by word concepts. The more extensive, the more precise one's vocabulary, the more exact one's thinking.

Undoubtedly this explains why there is such a high correlation between the results of a vocabulary and intelligence or "I.Q." test. Often a simple vocabulary test can be submitted for an intelligence test when circumstances make it impossible to administer a long test.

A simple vocabulary test can also reveal to a surprising extent one's educational attainment. This statement, of course, applies to the typical person, and not to that rare individual who without benefit of college education has managed to do a great deal of reading and who has, consequently, given himself the equivalent of a college education.

To see for yourself the high degree of relationship between educational attainment and vocabulary, try out the list of words given below.

These words have been carefully selected from general-magazine articles and from newspaper editorials. They are all useful words; not one can be properly described as a "trick" word.

Go over the list carefully and check the words that you think you know. Then look up the doubtful ones in the dictionary to be sure you are right before you credit yourself.

Here is the list:

elite	plebeian	enervate
obese	inane	laconic
ostracize	sagacious	nepotism
nostalgia	plebiscite	soporific
omnipotent	surfeit	recondite
avocation	banal	panegyric

If you are a high-school graduate you should know the correct meaning of two of these words. If you attended college, but left before graduation, you should be able to define five of these words. And if you are a college graduate, you should know eight of these words to equal the college average.

When this test was given to a national sample of high-school graduates it was found that one in every three could not define a single word correctly! And indicative of the lessened attention given to reading today, the most recent graduates tested had the lowest scores of all. On the average they knew only one word in the list, and fully half of those tested were unable to define correctly a single word!

Many parents are concerned about the lack of interest in reading displayed by their children. But they have found no easy way to induce these youngsters to read more. Only thirty years ago reading was one of the chief sources of entertainment—but that was before radio and television became so widely available.

Part of the blame for today's situation must be placed on parents. In far too many homes there is a tendency for the parents to urge young Johnny or Mary to "Run off to your room and read a good book" while papa and mamma sit glued to the TV set looking at an exciting Western or mystery.

If mothers and fathers have little time to give to reading—whether it be newspapers, magazines or books—they can be absolutely certain that their example will have a powerful impact on their children.

There is mounting evidence of a decline in reading interest in America, especially on the part of high-school and college graduates. In fact, some studies have brought to light the cases of college graduates who have not read a single book in at least a year. And in one survey it was found that more than half of those who were graduated from high school had not read a book during the previous twelve months.

It is a matter of national shame that new houses are being built without any provision for books. This lack of concern for a home library would have shocked earlier generations who prided themselves on the number and quality of books available in their own homes.

Each generation, of course, has its own special likes and dislikes. Books which were exciting to parents and to their parents can be frightfully dull to young people today—a fact which should be kept in mind in trying to induce the upcoming generation to spend more time reading.

Too often the reading lists recommended by our public schools include books which are boring and unpalatable to present-day students. Requiring children to read these books is self-defeating. Often the result of forcing a child to read a book for which he is not properly prepared or psychologically attuned is to develop in him a distaste for all books.

Reading is a habit and parents should not be too much concerned as to whether critics or authorities have recommended a given book. The prime objective is to get young people to read, and obviously it is easier to get them to read what they like than to get them to read what they don't like. In the latter case it will be only a short time until they read nothing at all.

For this reason, I believe that teachers, parents

and school librarians should co-operate in making up book lists, and these lists should be constantly revised. Books which students like, and books which they dislike, should be carefully identified. Equipped with this information, librarians can be reasonably certain that the book which they put into the hands of a student is one which he will enjoy, and having read it, he will be back next week for another book.

I would make it a regular order of business in parent-teachers meetings to discuss the success which those parents present are having with this problem of reading in their own homes. This exchange of ideas could be most valuable in discovering interesting books and the most effective measures for getting students to read them. And of equal importance is the regular reading of magazines and newspapers.

Many years ago I taught a course in freshman English at the University of Iowa. My students, I discovered, had read rather few books before they entered the university to start their college careers, a situation which is common throughout the country. The English Department at that time required these freshmen to read many books which were beyond their comprehension and appreciation. The result of this forced feeding was inevitable: literary indigestion. Most of these students, I am certain, came to think of "good" books as "dull" books, a fact which may account for the generally low interest in book reading displayed today by many of our college graduates.

I am certainly not opposed to "good" books. In fact, I am so desirous that such books be read in America that I do not want the interest in all books—both good and bad—killed by policies pursued for the right ends but by the wrong methods. The only certain way to get young people to spend more time reading is to make certain that the reading they do is both interesting and rewarding. The constant reader slowly but surely cultivates a taste for the "good" books.

A few years ago I enlisted the aid of teachers in some thirty high schools in various parts of the country in a study dealing with this problem. I suggested that they ask their students to list the most interesting and rewarding books they had ever read, and the age at which they had read each of these books. The results of this study were most revealing. Some books found on the recommended lists were mentioned, but most were books not on these standard lists. On the other hand, the books the students had liked best were not "cheap" or "trashy" books. They reflected the tastes and interests of a new generation brought up in entirely different circumstances from their elders, who had made up the lists.

Why all this fuss about reading? The answer has already been given. If students increase the amount of their reading of books, magazines, newspapers, then more of them will pass the college-board examinations, more will win scholarships, more will earn degrees.

Stated another way, persons who read more write better, speak better, think better. And it goes without saying that they know more. As a result of a knowledge of the past they can think better about the present and future.

Parents who despair of the quality of education their children are receiving can take new hope. It is in their province to do something about it. They need not reform the local school system, or move to a community which has a better one. All they have to do is find a way to get their own children to read a great deal more. The deficiencies of almost any school can be remedied by a carefully planned reading program.

If reading is all-important today for children, it is equally important for their parents. Reading is the one certain way to improve oneself. In a world which grows more complex, it is almost inconceivable that any person who wishes to keep himself well informed on matters vital to himself and his children and who wishes to improve his lot can achieve these goals without spending at least *two hours each day in reading.*

Some years ago I seriously considered starting what I called the hour-for-hour club. Persons who joined this organization would agree to spend one hour in serious reading or study for each hour they spend being entertained. I still think the idea is a good one. . . . We need always to remember that learning is a process which begins at birth and ends only with death. There is no better way to spend some of our leisure hours . . . than to devote a regular part of them to the reading of newspapers, magazines and books.

And this is not too much to ask. What we forget is that there is great excitement in learning, excitement which sometimes gets lost in our modern-day schools. We must find ways of bringing this excitement back to the learning process. We must recapture the spirit of Erasmus, who said, "When I get a little money, I buy books; and if any is left, I buy food and clothes."

Number of words 1880
See page 339 for questions
Reading time in seconds _______
See page 496 for conversion table

Section III

On Writing

How to Write Letters

Alma Denny

A millionaire without friends is poorer than a pauper with friends. As you will soon see, you make friends—and keep friends—with letters. Back in the seventeenth century, Lady Temple wrote, "All letters, methinks, should be as free and easy as one's discourse." In short, write as you speak. Does the following author agree?

Remember the sad song from 1935 (by Fred Ahlert and Joseph Young) that begins: "I'm gonna sit right down and write myself a letter, and make believe it came from you"? That spoke to the new decline of the Age of Correspondence, which may have started 2,500 years ago in Persia when the Empress Atossa, pining for news of her distant family, inscribed a parchment and dispatched a royal courier to Egypt with orders to wait for an answer. Shortly thereafter her father, Cyrus, established the first postal system, and people began to exchange letters.

But today, who writes letters? I mean *personal* letters, preferably handwritten, in which you really unfold, choosing your words and organizing your thoughts. The hey-day for that sort of letter came in wartime, during enforced separations, when warm words, penned on paper touched by the loved one, could bring a measure of comfort and closeness in a bleak world. Now people reach for the telephone, or even the car keys, to nourish ties with friends and family.

More's the pity. A telephone call ends and fades into thin air. Lawrence Durrell termed it a form of "noncommunication." But a letter has a long shelf life. It can be read quickly, then re-read at leisure, perhaps shared. It can be stored inside an empty candy-box or tied with a satin ribbon inside a bundle as part of a family history. But so few people bother. It means setting aside a quiet time, assembling stationery, stamp, and thoughts. Well, I bother. Helen Hayes bothers. I recall her telling an interviewer that she has kept track of friends "from kindergarten" through her correspondence. Actress Uta Hagan also writes letters. She credits one to Eva LeGallienne in 1937 with opening the door to her acting career. A new biography of Georgia O'Keeffe, the great American painter, credits her correspondence with Alfred Stieglitz, the eminent photographer, with fostering their romance and later marriage. Through letters they were able to work out a way to reconcile the demands of work and those of love.

Perhaps letter-writing scares some people. They may worry about "going on record" in an unretractable form, and not trusting the recipient to protect the privacy of the relationship. Others are daunted by the mechanics of putting together a proper "handmade" communication. Still others suffer letter-writer's block immediately after writing: "Dear Auntie Flo."

As for sitting down and getting the job done, you'll plunge in if you realize it's just *getting* a letter, as much as what's in it, that excites the recipient. The shortest one I heard of had just one word: "Come." It was carved in crayon by a six-year-old to his grandmother. The longest one I know of was 183 metres (200 yards) long on 10-centimeter (4-inch) teletype paper, handwritten by a young lady to her financé, a serviceman stationed overseas. And the laziest one was from a 10-year-old at summer camp, quoted here in its entirety: "Dear Mom and Dad. Can't think of a thing to write. Love, Joe."

Don't worry about spelling, or punctuation. Your participles may dangle like Pauline from a Peril, but it's a good letter if it adds up to: "Hello. I'm thinking of you." Legibility counts, of course, and handwriting is at risk although much preferred over typing. Thomas Bailey Aldrich addressed this reply to a "scribbler" whose penmanship he couldn't decipher: "There's a singular and perpetual charm in a letter of yours. It never grows old, it never looses its novelty. Other letters are read and thrown away and forgotten, but yours are kept forever—unread. One of them will last a reasonable man a lifetime."

As for what to say, start with the here and now. The words will come. Focus on old Uncle Bill living alone and household, hungry for mail. "Just had supper. Finished a watermelon. Took my shoes off." Boring to you, but to Uncle Bill it's a cozy visit. A page fills up. You ask a few questions and share something current in your own life, trivial or momentous. Getting new wallpaper for the bathroom? Enclose a sample of the design. Somebody graduating? Clip the news from the local paper. Items that sound dull to you serve to fill in the blanks about you, so that when you and your correspondent meet or talk, you are each more *au courant* about the other's status than if there'd been utter silence.

The main reward of maintaining a rich letter-to-letter relationship is the chance to know another person in ways no one else knows him and in ways he doesn't even know himself. Alone, addressing another human being in a one-to-one colloquy on paper, strange things happen. You become eloquent. Tongue-tied men wax poetic and compose love letters, without the aid of a Cyrano. My busy mother, with no time for patient answers and discussions with her 10 children, revealed herself as a talented raconteur and wit in the letters she wrote to my brother, the first child to attend an out-of-town college. This was a mother I'd never have known but for the letters he saved, and still has. Another brother, halting of tongue and dubbed "the silent one," blossomed into a 10-page written "chatterbox" during his Army stint. From Needles, California, we learned of his desert maneuvers and how to make one glass of water serve a dozen purposes!

I learned the power of a letter when I was eight years old and accompanied Auntie Bessie to the post office to mail letters to her three roving sons. She was stone-deaf and alone and lived with us. Letters were her link to her children and to life. Our mailman said he felt like forging a letter for her during a long wait between the envelopes from Singapore, Chicago, and Tennessee. He couldn't bear to look at her. And he quickened his steps when he carried one of the invigorating envelopes for her. In writing to each son, Auntie Bessie went through rituals akin to those of a Japanese tea ceremony. The stationery and color of ink were carefully chosen. The corner mailbox wouldn't do. We walked to the P.O. and Auntie Bessie kissed the departing envelope, asking me to do the same. Then came the wait for a reply.

Curious about what ever happened to U.S. National Letter-Writing Week, which I remembered reading about years ago, I called the postmaster. Yes, it is still on the calendar—the first week in November. But it's been years since it's been touted. The postal service must have muted the idea as an exercise in futility, noting that their pouches were filled with catalogs, form letters, bills, and periodicals, and contained fewer personal, hand-addressed, colorful envelopes from friends and relatives.

Is the Age of Correspondence really over? George O'Connell wrote in *The New York Times* that his Aunt Maude proclaims: "Ma Bell and even Cousin Hallmark have displaced the postman." She longs for "caring and literate letters" to hold a family together. Good letters will continue to be written, though only by people who enjoy getting them and who don't make a big deal about answering them. To bring others inside their orbit, these reach-out folks just sit down and write a few (or many) sincere lines, enclose a snapshot or a maple leaf or any artifact inside an envelope, and mail it. . . .

So why not, dear reader, dust off the old address-book and surprise someone who hasn't had a letter from you in years? You may surprise yourself, too, by producing a letter so excellent that you feel like an author who has clicked!

Number of words 1270
See page 343 for questions
Reading time in seconds _______
See page 496 for conversion table

The Hustle (How to Get Good Grades and Still Enjoy College)

Michael E. Gorman

Think of all the term papers, all the essay exams, all the compositions you write. Do you realize that as a student you literally write your way to either success—or failure? Slip into Mr. Gorman's class the first day of the semester and watch him arrange his notes. Then listen as he tells you how to get good grades.

I adjust the lectern, arrange my notes carefully, and watch my students watch me. It is the first class of the semester. Latecomers stick their heads in, study me for a moment, then race to an open seat.

At 4:10, I close the door. I return to the lectern, grip it firmly in both hands and stare at my notes. They are useless. I grin up at the class.

"Here we are, all ready to start, and I've got the wrong notes."

I shake my head, flip through my notebook and find the right outline. When I look up again, I am greeted by murmurs and worried frowns.

"Better get used to this. I do it all the time."

My students will learn to like me. I make fun of myself during lectures. I can hardly help it—I am a chronic chalkdropper, a classic fumblemouth. I charge off an quixotic digressions, even when I suspect that they interest no one but me. Because I never pretend to be anything other than a human being, most of my students forgive me.

But I am also a professional. If my students haven't guessed that already, they find out on the first exam. I sweat through the test with them, watching their anxious, thoughtful expressions. When a student looks up, I smile reassuringly. They rarely smile back.

As they are leaving, a few stop up at my desk to argue about particular questions. Sometimes they are right—I have included a poor question. I quickly concede. But we have become adversaries, locked in combat over points and grades.

When I return the exams, the class is worse. Most of the students look resentful—even the ones who have done well. I spend a lot of time going over the test. Several students argue with me; most just sit silently. The friendly atmosphere is gone.

The next week is full of conferences. Students come in to worry over their grades with me. Here is my chance to turn negative, post-test feelings into positive ones. I seize it eagerly.

I remind them that I am a student, too—even as I am grading them. I am being graded myself, in graduate courses. So I know how it feels to struggle for those points. I hustled grades for four years in college, where I learned all the tricks: how to take multiple-choice tests, how to read instructors and give them what they wanted, how to b.s. for twenty pages and get an A on a paper.

I ask my students if they are satisfied with their college grades. None of them is. So I teach them how to do better.

DIFFERENT STRATEGIES

I have their tests before me, so that's where I start. There are two kinds of questions on my exams: multiple-choice and short essay. Each requires a different strategy.

When the answer to a multiple-choice question isn't immediately obvious, I tell my students to eliminate all those alternatives that are clearly incorrect. If there are four choices following a given question, eliminating two of them will improve one's chances of getting the right answer to fifty-fifty.

The wording of each multiple-choice alternative is also important. Consider the following example:

1. The correlation between factors A and B is .92. One can safely infer that:
   (a) A causes B
   (b) B causes A
   (c) A third factor, C, may cause the relationship between A and B
   (d) A correlation of .92 is impossible

Even if the student knows nothing about correlation, the answer is obvious. Note the word "may" in item (c). All the other alternatives are definite statements. The question asks what one can *safely* infer. The safest inference is usually the one most cautiously worded. . . .

To rely solely on tricks like wording to answer multiple-choice questions is very dangerous. But if you know your material, a couple of tricks will help you over the tough spots.

One of my professors in college was a successful novelist who decided to go back to graduate school in mathematics. He inquired at U.C.L.A.; he assumed that they would give him special consideration because of his long, out-of-school career as a free-lancer.

No such luck. The people in the admissions office smiled politely at his story, then told him that only those students who scored in the top one per cent of the country on the math GRE were admitted to U.C.L.A. The GRE is a computer-graded, multiple-choice exam given nationwide.

My friend had been out of school for over 10 years. He would be competing with college students who were professional exam-takers. So he studied two things: mathematics and how to take multiple-choice tests.

On the exam itself, he quickly eliminated incorrect alternatives, paid careful attention to the way questions were worded and guessed at an answer only when the odds were in his favor. He finished first in the nation on the math GRE that year. His mathematics skill was the main reason for his success, but he confessed to me that his careful use of multiple-choice strategy helped him answer a number of tricky questions.

My professor-friend also told me that he was amazed at students' ability to answer essay questions on exams. As a professional writer, he was accustomed to spending several hours struggling to find the right opening sentence for a piece. A student on an exam may have fifteen minutes to write several coherent pages on a difficult question. My friend regarded it as a miracle that they produced anything at all.

Essays

There are three steps to answering an essay question. First, read the question carefully. The worst responses are always those that have no relationship to the question asked.

Second, before starting to write, outline your answer. Think before scribbling—you should know roughly what you want to say before you touch pen to paper. Don't panic and start writing everything you can remember that might relate to the question. Take the time to give a careful, focused answer.

Third, write clearly. If I cannot understand what a student is saying, I assume that he or she is wrong. I often get arguments on this point, but I refuse to budge. A vague, sloppy sentence indicates to me that the student has no idea what he or she is talking about.

I failed one of my graduate qualifying exams because I did not pay attention to these three steps, and because I ignored a fourth maxim: prepare for the type of question that will be asked. I studied the material, but I should have also studied the examiners. One of them asked broad, "What is reality?" type questions—but expected specific detailed answers.

When I saw his question, I hit the dump button. I started writing everything I knew that might relate even vaguely to the question I thought he was asking. I managed to violate all three maxims: I did not read his question carefully, I scribbled my thoughts at random and I produced a string of long, mangled sentences that no one could understand. I failed. I deserved to.

I was permitted to retake the test about six months later. This time, I worked with a close friend who was also trying to qualify. We picked out a set of potential questions and outlined answers to every one. There were no surprises on the test. I took my time and wrote careful answers that related directly to the questions. We both passed easily.

When studying for an essay exam, don't just read over your notes—practice answering potential questions. Work with one or two other people in the class. See if you can figure out what your instructor is likely to ask: look at what he or she has emphasized in lecture, talk to someone who has taken the course before, etc. Then outline answers to all the questions you can come up with. When you have trouble with an outline, you will know you have to review that material.

Term Papers

So much for exams. How about papers? Instructors are even more idiosyncratic about papers than they are about exams. Some insist on good grammar and spelling, others focus almost exclusively on content, still others insist that you write in a particular style.

Outside of English departments, most instructors attempt to grade for content independently of style. My strategy for handling those profs in college was to write a lot of 20 or 30 page papers. I got to the point where I could whip off 20 pages in two or three nights. The length of my efforts suggested to my profs that I was putting a great deal of time and effort into them.

Sometimes I was. I recall one 37-page physics paper that was a masterpiece of undergraduate clarity. That one took several weeks to write. It was my one and two night stands that were horrors—20 pages of the most alarming nonsense. Still, if I pushed up over 20 pages, I could be relatively sure of getting at least an A minus. Too many of my profs confused length with quality of content and amount of effort expended.

But there were times when this sort of strategy didn't work, when twenty pages of b.s. was recognized as just that. I had a few instructors whose major demand was clarity, both in thought and writing. Even the ones who didn't demand clarity appreciated it: I found that 12 careful pages would fetch me as good a grade as 20 sloppy ones.

As a novice instructor, I emphasize clarity and content about equally when I grade my students' papers. The two are not separable—even the most brilliant idea in the world is useless if it is written in such a way that no one can ever understand it. If you are writing a paper and you want to see if you're making sense, read portions of it to a friend. If they have no idea what you are talking about, you need to rewrite. Clarity comes before punctuation, grammar, and style.

Write so that someone else will understand what you are saying. (This assumes, of course, that you have done your research and have something to say.) If your instructor has certain stylistic fetishes, take them seriously—use the proper style manual for footnotes, consult a dictionary for spelling, type your papers whenever possible. If you have a long paper due at the end of the semester, start early and work a little bit each day.

The hardest thing students have to learn in college is organization. Most kids come out of a highly structured high school program where they have classes from eight to three and regular homework assignments. Their time is scheduled for them. In college you are free to skip classes, ignore assignments, and cram for exams at the last minute. Of course, students who do this will end up failing most of their classes.

A number of the freshmen in my introductory psychology class have complained about this lack of structure. My syllabus is quite detailed; it breaks up the readings into units, provides due dates for all assignments, and explains exactly how students will be evaluated in the course. But because I give only three major exams in my course, it is possible for students to put off doing the readings until just before the test. I also assign two papers; again, students can put off doing these until the last minute. What some of my freshmen would prefer is weekly quizzes and some kind of regular homework: they want me to force them to keep up in the class.

I won't. I tell them that's one of the most valuable lessons they will learn in college: how to structure their own time. Then I give them some suggestions.

As a student, you should get in the habit of doing a little work on each course every day—even if the only thing you do is spend ten minutes looking over your lecture notes, or reading a page in your text. This keeps the material you are learning fresh. Some weeks the requirements for one course will outweigh all the others—when there is an exam, or a paper due. Even so, you should set aside some time to keep up in your other classes.

Persistence of this sort is particularly useful in courses that require a paper. You should start working on it early in the semester and—when you have finished enough research to sit down at a typewriter—write for about half-an-hour every day. I am now taking a graduate-level course in writing; the instructor is a professional free-lancer who has published several novels and numerous articles. His time is limited: he can only write for a short period each day. His strategy is to make sure that he does just that *every* day, even if he can only sit down at the typewriter for fifteen minutes. He continues to produce quality material at a consistent rate.

Math courses require a similar persistence. You must do homework problems every week—even if none are assigned. I took a year of calculus in college and got A's in every class. I have no natural mathematical ability; equations terrify me. But I'm a good plodder; I did lots of problems. When I took my first graduate-level statistics course, there was no assigned homework. But I worked examples on my own, anyway, and made the instructor look at them.

Mathematics and writing, like tennis and piano-playing, are skills that require constant practice. I think that studying and taking exams are also skills that can be learned if practiced constantly. Work a little every day—read your text, ask yourself frequent questions, review lecture notes with a friend. You'll actually end up with more free time, because you won't waste it trying to study for six hours in a row. No one can do that. Reward yourself by taking frequent breaks—but only after you have completed a specified amount of work.

The best way to get good grades is to adopt a professional attitude toward your course work. It also happens to be the best way to learn and the best way to prepare for a career.

I took my last math class in college the term before I graduated. I was worried about maintaining my high G.P.A.: I was close to an A in the class when I took the final. There were several problems that involved a lot of arithmetic. I was sure I had screwed them up. I wrote a long apologetic note to the instructor on the back of my exam, arguing that I shouldn't lose much credit for arithmetic errors.

Turns out I aced the exam, but the prof threatened to give me a B in the class. He said that any student who apologized for his work deserved a lower grade. I should have taken the test, handed it in and accepted the consequences.

He was right. I deserved a B. Never apologize for your work. Do the best you can, hand it in and forget about it immediately afterwards.

That will leave you time to enjoy college.

Number of words 2540
See page 345 for questions
Reading time in seconds _______
See page 496 for conversion table

Selection 38

The Most Unforgettable Character I've Met

Henry Schindall

"Mint new coins—your own coins." For a would-be writer, that advice is as good today as it was back when Wilmer T. Stone stepped into a high school English class. Sometimes it takes an unforgettable character to make such insights come through.

I remember vividly that first English class in the last term of high school. We boys (there were no girls in the school) were waiting expectantly for the new teacher to appear. Before long, through the door came a tall, unimpressive-looking man of about 40. He said shyly, "Good afternoon, gentlemen."

His voice had a surprising tone of respect, almost as if he were addressing the Supreme Court instead of a group of youngsters. He wrote his name on the blackboard—Wilmer T. Stone—then sat on the front of his desk, drew one long leg up and grasped his bony knee.

"Gentlemen," he began, "we are here this semester—your last—to continue your study of English. I know we shall enjoy learning with—and from—one another. We are going to learn something about journalism and how to get out your weekly school paper. Most important, we are going to try to feel the joy of good literature. Maybe some of us will really get interested in reading and writing. Those who do, I venture to say, will lead far richer, fuller lives than they would otherwise."

He went on like that, speaking without condescension, voicing a welcome message of friendliness and understanding. An unexpected feeling of excitement stirred in me.

During the term that followed, his enthusiasm spread through us like a contagion. He would read one of Keats's poems, for instance, and then say musingly, "I wonder whether we can say that better. Let's see." Then we'd all chip in, and voices would grow high-pitched in the melee of thoughts and phrases. Soon would come a glow of wonderment as we began to discover that there *was* no better way of saying it. By such devices he led us to an appreciation of the beauty and perfection of language and literature.

There was little formality about our sessions, but he never had to discipline us. Since he treated us with unfailing courtesy, we couldn't very well do anything except return it; approached as adults, we couldn't show ourselves childish. Besides, we were much too interested and too anxious to participate in the discussions to have time for foolishness.

We would point things out to one another, each contributing an idea, a viewpoint. We examined the subject as a child studies a new toy, turning it over in our hands, peering underneath, feeling its shape and finding out what made it go.

"Don't be afraid to disagree with me," he used to say. "It shows you are thinking for yourselves, and that's what you are here for." Warming to such confidence, we felt we had to justify it by giving more than our best. And we did.

Mr. Stone abhorred sloppy speech and lazy writing. I remember a book review in which I wrote, "At the tender age of 17, he. . . ." Back came a sharp note: " 'Tender age' was a good phrase when first used, but now it's like a worn-out sock. Mint new coins—your own coins."

Mr. Stone gave us the greatest gift a teacher can bestow—an awakening of a passion for learning. He had a way of dangling before us part of a story, a literary character or idea, until we were curious and eager for more; then he would cut himself short and say, "But I suppose you have read so-and-so." When we shook our heads, he would write the title of a book on the blackboard, then turn to us. "There are some books like this one I almost wish I had never read. Many doors to pleasure are closed to me now, but they are all open for you!"

He was a great believer in wide reading outside class. "You know," he said once, "if I had to put all my advice into a single word, it would be: *browse*. In any library you will find awaiting you the best that has been thought and felt and said in all the ages. Taste it, sample it. Peek into many books, read a bit here and there, range widely. Then take home and read the books that speak to you, that are suited to your interests."

"How would you like to live in another century, or another country?" he went on. "Why not for a while live in France at the time of the French Revolution?" He paused and wrote on the blackboard: *Tale of Two Cities*—Dickens. "Or how would you like to take part in 14th-century battles?" He wrote: *The White Company*—Doyle. "Or live for a spell in the Roman Empire?" *Ben-Hur*—Wallace. He put the chalk down. "A man who reads lives many lives. A man who doesn't, walks this earth with a blindfold."

The end of the term came much too soon. The morning before graduation day the class suddenly and spontaneously decided to give Mr. Stone a literary send-off that afternoon—a good-bye party with poems and songs concocted for the occasion.

Bernie Stamm started a poem called "Farewell." We cudgeled our brains and each put in a line here and there. Then Herb Galen suggested a parody, and we went to work on Gilbert and Sullivan's "A Policeman's Lot Is Not a Happy One," changing it to "Poor Wilmer's Lot Is Not a Happy One." After we finished the verses Larry Hinds sang it in his premature baritone, and we howled in glee.

That afternoon when Mr. Stone walked slowly into Room 318 we made him take a seat in the first row. Do you remember those old-fashioned school desks that you had to inch into from the side, with a small seat and a slightly sloping top? Mr. Stone, a tall, big-boned man, sat with his gawky legs spread out into the aisles and waited to see what would happen.

One of the boys, sitting in the teacher's chair, started off with a speech; the rest of us were grouped around him. Mr. Stone sat tight-lipped, until toward the end when he slowly turned to the right and then to the left, looking at each of us in turn as if he wanted to register the picture on his mind.

When we got to the last chorus of the parody, we saw tears rolling down Mr. Stone's high cheekbones. He didn't brush them off but just blinked hard once or twice. We sang louder so that nobody would seem to be noticing. As we came to the end, every throat had a lump in it that made singing difficult.

Mr. Stone got up and pulled out a handkerchief and blew his nose and wiped his face. "Boys," he began, and no one even noticed that he wasn't calling us "men" any more, "we're not very good, we Americans, at expressing sentiment. But I want to tell you you have given me something I shall never forget."

As we waited, hushed, he spoke again in the gentle musing voice of the natural-born teacher. "That is one of the secrets of life—giving; and maybe it is a fitting thought to leave you with. We are truly happy only when we give. The great writers we have been studying were great because they gave of themselves fully and honestly. We are big or small according to the size of our helping hand."

He stopped and shook hands with each of us. His parting words were: "Sometimes I think teaching is a heartbreaking way of making a living." Then as he glanced down the line and saw the boys looking at him reverently, he added with a wistful smile, "But I wouldn't give it up for all the world."

Part of Wilmer Stone, I know, stays in the hearts of all of us who once faced him across the desks of Room 318.

Number of words 1300
See page 349 for questions
Reading time in seconds _______
See page 496 for conversion table

SELECTION 39

"The" First Word

Marlys Millhiser

When you're writing a letter, theme, report, research paper, story—yes—even a novel, what's the first step? Writing the first word! Here's one person's suggestion for getting that word on paper. She even tells you exactly what word to use.

I run for exercise and to keep down the pounds that add up so quickly in any sedentary occupation. I run different routes, most of them about four miles and most of them end at the top of the same steep hill. By the time I reach even the bottom of that hill my eyelashes are dragging.

When I begin my runs from my home, I try never to think of that hill and when I actually reach it, I try never to think of it either. I just lower my head and think of the next few feet and then the next and the next. (I lower my head so that I can't see the massive task ahead.) Pretty soon I'm at the top of the hill.

It has occurred to me from time to time that there is some similarity between writing and running. You feel so good when you stop. Sometimes if you dwell too long on what lies ahead you may not have the courage to start. But always, a four-mile run begins with the first step, and a novel begins with the first word.

For me, the thought of writing an entire novel approaches the madness of tackling the Boston Marathon with a broken leg. So I don't think of writing an entire novel; I think of writing a word. That word is usually "the." Not too exciting perhaps, but it certainly leaves the rest of the sentence open to an infinite number of possibilities.

The whole point, you see, is in getting started, and there are enough starts in this business to overwhelm beginner and pro alike. The decision to start writing novels at all can take some major reshuffling of your time and energies. But then you must decide where in the story to start the story, where to begin each new chapter. Then there's the problem of starting again each day or after your mind has blocked on the story and refuses to go on; after the break of a weekend, a phone call, a trip to the mail box.

Many of these starting problems stem, I suspect, from a basic lack of confidence that seems to plague those of us afflicted with the writing bug. But the mind and imagination will weary in any task of intense concentration, and reading about someone else's method can sometimes prove a useful tonic.

Where in a story do you begin a story? They are ongoing organisms, remember, that exist before your page one and long after you type, "The End." Even if your story follows one character from birth to death, your beginning and your end may not be that straightforward. Family, community, even world events such as war have shaped the environment into which that child is born and must grow. And the character's actions, decisions and relationships with others will have effect on your story world long after his death.

You can start a story with the first scene or first character that occurred to you, the germ that enticed you to write this particular novel to begin with. You may rearrange things before you're through, and that original opening may no longer be in the book or it might turn up in the middle.

You could begin with a major action scene, especially if it's to be a suspense novel, and then fill in the events that led up to it later. Or you can start at what you first perceived the ending to be and spend the rest of the book showing the reader how this came to pass.

These same ideas can apply to starting each chapter. Also, if you are like me and like to keep readers up all night, there's the classic device of ending a chapter in the middle of a harrowingly suspenseful scene. It makes it much easier for you to start the next chapter and let us hope excruciatingly difficult for the reader to turn out the light, go to sleep and await the outcome of your cliffhanger until the next day.

But no matter where you begin your story or your chapter, you will have to begin with the first word.

I have a lucky friend who received a contract for a juvenile mystery, on the basis of an outline, from a publisher who had already bought several of her novels. She must have known a great deal about her story to have fully outlined it beforehand, but when she sat down to begin one morning she just stared at a silent typewriter until four o'clock in the afternoon. Waiting for that first word.

About half the published writers I know have their stories mapped out before they begin, and the other half, like me, just sort of muddle along until they figure out what's going on—allowing the story to grow from what has come before it. I have noticed between the two groups about an equal number of disasters and successes. But both groups admit to having trouble with starts.

Try the word "the." I defy you to go off and leave it sitting on a page all by itself. It is so incomplete, silly, and helpless it cries out for the next word. "The" what? And "the" combined with that next word will create a complication that demands another word, and so on until you have a sentence. You will need another sentence to explain, clarify, or extend the first sentence and then another, until you have a paragraph, eventually a page. But what you really have is a start. It might not be any good and you might want to go back and fix it up and rearrange it later, but that's a good deal easier than getting started to begin with.

Suppose you have only a vague idea of what your story will be about. But you are sitting there staring at that ridiculous "the" and it occurs to you that one of your characters is a woman. So—"The woman—" The woman what? What's she doing? Eating? Running? Dying? Taking a shower?

I expect you've about given up hope, but now is when this inanely simple little exercise in self-deception begins to make some sense. Because, whether you're aware of it or not, inside your head there is a movie screen on which you visualize your thoughts.

How often have you met someone you'd heard much about beforehand and been surprised to find she looked different from what you had expected? That's because your movie screen had been flashing you images of that person—albeit incorrect—made up of tidbits of other people's opinions, your own assumptions and past experiences in meeting similar types. That movie is always running, when you're asleep or awake. It's running in Technicolor; it's how you see your dreams. It's how you see a story, whether you're reading it or writing it. It's how you see a sentence. It's automatic, like breathing, and you use it without particularly noticing it.

Unless you're a writer.

Writers (and everyone from painters to interior decorators) learn quickly to locate and concentrate on that screen; to order the scenes of the film that would otherwise be random; to stop, start, reverse, focus, and edit the film. I used to project onto the wall in front of my desk, but now I purposely locate my screen on the inside of my forehead. It's more portable and immediate and somehow less open to the influence of stray images.

So, because you've been staring at two words on an otherwise blank piece of paper for some time now, your movie screen has been flashing you the image of a woman, with a lot of other junk, and if you'll just stop feeling unsure, inadequate, preposterous, and defeated, and concentrate—you'll notice her. She isn't clear enough to describe, or know or sympathize with, perhaps, but it's obvious she's just standing there. (Not a terribly active way to begin but at least she's not lying dead.) And you have word number three. "The woman stood—"

Now if you can go off to sharpen pencils or raid the refrigerator with that half-formed sentence in your typewriter you're too incurious to be a writer. The woman stood where?

> The woman stood in the constant shadow of a cliff overhang in a gorge so deep and narrow the sun never reached the barren sand at her feet.

How do you know this? Because three weeks ago on your vacation you stood at the top of just such a gorge and felt almost sick looking down at the tiny black river below and wondered what it would be like being down there looking up. Remember now? That thought and accompanying visualization of this story germ have been imprinted on your mind film ever since, mixed up with all sorts of other images.

You have a whole sentence now, and you have another question to keep things going. You must know why that woman is standing at the bottom of a gorge.

> The voices of those who'd left her there faded and the sound of their paddles against the river . . . .

How do you know this? Well, you've stirred up some things in your head by now, and though there are no memory images to help you here, your imagination has become intrigued with the gaps and is offering suggestions for filling them in. Memory and imagination can combine to give you more on a mind film than you'd ever experience in a regular movie house. Besides sound and color and movement, they can offer smells, tastes and textures; the sensations of fear, loss, love, hunger—everything. It's all there. You just need a little confidence and a lot of sitting in that chair to find it. Memory and imagination can give you a sentence, a chapter, a novel. But don't worry about so steep a hill yet. Just think about completing that paragraph. You're already beginning to sort out what will prove useful, automatically beginning to edit and associate. You have a start. And it all began with the word, "the."

You'll notice this article did not.

That's because I had no trouble with this particular start. But it could just as well have been because I had gone back and rewritten it. I would probably not have allowed both the first two sentences to begin with "The" in the story about the woman in the gorge when I rewrote it, but for now I would hurry along with this start if I were you because it looks to be the beginning of a full dramatic scene. And what better way to begin a story?

What else is happening around that woman? Are there birds, insects, lizards? Is the river broad? Clear? Rushing? What shape would the sky have when seen from so deep a gorge? Why is she here? Who are the people who abandoned her? What are the colors, odors of this gorge? Is this story situated in the present or the past or the future? What is she feeling emotionally at this moment? What is she remembering? What is she planning to do? Who is she? Is she hungry? Does she hurt anywhere?

By the time you answer all these questions, you'll be into several pages and glad you didn't worry too long about that first word. You might run for hours, days or weeks on the momentum of this first scene but eventually you'll slow, become winded, wear down. That shouldn't stop you for long, though, because now you know where to catch your second wind or how to use your movie screen.

And your movie screen is just waiting for "the" first word.

Number of words 1950
See page 353 for questions
Reading time in seconds _______
See page 496 for conversion table

Selection 40

Ten Tips to Help You Write Better

Changing Times

We communicate 70 percent of our waking time. Of that total communication time, we spend 40 percent in listening, 30 percent in speaking, 16 percent in reading, and 9 percent in writing. Get the message? Develop added skill in writing, and you've got the most exclusive skill of all. Here's help!

1. Get to the point. Tell your reader right away what you plan to write about.

Ever notice how many writers tell you something else first, before getting to the business at hand? They recite anecdotes, allude to the classics, quote oft-quoted quotations, describe places, events or moods in loving detail—*anything* to avoid getting to the point.

One type of subject avoidance has been called NCD, noncommunicating discourse. NCD is talk that tells you nothing you don't know already. Examples: "We are gathered here tonight . . ." "I am writing you this letter . . ."

What audience nneds to be told that it has assembled, or where or when? What letter reader needs to be informed that the writer of the letter he holds in his hand has written a letter? Or, for that matter that the enclosed enclosure is enclosed?

A lot of opening wordage is mere warm-up material. Warming up is what a baseball pitcher does before he goes into the game. If you can't write without warming up, write your little warm-up—and throw it away. Don't ask your reader to catch before you're ready to pitch.

2. Get your facts together. Put everything on the same subject in the same place.

Some writers hate to tell all they know. They hoard facts, yielding them up one by one only as their text drives them to do so. This obliges the reader to piece the story together from scraps sprinkled sparsely along the way.

Some writers write piecemeal prose because they can't stick to the subject. At every opportunity they head out the exits hell-bent on unscheduled excursions. These side trips come to dead ends, of course. And then you read: "But, to get back to our story . . .".

There are fewer chances to digress when you put everything on the same subject in the same place. There are other advantages, too. A complete set of facts in one place helps your reader comprehend your meaning quickly and fully, which is a hallmark of good writing.

Just as important, putting facts together forces you, the writer, to consider whether all the necessary facts actually are present and in their proper order. If ends are left dangling, if items are omitted or arranged illogically, those faults will show in time for you to correct them.

3. Get your story in order. Remember, the object is exposition, not mystification. If you wish to tease and confuse, write a mystery. Then you can withhold facts, digress to mislead, relate events first and explain them later.

The purpose of exposition is to inform and clarify. Its aim is understanding. And there is no greater aid to understanding than logical sequence.

So put your thoughts in logical order even before you put them on paper. Then make an outline and tinker with it until you get it right. After that you can write. Then rewrite. Then write it all over again.

Laborious? Yes. Orderly thinking itself is hard work, and writing is nothing but the rigorous toil of analyzing and systematizing one's thoughts.

There is no way around it, either. Clear writing never came from a mind that had not yet overcome its natural-born muddle.

4. Write simple. Use ordinary, everyday words. Don't write "configuration" when you mean "shape." If you mean "idea," don't say "conceptualization." And if you mean "too long," don't write "inordinately protracted."

Two-dollar words represent inflation. They puff up what you say, making you sound stiff and pompous. Worse yet, they often turn solid, accessible ideas into difficult abstractions.

Beware of words of three syllables or more that sound like Latin once removed. Usually there is a shorter word that says the same thing better.

5. Write short. Why? Because time is precious and readers don't' want to have their time wasted by your long-windedness.

Pascal once wrote, "Please excuse such a long letter; I don't have time to write a short one." He was right. Brevity does take longer. And you have to sweat to achieve it.

There are three tricks to writing short. Point A, mentioned earlier, is to throw away everything you said before you got to your subject. Point C is to stop the instant you have said all you have to say. Point B is to be succinct en route from point A to point C.

And just in case you think that your normal writing style is sufficiently concise, here is a homework exercise to test yourself.

Write two pages on any subject. Then go back over it crossing out words and phrases you can do without, eliminating redundancies, replacing long words with short ones. Keep at it until your two-page piece will fit on one page *yet include every fact and idea that was in your two-page first draft.*

Then shorten the one-page version by another third. This process hurts, but from the pain you will learn plenty about brevity.

6. Keep moving. We call the most enthralling stories page-turners. An enthusiastic reader's highest praise is, "I couldn't put it down!"

But what keeps readers reading?

Unfulfilled promise, partly. Suggest to your reader that you will reveal something interesting or useful and he will keep reading to find out what it is.

Partly it's involvement. Talk to your reader about his interests rather than yours and you have a chance to grip his attention.

Promise and involvement together still aren't enough, however. Your writing must also have momentum, a steady sense of movement, of getting somewhere. Once the pace stalls, you risk losing your reader.

Short sentences help keep things moving. When sentences are short, one idea succeeds another swiftly. There is less chance for interest to lag.

Straightforward sentences help, too. Suppose you write: "My subject is the catching of fish." That sounds stiff, inert, pedantic. Change that clumsy "the catching of fish" to the straightforward "catching fish."

"My subject is catching fish" is better, but you're still talking about yourself rather than your reader and not promising him much reward for his attention.

So make your implicit promise clear, put a more active twist on "my subject is" and speak directly to your reader and his concerns: "I'm going to tell you how you can catch more fish."

Now you're moving. And you have probably hooked a reader. Just keep up the momentum.

7. Be specific. Name names. Wherever possible, use exact numbers instead of indefinite terms.

Specifics evoke more vivid images than generalized words do. Say "a Mercedes" and you give a different picture than if you say "an automobile." "Tawny" is more precise than the indefinite "dark-hued." "Three" makes a sharper and stronger statement than "a number of," "a few," "several" or "some."

Use specifics even when there can be no doubt of your exact meaning. There is but one President of the U.S. and you won't be misunderstood if you write "the President." Nevertheless, the image becomes more vivid with the specific "President Carter."

Good specifics can stand repeating, too. Having mentioned Carter once, it's all right to call him by name if you mention him again. There is no reason to back away to any such circumlocutory evasion as "the nation's chief executive." Just call him President Carter.

One nonspecific worth avoiding is "not all that," as in "the pileated woodpecker is not all that plentiful." This fad usage has a vaguely negative connotation, yet it states nothing definite. The trouble with "not all that" is that it isn't all that specific.

8. Be positive. If you have something to say, find the courage to say it forthrightly.

Don't express things tentatively, in cautious, half-hearted ways. Avoid weakening modifiers like "rather," "somewhat," "kind of," "perhaps," "slightly." Even the nominally forceful "very" has a weakening effect when it props an assertion that ought to stand on its own.

So strike out all such attenuators. If you don't have the strength to make a declarative statement, be silent until you do.

9. Be frugal. If one word will do, don't use two. For example, under guideline number 7 the phrase "circumlocutory evasion" appears. Since circumlocutions by definition are evasions, the phrase is redundant. Either "circumlocution" or "evasion" would have served as well as—or even better than—both.

Another example of superfluity: "an added plus." Think about that. A "plus" can only be something added, so "an added plus" adds up to an additional addition.

Redundancies aren't the worst type of spendthrift wordage, either. They at least mean 50 percent of what they say. Sometimes the ratio of content to volume is lower, as in the notorious "at this point in time," five words doing the work of "now."

10. Practice. No one ever learned to play the violin by attending seminars, taking courses, viewing training films, listening to cassettes or reading books and articles. It is the same with writing. To write better, you must practice, and practice a lot.

Workshops and courses may help if they force you to sit down and start writing. The instruction and criticism you get may be useful, too, depending on their quality, which is variable.

Books about writing can inspire, of course, and give you useful pointers. One book is invaluable, *The Elements of Style*, by William S. Strunk Jr. and E. B. White (Macmillan; paperback). If you're serious about writing better prose, study this small classic.

Still, the best instruction in the world and the sagest advice won't improve your writing one jot unless you work at your writing.

Practice, practice, practice.

Practice won't make you a great writer, but it may school you to become your own constant critic. And that is the first step toward making your writing better.

Number of words 1610
See page 357 for questions
Reading time in seconds _______
See page 496 for conversion table

Selection 41

The Road to Success in Writing

Madeleine L'Engle

What's the difference between an icon and an idol? An icon is a sacred image; an idol is a godlike image to be worshiped. And what is the road to success as a writer? Not easy to find or to travel, as you'll see. But when you win the prestigious Newbery Medal, as Madeleine L'Engle did, you're a success. Find out how an icon, not an idol, helped.

The various pressures of twentieth-century living have made it almost impossible for the young mother with preschool children to have any solitude. During the long drag of years before our youngest child went to school, my love for my family and my need to write were in acute conflict. The problem was really that I put two things first. My husband and children came first. So did my writing. Bump.

Crosswicks is isolated, which is one of the things we love about it, but it meant that if the children were to have playmates outside their own siblings, I had to drive them somewhere, or pick up some other children and bring them here. The house was usually full of kids, and that's the way we wanted it, but there were times when for at least a full minute I thought of following Gauguin: I needed a desert island, and time to write.

Well, somehow or other, like a lot of other women who have quite deliberately and happily chosen to be mothers, and work at another vocation as well, I did manage to get a lot of writing done. But during that decade when I was in my thirties, I couldn't sell anything. If a writer says he doesn't care whether he is published or not, I don't believe him. I care. Undoubtedly I care too much. But we do not write for ourselves alone. I write about what concerns me, and I want to share my concerns. I want what I write to be read. Every rejection slip—and you could paper walls with my rejection slips—was like the rejection of me, myself, and certainly of my *amour-propre*. I learned all kinds of essential lessons during those years of rejection, and I'm glad to have had them, but I wouldn't want to have to go through them again. (I'm getting to icons: wait.)

I was, perhaps, out of joint with time. Two of my books for children were rejected for reasons which would be considered absurd today. Publisher after publisher turned down *Meet the Austins* because it begins with a death. Publisher after publisher turned down *A Wrinkle in Time* because it deals overtly with the problem of evil, and it was too difficult for children, and was it a children's or an adults' book, anyhow? My adult novels were rejected, too. *A Winter's Love* was *too* moral: the married protagonist refuses an affair because of the strength of her responsibility toward marriage. Then, shortly before my fortieth birthday, both *Meet the Austins* and an adult novel, *The Lost Innocent*, had been in publishing houses long enough to get my hopes up. I knew that *The Lost Innocent* was being considered very seriously; one editor was strong for it; another was almost equally enthusiastic; a third hated it; and they were waiting for the opinion of a fourth editor who had just come back from Europe. I tried not to think about it, but this was not quite possible. And there was that fortieth birthday coming up. I didn't dread being forty; I looked forward to it. My thirties had been such a rough decade in so many ways that I was eager for change. Surely, with the new decade, luck would turn.

On my birthday I was, as usual, out in the Tower working on a book. The children were in school. My husband was at work and would be getting the mail. He called, saying, "I'm sorry to have to tell you this on your birthday, but you'd never trust me again if I kept it from you. _______ has rejected *The Lost Innocent*."

This seemed an obvious sign from heaven. I should stop trying to write. All during the decade of my thirties (the world's fifties) I went through spasms of guilt because I spent so much time writing, because I wasn't like a good New England housewife and mother. When I scrubbed the kitchen floor, the family cheered. I couldn't make decent pie crust. I always managed to get something red in with the white laundry in the washing machine, so that everybody wore streaky pink underwear. And with all the hours I spent writing, I was still not pulling my own weight financially.

So the rejection on the fortieth birthday seemed an unmistakable command: Stop this foolishness and learn to make cherry pie.

I covered the typewriter in a great gesture of renunciation. Then I walked around and around the room, bawling my head off. I was totally, unutterably miserable.

Suddenly I stopped, because I realized what my subconscious mind was doing while I was sobbing: my subconscious mind was busy working out a novel about failure.

I uncovered the typewriter. In my journal I recorded this moment of decision, for that's what it was. I had to write. I had no choice in the matter. It was not up to me to say I would stop, because I could not. It didn't matter how small or inadequate my talent. If I never had another book published, and it was very clear to me that this was a real possibility, I still had to go on writing.

I'm glad I made this decision in the moment of failure. It's easy to say you're a writer when things are going well. When the decision is made in the abyss, then it is quite clear that it is not one's own decision at all.

In the moment of failure I knew that the idea of Madeleine, who had to write in order to be, was not image.

And what about that icon?

During those difficult years I was very much aware that if I lost my ability to laugh, I wouldn't be able to write, either. If I started taking myself and my failure too seriously, then the writing would become something that was *mine*, that I could manipulate, that I could take personal credit—or discredit—for. When a book was rejected, I would allow myself twenty-four hours of private unhappiness. I'm sure I wasn't as successful in keeping my misery from the family as I tried to be, but I did try. Our house fronts on a dirt road—we didn't have the land with the brook, then—and I would go down the lane to do my weeping. I found that I could play games with the children during dinner (Buzz and Botticelli were our favorites), but I couldn't listen to Bach. But perhaps what was most helpful—and still is—is a white china laughing Buddha which sits on my desk in the Tower. He laughs at me, never with ridicule, but lovingly, tolerantly: you *are* taking yourself seriously, aren't you, Madeleine? What matters is the book itself. If it is as good a book as you can write at this moment in time, that is what counts. Success is pleasant; of course you want it; but it isn't what makes you write.

No, it's not. I found that out on the morning of my fortieth birthday.

My white china Buddha is an icon. He has never become an idol.

Number of words 1190
See page 359 for questions
Reading time in seconds _______
See page 496 for conversion table

SELECTION 42

Writing a Resumé That Gets the Job

Changing Times

What's the most important writing you'll ever do? Getting yourself on paper in a resumé for a much-wanted job. Actually you may repeat that writing assignment several times in your lifetime—whenever you want a different job. How do you best write that resume? You need to know.

A personal advertisement . . . a condensed self-analysis . . . a ledger of your accomplishments . . . the paper you. That's what a job resumé has been called. As such it's a key part of landing a job. Its purpose is to get you job interviews. To do that, it must attract the attention of prospective employers and interest them in what you have to offer as a potential employee.

"It used to be that people were hired for some jobs by word of mouth," said an employment counselor recently. "Now employers want a resumé on everybody from the janitor to the chairman of the board."

Your resumé is one of the first things you should get in order when you decide to look for a new job. You'll want to include a copy with every job-hunting letter you mail and with every answer to a want ad. You should have copies available for job interviewers and employment agency counselors. It's also a smart idea to give copies to friends, associates and people you've asked to be your references to bring them up-to-date on your job goals and qualifications so they can help in your hunt.

Organizing Your Story

A resumé is not a full-fledged autobiography but a shorthand sketch aimed at getting your foot in the door. If it works, you'll have time later, in a personal interview, to go into detail about your background. The shape your resumé takes will depend to some extent on your own experience and qualifications and the sort of job you are looking for. But there are some basic elements that every resumé should contain. Present them in a simple, uncluttered, eye-pleasing outline form, usually in this priority.

Identification. Right up at the top put your name, address and telephone number (office as well as home phone if you can take job calls at work).

Your objective or job goal. Handle this carefully. If you're too specific, you could rule yourself out for related jobs you'd actually want to consider. If you are vague about what you want to do, an employer might not bother to try to figure out where he could use you. One job counselor suggests that instead of a specific job title, such as "contract procurement officer," you include a one- or two-line summary of your abilities: "Comprehensive background in all phases of contract negotiation and administration."

Work experience. This is the heart of your resumé. Give it the most space and emphasis, and don't waste time getting to it. Describe briefly the development of your career to date. Work in this information about each job you've held: name and location of the firm (for a small or unknown company identify the type of business; for a giant corporation indicate the department you worked in); dates of your employment; your title and responsibilities if not apparent; and, above all, your specific accomplishments, presented so that they are immediately apparent, not buried in a long paragraph. Examples are money-saving innovations or promotions within one firm. Give the most space to your latest or highest-level position.

There are several ways of presenting this information. You can do it job by job in chronological order, starting with your present or last job and working backward. This format works best for most people and particularly well when you have held a series of progressively better jobs. On the other hand, you can outline your work experience by the kinds of positions you've held, giving first priority to your most important job function, lesser attention to other job functions regardless of actual employment chronology. This is a good idea with occupations where you perform several functions or where there are frequent changes of assignment in each job. Another possibility is to combine features of both formats.

Education and training. List your high school or college, degree and major. Also note postgraduate and special training courses or seminars you have completed. Cite special job-related skills, such as knowledge of foreign languages or specialized certification.

If you are a new graduate with little work experience, you might cover your educational background before your work experience. And flesh out the education section with more details to show how your studies and extracurricular activities relate to the work you seek. Note the areas of emphasis in your major.

Personal data. This is where you might include information on your age, marital status and health, especially if you think it has a bearing on your application, though in most cases it really isn't necessary. Do include such things as business, professional, social and civic affiliations; honors and awards; military service; hobbies or outside interests.

References. At the end of your resumé, include the statement, "References will be provided upon request."

Don't omit any of the sections noted above, no matter how meager you think your material is. The absence of any section will only raise questions and could eliminate you from consideration before you have a chance to explain. There's no reason to dwell on information you consider negative. Put it down in a way that minimizes its importance without misrepresenting the facts. A company sales manager might be embarrassed about being a fifth-grade dropout. But if he omitted any reference to his schooling, an employer would wonder why and might reject him on principle. Included, the fact of curtailed schooling would seem inconsequential in view of his career record, and it just might say something to the employer about his enterprise and initiative.

Putting it in Writing

Should you resort to a professional resumé-writer? Given the proper material, a professional can craft for you an attractive resumé with an excellent chance of catching the eye of an employer.

But that's only half the job of a resumé. It also tells an employer something of a person's ability to marshal and present facts. An employer who recognizes that your resumé was professionally prepared may decide not to take the time to test you in some other way. Writing your own covering letter could take the edge off a prepared resumé. One personnel manager says that if both a resumé and its covering letter are obviously factory-made, he wonders about the job applicant's ability to communicate. If you need advice from a pro, get it, but turn out the basic products yourself.

You don't have to pay for resumé-writing help. Look over ones that friends have used to get good jobs. Also check model resumés in books such as these, available in libraries and bookstores: *Job Resumés, How to Write Them, How to Present Them*, by J. I. Biegeleisen (Grosset & Dunlap), and *How to Get a Better Job Quicker*, by Richard A. Payne (Taplinger).

A word of caution about model resumés: Don't copy the format rigidly; use them as guides to write your own. The personnel director of a large company said he frequently receives—and rejects out of hand—resumés from different job applicants who've obviously used the same model.

Begin by collecting and jotting down on scratch paper all the data you'll need. Organize the material under the headings of the outline described earlier. Then you're ready to begin writing. Here are some tips to guide you:

- *Be positive.* Demonstrate a confidence in your abilities and your experience. Don't dwell on your adversities. One job applicant explained in her resumé that she wanted to leave her present job because she had to get up at 5 A.M. and take three different buses each way to and from work and she was exhausted when she got home at the end of the day. A prospective employer isn't interested in hearing about your problems; he wants to know if you can solve *his* problems. Also, never attempt to build yourself up by knocking a former employer or fellow employee. The only thing negative information can do for you is scotch your chance for the job.

- *Be brief.* One-page resumés are best; two-pagers are okay; longer ones are a poor idea unless there are extraordinary reasons for such length. An employer can't spend all morning studying your resumé. Make it easy for him to get at the key points of your background quickly and easily.

- *Stick to the facts.* Avoid flowery adjectives and personal opinions. What counts is what you have done ("Sales volume rose 34 percent during my control of the department"), not what you think about it ("I feel I contributed greatly to the over-all success of the company"). Don't lie. If you can't back something up, don't include it. Even little white lies have a way of tripping you up. Things you fudged on will seem much worse than they are when you have to explain why you tried to hide them.

- *Make yourself clear.* Use correct, straightforward English—active verbs, short and simple words. You needn't use complete sentences, but your phrases should read smoothly. Avoid using stilted language, abbreviations and obscure terms of your trade.

- *Keep things in focus.* Emphasize background and credentials that best establish your qualifications for the work you seek. Tailor your resumé as closely as you can to specific job fields or employers, even if it means writing several versions. For example, if you are interested in landing a job as a research assistant, a copywriter or an English teacher, don't use the same resumé for all three jobs. Write separate ones to emphasize your background related to each job goal.

- *Write, rewrite and polish.* Obviously, you'll go through a number of rough drafts before your resumé begins to fall into shape. When you think you've come up with a final draft, give it yet another once-over. See whether you can edit it a bit more, cut out every unnecessary word or phrase, and give it that extra punch.

- *Make it neat.* Be sure your resumé is expertly typed on standard-sized, good-quality paper. Use underlines and words in capital letters to set things off. Leave lots of white space in margins and between sections of type. Don't try to attract attention with wild gimmicks or somebody's idea of an unusual format. And make clean, legible copies—by offset printing or Xerox, for instance, not mimeograph or carbon copies.

The appearance of your resumé says perhaps as much about you as its content. One employment manager says about 15 percent of the ones he receives are rejected purely on the basis of their appearance—full of typos, smeared and smudged, coffee stained. Will your resumé identify you as a slob, or as a neat, organized individual with originality and the ability to get essential information across quickly and forcefully?

Number of words 1760
See page 363 for questions
Reading time in seconds _______
See page 496 for conversion table

Selection 43

How to Write with Style

Kurt Vonnegut

Doing things with style! According to the dictionary, that's performing with "distinction, excellence, originality, and character." Who wouldn't desire that? The famous writer Vonnegut gives you the very advice needed to help you write with style—with distinction.

Newspaper reporters and technical writers are trained to reveal almost nothing about themselves in their writings. This makes them freaks in the world of writers, since almost all of the other ink-stained wretches in that world reveal a lot about themselves to readers. We call these revelations, accidental and intentional, elements of style.

These revelations tell us as readers what sort of person it is with whom we are spending time. Does the writer sound ignorant or informed, stupid or bright, crooked or honest, humorless or playful—? And on and on.

Why should you examine your writing style with the idea of improving it? Do so as a mark of respect for your readers, whatever you're writing. If you scribble your thoughts any which way, your readers will surely feel that you care nothing about them. They will mark you down as an egomaniac or a chowderhead—or, worse, they will stop reading you.

The most damning revelation you can make about yourself is that you do not know what is interesting and what is not. Don't you yourself like or dislike writers mainly for what they choose to show you or make you think about? Did you ever admire an empty-headed writer for his or her mastery of the language? No.

So your own winning style must begin with ideas in your head.

1. Find a subject you care about. Find a subject you care about and which you in your heart feel others should care about. It is this genuine caring, and not your games with language, which will be the most compelling and seductive element in your style.

I am not urging you to write a novel, by the way—although I would not be sorry if you wrote one, provided you genuinely cared about something. A petition to the mayor about a pothole in front of your house or a love letter to the girl next door will do.

2. Do not ramble, though. I won't ramble on about that.

3. Keep it simple. As for your use of language: Remember that two great masters of language, William Shakespeare and James Joyce, wrote sentences which were almost childlike when their subjects were most profound. "To be or not to be?" asks Shakespeare's Hamlet. The longest word is three letters long. Joyce, when he was frisky, could put together a sentence as intricate and as glittering as a necklace for Cleopatra, but my favorite sentence in his short story "Eveline" is this one: "She was tired." At that point in the story, no other words could break the heart of a reader as those three words do.

Simplicity of language is not only reputable but perhaps even sacred. The Bible opens with a sentence well within the writing skills of a lively fourteen-year-old: "In the beginning God created the heaven and the earth."

4. Have the guts to cut. It may be that you, too, are capable of making necklaces for Cleopatra, so to speak. But your eloquence should be the servant of the ideas in your head. Your rule might be this: If a sentence, no matter how excellent, does not illuminate your subject in some new and useful way, scratch it out.

5. Sound like yourself. The writing style which is most natural for you is bound to echo the speech you heard when a child. English was the novelist Joseph Conrad's third language, and much that seems piquant in his use of English was no doubt colored by his first language, which was Polish. And lucky indeed is the writer who has grown up in Ireland, for the English spoken there is so amusing and musical. I myself grew up in Indianapolis, where common speech sounds like a band saw cutting galvanized tin, and employs a vocabulary as unornamental as a monkey wrench.

In some of the more remote hollows of Appalachia, children still grow up hearing songs and locutions of Elizabethan times. Yes, and many Americans grow up hearing a language other than English, or an English dialect a majority of Americans cannot understand.

All these varieties of speech are beautiful, just as the varieties of butterflies are beautiful. No matter what your first language, you should treasure it all your life. If it happens not to be standard. English, and if it shows itself when you write standard English, the result is usually delightful, like a very pretty girl with one eye that is green and one that is blue.

I myself find that I trust my own writing most, and others seem to trust it most, too, when I sound most like a person from Indianapolis, which is what I am. What alternatives do I have? The one most vehemently recommended by teachers has no doubt been pressed on you, as well: to write like cultivated Englishmen of a century or more ago.

6. Say what you mean to say. I used to be exasperated by such teachers, but am no more. I understand now that all those antique essays and stories with which I was to compare my own work were not magnificent for their datedness or foreignness, but for saying precisely what their authors meant them to say. My teachers wished me to write accurately, always selecting the most effective words, and relating the words to one another unambiguously, rigidly, like parts of a machine. The teachers did not want to turn me into an Englishman after all. They hoped that I would become understandable—and therefore understood. And there went my dream of doing with words what Pablo Picasso did with paint or what any number of jazz idols did with music. If I broke all the rules of punctuation, had words mean whatever I wanted them to mean, and strung them together higgledy-piggledy, I would simply not be understood. So you, too, had better avoid Picasso-style or jazz-style writing, if you have something worth saying and wish to be understood.

Readers want our pages to look very much like pages they have seen before. Why? This is because they themselves have a tough job to do, and they need all the help they can get from us.

7. Pity the readers. They have to identify thousands of little marks on paper, and make sense of them immediately. They have to *read*, an art so difficult that most people don't really master it even after having studied it all through grade school and high school—twelve long years.

So this discussion must finally acknowledge that our stylistic options as writers are neither numerous nor glamorous, since our readers are bound to be such imperfect artists. Our audience requires us to be sympathetic and patient teachers, ever willing to simplify and clarify—whereas we would rather soar high above the crowd, singing like nightingales.

That is the bad news. The good news is that we Americans are governed under a unique Constitution, which allows us to write whatever we please without fear of punishment. So the most meaningful aspect of our styles, which is what we choose to write about, is utterly unlimited.

8. For really detailed advice. For a discussion of literary style in a narrower sense, in a more technical sense, I commend to your attention *The Elements of Style*, by William Strunk, Jr., and E. B. White (Macmillan, 1979). E. B. White is, of course, one of the most admirable literary stylists this country has so far produced.

You should realize, too, that no one would care how well or badly Mr. White expressed himself, if he did not have perfectly enchanting things to say.

Number of words 1270
See page 365 for questions
Reading time in seconds _______
See page 497 for conversion table

On Learning How to Write

Benjamin Franklin

The allusions may be obscure, the style antiquated—after all, Franklin wrote this over 200 years ago—but it's still clear and vigorous writing. And what Franklin says about learning to write has been proved by experience, for he did work—and write—his way to fame. Why not try his method yourself?

From a child I was fond of reading, and all the little money that came into my hands was ever laid out in books. Pleased with the *Pilgrim's Progress*, my first collection was of John Bunyan's works in separate little volumes. I afterward sold them to enable me to buy R. Burton's *Historical Collections*; they were small chapmen's books, and cheap, forty or fifty in all. My father's little library consisted chiefly of books in polemic divinity, most of which I read, and have since often regretted that, at a time when I had such a thirst for knowledge, more proper books had not fallen in my way, since it was now resolved I should not be a clergyman. Plutarch's *Lives* there was in which I read abundantly, and I still think that time spent to great advantage. There was also a book of Defoe's, called an *Essay on Projects*, and another of Dr. Mather's, called *Essays to do Good*, which perhaps gave me a turn of thinking that had an influence on some of the principal future events of my life. . . .

And after some time an ingenious tradesman, Mr. Matthew Adams, who had a pretty collection of books, and who frequented our printing-house, took notice of me, invited me to his library, and very kindly lent me such books as I chose to read. I now took a fancy to poetry, and made some little pieces; my brother, thinking it might turn to account, encouraged me, and put me on composing occasional ballads. One was called *The Lighthouse Tragedy*, and contained an account of the drowning of Captain Worthilake, with his two daughters; the other was a sailor's song, on the taking of Teach (or Blackbeard), the pirate. They were wretched stuff, in the Grub Street ballad style; and when they were printed he sent me about the town to sell them. The first sold wonderfully, the event being recent, having made a great noise. This flattered my vanity; but my father discouraged me by ridiculing my performances, and telling me verse-makers were generally beggars. So I escaped being a poet, most probably a very bad one; but as prose writing has been of great use to me in the course of my life, and was a principal means of my advancement, I shall tell you how, in such a situation, I acquired what little ability I have in that way.

There was another bookish lad in the town, John Collins by name, with whom I was intimately acquainted. We sometimes disputed, and very fond we were of argument, and very desirous of confuting one another, which disputatious turn, by the way, is apt to become a very bad habit, making people often extremely disagreeable in company by the contradiction that is necessary to bring it into practice; and thence, besides souring and spoiling the conversation, is productive of disgusts and perhaps enmities where you may have occasion for friendship. I had caught it by reading my father's books of dispute about religion. Persons of good sense, I have since observed, seldom fall into it, except lawyers, university men, and men of all sorts that have been bred at Edinburgh. . . .

About this time I met with an odd volume of the *Spectator*. It was the third. I had never before seen any of them. I bought it, read it over and over, and was much delighted with it. I thought the writing excellent, and wished, if possible, to imitate it. With this view I took some of the papers, and making short hints of the sentiment in each sentence, laid them by a few days, and then, without looking at the book, tried to complete the papers again, by expressing each hinted sentiment at length, and as fully as it had been expressed before, in any suitable words that should come to hand. Then I compared my *Spectator* with the original, discovered some of my faults, and corrected them. But I found I wanted a stock of words, or a readiness in recollecting and using them, which I thought I should have acquired before that time if I had gone on making verses; since the continual occasion for words of the same import, but of different length, to suit the measure, or of different sound for the rhyme, would have laid me under a constant necessity of searching for variety, and also have tended to fix that variety in my mind, and make me master of it. Therefore I took some of the tales and turned them into verse; and, after a time, when I had pretty well forgotten the prose, turned them back again. I also sometimes jumbled my collections of hints into confusion, and after some weeks endeavored to reduce them into the best order, before I began to form the full sentences and complete the paper. This was to teach me method in the arrangement of thoughts. By comparing my work afterwards with the original, I discovered many faults and amended them; but I sometimes had the pleasure of fancying that, in certain particulars of small import, I had been lucky enough to improve the method or the language, and this encouraged me to think I might possibly in time come to be a tolerable English writer, of which I was extremely ambitious. My time for these exercises and for reading was at night, after work, or before it began in the morning, or on Sundays, when I contrived to be in the printing-house alone. . . .

Number of words 920
See page 367 for questions
Reading time in seconds _______
See page 497 for conversion table

SELECTION 45

Why I Write

Joan Didion

When you write, do you feel like a secret bully? Do you agree with Joan Didion that writing is an aggressive act? She should know. She's written novels and essays and collaborated on screenplays; she's a writer par excellence. *Find out why she writes—and why you might want to write.*

Of course I stole the title for this talk, from George Orwell. One reason I stole it was that I like the sound of the words: *Why I Write.* There you have three short unambiguous words that share a sound, and the sound they share is this:

I
I
I

In many ways writing is the act of saying *I*, of imposing oneself upon other people, of saying *listen to me, see it my way, change your mind.* It's an aggressive, even a hostile act. You can disguise its aggressiveness all you want with veils of subordinate clauses and qualifiers and tentative subjunctives, with ellipses and evasions—with the whole manner of intimating rather than claiming, of alluding rather than stating—but there's no getting around the fact that setting words on paper is the tactic of a secret bully, an invasion, an imposition of the writer's sensibility on the reader's most private space.

I stole the title not only because the words sounded right but because they seemed to sum up, in a no-nonsense way, all I have to tell you. Like many writers I have only this one "subject," this one "area": the act of writing. I can bring you no reports from any other front. I may have other interests: I am "interested," for example, in marine biology, but I don't flatter myself that you would come out to hear me talk about it. I am not a scholar. I am not in the least an intellectual, which is not to say that when I hear the word "intellectual" I reach for my gun, but only to say that I do not think in abstracts. During the years when I was an undergraduate at Berkeley I tried, with a kind of hopeless late-adolescent energy, to buy some temporary visa into the world of ideas, to forge for myself a mind that could deal with the abstract.

In short I tried to think. I failed. My attention veered inexorably back to the specific, to the tangible, to what was generally considered, by everyone I knew then and for that matter have known since, the peripheral. I would try to contemplate the Hegelian dialectic and would find myself concentrating instead on a flowering pear tree outside my window and the particular way the petals fell on my floor. I would try to read linguistic theory and would find myself wondering instead if the lights were on in the bevatron up the hill. When I say that I was wondering if the lights were on in the bevatron you might immediately suspect, if you deal in ideas at all, that I was registering the bevatron as a political symbol, thinking in shorthand about the military-industrial complex and its role in the university community, but you would be wrong. I was only wondering if the lights were on in the bevatron, and how they looked. A physical fact.

I had trouble graduating from Berkeley, not because of this inability to deal with ideas—I was majoring in English, and I could locate the house-and-garden imagery in "The Portrait of a Lady" as well as the next person, "imagery" being by definition the kind of specific that got my attention—but simply because I had neglected to take a course in Milton. For reasons which now sound baroque I needed a degree by the end of that summer, and the English department finally agreed, if I would come down from Sacramento every Friday and talk about the cosmology of "Paradise Lost," to certify me proficient in Milton. I did this. Some Fridays I took the Greyhound bus, other Fridays I caught the Southern Pacific's City of San Francisco on the last leg of its transcontinental trip. I can no longer tell you whether Milton put the sun or the earth at the center of his universe in "Paradise Lost," the central question of at least one century and a topic about which I wrote 10,000 words that summer, but I can still recall the exact rancidity of the butter in the City of San Francisco's dining car, and the way the tinted windows on the Greyhound bus cast the oil refineries around Carquinez Straits into a grayed and obscurely sinister light. In short my attention was always on the periphery, on what I could see and taste and touch, on the butter, and the Greyhound bus. During those years I was traveling on what I knew to be a very shaky passport, forged papers: I knew that I was no legitimate resident in any world of ideas. I knew I couldn't think. All I knew then was what I couldn't do. All I knew then was what I wasn't, and it took me some years to discover what I was.

Which was a writer.

By which I mean not a "good" writer or a "bad" writer but simply a writer, a person whose most absorbed and passionate hours are spent arranging words on pieces of paper. Had my credentials been in order I would never have become a writer. Had I been blessed with even limited access to my own mind there would have been no reason to write. I write entirely to find out what I'm thinking, what I'm looking at, what I see and what it means. What I want and what I fear. Why did the oil refineries around Carquinez Straits seem sinister to me in the summer of 1956? Why have the night lights in the bevatron burned in my mind for twenty years? *What is going on in these pictures in my mind?*

When I talk about pictures in my mind I am talking, quite specifically, about images that shimmer around the edges. There used to be an illustration in every elementary psychology book showing a cat drawn by a patient in varying stages of schizophrenia. This cat had a shimmer around it. You could see the molecular structure breaking down at the very edges of the cat: the cat became the background and the background the cat, everything interacting, exchanging ions. People on hallucinogens describe the same perception of objects. I'm not a schizophrenic, nor do I take hallucinogens, but certain images do shimmer for me. Look hard enough, and you can't miss the shimmer. It's there. You can't think too much about these pictures that shimmer. You just lie low and let them develop. You stay quiet. You don't talk to many people and you keep your nervous system from shorting out and you try to locate the cat in the shimmer, the grammar in the picture.

Just as I meant "shimmer" literally I mean "grammar" literally. Grammar is a piano I play by ear, since I seem to have been out of school the year the rules were mentioned. All I know about grammar is its infinite power. To shift the structure of a sentence alters the meaning of that sentence, as definitely and inflexibly as the position of a camera alters the meaning of the object photographed. Many people know about camera angles now, but not so many know about sentences. The arrangement of the words matters, and the arrangement you want can be found in the picture in your mind. The picture dictates the arrangement. The picture dictates whether this will be a sentence with or without clauses, a sentence that ends hard or a dying-fall sentence, long or short, active or passive. The picture tells you how to arrange the words and the arrangement of the words tells you, or tells me, what's going on in the picture. *Nota bene*:

It tells you.

You don't tell it.

Let me show you what I mean by pictures in the mind. I began "Play It As It Lays" just as I have begun each of my novels, with no notion of "character" or "plot" or even "incident." I had only two pictures in my mind, more about which later, and a technical intention, which was to write a novel so elliptical and fast that it would be over before you noticed it, a novel so fast that it would scarcely exist on the page at all. About the pictures: the first was of white space. Empty space. This was clearly the picture that dictated the narrative intention of the book—a book in which anything that happened would happen off the page, a "white" book to which the reader would have to bring his or her own bad dreams—and yet this picture told me no "story," suggested no situation. The second picture did. This second picture was of something actually witnessed. A young woman with long hair and a short white halter dress walks through the casino at the Riviera in Las Vegas at one in the morning. She crosses the casino alone and picks up a house telephone. I watch her because I have heard her paged, and recognize her name: she is a minor actress I see around Los Angeles from time to time, in places like Jax and once in a gynecologist's office in the Beverly Hills Clinic, but have never met. I know nothing about her. Who is paging her? Why is she here to be paged? How exactly did she come to this? It was precisely this moment in Las Vegas that made "Play It As It Lays" begin to tell itself to me, but the moment appears in the novel only obliquely, in a chapter which begins:

"Maria made a list of things she would never do. She would never: walk through the Sands or Caesar's alone after midnight. She would never: ball at a party, do S-M unless she wanted to, borrow furs from Abe Lipsey, deal. She would never: carry a Yorkshire in Beverly Hills."

That is the beginning of the chapter and that is also the end of the chapter, which may suggest what I meant by "white space."

I recall having a number of pictures in my mind when I began the novel I just finished, "A Book of Common Prayer." As a matter of fact one of these pictures was of that bevatron I mentioned, although I would be hard put to tell you a story in which nuclear energy figured. Another was a newspaper photograph of a hijacked 707 burning on the desert in the Middle East. Another was the night view from a room in which I once spent a week with paratyphoid, a hotel room on the Colombian coast. My husband and I seemed to be on the Colombian coast representing the United States of America at a film festival (I recall invoking the name "Jack Valenti" a lot, as if its reiteration could make me well), and it was a bad place to have fever, not only because my indisposition offended our hosts but because every night in this hotel the generator failed. The lights went out. The elevator stopped. My husband would go to the event of the evening and make excuses for me and I would stay alone in this hotel room, in the dark. I remember standing at the window trying to call Bogotá (the telephone seemed to work on the same principle as the generator) and watching the night wind come up and wondering what I was doing eleven degrees off the equator with a fever of 103. The view from that window definitely figures in "A Book of Common Prayer," as does the burning 707, and yet none of these pictures told me the story I needed.

The picture that did, the picture that shimmered and made these other images coalesce, was the Panama airport at 6 A.M. I was in this airport only once, on a plane to Bogotá that stopped for an hour to refuel, but the way it looked that morning remained superimposed on everything I saw until the day I finished "A Book of Common Prayer." I lived in that airport for several years. I can still feel the hot air when I step off the plane, can see the heat already rising off the tarmac at 6 A.M. I can feel my skirt damp and wrinkled on my legs. I can feel the asphalt stick to my sandals. I remember the big tail of a Pan American plane floating motionless down at the end of the tarmac. I remember the sound of a slot machine in the waiting room. I could tell you that I remember a particular woman in the airport, an American woman, a *norteamericana* , a thin *norteamericana* about 40 who wore a big square emerald in lieu of a wedding ring, but there was no such woman there.

I put this woman in the airport later. I made this woman up, just as I later made up a country to put the airport in, and a family to run the country. This woman in the airport is neither catching a plane nor meeting one. She is ordering tea in the airport coffee shop. In fact she is not simply "ordering" tea but insisting that the water be boiled, in front of her, for twenty minutes. Why is this woman in this airport? Why is she going nowhere, where has she been? Where did she get that big emerald? What derangement, or disassociation, makes her believe that her will to see the water boiled can possibly prevail?

"She had been going to one airport or another for four months, one could see it, looking at the visas on her passport. All those airports where Charlotte Douglas's passport had been stamped would have looked alike. Sometimes the sign on the tower would say 'Bienvenidos' and sometimes the sign on the tower would say 'Bienvenue,' some places were wet and hot and others dry and hot, but at each of these airports the pastel concrete walls would rust and stain and the swamp off the runway would be littered with the fuselages of cannibalized Fairchild F-227's and the water would need boiling.

"I knew why Charlotte went to the airport even if Victor did not.

"I knew about airports."

These lines appear about halfway through "A Book of Common Prayer," but I wrote them during the second week I worked on the book, long before I had any idea where Charlotte Douglas had been or why she went to airports. Until I wrote these lines I had no character called "Victor" in mind: the necessity for mentioning a name, and the name "Victor," occurred to me as I wrote the sentence. *I knew why Charlotte went to the airport* sounded incomplete. *I knew why Charlotte went to the airport even if Victor did not* carried a little more narrative drive. Most important of all, until I wrote these lines I did not know who "I" was, who was telling the story. I had intended until that moment that the "I" be no more than the voice of the author, a 19th-century omniscient narrator. But there it was:

"I knew why Charlotte went to the airport even if Victor did not.

"I knew about airports."

This "I" was the voice of no author in my house. This "I" was someone who not only knew why Charlotte went to the airport but also knew someone called "Victor." Who was Victor? Who was this narrator? Why was this narrator telling me this story? Let me tell you one thing about why writers write: had I known the answer to any of these questions I would never have needed to write a novel.

Number of words 2590
See page 369 for questions
Reading time in seconds _______
See page 497 for conversion table

SECTION IV

ON SPEAKING

Selection 46

Simple Secrets of Public Speaking

Dale Carnegie

Sometimes we speak without thinking, but we certainly ought not to speak in public that way. Shakespeare had a point. Remember? "Mend your speech a little, lest you may mar your fortunes. . . ." For most of us, public speaking does pose a problem. Here are some secrets that will make you more effective.

I am going to let you in on a secret that will make it easy for you to speak in public immediately. Did I find it in some book? No. Was it taught to me in college? No. I had to discover it gradually, and slowly, through years of trial and error.

Stated in simple words, it is this: *Don't spend ten minutes or ten hours preparing a talk. Spend ten years.*

Don't attempt to speak about anything until you have earned the right to talk about it through long study or experience. Talk about something that you know, and you know that you know. Talk about something that has aroused your interest. Talk about something that you have a deep desire to communicate to your listeners.

To illustrate, let's take the case of Gay Kellogg, a housewife of Roselle, New Jersey. Gay had never made a speech in public before she joined my class in New York. She was terrified: she feared that public speaking might be a hidden art way beyond her abilities. Yet at the fourth session of the course she made an impromptu talk that held the classroom audience in the palm of her hand.

I asked her to speak on "The Biggest Regret of My Life." Six minutes later, the listeners could hardly keep the tears back. Her talk went like this:

"The biggest regret of my life is that I never knew a mother's love. My mother died when I was only six years old. I was brought up by a succession of aunts and relatives who were so absorbed in their own children that they had no time for me. I never stayed with any of them very long. They never took any real interest in me, or gave me any affection.

"I knew I wasn't wanted by any of them. Even as a little child I could feel it. I often cried myself to sleep because of loneliness. The deepest desire of my heart was to have someone ask to see my report card from school. But no one ever did; no one cared. All I craved as a little child was love—and no one ever gave it to me."

Had Mrs. Kellogg spent ten years preparing that talk? No. She had spent twenty years. She had been preparing herself to make that talk when she cried herself to sleep as a little child. She had tapped a gusher of memories and feelings deep down inside her. No wonder she held her audience spellbound.

Poor talks are usually the ones that are written and memorized and sweated over and made artificial. A poor speaker, like a poor swimmer, gets taut and tense and twists himself up into knots—and defeats his own purpose. But, even a man with no unusual speaking ability can make a superb talk if he will speak about something that has deeply stirred him.

Do beginning speakers know that? Do they look inside themselves for topics? No; they are more likely to look inside a magazine. Some years ago, I met in the subway a woman who was discouraged because she was making little progress in a public-speaking course. I asked her what she had talked about the previous week. I discovered that she had talked about [the Middle East situation.]

She had gotten her information from a weekly news magazine. She had read the article twice. I asked her if she had some special interest in the subject, and she said "No." I then asked her why she had talked about it.

"Well," she replied, "I had to talk about something, so I chose that subject."

I said to her: "Madame, I would listen with interest if you spoke about how to rear children or how to make a dollar go the farthest in shopping; but neither

I nor anyone else would have the slightest desire to hear you try to interpret [the Middle East situation]. You don't know enough about it to merit our respect."

Many students of speaking are like that woman. They want to get their subjects out of a book or a magazine rather than out of their own knowledge and convictions.

You are prepared right now to make at least a dozen good talks—talks that no one else on earth could make except you, because no one else has ever had precisely the same experiences. What are these subjects? I don't know. But you do. So carry a sheet of paper with you for a few weeks and write down, as you think of them, all the subjects that you are now prepared to talk about through experience—subjects such as "The Biggest Regret of My Life," "My Biggest Ambition," and "Why I Liked (or Disliked) School." You will be surprised how quickly this list will grow.

Talking about your own experiences is obviously the quickest way to develop courage and self-confidence. But later you will want to talk about other subjects. What subjects? And where can you find them? Everywhere.

I once asked a class of executives that I was training for the New York Telephone Company to jot down every idea for a speech that occurred to them during the week. It was November. One man saw Thanksgiving Day featured in red on his calendar and spoke about the many things he had to be thankful for. Another man saw some pigeons on the street. That gave him an idea. He spent a couple of evenings in the public library and gave a talk about pigeons that I shall never forget.

But the prize winner was a man who had seen a bedbug crawling up a man's collar in the subway. He went to the library, uncovered some startling facts about bedbugs, and gave us a talk that I still remember after fifteen years.

Why don't you carry a "scribbling book"? Then, if you are irritated by a discourteous clerk, jot down the word "Discourtesy." Then try to recall two or three other striking examples of discourtesy. Pick the best one and tell us what we ought to do about it. Presto! You have a two-minute talk on Discourtesy.

Don't attempt to speak on some world-shaking problem like ["AIDS"]. Take something simple—almost anything will do, provided the idea gets you, instead of you getting the idea. Once you begin to look for topics for talks, you will find them everywhere—in the home, the office, the street.

Here are seven rules that will help immensely in preparing your speeches:

1. Don't Write Out Your Talks. Why? Because if you do, you will use written language instead of easy, conversational language; and when you stand up to talk, you will probably find yourself trying to remember what you wrote down. That will keep you from speaking with naturalness and sparkle.

2. Never Memorize a Talk, Word for Word. If you do, you are almost sure to forget it; and the audience will probably be glad, for nobody wants to listen to a canned speech. Even if you don't forget it, you will have a faraway look in your eyes and a faraway ring in your voice. If you are afraid you will forget what you want to say, then make brief notes and hold them in your hands and glance at them occasionally.

3. Fill Your Talk with Illustrations and Examples. By far the easiest way to make a talk interesting is to fill it with examples. Years ago, a congressman made a stormy speech accusing the government of wasting money by printing useless pamphlets. He illustrated what he meant by a pamphlet on "The Love Life of the Bullfrog." I would have forgotten that speech years ago if it hadn't been for that one specific illustration.

4. Know Forty Times as Much About Your Subject as You Can Use. The late Ida Tarbell, one of America's most distinguished biographers, told me that years ago while in London, she received a cable from McClure's Magazine asking her to write a two-page article on the Atlantic cable. Miss Tarbell interviewed the London manager of the Atlantic cable and got all the information she actually needed for a 500-word article. But she didn't stop there.

She went to the British Museum library and read articles and books about the cable, and the biography of Cyrus West Field, the man who laid it. She studied cross sections of cables on display in the British Museum; then visited a factory on the outskirts of London and saw cables being manufactured.

"When I finally wrote those two pages," Miss Tarbell said, "I had enough material to write a small book. But that vast amount of material which I had and did not use enabled me to write what I did write with confidence and clarity and interest. It gave me reserve power."

Ida Tarbell had learned through years of experience that she had to earn the right to write even 500 words. The same principle goes for speaking. Make yourself something of an authority on your subject. Develop that priceless asset known as reserve power.

5. Rehearse Your Speech by Conversing with Your Friends. Will Rogers prepared his famous Sunday-night radio talks by trying them out as conversation on the people he met during the week. If, for example, he were going to speak on the gold standard, he would wisecrack about it during the week. He would then discover which of his jokes went over with his listeners, which remarks elicited interest. That is an infinitely better way to rehearse a speech than trying it out with gestures in front of the bathroom mirror.

6. Instead of Worrying about Your Delivery, Get Busy with the Causes That Produce It. A lot of harmful nonsense has been written about delivery of a speech. The truth is that when you face an audience, you should forget all about voice, breathing, gestures, posture, emphasis. Forget everything except what you are saying.

Don't imagine that expressing your ideas and emotions before an audience is something that requires years of technical training, such as you have to devote to mastering music or painting. Anybody can make a splendid talk at home when he is angry. If somebody hauled off and knocked you down this instant, you would get up and make a superb talk. Your gestures, your posture, your facial expression would be perfect because they would be the expression of emotion.

To illustrate, a rear admiral of the Navy once took my course. He had commanded a squadron during World War I. He wasn't afraid to fight a naval battle, but he was so afraid to face an audience that he made weekly trips from his home in New Haven, Connecticut, to New York City to attend the course. Half a dozen sessions went by, and he was still terrified. So one of our instructors, Prof. Elmer Nyberg, had an idea that he felt would make the admiral forget himself and make a good talk.

There was a wild-eyed [radical] in this class. Professor Nyberg took him to one side and said: "Now, don't let anybody know that I told you to do this, but tonight I want you to advocate that we grab guns, march on Washington, shoot the President, [and take over] the government. . . . I want you to get the admiral angry, so he will forget himself and make a good talk."

The [radical] said: "Sure, I'll be glad to." He had not gone far in his speech, however, when the rear admiral leaped to his feet and shouted: "Stop! Stop! That's sedition!" Then the old sea dog gave [the speaker] a fiery lecture on how much he owed to this country and its freedom.

Nyberg turned to the officer and said: "Congratulations, Admiral! What a magnificent speech!" The rear admiral snapped back: "I'm not making a speech; but I am telling that little whippersnapper a thing or two."

This rear admiral discovered just what you will discover when you get stirred up about a cause bigger than yourself. You will discover that all fears of speaking will vanish and that you don't have to give a thought to delivery, since the causes that produce good delivery are working for you irresistibly.

7. Don't Try Imitating Others: Be Yourself. Act on the sage advice that the late George Gershwin gave to a struggling young composer. When they first met, Gershwin was famous while the young man was working for $35 a week in Tin Pan Alley. Gershwin, impressed by his ability, offered the fellow a job as his musical secretary at almost three times the salary he was then getting.

"However, don't take the job," Gershwin advised. "If you do, you may develop into a second-rate Gershwin. But if you insist on being yourself, some day you'll become first-rate on your own."

The young man heeded the warning, turned down the job and slowly transformed himself into one of the significant American composers of this generation.

"Be yourself! Don't imitate others!" That is sound advice both in music and in public speaking. You are something new in this world. Never before, since the dawn of time, has anybody been exactly like you; and never again, throughout all the ages to come, will there ever again be anybody exactly like you. So why not make the most of your individuality?

Your speech should be a part of you, the very living tissue of you. It should grow out of your experiences, your convictions, your personality, your way of life. In the last analysis, you can speak only what you are. So, for better or for worse, you must cultivate your own little garden. For better or for worse, you must play your own little instrument in the great orchestra of life.

Number of words 2310
See page 371 for questions
Reading time in seconds _______
See page 497 for conversion table

The 30,000 Words a Day We Talk

Virgil Baker

Are you having one of your ordinary, run-of-the-mill days? If so, how are you coming along with your scheduled 30,000 spoken words for the day? An even more important question to raise is this: Why are we such talkers? What do you think of this author's answers to that important question?

Do you have any idea how many words you speak in an ordinary, run-of-the-mill day?

Of course the figures varies with different people. Some are naturally "talkers." Others aren't. Then, too, some of us—teachers, salesmen and personnel workers, for instance—talk a lot because our jobs demand it, while those who work mostly alone don't talk nearly as much. But if your temperament, occupation, and other obvious factors make you an "average" talker, it isn't unusual for you to speak around 30,000 words a day.

Maybe that seems like a rash estimate, but here's the breakdown on it. Authorities figure that we talk about a third of the time we're awake. That's a third of 16 hours, or about $5^1/_2$ hours. But let's be conservative and say we spend only $3^1/_2$ hours a day talking. Not talking a blue streak. Just conversing casually. If we talk at the rate of 150 words a minute, which isn't unusually fast, we're using about 9,000 words an hour, or 31,500 words in a day's stint.

It hasn't been proved that the urge to talk is stronger in women than in men, either. I was pretty well convinced that it is when 30 women had a meeting in my living room while I tried to read a book at the back of the house, but I doubt if the evidence would stand up in statistical circles. Incidentally, my wife assures me that she heard not only what was being said right around her, but got the general drift of all the other conversations going on in the room at the same time! I don't think I could do it, but that's beside the point. Consider, if you're a man, all the small talk and shop talk that goes on at strictly male assemblies, and you'll probably agree that men are about as talkative as women.

What's back of all this verbal bombardment? We feel the urge to talk—but why? Speech specialists have dug into the matter and come up with some reasons that should help us to understand ourselves—and each other—a good deal better. Here is a simplified summary of their findings.

First of all, we talk to give vent to our feelings and emotions. According to psychologists, this is a perfectly natural and normal thing to do, particularly if the emotions are extremely pleasant or painful. If we bottle up those feelings too tightly—they call it "delaying our emotional responses"—we "blow our tops." Sometimes we give verbal expression to our emotions even when there's nobody else around.

Secondly, we talk to ourselves to find out what we mean. Some people talk to themselves aloud, of course, but usually this kind of talk isn't oral. It goes on silently within our minds. Confused by a fuzzy idea or a memory so vague that it refuses to come to the front, we probe with words to make it come clear. We also toss new ideas about in our minds to discover if the ideas "make sense." We even hold debates with the various facets of our personality, trying to find a satisfactory solution to our problems. And most of us often speak silently to God, receiving in return the inspiration, insights and satisfactions we couldn't get in any other way.

In the third place, we talk because we must break through the barrier of silence to one another. We've been able to work out an elaborate system of thought symbols—a language of words—to help us do this more effectively. A dog can "tell" us it is hungry by the way it looks and whimpers, but it can't tell us so by words. It's only a person who can say that he is hungry for ham and eggs.

Every time we say "hello" or "good morning" we feel less alone, for a moment less shut up within ourselves. If we're conscious of this fact, the little inanities with which we greet one another will have more warmth. At the very least, we'll never find them annoying. I remember how, when I was a child, my grandfather's morning greeting irritated me. He'd say "Well, are you up for all day?" I get the same feeling now when someone finds me with my head under the hood of my stalled car and says, "Stopped on you, eh?" My impulse is to turn around and say, "Does it look like it's clipping down the road?" But of course I don't say it because I know the stranger means something like this: "Hello, fellow human being. I see you're having car trouble and I want to be friendly and help you."

As for small talk, it is often aimless and rambling, but who cares? In reasonably small doses, it's a pleasant and wholesome way of maintaining contact with those around us.

So much for the basic reasons why we talk: the urge to give vent to our emotions, the desire to clarify our thoughts and establish contact with God by means of inner speech, and the need to break through the silence barrier.

Less fundamental than the three basic reasons why we talk but no less challenging and important are the drives to talk which spring from society. Because we live in a world where inter-action is imperative, we talk to develop inter-action.

No man is an island, it has been said. My life and experience—myself—overlaps your life and experience—yourself. And so we must reason together. We must inter-think. In this kind of talk, the other person gives back to us our own thoughts, plus his. Thus, ideas are enlivened and enriched.

Some years ago a friend of mine died. We had gone to college together and had always spoken freely to each other of what was on our minds and in our hearts. After he was gone I felt that a part of me was gone, too. No doubt you have had a similar experience. To practice this sort of inter-thinking—this kind of talk—is to experience friendship at its deepest level.

The "tightened-up" world we live in makes for an intimate and complex society. Except in a few highly specialized fields, not many individuals work alone these days. It is truly an age of teamwork. Domestic problems are tackled by committees, clubs, boards, unions, and on the international level by such organizations as the United Nations.

Fewer businesses are owned and operated by one man. Many are corporations controlled by managers appointed by stockholders who own the business. Even groups of scientists must team together in long-range programs to explore successfully the immensely complicated facts of nature and to put scientific knowledge into action.

Thus speech—the use of words as tools for inter-thinking—has become a crucial factor in today's world. Personal opinions expressed in thousands of conversations, speeches and discussions, merge into public opinion and laws. The urge to use words as tools for inter-thinking is a creative urge, pushing forward, we believe, toward a better society. A democracy—our democracy—is government through discussion.

Sometimes, we talk not to exchange opinions with others but to press our opinions upon them. This kind of speech is known as persuasion. It, too, came into our Western culture along with the art of discussion. The caveman didn't know how to use talk to persuade. He used his muscles, and if they couldn't get the job done he picked up a club. Dictators don't use the art of verbal persuasion, either. They try to control the actions of others by violence and threats.

Anytime we use words to "put across a point" we're practicing the art of persuasion. Politicians use it to get votes. Businessmen call it advertising and use it to promote sales.

There are some ethical points involved, of course. Each of us, as a persuader, should be sincere, dependable and honest. If we make promises we should be sure we can keep them. The "smooth talker," the "high-pressure personality" abuses the privileges of a citizen in a democratic society. His ethics are based on the faulty assumption that success depends not on what he is, but the appearance he makes, and the verbal web he can weave.

When the persuasive speech of one man or a few men does violence to the individual or to the group, speech has been used for an unethical purpose. No one has the right to seek absolute control. A person has only the right to present his honest convictions, with the good of the group at heart instead of his own selfish interests.

The urge to talk stems from various needs. Some of them are purely personal, and some are all wrapped up in the needs of other people. Those 30,000 words most of us speak in a day's time are a mighty force when turned loose along with everyone else's. Small talk and pleasantries, inter-thinking and persuasion are all a part of it; each part, if wisely used, serves a good and constructive purpose.

Do we talk too much? Each of us has to make that decision for himself. Some situations require a heap of listening and a firm rein on that urge to talk. It's a wise person who can spot such a situation, and a well-disciplined one who can adapt himself to it.

Number of words 1560
See page 373 for questions
Reading time in seconds _______
See page 497 for conversion table

Selection 48

Mark Twain's Speechmaking Strategy

Lydel Sims

You probably think of Mark Twain as the author of Tom Sawyer, Huckleberry Finn, *or* Connecticut Yankee in King Arthur's Court. *In his own day, however, he was equally well known for his ability as a speaker. You'll understand why when you read about his strategy.*

The schoolboy in the old story explained the technique nicely. "Strategy," he wrote, "means that when you run out of bullets you keep on firing." It hasn't caught on in military circles, but speechmakers have been practicing that kind of strategy for generations.

Consider the problem:

You're going to a sales conference, a convention, a testimonial dinner, a meeting of department heads. You're scheduled to speak, or you know you'll be called on. So you organize your thoughts, scribble notes on a piece of paper . . . and worry.

You worry, because like all good speakers, you want people to believe the words just flow out—all the humor, the motivation, the drive, the matchless grasp of detail, the fresh and sparkling anecdotes.

But speakers who hold audiences in the palm of their hand don't speak from notes. Are you going to pause and consult those plaguey notes, thus admitting mere mortality? Or are you going to wing it and risk forgetting your best story, omitting your most important point? And if you run out of ammunition, are you going to try to keep on firing?

Mark Twain faced that very same dilemma and solved it, becoming one of the most successful speakers in America's history.

In his early days on the lecture circuit, Mark Twain worked out a solution to the speechmaker's dilemma by trial and error, but he didn't explain it until years later in a little-known essay that was published after his death. The system was so good, he testified, that a quarter-century after he had given a lecture he could remember the whole thing by a single act of recall.

You have Twain's posthumous guarantee that it'll work for you.

When he first began his speaking career, Twain recalled, he used a full page of notes to keep from getting mixed up. He would write down the beginnings of key sentences, to take him from one point to another and to protect him from skipping. For a typical evening's lecture, he would write and memorize 11 key beginnings.

The plan failed. Twain would remember the sentences, all right, but forget their order. He would have to stop, consult his notes, and thereby spoil by spontaneous effect of the whole speech.

Twain then decided to memorize not only his key sentences, but also the first letter of each sentence. This initial-letter method didn't work either. Not even when, as he solemnly alleged, he cut the numbers of letters to 10 and inked them on his fingernails.

"I kept track of the fingers for a while," he wrote in his essay, "then I lost it, and after that I was never quite sure which finger I had used last."

He considered licking off the inked letters as he went along. People noticed he seemed more interested in his fingernails than his subject; one or two listeners would come up afterwards and ask what was wrong with his hands.

Then Mark Twain's great idea came—that it's hard to visualize letters, words and sentences, but *pictures* are easy to recall. They take hold. They can make things stick . . .

Especially if you draw them yourself.

Twain was no artist, mind you, but that didn't stop him. "In two minutes I made six pictures with a pen," he reported, "and they did the work of the 11 catch-sentences, and did it perfectly."

Having once drawn the pictures, he found he could throw them away. He discovered [and you can test it for yourself] that, having once made a crude series of drawings, he could recall their images at will.

He left us samples of three of those first six

pictures, and they are pathetic things, indeed, by artistic standards. But they got the job done.

The first was a haystack with a wiggly line under it to represent a rattlesnake—that was to tell him to begin talking about ranch life in the West. Alongside it, he drew a few slanting lines with what could just possibly be an umbrella and the Roman numeral II—that referred to a tale about a great wind that would strike Carson City at 2 o'clock every afternoon. Next, he drew a couple of jagged lines—lightning, of course—telling him it was time to move on to the subject of weather in San Francisco, where the point was that there *wasn't* any lightning. Nor thunder either, he noted.

From that day, Twain was able to speak without notes, and the system never failed him. Each portion of his speech would be represented by a picture. He would draw them, all strung out in a row, then look at them and destroy them. When the time came to speak, there was the row of images sharply in his mind.

Twain observed you can even make last-minute notes based on the remarks of an earlier speaker. Just insert another figure in your set of images.

The magic of the Twain technique should be immediately obvious to the speaker who organizes remarks around anecdotes. Are you introducing your first point with a story about a nervous doctor in Dubuque? Draw the doctor. Are you following that with the principle that's best illustrated with the tale of the fellow who treed a wildcat? Draw a tree alongside the doctor. And so on.

The remarkable things is that Twain's method can work just as well for concepts as it does for anecdotes. Sales must be increased? Draw a vertical arrow with a dollar sign. Something about productivity? A lopsided circle representing a wheel is sufficient. Research and development? Even you can draw what will be recognized—by you—as a mad scientist. And if you need figures, put them in the pictures, too, coming out of people's mouths, piled in pyramids, outlined in exclamation marks, lurking under bridges.

The wilder the image, the easier it'll be to remember. And once you have your scrawls in sequence and take a good look, you're fixed. Instant memory.

Mark Twain didn't mention it, but there's one more thing you might do. When you reach the end of your drawings, hence the end of your speech, you could add one more—a drawing of an octagonal sign: STOP!

That would be smart strategy, for then you really *are* out of bullets. No need to keep on firing.

Number of words 1050
See page 375 for questions
Reading time in seconds _______
See page 497 for conversion table

SELECTION 49

The 11 Toughest Job Interview Questions . . . and How to Answer Them

Bruce E. Moses

Getting a responsible job usually involves writing the kind of letter of application that opens the way to still another hurdle—the personal interview. Two you's *are thus revealed—you the writer and you the talker, or the social creature. Can you the talker handle an interview effectively? Here's a helpful article.*

As the food commercial jingle on TV suggests . . . "Anticipation . . .".

The job hunter must anticipate and be prepared for the so-called "curve" questions which no doubt will be thrown out during the interview. Everyone is vulnerable to "loaded" or "curve" questions. This is especially true if there is a "red flag" on your resume to call attention to a particularly delicate subject. But not everyone is vulnerable to the same questions in the same way because we all bring different strengths and weaknesses to an interview.

Following is my selection of the 11 toughest

questions which are asked during the interview . . . and how to answer them. It is based on composite feedback received from candidates I have recruited as well as corporate clients I have served during 15 years as an executive recruiter.

1. Several jobs in a short period of time. The best defense is an offense. As long as the "Dates Employed" are glaring at the interviewer from the resumé, you should explain why you had so many jobs *before* the question is even raised.

For instance, suppose you were fired for incompetence after just one year on a particular job. Depending on how long ago it was, you might indicate that, "Although the job did not work out, I gained quite a bit from it because . . ." and then proceed to tell why. You might also list some of your accomplishments, even though you were there only a short time. You might have taken some additional courses to help improve your background—so that you will be better prepared the next time around. Use empathy and make sure you are coming across in a sincere and positive manner. For all you know, the same thing may have happened to the interviewer at one time. Avoid transparent excuses—candor is refreshing!

2. Weak formal education. Turn the liability into an asset. Explain what responsibilities you had when you were young, and how you have studied on your own. If it is true, you might explain that no matter where you were employed, you were usually the only noncollege graduate at your job level. If there is a possibility of night school, tell that to the interviewer, too.

3. What are your long-range goals? This question seems to baffle a lot of people. Whatever you say, avoid indicating that "What I really want is a business of my own" . . . even if you do! You certainly will not encourage an employer by indicating you will give the company the privilege of training you for a couple of years, but then plan on going out on your own to compete with them. You may even change your mind once you begin to work for the company. Frequently, I will hear from an employee who has spent twenty or more years with his company who says, "When I first joined my employer more than twenty years ago, I had absolutely no intention of staying more than just a couple of years—just for the experience."

Answer the "long-range goal" question as you really believe . . . outside of "leaving the company." If you feel that someday you could become president of the company, then tell the interviewer so. Also, offer reasons that support your ambitious plans. Maybe you plan on obtaining your MBA, or some other positive accomplishment to help you meet your goals.

4. What is your greatest weakness? Nobody is perfect. When answering this question, you had better use empathy. The wrong answer could instantly disqualify you for the job.

I will never forget the candidate I once recruited for the position of corporate comptroller who told the president of the company that, "My greatest weakness is detail. I hate detail work!" Needless to say, that particular candidate was not hired. The irony of it all was that he had been a successful comptroller for almost fifteen years. Be honest, but try to think of a "greatest single weakness" which will not immediately eliminate you from any further consideration for the job.

5. Physical handicap or health problem. Not everyone is blessed with perfect health or appearance. If you have an obvious physical handicap or health problem, it is usually best to discuss it openly with the interviewer, provided it will not automatically disqualify you. Be honest with both the interviewer and yourself.

I once recommended a candidate who was confined to a wheelchair because of a childhood accident. He explained very positively that his handicap was really not a hindrance but a mere inconvenience. His attitude was marvelous. This man very candidly admitted that because of his handicap he always tried a little harder to overcome it . . . and most certainly did.

6. Recently divorced. This is a common subject which, when discussed with applicants, frequently causes discomfort—especially if there are children involved. Some companies will not hire a recent divorcee until after the so-called "adjustment period" (whatever that is) is completed. Some people never completely adjust to divorce, while others were never completely adjusted to marriage—and therefore become much better immediately after the divorce.

The trepidation employers sometimes have about the recently divorced is that any new job requires total concentration and commitment. If a new employee has to tackle, simultaneously, the adjustment to a new job plus putting life back together after a recent divorce, then the pressures may be too great.

When the subject comes up in an interview, it is best to be candid about it. If the divorce is fairly recent, try to explain to the interviewer that because your marital problems are now over, you are prepared to give 110% to the job. Be positive!

7. Recently retired military officers. The typical

"curve" question which may be thrown at a recently retired military officer: "Do you think you may have difficulty adapting to civilian life?" Your response could be: "The responsibility and exposure that I received in the military are directly applicable for the following reasons . . ." then proceed to explain those reasons. Try to draw analogies between what you accomplished in the military and what you perceive the job requiring.

If the interviewer brings up the fact that you are earning a handsome retirement salary and therefore should not require too much money . . . you might indicate politely, bur firmly, "My pension pay should have no bearing on the salary the employer has set for the job opening. I will contribute as much to the company as someone who is not on a pension, and therefore should be compensated appropriately."

You want to convince the interviewer that your military experience is an asset in fulfilling the requirements of the job. Use civilian terminology which you know will be positive. You want the interviewer to think of you as a "business executive" rather than a "retired officer looking for a way to spend his free time."

8. Why should the company hire you? This is one of the most frequently asked questions, yet most job hunters fail to take advantage of it. Prepare for this question prior to your interview and be ready to answer it with enthusiasm and in a manner of controlled confidence. Summarize your experience and accomplishments in a concise positive statement as to why you are the best qualified candidate for the job. Do not bore the interviewer with a long dissertation, but be sure to convey the benefits the company will receive by hiring you.

9. Why are you leaving your present position? The job may be dull, the boss a boor, and the pay low . . . however, you want to avoid the negative cliches and use more positive reasons. You might be seeking greater advancement opportunities where you could take on added responsibilities and earn more money. Your prospects for career development could be limited because of a lack of promotional opportunities. You do not want to appear as a job-hopper who is just running away from another problem. Use reasons which the interviewer can relate to and identify with.

10. Age—Too young or too old? If you are young, you want to come across as mature and level-headed. You want to illustrate that you have already handled business situations and possess the experience and good judgment to do an excellent job. Cite some examples of your success.

If you are "middle aged" or older (and I am not sure I know what "middle aged" is), you want to appear full of vim and vitality. Talk about your most recent accomplishments and the future goals you have set for yourself. Substantiate to the interviewer that your most recent years have been most productive. Highlight your most recent achievements.

11. Unemployed executive. If you are unemployed and there is no way you can cover yourself with your prior employer—like remaining on the payroll—then just indicate that you are unemployed . . . but have several offers pending.

It just does not pay to try and cover yourself with the "I am presently doing consulting" routine, unless you really are. Any astute interviewer will see right through your facade, and you will only further weaken your position.

One approach you may consider is that you found it difficult taking time off from work to explore other opportunities. You felt that as long as your prior employer was paying you, you owed him a fair day's work. So rather than lie or make excuses for taking time off, you elected to pursue your job campaign on a full-time basis.

The above subjects and questions are the 11 toughest, but there are many more which could be just as important, depending on your circumstances. Do not be caught by surprise. Make a list of every conceivable question an interviewer might ask. You will be amazed at what you come up with. Remember, these same questions could be thrown at you!

Successful interviews do not happen by chance. Everyone has the desire to do well in an interview, but the job hunter who will ultimately receive the offer is the one who has the greatest desire to prepare for the interview.

Number of words 1670
See page 377 for questions
Reading time in seconds _______
See page 497 for conversion table

You CAN Be Persuasive

Morton L. Janklow

One historic figure was said to have had "a head to contrive, a tongue to persuade, and a hand to execute." When you finish reading Zuke Berman's one-minute attempt to persuade, you may want to know more about his persuasive technique. It may help you develop the right head-tongue-hand combination yourself.

When Emile Zola Berman, the famous trial lawyer from New York, entered the Non-Commissioned Officers' Club at the Marine Corps boot camp at Parris Island, S.C., that hot, humid July night in 1956, the tension was immediate and palpable. The usually boisterous drill instructors were stunned into silence as Zuke Berman (as he was known to the legal world) strode into their sacred precincts as if he owned the place, went to the center of the room, climbed onto a table and, with steely-eyed gaze, stared out at the assembled noncoms.

The room grew silent. Then, with the skill of the great actor that he was, Berman spoke: "My name is Emile Zola Berman, I'm a civilian. I'm a Jew, and I'm a Yankee from New York City. I've come down here to save the Marine Corps. If no one helps me, I'm going back to New York to resume my life. If you care about the Corps, and if you care about the truth, come see us in our quarters tonight and help us keep you proud to be Marines."

With that, he scrambled down off the table and strode out of the room as silently as he had entered it.

The occasion for this high drama was the most famous Marine Corps court-martial in history. Sgt. Matthew McKeon—the embodiment of the professional Marine drill instructor—was on trial on the most serious charges stemming from the drowning deaths of six young recruits in his company during a disciplinary night-training exercise in the swamps of Ribbon Creek. Berman and I (then a young attorney with experience in the military justice system) had volunteered to defend McKeon.

The key to our defense to the most serious charge was to prove that what McKeon had done did not constitute cruelty against his troops but was, in fact, common practice among Marine Crops drill instructors training young men for combat.

When we had arrived at Parris Island a few days earlier, we had fully expected the drill instructors to cooperate with us in getting at the truth about combat training. What we met instead was a stone wall—set up, we learned, by the Marine Corps brass. Nobody would talk to us. We couldn't even get witnesses from other bases. Try as we would, we could not persuade the leadership of the Marine Corps or its drill instructors that the future and credibility of the corps was at stake.

Berman's one-minute appearance and dramatic statement at the NCO Club was his desperate effort to break through that wall of silence. "This will either make us or break us," he said to me as we left the club.

Back in our quarters, Berman went to sleep, having admonished me to sit up and wait in case, as we hoped, somebody showed up. At about 2 A.M., just as he had predicted, there was a light tap at the window. I let in an extremely frightened young drill instructor. "I think I know why you guys are here," he said, "and I'm prepared to tell you what really goes on in these boot camps." His testimony was the break in the dam. Before we were finished, dozens of drill instructors had come forward to testify that, indeed, the march in the swamp was common practice to discipline troops and that there was nothing "cruel or unusual" about this behavior.

Zuke Berman had persuaded a group of the toughest men in the world to do as he felt they should and as he wanted. He did it in the face of innate prejudices, which he addressed at once with his opening comments. I have never forgotten the lessons I learned that night at Parris Island. I've used them over and over in my law practice, my work as a literary agent and my life. In those few words were embodied some of the greatest rules of persuasiveness, and I'd like to share them with you.

1. Know precisely what you are trying to accomplish. First and foremost, when seeking to persuade, have your objective clearly in mind. It is amazing how many people do not have such a fixed goal when they try to talk other people into doing things. Berman was seeking to batter down the imposed wall of silence, to make those drill instructors understand that his goals and theirs were the same and to convince them that giving us the information with which to defend one of their number could only, in the long run, benefit them and the Marine Corps that they cherished.

2. Put yourself in the other person's shoes. Be aware of the specific reasons why the other person requires persuasion and perhaps has resisted it. What is there about your goals that he resists or resents? What need or priority of his is threatened by your needs? How can you alleviate that fear? At Parris Island, the non-coms were worried that if they came forward in defiance of the brass's policy to keep the story quiet, they might get into trouble.

Berman did not attempt to mislead them or tell them there was no risk—the risk was obvious. He chose, instead, to appeal to their pride as men and as Marines. He put himself on their side and made them realize that his objective was one they shared, namely, to save the Marine Corps. By putting yourself in the other fellow's shoes, you develop a sensitivity to that person's needs and can better address them. It is not easy to do, but it's usually necessary if you want to persuade someone.

3. Recognize that other people frequently have prejudices and points of view that they never examine and never question. You can argue with them, you can tell them they shouldn't have those beliefs, but you will rarely shake them. What you must do is confront these issues head on, as Berman did that night. To be a civilian, to be a New Yorker and to be Jewish were really not the ideal things for a defense counsel in South Carolina in a prominent Marine court-martial in July of 1956. To be a Catholic running for President in 1960 also flew in the face of many prejudices, which John F. Kennedy attacked at the start of his campaign in order to clear the decks for a discussion of issues.

4. Be prepared to take risks. Whenever you are attempting to change an opinion—whether of a jury in a homicide trial or of a friend, spouse or parent from whom you seek a personal favor—you're going to meet strong levels of resistance. There is a moment where you've made your best case and you must be prepared to take your stand. Most people, when attempting to advance a point of view persuasively, become fearful that they will fail, and that fear is conveyed to the person they are trying to persuade. It is the surest way to fail. If you can screw up your courage, as Zuke Berman did, tell somebody you've made the best case you can and walk away prepared for possible loss, you will most often be a winner. People have enormous respect for someone who says, "This is my best case, I've done the best I can, I've explained to you why I feel the way I do, and I hope that you will agree with me."

5. Convince the other fellow that your objective is decent and honorable. By going along with you, he will be demonstrating that he shares those values. Most people are inherently decent and fair and "want to do the right thing." They're not always sure, however, what fairness or rightness is, and they are often full of anxiety when forced to say yes or no.

It is your job, as the persuader, to make them understand the human values represented by your position. They must be made to feel empathy for what you are trying to do so that emotionally they want to give you the response you seek. Zuke Berman did this when he said, "I've come down here to save the Marine Corps." Those drill instructors understood that and admired his courage in taking them on.

The civil rights movement enjoyed its ultimate victory over bigotry when people saw for themselves on television the dogs being loosed on the marchers in Selma, Ala., and the police crashing into the crowds with their clubs. Suddenly, people understood what the real effects were of unfair and inhumane policies, their emotions were aroused in a positive way, and it wasn't long before the President and the Congress felt that the public would support a strong Voting Rights Act.

Even when dealing with everyday matters, you should try to create in the other person a worthy emotional reason to support your point of view. Imagine you are young Luke or Linda, wanting to borrow the car. Suppose you say, "Dad, may I borrow the car?" It's easy for Dad to reply, "What for? Why don't you stay home and study? You had the car the day before yesterday." Instead, you might try: "Dad, tomorrow night is Angela's birthday, and I would love to take her out to dinner. She loves the Old Mill Restaurant, and I'd really appreciate it, and so would she, if I could use the car. I'll be home at a decent hour, and I won't drink. Maybe you and Mom could take in a movie or watch HBO."

By seeking to persuade in this way, you have explained precisely what your goal is, why it is necessary, why your father should grant your wish before he takes any kind of negative stand, why he should have an emotional stake in the outcome, how reasonable the goal is and why it is not difficult to grant the wish (because there are acceptable alternatives). Perhaps most important, you have given the other fellow an opportunity to be generous at little cost to himself. You've been deferential to his authority and sensitive to his needs.

6. Know when to stop. More arguments are lost by not knowing when to quit than by any other single factor. There is a moment when you have marshaled all of the factual and emotional issues in your favor and have expressed them as best you can. If you continue to hammer away, you do nothing but build resentment in the person you are trying to persuade. How many times have you had discussions where the issue becomes not the merits of the question before you but whether you are raising your voice too much or "bulldozing" the other person? Great lawyers and great actors all know when enough is enough.

Zuke Berman could have said a lot more that night in the NCO Club. He could have talked about the attitudes of the brass, enumerated the issues in the case, talked about our suspicions that every man in the room had committed the same acts as did our defendant, taken questions from the audience. In fact, he did none of these things because he knew, intuitively and brilliantly, that to belabor his point would not be helpful.

Finally, there are times in life when nothing seems to work, and the other side just refuses to be persuaded. That is when I invoke *Rule No. 7 of the Art of Persuasion.* I call it "The Last Resort Rule." It was taught to me by a great teacher at Columbia Law School named Jerome Michael, who taught a course in appellate advocacy. At the last moment in the last class of the course, when he had taught us everything we knew, he said: "These are my final words on advocacy. If you have the facts on your side, hammer the facts. If you have the law on your side, hammer the law. If you have neither the facts nor the law, hammer the table."

Number of words 1990
See page 379 for questions
Reading time in seconds _______
See page 497 for conversion table

Selection 51

You Are the Next Speaker

Robert Haakenson

What's the number one fear among Americans? According to the Book of Lists*, it's "Fear of Public Speaking"! Fear of death ranks a distant seventh. The following selection should do wonders to stop those potentially shaking knees and butterflies in the stomach.*

One afternoon a Roman Emperor was entertaining himself at the Colosseum by feeding Christians to the lions. Several Christians were sacrificed and the crowd screamed for more.

The next martyr said something to the lion, and the beast slunk away. Then a second lion; same result. And a third. The amazed throng began to shift its sympathies to the Christian. The Emperor announced that the Christian's life would be spared. He insisted, however, that the martyr appear before him.

"I am sparing your life," said the Emperor, "but before I release you, I demand to know what it was that you said to those beasts."

"I merely said to each lion: 'After dinner, of course, you'll be expected to say a few words.'"

As American adults, each of us faces a pretty good likelihood he will be "asked to say a few words" at least once during the coming year. The audience may be eight or eight hundred—or more likely—thirty-five, a typical after-dinner audience. How do you feel about it? When someone says to you, "Of course, we'll expect you to say a few words after dinner," do you—like the lions—run in dismay?

You shouldn't. You should welcome the opportunity. Here are some helps. Let's start with three key phrases: (1) "Meat and potatoes"; (2) "Tell, tell and tell"; (3) "Conversationality."

First, "Meat and Potatoes"

The most important item in good speaking is *having something worthwhile* to say. This may take the form of new ideas, new information, a new slant on an old idea, or a new interpretation of existing information.

In a well-planned talk, we develop a single theme; that is, we talk about a single subject. We develop our theme with "specifics": specific examples, illustrative anecdotes, definitions, comparisons, contrasts and statistics. These are called the "meat and potatoes" of speaking. When the last vote is counted, it is the amount and quality of "meat and potatoes" that will determine how well an audience liked a speaker.

For our "meat and potatoes," we must do research, but it can be simple in nature and actually enjoyable. First, we must *reflect*; that is, with pencil and paper, summarize what we already know on the chosen topic. We often will surprise ourselves with the amount of information we have. Secondly, we must *read*—as extensively as possible. Thirdly, we must *converse*. We can discuss our subject with everyone who is willing to talk about it. Finally, if the subject is one that lends itself, we must *observe* directly. For example, if we are talking about a community problem such as zoning or parks, we can make direct observations and nothing is more useful.

We should gather at least three or four times as much material as we possibly can include in the talk. Then we can select the best items on the basis of: (1) relevance; (2) accuracy; (3) human interest. We know that people like stories. "Once upon a time," is one of the most magic phrases in our language; "for instance," is another. People also like action, emotion, conflict, novelty, and the familiar, with a new twist. These are the elements of human interest.

Dr. Russell Conwell, who founded Temple University, was famous for his "Acres of Diamonds." By giving this talk 7,000 times, he earned seven million dollars, many of which were devoted to the education of deserving young men at Temple University. "Acres of Diamonds" is made up of *one story after another*, demonstrating that opportunity lies everywhere about us if we will scratch the surface. Like a skilled composer, Dr. Conwell lost no opportunity to develop his theme.

A special kind of "meat and potatoes" is audio-visual aids: maps, photos, drawings, graphs, charts, models, objects, phonograph records, tape recordings. Flannelboards, blackboards and projectors are useful devices. When properly used, audio-visual aids enhance a talk because they clarify meaning, give it impact, heighten interest and spark the speaker's delivery. . . .

We have good content, then, when we have something worthwhile to say. It is worthwhile if we have a useful and interesting theme, and if we develop our theme with pertinent, accurate and interesting specifics gathered through reflection, reading, conversing and observing.

Now for our second major point—

"Tell, Tell and Tell"

People sometimes argue over which is the more important: *what* a speaker says, or *how* he says it. Often they fail to take into account that there is a third element that can improve both the *what* and the *how: how he puts it together*. Effective organization can make a mediocre speech good and a good one better.

How do we go about organizing the speech? Follow the rule for successful teaching: "First tell them what you're going to tell them; then tell them; then tell them what you've told them."

The following simple outline can be adapted to almost any talk:

- **I.** *Introduction*
  - A. "Icebreaker"
  - B. Preview
- **II.** *Body*
  - A. Theme or Thesis
    - 1. Main Point No. 1
    - 2. Main Point No. 2
    - 3. Main Point No. 3
- **III.** *Conclusion*
  - A. Summary
  - B. "Haymaker"

What is an "icebreaker"? A vessel with a reinforced prow that leaves Duluth in the spring? Yes. It's also an anecdote, an unusual definition, a rhetorical question, a quotation—anything that "breaks the ice" and establishes rapport between the speaker and his audience. Often the "icebreaker" is suggested by something that happens at the meeting, like the spilling of hot soup on a clergyman who was about to speak. The scalded clergyman asked: "Will some layman please make a few appropriate remarks?"

The ideal "icebreaker" should arouse interest in speaker and subject and audience; and create a friendly, receptive atmosphere for what the speaker has to say. Robert M. Hutchins, as president of the University of Chicago, once told a student audience that the secret of success was spelled out in four letters on the door by which he had entered the auditorium. The students roared, because their side of the door was marked "Pull." But that made it easy for Hutchins to get across his point that "Push" is as important as "Pull."

Perhaps the most useful "icebreaker," speech in and speech out, is a personal narrative. If the speaker has such a story that is pertinent, without being boastful, it will enable him to establish common ground between himself and his subject and his audience. When, as wartime President, Franklin D. Roosevelt spoke to the workers at the Bremerton shipyards, he reminded them of his last visit, years before, when he was Assistant Secretary of the Navy. This linked him with his audience and both with his subject, production to win the war.

After the "icebreaker" comes the preview, telling in a few words what the speech is to be about. In addition to announcing the theme, it is a good idea to enumerate the main headings, the main points that will be developed. "I want to talk with you about the importance of passing the school bond proposal. First, I propose to outline the problem of critical school needs. Secondly, I want to describe *your* children's losses while these needs are unmet. Thirdly and finally, let me suggest a plan for passing this proposal and reaping the educational benefits."

Why have a preview, since the audience will hear the speech itself anyway? Won't you destroy suspense? One purpose of the preview is to whet anticipation. Secondly, it helps understanding and retention, because it creates a frame of reference. Having a broad outline of what is to follow, the listener can fill in the pigeonholes, so to speak.

The preview should be as tantalizing as you can make it; but don't promise more than you can deliver. If you were to say, "Before I've finished speaking, I'm going to convince every man and woman in this room that the binomial theorem is based on a fundamental Newtonian misconception," I honestly doubt whether you could make good your promise.

In any case, the rule to avoid apology is solid gold. What a masterpiece of negative psychology to being, "Well, I'm really not prepared to speak on this subject. . . ." If the speaker expects his talk to be poor, listeners will too.

How do we go about working out the main headings? A simple way is to employ time-honored "stock speech designs." Here are a few:

A. *Time Sequence*

1. Past
2. Present
3. Future

"The Gettysburg Address" is a famous speech organized in this pattern.

B. *Spatial Pattern*

1. Left	or	1. Top	or	1. Near
2. Center		2. Middle		2. Middle-Distant
3. Right		3. Bottom		3. Far

C. *Topical Order*

1. Who	or	1. Political	or	1. Theory	or	1. Animal
2. What		2. Social		2. Practice		2. Vegetable
3. Where		3. Economic				3. Mineral
4. When						
5. How						
6. Why						

D. *Logical Order*

1. Problem	or	1. Cause
2. Damage		2. Effect
3. Solution		

Problem-Damage-Solution, or simply Problem-Solution, is perhaps the most useful of all organizational patterns.

In writing words to be read, we strive for smooth-flowing continuity without visible joints or seams. But in speaking, conspicuous transition is often desirable—even to the point of being abrupt or unexpected. The abrupt transition serves two purposes. First, it adds variety. Again we may use the analogy of the composer, bringing in his second subject in a related but quite different key. Secondly, since the logical place for a transition is between the topics you've promised to discuss, the transitions serve as checkpoints for your audience. When you say, "Let us move ahead to the second area of discussion," listeners can see that you're making progress, that you're following a well-charted course and you won't ramble aimlessly all night.

An especially strong transition is the partial summation: "We see then that there is a mounting problem of discharged mental patients needing to make a successful return to their communities. Secondly, let us examine the consequences if this problem continues unresolved." . . .

In the Body of the speech the speaker establishes his theme (or thesis) by developing his main headings, embellishing them with "meat and potatoes" specifics.

In the Conclusion, the speaker should first offer a strong and complete final summary of theme and headings. Then he should conclude on a note of triumph with a rousing "haymaker"—a hard-hitting, dramatic and memorable crystallization of his theme. The "haymaker" may be in the form of a statement, question, quotation, poem, resolution, challenge, etc. . . .

How long should a talk be? The best answer seems to be that of the veteran pastor who was asked by his new assistant, "How long should I preach when I give my first sermon next Sunday?"

"That's up to you," came the reply, "but we feel we don't save any souls after twenty minutes."

Most subjects can be covered reasonably in that time. The point of diminishing returns in the human attention span probably occurs within twenty minutes. A short speech often will permit a question and answer period, and many speakers feel they can "score the most points" in the Q&A. There are, in fact, speakers who believe the chief function of the talk is to be a springboard, stirring up questions and statements for the Q&A.

We've defined "meat and potatoes." We've explained what we mean by "tell, tell and tell."

Now for our third major point—

"Conversationality"

Did you ever analyze what you're doing in a very animated conversation, perhaps a friendly argument? First of all, you're assembling material. You're searching your memory for every instance, statistic, concrete example or emotional appeal that bears on the argument. Subconsciously, you're also selecting material, choosing those arguments which are most forceful and convincing. You're presenting your arguments with persuasive gestures and vocal inflections. And you're too interested in the reaction of your adversary—watching to see if you're winning the desired response—to be self-conscious yourself.

In short, you're communicating. Sound arguments, forcefully presented—these are the essence of communication, whether across the back fence or across the aisle in Congress.

Here a word should be said about stage fright. Everyone suffers from it at some time or other. Standing up in public to address our fellow man does take getting used to. The thing to remember is that stage fright, while uncomfortable, is very seldom fatal. We may not be able to prevent our knees from knocking, and our hands and voices from shaking, but if we've done our homework adequately and have the basic determination to say our say, our words will have authority. It is possible to be both *perspiring and persuasive.* The main thing is to show that, as the military put it, the "situation is well in hand."

It's important not to be thrown by the unexpected things that are bound to happen. Audiences are very forgiving about minor *faux pas* if the speaker doesn't call attention to them. Stumbling over a word or two won't spoil your speech. Nor will a waiter's dropping a tray of dishes, especially if you can think of an appropriate spur-of-the-moment comment. Recently, a clergyman in suburban Philadelphia was preaching on the Last Judgment when the church oil burner exploded. Looking up from his text, the clergyman commented: "This sermon may not be a minute too soon."

What sort of voice have you? Even if it's not good enough to get you into the Metropolitan Opera, it can be very effective for speaking. The most frequent fault of speakers is monotony. Vary the pitch of your speaking voice. Let it rise and fall to suit the words. Notice how skillfully this is done by fine speakers. An interesting experiment is to play a speech recording, moving far enough away so that you can't make out the words. Just listen to the sound. You'll be amazed by the vocal compass of someone like the late Franklin D. Roosevelt or—the greatest speaker I ever heard in person—Norman Thomas.

Avoid the extremes of shrill screech or cellar rumble, weary plod or machine gun staccato, mousey whisper or deafening blast. A common fault of speakers is speaking too quietly. Speakers tend to sound louder to themselves than they do their audiences. Speak up; don't be bashful. There is far greater danger of being too quiet than too loud. Anyone with normal vocal power should be able to make himself heard by an audience of forty, even in the midst of background noise. Have an ally at the back of the room to signal whether or not you can be heard. Or, simply ask your audience: "Can you hear me all right?" This can be a very effective "icebreaker." . . .

How a speaker looks is as important as how he sounds. Try to appear natural and comfortable. Mannerisms that call attention to themselves distract from what you are saying.

Bodily action, or physical expressiveness, includes movements around the platform, stance/posture, gesture, facial expression and eye contact. Bodily action should be: *plentiful, meaningful and spontaneous*. It is possible to have reasonable movement around the 2-foot by 2-foot square platform even when hemmed in by program chairman, president, head table and back wall. Posture should be comfortably erect. An uncomfortable "West Point brace" and a slovenly slouch are equally bad.

Use gestures—just as you do in a lively conversation. Not only arms and hands, but head, feet and the entire body can make movements which emphasize the points you are making. Physical expression attracts audience attention, communicates meaning (e.g., Charlie Chaplin, Harpo Marx), and stimulates the speaker to be a livelier communicator in all ways. Meaningless threshing about is bad, of course, but as beginning speakers we are far more apt to underdo than overdo. To get the habit of gesturing started, a few awkward movements may have to come first.

Keep facial expression alert and friendly. When we are nervous about making a speech, our fear tends to show in our faces as hostility. Remember the story of Toscanini and the philharmonic cellist. The cellist wore such a sour expression that Toscanini finally took the man aside and asked whether he had done anything to offend him.

"Oh, no, Maestro," the cellist replied. "I just hate music."

A good speaker will be alert from the time he enters the room. He will be attentive and responsive to everything that precedes his speech. Often the preliminary talks will give him valuable clues for his own.

One of the most important factors in communicating is maintaining eye contact with the audience. Eye contact should be direct and continuous. The speaker's eyes should "embrace" all listeners in a sort of irregular sweep, back and forth over the audience. Even when reading a speech, the speaker should be making eye contact with his audience 90 percent of the time.

In Sum . . .

We can summarize by saying that a speaker should have something worthwhile to say—"meat and potatoes." He should organize his material into a logical structure, making his points with emphasis—"tell, tell and tell." In the actual delivery he should try to eliminate all distractions that block communication with his listeners—and achieve "conversationality." By carefully observing these simple rules, almost anyone can be an acceptable speaker, and a little more practice may turn him from an acceptable speaker into an outstanding one.

Number of words 2860
See page 381 for questions
Reading time in seconds _______
See page 497 for conversion table

Ask, Don't Tell

Nardi Reeder Campion

Have you ever wondered why some people are such good company and others are not? Perhaps you'll find one reason as you read this article. Afterwards, start observing friends and acquaintances. See how many know how to unlock doors with questions.

> You start a question and it's like starting a stone. You sit quietly on the top of a hill; and away the stone goes, starting others.
>
> —Robert Louis Stevenson

How wonderful it is when a conversational stone we throw out brings an avalanche of response from those around us; when our interest and concern open a wide path to another's personality. How wonderful—and how rare! So often we feel shut out from the true thoughts of our friends and loved ones. They may be overflowing with ideas, but it is difficult for us to establish real contact. Yet each of us can learn the magical power of asking the right question at the right time, and gain the joy of unlocking the floodgates of true communication.

This exciting idea was first presented to me by the principal of our school. "When I talk to our 10-year-old son, Russell," I complained, "he pretends to be listening, but he's not. Later I find out that he didn't hear one word I said."

Miss Markham smiled and suggested, "Don't tell him, ask him—and then *you* really listen to what *he* says."

"Ask him what?" I countered.

"Well, what do you think he'd like to talk about?"

As I paused to mull over my answer, it suddenly dawned on me that Miss Markham was using the very technique she was telling *me* to use. Because she had answered my question with a question, I was thinking about the problem as I never would have if she had spelled out exactly what questions I should ask. Her apt question engaged my attention completely.

"It could be all the difference between sitting on a beach and swimming in the waves, if you can convince your son you'll heed any answer he gives you, no matter how unacceptable it seems. Genuine interest and acceptance . . . these are the keys to real communication."

Don't tell, ask. I doubted if such a simple suggestion could be of any real value, although I can understand that it is dangerous to "tell" too much. Most of us at some time have blundered into the booby-trap of repeating ideas until our children dial out.

Could it be possible, I asked myself, that Miss Markham's idea could really help me to bridge the gulf that separated me from others? I decided to test it by trying a few "asking" experiments in the laboratory of my own living room, to see whether the idea offered a fresh attack on "the disease of not listening."

I didn't have to wait long for an opportunity. Our 15-year-old daughter Cissa and I clash with clock-like regularity over the time she should come home at night. I usually say, "I want you to be in by 10:30."

"But, Mother," she moans, "*everybody* stays out until 11."

"How many times have I told you—everybody's business is nobody's business?" I answer. And then we are off on a collision course.

This Saturday when Cissa started out for the basketball game I tried Miss Markham's advice. I simply asked, "What time do you think you'll get back?"

"Oh," she said, "I'll make it by 10:30 all right."

I almost fell over. I felt as though I had been pushing against a door that was already open. Communications hadn't exactly flowed forth, but by asking one small question I had by-passed our usual head-on crash, and it left the door open between us.

I made up my mind right then to take as my motto those cheerful words from the Sermon on the Mount. "Knock, and it shall be opened unto you." My optimism increased when I read in a magazine that Norman Vincent Peale, who is more qualified than most of us to be a "teller," is a genius at the art of asking. When his children were growing up, Dr. Peale used to bring home letters people had written to him about their problems, and ask his children how they would answer them. He would say, "Here's a lady who's upset because her son lies to her. What advice can we send her?"

As Dr. Peale's children spelled out their answer they did some serious thinking about truth. Knowing their father valued their opinion made them clarify their own convictions. They knew he would give thoughtful consideration to their answers, however zany they might sound. If his son said, "I think it helps to be a good liar," Dr. Peale wouldn't register disapproval. He would say, "Can you explain what you mean?" And then the dialogue would begin.

Encouraged, I started asking questions right and left. At first I ran into a number of blank walls. Some questions, I discovered, come equipped with built-in discouraging answers. When our high school senior came home from the spring dance I asked eagerly, "How was the party, Toby?" The words were no sooner out of my mouth than I knew what the answer would be.

"Okay."

"Do you want to tell me about it?"

He shrugged his broad shoulders. "Not really."

End of conversation, if that's what you can call it.

I wasn't much more successful with Russell when I quizzed him about his new baseball club. He answered me patiently at first and then said, "Gosh, Mom, what is this? Twenty Questions?"

I'm glad to say my husband opened up much more freely than the boys had. When he came home from work I discarded the usual "What did you do today?" for a more definite question: "What was the most interesting thing that happened all day?"

"The cost control meeting."

"Cost control? Can you explain that to me?"

He eyed me skeptically. "You mean it?"

"Of course."

"Well, the whole area of cost control is sensitive..." and away he went. *Can you explain that?* turned out to be a leading question all right. Ten minutes later my husband said, "You're not listening."

"But I *want* to hear more about your work," I insisted.

"Don't try to bluff it," he laughed. "You're not all that crazy about cost control."

Clearly I had a lot to learn about the art of asking questions. Some of mine apparently closed more doors than they opened. Toby seemed to feel my questions didn't really concern him; Russell thought I was overly inquisitive; and my husband accused me of insincerity, however well-intentioned.

While brooding moodily over my ineptness, a picture suddenly flashed before my mind's eye. I was a young girl again, all dressed up for my first formal dance. My mother, who grew up in the southern-belle tradition, was counseling me, "Try to get your beau to do the talking, my dear. It's better for a girl to ask the right questions than to know all the answers."

"What *are* the right questions?"

"The ones that flatter your young man, of course. 'What's your opinion of this?' or 'Would you explain that?' Men like to feel important, and most of them can't resist a girl who asks leading questions and pays rapt attention to their answers."

My mother reassured me that the feminine "asking" role is marvelously effective. "It goes all the way back to Biblical times," she said, "and probably accounts for the Queen of Sheba's dazzling conquest of King Solomon. You remember in the Second Book of Chronicles it says the Queen of Sheba 'communed with him of all that was in her heart. And Solomon told her all her questions.' "

What was it, I asked myself, that the Queen of Sheba knew about the art of asking questions that I didn't know?

I am lucky to have as a friend and neighbor one of America's wisest men, a great preacher now in his eighties—Dr. Harry Emerson Fosdick. Like the rest of his friends, when I have a problem, I call on him. Dr. Fosdick had written: "My father's typical method in getting something done he wanted done was to ask us what we really thought about it ourselves, and even when I asked him for counsel I was fairly certain to have the question thrown back at me—what did I think myself? So from the beginning we were trained for independence." When I consulted him about the secret of asking good questions, he thought a minute and then said, "I suppose the secret, if there is one, is to realize that questioning and listening are inseparable. The asking of good questions represents listening on its highest plane, and of course true listening can never be faked or turned on. It must come from within. In order to sound sincere, a person has to *be* and *act* sincere, and I believe it's the quality of attention that makes all the difference."

I resolved to concentrate on the "quality of attention" with my husband, too. That evening, instead of too many eager-beaver questions, I waited for him to start our conversation when and where we wanted it to start. After years of plunging right in, this took a little doing, but I managed to keep quiet. At first there was a long silence, and then my husband said, "I'm quite concerned about a new committee I'm working on at the plant . . .".

As he talked I had no difficulty appearing interested, for I *was* interested—simply because what he was talking about was so important to him. After he finished he smiled at me and said, "You know, it's encouraging to have you listen to me like that." What a rewarding moment that was when I felt the magic of communication that grows out of a real concern for another!

What could actually be more encouraging than to make someone feel that you want to hear more fully what he thinks? A person who can do this naturally must have an invaluable gift. John F. Kennedy, for instance, was famous for the incisive questions he asked, and the intent way he listened to replies. Robert Saudek, who conferred with President Kennedy at the White House while he was producing *Profiles in Courage* for television, later told friends, "President Kennedy made you think he had nothing else to do except ask you questions and listen, with extraordinary concentration, to your answer. You knew that for the time being he had blotted out both the past and the future. More than anyone else I have ever met, President Kennedy seemed to understand the importance of *now*."

The phrase, "the importance of now" struck me like lightning. Suddenly I realized I had just been playing games with my family. If I were serious about trying to communicate with them, I would have to watch keenly for every fleeting chance to do so. Instead of trying to create those moments artificially, I would have to grasp every possible opportunity to bridge the gap by asking the right question at the right time.

I noticed how spontaneously my young neighbor responded to "the importance of now," even when the one asking questions was a small child. One day when we were having tea, her muddy 3-year-old son burst into the room, babbling about some question he wanted to ask. His mother excused herself, knelt down to get on an eye-level with the little boy, and listened carefully. Then she answered him as gravely as if he had been an adult. He nodded and trotted happily out of the room. When I commented on her patience with a rambling childish question she said, "I'm sure that question did sound silly, but right now it is the most important thing in the world to Peter." During their brief dialogue, the mother had conferred dignity on the child simply because she felt his needs to be as important as her own.

Thinking over my all-out attack on *Ask, don't tell*, I decided I had, by trial-and-error, learned a number of things. I sat down and made a list of what I now knew about the art of asking questions.

Rx For Good Questions

1. Grasp every possible chance to ask a searching question—*then keep quiet*. (When you're talking, *you're* not learning anything.)
2. One thoughtful question is worth a dozen inquisitive ones. The prod-and-pry approach makes people clam up fast.
3. Questions that come close to the other person's true interest get the best answers—provided the listener is interested, too.
4. Be prepared to wait. Sometimes a long silence can be more rewarding than plunging in with another question.
5. *In every case*, the quality of an answer depends on the quality of attention given by the questioner.
6. Questions must spring from honest inquiry, not from attempts at flattery or efforts to manipulate the other person's thinking.
7. Questions that deal with a person's *feelings* are more provocative than those dealing with *facts*.
8. A good questioner must really want to hear the answers, even if they are unpleasant.

I read and reread my list. It seemed all right, as far as it went, but something essential was lacking. To my surprise, it was my high school boy who supplied the missing ingredient. Toby came downstairs one night after he had finished studying and announced, "I think Hamlet's an idiot."

"Why?"

"Because he's putty in his mother's hands."

I asked him to explain what he meant and he launched into a diatribe that was the beginning of a long, often heated, dialogue. We started out with Hamlet and Queen Gertrude, and ended with a lively discussion of the mother-and-son relationship. It was one of those rare and wonderful interludes when communication flows like wine.

The next morning at breakfast I said, "I enjoyed our conversation, Toby."

"Me, too," he mumbled, addressing the cereal bowl.

"Why was it so good?" I said. "When I asked you about the spring dance, you gave me the old deep freeze. What was different last night?"

Toby grinned at me. "Well," he said, "I guess it was because you weren't just leading me on. For once I knew you really cared."

There, I submit, in a simple sentence, is the essence of true communication: "You really cared." To ask good questions we have to care, and care very much, about what the other person feels and says. True dialogue begins when we really want to share another's thoughts, for only a listening, loving heart has power to penetrate the coat of armor that encases us.

Number of words 2394
See page 383 for questions
Reading time in seconds _______
See page 497 for conversion table

SELECTION 53

Conversation Is More Than Talk

Gelett Burgess

*Conversation . . . is it really a lost art? What principles can you put to use to transform conversation into that rarity—*good *conversation? After all, you converse much more than you make public speeches. That's why it's well worth your attention.*

Good talkers are common, but good conversation is rare. Yet, like good manners, conversation is an essential requisite for anyone who wishes to be friends with those people who are usually most worthwhile. The man or woman who understands that good conversation is a social exchange of ideas is welcome everywhere.

There is a fundamental principle underlying good conversation. It is the basis of all good manners. This principle is the avoidance of friction in social contacts—a friction caused by irritation, boredom, envy, egotism, ridicule, and such emotions.

In San Francisco I once was a member of a small group which met weekly for the purpose, we proudly claimed, of reviving the lost art of conversation. Here are some of the rules we finally adopted that guided our talks and made our conversation a delightful game.

1. Avoid all purely subjective talk. Don't dilate on your intimately personal affairs—your health, your troubles, domestic affairs; and never, never discuss your wife or husband.

Streams of personal gossip and egotism destroy, in any group, all objective discussion—of art, science, history, timely topics, sports, or whatever. Such monologues not only bore the listener, but, as the talker is repeating only what he or she already knows, he learns nothing from others.

2. **Don't monopolize the conversation.** One of my friends long ago was a laughing, attractive person, who told stories well, with a mixture of highbrow terms and slang that was most amusing. But his stories were too long and too many. You roared with laughter, but after a while you grew restless and yearned for a more quiet, comfortable talk with plenty of give-and-take. You couldn't help remembering what old John Dryden said about those "who think too little, and who talk too much."

3. Don't contradict. Flat contradiction is another conversation-stopper. You may say, "I don't quite agree with that," but conversation, to be pleasant and profitable, should never descend to the level of emotional argument.

To get the most benefit from a conversation one should instead seek to find points of agreement. In that way, the subject develops in interest with each one's contribution to the discussion, and you both advance in knowledge. I had a postal-card correspondence with a friend, once, on the subject of God. We found we had so many ideas in common that, if I were not converted to his thought, my own thinking was considerably broadened.

4. Don't interrupt. Of course, when you toss a few grace notes into the talk such as, "How wonderful!" or "You mean she didn't know?" it doesn't throw the train of conversation off the track. But to interpolate views of your own is not only discourteous, but leaves what the speaker has to say unfinished when he perhaps hasn't yet made his point. Conversation is like an ordered dinner where each is served in turn. It should have rhythm and tempo to be gracious and truly social.

One perfect conversational dinner party is still alive in my memory. It was given in Boston by Mrs. James T. Fields, widow of the publisher who had entertained every visiting writer from Dickens to Kipling. There were present Mr. and Mrs. Thomas Bailey Aldrich; the brilliant Mrs. Bell, daughter of Rufus Choate; Bliss Perry, then editor of *The Atlantic Monthly*; and myself.

Six is the ideal number for an intimate dinner; if you have more, the conversation is apt to break up into separate side dialogues. At Mrs. Fields' each of us talked and each of us listened. No one interrupted; no one contradicted; no one monologued. The affair had the charm and pleasing restfulness of music.

5. Don't abruptly change the subject. Some people virtually interrupt, after patiently and painfully waiting for a talker to cease, by jumping into the conversation with a new subject.

In our Conversation Club it was an unwritten rule that after one person had stopped talking there should be half a minute or so of silence in which to reflect, digest, and appreciate what had been said. It is the proper tribute to anyone who has offered an idea for consideration.

There is no surer way to make people like you than to pay them the compliment of interest and sympathy. Prolong their subject, ask more about it, and they expand like flowers in the sun. Yet what usually happens is that, should you venture to describe some misfortune or accident that has happened to you, they immediately narrate a similar mischance that they have suffered.

6. Show an active interest in what is said. You need not only your ears to listen well, but your eyes, hands, feet, and even posture. I have often tested the merits of a story or an article I have written by reading it aloud to one or two friends. What they said about it never helped me much since one often liked what another didn't.

But if their eyes went up to the ceiling, or to a picture on the wall, if their fingers moved or their feet tapped the floor or swung from a knee, I had indisputable evidence that the manuscript wasn't holding their interest and I marked the dull spots for revision.

And so in good conversation your social duty is to manifest an alert interest in what is said. It brings out the best in the speaker and it insures his confidence in your sympathy.

7. After a diversion, return to the subject. There is no surer test of being able to converse well than this. Often while a subject is not yet fully considered it is completely lost in some conversational detour. To reintroduce this forgotten topic is not only polite and gracious, but it is the best evidence of real interest.

If it is your own story, it is futile for you yourself to bring it back to persons who have by-passed it. Let it go, and see that you don't commit their error.

8. Don't make dogmatic statements of opinion. The Japanese tea ceremony, when gone through according to the old rules, was perhaps the most refined and idealistic social form ever practiced. Everything about the special tea house, every stone on the path to it, every gesture in partaking of the tea was strictly prescribed. It was a cult of simplicity and self-effacement.

One of the rules of behavior concerned conversation during the ritual. It was considered vulgar and inartistic for host or guest to make any definite, decisive statement. One might speak of anything—the symbolism of the one *kakemono* on the wall, perhaps, or the beauty of a flower arrangement—but never with an expression of finality. The remark was left up in the air, so to speak, for the next guest to enlarge upon or add to, so that no one was guilty of forcing any personal opinion upon the others.

It is a good game, but difficult; try it some time with your friends. The principle applies well to almost any conversation where opinions are concerned. You may state facts as facts; but your application of them should be tentative, with such qualifications as "In my opinion," or "It seems to me," or "Isn't it possible that . . . ?"

If you associate with people of wisdom and understanding, you'll find they probably use such qualifying phrases, "with the meekness of wisdom," as St. James says, while the ignoramus is always for cut-and-dried pronouncements.

9. Speak distinctly. Even a bore can attain a certain consideration if he enunciates his words well, while another person with a great deal more intellect will not be listened to simply because he mumbles or whispers.

While I was a member of the executive committee of the Authors' League, I was fascinated by the fact that one or two men were always listened to, while the others often had to force their way into the conversation. Those who spoke slowly dominated the meeting. High, hurried voices simply couldn't compete with Ellis Parker Butler's deliberate words, and his voice helped him maintain his leadership for years.

If you observe a group talking, you'll find that the one with a low, controlled voice always gets the most respect. The eager, temperamental contenders dash up against him like waves against a rock, and the rock always withstands them.

10. Avoid destructive talk. Did you ever attempt to live for a single day without saying anything destructive in tone? At a house party, long ago, I was one of half a dozen guests who agreed to try it. If one of us went to the window and said, "It looks like rain," there would be a whoop of glee, and a fine of one dollar. If you said you didn't like bananas, another dollar; and so on.

At the end of the day we agreed that nothing but optimism and Pollyanna was a good deal of a bore, and we like a little pepper in our conversational soup; but we did realize for the first time how many quite unnecessary derogatory remarks we were all likely to make.

Evil, of course, must be condemned and opposed. But the unnecessary criticism, the desire to raise a laugh through ridicule, the general tendency to look on the unpleasant side of life, puts lines and a cynical expression in your face, and makes people shun you no matter how clever you are.

Now this little decalogue may seem simple, even axiomatic. But you will be amazed to find how often these primary rules are violated even by those who are supposed to be cultivated people, and how often their infringement causes unpleasantness.

So much for the negative side. What about the constructive view? How to create and maintain an agreeable conversation?

The secret is simple. To talk well one must think well. If you merely relate an incident that has happened—the facts in the case—it is nothing but anecdote. To make good conversation you must think underneath, above, and all around the subject.

This kind of thinking is well illustrated in the conversation of baseball enthusiasts. Are they content with telling the score, the number of base hits, errors, and home runs? Not at all. They discuss a team's potentialities, its comparison with another, the characteristics of the different players and their values, the theory and technique of the game. The same principle applies to all kinds of conversation.

Anyone who finds it hard to talk should learn to think about what he sees and hears and reads, and get something out of it. Ask why, and what it means. Discover what you can learn from it.

As you ponder, try to associate the subject with your own experience and observations and with ideas previously acquired.

Furthermore, if you mingle only with your own set or trade, your conversation inevitably degenerates into shop talk, or sport talk, or dress talk.

Get out of your rut and enlarge your interests by making acquaintances engaged in other pursuits. Develop a genuine curiosity about what is outside your ken, not a cheap inquisitiveness with regard to personalities. Join clubs. Join the church actively. Develop a hobby. Read up on subjects that have interested you. Study Spanish or nature or numerology—anything that has been outside your field of view.

If you fertilize and enrich your thinking in such ways, you need not worry about being able to converse well. Every new experience will make your talk more interesting and more valuable.

Number of words 1910
See page 385 for questions
Reading time in seconds _______
See page 497 for conversion table

America's Penniless Millionaire

Farnsworth Crowder

What do you do to become a millionaire? Do as Russell Conwell did. Just develop a speech so inspiring that it earns you a fortune of five million. Then, once you're a millionaire, what do you do to become a "penniless millionaire"? Read on. You'll soon find out exactly how that's done, too.

Statistically, the most extraordinary speech of all time was a collection of two dozen true stories woven into an inspirational lecture called *Acres of Diamonds*. It had a "run" of fifty years; it was repeated no less than 6,000 times to an audience of millions throughout the world. It crowded little provincial churches and packed the largest auditoriums in the biggest cities. It hypnotized gatherings of the widest diversity, from handfuls of prairie homesteaders in crossroads school houses to metropolitan assemblies of the elect. It drew fees ranging from a chicken dinner to $9,000. Its net earnings, conservatively husbanded, easily could have built for its author a fortune of five million. That it did nothing of the sort was due to the fact that, as rapidly as the money rolled in, the author gave it away. During certain long periods, though he was making tens of thousands, he would rarely have more than a hundred ready dollars of his own at one time. Russell Herman Conwell was "America's penniless millionaire."

His fabulous lecture was a defense, by means of anecdotes, of the theme that the world is a vast acreage strewn with diamonds. The wise man snatches up the dull stone that others have been kicking around. He chips a corner to find an eye of blue-white fire looking at him and then laboriously polishes it down to the form of a splendid jewel.

Opportunity, said Conwell, is no chance visitor who knocks but once and flees. It stands, very possibly, in our own boots, wearing our own socks. It is in our own back yard. It sits on the door step beside the milk bottle, waiting to be brought in. It is here, now; not over the horizon, tomorrow. It wanders about in unlikely and forlorn and even trampish guises, while heedless people kick it aside in their frantic rush to find a spectacular golden goddess called Luck.

With respect to this particular deity, Russell Conwell was an atheist. "The most hopeless proposition in the world," he would say, "is the fellow who thinks that success is a door through which he will sometime stumble if he roams around long enough." Good Luck he would define as a product of purpose, will, training and industry, Bad Luck as a face-saving excuse rather than an explanation. Golden Apples were to him a harvest from hard work, not chance sports on neglected trees.

To support his thesis, he scarcely could have found a more pat illustration than his own life. He mined and minted his own Good Luck. It was said of him that he could see the promise and design of a mountain in a molehill and then bring the mountain into being. He uncovered opportunities on the most unexpected and discouraging sites. He could snatch up thin suggestions and develop them into monuments.

From earliest youth, he seemed to realize, with some compelling intuitive wisdom, that he must make the best of whatever raw material was under his own hat and within immediate reach of his hands. He might have to live in poverty on a Massachusetts rock pile that his father called a farm. He might have to get up at four in the morning and work like a man. There might be no well-staffed neighborhood school with a rich curriculum. But he could learn to read. He carried a book wherever he went, down the furrows, to the pasture, out to the barn. It was a habit he never broke and never ceased to advocate: "Remember, you can carry a university in your coat pocket."

He so far developed the power to read, and with it his memory, that he could fix a page in mind and later recall it, word for word, as if he held the book in his hand. The capacity of his memory became an astonishment to his friends, though he believed he had only an average memory given an extraordinary discipline.

He never allowed it to break training. He never practiced the gentle vices of loafing and wool-gathering. During his services with the Union Army, he employed idle hours to commit the whole of Blackstone. Years later, while commuting by train to and from his law offices in Boston, he learned to read five languages.

No time, no occasion, no suggestion was ever left unexploited. As a boy, he made the farm livestock his first audience. The power, as orator and preacher, which was to make him the platform peer of William J. Bryan, was first exercised in the chicken house.

By the time he entered Yale College, his habits of application and self-command enabled him to carry the academic and law courses simultaneously, while supporting himself with employment in a New Haven hotel. When the Civil War broke, it was as if he had anticipated the opportunity to become "the recruiting orator of the Berkshires." He raised and captained the Mountain Boys of Massachusetts and was later returned from the South to assemble a company of artillery.

There is an event of his military service which demonstrates his facility for laying hold of symbols, suggestions and incidents and fixing them tenaciously into the dynamic pattern of his life. A diminutive orderly, John Ring, attached to the company, became profoundly devoted to big fine-looking Captain Conwell—and to the Captain's sword, which represented, to John, both his beloved officer and all the glory of war. One day, near New Bern, a surprise Confederate advance routed the company from its position. Retreating across a river, the men fired a wooden bridge to cut off their pursuers. They had also cut off escape for their orderly: Johnnie Ring had dashed back to bring the Captain's sword. He appeared with it at last and gained the blazing bridge. But with clothes in flames he fell into the river. Dragged out and returned to consciousness, his first thought was for his Captain and the sword. He smiled to find it safe beside him, took it in his arms and died.

"When I stood over his body," Conwell recollected, "and realized that he had died for love of me, I made a vow that I would live, thereafter, not only my own life, but also the life of John Ring, that it might not be lost."

And from then on, for sixty years, Russell Conwell literally worked a double day—eight hours for himself and eight for Johnnie. And always over the head of his bed hung the sword to keep bright his extravagant vow. That he kept it, one can well believe after a glance at a mere catalogue of his activities.

Following a European interlude to recover his health, broken by war injuries, he settled down to an intensive, versatile career in Boston. He opened two law offices in Boston. He lectured. He launched the Boston Young Men's Congress. He wrote editorials for the *Traveler*, corresponded for outside newspapers and went abroad frequently to interview celebrities. He managed a political campaign. He made money in real estate. He founded the *Journal* in suburban Somerville and maintained a free legal clinic for the poor.

Conwell had lost his first wife and had married again, a woman who freshened his interest in religious work. One day, an elderly lady visited his office for legal counsel on selling a distressed church property in Lexington. To give his advice, he journeyed out to a meeting of the discouraged and pastorless congregation. There was such melancholy in the little group, some of whom had worshipped there all their lives, that Conwell was moved to blurt, "Why sell it? Why not start over again!"

They objected that the structure was too dilapidated and money too dear. But young Conwell's eye for the hidden chance was wide awake and challenged. "You can make repairs," he shouted. "I'll help you!"

On the appointed day he borrowed tools and came out. No one else showed up, but he pitched in on the rickety front steps. A livery-stable proprietor of the town paused to ask what he was going to do. "Build a new church," Conwell answered. They fell to chatting and before he left, the man had pledged $100 toward a new building.

It was all the prospect that Russell Conwell needed to set imagination and energy to working. He made the hundred-dollar kernel grow. While the new church was going up, he preached to the congregation in rented rooms. Within eighteen months he had been ordained as their minister and had built around them a flourishing institution.

From Lexington he was invited to another hapless, debt-ridden little church in Philadelphia. He accepted and, characteristically, saw great possibilities in the discouraging new scene. The salary offered him was only $800, but the trustees stipulated that every time he could double the congregation, they would match the feat with a doubled salary. Six weeks after taking charge, Conwell had done it. Within six years he was drawing $10,000. Thereafter, he mercifully excused the trustees from their agreement. Had he held them to it, his salary would have climbed to over $25,000.

The popularity of his services was soon straining the capacity of the auditorium. One Sunday, from the many being turned away, he rescued a particularly unhappy little girl and saw her to a place inside. She was so grateful for the kindness and so distressed at the smallness of the room that she resolved to save her money for a building that would be big enough. Before she had advanced far on her grand project, she died. Her father turned over her fund, just fifty-seven cents in pennies.

Conwell reported the gift to his trustees. They were touched, but he was inspired. If $100 could be the nucleus of a building fund in Lexington, fifty-seven cents could do similar duty in Philadelphia! Accordingly, he went to the owner of a certain fine lot on Broad Street. The price was $10,000. Conwell made the outrageous offer of a down payment of fifty-seven cents. It was accepted. In due time the balance was paid off and upon that property, in 1891, was dedicated the largest church auditorium of its day.

The design of Russell Conwell's achievements might be called horticultural—the discovery of a seed; an uncanny insight into its fertility; a prodigious amount of work to make it grow.

From the modest ambitions of a young man came a university. Conwell was solicited for advice by a student who wanted to better his education, but was handicapped by having little money and a mother to support. As to all such, Conwell's first admonition was: "Read. Make a traveling library of your pocket." And then he added: "Come to me one evening a week and I'll begin teaching you to be a minister myself."

The first week, the student appeared with six friends in tow. The second week, forty were in the class. More volunteer teachers had to be invited. A house was rented. By the end of the first year, 250 were studying in this informal night college. A second house was hired. Buildings rose beside the great Temple church into the physical form of Temple University. "Our aim from the first," said President Conwell, "was to give education to those unable to get it though the usual channels." He lived to see more than 100,000 such pupils take work in his school.

Similar and equally unpretentious was Conwell's founding of Philadelphia's big Samaritan Hospital. Two rented rooms, one nurse, one patient. That was all. But it was enough for a beginning. In its expansion, the Samaritan acquired Goodheart Hospital and Garretson in the industrial quarter of the city and all became affiliated with Temple University.

But the heading up of a huge institutional church, a University and three hospitals was not enough for the dual capacities of Russell Conwell-Johnnie Ring. Out of the daily stint of sixteen hours was found the time to go on the platform for more than 8,000 lectures—usually *Acres of Diamonds*; to maintain contacts with scores of the leading men of his time and with hundreds of the boys and girls he was helping through school; and to write thirty-seven volumes—biographies, travel books and legal treatises. In authorship, his vast reading and disciplined memory served him like a reference library. It was told that, on the train between lecture dates, without notes or books, he dictated a best-selling biography of Charles H. Spurgeon, the eminent evangelist, in twelve days.

His famous lecture was one more work developed from a rudiment. Any number of people might have heard—did hear—the story which an Arab guide along the Euphrates River was fond of telling. They might have thought it interesting, even worthy a place in their repertoire of traveler's tales. But to Russell Conwell's ears, it was dramatically suggestive; its lesson squared with his own philosophy of success; it could be made the germinal anecdote of a strong lecture.

The Arab's story was that of the wealthy and contented farmer, Ali Hafed, who was made to feel wretchedly poor and miserable by a visitor who infected him with a passion for diamonds. So covetous did Ali become that he sold the farm, abandoned his family and set out to prospect the world. And while he found no precious stones and at last threw his spent and starving body into the sea, the man who had purchased his farm discovered along its familiar stream beds the diamond mines of Golconda. "Ali would have been better off to remain at home and dig in his own cellar."

Throughout his lecture, Conwell hammered with his massive force at that simple moral. The impact of the message on many lives was crucial. As the years went by, testimonials poured in on him from governors, mayors, teachers, merchants, engineers and professionals, thanking him for the impetus his lecture had given their lives.

And from the thousands of college young people benefited by his largess came testimonials even more gratifying. Conwell was only thirty-three, and far from rich, when he determined to devote the proceeds of his lecturing to students fighting the kind of material odds and social discriminations he had experienced at Yale. His program of donations was continued for over forty years. He always kept a list of candidates for aid, most of them recommended by college presidents. His one rigid and unvarying requirement before extending help was that a student must be trying to help himself. He wanted his gifts to be, not chance windfalls, but premiums for diligent effort already made.

When, in 1925, Russell Conwell entered his eighty-second and last year, with all his enormous work behind him, books written, institutions founded and prospering, honors, degrees, prizes and medals to his name, there was one old-man satisfaction that he could not have. He could not mull over huge bank accounts and vast accumulated investments. He had distributed his fortune as he made it. He remarked, shortly before his death, that his riches lay in the men and women he had started on the road to accomplishment and happiness; and that was all, in the way of assets, he needed now.

Number of words 2530
See page 387 for questions
Reading time in seconds _______
See page 497 for conversion table

Selection 55

Your Voice Gives You Away

John E. Gibson

When you read a Sherlock Holmes story, you're supposed to be amazed at how the greatest detective notices things others never see. Take that intimate part of yourself, your voice. Does it take a Sherlock Holmes to unravel its secrets? No—apparently it reveals more about you than you think, much more than what you say.

Did you know that your voice can reveal how old you are, whether you're short or tall, fat or thin; whether you are an introvert or an extrovert? It's true! In fact, research conducted at leading universities and research centers has shown that in a surprisingly large percentage of cases, a person's voice even can reveal the general type of work he is engaged in. And tests at Harvard's psychological laboratories show that another person, just by listening to your voice, can judge your personality traits—and be right 90 per cent of the time!

It has been scientifically established by studies conducted both in the U.S. and Britain that a person's voice can give an incredibly accurate picture of many of his mental and physical characteristics. To test these findings, the Psychological Institute of the University of Vienna conducted a fascinating experiment.

The voices of nine persons who differed widely in age, personality, and occupation, were broadcast from a radio station. Questionnaires were distributed in advance to the radio audience, announcing the experiment, and requesting the audience to listen carefully to each of the nine voices, and then judge the age, physical appearance, personality, and vocation of the speakers. This information was to be written on the questionnaire form, and mailed back to the university.

The speakers whose voices were broadcast were: a stenographer (age 27), a college professor (age 48), a tavern keeper (age 53), a minister (age 58), a grade-school teacher (age 39), a mathematician (a woman, age 46), a taxi driver (age 30), a boy age (age 12), and a girl (age 14).

At the time set for the broadcast, each of these persons stood before a microphone and read aloud from a script for two minutes. Then followed a period of organ music, during which members of the listening audience were requested to write down their judgments on the form provided for the purpose.

Twenty-seven hundred listeners sent in completely filled-out questionnaires. Analysis of these revealed a strikingly large percentage of correct judgments. The average estimate of the age of the speakers was almost "on the nose" in a number of cases. For example, the average guess for the 27-year-old stenographer was 26; average guess for the 39-year-old school teacher was 38; and most listeners were only two years off in estimating the boy's age.

In judging the age of the persons who were over 45 however, the estimates tended to be less accurate. The investigators' conclusions: age can be judged by a person's voice with a high degree of accuracy until he or she reaches middle age. After that the voice tends to sound younger than the person actually is.

So far as judging temperament and physique were concerned, the psychologists found that the average guess was remarkably accurate—except in the case of the taxi driver and the two children. In all of the other cases the listeners were able to classify the speakers' builds correctly and make accurate judgments as to their personality characteristics.

An astonishingly high percentage of the radio listeners was able to correctly classify the speakers' occupation—just, mind you, by listening to their voices. Almost half judged the professor to be a member of the academic profession.

From 27 percent to 35 percent of the listeners put the mathematician, tavern keeper, minister, and the school teacher in the right occupational bracket. And as for the taxi driver—out of the 2,700 persons who filled out the questionnaires, over *2,000* judged his occupation correctly!

The only one they didn't do so well on was the stenographer. Ninety-three percent guessed her to be just about everything but what she was. Most, however, did come within a year of guessing her age—and made substantially accurate judgments as to her body build and temperament.

A number of the radio listeners who participated in the experiment were totally blind. And it is extremely interesting to note that they were invariably more accurate in their judgments than the others. This fact is easily explained. When a person loses his sight, his other senses, including hearing, seem to become more sensitive and acute because he places greater reliance upon them.

Impressed by the findings of the Vienna study, Harvard University scientists conducted a similar test in the United States. They installed complete broadcasting equipment in the psychological laboratory and broadcast the voices of 18 speakers—each carefully selected for the experiment. Listeners were asked to make judgments regarding each speaker's age, temperament, vocation, etc. A total of 587 responded.

The results more than corroborated the conclusions of the University of Vienna investigators. In the majority of cases, the average guess for a speaker's age came within a year of hitting the exact mark—when the speakers were under 40.

But, as in the Vienna experiment, speakers past middle age tended to sound younger than they were. The listeners also showed a marked ability to classify occupations correctly. They also were able to successfully match sketches of the speakers—which were distributed—with their voices. And a majority were able to judge which of the voices belonged to introverts and which to extroverts.

Most striking evidence of the extent to which a person's voice reveals both appearance and personality was furnished by a further test in which the judges were asked to decide whether each speaker was "moody," "nervous," "precise," "dapper," and so on. *Ninety-one percent of the judgments were wholly correct!*

Another interesting point brought out by the Harvard study was that when tests were repeated, using a curtain rather than the radio to conceal the speaker, the listeners were about seven percent more accurate in their judgments. This finding, the investigators believe, indicates that a slight degree of distortion was produced when the voices were transmitted over the radio.

Another test to determine what your voice reveals about you was conducted at DePauw University. Voices were broadcast over a public address system, and students were asked to identify the body build of the speakers. It was found that the easiest type to identify by voice alone was the person who is tall and slender; the short, stocky type ranked a close second.

The only type that couldn't be identified with a high degree of accuracy was the well-proportioned, or "athletic" build. That the tone of a short, stocky (pyknic type) individual tends to differ appreciably from the leptosome (tall, thin), and from the athletic type, was borne out by the DePauw tests. (*Editor's note:* However, the nuances of timbre, modulation and tonal qualities are too subtle for accurate verbal description in this article.)

The study also showed that certain professions can be judged better than others from the individual's voice. It was found, for example, that it's easier to identify a preacher or a lawyer than it is a musician or a detective.

To what extent a man's voice gives away his thoughts has not yet been scientifically established. But university tests have shown that in most cases you can tell whether a person is lying or not—just from the way his voice sounds!

Student subjects at DePauw were asked to label the statements of hidden speakers as "the truth" or "a lie." The speakers then made statements about themselves, such as "I'm wearing a green tie," or "My name is Fred," or "I had ham and eggs for breakfast," etc. In the majority of instances the listeners were able to correctly label each statement as being true of false.

The women subjects turned in a higher percentage of correct judgments than the men did. And another phase of the test showed that when a woman tells an untruth, her voice doesn't give her away to the extent that a man's does!

Psychologists have demonstrated that a person's voice frequently reveals things about him which ordinarily could be ascertained only by psychoanalysis. Studies at Kent State University, Kent, Ohio, for example, have shown that an unpleasant voice indicates the likelihood of neurotic tendencies.

Analysis of hundreds of men and women showed that pleasant-voiced individuals tend to be better adjusted. The studies indicated that voices of persons with neurotic tendencies tend to fall into three different categories: (1) breathy, (2) nasal whine, (3) harsh and metallic. The whiny-voiced individuals are found to be the most emotionally unstable.

At Brooklyn College, students whose voices were classified as harsh and unpleasant were given clinical examinations. In about three-fourths of the cases investigators found no direct physical cause. But when personality tests were administered, almost half of the subjects were found to be definitely maladjusted. The study further showed that when better personality adjustment was brought about, the unpleasant quality in the subject's voice tended to disappear.

There are many types of unpleasant voices, and all of them have been found to indicate, to a greater or lesser extent, the likelihood of neurosis. Take, for example, the person who speaks in a dull monotone. Stanford University investigations show that these individuals are, more often than not, lacking in mental and emotional stability.

In a recent Smith College study, a group of fifth-grade children who spoke in a continuous and unvaried monotone, was selected for careful personality analysis. *It was found that 100 percent of the group was definitely maladjusted!* This does not mean, of course, that every person who speaks in a monotone possess neurotic tendencies. But it does suggest that a strong likelihood does exist in a high percentage of the cases.

Dr. Paul J. Moses of Stanford University Medical School has made a study of thousands of voice recordings and related them to the personal characteristics of the speakers. His conclusions are in general agreement with those of other studies cited in this article.

Indeed, he finds that the human voice offers so many vital clues to an individual's make-up and temperament, as to be of value to both layman and specialist in assessing the personality of their fellowmen!

Number of words 1660
See page 389 for questions
Reading time in seconds _______
See page 497 for conversion table

Section V

On Listening

We Quit Talking—and Now the Cupboard Is Bare

Ewart A. Autry

Ambrose Bierce, in his Devil's Dictionary, *defines a bore as "a person who talks when you want him to listen." That suggests that listening is the key to social acceptance. This married couple shows you both the advantages and disadvantages of less talking, more listening.*

"We're talking too much," my wife announced one morning at breakfast. "But these are the first words we've said since we sat down," I protested. "I mean when we're out in public or have company," she explained. "We carry too much of the conversation. It must bore others."

I thought it over. "Well," I finally agreed, "it's true we rarely run out of words."

"And we're always eager to get them in," she continued. "We talk so much that people learn everything about us while we're learning nothing about them. So let's do something about it."

"Tape our lips?" I suggested.

She ignored that, with reason. "Let's agree to limit our part of the conversation when others are around," she said. "We'll set up some signals. When you think I'm talking too much just touch your forehead and I'll slow down. When I think you're talking too much, I'll use the same signal."

I was skeptical but willing to try. So we did. On our very next visitor.

It wasn't a successful experiment. He was a phlegmatic neighbor who never used any more words than were absolutely necessary. That, coupled with our resolve to let guests carry most of the conversation, produced long, awkward silences. Intermittently the three of us stared into our open fire and there was little sound except the crackling of my hickory logs. When our visitor had gone, my wife looked chagrined. "I kept hoping you'd talk," she said, "but I didn't know how to get you started. The only signal we agreed on was the one to cut down on the talking."

There was another repercussion from that fiasco. Our visitor reported to the neighbors that we weren't well and they kept calling to inquire about our health. "That's some reputation to have," I grumbled. "When we don't rattle on all the time, people think we're sick."

Most visitors, though, unknowingly cooperated with our new scheme. They kept the conversation rolling with no more than an occasional word from us. It was amazing how much some people talked. I commented on it one day after a visit from Dan and Ina Blake. "Dan was really wound up," I said. "I thought he'd never finish that story about the big bass he caught Christmas day."

"This is the first chance he's had to finish it," advised my wife. "Always before you've interrupted to tell some wild fish story of your own."

"And I noticed Ina got in the full account of her latest operation," I retorted. "Other times you've put your stitches in before she could even begin on hers."

"It takes will power to keep your mouth shut," said my wife thoughtfully. "Especially when you have something more interesting to tell than what's being told."

The signals actually worked well and we didn't have to use them too often. But sometimes we'd let our tongues get ahead of our brains. Like when I was telling Don Duke about a bass I'd hooked. The fish was weighing about nine pounds and I had him on the way to the boat when I saw my wife touch her forehead. I immediately cut the bass down to three pounds and let him get away.

Then there's the time my wife was telling some friends about a recent vacation trip to the ocean. She was waxing poetic as she described a sunset over the water. I noticed our visitors beginning to wiggle restlessly, so I caught her eye and touched my forehead. You never saw a sun drop so quickly into the sea.

There were times when others noticed our signals. Once we were visiting friends and I was talking too much. My wife touched her forehead. When I didn't react immediately she kept touching it. In a few minutes our hostess left the room and returned with a glass of water and an aspirin. "You poor thing," she said to my wife. "You have a headache. Take this."

A few days later I had a bad crick in my neck. I went to a doctor who is a family friend. At his invitation my wife came into the consultation room. She began to tell him my various symptoms. I thought she was telling too much so I touched my forehead. The doctor noticed it immediately. "Ah, ha," he said. "Just as I thought. You have sinus trouble."

He tilted my chin and sprayed my nose with the hottest stuff I ever felt. My eyes watered for an hour. But I must have touched the right spot. My neck was better before we got home.

Our talk curb has been in effect for a year now. We've talked less and heard more. Not all of it has been worthwhile but at least it's been as good as some of the stuff we were putting out.

And we've learned one thing for certain—talk less and you'll have more company. More people came to our house this past year than in any of the thirty we've been married. One of our regular visitors said why. "I like to visit here," he beamed. "You're interesting people to talk to."

"To." Not "with."

We have a problem though. Much of our company has been at mealtime. Sometimes our pantry has been stripped to the danger point. Right now we're trying to decide whether to buy more groceries each week or forget our conversation moratorium.

When I mention the second possibility, my wife gets an eager gleam in her eyes. And come to think of it, there are a few things I'd like to say too. So, if you're planning to come to our house, you'd better hurry. Before we start talking again.

Number of words 950
See page 391 for questions
Reading time in seconds ________
See page 497 for conversion table

SELECTION 57

On Listening and Not Listening

Lyman K. Steil

In 1979, interest in listening led the author of this article to organize the International Listening Association. Its purpose? To promote the study and development of effective listening. How important is listening? Let Dr. Steil answer that question. He's uniquely qualified to do just that.

An insurance agent called his company for background on a potential client and received instructions not to insure him—he was a bad risk. But the agent misunderstood. He thought his company had given him the go-ahead, and drew up a contract for multimillion dollar coverage. A few months later the client filed a substantial claim. The insurance company was forced to pay and the agent lost his job.

A phone conversation overheard in the Seattle airport: "Guess what!" said the man in the booth next to mine. "I'm not supposed to be here until tomorrow. I could have sworn they told me to come today." "What will you do?" the voice at the other end must have asked. "What can I do?" said the man. "I'll stay overnight and absorb the cost."

On an airplane recently, I talked with the president of a small company. I asked whether his firm had experienced any problems because of employees' inability or failure to listen. The man's eyebrows went up. He told me how the company had recently lost a million dollar sale. "Two of my employees were involved," he said. "One didn't hear the important message at all, and the other one misinterpreted it. The upshot was that we lost out on a bid that we should have won hands down."

The incidents differ, but there is a common denominator: In each case someone failed to listen. A mistake was made. Money was lost. With more than 100 million workers in this country, a simple $10 mistake by each of them as a result of poor listening adds up to a cost of a billion dollars. And most people make more than one listening mistake every day.

My point is this: The failure or the inability to

listen has costs associated with it—in time, relationships and productivity. And what is the price of an idea not heard? These are avoidable costs, which, to the extent avoided, have a direct impact on the profit and loss statement.

Don't be misled: Listening problems aren't limited to the workaday world. Actually, bad listening habits encroach deeply into the territory of our personal lives too. It's just that business is more noticeably vulnerable to the quantitative results of a bad habit. Dollars are lost, and that affects the bottom line. With all of the computerization in businesses today, large and small, the automation, and the organizational and management counseling that is available, it's both heartening and discouraging to know that a simple human error, an "I forgot," or "I thought you said you were going to mail the proposal," are still at the heart of our enterprise.

Indeed, the effects of bad listening are to be seen all around us: The sinking of the *Titanic*, Pearl Harbor, the Jonestown, Guyana incident, the MGM Grand fire and some of the recent airplane disasters, though dramatic, are classic examples of a breakdown in communication. A message was sent, listening failed, and lives were lost.

And poor listening affects our emotional lives. Parenting and marriage provide examples most of us understand. Listening audits show that respondents usually rate themselves as poorer listeners with spouses than with friends or business associates. But even sadder is that while newlyweds rate each other very highly as listeners—close to the level of best friend, which ranks highest—that ranking falls steadily downhill as the marriage goes on. In a household where the couple has been married for 50 years, chances are that while there may be a lot of talking going on, very little listening will be going on to reciprocate. The result? Clearly, a great many of the one million divorces each year are related to the inability or unwillingness to listen.

With all the talk about poor communication being at the root of so many ills, there is surprisingly little thought given to what that means. Communication is most often considered something we do unto others, when actually about half of that activity has to do with the willingness to receive from others: People spend about 80 percent of their waking hours communicating, and about 45 percent of that time is spent listening. And most people, even by their own admission, are at best average listeners.

After hearing a ten-minute oral presentation, the average listener has heard, understood, properly evaluated and retained only half of what was said, according to some studies. Within another 48 hours that drops off another 50 percent, meaning that an audience only effectively comprehends and retains one-quarter of what is said.

Back to business. Add the chain of command of a large corporation to the statistics on how humans misconstrue messages: Ideas can be distorted by as much as 80 percent as they're stretched, condensed, twisted and hurried along the sometimes tortuous organizational path. The cost of that distortion is more than dollars. Productivity is affected and profits suffer. Letters have to be retyped, appointments rescheduled, shipments rerouted. And as many married couples feel increasingly distant and alienated from one another, employees can feel distant from the objectives of a department or the goals of a corporation, and ultimately feel alienated from its day-to-day operations.

For each of us, one of our greatest needs is to be listened to.

The solution? Unfortunately, that activity which we do most in life—listening—is taught least. This is unfortunate because listening is so much more complex than, say, reading. What we read is locked on the printed page. If you're distracted, you can put it aside and return to it later. If you don't understand, you can read it over again. But in listening, the message is written on the wind. If you don't get it the first time, there's no going back.

Fortunately, listening *can* be taught. People aren't born good listeners. Listening is learned. If you exercise the listening muscles, your listening skills will improve. A number of primary and secondary schools—still the exceptions—are teaching listening, along with the old standards reading, writing, and arithmetic. After all, students spend 60–70 percent of classroom time *listening* to what the teacher is saying. Hundreds of companies are recognizing the same need.

One study of the 20 most critical managerial competencies lists "Listen Actively" at the very top. In comparison, number two on the list is "Give Clear, Effective Instructions." Number five, "Manage Time and Set Priorities"; number twelve, "Write Effectively"; and number twenty, still listed as a critical activity, "Participate in Seminars and Read."

The higher one advances in management, the more critical listening skill becomes. It's the heart of success. But like everyone else, managers often don't hear the messages of others. They may be busy, preoccupied, distracted, or they misunderstand and don't respond.

Poppycock to the individual who says, "When I need to listen well, or when I want to listen well, I can will myself to listen." More than three decades of research proves that we can only listen at any moment at the level of skill we've developed. For most of us, that's simply not good enough. We cannot simply "will" ourselves to listen well.

Listening is more complex than will's and won'ts and do's and don'ts. *There is no quick fix.* Hearing is only the beginning. There's also interpretation, which leads to understanding or misunderstanding. There's evaluation, which is when you decide how to use the information, and then there's the reaction itself. Taken together, that's listening.

Whether it be a company-wide effort, sales training, or a separate group project, much can be done to improve one of the most mutually endearing—and necessary—of our human attributes, the ability to listen. And the benefits of better listening far outweigh the costs.

Semper bene ausculpabis!

Number of words 1290
See page 393 for questions
Reading time in seconds ________
See page 497 for conversion table

Selection 58

Listening Is a 10-Part Skill

Ralph G. Nichols

When you sit down by Dr. Nichols at his desk, what do you see? A sign of nameplate size that reads, "I'm listening"! For the first time you may realize the significance of listening in interpersonal relations. It's important to be listened to—and to listen.

White collar workers, on the average, devote at least 40 percent of their work day to listening. Apparently 40 percent of their salary is paid to them for listening. Yet tests of listening comprehension have shown that, without training, these employees listen at only 25 percent efficiency.

This low level of performance becomes increasingly intolerable as evidence accumulates that it can be significantly raised. The component skills of listening are known. They boil down to this:

Learning through listening is primarily an inside job—inside action on the part of the listener. What he needs to do is to replace some common present attitudes with others.

Recognizing the dollar values in effective listening, many companies have added courses in this skill to their regular training programs. Some of the pioneers in this effort have been American Telephone & Telegraph Co., General Motors Corporation, Ford Motor Company, The Dow Chemical Company, Western Electric Co., Inc., Methods Engineering Council of Pittsburgh, Minnesota Mining & Manufacturing Co., Thompson Products, Inc., of Cleveland, and Rogers Corp. of Connecticut.

Warren Ganong of the Methods Engineering Council has compared trainees given a preliminary discussion of efficient listening with those not provided such discussion. On tests at the end of the courses the former achieved marks 12 to 15 percent higher than did the latter.

A. A. Tribbey, general personnel supervisor of the Wisconsin Telephone Company, in commenting on the results of a short conference course in which effective listening was stressed, declared: "It never fails to amaze us when we see the skill that is acquired in only three days."

The conviction seems to be growing that upper-level managers also need listening skill. As Dr. Earl Planty, executive counselor for the pharmaceutical firm of Johnson & Johnson, puts it: "By far the most effective method by which executives can tap ideas of subordinates is sympathetic listening in the many day-to-day informal contacts within and outside the work place. There is no system that will do the job in an easier manner. . . . Nothing can equal an executive's willingness to hear."

A study of the 100 best listeners and the 100 worst listeners in the freshman class on the University of Minnesota campus has disclosed ten guides to improved listening. Business people interested in improving their own performance can use them to analyze their personal strengths and weaknesses. The ten guides to good listening are:

1. Find Areas of Interest

All studies point to the advantage in being interested in the topic under discussion. Bad listeners usually declare the subject dry after the first few sentences. Once this decision is made, it serves to rationalize any and all inattention.

Good listeners follow different tactics. True, their first thought may be that the subject sounds dry. But a second one immediately follows, based on the realization that to get up and leave might prove a bit awkward.

The final reflection is that, being trapped anyhow, perhaps it might be well to learn if anything is being said that can be put to use.

The key to the whole matter of interest in a topic is the word *use*. Whenever we wish to listen efficiently, we ought to say to ourselves: "What's he saying that I can use? What worthwhile ideas has he? Is he reporting any workable procedures? Anything that I can cash in, or with which I can make myself happier?" Such questions lead us to screen what we are hearing in a continual effort to sort out the elements of personal value. G. K. Chesterton spoke wisely indeed when he said, "There is no such thing as an uninteresting subject; there are only uninterested people."

2. Judge Content, Not Delivery

Many listeners alibi inattention to a speaker by thinking to themselves: "Who could listen to such a character? What an awful voice! Will he ever stop reading from his notes?"

The good listener reacts differently. He may well look at the speaker and think, "This man is inept. Seems like almost anyone ought to be able to talk better than that." But from this initial similarity he moves on to a different conclusion, thinking,: "But wait a minute. . . . I'm not interested in his personality or delivery. I want to find out what he knows. Does this man know some things that I need to know?"

Essentially we "listen with our own experience." Is the conveyer to be held responsible because we are poorly equipped to decode his message? We cannot understand everything we hear, but one sure way to raise the level of our understanding is to assume the responsibility which is inherently ours.

3. Hold Your Fire

Overstimulation is almost as bad as understimulation, and the two together constitute the twin evils of inefficient listening. The overstimulated listener gets too excited, or excited too soon, by the speaker. Some of us are greatly addicted to this weakness. For us, a speaker can seldom talk for more than a few minutes without touching upon a pet bias or conviction. Occasionally we are roused in support of the speaker's point; usually it is the reverse. In either case overstimulation reflects the desire of the listener to enter, somehow, immediately into the argument.

The aroused person usually becomes preoccupied by trying to do three things simultaneously: calculate what hurt is being done to his own pet ideas; plot an embarrassing question to ask the speaker; enjoy mentally all the discomfiture visualized for the speaker once the devastating reply to him is launched. With these things going on subsequent passages go unheard.

We must learn not to get too excited about a speaker's point until we are certain we thoroughly understand it. The secret is contained in the principle that we must always withhold evaluation until our comprehension is complete.

4. Listen for Ideas

Good listeners focus on central ideas; they tend to recognize the characteristic language in which central ideas are usually stated, and they are able to discriminate between fact and principle, idea and example, evidence and argument. Poor listeners are inclined to listen for the facts in every presentation.

To understand the fault, let us assume that a man is giving us instruction made up of facts A to Z. The man begins to talk. We hear fact A and think: "We've got to remember it!" So we begin a memory exercise by repeating "Fact A, fact A, fact A. . . ."

Meanwhile, the fellow is telling us fact B. Now we have two facts to memorize. We're so busy doing it that we miss fact C completely. And so it goes up to fact Z. We catch a few facts, garble several others and completely miss the rest.

It is a significant fact that only about 25 percent of persons listening to a formal talk are able to grasp the speaker's central idea. To develop this skill requires an ability to recognize conventional organizational patterns, transitional language, and the speaker's use of recapitulation. Fortunately, all of these items can be readily mastered with a bit of effort.

5. Be Flexible

Our research has shown that our 100 worst listeners thought that note-taking and outlining were synonyms. They believed there was but one way to take notes—by making an outline.

Actually, no damage would be done if all talks followed some definite plan of organization. Unfortunately, less than half of even formal speeches are carefully organized. There are few things more frustrating than to try to outline an unoutlineable speech.

Note-taking may help or may become a distraction. Some persons try to take down everything in shorthand; the vast majority of us are far too voluminous even in longhand. While studies are not too clear on the point, there is some evidence to indicate that the volume of notes taken and their value to the taker are inversely related. In any case, the real issue is one of interpretation. Few of us have memories good enough to remember even the salient points we hear. If we can obtain brief, meaningful records of them for later review, we definitely improve our ability to learn and to remember.

The 100 best listeners had apparently learned early in life that if they wanted to be efficient note-takers, they had to have more than one system of taking notes. They equipped themselves with four or five systems, and learned to adjust their system to the organizational pattern, or the absence of one, in each talk they heard. If we want to be good listeners, we must be flexible and adaptable note-takers.

6. Work at Listening

One of the most striking characteristics of poor listeners is their disinclination to spend any energy in a listening situation. College students, by their own testimony, frequently enter classes all worn out physically; assume postures which only seem to give attention to the speaker; and then proceed to catch up on needed rest or to reflect upon purely personal matters. This faking of attention is one of the worst habits afflicting us as a people.

Listening is hard work. It is characterized by faster heart action, quicker circulation of the blood, a small rise in bodily temperature. The overrelaxed listener is merely appearing to tune in, and then feeling conscience-free to pursue any of a thousand mental tangents.

For selfish reasons alone one of the best investments we can make is to give each speaker our conscious attention. We ought to establish eye contact and maintain it; to indicate by posture and facial expression that the occasion and the speaker's efforts are a matter of real concern to us. When we do these things we help the speaker to express himself more clearly, and we in turn profit by better understanding of the improved communication we have helped him to achieve. None of this necessarily implies acceptance of his point of view or favorable action upon his appeals. It is, rather, an expression of interest.

7. Resist Distractions

The good listeners tend to adjust quickly to any kind of abnormal situation; poor listeners tend to tolerate bad conditions and, in some instances, even to create distractions themselves.

We live in a noisy age. We are distracted not only by what we hear, but by what we see. Poor listeners tend to be readily influenced by all manner of distractions, even in an intimate face-to-face situation.

A good listener instinctively fights distraction. Sometimes the fight is easily won—by closing a door, shutting off the radio, moving closer to the person talking, or asking him to speak louder. If the distractions cannot be met that easily, then it becomes a matter of concentration.

8. Exercise Your Mind

Poor listeners are inexperienced in hearing difficult, expository material. Good listeners apparently develop an appetite for hearing a variety of presentations difficult enough to challenge their mental capacities.

Perhaps the one word that best describes the bad listener is "inexperienced." Although he spends 40 percent of his communication day listening to something, he is inexperienced in hearing anything tough, technical, or expository. He has for years painstakingly sought light, recreational material. The problem he creates is deeply significant, because such a person is a poor producer in factory, office, or classroom.

Inexperience is not easily or quickly overcome. However, knowledge of our own weakness may lead us to repair it. We need never become too old to meet new challenges.

9. Keep Your Mind Open

Parallel to the blind spots which afflict human beings are certain psychological deaf spots which impair our ability to perceive and understand. These deaf spots are the dwelling place of our most cherished notions, convictions, and complexes. Often, when a speaker invades one of these areas with a word or phrase, we turn our mind to retraveling familiar mental pathways crisscrossing our invaded area of sensitivity.

It is hard to believe in moments of cold detachment that just a word or phrase can cause such emotional eruption. Yet with poor listeners it is frequently the case; and even with very good listeners it is occasionally the case. When such emotional deafness transpires, communicative efficiency drops rapidly to zero.

Among the words known thus to serve as red flags to some listeners are: mother-in-law, landlord, redneck, sharecropper, sissy, pervert, automation, clerk, income tax, communist, Red, dumb farmer, pink, "Greetings," antivivisectionist, evolution, square, punk, welsher.

Effective listeners try to identify and to rationalize the words or phrases most upsetting emotionally. Often the emotional impact of such words can be decreased through a free and open discussion of them with friends or associates.

10. Capitalize on Thought Speed

Most persons talk at a speed of about 125 words a minute. There is good evidence that if thought were measured in words per minute, most of us could think easily at about four times that rate. It is difficult—almost painful—to try to slow down our thinking speed. Thus we normally have about 400 words of thinking time to spare during every minute a person talks to us.

What do we do with our excess thinking time while someone is speaking? If we are poor listeners, we soon become impatient with the slow progress the speaker seems to be making. So our thoughts turn to something else for a moment, then dart back to the speaker. These brief side excursions of thought continue until our mind tarries too long on some enticing but irrelevant subject. Then, when our thoughts return to the person talking, we find he's far ahead of us. Now it's harder to follow him and increasingly easy to take off on side excursions. Finally we give up; the person is still talking, but our mind is in another world.

The good listener uses his thought speed to advantage; he constantly applies his spare thinking time to what is being said. It is not difficult once one has a definite pattern of thought to follow. To develop such a pattern we should:

- *Try to anticipate what a person is going to talk about. On the basis of what he's already said, ask yourself: "What's he trying to get at? What point is he going to make?"*
- *Mentally summarize what the person has been saying. What point has he made already, if any?*
- *Weight the speaker's evidence by mentally questioning it. As he present facts, illustrative stories, and statistics, continually ask yourself: "Are they accurate? Do they come from an unprejudiced source? Am I getting the full picture, or is he telling me only what will prove his point?"*
- *Listen between the lines. The speaker doesn't always put everything that's important into words. The changing tones and volume of his voice may have a meaning. So may his facial expressions, the gestures he makes with his hands, the movement of his body.*

Not capitalizing on thought speed is our greatest single handicap. The differential between thought speed and speech speed breeds false feelings of security and mental tangents. Yet, through listening training, this same differential can be readily converted into our greatest asset.

Number of words 2490
See page 395 for questions
Reading time in seconds ________
See page 497 for conversion table

Selection 59

"After This Manner, Therefore, Listen"

B. W. Overstreet

Here's General George Marshall's formula for success in dealing with people: (1) listen *to the other person's story; (2) listen to the other person's* complete *story; (3) listen to the other person's complete story* first. *Do you think Overstreet would agree with such a formula? And where does reading fit into the picture? Listen, and you shall hear.*

Stop—Look—Listen. That is good advice at a railroad crossing; and equally good advice in a lot of other places: places where there are things to see that we do not see; things to hear that we do not hear; things which, if they could hold our attention and become part of our understanding, would make us more safe to be allowed at large in a worried and suffering world. It is good advice. Particularly the word "listen." For most of us do not listen.

This need not mean that we do more than our share of the talking. It may mean that. But quite as likely it means that we are mentally awake only when we are doing the talking—that we slide into a coma when it comes our turn to keep still. Our comatose state may be disguised—if we are expert in the use of the fixed bright expression; the eager smile; the little nod that says, "Of course," and the shake of the head that says, "Oh, dear, what a shame!" I have even known people who could appear to be thinking—weighing carefully every word that was being said—with the effect achieved by their muscles instead of their minds. This accomplishment involves a certain furrowing of the brow, and a rhythm of smoothing and deepening the furrows; a certain drooping of the jowls as though under the weight of a problem. It does not, however, involve thinking. Nor real listening. Just enough clue-listening to be sure that the muscular responses hit the right rhythm.

Wordsworth, in brief, was more of an optimist than a psychologist when he wrote:

> The eye—it cannot choose but see;
> We cannot bid the ear be still. . . .

Eyes that are not seeing and ears that are not hearing are the rule rather than the exception—if we take seeing and hearing to be mental and emotional, as well as purely physical, experiences.

There is a kind of common notion that talking is a more active form of behavior than listening: that more of the self is engaged. Probably this error stems from the fact that our lips move when we talk, but our ears do not wiggle when we listen. So far as the active involvement of the brain is concerned, however, the two processes—talking and listening—should be equal parts of one experience: the experience of breaking down our own separateness, our own psychological isolation, and linking ourselves in mutual understanding with other people.

Sometimes even our talking seems curiously related to mental activity. Words keep on coming out of the mouth for no better reason, apparently, than because nothing has happened to stop them. But even more frequent is a condition of imitation listening: of silence that is not the silence of mental receptivity.

Real listening is a very active business. Rightly understood, our power to listen is the power to escape the limitations of our own experience and learn more about life than we can ever have a direct, personal chance to learn.

We are all partial, narrow, biased, walled around by our own memories and habits. We cannot help being so. For very few of the whole multitude of things that can happen to human beings ever happen to any one of us. And since it is what happens to ourselves that we feel most vividly, we easily think of our partial experience as typical experience. Listening—listening with the mind and heart, as well as with the ears—is the best means we have of supplementing our narrow experience with the wider experience of the race.

But to listen in this fashion we have to lend

ourselves fully to the speaker. Hearing his words, we have also to feel the person who speaks them: the person for whom they represent experience and value. This person-who-is-not-ourselves may be talking about the house where he grew up; or about the high cost of living; or about refugees from Europe; or about Congress, or the younger generation, or a trip across country, or a new hat. But always and inevitably he is describing himself. By talking about a subject, he is telling what he thinks is worth talking about. By choosing to say one thing rather than another about a person he knows or a magazine article he has read, he is telling what he values. The art of listening, then, is the art of imaginatively moving ourselves over into the speaker's mind, the art of locating his few spoken words in the context of all his memories and hopes, beliefs, and doubts. If we form the habit of thus actively listening when others talk, we will be continually broadening and deepening our knowledge of what it feels like to be human, what it feels like even in situations utterly different from our own.

Perhaps it is stretching a point to say that the art of reading is actually the art of listening—just another form of it: a form that allows us to cock a receptive ear toward a speaker a world away from us in space or centuries away from us in time. Yet that is how I myself like to think of reading.

After all, it is still a new thing for the human race to be able to read. For more generations than we can number, listening was the only means man possessed of enlarging his own experience by the borrowed experience of others. Philosophy, religion, drama, history, story, poetry: these no less than the small incidents of his friends' lives came to man, if at all, because they were spoken by someone and he listened to them. He listened to them and built up feelings around them and used them as a measure of his own behaviors, as company for himself when he was alone, as a stimulus to his own powers when they needed stimulus, as wisdom to pass on in his turn to other folk. The individual who, in the long preliterate stages of history, had no keen ability as a listener must have remained a prisoner within his own small cell of experience.

But we learned after a while, after many centuries. We learned, as it were, to take liquid speech and freeze it on the printed page: fix it there for keeps, fix it there so that people could look with their eyes at what was formerly accessible only to their ears. But this meant that the reader had to know how to listen—with mind and heart—to whoever was speaking to him in the soundless code of print. Here, again, he had to learn how to imagine his way into the other person's mind; he had to learn the art of looking out at life from the angle of the other person's experience. He had to listen with his eyes.

When we do thus learn to listen to the printed page, we move into a far wider company of talkers than we can ever expect to know by just listening with our ears to audible voices. We can open a novel and listen to people worrying their way through problems that we never thought about before, but that suddenly become real to us: the problems, perhaps, that are faced by sharecroppers, or members of some minority group, or men and women who earn their living at jobs we have never tackled. We can open a book of philosophy and listen to Socrates talking on an Athenian street corner. We can open a book of poetry and hear voices that astonish us with beauty, or stab us with a new sense of the world's old sorrow. We can, in brief, invite into our own living room any speaking company to which we choose to lend the ears of our understanding.

And these people who speak to us from books speak with an astonishing lack of inhibition. They tell us, in the first half-hour that we spend with them, more about their own inner thoughts and their past lives than even our intimate friends ever bring themselves to tell. By listening, then, to those who speak from the pages of novels, histories, and dramas, we acquire a store of insight about human experience and feeling that it would take many lifetimes to acquire from words that reach the ear from the speaking lips of our own acquaintances.

It is a rich and subtle art, this art of listening. He who learns it well may also learn well, as a by-product, the art of speaking with wisdom.

Number of words 1434
See page 397 for questions
Reading time in seconds ________
See page 497 for conversion table

Selection 60

Are You Listening?

Stuart Chase

You aren't learning anything when you're talking! Why not? Traffic is going the wrong way. On a four-lane highway, two lanes bring traffic south, two take traffic north. It's the same with communication: reading and listening bring information in; speaking and writing carry it out. Are you listening?

Listening is the other half of talking. If people stop listening it is useless to talk—a point not always appreciated by talkers.

Listening isn't the simple thing it seems to be. It involves interpretation of both the literal meaning of the words and the intention of the speaker. If someone says, "Why, Jim, you old horse thief!" the words are technically an insult; but the tone of voice probably indicates affection.

Americans are not very good listeners. In general they talk more than they listen. Competition in our culture puts a premium on self-expression, even if the individual has nothing to express. What he lacks in knowledge he tries to make up for by talking fast or pounding the table. And many of us while ostensibly listening are inwardly preparing a statement to stun the company when we get the floor. Yet it really is not difficult to learn to listen—just unusual.

Listening is regarded as a passive thing, but it can be a very active process—something to challenge our intelligence. A stream of messages is coming in to be decoded: How close can we come to their real meaning? What is the speaker trying to say? . . . How does he know it? . . . What has he left out? . . . What are his motives?

Sometimes only about a quarter of an audience understands clearly what a speaker has said. To sharpen the ears of its members, the New York Adult Education Council has inaugurated "listening clinics." One member reads aloud while the others around the table concentrate on what he is saying. Later they summarize what they have heard and compare notes—often to find that the accounts differ widely. Gradually the listeners improve, and often they find themselves transferring the skill to business and home affairs. As one member said:

"I became aware of a new attitude. I found myself attempting to understand and interpret the remarks of my friends and associates from *their* viewpoint, and not from my own as I had done previously."

Some years ago Major Charles T. Estes of the Federal Conciliation Service was called in to help settle a long-term dispute between a corporation and its unions. The Major proceeded to invent a technique for listening that has since had wide application in the labor field. He asked delegates from both union and management to read aloud the annual contract which was in dispute. Each man read a section in his turn; then all discussed it. If a dispute began to develop, the clause was put aside for later examination.

In two days the delegates really knew what was in the contract, and were competent to go back and tell their fellow managers or fellow workers what it contained. "We had conditioned them to communicate," said the Major. The contract was not rewritten but has continued in force with very few changes for ten years. Good listening had transformed bad labor relations into good ones.

Carl R. Rogers, University of Chicago psychologist, suggests a game to be played at a party. Suppose a general discussion—say on the French elections—becomes acrimonious. At this point Rogers asks the company to try an experiment. Before Jones, who is on the edge of his chair, can reply to the statement just made by Smith, he must summarize what Smith has said in such a way that Smith accepts it. Any attempt to slant or distort is instantly corrected by the original speaker. This means careful listening, during which emotion is likely to cool.

The result is that everyone in the circle, by listening and rephrasing, acquires a working knowledge of the other fellow's point of view, even if he does not agree with it. The players are quite likely to increase their knowledge of the subject—something that rarely happens in the usual slam-bang argument. The experiment takes courage, says Rogers, because in restating the other man's position one runs the risk of changing one's own.

F. J. Roethlisberger of the Harvard Business School, in a recent study of training courses for supervisors, describes a significant contrast in listening. An executive calls foreman Bill to his office to tell him about a change in Bill's department. A casting will be substituted for a hand-forged job, and the executive tells Bill how to do it.

"Oh yeah?" says Bill.

Let us follow two steps which the boss might take at this point. First, suppose he assumes that "Oh yeah" means Bill does not see how to do the new job, and it is up to the boss to tell Bill. This he proceeds to do clearly and logically. Nevertheless, Bill is obviously freezing up, and presently things begin to happen inside the boss. "Can it be," he asks himself, "that I have lost my power to speak clearly? No, Bill just doesn't understand plain English; he's really pretty dumb." The look which accompanies this unspoken idea makes Bill freeze up even harder. The interview ends on a note of total misunderstanding.

But, says Roethlisberger, suppose the boss sees from the "Oh yeah" that Bill is disturbed, and he tries to find out why. He says: "What's your idea about how the change-over ought to be made, Bill? You've been in the department a long time. Let's have it. I'm listening."

Things now begin to happen inside Bill. The boss is now laying it on the line, he's willing to listen. So ideas come out, slowly at first, then faster. Some are excellent ideas and the boss becomes really interested in Bill's approach—"Smarter man than I thought!" A spiral reaction is set up, as Bill begins to realize that he never appreciated the boss before. The interview ends on a note of close harmony.

In the first case, the boss did not listen to Bill, he *told* Bill; and though the telling was clear enough, the goal moved farther away. In the second case, the boss listened until he had located what was worrying Bill; then they went along together.

So far, we have been talking about sympathetic listening in face-to-face situations, to make sure we grasp the speaker's full meaning. But critical listening, too, is needed in a world full of propaganda and high-pressure advertisers. Here are some techniques which help to develop critical listening to a speech or a conversation, a sales talk at your door or the testimony of a witness before a jury:

Look for motives behind the words. Is the speaker talking chiefly in accepted, appealing symbols—Home, Mother, the Founding Fathers, Our Glorious Heritage, and so on—avoiding the need for thought, or is he really trying to think? Speeches are often solidly larded with symbols, and the well-trained ear can identify them a long way off.

Is the speaker dealing in facts or inferences? With practice you can train your ear to find this distinction in political and economic talk, and to follow the shifts from one level to the next.

The listener should also consider his own attitude toward the speaker. Is he prejudiced for or against him? Is he being fair, objective, sympathetic?

The sum of careful listening is to work actively to discover how the speaker feels about events, what his needs and drives appear to be, what kind of person he is. The appraisal can only be rough, but it can be a decided help in dealing with him, in giving him a fair answer.

One other thing: I find that careful listening also helps me to keep quiet rather than sound off foolishly. The best listeners listen alertly, expecting to learn something and to help create new ideas.

Are you listening?

Number of words 1275
See page 399 for questions
Reading time in seconds ________
See page 497 for conversion table

Selection 61

What Has Listening Done for Us?

James I. Brown

We usually think of what we do *to communicate—to read, to listen, to speak, and to write. But shouldn't we turn that question around once in a while? Shouldn't we ask what reading, speaking, and writing have done for us? And, especially, what has listening done for us? We need to know.*

Listening has worked a miracle—probably an unrecognized miracle. It has given us language—the basis for all subsequent communication—the foundation for lifelong reading, writing, speaking, and listening activities.

As adults in a foreign country, we feel confused and uncomfortable when surrounded by a totally strange language. To pick out separate words, recognizable letters or syllables in such gibberish seems impossible. Yet at birth, all of us face a similar but far more difficult task. It's more difficult because at birth we lack basic concepts. At first, we do not know there are such things as letters, syllables, words, sentences, or grammar. We don't know that letters have sounds and words have meanings. In short, we know absolutely nothing about language—not even what it is.

Amazingly enough, however—usually in our first five years—we will complete the greater part of the basic language acquisition process, with no formal instruction—depending solely on listening. That means discovering the basic underlying concepts of language. It means analyzing the language completely, discovering the rules of phonology needed to put sounds together into words, the rules of syntax needed to put words together into meaningful sentences, the rules of semantics needed to interpret word and sentence meanings, and the rules of pragmatics needed to manage the intricate patterns of taking turns in dialogue in a variety of social situations.

The learning through listening that goes on during those early formative years seems almost miraculous. Of course a child who hears no language, learns no language. In France, in 1797, a twelve-year-old boy was captured—the "Wild Boy of Aveyron." Up to that time he had apparently lived his life as an animal, completely isolated from people. He trotted along on all fours, not walking erect as a person—and he was inarticulate. A young French physician, not believing the boy was an incurable idiot, set out to instruct him to speak. After five years of patient endeavor, the doctor discovered that the boy had the ability to learn many things—but not language. He never learned to speak. The conclusion was that a child who had never heard language in his early years lost forever the ability to speak. A deaf child will coo and babble for the first six months of life but cease at that time. Normal children will continue to babble. Listening to language apparently makes the difference.

Through listening, children learn the most important ability needed—the ability to communicate by words—an activity that will eventually take up about 70 percent of our waking time. And this highly complex task is done solely through listening. It is done so rapidly that one linguist wrote: "Ten linguists working full time for 10 years to analyze the structure of the English language could not program a computer with the ability for language acquired by an average child in the first 10 or even 5 years of life." This accomplishment immediately elevates listening to a position of foremost importance as a learning channel.

It also raises many unanswered questions. During those language-learning years can parents contribute added language facility? We know that great differences in language fluency and mastery exist from person to person. How many of those differences are attributable to heredity and how many to environment? Can a greater awareness of the key role of listening in language acquisition bring increased mastery? Can an enhanced language environment make a measurable difference?

The recent book, *A Mother's Work* by Deborah Fallows, has as its first principle that mothers who leave their children in others' care are jeopardizing their formative years and that the 50 percent of American mothers who think they can both work and raise happy kids are fooling themselves and harming their children. Is it language acquisition that suffers from such a situation?

In the article "Becoming a Nation of Readers," published by the International Reading Association, reading aloud to children is called "the single most important activity for building the knowledge required for eventual success in reading." Does this way of enriching language environment have a heightened effect on language acquisition as well as on subsequent reading and listening development?

The rapidity of language acquisition leads some to say that the human brain is programmed at birth for learning language—a programming that is lost later in life, as evidenced by difficulties in learning another language, despite the variety of instructional aids available. Is this so, or have we just lost our early listening ability through neglect? Could the educational system be so restructured as to retain all or most of that initial listening effectiveness as well as develop the ability to read? . . .

These are but a few of the many unanswered questions arising from this most important early learning-by-listening experience.

If listening provides the primary learning channel for early informal education, what about subsequent formal education from kindergarten through college and graduate school?

When we begin school, since we can neither read nor write, the major part of instruction still, of necessity, comes through listening. Through its use, we gradually learn to connect sounds with letters and words until we are able to read words with understanding as well as listen to them. Early research by Wilt determined that 57.7 percent of the class time from grades one through seven was spent in listening. Interestingly enough, when teachers were asked to estimate the time pupils spent in listening, they said 74 minutes a day. Actual timed observations showed they listened 158 minutes a day—more than twice the estimated figure. Listening seemed almost unnoticed by the very individuals who should be most aware of it.

Studies suggest that up to about the sixth grade, listening is the most efficient learning channel. From the sixth to the ninth grade levels listening and reading seem about equally efficient. Gradually as students learn to read better and make greater use of that channel, their listening ability begins a slow deterioration. By the time they enter college as freshmen, their ability as listeners has dropped back to a lower level.

What about high school? Even there most class instruction still comes orally. The inevitable learning loss, resulting from the diminution of listening ability, has to be compensated for by heavier reliance on reading as the major learning channel.

In higher education—both undergraduate and graduate—the lecture system remains the norm, with some classes of up to two or three hundred students. This demands highly-developed listening ability. Students themselves in three different surveys rated listening as more important than reading as a factor in achieving academic success. For all too many, however, listening is relatively inefficient—at the 25 to 35 percent level. A check of those students graduating "with high distinction" and "with distinction" on the St. Paul campus of the University of Minnesota provides additional evidence of this relationship. Of those graduating "with high distinction," the average percentile rank in reading, as measured by the *Nelson-Denny Reading Test*, was 78; the average percentile rank in listening, as measured by the *Brown-Carlsen Listening Comprehension Test*, was 92. Of those graduating "with distinction," the average percentile rank in reading was 78, in listening 81. Performance levels in those two assimilative areas apparently contribute measurably to academic success.

As incoming freshmen, only two students in those two groups had scores in listening below the 50th percentile. Both were given special training in listening for one quarter in Freshman Communication, one progressing from the 8th to the 96th percentile, the other from the 34th to the 85th percentile. In one quarter they apparently recovered sufficient ability in listening to manage all college courses for their remaining three years with better than average success.

Again, many unanswered questions arise. In life, when we make little use of any ability, it tends to diminish or atrophy through disuse. When we practice reading and use reading more and more frequently, would it not be natural to lose much of the listening ability that we had relied on so heavily and exclusively early in life? Look more closely at what happens during those first years of schooling. Primary attention is on making a nation of readers with little or no attention on listening. What about making a nation of listeners? What would happen if both reading and listening were taught with equal emphasis? We need to know. How much does our neglect of listening contribute to its loss of effectiveness? We do know that students weak in reading rely more strongly on listening and seem to retain sufficient ability to make it their major channel of learning. Again, in building added skill in reading are we sacrificing effectiveness in listening? Why lose effectiveness in either of the two learning channels?

With evidence of the importance of listening and reading in formal education, you might expect universities to offer courses in those fields. Yet composition and speech courses are still far more common. Strangely enough, at one university where state funds were in short supply, the strong program of instruction in listening and reading was severely cut, but not courses in writing and speaking. Why offer students educational opportunities with one hand and deprive them of the skills needed to take maximum advantage of them with the other? To be sure, we need scientists, historians, educators, economists, mathematicians, statesmen and the like. But to get them, reliance must be placed on the dual channels of listening and reading. If those two learning channels are not in good condition, all education—all learning—suffers. . . .

Listening ability lies at the very heart of all our growth, from birth through the years of formal education. The better those learning skills are developed, the more productive our learning efforts.

After our years of preparation—of informal and formal education—the time comes to step out into the world of work, our eyes fixed firmly to the future. What will listening do for us for the rest of our lives?

Listening still holds as ubiquitous a place as ever. But we still may overlook its importance. Listening may be like the concealed letter in Poe's famous story, "The Purloined Letter"—hidden so obviously that it goes unnoticed—concealed in plain sight, so to speak. Listening may indeed be so omnipresent that we overlook it, failing to appreciate the rich wealth of untapped resources it provides for daily living.

Whatever we turn to, whether of major or minor concern, seems to have implications for and connections with listening. In Toffler's book, *Future Shock*, he states that the "average American adult is assaulted by a minimum of 560 advertising messages each day. Of that number, he notices only seventy-six, in effect blocking out 484 messages a day to preserve his attention for other matters." Toffler sees this blocking out of messages as a way of preventing future shock at the most personal level—of keeping stimulation from pushing us beyond our natural adaptive limit. This matter of impinging stimuli would seem a major factor in understanding, controlling, and developing listening potential. How much of our waking time is spent in listening to radio, TV, phone, and others; and what effect does this almost solid flow of stimuli have on our listening skills and habits? Should we ration our flow and make it more selective to provide added control?

Furthermore, as our culture has grown more complex, the kinds of messages received by the ordinary person have changed markedly. For villagers in the agricultural society of the past, most messages were casually structured—banter, griping, complaining, boasting, factual. The messages received by the average person today, mainly from the mass media, which didn't exist in early days, are artfully and scientifically fashioned by communication experts to make a heightened appeal. We listen to the news, watch carefully scripted plays, telecasts, and movies, hear frequent speeches. These bombard us with ever-increasing force and demands on attention. How do we cope with such changes?

According to Toffler, the median time spent by adults in reading newspapers is 51 minutes a day. That same adult spends additional time reading magazines, books, signs, billboards, recipes, memos, and letters, ingesting between 10,000 and 20,000 edited words per day of the many times that number of words surrounding him. The same adult spends at least an hour and a quarter a day listening to the radio—news, commercials, commentary, hearing about 11,000 processed words—plus perhaps another 10,000 words or more in watching TV. What effect does this flood of words have on his listening habits and abilities? These are matters we desperately need to understand if we are to deal with individual listening problems. Toffler may be appalled by how little we actually know about our level of adaptability and the danger of future shock. We have reason to be appalled by how little we still know about the visible yet invisible world of listening.

Perhaps the four lines written by the poet Francis Thompson are apropos:

> O world invisible, we view thee,
> O world intangible, we touch thee,
> O world unknowable, we know thee,
> Inapprehension, we clutch thee.

Certainly listening still seems invisible, intangible, and unknowable. Our challenge, as we face our listening-centered world, is to learn to view it, to touch it, and to know it—to turn what is inapprehension to apprehension. That means recognizing its key importance and learning to listen more effectively—educationally, socially, politically, nationally, and internationally.

Number of words 2240
See page 401 for questions
Reading time in seconds ________
See page 497 for conversion table

SELECTION 62

How to REALLY Talk to Another Person

Malcolm Boyd

Someone once said, "There are very few people who don't become more interesting when they stop talking." Is that, in essence, what the author of the following selection is saying? At any rate, we should know how to really *talk to people. And that's what you'll soon find out.*

One of my favorite news clippings of all time was written early in the century and concerns the first two automobiles ever to have appeared on the streets of a major American city. Its opening sentence went something like this:

"The only two automobiles in town collided today at the intersection of State and Main."

But we don't need to be in cars to collide. People bump into one another all the time—in their families, their jobs, their social relationships and in the public arena. Somehow, we get our signals crossed because we just don't communicate clearly. This article will offer seven basic rules to help keep you collision-free when exchanging ideas.

Communication failures are stumbling blocks to good living. We hear examples of them every day: "I didn't mean to say that." "She misunderstood me." "He lied."

The resultant damage to human feelings, to business, to property and finances—even to international relations—is inestimable. We can avoid all this only by communicating clearly, honestly and effectively.

Strangely enough, I have found that the secret of being heard—of how to really talk to another person—is, for the most part simply to *listen.*

Listening to others is a sure way to get yourself heard—and it can capture more attention than a string of crackling firecrackers. Picture a roomful of people all shouting their message. Finally, a gavel pounds, order is restored. One by one, each shouter is given a chance to speak. The first, Bill, arrogantly insists that only his argument is valid. He bars any compromise. Eileen, a speaker with an opposing point of view, watches sullenly as Bill holds forth. Gene, waiting for his turn to grab the spotlight, rehearses what he will say. Among them, *nobody is listening!* You can bet that, even as each takes a turn at the microphone, he or she will not be heard by the others. You'd have an even surer bet that, if John Doe got up and recapped each position given and then addressed them, the shouters *would* listen to John Doe. Why? Because John would have practiced one of the prime rules of communication.

One of the first lessons taught most schoolchildren is, "Stop, look and listen before you cross the street." That way, they're told, they'll avoid accidents. If, before we talk, we learn to stop, look (at how people talk, both with their faces and bodies) and listen (to the sounds of people's voices as well as their words), we'll probably avoid collisions in communications.

Sometimes we hear more with our eyes than with our ears and hear more from tones than from words. That's why it is important to follow this rule:

1. Listen with an inner ear—to hear what actually is meant, rather than what is said with words. War, peace, love, hate—at crucial times, everything may hang on this ability. Of course, people should say what they mean, but sometimes they just can't. Only by listening carefully and deeply to others—and observing their actions, as well as their words—can we truly communicate.

2. Listen to the concerns of others. Don't con-

centrate solely on your own ideas. You already *know* what *you* think. Find out what others think and address *their* ideas. You might learn something, and others, seeing that you take them seriously, may be moved to take you seriously in return. Nothing is more deadly than I-I/me-me. Make it *we* and *us*. You'll get a bigger audience than a skywriter does—and people may even be willing to help you cross your Ts in the process.

3. It is important to know when *just* to listen. Sometimes, a barrier suddenly falls between two people with a very close relationship. When it happens to you, try not to panic. No matter how close two people may be with one another, there are times when one person withdraws. This may occur for any reason—from midlife crisis to job anxiety to personal pain to a deep sense of loss. Usually it has nothing to do with *you*, specifically. Yet it affects you acutely.

Suddenly, words fail. Coldness replaces warmth. Silences seem threatening: You wonder: "Is this the end? Can I possibly save this situation?" Familiar ways of bonding are met with indifference. Your signaled need for closeness meets with rejection. You feel vulnerable, and the sense of alienation grows.

If ever there was a time to listen, this is it. Be patient and supportive. Be quiet and wait. Be ready to respond to communications the other person initiates. Sometimes, by simply listening, you say more about how you feel than any words could say. The other person will hear you and be grateful.

Try always to listen with a clear head and an open mind, which leads to the next rule:

4. Assume nothing. Too often we assume something is one thing and later find that it is something else entirely.

We all have found that appearances are deceptive. We assume: *This* person couldn't possibly cheat. (But he does!) *That* relationship is more solid than the Rock of Gibraltar. (But it isn't.) Pat, the well-groomed, smiling man, obviously is bright, and Mike, the thrown-together one, is a dolt. (The reverse is true.)

Making assumptions in human relations—and letting them affect our point of view, untested—can be fatal. Did you ever have a feeling that someone was out to "get" you? It's too easy to persuade ourselves that someone is telling a lie, gossiping maliciously, being unfaithful or trying to get our job. However, if we act on an assumption as though it were fact and make a false judgment, not only might we end up with egg on our faces, but we also could create very real losses for ourselves.

Misreading signs of humans behavior can have very serious repercussions. I learned long ago that a seemingly unfriendly attitude might indicate nothing more than that someone is suffering—from a toothache or a troubled life at home. Look for the real (not the assumed) person behind the stranger you meet. It's important to remember always that we're communicating with another distinctively individual human being who lives and breathes and feels the need to like and be liked.

An elderly woman, blind and nearly deaf, lived in a retirement home I visited. She scared me by acting scared when I drew near. But, one day, I greeted her gently.

"Who are you?" she whispered.

"I've come to visit you," I said.

"Oh, how nice," she responded.

I described her dress, so she too could "see" its hues of bright turquoise, burnt orange and gold. Her face lit up.

"People do need each other," she said. "Together, we're not so lonely."

We've explored listening as a surefire way to be heard. Now let's address *how to talk to another person*. And the cardinal rule here is this:

5. Say what you mean. It never ceases to amaze me that some people offhandedly tell such outright lies as: "I like it." "Your job is safe." "I'll be back in five minutes." They say things they don't mean. Result: hurt, confusion, resentment. Once we stop telling the truth about small things, it's just a small step to spinning a veritable spiderweb of falsehoods. Then, finding we're caught in that web, we start to tell bigger lies. Saying what we mean keeps confusion to a minimum.

At a recent meeting, a dozen professional men and women gathered to draft a statement about long-range plans. It became painfully clear that the discussion was getting nowhere, growing ever more abstract and unrealistic. Finally, I asked: "Why don't we say what we mean?" A silence fell. Then someone laughed sheepishly and said, "But that's so hard to do."

6. Before speaking, always ask yourself: What is the message that's needed? It wouldn't be quite so hard to communicate clearly if we first answered these questions: What do those I'm talking to need to know? What is the best way for me to say it and to get straight to the point? How do I get them to listen?

The rules for talking and listening are very similar. the key to the deepest secret of communication lies in *truly understanding what must be communicated*. If, for example, you are trying to *give* information to others, you must first find out what they need to know. If you are trying to *get* information, ask clearly for what you need to know. If, after listening carefully, you don't get what you need—or you don't understand what you get—say so and ask questions to clarify matters. Too often, we short-circuit our messages by telling people what we think they ought to know, rather than finding out what it is they need to know.

7. Remember that communication is in the present. "I should've said" just doesn't cut it. This moment—now—might change your life forever. Be open to communicating with that person who comes your way today. Don't miss your chance!

Number of words 1510
See page 403 for questions
Reading time in seconds ________
See page 497 for conversion table

SELECTION 63

Basic Building Blocks for Total Listening

Robert L. Montgomery

Zeno, the Classical Greek philosopher, once argued the importance of listening with strange logic—"We have two ears and one mouth that we may listen the more and talk the less." Zeno was right! We actually do listen more. That brings up a question. Since we listen more often, how can we listen more effectively?

Here are six basic guidelines for better listening. You can improve your listening the day you start practicing them. . . .

A stepladder has a number of rungs on it to help you move upward. I'm going to use the ladder idea to help you progress upward in the ability to be an active listener. I'm going to spell out L A D D E R with the six rules. This will make it easier to remember them.

The Eyes Have It

First, the *L* stands for: **Look** at the other person. Look at the person who is talking to you. Also, always look at the person you're talking to. Looking directly at the person who is speaking shows dynamic interest. I don't mean staring at the other person, just looking into his or her eyes, but looking toward the person as he or she talks to you. You can look at the hairline, the neckline, watch the mouth as the person speaks, even notice the color of the eyes of the speaker.

But don't look at the floor or ceiling or out the window. And don't turn your eyes to view every distraction around you. People tell me they don't trust the person who doesn't look at them. They also sense suspicion, trickery, or distrust from such people. And distrust will block communication. It's a huge block also to motivation. There's little or no motivation when there is no respect. Concentrate on the other person as you listen. Looking at the person will enable you to judge the intent of the message as well as the content. So give your undivided attention as you listen to others. If you project genuine, active attention, you will convey sincere interest.

I was visiting a friend of mine who is also in the education field. She told her seven-year-old daughter to clean her room before dinner. At that moment, the child inquired, "Mommy, I wasn't looking when you said that. Did you say it with a smile or a frown?"

So, even first graders are already keenly aware of the importance of facial expression and body language. This seven-year-old wanted to know her mother's true intent. That is, did her mother really mean what she said? Likewise, you will know more when you observe the body language and facial expressions of others.

Again Rule 1, always look at the person you're talking to—and always look at the person who is talking to you. When the eyes are elsewhere, the mind is elsewhere.

The Art of Asking Questions

Moving up the ladder to better listening, Rule 2 starts with *A*. Ask questions. This is the best way for anyone to become a better listener fast. It's a necessity for parents, teachers, managers, and salespeople. To keep from doing all the speaking yourself and to get the other person talking, develop the tools of the reporter, the art of asking questions. Master the different types of questions you'll learn now. Start using them today. Practice is the best instructor.

Some types of questions help you discover facts. You might want to know where someone works or lives, what they do, where they're from. Questions that get specific, concise facts for answers are called *closed-end questions*. You rarely get more than a word or two in reply. "What is your name?" is one example. "How old are you?" is another.

The opposite type is called *open-ended questioning*. You can find out most of the facts about a person by asking just one or two open-ended questions. For example, I might ask you, "How did you get into the line of work you're in now?" That question will usually get a person talking for at least 5 minutes and more likely for 15. Of course, you could simply say to someone, "Tell me about yourself." That's open-ended and will accomplish the same purpose.

Try to develop a skill for questioning others in conversation and in business communications. Naturally, you won't ask a lot of questions if you don't have the time and it isn't necessary. But when you have the time, try out these different types of questions and become accustomed to using them. We really don't take anything for our own without practice.

You might ask someone, "How did you get into the job you have now?" and even though it's an open-ended question, the person might simply answer, "By accident." Now what do you do? You ask a follow-up question, such as "What happened?" Then you'll get the person talking in depth.

We can learn a lesson from doctors, lawyers, and dentists on questioning skills. None of them would be able to help you unless they asked a few questions. Once the questions have been asked and the answers given, a lawyer may decide not to handle your case. Doctors and dentists can't help you at all until they find out what's wrong.

Doctors especially develop a skill for questioning. Perhaps psychiatrists, most of all, need the tools of questioning to help discover a patient's problem. Psychiatrists are paid $100 an hour and more to listen to the problems of patients and try to help solve them. So in their training as therapists, they are taught to use skillful, open-ended questioning to get the whole story from a patient. Once the problem has been stated, the doctor might say, "That's interesting! Tell me more." Or "I don't understand. Could you give me an example?" This kind of questioning produces the answers needed to enable the doctor to help others.

First, ask fact-finding questions to discover what the problem is. Then, just as the medical doctor might, ask a question to discover how the person feels. People love to explain how they feel. Parents, managers, salespeople, anyone can learn more and get along better with other people by discovering how those people feel about things. Additional questions will also help gain an understanding of why they feel as they do.

I've often wondered how many sales are lost each week because the salesperson doesn't listen to the prospect or customer. There's been a revolution in selling. The change has taken us from the product-pusher of the past to the counselor-type salesperson who asks questions first. Contrary to the belief of many people, you actually save time and make the sale faster by asking the prospect some questions to discover his or her needs, problems, or objectives. I've conducted hundreds of role plays on videotape with salespeople over the years and have used a stopwatch to time their sales interview. I've discovered that it takes a shorter time to sell by using the questioning approach.

Besides, I've noted that the sale is almost always made when questions are asked and the prospect participates. And the sale is rarely made when it's a one-way sellathon, with the salesperson spouting facts, features, benefits, and advantages without learning the definite needs or wants of the prospect.

People don't have time to listen to others rave on and on about their product or service in person or on the telephone. But they are willing to spend time with someone who is interested in their ideas, needs, and problems. Besides, it doesn't take long to find out what a person feels, needs, or wants.

To illustrate the power of questions, I think of the experience of a famous sales trainer and speaker, the late Fred Herman. Herman was introduced on the Mike Douglas television show one day as "the greatest salesman in the world." What happened next was purely spontaneous; Herman vowed he had no idea what Mike Douglas would ask him.

Douglas began by saying, "Fred, since you're hailed as the Number 1 salesman in the world, sell me something!" Without any hesitation, Fred Herman responded instantly and instinctively with a question: "Mike, what would you want me to sell you?"

Mike Douglas, who is paid a couple of million dollars a year for asking questions, was now on the defensive. Surprised, Douglas paused, looked around, and finally answered, "Well, sell me this ashtray."

Fred Herman again spoke instantly, "Why would you want to buy that?" And again, Mike Douglas, surprised and scratching his head, finally answered, "Well, it's new and shapely. Also, it's colorful. And besides, we are in a new studio and don't want it to burn down. And, of course, we want to accommodate guests who smoke."

At this point, Mike Douglas sat back in his chair, but not for long. Instantly Fred Herman responded, "How much would you pay for the ashtray, Mike?"

Douglas stammered and said, "Well, I haven't bought an ashtray lately, but this one is attractive and large, so I guess I'd pay $18 or $20." And Fred Herman, after asking just three questions, closed the sale by saying, "Well, Mike, I'll let you have the ashtray for $18."

That's selling by questioning and listening. I call it selling with a professional ear. The whole sale took less than one minute. Fred Herman said he simply reacted as he always does in selling, by asking questions.

Follow the method of professional listeners. Learn to ask questions and develop a big ear for listening.

Rudyard Kipling, the famous author, summed up the skill of questioning in these words: "I have six honest servants. They've taught me all I know. Their names are who, what, where, when, why and how."

You'll find that who, where, and when are opening words for closed-end questions that produce monosyllabic replies. Whereas what, why, and how generally begin open-ended questions and produce much more detailed information.

Practice Rule 2 every day. Make it your personal goal to ask a lot of questions. But have a purpose for each question. There are two basic categories: to get specific information or to learn opinions and feelings. It's easier to gain a rapport and get a person to open up by relating your questions to the other person's background or experience. Use open-ended questions to draw out. Remember, closed-end questions will make it difficult to get another person to speak and share ideas or information. Nobody likes to feel they're being investigated.

Finally, remember the advice of the famous statesman of some years ago Bernard Baruch, who said: "You can win more friends in two months by showing interest in others than you can in two years by trying to interest others in you." Looking at people as you converse with them and asking questions will help show genuine interest.

Don't Interrupt

Continuing up the ladder of success in listening, Rule 3 is the first of the two *D*'s: **D**on't interrupt. It's just as rude to step on people's ideas as to step on their toes.

It's a human tendency to want to jump right into a conversation when we get an idea or are reminded of something by someone's words. And that's why there's a problem. We need to continually practice letting other people finish their sentences or ideas. Speak only in turn is the answer.

Most of us avoid interrupters. We even go out of our way to avoid them. In fact, a desire to prevent interruptions motivated Thomas Jefferson to invent the dumbwaiter, a mechanical lift to take food and drink by pulley from the kitchen to an upstairs dining room. Jefferson disliked being interrupted in conversation by servants; with the dumbwaiter, no servants were necessary and he couldn't be interrupted.

Nobody likes to be cut off while speaking. So work at letting others finish what they have to say. Bite your tongue and count to 10 if you have to, but practice Rule 3.

Don't Change the Subject

Rule 4 for better listening is the second *D*: **D**on't change the subject. This is a little different from Rule 3. Interrupting is bad enough, but going right on and changing the subject at the same time is positively rude. Some people do this so much they are dodged by others who don't want to be their next victim.

Consider a group of people who are talking and one of the members says, "I was watching television the other night and Senator Hayakawa of California spoke about . . . ." Now at this point, another member of the group, hearing the word *California*, interrupts immediately and changes the subject. "Oh, California, have you been out there to Disneyland? It's terrific! We took the kids there last summer and had a ball. You know, they have an island there, Tom Sawyer Island. And they have tree-houses, caves, all kinds of things to do. Why, you could spend a couple of days there. You get to the island on a raft or on one of those old Mississippi steamboats. Boy, it was just like being Robinson Crusoe on that island. Now what were you saying?"

Well, the speaker who was going to say something about Senator Hayakawa of California has no doubt buried that idea forever. In fact, the person who was cut off will not offer any more ideas and will probably find a reason to get out of the presence of the interrupter who also changed the subject.

Interrupting and changing the subject are sure ways to alienate people quickly. So try to curb both tendencies. You can be certain of this: If you cut people off while they're speaking and also change the subject, you'll be cutting them out of your life as friends or associates as well. A little restraint will pay big dividends.

Check Your Emotions

Going on up the ladder to success in listening, our next rung is the letter *E*, for **E**motions. Rule 5 is to check your emotions. Some people are prone to anger and get excited about certain words.

It doesn't pay to get overstimulated and overreact to the words and ideas of others. Words such as gasoline, taxes, 7 percent, abortion, and communism can stir one's emotions instantly. Curb your emotions. Control your urge to interrupt and stifle the other person's idea. It's a free country. People are entitled to their opinions and the right to complete their thoughts. Hear others out.

Let others explain their points of view, ideas, or convictions. Cutting them off won't accomplish anything. Try to understand them first. Then give your own ideas in a controlled manner. Little is gained through arguing and fighting. On the contrary, usually loss of time and injured relationships result.

Evaluate when the idea is complete, not before, or only when you fully understand the other person's meaning. . . .

I know a fellow who went storming into his boss's office. He was shouting and complaining that someone not as long with the company had received a promotion he thought he should have gotten. The boss told him that because of his quick temper he couldn't be trusted to manage others.

Besides, getting overly excited causes us to mentally debate or fight any idea that differs from our personal conviction, experience, or bias. So we don't hear what the speaker is saying at these times. Remember, the biggest problem in listening is failing to concentrate on the other person's communication. Getting overly emotional about something is one of the causes of the problem. Following the LADDER will help us avoid the pitfalls of poor listening. Check your emotions. Hear the other person out first.

Listen Responsively

Finally, the top rung of the ladder. The *R* stands for an essential principle of better listening and therefore better understanding: **R**esponsiveness. Be a responsive listener. Be responsive in your demeanor, posture, and facial expression. Let your whole being show you are interested in other people and their ideas.

As you listen, look at the other person and show some signs of hearing and understanding. Nod your head occasionally—gently, not vigorously. Nod slightly with a yes for agreement or a no when it's something sad or unhappy. Show through your posture, whether seated or standing, that you are concentrating on listening totally.

We show our interest in others also when we say occasionally "Um-mm" or "Uh-huh." These simple signs encourage speakers. They show we're interested in them and that we're listening to what they're saying. However, others won't talk long unless we are responsive in our listening and offer some nonverbal and even some slight verbal signs of understanding.

To understand this important principle of being responsive, it helps to ask, "How do we turn people off?" The answers come quickly: by not looking at them, not asking questions, not showing any positive response; by looking at our watch or out the window, shuffling papers, interrupting, and giving other negative types of feedback.

But we want to turn people on, not off. Whether we're teachers, managers, doctors, parents, or salespeople, we want to encourage others to communicate with us so we can gain understanding.

And there's one more important part to being responsive in listening to others: The one time it is all right, even desirable, to interrupt is to clarify what is said. For example, as soon as you hear someone's name when you are introduced, inquire right at that moment how to spell the name if it is a difficult one. Or if you aren't sure of a statistic, date, place, or other fact someone mentions, it shows responsive, concentrated listening to interrupt to clarify.

You can cushion your interruption with "Pardon me." But sometimes that isn't necessary. You might simply inquire "How many?" or "When did it happen?" or "What's the name?" The interruption to clarify will actually help you focus on the other person's message more actively.

Number of words 2910
See page 405 for questions
Reading time in seconds ________
See page 497 for conversion table

SELECTION 64

Four Strategies for Improving Evaluative Listening

Florence I. Wolff, Nadine C. Marsnik, William S. Tacey, and Ralph G. Nichols

Both in school and out, messages bombard us—messages that demand evaluation. One strategy seems hardly enough. Read on to discover four strategies that you can put to immediate use.

Mortimer Adler cautioned that when readers evaluate a book the first step must be understanding and the second step judgment. It is useful advice for evaluative listeners. We would be wise to put into practice all the strategies for discriminative listening so that we understand the persuasive message, then practice strategies for evaluative listening so that we judge the message intelligently after the listening experience.

We often change our attitudes, beliefs, or behavior as a result of persuasion. However, most of us would say, "I changed my mind," or "I decided to act." We seldom think, "That speaker convinced me to change my mind," or "That speaker convinced me to act thus." We are correct. Speakers may persuade but we become convinced. . . . Let us consider specific practices which can improve that participation.

1. Increase Our Knowledge in Specific Areas. Anderson suggests that increasing our personal knowledge should be considered a key strategy for planning a system of response to persuasive efforts. If we systematically read and listen to deepen our understanding of a field, we prepare ourselves to make more accurate immediate analyses of points of persuasion that touch on that subject. We might choose the field of public affairs, politics, history, a hobby, or a sport and develop expertise in this area. Whenever we hear persuasive messages in this area we will immediately be able to analyze individual points of evidence with accuracy. We will operate much like the sports fan who knows the batting averages and pitching records of major league baseball players. This fan can immediately recognize and set aside irrelevant data on the subject of baseball.

Each of us who chooses to develop extensive knowledge in a specific area has added one more field in which we can make more intelligent immediate and delayed appraisals. . . .

2. Learn to Recognize Strategies Used by Persuaders. Generally, persuaders use logical procedures, such as reasoning and evidence, and procedures that are not logical, such as suggestion and motivational appeals.

Reasoning is the process of inferring conclusions from a series of premises. The persuader may employ *deduction*, reasoning from premises accepted as true to a conclusion, or *induction*, reasoning from bits of evidence to a conclusion. If we learn as much as we can about these two processes of reasoning, we can employ this knowledge when we evaluate a persuader's message.

Evidence is the information that convinces us that premises or conclusions are true. This supporting material usually takes the form of statistics or a statement from an alleged authority. Speakers can express it as explanation, anecdote, quotation, example, or testimony. We can test all evidence used by a persuader by asking these three questions. "Is it recent?" "Is it competent?" and "Does it come from an unprejudiced source?" Recent evidence is as up-to-date as possible. Competent evidence comes from a source recognized to be authoritative. Evidence that is free from prejudice is objective and not slanted in such a way that the speaker stands to gain from our acceptance of it.

Suggestion in persuasion refers to the way a persuader moves us to think or act without deliberating. Persuaders use suggestion by associating verbal or nonverbal symbols with something else. Interviewees who anticipate the kinds of questions an interviewer might ask, who dress in a businesslike manner, and who make sure their voices are well modulated persuade by suggestion. They suggest to interviewers that they ar capable, intelligent, and good communicators.

Persuaders direct *motivational appeals* to wants, desires, or needs that they perceive ir persuader may address in either a positive or manner such needs as self-preservation, affection and esteem, freedom, pleasure and fulfillment, power and control, and achievement. Most of us exhibit several of these needs and can expect to find motivational appeals directed toward them. We can learn to recognize them and carefully monitor our response as we evaluate.

If we wish to develop competency in recognizing individual strategies used by persuaders, it is wise to study the art of persuasion and specific procedures used by persuaders. Whenever we spend time in delayed appraisal, we can review the ways a persuader has employed specific strategies and our reaction to each of them.

3. Learn to Identify Commonly Used Fallacies and Propaganda Techniques. Many times persuaders make hasty extrapolations or deliberately use fallacious reasoning and propaganda in attempting to elicit change. Three common fallacies appear fairly often in persuasion and careful evaluators learn to recognize them. They are the "always has, always will" fallacy, the hasty generalization, and the hidden variable.

"Always has, always will." refers to the false reasoning that because something has existed unchallenged in the past, it is good and ought to be continued in the present and future. We might hear this fallacy presented in a manner similar to this: "We have always appointed a person with a Ph.D. to this position. The appointees have always worked out very well. Let's not change our successful policy." The converse form of this fallacy is equally misleading. For example, "Taking drugs is as old as humanity itself. We've never been able to eliminate it, and we never will."

The hasty generalization describes conclusions reached from considering only a few cases. Personnel managers who state, "We are not eager to hire women as laborers in this company because we have found that women demand extra privileges," are undoubtedly saying what they believe to be true. However, this conclusion is probably based upon a generalization made from only a few examples.

When persuaders suggest that when two things follow in sequence one is somehow responsible for the other, they exhibit the fallacy of the hidden variable. An argument such as, "We urge our associates to join a church because we've found that church-going members are our best workers," exhibits this kind of fallacy. This conclusion overlooks the fact that the dedicated workers might also possess other virtues that inspire them to join churches, rather than that their church membership is responsible for perfecting their work habits.

Many years ago, after U.S. citizens discovered that they had been victims of unscrupulous propaganda during World War I, the Institute for Propaganda Analysis defined several basic techniques of propaganda. Strictly speaking, propaganda may be used in any attempt—good or bad—to change opinion. We do not suggest that it is universally unfair; however, it is often used unfairly in persuasion. Although we are far more propaganda-wise than we were a few decades ago, it is profitable to learn to recognize some of these techniques because they still surface in persuasion. Propaganda makes use of such approaches as name calling, glittering generalizations, transfer, testimonial, "plain folks," card stacking, and bandwagon appeals. . . .

If we learn, by reading and listening, as much as we can about fallacies in reasoning and about propaganda techniques, we can recognize and disregard each as we encounter it during some persuasive efforts.

4. Identify Any Changes in Belief or Attitude. During delayed appraisal each day, we can consider and evaluate any changes we perceive in our own beliefs and attitudes that result from listening to persuasion. We can often facilitate this process by asking ourselves these questions.

"What was my original position?" We can pinpoint our original belief or attitude and write it down. We can then rank the strength of that belief or attitude on a scale of one to ten.

"To what did I respond?" We can recall what specific evidence, reasoning, motivational appeals, or suggestions the speaker used to encourage a change in our thinking. We can note each bit of evidence and reappraise its recency, competence, and freedom from prejudice. We can decide whether the speaker used propaganda or suggestions.

"Was I objective?" Often our attitude toward the speaker can move us to abandon objectivity and respond to the speaker's personality. We can consider whether our positive feelings toward the speaker caused us to change. Similarly, we can consider whether our negative feelings toward a speaker caused us to refuse to change.

"Was I persuaded?" We can decide whether our attitude or belief has altered sufficiently to justify a change in action. If we think and weigh both during and after persuasion, we find our evaluation of spoken persuasion improving.

Number of words 1370
See page 407 for questions
Reading time in seconds ________
See page 497 for conversion table

SELECTION 65

Empathic Listening

Florence I. Wolff, Nadine C. Marsnik, William S. Tacey, and Ralph G. Nichols

Problem: with only two ears, how do you do four different kinds of listening? There's discriminative listening, evaluative listening, appreciative listening, and empathic listening. The first three have something in common. Empathic listening is totally different, as you'll soon discover. Lend the author your ears.

All of us have been motivated by a need to talk to someone who will listen to us. When speakers turn to us for this purpose we do . . . *empathic listening*. It differs from the [other] kinds because of our intent. We listen discriminatively, evaluatively, or appreciatively for intrinsic reasons. In one way or another, we expect to grow personally or to profit from it. We listen empathically primarily for extrinsic reasons. We reap several personal rewards from empathic listening, but we do it principally so that another person—the speaker—may grow and profit from it.

Empathic means characterized by empathy, and comes from the word *empathy*, "an understanding so intimate that the feelings, thoughts, and motives of one are readily comprehended by another." Kennedy suggests that empathy arises from entering into the experience of others, ". . . being able to stand there with them as they explore themselves, not backing away when the experience threatens to become hard on us." This entering into the exerpience of others occurs both formally and informally.

Formal empathic listening occurs in prearranged meetings for the purpose of therapy. We commonly arrange this with trained professionals in the helping professions. Other professionals, such as clergymen, teachers, general physicians, and lawyers, often listen empathically in formal situations. But if they are untrained in these skills, they may provide only frustration for their clients.

Empathic listening is not easy; it is perhaps the pinnacle of listening. It demands fine skill and exquisite tuning to another's mood and feelings. Presumably, only psychiatrists, psychologists, and counselors perfect it and possess the necessary training to help clients find curative power by talking. Unless we have the kind of intensive training that helping professionals acquire, we cannot presume to predict healing results from listening.

However, very few people go to psychiatrists with their problems. But many people take their troubles to close friends and relatives. We cannot, as laymen, possibly offer our friends the help that a psychiatrist gives to a patient. But there is no reason that we cannot become helpful empathic listeners. We can provide a listening ear to our friends in informal situations.

We listen empathically almost daily in informal encounters with friends, family, and co-workers who need someone to listen. When a friend calls to report feelings of rejection at not being accepted by a prestigious graduate school, when a co-worker stops to share feelings of inadequacy because a suggestion was overlooked, when members of our family come home angry because they had frustrating days, we encounter opportunities for informal empathic listening. We cannot cure these problems by listening. However, these people are looking for neither therapy nor advice. They ar looking for someone who is willing to sit still and list

These speakers wish to talk freely and, by listening to their own thoughts as they put them into words, arrive at their own solutions or come up with their own advice.

The Empathy-Seeking Speaker's Goals

Just as we did with the other three kinds of listening, we will consider the speaker's goals in seeking a listening ear. Usually the speaker intends to explain inner feelings about something. If the speaker put a goal into words, it might be, "I want to talk about my fears about my mother's illness," or "I want to talk about how I feel about my son's leaving home." The purpose centers around the speaker's own feelings about the subject.

Because speakers identify goals in terms of listeners, they focus on anticipated results. They hope listeners will understand not only what they say but how they feel about it. They could identify the behavior they look for in a listener by saying, "I hope Bill will understand how I feel," or "I want Joan to understand why I am upset."

Speakers may also expect to observe both verbal and nonverbal indications that the listener understands. They may watch for sympathetic looks, eye contact, nods, or even comments that communicate that the listener intimately comprehends the speaker's feelings and thoughts.

The Empathic Listener's Goals

In this helping relationship we gather information, but the process differs from the kind we do in discriminative listening. We wish to understand both the verbal and the nonverbal messages the speaker sends, and also to comprehend the speaker's feelings about it. If we wish to verbalize our goal we might say, "I want to comprehend exactly what Jean is saying about her mother's illness and to understand how she feels about it."

However, we ultimately aim toward not only understanding the message and the feelings about the message, but also toward communicating this understanding to the person seeking help. We must help the speakêr experience being understood. We must add this dimension to our goal. We would then state it thus, "I want to understand Fred, and I want him to know he is being understood," or "I want Bill to realize that I understand how he feels about this."

Carl Rogers, originator of the concept of empathic listening, said, "If I can listen to what he tells me, if I can understand how it seems to him, then I will be releasing potent forces of change within him." We would add one step to Dr. Rogers' injunction, "If I can also let him know that I understand, I will be listening empathically."

Let us look at some strategies that might increase our effectiveness in this helping role.

Some Strategies to Improve Empathic Listening

We can do several things to improve the way we listen empathically to our friends, co-workers, and family. These strategies will not turn us into counselors. They will help us facilitate day-to-day communication when speakers need the help of someone who tries to understand the way they feel.

1. Avoid Judgment. Most of us have a natural tendency to pass judgment on the world around us. We leave a movie, training session, or even a social event making a judgment such as, "I liked that," "That was a waste of time," or "Wasn't that boring?" We certainly recognize the positive impact of weighing evidence and deciding its value when listening to extend our field of knowledge and to evaluate persuasion. However, such evaluation interferes with empathic listening.

Making judgments about what we receive places us outside the message; figuratively, we stand back and look at it. This limits us to considering the content of a message rather than considering how the speaker feels about it. This is precisely what we wish to avoid. We cannot help a speaker experience being understood while we provide the experience of being judged. If we judge, we force speakers to do one of two things. First, we place them in the position of defending and justifying what they said, in which case they are no longer aiming toward their goal. Second, when speakers realize we communicate no empathy they end the conversation.

If our friend, distraught over a new experience, confides, "I can't do anything right for my boss," that friend wants to be understood. We can make judgmental responses such as, "Are you trying to talk to your boss?" "Are you working as hard as you can?" But we make these observations by standing outside and judging the content of the remark. We can respond to the speaker or to ourselves thus, "You are feeling like a failure." This focuses on the speaker's feelings without judgment.

All of us have experienced critical evaluation almost from birth. When we are babies, our mothers evaluate our physical progress by comparing us to the neighbor's baby. In school, our teachers give us report cards that evaluate our progress by comparing us to others in the class. On the job, our superiors evaluate our work by comparing it to what something else has done. Most of us are judged and found wanting during most of our lives. It is no wonder that when speakers find a listener who merely listens and does not judge, they often feel as if they could talk all day. In empathic listening we must, at all costs to our own feelings, avoid making comparisons or passing moral judgments.

2. Give the Speaker Time. We must allow the speaker time to tell the entire story. When people come to us because they want to talk, they want us to allow them to proceed without interruption and arrive at a clearer understanding of their own feelings and perceptions. Impatience is a powerful deterrent to this. When we are short of patience, we want to jump ahead and assume that we know what the speaker means. It is tempting to nod, interrupt, or attempt to finish sentences when we think we know what the speaker is going to say. This is the last thing people groping their way toward an accurate description of their feelings need. Be patient. Even if we think we know, we should wait. Remain quiet.

We suggest, in fact, that empathic listeners limit responses to these three kinds only. First, as the talker proceeds, the listener may employ a series of eloquent and encouraging grunts, "Hmmmm," "Oh," or "I see."

Second, if the talker becomes wild and unreasonable, the listener should restate what has just been said, putting it in the form of a question. We might say, "You really think, then, that all middlemen are dishonest?" or "You believe your mother-in-law is deliberately trying to ruin your marriage?" In no case should we give relief-seeking speakers advice—even when they request it.

Third, if the talker pauses momentarily, we should remain silent, continuing to make eye contact, perhaps nodding to indicate understanding. Silence is an important part of empathic listening. Speakers who are not interrupted by questions can concentrate on sorting out the parts of the message they wish to send. They are not forced to respond to our message, thereby are not forced to diffuse their focus.

Our remaining silent also allows speakers to remain silent. They may need time for quiet thinking. In their own silence, they can probe more deeply into their feelings and thoughts, and perhaps even perceive the truth about their own problems.

Several years ago a colleague discovered the importance of silence in communication. She solved a difficult problem for herself when another used and allowed her to use silence. For months she had tried to ignore her problem by refusing to speak of it. During this time—perhaps coincidentally, perhaps not—she suffered from headaches that did not respond to any of her doctor's prescriptions. One day, after describing her headache to her doctor, he simply sat silent when she stooped talking. After a while she began to enlarge upon her symptoms and, then, her general state of mind. Before she stopped, she had identified and described how she felt about her personal problem. "Suddenly I realized," she said, "I had needed to tell someone how rejected and abandoned I felt. Once I put it into words, I was able to sort out my own feelings toward what I saw as a crushing burden." Coincidentally or not, when her problems became lighter her headaches subsided. Because her doctor had remained silent, he had allowed her to resolve her own problem.

Our need for silence in communication certainly is not new. The ancient Egyptian pharaoh, Ptahhotep, 5,000 years ago, reminded us of the power of silence when he cautioned those around him: "Be silent—this is better than teftef flowers. Speak only if thou knowest that thou canst unravel the difficulty."

3. Focus on the Speaker. The extrinsic nature of emphatic listening suggests that we do it primarily for the benefit of another. Therefore, as we listen, we must remember to focus attention on the speaker no matter how tempting it may be to draw a parallel between his situation and our own life.

Several months ago Ellen, a college student, illustrated just what happens when we draw the focus away from the speaker to ourselves during empathic listening. In recounting the incident she said, "I like Tim, but he never listens." We thought of Tim as an excellent communicator, so we asked her why she felt this way. She said, "I told him that I was thinking of dropping my business major because I was so depressed about accounting, and he just said, 'I know what you mean, I'm thinking of switching to physical education myself.' " In fact, Tim was equally disturbed by serious doubts about his own engineering major. When he made what he thought was a supportive "I understand" remark, he turned the subject back to himself, which made his friend feel abandoned and as if he had not listened.

Truly empathic listeners attempt to set aside thei own worries in order to see from the viewpoint another. Speakers who need to talk through a pro have chosen us to be empathic listeners. The s who does so believes that we are sensitive and capable of accepting trust. At that moment speakers do not care at all about our problems or our point of view. They only want us to accept them and listen.

Karl Menninger described this acceptance by saying, "Listening is a magnetic and strange thing, a creative force. The friends who listen to us are the ones we move toward, and we want to sit in their radius. When we are listened to, it creates us, makes us unfold and expand."

Number of words 2230
See page 409 for questions
Reading time in seconds ________
See page 497 for conversion table

SECTION VI

ON VOCABULARY

Test Your Vocabulary

William Morris

It pays to increase your vocabulary. Where have you heard that before? But before you start, why not find out how much you need to improve? Would you call your vocabulary average, above-average, or below average? Check up on yourself. Work through this article and test.

If you think you have a pretty good vocabulary, you feel pleased with yourself. You may keep this pride hidden, of course, but it is there all the same. If, however, you are a little uncertain of your word prowess—as most of us are—you may be one of the reasons why vocabulary-building books sell so well, even though they aren't much help.

The basic reason for this interest in words is the big American urge for self-improvement. We all admire the person who has a ready command of words. We instinctively feel that to know more words ourselves would increase our self-confidence and prestige. We also hear that people who rise to the top usually are those who express their ideas easily and accurately, and we see a correlation between the size of vocabulary and the size of pay check.

Naturally we want all these good things. If words will give them to us, let's learn more.

How many words do you know, and how many ought you to know?

Accompanying this article is a quiz which will answer the first part of that question. The test was devised exclusively for *Changing Times* by William Morris, editor-in-chief of Grosset & Dunlap, New York book publishing firm, and author of a syndicated column on words.

If you score high, you can give yourself a pat on the back. If you don't, don't worry too much. Vocabularies can be improved, as you will see.

Nobody knows exactly how many words there are in the English language, but the figure 750,000 is widely accepted. A foreigner probably could get along here on about 350, and Basic English—an English for international use—depends on only 850.

But all of us use many times that number. A child of eight, for example, knows about 3,600 words and a child of fourteen, about 9,000. Men and women with little formal education probably recognize between 9,000 and 10,000 words.

Shakespeare used some 24,000 different words in his plays and undoubtedly knew many more than that. The total recognition vocabulary for the adult high school graduate has been placed as high as 25,000 words. The literate college graduate who reads a few books a year knows 35,000 or more.

How do you go about increasing your fund of words? The word-building books have it all figured out. They offer word-a-day plans, 30-day plans, or even lists of 5,000 or so supposedly high-powered words which, if learned, will give you a vocabulary second to none.

The trouble with these plans is that they don't work. You buy a book and study it faithfully—15 or 30 minutes a day, whatever is called for. But the words don't stick. The system is too artificial.

Crossword puzzles are equally useless. They are concerned too much with freak words. Magazine and newspaper word columns are more helpful, and so is the plan of writing down unfamiliar words when you come across them and looking them up in a good dictionary.

But the sure way to increase your vocabulary—and, say the experts, the only real, workable way—is to read.

Vocabulary building is a process of mental absorption. You soak up words automatically if you see or hear them frequently enough. Their meaning becomes clear through context, and your mind retains them.

The next question is what to read. Here is where most articles on vocabulary building stop short. But despite the fact that reading is largely a matter of personal preference, there is some good advice to be had.

If you happen to have read *A Tree Grows in Brooklyn*, you may recall that Katie's mother advised Katie to read Shakespeare and the King James Version of the Bible if she wanted to raise herself by her bootstraps.

That's still good advice. You couldn't get better. Only you've heard this before.

Here is some other reading you can do. Start on the

classics. Yes, it will take a little more effort than reading the sports or women's pages. But it is not as formidable as you may think, and if you are really serious about building up your vocabulary, this is the best way to do it.

Take Washington Irving, the first great American stylist. You probably read *The Sketch Book* in high school. But get it out and read it again. Not just *Rip Van Winkle* and *The Legend of Sleepy Hollow*. Read the essays too.

In the novel, the possibilities are, of course, endless. Read *Treasure Island* again, or anything by Stevenson. Or perhaps Thomas Hardy's *Return of the Native*, Henry James's *Turn of the Screw*, Conrad's *Lord Jim*, Thackeray's *Vanity Fair*, Trollope's *Barchester Towers*, Emily Brontë's *Wuthering Heights*, George Eliot's *Adam Bede*.

Then go into other fields—history, biography, political science. Try Parkman's *The Oregon Trail*; Strachey's *Queen Victoria*; *The Federalist*; or H. G. Wells's *Outline of History*.

All these books are readily available. Your library has them. Your bookstore has them. Many can be had in paper-bound editions.

Does it all sound too highfalutin? It isn't really. If you had thought of spending 30 minutes a day studying words, try using the 30 minutes to read books like these instead. Their authors had a fine command of the English language, and some of it is bound to rub off on you.

[Now turn to page 000 and check your comprehension of this selection before going ahead with the test which follows.]

Number of words 890
See page 413 for questions
Reading time in seconds ________
See page 498 for conversion table

Self-Scoring Vocabulary Test*

This is really tough, no fooling. You probably have never seen a lot of these words. The test has to be made hard in order to accommodate the few individuals who are whizzes with words. So don't get discouraged—even people with sizable vocabularies may miss half the words.

Another thing: Speed does not count, so take your time. But no peeking into the dictionary, or at the answer key on p. 000.

Directions for Section I and II: Before each word in column A write the letter of the word from column B that most nearly matches it in meaning. You will find it helpful to strike out words in column B as you use their letters in column A.

SECTION I

A		B	
1.	_____*amenable*	a.	amnesty
2.	_____*bizarre*	b.	confident
3.	_____*captious*	c.	faultfinding
4.	_____*commensurate*	d.	grotesque
5.	_____*compassionate*	e.	incipient
6.	_____*contumacious*	f.	inflexible
7.	_____*guileless*	g.	inherent
8.	_____*immanent*	h.	irresolute
9.	_____*inane*	i.	lively
10.	_____*incessant*	j.	insipid
11.	_____*inchoate*	k.	perverse
12.	_____*jejune*	l.	prank
13.	_____*lachrymose*	m.	proportionate
14.	_____*monkeyshine*	n.	risky
15.	_____*obdurate*	o.	showy
16.	_____*ostentatious*	p.	sincere
17.	_____*palpable*	q.	sympathetic
18.	_____*pardon*	r.	tangible
19.	_____*precarious*	s.	tearful
20.	_____*renegade*	t.	toady
21.	_____*salubrious*	u.	tractable
22.	_____*sanguine*	v.	turncoat
23.	_____*sprightly*	w.	uninterrupted
24.	_____*sycophant*	x.	vacuous
25.	_____*vacillating*	y.	wholesome

SECTION II

1.	_____*abrogate*	a.	annihilate
2.	_____*aggravate*	b.	annul
3.	_____*ameliorate*	c.	antiquated
4.	_____*augur*	d.	boldness
5.	_____*contravene*	e.	cunning
6.	_____*crotchety*	f.	dexterous
7.	_____*dawdling*	g.	elicit
8.	_____*deft*	h.	enervated
9.	_____*diminutive*	i.	enthusiastic
10.	_____*ebullient*	j.	exact
11.	_____*educe*	k.	favorable

*Prepared especially for *Changing Times* Magazine by William Morris, noted editor and lexicographer.

12. _____*effrontery*
13. _____*extirpate*
14. _____*haphazard*
15. _____*irascible*
16. _____*laconic*
17. _____*naive*
18. _____*obdurate*
19. _____*precise*
20. _____*propitious*
21. _____*senile*
22. _____*shipshape*
23. _____*slovenly*
24. _____*spiritless*
25. _____*wily*

l. foretell
m. intensify
n. laggard
o. minute
p. mitigate
q. mulish
r. odd
s. random
t. splenetic
u. verse
v. tidy
w. unkempt
x. unsophisticated
y. violate

SECTION III

Check the lettered word or phrase nearest in meaning to the numbered words below.

1. *banal* (a) vivid; (b) imaginative; (c) fraternal; (d) commonplace.
2. *chicanery* (a) poultry; (b) admiration; (c) petty trickery; (d) stubborn pride.
3. *diffident* (a) unusual; (b) unconfident; (c) various; (d) routine.
4. *quixotic* (a) swift; (b) insane; (c) practical; (d) romantically idealistic.
5. *potable* (a) drinkable; (b) transportable; (c) elementary; (d) poisonous.
6. *mundane* (a) pecuniary; (b) worldly; (c) municipal; (d) weekly.
7. *necropolis* (a) a large city; (b) cemetery; (c) lovers' lane; (d) site of a guillotine.
8. *didactic* (a) poetic; (b) entertaining; (c) instructive; (d) pertaining to diets.
9. *truculent* (a) portable; (b) amiable; (c) stiffly formal; (d) fiercely resentful.
10. *opulent* (a) wealthy; (b) industrious; (c) overweight; (d) impoverished.
11. *effulgent* (a) filling to overflowing; (b) feeding until corpulent; (c) pouring out a stream of radiant light; (d) retiring in nature.
12. *euphony* (a) repetitious sound; (b) musical variation; (c) characteristic of organization; (d) sweet sound.
13. *prescience* (a) preliminary investigation; (b) a phase of science; (c) crystal clear; (d) foresight or knowledge of the future.
14. *postulate* (a) protest; (b) reply to a statement; (c) a musical phrase; (d) proposition taken for granted.
15. *ephemeral* (a) effeminate; (b) lasting; (c) interesting; (d) short-lived.
16. *persiflage* (a) light raillery; (b) disguise; (c) anger; (d) thermal.
17. *desultory* (a) dreary; (b) designing; (c) aimless; (d) lonely.
18. *profligate* (a) set fire to; (b) recklessly extravagant; (c) humdrum; (d) hateful.
19. *blatant* (a) dark; (b) bland; (c) flattering; (d) noisy.
20. *foment* (a) extinguish; (b) smooth out; (c) nurse to life; (d) make bubblelike.
21. *soporific* (a) dreamy; (b) sleep-inducing; (c) of exceptional swiftness; (d) viscous.
22. *collate* (a) to eat a meal; (b) gather and compare; (c) clot; (d) add.
23. *uxorious* (a) slavishly devoted to one's wife; (b) urgent; (c) usurping; (d) laborious.
24. *pariah* (a) father; (b) an outcast; (c) an ancient; (d) a foreigner.
25. *vestige* (a) power of office given to officials; (b) a trace of something no longer existent; (c) early sign of sprouting seeds; (d) evidence of destruction.
26. *accolade* (a) an award or decoration; (b) a verdict handed down by courts; (c) decision rendered by international court; (d) a special dispensation.
27. *redolent* (a) harsh in scent; (b) pleasingly fragrant; (c) overflowing; (d) repetitious in nature.
28. *anomalous* (a) similar to another; (b) routine and regular; (c) diminutive; (d) out of the ordinary.
29. *hebdomadal* (a) occurring at intervals of seven days; (b) varying at long intervals; (c) any idolatrous worship; (d) a seasonal variation.
30. *insensate* (a) undeveloped; (b) small in size; (c) with high sensory reaction; (d) without sensation.
31. *calumny* (a) catastrophic action; (b) false accusation; (c) just accusation before a court; (d) a settling of guilt.

32. *porcine* (a) characteristically hoggish in appearance; (b) round-bodied and smooth; (c) high-handed; (d) lacking energy.
33. *tautology* (a) to pull something taut or tight; (b) a kind of philosophy; (c) terseness in diction; (d) needless repetition of meaning in other words.
34. *lucubration* (a) system of oiling machinery; (b) state of being slippery; (c) laborious study; (d) process of cultivating land.
35. *enucleate* (a) to tie things together; (b) to raze a structure; (c) to peel out of a shell; (d) to break something.
36. *verisimilar* (a) closely resembling; (b) related mathematically; (c) contrary to reality; (d) appearing to be true.
37. *depurate* (a) to appoint a deputy; (b) to free of impurities; (c) to delegate authority; (d) to incorporate a group.
38. *lustrate* (a) to make pure by offerings; (b) to point out something; (c) to show by illustration; (d) to pay homage.
39. *cozenage* (a) study of family relations; (b) a type of humorous play; (c) organized play; (d) art or practice of fraud.
40. *polyandry* (a) a kind of mischievous ghost; (b) having more than one husband; (c) having more than one wife; (d) having many names.
41. *ominous* (a) thunderous or noisy; (b) inauspicious; (c) vacillating in action; (d) definitely true.
42. *hegemony* (a) leadership in government; (b) marriage between reigning families; (c) line of succesion; (d) organization of political adherents.
43. *flatulent* (a) explosive; (b) without order or plan; (c) pretentious; (d) flat.
44. *pother* (a) to confuse; (b) to be contrary; (c) to plan; (d) to organize.
45. *fecund* (a) sourish; (b) hateful; (c) miserly; (d) prolific.
46. *apostatize* (a) to proclaim a saint; (b) to request; (c) to renounce one's faith; (d) to petition.
47. *cortege* (a) a procession; (b) a jury for a high court; (c) flowers worn on a dress; (d) a funeral.
48. *eleemosynary* (a) electing by popular vote; (b) receiving alms or favors; (c) sanguine in disposition; (d) apathetic in attitude.
49. *pertinacious* (a) loosely held; (b) with a tendency to give up; (c) proceeding on a straight line; (d) unyielding.
50. *tumid* (a) swollen; (b) dampish; (c) gigantic; (d) characterized by tumult.

[Now turn to the key on page 414 and check your answers.]

Selection 67

Words That Laugh and Cry

Charles A. Dana

Mark Twain sensed the physical power of words when he wrote: "A powerful agent is the right word." Whenever we come upon one of those intensely right words in a book or a newspaper, the resulting effect is physical as well as spiritual and electrically prompt.

Did it ever strike you that there was anything queer about the capacity of written words to absorb and convey feelings? Taken separately they are mere symbols with no more feeling to them than so many bricks, but string them along in a row under certain mysterious conditions and you find yourself laughing or crying as your eye runs over them. That words should convey mere ideas is not so remarkable. "The boy is fat," "the cat has nine tails," are statements that seem obviously enough within the power of written language. But it is different with feelings. They are no more visible in the symbols that hold them than electricity is visible on the wire; and yet there they are, always ready to respond when the right test is applied by the right person. That spoken words, charged with human tones and lighted by human eyes, should carry feelings, is not so astonishing. The magnetic sympathy of the orator one understands; he might affect his audience, possibly, if he spoke in a language they did not know. But written words: How can they do it! Suppose, for example, that you possess remarkable facility in grouping language, and that you have strong feelings upon some subject, which finally you determine to commit to paper. Your pen runs along, the words present themselves, or are dragged out, and fall into their places. You are a good deal moved; here you chuckle to yourself, and half a dozen lines farther down a lump comes into your throat, and perhaps you have to wipe your eyes. You finish, and the copy goes to the printer. When it gets into print the reader sees it. His eye runs along the lines and down the page until it comes to the place where you chuckled as you wrote; then he smiles, and six lines below he has to swallow several times and snuffle and wink to restrain an exhibition of weakness. And then some one else comes along who has no feelings, and swaps the words about a little, and twists the sentences; and behold the spell is gone, and you have left a parcel of written language duly charged with facts, but without a single feeling.

No one can juggle with words with any degree of success without getting a vast respect for their independent ability. They will catch the best idea a man ever had as it flashes through his brain, and hold on to it, to surprise him with it long after, and make him wonder that he was ever man enough to have such an idea. And often they will catch an idea on its way from the brain to the pen point, turn, twist, and improve on it as the eye winks, and in an instant there they are, strung hand in hand across the page, and grinning back at the writer: "This is our idea, old man; not yours!"

As for poetry, every word that expects to earn its salt in poetry should have a head and a pair of legs of its own, to go and find its place, carrying another word, if necessary, on its back. The most that should be expected of any competent poet in regular practice is to serve a general summons and notice of action on the language. If the words won't do the rest for him, it indicates that he is out of sympathy with his tools.

But you don't find feelings in written words unless there were feelings in the man who used them. With all their apparent independence they seem to be little vessels that hold in some puzzling fashion exactly what is put into them. You can put tears into them, as though they were so many little buckets; and you can hang smiles along them, like Monday's clothes on the line, or you can starch them with facts and stand them up like a picket fence; but you won't get the tears out unless you first put them in. Art won't put them there. It is like the faculty of getting the quality of interest into pictures. If the quality exists in the artist's mind, he is likely to find means to get it into his pictures, but if it isn't in the man no technical skill will supply it. So, if the feelings are in the writer and he knows his business, they will get into the words; but they must be in him first. It isn't the way the words are strung together that makes Lincoln's Gettysburg speech immortal, but the feelings that were in the man. But how do such little, plain words manage to keep their grip on such feelings? That is the miracle.

Number of words 800
See page 415 for questions
Reading time in seconds ________
See page 498 for conversion table

SELECTION 68

How to Improve Your Vocabulary

Edgar Dale

It's not enough just to recognize the importance of word power. The next step is much more important. Exactly how do you improve your vocabulary? In this selection you'll find seven specific suggestions. Put them to immediate use and start enjoying the added confidence that follows.

The best readers usually have the best vocabularies. No really good reader has a poor one. A good reader is word-conscious, word-sensitive; he knows that words are an excellent way to share ideas and feelings. So one way to improve our reading is to improve our vocabulary, and vice versa.

What is an improved vocabulary? Certainly it is larger and broader. But also it has greater depth and precision. What can we do to develop a richer vocabulary?

Let's look first at the difference in size between an inadequate, poverty-stricken vocabulary and the rich vocabulary of an able, mature reader. About how many words are known by the average eight-grader, the high-school graduate, the college graduate? How many does the ablest reader know?

There are about 600,000 words in a big, unabridged dictionary such as *Funk and Wagnalls New College Standard* or *Webster's New International. Webster's New Collegiate Dictionary* has more than 125,000 entries, and the 896-page *Thorndike-Barnhart Comprehensive Desk Dictionary* includes over 80,000.

The big, unabridged dictionaries, however, contain many forms of the same word, as well as many rare and obsolete words, and names of thousands of places, persons, rivers, and towns. So I find it more useful to think in terms of the 80,000-word Thorndike-Barnhart dictionary.

The average eighth-grader knows at least 10,000 of these words, the average high-school graduate about 15,000, and the average college graduate not fewer than 20,000. But even college graduates have trouble with such words as *adumbrate*, *attenuate*, *avuncular*, *deprecate*, *egregious*, *germane*, *ingenuous*, *jejune*, *plethora*, *temerity*, *unconscionable*, *unctuous*. An able reader increases his vocabulary well beyond the college graduate's 20,000 words.

The best way to improve your vocabulary is through firsthand experiences. If you have had experience in cooking, you know such words as *dredge*, *sear*, *draw*, *marinate*, *parboil*, *sauté*, *braise*, *frizzle*, *coddle*. A sports fan will know baseball terms, such as *fungo*, *Texas leaguer*, *infield fly*. You don't usually learn such vocabularies by reading books or magazines. But cooks and sports fans do read in these fields and thereby increase the range and depth of their vocabularies.

So a first rule in improving your vocabulary is to improve the range and depth of your experiences. Visits to museums, art exhibits, the legislature, or Congress bring increased vocabulary. So do working with the Community Chest, a nature hike, political activity, or a visit to the seashore. Think of the terms that sailing may bring into your active vocabulary: *scupper*, *topsail*, *dinghy*, *starboard*, *luff*.

A second suggestion is to work at your vocabulary a little every day. You can do this in several ways. Underline in pencil the hard words you run across in magazines, books, or newspapers. You need not even look them up. Just fix your attention on them, guess their meaning, and go right ahead with your reading. The next time you see one of these words, test your previous guess about its meaning. Maybe your guess fits now, and maybe it doesn't. Check it with your desk dictionary. You might also note its origin and get an additional memory hook on which to hang this word. If you check the pronunciation and say the word aloud, you get another boost in remembering it. You can also check on words you may mispronounce, such as *acclimate*, *archipelago*, *niche*, *orgy*, *schism*, *succinct*.

Third, you can sharply improve your vocabulary by reading more. You will see the hard words more often and in a variety of contexts. Of the many ways to increase your vocabulary by indirect experience, reading is the best.

Fourth, start using some of your "new" words in ordinary conversation.

Fifth, read aloud. Years ago, when I started to read "Penrod and Sam" to a seventh-grade class, I discovered that my speaking vocabulary was way behind my reading vocabulary. I did not know how to pronounce such words as *conversant*, *dolorous*, *primordial*, *flaccid*, *solaced*.

Sixth, you can increase your word power by becoming conscious of key roots and important suffixes and prefixes. A root such as *folium*, meaning *leaf*, gives us *foil*, *cinquefoil*, *foliaceous*, *foliage*, *foliate*, *folio*, *portfolio*, *trefoil*.

Do you know the prefixes *crypto-*, *hyper-*, *hypo-*, *neo-?* They appear in words like *cryptocommunist*, *cryptograph*, *hyperbole*, *hypertension*, *hypertrophy*, *hypochondriac*, *neoclassic*, *neologism*, *neophyte*.

A single root such as the Greek *nym*, meaning name, yields *antonym*, *homonym*, *acronym*, *pseudonym*, *synonym*, *anonymous*. *Nom*, from the Latin *nomen*, also meaning name, gives us *nominate*, *nominative*, *nomination*, *denomination*, *nomenclature*, *nominee*.

A seventh way to improve your vocabulary is to develop an interest in the origins of words. Thus you learn that a *nightmare* is not a night horse but an evil spirit formerly supposed to cause bad dreams. A *nasturtium* is a nose twister. *Recalcitrant* means kicking back. *Excoriate* means to take the hide off. The *devil* in "between the devil and the deep blue sea" is a part of a boat.

Finally, it will help if you become conscious of the four stages by which vocabulary grows.

In the first stage, you see a word and are certain you have never seen it before. You never saw *shug* and *bittles*, hence don't know them. They are not words at all; I just made them up.

But you probably have seen words like *lethargic*, *lissome*, *serendipity*. If so, you may be in the second stage and may say, "I've seen these before, but I haven't any notion what they mean."

In the third stage, you are able to place the word in a broad classification. You may say, "I know that *lethargic* is an unfavorable word, that *lissome* and *serendipity* are attractive, favorable words, but I don't know exactly what they mean."

You are in the final stage when you know the word accurately.

Many of us have a large number of words in stage three, the twilight zone between words being known and yet not known. Are some of the following words in your twilight zone: *lares and penates*, *abscond*, *garrulous*, *dolorous*, *ingenuous*, *friable*, *tedium*, *savant*, *sedulous*, *sine qua non*?

Also, you may move a word toward a more scientific definition. You may have used *respiration* as a synonym for breathing; later you may learn it is the name for the body's process of absorbing oxygen and giving off carbon dioxide and water. A child may think of a *whale* as a fish, but the adult thinks of it as a mammal that nurses its young. A *spider* is not an insect. A *star* is not a planet. Botanically, a *tomato* is a fruit.

And there is precision of vocabulary—Wordsworth's "choice word and measured phrase." A tree isn't just a tree; it is a *cryptomeria*, a *locust*, a *white pine*, a *yellow poplar*. The ground may be *moist*, *sodden*, *arid*, or *parched*. Is a person *sulky*, *petulant*, or perhaps *bilious*? Why not learn the difference between a *jackanapes* and a *jackal*, a *winch* and a *wench*, *pretentious* and *portentous*? The educated person is one who sees life with increasingly finer discriminations. And certainly this applies to his discrimination about the words he uses in speech and recognizes in reading.

Sometimes we may say, "Why should I study words before I need to use them? If I meet them in my reading, I'll look them up." But, curiously, a brief acquaintance with a word may cause us to see it later. Haven't you ever looked up an unusual or rare word and then suddenly found it in later reading?

Once, to illustrate an article, I chose four words from a list—*alb*, *valerian*, *periwinkle*, and *fichu*. I didn't know what they meant, but within three months I had "accidentally" seen and learned all of them. *Alb* appeared on a label in an exhibit of religious garments, *fichu* on a label describing the neckerchief worn by a young women in a painting. I saw *valerian* in a display at the old country drugstore in the Farmers' Museum in Cooperstown, New York. And the color *periwinkle* blue turned up in the film *Artists and Models*.

I can draw two conclusions. First, just looking carefully at an unknown word and noting its spelling, as I suggested earlier, may cause us to be ready to see it later. And second, exhibits, galleries, and museums are good places to improve our vocabularies. Just looking sharply at an unknown word can thus be the cause of further experience as well as a result. A chance acquaintance with words sometimes brings them into our vocabulary. We become restless when we don't know what a *pied piper* is, the difference between a *monogram* and a *monograph*, between a *connoisseur* and a *diletante*, between *ingenious* and *ingenuous*.

The best way of all to improve your vocabulary is to get fun out of words. I enjoy collecting interesting misuses and mispronunciations, such as: "He stepped on the exhilarator." "We are studying jubilant delinquency." "I don't deserve all this oolagoozing." "I don't like to sing solo; I like to sing abreast." "Minch pie." "My boy can't come to school. He has indolent fever."

If we accept the late John Erskine's theory that we have a moral obligation to be intelligent, we should improve our vocabularies. Then, we can read magazines and books that wake us up mentally. We can "argue" with the authors. We can discuss what we have read, improve our dinner-table conversation, be more interesting people.

Your vocabulary gives you away. It may suggest that you are a person with a rich and varied experience, for it tells where you have been, what you have read, talked about, reflected upon. And it tells how far you have traveled along the road to intellectual maturity and discriminating living.

Number of words 1600
See page 419 for questions
Reading time in seconds ________
See page 498 for conversion table

SELECTION 69

In Defense of Gender

Cyra McFadden

In the English language we're blessed with three genders—masculine, feminine, and neuter. And that's where we have the problem of desexing English. He/She/It must not feel slighted, of course. Take a closer look at the desexing problem.

So pervasive is the neutering of the English language on the progressive West Coast, we no longer have people here, only persons: male persons and female persons, chairpersons and doorpersons, waitpersons, mailpersons—who may be either male or female mailpersons—and refuse-collection persons. In the classified ads, working mothers seek childcare persons, though one wonders how many men (archaic for "male person") take care of child persons as a full-time occupation. One such ad, fusing nonsexist language and the most popular word in the California growth movement, solicits a "nurtureperson."

Dear gents and ladies, as I might have addressed you in less troubled times, this female person knows firsthand the reasons for scourging sexist bias from the language. God knows what damage was done me, at 15, when I worked in my first job—as what is now known as a newspaper copyperson—and came running to the voices of men barking, "Boy!"

No aspirant to the job of refuse-collection person myself, I nonetheless take off my hat (a little feathered number, with a veil) to those of my own sex who may want both the job and a genderless title with it. I argue only that there must be a better way, and I wish person or persons unknown would come up with one.

Defend it on any grounds you choose; the neutering of spoken and written English, with its attendant self-consciousness, remains ludicrous. In print, those "person" suffixes and "he/she's" jump out from the page, as distracting as a cloud of gnats, demanding that the reader note the writer's virtue. "Look what a nonsexist writer person I am, avoiding the use of masculine forms for the generic."

Spoken, they leave conversation fit only for the Coneheads on "Saturday Night Live." "They have a daily special," a woman at the next table told her male companion in Perry's, a San Francisco restaurant. "Ask your waitperson." In a Steig cartoon, the words would have marched from her mouth in the form of a computer printout.

In Berkeley, Calif., the church to which a friend

belongs is busy stripping its liturgy of sexist references. "They've gone berserk," she writes, citing a reading from the pulpit of a verse from I Corinthians. Neutered, the once glorious passage becomes "Though I speak with the tongues of persons and of angels . . ." So much for sounding brass and tinkling cymbals.

The parson person of the same church is not referring to God as "He/She" and changing all references accordingly—no easy undertaking if he intends to be consistent. In the following, the first pronoun would remain because at this primitive stage of human evolution, male persons do not give birth to babies: "And she brought forth her firstborn son/daughter, and wrapped him/her in swaddling clothes, and laid him/her in a manger; because there was no room for them in the inn. . . ."

As the after-dinner speaker at a recent professional conference, I heard a text replete with "he/she's" and "his/her's" read aloud for the first time. The hapless program female chairperson stuck with the job chose to render these orally as "he-slash-she" and "his-slash-her," turning the following day's schedule for conference participants into what sounded like a replay of the Manson killings.

Redress may be due those of us who, though female, have answered to masculine referents all these years, but slashing is not the answer; violence never is. Perhaps we could right matters by using feminine forms as the generic for a few centuries, or simply agree on a per-woman lump-sum payment.

Still, we would be left with the problem of referring, without bias, to transpersons. These are not bus drivers or Amtrak conductors but persons in transit from one gender to the other—or so I interpret a fund-drive appeal asking me to defend their civil rights, along with those of female and male homosexuals.

Without wishing to step on anyone's civil rights, I hope transpersons are not the next politically significant pressure group. If they are, count on it, they will soon want their own pronouns.

In the tradition of the West, meanwhile, feminists out here wrestle the language to the ground, plant a foot on its neck and remove its masculine appendages. Take the local art critic Beverly Terwoman.

She is married to a man surnamed Terman. She writes under "Terwoman," presumably in the spirit of *vive la différence*. As a letter to the editor of the paper for which she writes noted, however, "Terwoman" is not ideologically pure. It still contains "man," a syllable reeking of all that is piggy and hairy-chested.

Why not Beverly Terperson? Or better, since "Terperson" contains "son," "Terdaughter"? Or a final refinement, Beverly Ter?

Beverly Terwoman did not dignify this sexist assault with a reply. The writer of the letter was a male person, after all, probably the kind who leaves his smelly sweat socks scattered around the bedroom floor.

No one wins these battles anyway. In another letter to the same local weekly, J. Seibert, female, lets fire at the printing of an interview with Phyllis Schlafly. Not only was the piece "an offense to everything that Marin County stands for," but "it is even more amusing that your interview was conducted by a male."

"This indicates your obvious assumption that men understand women's issues better than women since men are obviously more intelligent (as no doubt Phyllis would agree)."

A sigh suffuses the editor's note that follows: "The author of the article, Sydney Weisman, is a female."

So the war of the pronouns and suffixes rages, taking no prisoners except writers. Neuter your prose with all those clanking "he/she's," and no one will read you except Alan Alda. Use masculine forms as the generic, and you have joined the ranks of the oppressor. None of this does much to encourage friendly relations between persons, transpersons or—if there are any left—people.

I also have little patience with the hyphenated names more and more California female persons adopt when they marry, in the interests of retaining their own personhood. These accomplish their intention of declaring the husband separate but equal. They are hell on those of us who have trouble remembering one name, much less two. They defeat answering machines, which can't handle "Please call Gwendolyn Grunt-Messerschmidt." And in this culture, they retain overtones of false gentility.

Two surnames, to me, still bring to mind the female writers of bad romances and Julia Ward Howe.

It's a mug's game, friends, this neutering of a language already fat, bland and lethargic, and it's time we decide not to play it. This female person is currently writing a book about rodeo. I'll be dragged behind a saddle bronc before I will neuter the text with "cowpersons."

Number of words 1125
See page 421 for questions
Reading time in seconds ________
See page 498 for conversion table

My Alma Mater

Malcolm X

Have you ever observed, personally, a man who commanded total respect with his words? Malcolm X once did. That started him on a word-building program without parallel. The heart of his program was the dictionary. Here's what he did with it.

The first man I met in prison who made any positive impression on me whatever was a fellow inmate, "Bimbi." I met him in 1947, at Charlestown. He was a light, kind of red-complexioned Negro, as I was; about my height, and he had freckles. Bimbi, an old-time burglar, had been in many prisons. In the license plate shop where our gang worked, he operated the machine that stamped out the numbers. I was along the conveyor belt where the numbers were painted.

Bimbi was the first Negro convict I'd known who didn't respond to "What'cha know, Daddy?" Often, after we had done our day's license plate quota, we would sit around, perhaps fifteen of us, and listen to Bimbi. Normally, white prisoners wouldn't think of listening to Negro prisoners' opinions on anything, but guards, even, would wander over close to hear Bimbi on any subject.

He would have a cluster of people riveted, often on odd subjects you never would think of. He would prove to us, dipping into the science of human behavior, that the only difference between us and outside people was that we had been caught. He liked to talk about historical events and figures. When he talked about the history of Concord, where I was to be transferred later, you would have thought he was hired by the Chamber of Commerce, and I wasn't the first inmate who had never heard of Thoreau until Bimbi expounded upon him. Bimbi was known as the library's best customer. What fascinated me with him most of all was that he was the first man I had ever seen command total respect . . . with his words.

Bimbi seldom said much to me; he was gruff to individuals, but I sensed he liked me. What made me seek his friendship was when I heard him discuss religion. I considered myself beyond atheism—I was Satan. But Bimbi put the atheist philosophy in a framework, so to speak. That ended my vicious cursing attacks. My approach sounded so weak alongside his, and he never used a foul word.

Out of the blue one day, Bimbi told me flatly, as was his way, that I had some brains, if I'd use them. I had wanted his friendship, not that kind of advice. I might have cursed another convict, but nobody cursed Bimbi. He told me I should take advantage of the prison correspondence courses and the library.

When I finished the eighth grade back in Mason, Michigan, that was the last time I'd thought of studying anything that didn't have some hustle purpose. And the streets had erased everything I'd ever learned in school; I didn't know a verb from a house. . . .

Many who today hear me somewhere in person, or on television, or those who read something I've said, will think I went to school far beyond the eighth grade. This impression is due entirely to my prison studies.

It had really begun back in the Charlestown Prison, when Bimbi first made me feel envy of his stock of knowledge. Bimbi had always taken charge of any conversation he was in, and I had tried to emulate him. But every book I picked up had few sentences which didn't contain anywhere from one to nearly all of the words that might as well have been in Chinese. When I just skipped those words, of course, I really ended up with little idea of what the book said. So I had come to the Norfolk Prison Colony still going through only book-reading motions. Pretty soon, I would have quit even these motions, unless I had received the motivation that I did.

I saw that the best thing I could do was get hold of a dictionary—to study, to learn some words. I was lucky enough to reason also that I should try to improve my penmanship. It was sad. I couldn't even write in a straight line. It was both ideas together that moved me to request a dictionary along with some tablets and pencils from the Norfolk Prison Colony school.

I spent two days just riffling uncertainly through the dictionary's pages. I'd never realized so many words existed! I didn't know which words I needed to learn.

Finally, to start some kind of action, I began copying.

In my slow, painstaking, ragged handwriting, I copied into my tablet everything printed on that first page, down to the punctuation marks.

I believe it took me a day. Then, aloud, I read back, to myself, everything I'd written on the tablet. Over and over, aloud, to myself, I read my own handwriting.

I woke up the next morning, thinking about those words—immensely proud to realize that not only had I written so much at one time, but I'd written words that I never knew were in the world. Moreover, with a little effort, I also could remember what many of these words meant. I reviewed the words whose meanings I didn't remember. Funny thing, from the dictionary first page right now, that "aardvark" springs to my mind. The dictionary had a picture of it, a long-tailed, long-eared, burrowing African mammal, which lives off termites caught by sticking out its tongue as an anteater does for ants.

I was so fascinated that I went on—I copied the dictionary's next page. And the same experience came when I studied that. With every succeeding page, I also learned of people and places and events from history. Actually the dictionary is like a miniature encyclopedia. Finally the dictionary's A section had filled a whole tablet—and I went on into the B's. That was the way I started copying what eventually became the entire dictionary. It went a lot faster after so much practice helped me to pick up handwriting speed. Between what I wrote in my tablet, and writing letters, during the rest of my time in prison I would guess I wrote a million words.

I suppose it was inevitable that as my word-base broadened, I could for the first time pick up a book and read and now begin to understand what the book was saying. Anyone who has read a great deal can imagine the new world that opened. Let me tell you something; from then until I left that prison, in every free moment I had, if I was not reading in the library, I was reading on my bunk. You couldn't have gotten me out of books with a wedge. Between Mr. Muhammad's teachings, my correspondence, my visitors—usually Ella and Reginald—and my reading of books, months passed without my even thinking about being imprisoned. In fact, up to then, I never had been so truly free in my life. . . .

As you can imagine, especially in a prison where there was heavy emphasis on rehabilitation, an inmate was smiled upon if he demonstrated an unusually intense interest in books. There was a sizable number of well-read inmates, especially the popular debaters. Some were said by many to be practically walking encyclopedias. They were almost celebrities. No university would ask any student to devour literature as I did when this new world opened to me, of being able to read and *understand*.

I read more in my room than in the library itself. An inmate who was known to read a lot could check out more than the permitted maximum number of books. I preferred reading in the total isolation of my own room.

When I had progressed to really serious reading, every night at about ten P.M. I would be outraged with the "lights out." It always seemed to catch me right in the middle of something engrossing.

Fortunately, right outside my door was a corridor light that cast a glow into my room. The glow was enough to read by, once my eyes adjusted to it. So when "lights out" came, I would sit on the floor where I could continue reading in that glow.

At one-hour intervals the night guards paced past every room. Each time I heard the approaching foot-steps, I jumped into bed and feigned sleep. And as soon as the guard passed, I got back out of bed onto the floor area of that light-glow, where I would read for another fifty-eight minutes—until the guard approached again. That went on until three or four every morning. Three or four hours of sleep a night was enough for me. Often in the years in the streets I had slept less than that.

I have often reflected upon the new vistas that reading opened to me. I knew right there in prison that reading had changed forever the course of my life. As I see it today, the ability to read awoke inside me some long dormant craving to be mentally alive. I certainly wasn't seeking any degree, the way a college confers a status symbol upon its students. My homemade education gave me, with every additional book that I read, a little bit more sensitivity to the deafness, dumbness, and blindness that was afflicting the black race in America. Not long ago, an English writer telephoned me from London, asking questions. One was, "What's your alma mater?" I told him, "Books." You will never catch me with a free fifteen minutes in which I'm not studying something I feel might be able to help the black man. . . .

Every time I catch a plane, I have with me a book that I want to read—and that's a lot of books these days. If I weren't out here every day battling the white man, I could spend the rest of my life reading, just satisfying my curiosity—because you can hardly mention anything I'm not curious about. I don't think anybody ever got more out of going to prison than I did. In fact, prison enabled me to study far more intensively than I would have if my life had gone differently and I had attended some college. I imagine that one of the biggest troubles with colleges is there are too many distractions, too much panty-raiding, fraternities, and boola-boola and all of that. Where else but in prison could I have attacked my ignorance by being able to study intensely sometimes as much as fifteen hours a day?

Number of words 1720
See page 425 for questions
Reading time in seconds ________
See page 498 for conversion table

SELECTION 71

Two Words to Avoid, Two to Remember

Arthur Gordon

Back near the turn of the century, French psychotherapist Emile Coué devised a system of autosuggestion, which he brought to America. To start the day his way, you say three times, "Every day in every way I'm getting better and better." It's the verse from the Bible all over again: "As a man thinketh in his heart, so is he." Here's still another example to apply.

Nothing in life is more exciting and rewarding than the sudden flash of insight that leaves you a changed person—not only changed, but changed for the better. Such moments are rare, certainly, but they come to all of us. Sometimes from a book, a sermon, a line of poetry. Sometimes from a friend. . . .

That wintry afternoon in Manhattan, waiting in the little French restaurant, I was feeling frustrated and depressed. Because of several miscalculations on my part, a project of considerable importance in my life had fallen through. Even the prospect of seeing a dear friend (the Old Man, as I privately and affectionately thought of him) failed to cheer me as it usually did. I sat there frowning at the checkered tablecloth, chewing the bitter cud of hindsight.

He came across the street, finally, muffled in his ancient overcoat, shapeless felt hat pulled down over his bald head, looking more like an energetic gnome than an eminent psychiatrist. His offices were nearby; I knew he had just left his last patient of the day. He was close to 80, but he still carried a full case load, still acted as director of a large foundation, still loved to escape to the golf course whenever he could.

By the time he came over and sat beside me, the waiter had brought his invariable bottle of ale. I had not seen him for several months, but he seemed as indestructible as ever. "Well, young man," he said without preliminary, "what's troubling you?"

I had long since ceased to be surprised at his perceptiveness. So I proceeded to tell him, at some length, just what was bothering me. With a kind of melancholy pride, I tried to be very honest. I blamed no one else for my disappointment, only myself. I analyzed the whole thing, all the bad judgments, the false moves. I went on for perhaps 15 minutes, while the Old Man sipped his ale in silence.

When I finished, he put down his glass. "Come on," he said. "Let's go back to my office."

"Your office? Did you forget something?"

"No," he said mildly. "I want your reaction to something. That's all."

A chill rain was beginning to fall outside, but his office was warm and comfortable and familiar: book-lined walls, long leather couch, signed photograph of Sigmund Freud, tape recorder by the window. His secretary had gone home. We were alone.

The Old Man took a tape from a flat cardboard box and fitted it onto the machine. "On this tape," he said, "are three short recordings made by three persons who came to me for help. They are not identified, of course. I want you to listen to the recordings and see if you can pick out the two-word phrase that is the common denominator in all three cases." He smiled. "Don't look so puzzled. I have my reasons."

What the owners of the voices on the tape had in common, it seemed to me, was unhappiness. The man who spoke first evidently had suffered some kind of business loss or failure; he berated himself for not having worked harder, for not having looked ahead. The woman who spoke next had never married because of a sense of obligation to her widowed mother; she recalled bitterly all the marital chances she had let go by. The third voice belonged to a mother whose teen-age son was in trouble with the police; she blamed herself endlessly.

The Old Man switched off the machine and leaned back in his chair. "Six times in those recordings a phrase is used that's full of subtle poison. Did you spot it? No? Well, perhaps that's because you used it three times yourself down in the restaurant a little while ago." He picked up the box that had held the tape and tossed it over to me. "There they are, right on the label. The two saddest words in any language."

I looked down. Printed neatly in red ink were the words: *If only*.

"You'd be amazed," said the Old Man, "if you knew how many thousands of times I've sat in this chair and listened to woeful sentences beginning with those two words. 'If only,' they say to me, 'I had done it differently—or not done it at all. If only I hadn't lost my temper, said that cruel thing, made that dishonest move, told that foolish lie. If only I had been wiser, or more unselfish, or more self-controlled.' They go on and on until I stop them. Sometimes I make them listen to the recording you just heard. 'If only,' I say to them, 'you'd stop saying *if only*, we might begin to get somewhere!' "

The Old Man stretched out his legs. "The trouble with 'if only,' " he said, "is that it doesn't change anything. It keeps the person facing the wrong way—backward instead of forward. It wastes time. In the end, if you let it become a habit, it can become a real roadblock, an excuse for not trying anymore."

"Now take your own case: your plans didn't work out. Why? Because you made certain mistakes. Well, that's all right: everyone makes mistakes. Mistakes are what we learn from. But when you were telling me about them, lamenting this, regretting that, you weren't really learning from them."

"How do you know?" I said, a bit defensively.

"Because," said the Old Man, "you never got out of the past tense. Not once did you mention the future. And in a way—be honest, now!—you were enjoying it. There's a perverse streak in all of us that makes us like to hash over old mistakes. After all, when you relate the story of some disaster or disappointment that has happened to you, you're still the chief character, still in the center of the stage."

I shook my head ruefully. "Well, what's the remedy?"

"Shift the focus," said the Old Man promptly. "Change the key words and substitute a phrase that supplies lift instead of creating drag."

"Do you have such a phrase to recommend?"

"Certainly. Strike out the words 'if only'; substitute the phrase 'next time.' "

"Next time?"

"That's right. I've seen it work minor miracles right here in this room. As long as a patient keeps saying 'if only' to me, he's in trouble. But when he looks me in the eye and says 'next time,' I know he's on his way to overcoming his problem. It means he had decided to apply the lessons he has learned from his experience, however grim or painful it may have been. It means he's going to push aside the roadblock of regret, move forward, take action, resume living. Try it yourself. You'll see."

My old friend stopped speaking. Outside, I could hear the rain whispering against the windowpane. I tried sliding one phrase out of my mind and replacing it with the other. It was fanciful, of course, but I could hear the new words lock into place with an audible click.

"One last thing," the Old Man said. "Apply this little trick to things that can still be remedied." From the bookcase behind him he pulled out something that looked like a diary. "Here's a journal kept a generation ago by a woman who was a schoolteacher in my hometown. Her husband was a kind of amiable ne'er-do-well, charming but totally inadequate as a provider. This woman had to raise the children, pay the bills, keep the family together. Her diary is full of angry references to Jonathan's weaknesses, Jonathan's shortcomings, Jonathan's inadequacies."

"Then Jonathan died, and all the entries ceased except for one—years later. Here it is: 'Today I was made superintendent of schools, and I suppose I should be very proud. But if I knew that Jonathan was out there somewhere beyond the stars, and if I knew how to manage it, I would go to him tonight.' "

The Old Man closed the book gently. "You see? What she's saying is 'if only'; if only I had accepted him, faults and all; if only I had loved him while I could." He put the book back on the shelf. "That's when those sad words are the saddest of all: when it's too late to retrieve anything."

He stood up a bit stiffly. "Well, class dismissed. It has been good to see you, young man. Always is. Now, if you will help me find a taxi, I probably should be getting on home."

We came out of the building into the rainy night. I spotted a cruising cab and ran toward it, but another pedestrian was quicker.

"My, my," said the Old Man slyly. "If only we had come down ten seconds sooner, we'd have caught that cab, wouldn't we?"

I laughed and picked up the cue. "Next time I'll run faster."

"That's it," cried the Old Man, pulling his absurd hat down around his ears. "That's it exactly!"

Another taxi slowed. I opened the door for him. He smiled and waved as it moved away. I never saw him again. A month later, he died of a sudden heart attack, in full stride, so to speak.

More than a year has passed since that rainy afternoon in Manhattan. But to this day, whenever I find myself thinking "if only," I change it to "next time." Then I wait for that almost-perceptible mental click. And when I hear it, I think of the Old Man.

A small fragment of immortality, to be sure. But it's the kind he would have wanted.

Number of words 1596
See page 427 for questions
Reading time in seconds ________
See page 498 for conversion table

SELECTION 72

A Master-Word Approach to Vocabulary

James I. Brown

A master word is like a master key. An ordinary key unlocks only one or two doors. A master key for a building may unlock over a hundred doors. Master words provide that same kind of comprehensive help in unlocking not one word meaning but hundreds.

How would you like a way of getting acquainted with words, a thousand at a time?

A few minutes with each of the following fourteen words will help you master well over 14,000 words. These words, the most important in the language to speed you along a superhighway toward vocabulary and success, do even more. They furnish invaluable background for further word study and give you a technique, a master key, which has endless possibilities.

You see, most of our English words are not English at all, but borrowings from other languages. Eighty percent of these borrowed words come to us from Latin and Greek and make up approximately 60 percent of our language.

Since this is so, the most important of these classical elements offer amazingly useful shortcuts to a bigger vocabulary. The words in the list at the end of this article contain twelve of the most important Latin roots, two of the most important Greek roots, and twenty of the most frequently used prefixes. Over 14,000 relatively common words, words of collegiate dictionary size, contain one or more of these elements (or an estimated 100,000 words of unabridged dictionary size).

Now, how to put these words to work, converting them into keys to the meanings of thousands of related words?

First, look up each of the fourteen words in the dictionary, noticing the relationship between derivation and definition. For example, take the word "intermittent." Let's chop it in two and chase it back to its birthplace. The two halves you come up with are a Latin prefix "inter-," which means "among" or "between," and a root word "mittere," which to a Roman meant "to send." To send between!"

That does it. That drags the ghosts out of the Latin closet and arranges their bones so you can tell what goes on. An *intermittent* sound is one that is "sent between" periods of silence. Maybe those Romans had something, when you dust away the cobwebs caused by a dislike of high-school Latin. Now compare that derivational meaning, "to send between," with the dictionary definition, "coming or going at intervals."

This step develops an understanding of the many relationships existing between derivation and definition, relationships from almost exact agreement—as with *prefix*, by derivation and definition meaning "to fix before,"—to varied extensions and restrictions of the derivational meaning.

THE FOURTEEN WORDS:
KEYS TO THE MEANING OF OVER 14,000 WORDS

	WORDS	PREFIX	COMMON MEANING	ROOT	COMMON MEANING
1.	*Precept*	pre-	(before)	capere	(take, seize)
2.	*Detain*	de-	(away, from)	tenere	(hold, have)
3.	*Intermittent*	inter-	(between)	mittere	(send)
4.	*Offer*	ob-	(against)	ferre	(bear, carry)
5.	*Insist*	in-	(into)	stare	(stand)
6.	*Monograph*	mono-	(alone, one)	graphein	(write)
7.	*Epilogue*	epi-	(upon)	legein	(say, study of)
8.	*Aspect*	ad-	(to, towards)	specere	(see)
9.	*Uncomplicated*	un- com-	(not) (together with)	plicare	(fold)
10.	*Nonextended*	non- ex-	(not) (out of)	tendere	(stretch)
11.	*Reproduction*	re- pro-	(back, again) (forward)	ducere	(lead)
12.	*Indisposed*	in- dis-	(not) (apart from)	ponere	(put, place)
13.	*Oversufficient*	over- sub-	(above) (under)	facere	(make, do)
14.	*Mistranscribe*	mis- trans-	(wrong) (across, beyond)	scribere	(write)

Next, look up each prefix. When you look up "pre-," for example, you'll find five somewhat different specific meanings, all denoting priority—priority in time, space, or rank. The dictionary entry will fix those meanings in mind and will often indicate assimilative changes.

The third step is to list at least ten words containing the prefix, checking each with the dictionary to avoid mistakes. You'll find some prefixes as changeable as chameleons. *Offer* is really *ob-fer*, but *offer* is easier to say. And there's the word *cooperation*, "to operate or work together." But doesn't *com-* mean "together?" Yes, but *comoperation* is awkward to say, so we say *cooperation*. This prepares you for the changes that occur when *com-* is combined with *-stant*, *-relation*, *-laboration*, and *-cil* to make *constant*, *correlation*, *collaboration*, and *council*. There's your background for recognizing similar chameleon-like changes of *ob-*, *ad-*, *ex-*, and others.

Finally, list at least ten words containing the root, checking each carefully with the dictionary. A few examples are listed for each root which should suggest others. Try to discover less common forms by some intelligent guessing.

Take the root *plicare*, "to fold"—the one that's part of *complication*. First of all, you'll think of *application*, *implication*, and *duplication*. *Duplication* may suggest *duplex* as well as *perplex* and *complex*. *Complex* may open the way to *comply*, which may in turn remind you of *apply*, *imply*, *pliant*, *supply*, *deploy*, and *employ*. Each discovery you make of a variant form adds that much to your background and understanding of the large family of words for which that root is key. Your dictionary will keep your guesses in line with the facts.

So much for method. Now, just how useful is your newly acquired knowledge of roots and prefixes?

Suppose you see the strange word *explication*. You know *ex-* means "out" and you know *plicare* means "to fold"—"to fold out." With the help of the sentence—"his explication was confused and difficult to follow"—you see that explication refers to un unfolding or folding out of meaning—or an explanation, in other words. Sometimes knowing only part of the word is enough. A student reading of a man's *predilection* for novels need only notice the *pre-* to assume that the man places novels "before" other books, that he has a "preference" or "partiality" for novels. Take another example. Is a *precocious* child one who has matured before or later than the average child? Again the prefix is your key to the meaning.

This procedure puts certain psychological laws of learning to work for you overtime. It forces you to discover meaningful relationships between derivation and definition. It stimulates you to use your knowledge to analyze strange words and understand familiar words better. It leads you to discover important principles of language development. In short, it forces you to take the initiative necessary to speed toward vocabulary and success.

And spelling is easier. If you continually misspell *prescription*, spelling it with a *per-*, you have only to remember the meanings of the prefixes, Since a prescription is written *before* being filled, you'll have to spell it with a *pre-*. You'll also know how to spell such demons as *misspell* or *misstep*, for you know they're combinations of *mis-* with *spell* and *step*. And what about someone who migrates into this country? Is he an *immigrant* or *emigrant*? Since he's coming *into* the country, he is an *inmigrant* or by assimilation an *immigrant*.

In this way you begin to understand the intricacies of our language. At first you'll have trouble spotting the root *facere* in such a word as *benefactor*. But soon you'll be a regular Sherlock Holmes, able to ferret out that root in such varied disguises as *artifice*, *affair*, *feature*, *affection*, *facsimile*, *counterfeit*, *fashion*, *facilitate*. You'll soon have no trouble finding the prefix *ex-* in *effect*, or *in-* in *illiterate*, or *dis-* in *differ*.

And best of all, you'll have a master key to unlock the meanings of thousands of other words, a technique to use with other classical elements. Yours is the magic touchstone, curiosity about derivations, which will bring words to life and lead you eventually to an awareness and understanding of words reached by relatively few.

Number of words 1090
See page 429 for questions
Reading time in seconds ________
See page 498 for conversion table

SELECTION 73

Warming Up to Words

Frank G. Jennings

Who hasn't heard it said—"The pen is mightier than the sword"? But is that always true? No! It's true only *when the pen writes the right words—words of power, of feeling, and of force. The importance of words demands that we take a closer look at our first childish efforts to discover and produce them.*

The experiments in sound that the child engages in during the first months of life are interesting and exciting to itself and to the adults around it but it is nothing like the great adventure that begins when the child produces its first word.

There is a lot of delightful nonsense about the first word. Parents will argue that the labial noises combined with vowel sounds *means* Mama or Papa depending on which parent is more anxious, aggressive and acquisitive. *Mama* usually wins out in most languages. Why shouldn't it. She hovers lovingly over her child, feeding it cues and grasping at even remotely familiar sounds. The child, being intelligent, of course catches on. After all, he does want to become a member of the club and this giant creature seems to be offering easy initiation. It makes the noise *mama*. She is transported; she caresses, feeds and fondles the child who immediately senses the positive quality of this wondrous emotion. That the child may use the noise *mama* rather indiscriminately for a little while is overlooked. By dint of high-pressure teaching it finally attaches the "word" to the "proper" object. . . .

The great infant discovery in language is that words control things even when the thing is as great and as powerful as *Mama*. When it produces another sound, in our culture it may often be a word like *ball*, the infant is on its life-long way to control of the universe. For the infant, the word *ball* becomes a word-sentence. It can have many meanings depending on the way it is produced. It can mean, "there is a ball," "that is a ball," "I want the ball," "where is the ball?" and so on. With the word-sentence language becomes a tool. And learning the use of this tool is an accomplishment greater than all other learning.

After the first word, the rest is easy, or it appears so. Yet the infant has been learning the wonder of words for a long time before it begins to apply its knowledge. For words are understood long before the power to utter them develops. The words that come first may look like names, they are in fact really action words. A quick examination of the "ball" sentences above demonstrates this. These grammatical terms are scientific counters by which sophisticated adults organize their knowledge about language, after the fact. Some investigators insist however that "the quickness with which an infant grasps the possibility of expressing the idea of change, desired or resented, by the addition of a verb (or some part of it) to a noun is usually an indication of the quality of his intelligence."*

The awareness of change is the great marker of awakening to the nature of the world about us. For the child it is the beginning of time. It is the way the world starts spinning. It makes possible the mental "seeing" of here and there, then and now. When the infant knows change, life-in-motion really begins. This is the time when the greatest word care is, and rightly must be, lavished on the child. Objects must be shown to it, and actions demonstrated and the words attached thereto. It is a wonderful play time for the parents and the child. It is the great learning time, if the child is healthy and the environment rich in joyous occasions. But it is a time of danger too. The word causes the thing to be produced. It is easy to begin by thinking that the word and thing are inseparable and then to act as if the word itself were the thing. This is a dangerous disease from which too many of us suffer most of our lives. Consider how violently we sometimes react to words themselves. Think of the last argument you had. Remember how you hurt and were hurt by words. But the child is insulated from this by ignorance, by lack of experience. In the early months of its life it responds to a stimulus outside its body much as an electric bell responds to its button being pushed.

Children don't invent words, at least not in the beginning. They might get in the habit of saying *ba-ba* right after a bath or a feeding or some other pleasant affair. Perhaps the mother has made it a practice of giving him a ball at this time every day. Mama may seize upon this sound and decide that "he wants his ball." She gives it to him and then gets into the habit of associating the sound the child makes with his "wanting" the ball. If she forgets the ball one day and he continues to cry *ba-ba* she will say, "He is asking for his ball." And at this point she is probably right since her "asking" or "wanting" something is probably only a more complicated way of responding to a similar situation. The infant has now made another giant step forward in his management of his language and his world. Bloomfield calls it abstract or displaced speech in which the infant names things even when they are not present.

Actions are perfected by their results and so it is with speech. As he gains skill in making the sound for *ball*, he is understood. He gets what he wants. He is satisfied. And the polishing process continues. Parents and older children constantly feed him cues for more effective language usage. He learns. They are delighted. His wants are met more readily. He eagerly matriculates in the school of human speech. The curriculum is complicated but never boring. He receives the best teaching he will ever get and in fact all other teaching he experiences will be measured against this in terms of satisfaction and effectiveness.

All this is prologue. Mind is now in high gear. *Homo* is joined for life to *sapiens*, and the human being truly has been born. Now he can rehearse things that never were and ask, "Why not?" Now he can proceed to catalogue the universe of things and acts and conditions. He begins to learn to plan, which means he begins to learn to select from what he *thinks* are possible outcomes of what he proposes to do. He *takes*, literally handles, thought as he has learned to handle things, and his reading of the charts and dials of life become more and more precise.

This is the kind of reading that the schools in our society eagerly wait to teach him. This is why the women in the children's garden teach their charges the wonderful game of "show-and-tell." For all his learning has been with the wholes of his experience. The after-learning, much like the after-burner in a jet engine, gives after-power to his ideas. This after-power is his ability to abstract, to take the mind sign for *ball* and measure it against *orange* and see differences; to take the shock of recognition of these differences not as a hurt but as an opportunity to find out more about things and their relationships. He has learned the whole sound for ball, the whole picture for ball, now he learns the whole printed "word" for ball. It will still be a long time before it is worth his while, and his skill in abstracting is equal to the task of taking the word apart in sounds and signs and putting it back together the way it was.

By the time the child arrives at school for the first time, he has acquired a huge operating vocabulary. Dr. Mary K. Smith, in her study of the vocabularies of public school children estimated in 1941, that this was about 24,000 words. Today, after more than a decade of the mass

*A. F. Watts, *The Language and Mental Development of Children*. London: D. C. Heath, 1944, pp. 37–38.

use of television, this estimate must be revised upwards by many percent. These are the resources the child brings to the learning of reading. He is, by any count, immensely skilled in the basic uses of his language.

Number of words 1330
See page 433 for questions
Reading time in seconds _______
See page 498 for conversion table

SELECTION 74

Vocabulary First-Aid

Paul Witty

For a student, a new word a day keeps the low grades away. For someone in business, a new word a day speeds success on its way. And for all of us, a new word a day adds zest right away. Words are indeed important. Vocabulary first-aid deserves major attention.

Before you attempt to build your vocabulary, consider for a moment what words really are. Words are similar to money, as the following comparison shows.

You may have heard someone say that money is "a medium of exchange." Money itself—the paper and metal out of which bills and coins are made—has only a small actual value. The real value of money is in what it stands for. And that *what* includes among other things groceries, clothing, shelter, automobiles, movies, and medical care.

Words, like money, have little value in and of themselves. They are important because they stand for real things—objects, actions, sounds, thoughts, and feelings. They are also important because they are a medium for the exchange of ideas.

If you want to get a clearer notion of what words mean to you every day, try getting along without them. When you sit down to dinner this evening, "tell" your family something you did today. Instead of using words, try to use sign language only. You will find it difficult if not impossible to exchange many ideas. Then, tell your story in words. You will quickly decide that, as a medium of communication, words are truly wonderful.

Words Promote Better Living

If you are short on words, you may also be short on ideas. This will handicap you in school or college, on the job, at home, or elsewhere. But if you know many words, you are likely to have a wealth of ideas. You are better able to understand what you read or hear. You are also better able to express yourself when you talk or write.

Studies of successful people clearly show that they usually have large vocabularies. They know the exact meanings of words. And they use the right word in the right place at the right time.

Because words are an aid to good living, you will want to build your vocabulary. As you do so, you will improve your reading.

Words Can Be Walls or Gateways to Understanding

Assume that you have a very small vocabulary. Also assume that you do not know how to get the meanings of new words. When you come across an unfamiliar word, that word may block, like a wall, your understanding of the material. Your eyes pause too long on the word as you try to get its meaning. You go back and read the word again trying to obtain its meaning from the context—the words in the sentence where the word appears. As a result, you read much more slowly than you should—and you find that the hard word is a wall to your comprehension.

Suppose, however, that you know many words and that you are skilled in finding the meanings of new words. Then, your eyes move quickly and you read rapidly. You comprehend instantly what you are reading. To you, words are gateways which lead to better understanding.

If you have a good vocabulary, moreover, you are more likely to read for ideas. As your eyes move along a line of print, you do not think of words as words. When you see a word group, you think an idea—the idea for which the word group stands.

You Can Master New Words

No matter how good your vocabulary may be, you can always improve it. To strengthen your word power, you should set up your own program. This lesson will suggest ways to do it.

After you finish this lesson, you will want to continue your word-building program. If you do, you will maintain your interest in vocabulary growth. You will expand your vocabulary. And this will challenge your thinking, broaden your ideas, and increase the information and enjoyment that you get from reading.

Your bigger and better vocabulary will also help you increase the speed and accuracy of your reading. New and hard words will no longer master you, for you will have become their master.

What Are the Main Types of Vocabulary?

If you take a close look at the words you use, you will find that you really have two main types of vocabulary. The first type is your general vocabulary; the second type is made up of your technical vocabularies.

Your general vocabulary includes the words you commonly use in conversation and correspondence, and the words you read in newspapers, books, and magazines. Your technical vocabularies include the words you find in specialized subjects or fields such as English history, chemistry, engineering, medicine, farming, auto repair, and cooking.

You can build your general vocabulary indirectly through extensive reading—that is, through reading widely in different fields. You can also increase your general vocabulary directly through studying words.

Through your reading and your other experiences, you can develop your technical vocabularies. You, of course, do not want to master the technical vocabularies of all the different professions or trades, for example. In fact, you could not learn all these vocabularies even though you spent a lifetime trying to do so. Yet, you will need to acquire a technical vocabulary in each subject or field in which you are especially interested.

How Can You Best Learn the Meanings of New Words?

. . . You use words in four main ways:

1. Your read what other people have written.
2. You listen to other people.
3. You talk to other people.
4. You write to other people.

In each of these ways, you can increase your word power. With this greater word power, you can improve your reading, your conversation, and your writing.

Because you are using this book to become a better reader, this lesson tells you how you can build your vocabulary through reading and for reading. To increase your word knowledge, here are some suggestions:

1. *Look and listen for new words.* Keep your eyes and ears open for words that you do not know. You will see them in reading. You will hear them in talking with other people, in watching movies, and in listening to radio or television programs.
2. *Write down your new words.* Get yourself a pocket notebook and label it, "My Vocabulary Notebook." Carry this notebook with you. In it, write down every new word that you see or hear. Do this immediately. If you wait, you may forget the new word.
3. *Find the meanings of new words.* In the dictionary, look up the meanings of the new words that you have written in your vocabulary notebook. At the right of each word, write the dictionary definition or meaning that applies to the word as it was used in what you read or heard.
4. *Make the new words your own.* Use each new word in talking with your family or friends. Pronounce the word accurately. Also, use this word in what you are writing. Spell the word correctly. In speaking or writing, be sure that you use the word as it should be used.
5. *Enter several new words in your vocabulary notebook each day.* Keep building your word power. At the end of the week, quickly review the new words you entered during the seven-day period just ended. This review will help you remember the meanings of these words.

Build Your Vocabulary While You Read

When you meet a new word in your reading, guess its meaning. Using your pencil, mark a check near the word so that you can find it later. Then keep on reading until you finish the entire story or part of the story. In this way, you do not allow a new word to slow down your reading speed or to interrupt your understanding of the flow of the story.

After you finish the story or part of it, go back and find the new words that you did not know. Write each word in your vocabulary notebook. Then take these steps.

1. Try to guess the meaning of the word. Write down your guess.
2. Try to get the word's meaning by reading again the sentence in which the word appears. Copy the sentence.

3. Look up the word in the dictionary. Find the definition or meaning that applies to the sentence in which the word appears. Then write down this meaning.
4. Write your own sentence that includes this word.

Number of words 1380
See page 437 for questions
Reading time in seconds ________
See page 498 for conversion table

SELECTION 75

Do You Know How Words Can Make You Rich?

Morton Winthrop

To earn more money, learn more words! That pretty well sums up the following selection. You can even determine your probable top salary by trying the vocabulary test that follows. If you're disappointed, just give yourself a raise! Increase your vocabulary, beginning right now.

If you are not earning enough money, perhaps it's because you don't know the meanings of enough words.

More than any other single factor yet known, vocabulary predicts financial success!

This is the finding of the Human Engineering Laboratory, a leading nationwide psychological testing service, which has been exploring the aptitudes and careers of people f or the last 38 years.

Now, with a short 20-word test developed for *This Week* by the Laboratory, you can fairly accurately predict your top income.

Don't leap to the conclusion that a large vocabulary by itself—and a good score on our quiz—will guarantee you success. Vocabulary, which is really a measure of your potential—must be linked with good work habits, initiative and responsibility.

Dizzy Dean Speaks Up

As Dizzy Dean, baseball's master of malapropism (need to look that one up?) said: "There's a lot of guys that know how to read and write but that ain't making a living."

All the same, 30,000 vocabulary tests given each year by the Human Engineering Laboratory prove that big incomes and big vocabularies go together—and the same goes for small ones.

The Laboratory was founded in 1922 by a Harvard philosophy major named Johnson O'Connor. The Lab's first home was at the West Lynn, Mass., plant of General Electric, where O'Connor was in charge of selecting capable engineers. So successful was he in matching the man with the job through a battery of carefully developed tests that high-school students began asking to take them for career guidance. As these requests multiplied, O'Connor began giving tests evenings and Saturdays. Eventually the Laboratory expanded to the present huge, independent, non-profit outfit with branches in major cities throughout the country. It has developed dozens of tests to help a person find where his abilities lie, but the single most important is the vocabulary test, similar to that on these pages.

Husbands and wives taking our test needn't be surprised if their scores come close to matching. The Laboratory has discovered that married couples tend to know the same words because of the similarity of their educations, interests and backgrounds.

Men tend to marry girls with similar-sized vocabularies. So women who aren't married yet can fairly accurately predict the earning power of their husbands-to-be by word-testing themselves.

Vocabulary is an indication of precise as well as broad knowledge, and does not depend solely upon education but upon wide reading and wide experience as well.

"I once tested the president of a coal-mining company in Pennsylvania," says O'Connor. "He was a man who had worked his way up from the pits and his grammar was terrible. Yet, in all the vocabulary tests, he got only two words wrong. The best score that any college graduate in that town could make was thirteen words wrong."

A 40-year-old woman tested recently in Chicago

had only gone through the eight grade, yet she scored extremely high in laboratory vocabulary tests. She is an avid reader, interested in philosophy, semantics and logic. For the past five years she has headed a group of 60 accountants, although she is not an accountant herself.

Even among college graduates, vocabulary differences can be startling. In 1955, a group of college seniors selected by a large industrial plant as executive material was hired by the company to go to work after graduation.

The men were given a group of vocabulary tests. At work, each man was shifted around so that he had an equal opportunity to learn and to assume responsibility. *By last June, all of those men who had been tested in the top 10 percent in vocabulary had become executives. Not a single man who had tested in the bottom 25 percent is an executive!*

If you should score poorly on our test, all is not lost. According to Mr. O'Connor, you can work at building your vocabulary—and with it your chances for a larger income. Wide reading is an invaluable aid. The following techniques will pay off for you:

1. Set a goal of at least one serious book a month.
2. When you read, have a dictionary at hand. When you meet a difficult word, look it up.
3. Examine carefully how you heard or saw the word used. As O'Connor says, "People often try to use terribly difficult words and, of course, they wind up using them wrong. Other people laugh and the incentive to learn more new words is often lost."

No matter how you choose to build your vocabulary—through crossword puzzles, books, or reading the dictionary—*the point is you should do it!*

Not only is the reward a much greater possible income, but greater insight and confidence in yourself and what you can do.

Number of words of 790
See page 441 for questions
Reading time in seconds ________
See page 498 for conversion table

Vocabulary Test

This 20-word test will give you a fairly accurate idea of what your top income will be. Circle one of the five words that comes closest to the meaning of the first word in italic type. Be sure to read all five choices and, where you have no idea, guess. After you finish the test, turn to page 000 for the answers and your future top income.

1. Did you see the *clergy? / funeral / dolphin / churchmen / monastery / bell tower*
2. Fine *louvers. / doors / radiators / slatted vents / mouldings / bay windows*
3. Like an *ellipse. / sunspot / oval / satellite / triangle / volume*
4. *Dire* thoughts. */ angry / dreadful / blissful / ugly / unclean*
5. It was the *affluence. / flow rate / pull / wealth / flood / bankruptcy*
6. Discussing the *acme. / intersection / question / birth mark / perfection / low point*
7. How *odious. / burdensome / lazy / hateful / attractive / fragrant*
8. This is *finite. / limited / tiny / precise / endless / difficult*
9. Watch for the *inflection. / accent / mirror image / swelling / pendulum swing / violation*
10. The *connubial* state. */ marriage / tribal / festive / spinsterly / primitive*
11. See the *nuance. / contrast / upstart / renewal / delinquent / shading*
12. Where is the *dryad? / water sprite / fern / dish towel / chord / wood nymph*
13. Will you *garner* it? */ dispose of / store / polish / thresh / trim*
14. A sort of *anchorite. / religious service / hermit / marine deposit / mineral / promoter*
15. *Knurled* edges. */ twisted / weather beaten / flattened / ridged / knitted*
16. Is it *bifurcated? / forked / hairy / two wheeled / mildewed / joined*
17. Examining the *phthisis. / cell division / medicine / misstatement / dissertation / tuberculosis*
18. *Preponderance* of the group. */ absurdity / heaviness / small number / foresight / majority*
19. Ready to *expound. / pop / confuse / interpret / dig up / imprison*
20. Staring at the *relict. / trustee / antique table / corpse / widow / excavation*

Section VII

Current Problems

Was There Something I Was Supposed to Do with My Life?

Harold S. Kushner

Most people wonder, "What am I doing? Where am I going? Is this all there is to life?" The problem is, there are no easy answers. As society becomes more complex, do our lives have less and less meaning?

Ask the average person which is more important to him, making money or being devoted to his family, and virtually everyone will answer *family* without hesitation. But watch how the average person actually lives out his life. See where he really invests his time and energy, and he will give away the fact that he does not really live by what he says he believes. He has let himself be persuaded that if he leaves for work earlier in the morning and comes home more tired at night, he is proving how devoted he is to his family by expending himself to provide them with all the things they have seen advertised.

Ask the average person which means more to her, the approval of strangers or the affection of people closest to her, and she won't be able to understand why you would even ask such a question. Obviously, nothing means more to her than her family and her closest friends. Yet how many of us have embarrassed our children or squelched their spontaneity, for fear of what neighbors or strangers might think? How often have we poured out our anger on those closest to us because we had a hard day at work or someone else did something to upset us? And how many of us have let ourselves become irritable with our families because we were dieting to make ourselves look more attractive to people who do not know us well enough to see beyond appearances?

Ask the average person what he wants out of life, and he will probably reply, "All I want is to be happy." And I believe him. I believe that most people want to be happy. I believe that they work hard at making themselves happy. They buy books, attend classes, change their lifestyles, in an ongoing effort to find that elusive quality, happiness. But in spite of all that, I suspect that most people most of the time do not feel happy.

Why should that sense of happiness be so elusive, eluding both those people who get what they want in life and those who don't? Why should people with so many reasons to be happy feel so acutely that something is missing from their lives? Are we asking too much of life when we say, "All I want is to be happy"? Is happiness, like eternal youth or perpetual motion, a goal that we are not meant to reach, no matter how hard we work for it? Or is it possible for people to be happy, but we are going about it in the wrong way?

Oscar Wilde once wrote, "In this world there are only two tragedies. One is not getting what one wants, and the other is getting it." He was trying to warn us that no matter how hard we work at being successful, success won't satisfy us. By the time we get there, having sacrificed so much on the altar of being successful, we will realize that success was not what we wanted. People who have money and power know something that you and I do not know and might not believe even when we are told. Money and power do not satisfy that unnameable hunger in the soul. Even the rich and powerful find themselves yearning for something more. We read about the family problems of the rich and famous, we see their fictionalized conflicts on television, but we never get the message. We keep thinking that if we had what they have, we would be happy. No matter how hard we work at being popular and no matter how good we are at it, we never seem to reach the point where we can relax and feel we have arrived. If our sense of who we are depends on popularity and other people's opinions of us, we will always be dependent on those other people. On any day, they have the power to pull the rug out from under us.

I remember reading of a young man who left home to find fame and fortune in Hollywood. He had three dreams when he set out—to see his name in lights, to own a Rolls-Royce, and to marry a beauty contest winner. By the time he was thirty, he had done all three, and he was a deeply depressed young man, unable to work creatively anymore despite (or perhaps because of) the fact that all of his dreams had come true. By thirty, he had run out of goals. What was there for him to do with the rest of his life?

Several recent authors have written of "the imposter phenomenon," describing the feeling of many apparently successful people that their success is undeserved and that one day people will unmask them for the frauds they are. For all the outward trappings of success, they feel hollow inside. They can never rest and enjoy their accomplishments. They need one new success after another. They need constant reassurance from the people around them to still the voice inside them that keeps saying, If other people knew you the way I know you, they would know what a phony you are.

So, the woman who dreamed of marrying a successful doctor or corporate executive and living in a fancy house in the suburbs may find herself well married and living in her dream house but cannot understand why she goes around every morning saying to herself, Is this all there is to life? There has to be something more. She makes lunch dates with friends, works to raise money for charity, perhaps opens a boutique, hoping that if she fills her days, she will also fill the gnawing emptiness in her soul. But no matter how busy she keeps herself, the hunger within her is never sated.

Our souls are not hungry for fame, comfort, wealth, or power. Those rewards create almost as many problems as they solve. Our souls are hungry for meaning, for the sense that we have figured out how to live so that our lives matter, so that the world will be at least a little bit different for our having passed through it.

I was reading Carl Jung's book *Modern Man in Search of a Soul* one day, when I came across several passages which startled me with their insight. They gave me the feeling that a man who lived before I was born knew me better than I knew myself. The first passage was, "About a third of my cases are suffering from no clinically definable neurosis, but from the senselessness and emptiness of their lives. This can be described as the general neurosis of our time."

I had to admit that he was right. He was right about the 1980s as surely as he was about the 1920s and 1930s when he wrote those lines. What frustrates us and robs our lives of joy is this absence of meaning. Our lives go on day after day. They may be successful or unsuccessful, full of pleasure or full or worry. But do they *mean* anything?

Is there anything more to life than just being alive—eating, sleeping, working, and having children? Are we no different from insects and animals, except that we are cursed with the ability to ask, What does life mean? and as far as we know, other creatures don't have that problem? It is a hard question to answer, but an even harder one to avoid answering. For a few years, perhaps, we can put off answering it while we are distracted with educational, career, and marriage decisions. In those early decades, other people have more say in our lives than we do. But sooner or later, we will come face to face with the questions, What am I supposed to do with my life? How shall I live so that my life will mean something more than a brief flash of biological existence soon to disappear forever?

The curator of a butterfly museum in South Wales once introduced me to the "moth with no mouth," a species of caterpillar that lays its eggs and then changes into a moth that has no digestive system, no way of taking in food, so that it starves to death in a few hours. Nature has designed this moth to reproduce, to lay eggs and pass on the life of the species. Once it has done that, it has no reason to go on living, so it is programmed to die. Are we like that? Do we live only to produce children, to perpetuate the human race? And having done that, is it our destiny to disappear and make way for the next generation? Or is there a purpose to our existence beyond simply existing? Does our being alive matter? Would our disappearance leave the world poorer, or just less crowded? As Jung correctly understood, these are not abstract questions suitable for cocktail party conversation. They are desperately urgent questions. We will find ourselves sick, lonely, and afraid if we cannot answer them.

A man sat opposite me in my study one evening. He had called me the day before for an appointment, sounding agitated and saying only that he had a religious question to discuss with me. In my line of work, a religious question can mean anything from the issue of why God permits evil to the question of where the parents of the groom stand during a wedding ceremony. After some suitably vague remarks about his childhood and his early religious training, he told me what was on his mind.

"Two weeks ago, for the first time in my life I went to the funeral of a man my own age. I didn't know him well, but we worked together, talked to each other from time to time, had kids about the same age. He died suddenly over the weekend. A bunch of us went to the funeral, each of us thinking, "It could just as easily have been me." That was two weeks ago. They have already replaced him at the office. I hear his wife is moving out of state to live with her parents. Two weeks ago he was working fifty feet away from me, and now it's as if he never existed. It's like a rock falling into a pool of water. For a few seconds, it makes ripples in the water, and then the water is the same as it was before, but the rock isn't there anymore. Rabbi, I've hardly slept at all since then. I can't stop thinking that it could happen to me, that one day it *will* happen to me, and a few days later I will be forgotten as if I had never lived. Shouldn't a man's life be more than that?"

If a tree falls in the forest and there is no ear to hear

it, does it make a sound? If a person lives and dies and no one notices, if the world continues as it was, was that person ever really alive? I am convinced that it is not the fear of death, of our lives ending, that haunts our sleep so much as the fear that our lives will not have mattered, that as far as the world is concerned, we might as well never have lived. What we miss in our lives, no matter how much we have, is that sense of meaning.

Number of words 1810
See page 445 for questions
Reading time in seconds _______
See page 498 for conversion table

Selection 77

From *The Road to Wigan Pier*

George Orwell

Machines—we'd be lost without them, wouldn't we? Or, as Orwell suggests, are we actually lost **with** *them? Are you convinced by his reasoning? How do we manage the technological monster we have created?*

The function of the machine is to save work. In a fully mechanized world all the dull drudgery will be done by machinery, leaving us free for more interesting pursuits. So expressed, this sounds splendid. It makes one sick to see half a dozen men sweating their guts out to dig a trench for a water-pipe, when some easily devised machine would scoop the earth out in a couple of minutes. Why not let the machine do the work and the men go and do something else? But presently the question arises, what else are they to do? Supposedly they are set free from "work" in order that they may do something which is not "work". But what is work and what is not work? Is it work to dig, to carpenter, to plant trees, to fell trees, to ride, to fish, to hunt, to feed chickens, to play the piano, to take photographs, to build a house, to cook, to sew, to trim hats, to mend motor bicycles? All of these things are work to somebody, and all of them are play to somebody. There are in fact very few activities which cannot be classed either as work or play according as you choose to regard them. The laborer set free from digging may want to spend his leisure, or part of it, in playing the piano, while the professional pianist may be only too glad to get out and dig at the potato patch. Hence the antithesis between work, as something intolerably tedious, and not-work, as something desirable, is false. The truth is that when a human being is not eating, drinking, sleeping, making love, talking, playing games or merely lounging about—and these things will not fill up a lifetime—he needs work and usually looks for it, though he may not call it work. Above the level of a third- or fourth-grade moron, life has got to be lived largely in terms of effort. For man is not, as the vulgarer hedonists seem to suppose, a kind of walking stomach; he has also got a hand, an eye and a brain. Cease to use your hands, and you have lopped off a huge chunk of your consciousness. And now consider again those half-dozen men who were digging the trench for the water-pipe. A machine has set them free from digging, and they are going to amuse themselves with something else—carpentering, for instance. But whatever they want to do, they will find that another machine has set them free from *that*. For in a fully mechanized world there would be no more need to carpenter, to cook, to mend motor bicycles, etc., than there would be to dig. There is scarcely anything, from catching a whale to carving a cherry stone, that could not conceivably be done by machinery. The machine would even encroach upon the activities we now class as "art"; it is doing so already, via the camera and the radio. Mechanize the world as fully as it might be mechanized, and whichever way you turn there will be some machine cutting you off from the chance of working—that is, of living.

At a first glance this might not seem to matter. Why should you not get on with your "creative work" and disregard the machines that would do it for you? But it is not so simple as it sounds. Here am I, working eight hours a day in an insurance office; in my spare time I want to do something "creative," so I choose to do a bit of carpentering—to make myself a table, for instance. Notice that from the very start there is a touch of artificiality about the whole business, for the factories can turn me out a far better table than I can make for myself. But even when I get to work on my table, it is not possible for me to feel towards it as the cabinet-maker of a hundred years ago felt towards his table, still less as Robinson Crusoe felt towards his. For before I start, most of the work has already been done for me by machinery. The tools I use demand the minimum of skill. I can get, for instance, planes which will cut out any moulding; the cabinet-maker of a hundred years ago would have had to do the work with chisel and gouge, which demanded real skill of eye and hand. The boards I buy are ready planed and the legs are ready turned by the lathe. I can even go to the wood-shop and buy all the parts of the table ready-made and only needing to be fitted together, my work being reduced to driving in a few pegs and using a piece of sandpaper. And if this is so at present, in the mechanized future it will be enormously more so. With the tools and materials available *then*, there will be no possibility of mistake, hence no room for skill. Making a table will be easier and duller than peeling a potato. In such circumstances it is nonsense to talk of "creative work." In any case the arts of the hand (which have got to be transmitted by apprenticeship) would long since have disappeared. Some of them have disappeared already, under the competition of the machine. Look round any country churchyard and see whether you can find a decently-cut tombstone later than 1820. The art, or rather the craft, of stonework has died out so completely that it would take centuries to revive it.

But it may be said, why not retain the machine *and* retain "creative work"? Why not cultivate anachronisms as a spare-time hobby? Many people have played with this idea; it seems to solve with such beautiful ease the problems set by the machine. The citizens of Utopia, we are told, coming home from his daily two hours of turning a handle in the tomato-canning factory, will deliberately revert to a more primitive way of life and solace his creative instincts with a bit of fretwork, pottery-glazing or handloom-weaving. And why is this picture an absurdity—as it is, or course? Because of a principle that is not always recognized, though always acted upon: that so long as the machine *is there*, one is under an obligation to use it. No one draws water from the well when he can turn on the tap. One sees a good illustration of this in the matter of travel. Everyone who has traveled by primitive methods in an undeveloped country, knows that the difference between that kind of travel and modern travel in trains, cars, etc., is the difference between life and death. The nomad who walks or rides, with his baggage stowed on a camel or an ox-cart, may suffer every kind of discomfort, but at least he is living while he is traveling; whereas for the passenger in an express train or a luxury liner his journey is an interregnum, a kind of temporary death. And yet so long as the railways exist, one has got to travel by train—or by car or airplane. Here am I, forty miles from London. When I want to go up to London why do I not pack my luggage on to a mule and set out on foot, making a two days' march of it? Because, with the Green Line buses whizzing past me every ten minutes, such a journey would be intolerably irksome. In order that one may enjoy primitive methods of travel, it is necessary that no other method should be available. No human being ever wants to do anything in a more cumbrous way than is necessary. Hence the absurdity of that picture of Utopians saving their souls with fretwork. In a world where everything could be done by machinery, everything would be done by machinery. Deliberately to revert to primitive methods, to use archaic tools, to put silly little difficulties in your own way, would be a piece of dilettantism, of pretty-petty arty and craftiness. It would be like solemnly sitting down to eat your dinner with stone implements. Revert to handwork in a machine age, and you are back in Ye Olde Tea Shoppe or the Tudor villa with the sham beams tacked to the wall.

Number of words 1380
See page 449 for questions
Reading time in seconds ________
See page 498 for conversion table

Selection 78

How to Live 24 Hours a Day

Arthur Gordon

To live fully is, of course, a major problem. A Gallup Poll asked, "Do you find life exciting, pretty routine, or dull?" Of the 1,521 questioned, 51 percent found life "dull" or "routine." Going to college makes the most difference; only 24 percent of the college-educated replied "dull" or "routine." What else helps 24 hours a day?

Like several million other people, my wife is a faithful reader of a lady columnist who gives advice on all subjects. Pretty good advice, too, most of the time. But the other night I noticed the faithful reader frowning over the newspaper. "Here," she said, "take a look at this."

In the column, a married woman in her mid-30s was voicing a wistful complaint. She got on well with her husband, they had three well-adjusted children, there were no great health or financial problems. But something was wrong. There was busyness in her life, but no fulfillment. There was a coping with day-to-day problems, but no sense of adventure or joy. She had every reason to be contented, but she felt only half alive. What should she do? What *could* she do? She signed herself, *The Unenviable Mrs. Jones.*

In reply, the columnist urged the woman to be satisfied with what she had. Other people, she pointed out, had far more serious difficulties. "Count your blessings," she advised . . . and moved on to the next problem.

"The trouble with that reply," my wife said, "is that it doesn't answer the question. And the question needs to be answered, because it's just about the most important one there is. I know exactly how that woman feels. She wants to overcome her sense of futility. She wants somebody to tell her how to escape from ordinariness and start living—really be alive—24 hours a day."

"Can anyone," I said skeptically, "really be alive every single hour?"

"Oh," said my wife impatiently, "you know what I mean. In terms of time we all live 24 hours a day, but that's just horizontal living. In terms of emotions, people live vertically. At least, they should. That's what this Mrs. Jones is groping for: Depth in living and feeling. Intensity—that's the word, I guess. If you ask me, the main enemy in most marriages today isn't cruelty or infidelity or poverty or alcoholism. It's monotony. And frustration. I feel very sorry for Mrs. Jones."

"So do I." I said.

"Well," my wife said, "why don't you *do* something about it? In your work you meet all sorts of people who are supposed to be experts in the field of human behavior. Surely, they'd have something to offer that would be helpful. Why don't you pick a psychiatrist and a minister and ask them what they'd say if Mrs. Jones came to them with her problem?"

"I might talk to Herb Smith about it." I said, "the next time we go fishing. He's about as good a psychiatrist as I know. And the next time I go to New York I could ask Norman Peale what he would say."

"Do that," my wife replied. "This is a tough question. People need some answers."

"It's a very widespread thing," Dr. Herbert D. Smith said, "this nagging uneasiness, this feeling that life is hiding from you, that you've lost the capacity to enjoy or appreciate the ordinary pleasures of existence. I think women are more susceptible to it than men—partly because men tend to be absorbed in their work, partly because, being more emotional, women can become emotionally starved more easily."

"Now, what would I say to Mrs. Jones? I think I'd start by trying to reassure her a little. I'd tell her that her feelings are understandable, that many people have similar ones, that it takes courage to admit that you're dissatisfied with your life."

"Next, I'd try to inject some realism into her thinking. I'd say, 'Mrs. Jones, let's talk for a moment about something called acceptance. It's important, because unless you start with a degree of acceptance, you're going to go right on being discontented no matter what I say to you.

We all have certain limitations in our lives. We all yearn for more excitement and pleasure than we have. There are times when I wish I were an explorer or an astronaut, but I'm just a doctor, you're just a housewife, and I can't radically change my circumstances any more than you can. What I *can* change—if I work at it—is my attitude toward these circumstances, and, to some degree, my performance within those circumstances.'

"Finally, I'd give Mrs. Jones three specific suggestions to follow. She's really in a prison, partly of her own making. These three suggestions are designed to help her break out. Here they are:

"1. Pay more attention to people. Attention is a dialogue, and a dialogue is an escape from self. You can't be totally self-imprisoned when you pay deep attention to what another person feels, or says, or is.

"It doesn't matter who the other person is. Let's say your neighbor Martha drops in from next door for a cup of coffee. You're fond of Martha, but you take her completely for granted, and at times you feel she's a bit of a trial because she's always complaining about something.

"But take a new look at Martha. Why is she the way she is? What is she trying to say to you that she doesn't know how to say in words? What needs does she have that you might possible supply? Ask yourself, 'Who is this person?' On the surface she may seem like the same old Martha, complaining this time because her feet hurt or her husband snores. But actually, you have, right there in your kitchen, sitting at your table, a creature so fantastically complex that all the psychiatrists in the world couldn't fully explain her to you—or to herself.

"And don't limit yourself to Martha. Learn to observe and study all kinds of people. It's endlessly fascinating—and it will take your mind off yourself.

"2. Give your emotions more elbowroom. You can't expect them to have much vitality if you're constantly overcontrolling them. Too many of us are hesitant about expressing affection—we're afraid it may be misinterpreted or even rejected. Too many of us are ashamed of flashes of anger even when there's a valid cause. Too many of us have forgotten how to roar with laughter. These stifled emotions fence us in, cut us off from life and people. If Mrs. Jones would let herself go occasionally, instead of mutely enduring her frustrations, she might be a lot better off.

"3. Start a one-woman rebellion against routine. This is the greatest single cause of emotional numbness: The unvarying repetition of basically uninteresting tasks. Life tries to clamp a pattern down on all of us, and it's not easy to fight back. But it's imperative to try, even in small things. I remember I once ordered a man to drive to work by a different route every day, no matter how much extra time it consumed. He thought this was foolish, but it wasn't. He was encrusted with old, stale habits. We had to start somewhere.

"So I would say to Mrs. Jones, 'When routine begins to stifle you, look for new ways of doing things. Even with chores that have to be done, try to dramatize them somehow. Set new performance goals. Try to cut your shopping time or your vacuuming time in half; compete with yourself.

" 'Force yourself to do something unexpected now and then. Walk in the summer rain without an umbrella or a raincoat. Get up before dawn and watch a sunrise. Strike up a conversation with a stranger. Write a letter without using the words *I* or *me*, *my* or *mine*. In a restaurant, order a meal consisting exclusively of things you have never tasted before.

" 'In other words, Mrs. Jones, fight deadening routine as if it were your mortal enemy. Because it is.'

"If Mrs. Jones or anyone like her will take those suggestions seriously," Dr. Smith concluded, "I think she'll find that her problems grow less."

"What this Mrs. Jones is suffering from," Norman Vincent Peale said thoughtfully, "is a form of soul-sickness that is a peculiarly modern disease. Part of it, I think, is the result of a kind of emotional isolation. One or two generations ago, children grew up in large families with uncles and aunts scattered up and down the block and grandparents readily available. There wasn't so much shifting around; people knew and counted on their neighbors. But now we tend to live in tight family units—two antagonistic generations crowded together with all the interpersonal strains concentrated relentlessly day after day. Just parents and kids, no buffer personalities at all. No wonder people feel stifled and depressed.

"As for Mrs. Jones, I would make a few suggestions designed to get her into better alignment with the universe that surrounds her, I'd try to keep them practical, not pious. And I'd try to make them short.

"I'd say to her. 'Mrs. Jones, one of the things you need most is a heightened sense of awareness. This is not a gift that anyone can hand you; you must develop it yourself. You must make a conscious and deliberate effort to become more sensitized to the beauty and mystery and magic of things. Take life to pieces and what do you have? Miraculous fragments of reality. Not one of them is really commonplace. It's our reactions to them that grow dull if we let them.

" 'Learn to look beyond the obvious. If, let's say, you see a furry caterpillar walking on your windowsill, you must sometimes—not always, but *sometimes*—regard it not just as an unwelcome intruder that deserves to be squashed, but as a manifestation of the life force that in its own way is just as remarkable as you are.'

"I knew a woman once who had a serious illness followed by a long convalescence. Day after day she lay in bed, weak and listless. Her doctors were very concerned; the vital spark seemed almost to have flickered out. Then, suddenly, she began to improve dramatically.

"Later, when asked about her recovery, she pointed to a magnifying glass, small but powerful. 'This has a lot to do with it,' she said. 'When a friend brought it to me, I had almost lost interest in living. But when I began to look through it, commonplace things became astonishing. You have no idea what you can see in a simple flower, or a leaf, or a piece of cloth. I believe that something in me decided that this world was too beautiful to leave—and so I began to get well.'

"I would say to Mrs. Jones that this kind of discovery is available to all of us. Not everyone can be a Thoreau, perhaps, and live by a remote lake with no companionship but his own thoughts. But it should be possible for each of us to find his own small wilderness in a garden or a seashore or even a cramped backyard—any place where things grow and the seasons change and small creatures exist in their own tiny worlds. Even a city dweller can go up on the roof at night, or out into the street and stare at the stars and think about the incomprehensible distances and magnitudes involved. I remember once being told by an astronomer about one star so huge that if a creature existed on it in the same proportion to his star as we are to our Earth, he could swallow our sun without burning his throat. 'Ponder that, Mrs. Jones, and feel your mind reel—as it should!'

"What else can you do to develop a sense of wonder? All sorts of mental tricks! Imagined scarcity, for example. Suppose the common alley cat you see crossing the road were the *only* cat in existence. What a fabulous creature it would be considered—beautiful, sinuous, superb and priceless. Or suppose this were the last time you could ever see a sunset, or hear great music, or tuck your child into bed. Just a supposition, sure—but it creates a sense of wonder and gratitude.

"I would also advise Mrs. Jones to align herself with goodness now and then. I know that's what a preacher is expected to say, but there's more to it than that. 'This is an ethical universe,' I'd say. 'You are part of it, Mrs. Jones. Therefore it's important to put yourself in tune with those powerful unseen forces.'

"How do you do this? It's simple. Visit a sick friend. Take on some worthwhile civic responsibility. Help someone less fortunate. Give somebody an unexpected gift. Put yourself out when you'd much rather not. Do these things as often as you can.

"What does this have to do with intensity of living? Just this: The person who is bored or unfulfilled is almost always the person who in uninvolved. And often he's uninvolved because his self-esteem and, consequently, his self-confidence are low. Performing a kindness, helping another person makes you like yourself better. And the more you like yourself, the more outgoing and unbored you are going to be.

"Finally," the minister said, "I'd talk to Mrs. Jones about love, because this is the key that will open the doors that she feels are closed to her. I'd probably talk to her mainly about married love, which someone has called 'the persistent effort of two persons to create for each other conditions under which each can become the person God meant him to be.' If a woman—or a man, for that matter—can even come close to this ideal, *everything* is going to be colored by it. Every one of the 24 hours in a day is going to be richer and brighter.

"I rather suspect that if Mrs. Jones ever had this kind of relationship, it has become dimmed by the dust of daily living. That's what's at the heart of her discontent. And so I would recommend that she and her husband find a quiet place and quiet time and ask themselves three basic questions. Perhaps they could think them over alone at first.

" '1. In the life that you are leading today, what gives you most satisfaction, what seems most worthwhile? Is it sex, religion, children, work, some form of recreation? Do you agree, between yourselves, as to what it is? Do you share it—or does it separate you? Don't try in one sitting to solve the problems the question may raise. Just look at them honestly.

" '2. Thirty years from now, when you look back at your life as it is today, how will you feel about the way you are investing your time? Will you think some of your activities were unnecessary and meaningless? Will you wish you had used the priceless days of hours differently? Sit quietly—and discuss—and think.

" '3. If you could change just one thing in your husband-wife relationship, if each of you had one magic wish that could be instantly granted, what would that wish be? Listen carefully to what your partner says, because in it may lie a clue to your own happiness—or to what is keeping you from it.'

"And that," Dr. Peale concluded, "is approximately what I'd say to the unhappy Mrs. Jones."

"Well," I said later, when I had put their thoughts on

paper and showed them to my wife, "what do you think?"

"They're good answers," she said. "But it's still an enormous question."

"Of course it is," I said. "People have been wrestling with it since the beginning of time."

"Maybe," she said, "maybe there are no complete blueprints. Maybe each of us has to grope and struggle and find the answers for ourselves as we go along."

"Perhaps," I said.

"I think your minister friend came closest when he said that the central love-relationship is the main thing. If that's right, everything else will follow. If it's wrong, everything else will be in shadow."

"So we sit here in the sunshine counting our blessings, eh?"

She laughed. "As a matter of fact," she said, "sometimes I do."

Number of words 2654
See page 453 for questions
Reading time in seconds ________
See page 498 for conversion table

SELECTION 79

Too Many Divorces, Too Soon

Margaret Mead and Rhoda Metraux

Let me not to the marriage of true minds
Admit impediments. Love is not love
Which alters when it alteration finds. . . .

From Shakespeare on, marriage has been a favorite subject. What about divorce, the other side of the coin? Why the shift of attention?

In our generation divorce has become part of the American way of life.

We have not stopped believing in marriage. We are still among the most married people in the world, and increasingly Americans are willing to try a second, a third and even a fourth marriage. But over the past 30 years the proportion of women whose first marriage has broken down in divorce has continued to increase and in the last ten years alone the total annual number of divorces has risen steeply.

What has changed is not our belief that a good marriage is the most important adult relationship, but our expectation about the durability of marriage. We no longer deeply believe that two people who once have made the choice to marry necessarily should try to weather the storms that shake any vital, intimate relationship. Instead, and more and more, our answer to a difficult marriage is: Try it again—with someone else. And marriages are dissolved even though in reality, for too many people—particularly young mothers with children to care for and nowadays young fathers with children to rear—divorce means going it alone.

It is true that many young people in their 20s are deciding to remain single or are experimenting with alternatives to marriage. As yet we cannot know whether they will succeed in setting new styles in relationships between men and women or what the consequences will be for the kind of fragile marriage we now have.

One thing we do know is that these experiments with new styles have not yet reached down to a still younger age group—to the adolescents who fall in love and want to establish an exclusive pair relationship. For them marriage remains the answer they prefer—indeed, the only answer that promises freedom from parental control and the right always to be together. Equally important, it is the only solution—aside from breaking off the relationship—that most parents will tolerate. Whatever their reservations may be, where their adolescent sons and daughters are concerned, parents usually accept marriage with the idea that it may help—or force—the young pair to "settle down." And if it doesn't work out, they can always get divorced.

Certainly this is not the point of view of two young people deeply in love for the first time. They enter marriage, however hurriedly, with the happy conviction that it will work, that they are different from those who fail. Some of them *are* different and *do* succeed magnificently in growing into adulthood and parenthood serene and confident.

But many do not—too many, especially when there are children who later are shuffled about from one parent to the other. Especially when a second marriage with a second baby or a third does not work either—and unsuccessful second marriages tend to have a shorter life span than the first. Especially when the young mother does not find a new partner and, totally inexperienced and saddened, must both work and try, alone, to do what it has always taken two parents to do well, and then often with the help of other adults—to bring up children to be full human beings.

Knowing that the proportion of early marriages has dropped, many people simply shrug off the problems of early marriage and divorce. But the fact is that in absolute numbers teen-age marriages are increasing. The children of the "baby boom" are growing up and very many of them are marrying early. By ignoring their problems we are creating new difficulties, I think, for their generation and the next as well.

For their marriages are the most fragile of all. Compared to the marriages of young people in their 20s, statistics show, the marriages of teen-agers are of shorter duration and end in the catastrophe of divorce more than twice as frequently. And even when such marriages survive for many years, they carry a high risk. After ten years and 20 years, the likelihood that they will end in divorce remains twice as high as the marriages of young people who were only a few years older when they married.

Whatever we may think about divorce in general, I believe it is crucially important that we think very hard about the fate of the thousands of young people whose marriages falter and fail before they reach their mid-20s. It is not enough to say: They were too immature to make so important a decision, too inexperienced to handle their problems. This may well be true—in our society. But need it be?

Statistics tell part of the story of the hazards in early marriage:

Marriage and early pregnancy are the main reasons today why girls drop out of school, perhaps never to return. In most communities there is no place in the high-school system for a young married woman, let alone for a young mother. Often, too, young husbands fail to go on with their education. The freedom gained by leaving home and school becomes the obligation to work—to be self-supporting and, for a young father, to support a family. Lack of education in turn means that a very large proportion of the very young married live at the poverty level without any reserves to fall back on or any hope of getting out of poverty and debt by getting jobs that require greater skills and practice in using those skills.

There are, of course, young families that are supported by parents. Sometimes this works out happily, particularly when parents are furthering the education of their married children so that they can better make their own way. But mere financial support can mean a prolongation of parental control and childhood dependence and lead to resentment that invades all the family relationships.

In young marriages there is also the problem of health for mothers and their babies. Childbirth can be very safe today. But for many mothers under 20 there are still heavy risks in carrying and bearing a child. And the chances for that baby to be well-born are far less than for those whose mothers are only a few years older. Today 25 percent of the low-birth-weight babies are born to mothers in their teens. We know this, and yet it is very difficult for teen-aged adults to get the counseling they need or the medical care and support young mothers especially should have.

But such statistics can tell only part of the story of why so many young marriages end up as young divorces.

More significant is the dull and frightening sense of isolation that so often takes the place of feelings of freedom and the delight in being alone with a loved partner. Married and living alone, the young husband and wife no longer move among older adults, whose concerns they no longer share, and they have no place among their unmarried peers. All the social supports of their lives fall away in their total dependence on each other.

In most societies in which there is teen-age marriage, the young couple are given a great deal of time to find themselves in their new life. The young wife goes back and forth between her parents' home and her own, and when the first baby comes she is in the center of a group of mothering women while she gains her own experience of motherhood. The young husband too can count on help and companionship.

But with our insistence that marriage, as an adult relationship, means living in and fending for one's own home, the high price of early marriage too often is unprotected isolation and extreme loneliness. Unprepared for parenthood, two young people who have become very close may see the new baby as an interloper. Or if they are already restless, the baby may become just one more obstacle to pleasure and freedom. The mother is permanently stuck at home. The father is almost equally confined—or goes out alone. There is no money now for pleasure and almost nowhere the young couple can go for amusement with the baby.

Then our current belief that a speedy divorce is the way out of the dilemma begins to take effect. From the time a young wife gets pregnant, fear of divorce hangs over her. Will he stay with her? Will he help take care of the baby? Will he still love her? Or will he, like so many other young fathers, throw up his responsibilities because the load is too heavy, the future too bleak? And her anxieties feed his. Looking around, she becomes much more aware of the fatherless families she knows about; looking around, he sees the defecting fathers who are going their own way. And each accuses the other of things they both fear and long for—freedom from responsibility, a chance to get away, longing for better opportunities in life, a way out of their unhappy situation.

But is the divorce that so often follows the only solution? For a marriage that has irretrievably failed, it may be. But need it have failed?

The greatest enemy of young marriages, I believe, is the fact that from the beginning we anticipate their failure. Almost no one—neither the friends of the young couple nor their parents, teachers, and employers—expects a very young marriage to grow in stability and happy mutuality. When it does fail, most people say: "I told you so!" And the failure is the more poignant because of this ultimate rejection.

Where primitive peoples waited for young married couples to attain some maturity before they settled down, we all too often use marriage as the means of getting young people to settle down—the girl safely in her home, the boy firmly tied to his job. Since they are married, we expect them to behave as adults. But at the same time, because they are so young and inexperienced, we expect them to fail.

It is this ambivalence in our social attitudes toward young marriage that sets it apart from other marriages and compounds the problems of early-marriage failure and early divorce. It is also this ambivalence that prevents us from considering in all seriousness what can be done to protect these marriages while a young husband and wife are growing each other up, are learning to become parents before they are fully adult and are searching for a significant place for themselves in a world they have only begun to explore.

We shall not solve the problems of early marriage and early divorce until the climate of opinion about marriage and divorce in general changes. This may involve a much stronger feeling that it is valuable to remain single in the years in which a man and a woman are finding themselves as individuals. It may include a fresh appreciation of friendship as a basic adult relationship. Almost certainly, as we continue to value marriage we shall realize that a good marriage—and a good divorce too—does take a lot of devotion and hard work.

All that will help. But for young marriages it will not be enough.

Looking at young people who are trying to make a go of it, the thing that is most obvious is that they exist in a kind of limbo. They are treated neither as full adults nor as children. They are accorded neither the full rights that go with adult responsibilities nor the protections that go with childhood dependence. So they are left without the major sources of support provided in our kind of society.

Communities, educators, counselors and families all can contribute to providing a legitimate place in life for those who enter marriage early. They need to live where they can keep in touch with their peers, married and single, and where they have some continuing communication with older adults. Group living—as married students live close together during their college years—can keep them in touch with each other and give some unmarried young people a way to try out living away from home. Facilities for continuing their education and access to the kinds of education that will help them find their way as young adults are essential, both for their future and to keep them moving with their peers. The right to family counseling and medical care—without adult intervention—can ease many of their difficulties.

But above all they need opportunities to belong—to have the support of small groups of their own choice. They need to know that other people, young and not so young, have trouble getting adjusted to each other; they need to learn how to talk things out. Consciousness-raising for young couples is a much safer and more constructive enterprise than consciousness-raising for one sex, where women—or men—talk about their spouses who aren't present until often they are turned into monsters. They need to know what their spouses are troubled about as a first step in reaching out to help each other. And they need ideas—things to think about and things to do together outside the narrow walls of their marriage.

Young couples need a chance to continue to become persons. Some will grow together; some will grow apart. But whatever the outcome for the marriage, they will have had a *good* experience of being and living with a growing human person.

Number of words 2225
See page 457 for questions
Reading time in seconds ________
See page 498 for conversion table

Selection 80

None of This Is Fair

Richard Rodriguez

As America becomes more diverse, are laws that once attempted to ensure equal opportunities for all citizens still fair? Were they ever? Should such laws exist, and if so, who should be entitled to protection under Affirmative Action legislation?

My plan to become a professor of English—my ambition during long years in college at Stanford, then in graduate school at Columbia and Berkely—was complicated by feelings of embarrassment and guilt. So many times I would see other Mexican-Americans and know we were alike only in race. And yet, simply because our race was the same, I was, during the last years of my schooling, the beneficiary of their situation. Affirmative Action programs had made it all possible. The disadvantages of others permitted my promotion; the absence of many Mexican-Americans from academic life allowed my designation as a "minority student."

For me opportunities had been extravagant. There were fellowships, summer research grants, and teaching assistantships. After only two years in graduate school, I was offered teaching jobs by several colleges. Invitations to Washington conferences arrived and I had the chance to travel abroad as a "Mexican-American representative." The benefits were often, however, too gaudy to please. In three published essays, in conversations with teachers, in letters to politicians and at conferences, I worried the issue of Affirmative Action. Often I proposed contradictory opinions, though consistent was the admission that—because of an early, excellent education—I was no longer a principal victim of racism or any other social oppression. I said that but still I continued to indicate on applications for financial aid that I was a Hispanic-American. It didn't really occur to me to say anything else, or to leave the question unanswered.

Thus I complied with and encouraged the old bureaucratic logic of Affirmative Action. I let government officials treat the disadvantaged condition of many Mexican-Americans with my advancement. Each fall my presence was noted by Health, Education, and Welfare department statisticians. As I pursued advanced literary studies and learned the skill of reading Spenser and Wordsworth and Empson, I would hear myself numbered among the culturally disadvantaged. Still, silent, I didn't object.

But the irony cut deep. And guilt would not be evaded by averting my glance when I confronted a face like my own in a crowd. By late 1975, nearing the completion of my graduate studies at Berkeley, I was so wary of the benefits of Affirmative Action that I feared my inevitable success as an applicant for a teaching position. The months of fall—traditionally that time of academic job-searching—passed without my applying to a single school. When one of my professors chanced to learn this in late November, he was astonished, then furious. He yelled at me: Did I think that because I was a minority student jobs would just come looking for me? What was I thinking? Did I realize that he and several other faculty members had already written letters on my behalf? Was I going to start acting like some other minority students he had known? They struggled for success and then, when it was almost within reach, grew strangely afraid and let it pass. Was that it? Was I determined to fail?

I did not respond to his questions. I didn't want to admit to him, and thus to myself, the reason I delayed.

I merely agreed to write to several schools. (In my letter I wrote: "I cannot claim to represent disadvantaged Mexican-Americans. The very fact that I am in a position to apply for this job should make that clear.") After two or three days, there were telegrams and phone calls, invitations to interviews, then airplane trips. A blur of faces and the murmur of their soft questions. And, over someone's shoulder, the sight of campus buildings shadowing pictures I had seen years before when I leafed through Ivy League catalogues with great expectations. At the end of each visit, interviewers would smile and wonder if I had any questions. A few times I quietly wondered what advantage my race had given me over other applicants. But that was an impossible question for them to answer without embarrassing me. Quickly, several persons insisted that my ethnic identity had given me no more than a "foot inside the door"; at most, I had a "slight edge" over other applicants. "We just looked at your dossier with extra care and we like what we saw. There was never any question of having to alter our standards. You can be certain of that."

In the early part of January, offers arrived on stiffly elegant stationery. Most schools promised terms appropriate for any new assistant professor. A few made matters worse—and almost more tempting—by offering more: the use of university housing; an unusually large starting salary; a reduced teaching schedule. As the stack of letters mounted, my hesitation increased. I started calling department chairmen to ask for another week, then 10 more days—"more time to reach a decision"—to avoid the decision I would need to make.

At school, meantime, some students hadn't received a single job offer. One man, probably the best student in the department, did not even get a request for his dossier. He and I met outside a classroom one day and he asked about my opportunities. He seemed happy for me. Faculty members beamed. They said they had expected it. "After all, not many schools are going to pass up getting a Chicano with a Ph.D. in Renaissance literature, " somebody said laughing. Friends wanted to know which of the offers I was going to accept. But I couldn't make up my mind. February came and I was running out of time and excuses. (One chairman guessed my delay was a bargaining ploy and increased his offer with each of my calls.) I had to promise a decision by the 10th; the 12th at the very latest.

On the 18th of February, late in the afternoon, I was in the office I shared with several other teaching assistants. Another graduate student was sitting across the room at his desk. When I got up to leave, he looked over to say in an uneventful voice that he had some big news. He had finally decided to accept a position at a faraway university. It was not a job he especially wanted, he admitted. But he had to take it because there hadn't been any other offers. He felt trapped, and depressed, since his job would separate him from his young daughter.

I tried to encourage him by remarking that he was lucky at least to have found a job. So many others hadn't been able to get anything. But before I finished speaking I realized that I had said the wrong thing. And I anticipated his next question.

"What are your plans?" he wanted to know. "Is it true you've gotten an offer from Yale?"

I said that it was. "Only, I still haven't made up my mind."

He stared at me as I put on my jacket. And smiling, then unsmiling, he asked if I knew that he too had written to Yale. In his case, however, no one had bothered to acknowledge his letter with even a postcard. What did I think of that?

He gave me no time to answer.

"Damn!" he said sharply and his chair rasped the floor as he pushed himself back. Suddenly, it was to *me* that he was complaining. "It's just not right, Richard. None of this is fair. You've done some good work, but so have I. I'll bet our records are just about equal. But when we look for jobs this year, it's a different story. You get all of the breaks."

To evade his criticism, I wanted to side with him. I was about to admit the injustice of Affirmative Action. But he went on, his voice hard with accusation. "It's all very simple this year. You're a Chicano. And I am a Jew. That's the only real difference between us."

His words stung me: there was nothing he was telling me that I didn't know. I had admitted everything already. But to hear someone else say these things, and in such an accusing tone, was suddenly hard to take. In a deceptively calm voice, I responded that he had simplified the whole issue. The phrases came like bubbles to the tip of my tongue: "new blood"; "the importance of cultural diversity"; "the goal of racial integration." These were all the arguments I had proposed several years ago—and had long since abandoned. Of course the offers were unjustifiable. I knew that. All I was saying amounted to a frantic self-defense. I tried to find an end to a sentence. My voice faltered to a stop.

"Yeah, sure," he said. "I've heard all that before. Nothing you say really changes the fact that Affirmative Action is unfair. You see that, don't you? There isn't any way for me to compete with you. Once there were quotas to keep my parents out of certain schools; now there are quotas to get you in and the effect on me is the same as it was for them."

I listened to every word he spoke. But my mind was really on something else, I knew at that moment that I would reject all of the offers. I stood there silently surprised by what an easy conclusion it was. Having prepared for so many years to teach, having trained myself to do nothing else, I had hesitated out of practical fear. But now that it was made, the decision came with relief, I immediately knew I had made the right choice.

My colleague continued talking and I realized that he was simply right. Affirmative Action programs *are* unfair to white students. But as I listened to him assert his rights, I thought of the seriously disadvantaged. How different they were from white, middle-class students who come armed with the testimony of their grades and aptitude scores and self-confidence to complain about the unequal treatment they now receive. I listen to them. I do not want to be careless about what they say. Their rights are important to protect. But inevitably when I hear them or their lawyers, I think about the most seriously disadvantaged, not simply Mexican-Americans, but of all those who do not ever imagine themselves going to college or becoming doctors: white, black, brown. Always poor. Silent. They are not plaintiffs before the court or against the misdirection of Affirmative Action. They lack the confidence (my confidence) to assume their right to a good education. They lack the confidence and skills a good primary and secondary education provides and which are prerequisites for informed public life. They remain silent.

The debate drones on and surrounds them in stillness. They are distant, faraway figures like the boys I have seen peering down from freeway overpasses in some other part of town.

Number of words 1790
See page 459 for questions
Reading time in seconds ________
See page 498 for conversion table

Selection 81

The Fifth Freedom

Seymour St. John

"If a nation values anything more than freedom, it will lose its freedom; and the irony of it is that if it is comfort or money that it values more, it will lose that too"—so said Somerset Maugham. Is the fifth freedom one that addresses itself to that very problem?

More than three centuries ago a handful of pioneers crossed the ocean to Jamestown and Plymouth in search of freedoms they were unable to find in their own countries, the freedoms we still cherish today; freedom from want, freedom from fear, freedom of speech, freedom of religion. Today the descendants of the early settlers, and those who have joined them since, are fighting to protect these freedoms at home and througout the world.

And yet there is a fifth freedom—basic to those four—that we are in danger of losing: *the freedom to be one's best*. St. Exupéry describes a ragged, sensitive-faced Arab child, haunting the streets of a North African town, as a lost Mozart: he would never be trained or developed. Was he free? "No one grasped you by the shoulder while there was still time; and nought will awaken in you the sleeping poet or musician or astronomer that possibly inhabited you from the beginning." The freedom to be one's best is the chance for the development of each person to his highest power.

How is it that we in America have begun to lose this freedom, and how can we regain it for our nation's youth? I believe it has started slipping away from us because of three great misunderstandings.

First, the misunderstanding of the meaning of democracy. The principal of a great Philadelphia high school is driven to cry for help in combating the notion that it is undemocratic to run a special program of studies for outstanding boys and girls. Again, when a good independent school in Memphis recently closed some thoughtful citizens urged that it be taken over by the public-school system and used for boys and girls of high ability; that it have entrance requirements and give an advanced program of studies to superior students who were interested and able to take it. The proposal was rejected because it was undemocratic! Out of this misunderstanding comes the middle-muddle. Courses are geared to the middle of the class. The good student is unchallenged, bored. The loafer receives his passing grade. And the lack of an outstanding course for the outstanding student, the lack of a standard which a boy or girl must meet, passes for democracy.

The second misunderstanding concerns what makes for happiness. The aims of our present-day culture are avowedly ease and material well-being: shorter hours; a shorter week; more return for less accomplishment; more softsoap excuses and fewer honest, realistic demands. In our schools this is reflected by the vanishing hickory stick and the emerging psychiatrist. The hickory stick had its faults, and the psychiatrist has his strengths. But the trend is clear: *Tout comprendre c'est tout pardonner*. Do we really believe that our softening standards bring happiness? Is it our sound and considered judgment that the tougher subjects of the classics and mathematics should be thrown aside, as suggested by some educators, for doll-playing? Small wonder that Charles Malik, Lebanese delegate at the U.N., writes: "There is in the West"—in the United States—"a general weakening of moral fiber. [Our] leadership does not seem to be adequate to the unprecedented challenges of the age."

The last misunderstanding is in the area of values. Here are some of the most influential tenets of teacher education over the past fifty years: there is no eternal truth; there is no absolute moral law; there is no God. Yet all of history has taught us that the denial of these ultimates, the placement of man or state at the core of the universe, results in a paralyzing mass selfishness; and the first signs of it are already frighteningly evident.

Arnold Toynbee has said that all progress, all development come from challenge and a consequent response. Without challenge there is no response, no development, no freedom. So first we owe to our children the most demanding, challenging curriculum that is within their capabilities. Michelanglo did not learn to paint by spending his time doodling. Mozart was not an accomplished pianist at the age of eight as the result of spending his days in front of a television set. Like Eve Curie, like Helen Keller, they responded to the challenge of their lives by a disciplined training: and they gained a new freedom.

The second opportunity we can give our boys and girls is the right to failure. "Freedom is not only a privilege, it is a test," writes De Nöuy. What kind of a test is it, what kind of freedom where no one can fail? The day is past when the United States can afford to give high-school diplomas to all who sit through four years of instruction, regardless of whether any visible results can be discerned. We live in a narrowed world where we must be alert, awake to realism; and realism demands a standard which either must be met or result in failure. There are hard words, but they are brutally true. If we deprive our children of the right to fail we deprive them of their knowledge of the world as it is.

Finally, we can expose our children to the best values we have found. By relating our lives to the evidences of the ages, by judging our philosophy in the light of values that history has proven truest, perhaps we shall be able to produce that "ringing message, full of content and truth, satisfying the mind, appealing to the heart, firing the will, a message on which one can stake his whole life." This is the message that could mean joy and strength and leadership—freedom as opposed to serfdom.

Number of words 934
See page 461 for questions
Reading time in seconds ________
See page 498 for conversion table

SELECTION 82

Seven Keys to the Puzzle of Coping with Life

Roy Menninger, M.D.

Coping with life happens to be a universal problem. A psychiatrist is perhaps especially well qualified to share with us insights that will provide significant help. Menninger gets us back to the basics. As the Greeks put it, "Know thyself." Menninger adds, "in seven ways."

In this incredibly complex world each of us needs to examine ourselves—our motivations, our goals. As a search for a clearer idea of what we stand for, toward what we are headed, and what we think is truly important, this kind of continuing self-scrutiny can help to stabilize us in a world of explosive change. A close look at ourselves contributes to that sought-after capacity for autonomy, and gives us greater ability to make wise and useful choices, to exert some control over our own destiny.

It is never easy for any of us to look closely at ourselves—the ancient aphorism of "physician, heal thyself" notwithstanding. Most of us do so only when forced by crisis, anxiety, or a blunt confrontation with reality. Some of us have spouses or friends who help us look at the sore spots within, the personal rough spots which cause us and other pain. But for most of us, it is far easier to look outside, to look at others, whether to admire or to find fault, whether to seek guidance or to castigate.

As important as this self-knowledge is, the daily pressures to act, to do, to decide make it difficult to stop and think, to consider, to examine one's life goals, one's directions, one's priorities—the basic choices one faces in managing his own world. Indeed, it is more than probable that few of us would pause to undertake such a vital inventory unless someone else said, as I am saying now, "Stop! Think about these issues for a while; defer those other 'important' things that pre-empt your daily routine!"

How are we to go about this? I ask you to focus on several rhetorical questions—rhetorical because the answers are to be offered to yourself, not to the public scene. The questions are intended to be a framework around which you may organize ideas about yourself and your relationships with your environment. Though they are questions which focus on the inner world, though they are here raised by a psychiatrist, and though they might be considered a kind of "mental health check-up," they will unquestionably strike you as rather nonmedical and perhaps even more philosophic than scientific. But pre-eminently they are intended to provoke honest thought—never an easy task in relations to one's self.

I

The first of these questions is perhaps the most global for it invites a review of your basic life direction: What are your goals in life? Put otherwise, toward what objectives are you aiming and how realistic are they? How well do they incorporate what is *really* important to you, and how well do they accurately express your values? Are they for real, or only for show?

The network of queries arising from the central question provokes several observations. In an era when planning and setting objectives are bywords for every organization, it is ironic to see how few people have adopted the same strategy for themselves. Perhaps only in late middle-age does the lack of a clear sense of direction and the absence of specific goals become an appalling reality. Many people reach that point in life with a bitter sense of loss and regret, wondering where time and opportunity have gone. The lack of intrinsic value in the materialistically oriented goals some people adopt is obvious when they helplessly wonder what to do next with their lives, now that they have the million dollars they planned to make. The acquisition of a bigger house, a bigger car, and a bigger boat, plus all the status that money will buy has taken on the appearance of a logical goal for many—but would that truly represent your central values?

One cannot think about one's own life goals without asking still other difficult questions: To what purposes do you dedicate your efforts and your life? What are your personal priorities, and how well does your life's work reflect those priorities? Most of us find such difficult questions easy to avoid, presuming that time will answer them—as indeed it will, though not necessarily to our ultimate satisfaction. A close, comfortable, and accepting relationship with another person—a spouse, a colleague, a friend, or even a psychotherapist—can be of great help in considering such questions. The dilemma is, will you find such an opportunity?

II

Closely related to the question about goals is one which bears on your use of time and energy: Does your use of your vital resources truly reflect your priorities? Without much thought most of you would certainly answer "yes," failing to appreciate that for 90 percent of us the answer is almost assuredly "no." Executives with broad responsibilities are presumed to use their time for the things that are important—such things as planning, policy preparation, and the "big" decisions. With a consistency that is hard to believe, studies have repeatedly shown that this is rarely true, and that much more often the busy executive is spending 90 percent of his time on matters that could better be done by others, are simply a part of the daily routine, and have limited relation to the vital responsibilities which he carries.

Most of us will recognize in a moment of more somber thought that the "important things" in our lives are frequently deferred with some comforting but self-deceiving assumption that there will always be time tomorrow.

From yet another perspective, there is a high probability that your use of time and energy reflects serious imbalances within the life space of each of you. In spite of public protestations about the importance of the family, about the needs of the community, about the troubles in our world, most of us devote the smallest proportion of our time to these areas, Indeed, it could be fairly said of many of you that you are married to your jobs, not your husbands or wives, that you are invested in your colleagues, not your children, that you are committed to your business, not your society. The point is not that these imbalances are wrong, but that it is quite probable that they are deeply inconsistent with your own statements about what is important and what constitute your personal priorities.

It is this inconsistency which produces a subtle but corrosive tension as your conscience cries out for one commitment while your activities express another. At times this reflects a distorted conception of responsibility, at times an impulsive response to the demands of others, but most often it is the outcome of unthinking behavior, the consequence of a general failure to consider your goals, your priorities, and your plans for reaching them.

Nowhere is the imbalance in the use of time and energy more obvious than in regard to ourselves. Executives are dedicated people, and for many this dedication implies and finally comes to mean considerable self-sacrifice. Time for one's self is discouraged, pleasure is deemed to be selfish, and one's own needs come last.

Again drawing upon information from a study of executives, I can report that less than 40 percent of some 4,000 executives studied had an avocational pursuit. They appeared to have had few sources of personal gratification and gave themselves few opportunities for fulfilling personal pursuits. Why do they not think better of themselves than that, and are they so different from you?

III

The third question is to ask if your sense of responsibility is also out of balance. In its extreme forms, it is easy to find examples of those who will assume no more responsibility for anything than absolutely necessary; certainly the fragmentation of our contemporary culture encourages us to restrict our efforts to smaller and smaller sectors of the human community. Executives demonstrate that same pattern, pointing out that the quality of information is so great that fragmented specialization is inevitable and even advisable. And perhaps it is, but are we guilty of hiding an unduly narrow concept of our responsibility to others behind that rationalization?

Considerably more common in the field of industry is a pattern that reflects the other extreme: an excessive sense of responsibility that keeps us moving like a driven animal. Again, the needs of our organization and the endless call for our services make it hard to define a sense of responsibility which simultaneously expresses our commitment to our organization, to ourselves, and to our family and world as well. Failing to do so exposes us to the ravages of guilt feelings and failure, and of all the feelings known to the human psyche, guilt is probably the most painful.

It is easy to confuse a concept of responsibility with a command for action, connecting a notion of obligation with a need to do something about it. When one begins to discover how big the problem is about which he is worrying, his growing sense of helplessness leads him to turn away, disconnect, and assume that someone else will worry instead.

A more difficult but more effective concept of responsibility is an acknowledgement of the importance of continuing to think about problems and dilemmas, neither turning away in frustration nor hurling one's self forward into them under the pressure of guilt. Continuing to think about the problems of delinquency in one's community, the need for better school programs for the limited as well as the gifted, and the hundreds of other things for which responsible concern is needed is a way of staying engaged, remaining open to alternatives and opportunities, and being ready to respond when the occasion permits.

In more personal terms, the concept of balanced responsibility implies a willingness to accept the responsibility for one's own attitudes, feelings, failures and prejudices, forsaking the easier and unfortunately more frequent tendency to protect or displace these feelings and attitudes onto persons or focuses external to one's self. It is worth asking: Do each of you demonstrate a readiness to acknowledge your anger, your bias, or your limitations—at least to yourself, and to others when this is germane to the situation?

IV

My fourth query is to ask about your courage—not the sort more commonly associated with the battlefield, challenging or embarrassing situations or the like—important though that is. I refer to the courage we need to face the internal foe, for we are in most cases our own worst enemies. In the inimitable words of Pogo, "We have met the enemy—and they is us." This kind of courage is exemplified in an ability to look at yourself honestly and fairly—an expression of the responsibility I noted earlier. It is not easy to entertain the questions I am posing without fluctuating wildly between extremes of excessive personal criticism and total denial that these thoughts have any bearing on you at all.

It is this courage which enables us to face, to articulate, and finally to accept our disappointments and losses—one of the most difficult tasks the human psyche faces.

Perhaps this is not so apparent until one stops to realize that life itself is a succession of losses—beginning with the loss of the warmth and comfort of the uterus which nurtured us for the first nine months of our existence; progressing through childhood and its many losses: dependent infant status, our favorite childhood toys, our privileged status; the loss of the family as adolescence separates us from childhood; the loss of irresponsible pleasures of youth with the advent of maturity; the loss of jobs, or positions, or self-esteem, money, opportunity; the loss of one's friends with advancing age; these and a million others, and finally the ultimate loss of life itself. It is something to ponder how extensive the experience of each of us is with loss, big and small, and to note that these are experiences with profound effects upon our mental health. Even as losses vary in their impact upon us, our psychic structure varies in its capacity to handle them, and not all of us do it with equal success.

It has been said that the quality which distinguishes a great man from another otherwise like him is his capacity to manage disappointment and loss. One thinks of the experiences of Winston Churchill and the crushing disappointments of his early career, or those of Franklin Roosevelt with a disabling onslaught of polio, and begins to realize the wisdom in that observation.

Accepting loss is to accept the reality of it, to allow one's self to feel the pain and anguish of it. One can then come to terms with its meaning. Doing so is vital if the spirit is to continue to grow, and in some cases even to survive. It is relevant to note that the successful rehabilitation of a person newly blind depends upon his first having accepted the painful reality of his loss of vision, in a process of mourning akin to grieving the loss of a loved one.

It brings me to ask: What can you say about your courage to face and to accept the anguish of loss?

V

The fifth query is to ask you to examine the consistency and the quality of your personal relationships. Most of us accept the truism that people are important to people, yet we fail to perceive how often human relationships are superficial, meager, and unrewarding. Is this true of your own? Which of your relationships can you say has a quality of involvement with the other, expressing a depth of emotional investment which is real and mutually experienced? It is again too easy to explain that the pressures of our lives and the demands upon us, the superficial materialism of the age and all the rest are what account for a deep sense of poverty in our relationships with others. To call again upon that element of courage to which I earlier referred, can we examine the quality of the relationships of those who are closest to us to question how honest, how open, how real they are?

It is clear that the capacity to establish close, significant emotional ties with others is characteristic of emotional maturity. It is clear, moreover, that the work, the effort, and sometimes the pain of doing so is quite enough to discourage many, especially when the trends in our society are moving in the same direction. And yet we are still disdainful of the empty superficiality of the cocktail party, even when lessened by the illusion of intimacy which alcohol can provide.

The phenomenon of parallel play in the nursery school—two children in close physical contact with each other but playing entirely alone—is expectable at the age of 2 or 3. When it can be said to characterize a pattern of living at the age of 20 to 40, it hints at relationships eroded by infantile expectations and a lack of mutual commitment. Relationships which show a depth of emotional involvement require a willingness to engage, to share, to listen, to give. What can you say about these qualities in your human relationships?

VI

Not unrelated to a question about your human relationships is a query about sources of your emotional support: From whom do you receive it and to whom do you give it? I have referred to the lack of fulfilling avocation in the lives of many executives—the absence of a rewarding investment in art, in music, in physical activity, in stamp collecting, or a hundred others. Does this also describe you?

It is also clear that many people who are imbued with an especially strong sense of responsibility have great difficulty in seeking or accepting support from others. For some, this is reminiscent of a profoundly unpleasant sense of helplessness from an earlier phase of life. For some it is an unacceptable admission of weakness, of inadequacy; for some it is a contradiction of one's sense of strength and commitment to help others. Ironically, those whose careers lead to increasing responsibility to others must therefore provide increasing support for others at the very moment when they are progressively more isolated, less able to fend for help for themselves, and less able to receive it when it is available. Greater responsibility generates greater personal need—and greater obstacles to receiving it.

VII

Lastly, any survey of your mental health must ask about the role of love in your lives. For most of us the very use of this word threatens a deluge of sentimentality. It is a word which too readily conjures images of Technicolor Hollywood and cow-eyed adolescents. But it is a respectable feeling. I use it to refer to a capacity to care. Perhaps we are not fully aware that it implies a willingness to invest ourselves in others, to be involved with them, to listen to them—in short, to care about them. It should therefore be a hallmark of all our relationships with others. This is the true sense of helping, for it is the only antidote to hate we know, and it is also the foundation stone for that indispensable pillar of good human relationships—trust. Both are always in short supply.

Without intending to promote egocentricity, I would have to ask how truly and how well you love yourself—not in irrational or narcissistic and overblown terms, but as an object of pride and self-esteem, a thing of value, a person of worth. As one can love himself in this mature and realistic way, so he is able to extend the help of love to others in ways which are not demeaning, not controlling, not condescending or patronizing, but respectful and genuinely caring.

Your relationships to others do indeed mirror your relationship to yourself. How well you deal with others may depend upon your success in managing yourself in relation to the provocative and difficult questions I have posed for you today. No one has suggested these questions are easy; in some sense they may be unanswerable. But they do need to be thought about by each of you, talked about with those you love and are close to, and examined repeatedly in the months and years ahead.

Number of words 3010
See page 463 for questions
Reading time in seconds _______
See page 498 for conversion table

SELECTION 83

Presumed Innocents

Susan Goodman

Some problems come in small packages. Newborns are complex little human beings who are capable of more than most people expect. Exactly, how much do babies know at birth?

Not all that long ago, people pictured the newborn as a helpless blob, a tabula rasa waiting to be molded into a human being. Experts presumed infants spent their first weeks not only unable to speak, but also unable to see, hear or think. In the 1940s, even as progressive a scientist as Arnold Gesell, M.D., of the Yale Clinic of Child Development didn't begin studying a baby's development until he or she reached one month of age. He noted in the book *The First Five Years of Life:* "In a sense, he [the human infant] is not fully born until he is about four weeks of age. It takes him that long to attain a working physiological adjustment to his postnatal environment."

Then, about 25 years ago, scientists started taking a more careful look at the newborn—and realized the babies were looking right back!

These specialists are now in the midst of documenting what mothers have always suspected: Newborns are very complex, competent little creatures. Actually, not creatures at all. They are quintessentially human from day one.

Although the doctor standing in the corner of the delivery room may be blurred, neonates see quite distinctly up close. They can also tell the difference between bright and dim light. They can distinguish and favor patterns over solids, moving objects over still ones. They see the world in color, preferring pure tones over "boundary" colors such as red-orange. By three or four months of age, they see color as well as adults.

Deaf? Research now shows babies start hearing their mother's heartbeats and growling stomachs by the fifth month in utero. By month seven, they will startle at the clap of a cymbal from the outside world.

Experts have found that four-day-olds not only detect odors but discriminate among them. An experiment by Elliot Blass, Ph.D., professor of psychology and nutrition at Cornell University, proves the newborn also has functioning tastebuds, learning capacities and a sweet tooth. Consistently approaching from their left, Blass would stoke babies' foreheads, then give them a drop of sugar-water. Even a two-hour-old learned to turn and stick out a tongue in anticipation. No random event here; if a forehead was stroked and no sugar followed, most of the babies cried in protest.

To Interact Is Human

"Newborns are a wonderful combination of development and potential development. They come out of the womb with senses sufficiently developed to take in information and take advantage of their new world," explains Marc Bornstein, Ph.D., of the National Institute of Child Health and Human Development in Bethesda, Maryland. "But unlike many other species (with behavior preset by instinct), we are born 'cognitively flexible.' Babies can adapt to the environment they're confronted with."

An individual baby might take nine months in utero to ready this combination, but evolution has taken eons to perfect it. Too simply put, the human evolutionary process has created new problems as well as solutions. Standing erect and having a brain capable of integrating thought and feeling make us human. They also make birthing tough. In fact passage down the birth canal would be impossible if a baby's brain was allowed to completely develop in utero. The evolutionary solution was to deliver our infants extraordinarily immature and dependent upon a caregiver for years.

Nonetheless, human babies come amazingly ready and able to tackle their most important task: living in a social world. In fact, much of their innate equipment is geared toward this end.

"Babies are purely social," says Edward Z. Tronick, Ph.D., chief of the Child Development Unit at Children's Hospital in Boston. "The things that attract neonates to the inanimate environment are those that mimic the social environment like a teddy bear's face or the low-pitched sound of a rattle that echoes the frequencies of the human voice. Being tuned into the inanimate environment doesn't solve any of the infant's problems, you see. The social environment, on the other hand, provides food, warmth, comfort, everything. From the start, babies have enormous abilities they use to garner these resources."

The social environment's primacy becomes stunningly clear with a second look at the newborn's senses. Until the lenses of their eyes become more flexible at age two months, newborns can only focus well upon objects about eight inches away. This spot marks the distance caregivers naturally zoom in to when trying to attract a baby's attention, also the typical distance separating a nursing infant's face from his/her mother's.

And forget mobiles. Carolyn Goren, M.D., Ph.D., and her colleagues found that faces are exactly what neonates are born wanting to see. She and her associates gave newborns a choice of three pictures: a schematic face, a scrambled version, and a blank square. Before they had ever seen a real human face, many minute-old infants would turn a full 180 degrees to keep the most-human drawing in view.

By ten days of age babies will rapidly turn to sniff a pad doused with their mothers' milk over one donated by another mother. They learn their mother's voice even faster than her scent. Anthony DeCasper, Ph.D., currently at the University of North Carolina at Greensboro, devised a hookup between a pacifier and a tape recorder so a newborn's rate of sucking would determine what voice would be played. He found that the babies would suck at the rate necessary to hear their mothers' voices—and this was true even of babies only 36 to 72 hours old.

Born to Socialize

Neonates don't just passively absorb the social environment. In keeping with our evolutionary heritage they are born ready to take part in humanity's most crucial adaptation—social interaction. Physical tasks like picking up a ball or toddling around a room are mere child's play compared to the complexity of orchestrating a social interchange. Yet from birth infants communicate needs and respond to people around them, influence and are influenced by others.

This communication begins with the first cry that brings Mom running. "Babies use crying as part of their signaling system to communicate needs, wishes, their very state of being," explains Barry Lester, Ph.D., professor of psychiatry and pediatrics at Brown University and Bradley Hospital in Providence, Rhode Island. "Newborns have a hunger cry and their acoustically different pain or distress cry. By four to six weeks when they have more control over their vocal cords, babies develop a cry to communicate frustration and the 'fake' cry that is a bid for attention."

The early infant's signaling system, according to Lester, also includes a repertoire of postures, gestures and facial expressions. Fisted hands for example, convey anger or tension. Tracking something visually signals intrigue. Conversely, averting the gaze can express that a newborn is upset or overloaded by stimuli.

"I have videotape of me interacting with a six-week-old infant," says Tronick. "When I purposefully get too close, the baby narrows his eyes, looks off to the side and sort of purses his mouth. He won't look at me. I get even closer and the baby turns his head away. When I move back, he starts to peek at me. I keep talking to him and move back a little farther. He makes eye-to-eye contact and, since he can't yet fully smile, he gives me a sort of half smile. Then, when I come closer again, he looks off to the side.

"The infant is not only responding, he is actively behaving in a way to modify what I do," Tronick says. "When I am too intrusive and fail to respond to his signals, he turns away. When I am sensitive to his needs, I am rewarded by his looking at me, smiling and vocalizing—behavior that would encourage me."

Another study by Tronick and associates shows that even the youngest babies understand how human interaction is choreographed. Mothers sat face-to-face with their infants, neither moving nor speaking for three minutes. By facing their children yet refusing to engage, these "still-faced" mothers were sending contradictory messages. Baby after baby was confounded and disturbed by the event, confirming they understood exactly what a normal social interaction with Mom or anyone should be. Although their responses were limited, even two-week-olds appeared to be perplexed by a mother's stone-face reaction.

Like any other competent social partner, babies can actively work to keep exchanges running smoothly. Even when mothers aren't stonewalling for an experiment, caregivers and babies can fall out of sync for any reason from unclear signals to simple differences in mood. Yet studies by Tronick and Andrew Gianino, Ph.D., show that when babies attempted to repair these mismatches, 34 percent of the time they created a matching behavior state—mother and baby both playing, each looking at the other—on their first try. The second interactive step repaired 36 percent of the remaining mismatches.

The sophistication is astounding, but perhaps nothing compares to an infant's readiness to perceive speech, our most complicated communication system. "Studies show that young infants have the capacity to distinguish phonemes, the smallest significant units of sound in words, for example, the 'p' and 'm' in 'papa' and 'mama,' " explains Bornstein.

The Dance of Language

With any dance, including the dance of language, timing is crucial. In everyday conversation people alternate words with pauses that mark the boundary and switch of their turn. "The timing of these pauses is very important in terms of communication," explains Beatrice Beebe, Ph.D., associate professor of psychology at Yeshiva University in New York City. "People are very sensitive to the duration of these switching pauses. Strangers will unknowingly match each other's rhythms and will like each other better the more they match."

Beebe and her associates Joseph Jaffe, M.D., Stanley Feldstein, Ph.D., Cynthia Crown, Ph.D., and Michael Jasnow, Ph.D., have looked at the infant's capacity to participate in dialogue's essential rhythm. Babies don't start vocalizing much until around three months, but when Beebe and her colleagues measured vocal exchanges between mothers and their four-month-old infants, they found the partners dancing in step. When mothers used longer pauses, the babies did too. When the babies used shorter pauses, mothers followed along.

Still, a Fragile Being

Newborns are a far cry from the helpless blobs they were portrayed as 30 years ago. They have a new official baby picture as active human beings eager to understand and engage in their social world. Regardless, as Lester points out, they are still babies. "Despite their astounding capacities, newborns are relatively fragile," he says. "They have amazingly difficult tasks in front of them." They may have quite an impressive list of accomplishments—but parents should remember to give them plenty of quiet, protected time to acquaint themselves with their new world.

Number of words 1790
See page 467 for questions
Reading time in seconds ________
See page 498 for conversion table

SELECTION 84

The Great Paradigm Shift

Gloria Steinem

Steinem helps us analyze a perplexing problem: why people think as they do. She explores the organizing principles that determine how people interpret their world. Which paradigm governs your decision making?

"You can't beat something with nothing." That street wisdom also applies to habits of the mind. You can't lose old and negative ways of thinking until new and positive ones replace them.

The biggest and most far-reaching kind of cognitive therapy is a paradigm shift: a change in the organizing principle that underlies the way we think about ourselves and the world. It is a pattern so ingrained that we may consider it "natural" and be unaware of its existence.

In societies shaped by patriarchy and racial divisions, the prevailing paradigm comes in three parts.

The first is the either/or way of thinking that divides almost everything in two. "Masculine" and "feminine," subject and object, light skin and dark skin, dominant and passive, intellect and emotion, mind and body, winner and loser, good and evil, the idea that there are "two sides to every question"—all these are the living results of bipartite thinking. In older and more subtle cultures, each half was equally necessary to the other (as in the yin and yang of Eastern thought), but even that division had its origins in the division of human qualities into "masculine" and "feminine." The more unequal this genderized dyad became, the more it turned into the next part of the paradigm: linear thinking. Rating and grading people, the notion that all accomplishment lies in defeating others, even a linear view of abstractions like time and history—all these things were organized by the same paradigm. Since a straight line was too simplistic to be practical for most human interactions, however, it split into the third and last part of the paradigm: hierarchy. The pyramid or the classic organizational chart became the grid through which many cultures were to see the world for centuries: from a "male-headed" household to corporate structures in which all authority flows from the top from hierarchical classrooms to religions in which God's will is interpreted by a pope or ayatollah.

It isn't that a binary, linear, and then hierarchical paradigm is always wrong. Some things really have two parts, competition can be used to press individual boundaries, and a hierarchy is well-suited to firefighting, surgery, or anything else that requires quick action.

But as a universal pattern with almost no alternatives, this paradigm limits us at best and destroys us at worst. It turns most human interactions into a contest that only one or a few at the top can win, and it teaches us that there is a limited amount of self-esteem to go around; that some of us can only have it if others do not.

Fortunately, this is just a cognitive construct. There is nothing biological or immutable about it, and therefore it can be changed. In other times and cultures, there have been cyclical and regenerative paradigms, unitary paradigms, and pantheistic ones in which each living thing had a spirit of its own—to name just a few. Especially for those of us who have been looking at everything through a linear and hierarchical grid—perhaps no more aware of alternatives than a fish is aware of alternatives to water—it's important to let other possibilities into our minds. Since we are living in a time when the foundations of the old paradigm are cracking anyway, there are motives for changing it and glimpses through the cracks of what the future could be. Perhaps the most obvious motive for change is the ecological crisis. Disasters like pollution, a new species extinction every few hours, biospheric degradation, and the threat of nuclear annihilation are all powerful reasons to overturn the centuries of the either/or, Man-against-Nature paradigm that got us here. To think about taking our place in nature instead of conquering it is a deep change in the way we see ourselves and the world. It means changing from binary and linear thinking to a cyclical paradigm that is a new declaration of interdependence.

Another motive is the movement against internal

colonialisms of sex and race. Superior/inferior, light skin/dark skin, masculine/feminine divisions are being replaced with the idea that each person has a full circle of human qualities in unique combination. Instead of defining power as domination, it is being redefined as self-determination. Instead of outstripping others, the goal is completing oneself. Since the sexual caste system is the most ancient form of oppression and the one on which all others are based, changing it is like pulling the rug from under the whole hierarchy. As physicist Fritjof Capra writes in *The Turning Point*, feminism "will have a profound effect on further evolution" because patriarchy "is the one system . . . whose doctrines were so universally accepted that they seemed to be the laws of nature."

The communications revolution has eroded hierarchy by giving the bottom as much information as the top—and also by letting all parts of the hierarchy *see* each other (which is why computers and photocopiers are outlawed in totalitarian regimes, and access even to phone lines extremely restricted). Long-term hierarchies have produced a few people at the top who use power poorly, a lot of people in the middle who wait for orders and approval, and many more at the bottom who feel powerless and resentful. But from Eastern Europe to South Africa, democratic uprisings are softening and humanizing hierarchies into more circularity. Smaller, more lateral and cooperative units are emerging for diverse purposes, from Japanese corporate management to Gandhian village economies.

Even the sacred cow of competitiveness is getting to be less sacred. In *No Contest*, psychologist Alfie Kohn poses the question: *"Do we perform better when we are trying to beat others than when we are working with them or alone?"* After looking at many studies, he concludes: "The evidence is so overwhelmingly clear and consistent that the answer to this question already can be reported: *almost never*. Superior performance not only does not *require* competition; it usually seems to require its absence." In fact, a competitive system perpetuates itself by keeping self-esteem low and making even the winners constantly needy of more success. As Kohn writes, *"We compete to overcome fundamental doubts about our capabilities and, finally, to compensate for low self-esteem."*

Rather than finding a source in competition, self-esteem and excellence both come from the excitement of learning and pressing individual boundaries; a satisfaction in the task itself; pleasure in cooperating with, appreciating, and being appreciated by others—and as much joy in the process as in the result.

As each person completes herself or himself and contributes what is authentic, a new paradigm emerges: circularity. At rest, it is a circle, and in motion, a spiral. When we look more closely at each part, it is a microcosm of the whole. If we consciously take this as our organizing principle, we come up with very nonbinary, unlinear, nonhierarchical results. For instance:

If we think of ourselves as circles, our goal is completion—not defeating others. Progress lies in the direction we haven't been.

If we think of families and nurturing groups as circles, the sum means maximizing each part—not restricting others or keeping secrets. Progress is appreciation.

If we think of work structures as circles, excellence and cooperation are the goal—not competition. Progress becomes mutual support and connectedness.

If we think of nature as a circle, then we are part of its reciprocity. Progress means interdependence.

If we respect nature and each living thing as a microcosm of nature—then we respect the unique miracle of ourselves.

And so we have come full circle. Self-esteem is not a zero-sum game: by definition, there is exactly enough to go around. By making the circle the organizing image in our minds, a prison of lines and limits will gradually disappear.

Number of words 1310
See page 469 for questions
Reading time in seconds ________
See page 498 for conversion table

Tactics That Win Good Part-Time Jobs

Nancy Henderson

More and more people are employed in part-time jobs—by choice. Finding good part-time employment is often a problem. But by heeding Henderson's advice, you might land the part-time job of your dreams.

In 1973, when Ronnie Fox's first child was born, the computer programmer quit her full-time job at IBM because the company wouldn't convert her position to a part-time one. After four years of hunting for part-time work, Fox finally landed a five-hour-a-day job as a programmer at Control Data Corp. in Sunnyvale, Cal.

When Fox's department at CDC was reassigned to Minneapolis in November 1988, it took her only a month to find a 30-hour-per-week job with Tandem Computers, in Cupertino, Cal.

Part-time employment has grown 21% since 1980, according to the National Planning Association. The Bureau of Labor Statistics reports that about 20% of employed women and 6% of employed men voluntarily work a permanent part-time schedule. And almost 20% of part-time jobs are for professionals, which generally means the jobs require a college degree or equivalent experience.

Hundreds of companies are interested in following the lead of firms like US Sprint, which last August began a nationwide program to encourage part-time and job-sharing arrangements among its 16,000 employees. "Demographics show we will need flexible work arrangements to get employees with the right skills," says Deb Holt, human resources manager at US Sprint in Kansas City. "Organizations starting to do this now will be a good competitive position later on."

Women returning from maternity leave make up a large portion of part-time professionals, but a short workweek also appeals to employees who provide care for a disabled spouse or elderly parents.

Retirees, such as John Collins, make up one of the fastest-growing groups within the part-time work force. After 22 years of service Collins retired from the State Department in 1983. Since then, he has discovered that "there are all sorts of exciting careers you can poke around in."

His latest part-time assignments included directing educational programs at the Association of Telemessaging Services International and doing contract work for Resumes Plus, a résumé-writing and personnel firm in Alexandria, Va.

Where the Jobs Are

Despite an increased interest among employers, finding part-time work can be a job in itself, especially if you're looking for a new position rather than converting the full-time job you already hold to part-time status. There is no comprehensive listing of companies that offer opportunities for part-time employment, so you're pretty much on your own.

You'll find plenty of opportunities to flip hamburgers, but your chances of getting a professional position depend largely on your field and the companies you approach.

The best opportunities are in jobs that can be independent or project-oriented. If your experience includes writing or computer programming, for example, those would be attractive skills to emphasize. High-stress fields, such as social work, often offer part-time hours to avoid employee burnout. At US Sprint, part-time schedules are available in customer service, field sales, telemarketing and technical positions. Aetna Life & Casualty is using part-time schedules to help recruit accountants, auditors and bond raters.

Tougher to mold to a part-time schedule are jobs that require extensive staff management or client contact. Job-sharing—which is splitting the responsibilities of a full-time job with another employee—is one way to make part-time schedules feasible for many legal, advertising and financial-services positions. US Sprint offers job-sharing as an alternative for company attorneys. Kaiser Permanente, the nation's largest group-practice health maintenance organization, is developing a pilot job-sharing program for physicians in its northern California region.

Whatever your field, you'll improve your odds if you focus your search in these areas:

- **Your current employer.** Chances for negotiating a part-time schedule are usually best when you already know the company and the job. Your employer has made an investment in you, and hiring and training a replacement would be costly.

- **High-growth, high-tech companies.** Firms that have to compete for scarce talent need to be accommodating. AT&T, Apple Computer, Digital Equipment, Hewlett-Packard, IBM and Xerox are among the high-tech companies included in *Working Mother* magazine's October 1989 list of 60 best companies for working mothers.

- **Nonprofit organizations.** Many of the best part-time opportunities can be found in the nonprofit sector—libraries, museums, universities and human-service organizations, for instance. Unable to pay corporate-level salaries, they offer flexibility instead.

- **Small businesses.** Like nonprofit groups, small companies with salary constraints often compete with other firms by offering flexible schedules. And managers can usually negotiate more freely than in large organizations, where personnel policies sometimes seem set in stone.

- **Federal government.** A 1978 law required federal agencies to expand high-level part-time positions and prorate salaries and benefits according to the number of hours worked. In practice, some government employers, such as the Department of Labor and the Smithsonian Institution, encourage part-time hiring more than others. Part-time opportunities are expanding after a decline during the Reagan administration, when temporary or contractual arrangements were favored. However, professional slots are often restricted to applicants who have worked for the government at least three years.

- **State and local government.** Most state governments have at least one agency with part-time positions; Massachusetts, New York and North Carolina have formal plans promoting part-time employment. State and local governments often give part-timers generous benefits. Milwaukee, for example, encourages job-sharing among its city and county employees by offering full health insurance to job-sharers who contribute half of the premium.

Where To Get Help

The key is to zero in on employers who show evidence of being open to new ideas such as allowing employees to work at home using computer terminals. Companies with a relatively young work force or a large proportion of women in management tend to have employees with family responsibilities, which makes them more receptive to flexible scheduling.

Linda Marks, a career consultant in San Francisco who specializes in advising clients about part-time employment, suggests scrutinizing a company's annual reports. "Look for a company that emphasizes things like a new gym for employees or a parental-leave policy, not just new machinery," says Marks. . . .

Most colleges and universities have career-counseling centers that post job openings. A counseling center for women or senior citizens is especially likely to have leads on part-time positions. . . .

Don't neglect help-wanted ads, but don't concentrate on the "part-time" listings. You'll have better luck checking for part-time positions among the full-time listings in your field.

Sharpen Your Sales Pitch

Once you have a good prospect in sight, you may have to use some creative salesmanship to land the position you want. For example, you might apply for a full-time job and, during the interview, try to persuade the boss to make the position part-time. You might get somewhere if, say, the job requires 37 hours per week and you propose to work 33 hours. But if you want to work fewer than 30 hours a week, suggest job-sharing instead.

The less experience a prospective employer has in hiring part-time professionals, the more resistance you're likely to face. But don't be intimidated. If you're told that others in the department would resent your reduced hours, focus on your reduced pay. If the company has never hired anyone part-time and is afraid to take the risk, suggest a trial period.

Consider it your responsibility, not your employer's, to work out scheduling and logistical problems. Be available for clients or staff who need to reach you during your off hours. Get a telephone-answering machine to take messages at home. Be willing to come to the office for emergencies or meetings on your day off.

Come armed with some eye-opening statistics. A recent study by Catalyst, a New York research and business advisory group, examined part-time employment, job-sharing and telecommuting at 47 companies, mostly Fortune 500 firms. Sixty-five percent of personnel managers surveyed said that flexible schedules are boosting productivity, and 60% expect better work options to help the company recruit top professionals. Employees are happy, too; 88% reported their arrangements are working well.

Is It Worth It?

Getting a salary proportional to a job's full-time equivalent is usually tougher when you join a new company part-time than when you convert a full-time position to part-time. When you negotiate a salary, guard against working extended hours without compensation. If a company's official work week is 40 hours but most professionals work about 60, a half-time position will probably require 30 hours, not 20. In general, part-time and job-sharing arrangements are salaried; contractual or free-lance employees are paid by the hour.

Even if you work out an acceptable salary, you may still fall short on benefits. Fringes typically are worth more than one-third of a full-time worker's total compensation, but some part-time positions offer little more than what is required by law. All employees must get social security, unemployment insurance and worker's compensation. If a firm offers a pension plan, all employees over age 21 who have one year of service and work at least 1,000 hours per year must be eligible.

Most employers give part-time workers some paid holidays, partial vacation and sick leave based on the number of hours worked, but they are not required to do so.

Insurance coverage is less common. In a 1985 study by Hewitt Associates, only about half of 484 firms surveyed provided life insurance and partial medical and dental benefits to part-timers working from 20 to 29 hours a week. Short-term disability coverage was offered by 30% of the companies and long-term disability insurance by 25%. Five states—California, Hawaii, New Jersey, New York and Rhode Island—require disability insurance, and Massachusetts requires health insurance for employees working more than 20 hours a week.

Many health-insurance providers limit group coverage to employees who work more than 30 hours a week, so part-timers may not be eligible. If they are, they may be asked to pay a portion of the premium. . . .

Other Options

Sharing a job may give you a break on benefits. Because job-sharers split the responsibilities of a single full-time position, compensation and benefits are usually divided between them or prorated based on the total number of hours each person works.

Other strategies for keeping part-time hours include:

- **Independent contracting.** As a self-employed consultant or free-lancer you set your own schedule, but your income might be irregular and you receive no benefits. You are responsible for paying your own social security tax, which this year is 15.3% of income from self-employment. To avoid paying social security, unemployment insurance and pension benefits, some companies have hired independent contractors who function like regular employees. But the IRS is taking a look at that practice.
- **Temporary work.** No longer confined to clerical work, temporary positions are opening up in accounting, health care, engineering and other professional areas. You're generally an employee of an agency, which finds you work and pays social security, unemployment and possibly other benefits. Temporary work is usually full-time for a set period, which makes it more attractive for retirees than for parents with child-care needs.

Number of words 2520
See page 471 for questions
Reading time in seconds ________
See page 498 for conversion table

Selection 86

Understanding Self-Segregation on the Campus

Troy Duster

Becoming a part of campus life is a problem for many college students. Some choose to segregate themselves according to ethnic, racial, or cultural identity. Buy why? Don't all students want to fit in?

In the last decade, the increasing social and ethnic heterogeneity of the nation's college campuses has captured the attention of media pundits, higher-education administrators, and many faculty members. Unfortunately, the troublesome aspects of this development have dominated most of the public debate.

One major issue that has absorbed the media is that many students' social lives are segmented in ways that reaffirm their ethnic, racial, and cultural identities. This segmentation, now routinely referred to as "Balkanization," causes surprise, chagrin, and even some derision. It is characterized as an unseemingly reversion to "tribalism" that gets in the way of the search for common ground.

There is something both old and new here. Although typically treated as a new and alarming development, such segmentation is quite an old phenomenon and has been replayed throughout the history of higher education in America. Social historians who study U.S. colleges and universities know that the Hillel and Newman foundations played similar important roles for Jewish and Catholic students, respectively, for much of this century. With the assistance of such organizations, parties, dances, recreation, study groups, and sometimes residences were routinely "self-segregated," often in response to active discrimination against Jews and Catholics elsewhere on campus.

Today's critics are suffering from a selective cultural amnesia when they portray African-American theme houses and Chinese student associations as newly created enclaves that destroy the search for common ground. Even into the last decade, the most prestigious fraternities at Yale, Michigan, Harvard, and Berkeley had never admitted a Jew, much less an African American or an Asian. The all-Jewish fraternity was common as late as the 1960's, and when a Chinese American, Sherman Wu, pledged a fraternity at Northwestern in 1956, it was such a sensation that it made national news and generated a folk song. Over the years, some mild hand wringing occurred about such discrimination, but no national campaign was launched against the "self-segregation" of the all-white, all-Anglo fraternities.

Yet, despite this long tradition, I believe something new *is* occurring on campuses that may help explain the hysterical response that we have been hearing. The new development is a demographic shift that the long-dominant white majority sees as threatening its cultural hegemony.

At the Berkeley campus of the University of California, the undergraduate student body has been rapidly and dramatically transformed. In 1960, more than 90 per cent of the students were white. In 1980, the figure was about 66 per cent. Today, it is about 45 per cent. The freshman class this fall signals an even more striking change for those who still think of Berkeley in 1960's terms. For the first time in history, whites do not make up the largest proportion of the incoming class; instead, it is Asian Americans, who account for about 35 per cent. Only 30 per cent of the class are Americans of European ancestry. In addition, nearly 20 per cent of the class are Chicanos/Latinos, and nearly 8 per cent African Americans. If this pattern holds, well over 60 per cent of Berkeley students will be "of color" within the next five years.

Although it will not be quite as dramatic in some other regions of the country, this coloring of the campus landscape reflects a vital and constantly unfolding development in American social life. Although symbolized by dramatic figures such as those at Berkeley, the ramifications go far beyond the percentages of different ethnic and racial groups admitted to college campuses. The ramifications of demographic change certainly tug at the curriculum and challenge the borders of faculty turf and expertise. But the fundamental issues tapped by this change go to the heart of American identity and culture.

Bubbling just beneath the surface of all the national attention devoted to "political correctness" and "quotas" is a complicated question that, stated most simply, is: "What does it mean to be an American?" And the related question is, "How does one become an American?"

The controversy over diversity at Berkeley, much like the battle over the social-studies curriculum in New York State, is a struggle over who gets to define the idea of America. Are we essentially a nation with a common—or at least dominant—culture to which immigrants and "minorities" must adapt? Or is this a land in which ethnicity and difference are an accepted part of the whole; a land in which we affirm the richness of our differences and simultaneously try to forge agreement about basic values to guide public and social policy?

Critics of the current, visible wave of segmentation argue that "Balkanization" threatens the ties that bind civil society. But civil society in a nation of immigrants is forever in flux, and the basic issue always has been which group has the power to define what the values and structures of that common society will be. We should learn something from our history.

Being an American is different from being French or Japanese or almost any other nationality because, except for Native Americans, there actually is no such thing as an American without a hyphen. We are a nation of immigrants. Generations of immigrants have struggled to balance both sides of the hyphen, to carry on some aspects of the culture of the old country while adopting the norms and customs of the new. Today, many of their descendants continue to find comfort in an identification with the old country, however tenuous it may be. In a diverse nation, such identification can provide a sense of belonging to a recognizable collectivity. It helps give a sense of belonging—of being one with others like oneself—that helps to overcome the isolation of modern life, while paradoxically also allowing a sense of uniqueness.

This is the same phenomenon we see being reenacted on campuses all over the country today, the difference being that the actors are no longer all white.

At a place like Berkeley, there is no longer a single racial or ethnic group with an overwhelming numerical and political majority. Pluralism is the reality, with no one group a dominant force. This is completely new; we are grappling with a phenomenon that is both puzzling and alarming, fraught with tensions and hostilities, and yet simultaneously brimming with potential and crackling with new energy. Consequently, we swing between hope and concern, optimism and pessimism about the prospects for social life among peoples from differing racial and cultural groups. Are members of particular groups isolated or interacting, segregating or integrating, fighting or harmonizing? Who is getting ahead or falling behind?

It may well be that we have too narrowly conceived the options as *either/or*. It may be that as a nation we have cast the problem incompletely and thus incorrectly by posing the matter as either one of assimilation to a single, dominant culture where differences merge and melt away—or one of hardened, isolated, and self-segregated groups retreating into ethnic and racial enclaves, defeating the very purpose of trying to achieve diversity.

The findings from a two-year study of student life on the Berkeley campus in which I participated strongly suggest that these are not the only two alternatives before us. Other avenues are possible. In that research, we discovered an emerging vision of one of these options, a "third experience" of diversity. In this "third experience," the whole is greater than the sum of the various parts. In it, for example, collective problem solving by individuals from different backgrounds produces superior results precisely because of the synergy that develops from different approaches being brought to bear on the same problem.

At the public level, we see the possibility of people with strong ethnic and racial identities (including ethnically homogeneous affiliations and friendships) also being able to participate effectively in heterogeneous educational or work settings. These public spheres are enriched precisely because people bring to them the strengths of different cultural and ethnic identities forged out of their unique experiences and "separateness."

In the private arena, individuals with strong ethnic and racial identities also can form friendships that cross racial lines, for example, as students meet each other as equals in the dorms, classrooms, and quads. Although only a small proportion of students currently achieve this, students from different backgrounds can come to see one another as resources by recognizing different, yet complementary, competencies.

One of my favorite examples at Berkeley is an advanced student in computer sciences, an African American, who is acting as a mentor to two first-generation Asian émigrés. He is teaching them computer technology and such nuances of American culture as the unique role of charitable organizations. The Asian students, in turn, are teaching him about subjects ranging from traditional Chinese medicine to the symbolic importance of gift giving among Koreans. While this kind of learning has always occurred when there is contact between people from different cultures, the potential scale of this contact among "equals" at places like Berkeley is quite new—and holds out the promise of significant changes in social interaction over the long term.

Some of our students, no less than some of our leading pundits, such as George Will and Arthur Schlesinger, Jr., see "self-segregation" as an assault upon their idea of a common community. But other students understand that people living among their ethnic or racial peers are trying to forge an identity and support group to help them in a difficult and often alien world.

The all-black dining table in the dormitory or the all-Asian dance is visually striking, it is true, and stands in sharp relief against student life in earlier periods, when the social segregation among white ethnic students was much less obvious. We should not forget the invidious distinctions made in earlier periods, however. When I was an undergraduate at Northwestern University, I learned about the virulence of anti-Semitism from Christians and about vicious anti-Irish and anti-Italian sentiment from the Anglo upper crust in Evanston. But those distinctions did not reach *Time* and *Newsweek* or the national television networks, and columnists did not talk about the "Balkanization" of our college campuses. Race somehow matters more.

Wholesale condemnation of self-segregation is too simple and simple-minded. Just as Jewish students have found Hillel and a common ethnic/cultural identity the basis for self-affirmation, so too do today's ethnic and racial "minorities" often need to draw upon the social, cultural, and moral resources of their respective communities.

We must also remember that the European ancestry of the Jewish and Catholic students segregated into enclaves in the earlier part of the century was rather better reflected in the existing curriculum than are the ancestries of today's Asian, Latino, or African-American students. While the earlier "out" groups were generally content to receive the established curriculum, today's students are likely to challenge both the curriculum and the pedagogy used to deliver it.

What ultimately bothers today's critics most is not the racial or ethnic segregation of students' social lives, but the challenges that the growing numbers of Asian, Latino, and African-American students pose to the faculty once they find their ancestors' histories and contributions largely ignored in the classroom. That is what really rankles the critics and explains the depth of their anxiety; they recognize that the challenges to the curriculum represent a real and powerful confrontation over who answers, "What does it mean to be an American?"

Number of words 1900
See page 473 for questions
Reading time in seconds ________
See page 498 for conversion table

SELECTION 87

Which Career Is the Right One for You?

David P. Campbell

More than anything else, your choice of career is going to determine how you live—and probably even where you live. The following article, excerpted from Campbell's book, If You Don't Know Where You're Going, You'll Probably End Up Somewhere Else, *should help you see yourself from a different angle. (Before reading the article, you should turn to page 000 and take the Self-scoring Career Compatibility Test. You can then be your own career counselor.)*

When you are trying to plan your career, try out a variety of jobs, work in many different settings, volunteer for different tasks.

There are six basic categories of occupations. The six types of jobs, as developed by Professor John L. Holland, a psychology professor from Johns Hopkins University, are described here in some detail. Recognize that when I talk about the characteristics of people in the jobs, no one person has all of these characteristics. I am talking about trends, but they are strong trends.

TYPE A—REALISTIC JOBS

These are mainly skilled trades or technical jobs, usually involving work with tools or machines, frequently called "blue-collar" positions.

People who are attracted to realistic jobs are usually rugged, robust, practical, physically strong and frequently competitive in outlook. They usually have good physical coordination, but sometimes they have trouble expressing themselves in words or in talking with others. They prefer to deal with things rather than with ideas or with people. They enjoy creating things with their hands. They have good motor coordination, but they are frequently uncomfortable in social settings, and lack verbal and interpersonal skills. They usually see themselves as mechanically and athletically inclined and are stable, natural and persistent. They prefer concrete to abstract problems. Realistic people tend to see the world in simple, tangible and traditional terms. Possessions are important to them, and they usually put their recreational money into cars, boats, campers, snowmobiles, motorcycles, airplanes or other machinery.

Realistic people describe themselves in interviews as "conforming, frank, genuine, normal, persistent, practical, stable, thrifty, materialistic, shy and uninvolved."

One unique reward of most realistic jobs is that the worker can quickly see the results of her labors.

In general, in realistic jobs, life is not complicated by intricate problems between people or organizations, nor by troublesome choices between conflicting philosophies.

TYPE B—CONVENTIONAL JOBS

These are usually office jobs where people work with organizations, files and regular schedules.

Conventional occupations include bookkeeper, statistician, bank teller, inventory controller, payroll clerk, secretary, financial analyst, office manager, computer operator, bank cashier and accountant. Conventional jobs usually require a fair amount of writing, but it is usually the writing of business letters and regular reports.

People who enjoy conventional jobs describe themselves as "conforming, conscientious, efficient, inhibited, obedient, orderly, persistent, practical and calm."

They like for life to be orderly and to go according to plan. They like to know what is expected of them, and they enjoy carrying out their assignments.

Conventional people prefer the highly ordered activities, both verbal and numerical, that characterize office work. They dislike ambiguity and prefer to know precisely what is expected of them. They describe themselves as "conventional, stable, well-controlled and dependable." They have little interest in problems requiring physical skills or intense relationships with others and they are most effective at well-defined tasks. They value material possessions and status, although they usually prefer conforming and subordinate roles.

The rewards of working in conventional jobs center around seeing offices and organizations run smoothly, and in understanding how the individual's contribution helps in making that happen.

People in conventional positions are frequently the glue that holds the entire operation together. Because of the nature of their work, they are not always publicly recognized as much as perhaps they should be, but they themselves have some appreciation of the contribution they are making to the organization, and this is one of the pleasant aspects of conventional occupations.

Type C—Investigative Jobs

These are scientific and laboratory jobs, jobs where people investigate how the world is put together.

The tasks involved in investigative jobs are scientific or laboratory in nature, and usually involve trying to solve some puzzles, whether the puzzle is a large, mysterious problem such as how the universe came into being, or a more normal, daily problem such as figuring out the composition of a sample of blood taken from a patient in a medical clinic.

Investigative workers are usually found in research laboratories or clinical settings, but they also work in a wide range of other places—highway departments where they study issues such as traffic control and composition of highway materials; in advertising agencies where they work on market surveys; in food-producing companies where they work on nutritional aspects of food; in military settings where they work on new weapons or new military strategies; in financial departments where they work on questions of economic strategy, money flow and inventory problems—in general, in any place where problems are being attacked in a systematic, scientific way.

Investigative tasks frequently involve the use of computers, microscopes, telescopes, high-speed centrifuges or any of an incredible array of other laboratory and scientific equipment. The investigative job differs from the realistic job in that the realistic job is usually more concerned with machines that produce products, while the investigative job is concerned with machines that produce data or information.

People in investigative jobs are task-oriented, which means they get all wrapped up in the problem they are working on. They sometimes perceive themselves as lacking in leadership or persuasive abilities, but they are confident of their scholarly and intellectual abilities.

They prefer to think through problems rather than act them out. They enjoy ambiguous challenges and do not like highly structured situations with lots of rules. They frequently have unconventional values and attitudes and tend to be original and creative, especially in scientific areas.

They describe themselves as "analytical, curious, independent and reserved." They especially dislike repetitive activities and sales activities. They are very curious.

The unique reward of many investigative jobs is the worker's opportunity to satisfy an innate curiosity, analyzing situations, trying to understand what is going on in whatever field they are working.

Type D—Artistic Jobs

These are creative jobs where people work with words or music or art.

The tasks involved in artistic occupations usually involve working with words, music or other art forms. Decorating rooms, designing homes, or doing portrait photography are other examples of artistic activities.

Artistic jobs are found in settings such as art museums, art galleries, music departments, interior decorating offices, music stores, theater groups, photographic studios, radio and television studios and any place where artistic skills are used and/or taught.

People who enjoy working in artistic jobs describe themselves as "complicated, disorderly, emotional, idealistic, imaginative, impractical, impulsive, independent, introspective, intuitive, nonconforming and original." They like to work in free environments that allow them to express themselves in a wide variety of media—writing, music, drawing, photography, fabrics—in general, any art form.

They value beauty and aesthetic qualities, and don't care much for social entanglements. They like to make things, especially new and different things, and are willing to take risks to try something new, even if the chances of failure are high.

The artistic person has a distaste for appearing conventional or undistinguished. Such people like to use their creativity to help them stand out from the crowd.

Artistic people have little interest in problems that are highly structured or that require a lot of physical strength, preferring those problems that can be dealt with self-expression and artistic media. They resemble investigative people in preferring to work alone, but have a greater need for individualistic expression, are usually less assertive about their own capabilities, and are more sensitive and emotional.

The continual stimulation for the new and the different, for quality in creativity, is a primary reward of artistic jobs.

Type E—Social Jobs

These are jobs where people work with people—healing them, teaching them, helping them.

The tasks involved in social job are those concerned with working with other people, teaching them, or training them, or curing them, or leading them, or organizing them or enlightening them. Social tasks include explaining things to others, entertaining other people, planning the teaching of other people, helping other people solve their difficulties, organizing and conducting charities, and straightening out differences between people.

People who enjoy working in social jobs describe themselves as "cooperative, friendly, generous, helpful, idealistic, responsible, social, tactful and understanding." They like to work in groups, especially small groups that are working on problems common to individuals in the group.

They dislike working with machines or in highly organized situations such as military units. They like to discuss philosophic questions—the purpose of life, what constitutes right or wrong.

They like attention and seek situations that allow them to be at or near the center of the group. They prefer to solve problems by discussions with others, or by arranging or rearranging relationships between others. Social people also describe themselves as "cheerful, popular, achieving and good leaders."

The rewards of working in social jobs center around the warm glow that comes from helping other people solve their problems or improve themselves. People in social jobs usually have co-workers who are like themselves, and these groups are usually warm and supportive of each other. They make each other feel wanted, have great respect for each other's abilities, and have many opportunities for close interpersonal relationships.

Type F—Jobs of Leadership

These are jobs where people persuade other people to do something—sales jobs, political jobs, merchandising jobs.

Also included are many business executive jobs, making speeches, running for an elected office, heading up a fund-raising campaign and many other jobs of leadership, as well as taking a course in leadership development.

Other examples of jobs of leadership include public relations directors, stock and bond brokers, buyers, hostesses, retailers, fashion merchandisers and industrial consultants.

People who enjoy working in jobs in leadership describe themselves as "adventuresome, ambitious, argumentative, domineering, energetic, flirtatious, impulsive, optimistic, self-confident, sociable and talkative."

Such people enjoy competitive activities and like to work in groups where they can have some influence over what the group is doing. They are self-confident and usually see themselves as good leaders.

Generally, such enterprising people dislike science and systematic thinking.

People in leadership jobs usually have a great facility with words, which they put to effective use in selling, dominating and leading. They are impatient with detail work or work involving long periods of heavy thinking. They have strong drives to organizational goals or economic aims. They see themselves as aggressive, popular, self-confident, cheerful and sociable. They generally have a high energy level and lots of enthusiasm.

The unique reward from jobs of leadership is the sense of achievement that comes from making things happen, whether it is conducting a sales campaign, or winning an election, or persuading a board of directors to accept new policies.

Number of words 1750
See page 475 for questions
Reading time in seconds ________
See page 498 for conversion table

Comprehension and Vocabulary Check Questions and Exercises

Perhaps the best measure of reading comprehension is your ability to re-express with a minimum of loss or distortion what you have just read. That is, however, a very time-consuming process and does not lend itself to easy objective evaluation. The ten objective COMPREHENSION CHECK QUESTIONS are intended to provide a quick, convenient approximation or supplement to any such re-expression.

Your score on the first five questions will suggest how well you note details and is spoken of as *Receptive Comprehension*. Your score on the last five questions will suggest how well you get the central idea, draw inferences, reach conclusions, note relationships, and recognize pattern and organization. These last five questions come under the heading of *Reflective Comprehension*. The sixth question is always on the central idea. Indicate your answer by entering the number of the correct choice in the space following the question. When you have finished, check your answers with the key on page 493.

The VOCABULARY CHECK QUESTIONS are meant to encourage increased attention to context. In a general way they parallel the twofold division of the COMPREHENSION CHECK QUESTIONS. The distinction here is between knowing a word without further study, and having to depend upon a reflective analysis of context in order to arrive at an accurate understanding of its meaning. Low comprehension, in both reading and listening, is often attributable to inadequate vocabulary (Column I score) or to inability to make effective use of contextual clues in arriving at word meanings (Column II score).

Without looking back at the selection, you are to enter a set of answers in Column I, headed *without context*. This provides a measure of your word knowledge without the help of context. Next, turn back to the selection containing the words, find the word, and study it in its full context to see if you can arrive at a better understanding of its meaning. Use Column II, headed *with context,* for entering your second set of answers. When you have completed both sets, check your results by using the key on page 493 or by referring to your dictionary.

If you are as skilled as you should be in using contextual clues to word meanings, your scores in the second column should be almost perfect. If they are low, you have particular reason for developing added skill with context to facilitate your mastery of new words and improve comprehension. In the first few selections you read, if your answers in Column I are all correct, you may wish to omit working through the items a second time with the help of context. In that case, take 20 off for each mistake to get your WORD COMPREHENSION SCORE.

A careful record of your performance as you work through the various tests should do much to hasten your progress. Enter all your test results on the PROGRESS RECORD at the end of the book, beginning on page 499.

The eighty-seven EXERCISES immediately following each set of CHECK QUESTIONS provide for added practice, reinforcement, and extension of communication and study-related skills, with special emphasis on reading. Eleven of the twelve exercises for the selections in Section VII introduce special test-related material, patterned after the widely used *Nelson-Denny Reading Test,* to provide you with a more accurate assessment of your reading ability.

Index of Exercises

(By Selection)

Because of the close interrelationship among the four communication skills, some exercises cover more than one skill.

*from Nelson-Denny Reading Test national tryouts

Special Index of Reading-related Exercises, Grouped to Facilitate Maximum Progress

Individual differences are the norm. You are unique—as a person and as a reader. The grouping that follows lets you zero in on those specific exercises that best meet our own individual needs. Use them to speed your efforts to improve comprehension, to enhance vocabulary, to develop maximum flexibility of rate, and to cultivate added test-taking ability.

I. Exercises for Diagnosis

If, as a reader, you don't know what your problems are, how can you expect to solve them? "Know thyself"—so said the ancient Greeks. And that's still most important today. Here are exercises in discovery and diagnosis. Do them thoughtfully. They touch on almost all potential problem areas. To be sure, standardized tests provide the only statistically valid measures of your ability, but you still need to supplement such tests by additional informal checks, such as those in the following diagnostic exercises. Knowing yourself as a reader deserves top priority. Discover your individual needs.

II. Exercises to Improve Comprehension

A. Of the main idea

B. Of organization

C. Of paragraphs

D. Of narratives

E. By drawing inferences

F. By heightening interest

G. By improving memory

H. By general moves

28. "Use the SSQ Formula": Exercise 32, pages 328–329.
29. "Make Purpose Prevail": Exercise 34, pages 336–337.
30. Levels in the cognitive domain: Exercise 3, page 248.
31. Using your time effectively: Exercise 5, page 252.
32. Developing skill in interpretation: Exercise 6, page 254.
33. Creativity in learning: Exercise 8, page 258.
34. Dealing with synthesis and analysis: Exercise 9, page 260.
35. Reading for imagery: Exercise 11, page 264.
36. Developing an idea: Exercise 11, page 264.
37. Seeing cultural literacy at work; Putting cultural literacy to work: Exercise 13, pages 268–269.
38. Reading punctuation: Exercise 17, page 278.
39. Introducing SQ3R; Applying SQ3R: Exercise 21, page 290.
40. Perceptual development: Exercise 22, pages 292–293.
41. Word grouping exercises: Exercise 23, page 296.
42. Developing specialized reading skills: Exercise 24, page 298.

III. Exercises to Improve Rate Flexibility

43. "A New Look at an Old Method": Exercise 31, pages 324–325.
44. "Swing Three Bats": Exercise 26, pages 304–305.

IV. Exercises to Improve Test-Taking Ability

45–47. Exercises 77 and 78, pages 450–451 and 454–455.

48–55. Exercises 79, 80, 81, 82, 83, 84, 85, and 86, pages 458, 460, 462, 464–465, 468, 470, 472, and 474.

(These last eight exercises contain passages drawn from those included in the preliminary national tryouts for new forms of the *Nelson-Denny Reading Test*. In addition to providing valuable experience in handling reading tests, these passages serve an important diagnostic function: letting you see exactly how you compare with a cross-section of college and university freshmen across the country.)

NAME ______________________ DATE ______________ READING RATE ______________ WPM

COMPREHENSION CHECK QUESTIONS

1. Ogden claims knowledge is doubling every (1) 20 months; (2) 25 months; (3) 30 months; (4) 35 months 1. ______
2. Ogden lives and works (1) in a motor home; (2) in a small office; (3) in his house; (4) on a houseboat. 2. ______
3. The Japanese were said to grow how many tomatoes from one seed? (1) 5,000; (2) 10,000; (3) 15,000; (4) 20,000. 3. ______
4. Specific mention was made of (1) Mighty Mouse; (2) Batman; (3) Buck Rogers; (4) Superman. 4. ______
5. Ogden said we're using how much of our brain? (1) 1 percent; (2) 2 percent; (3) 10 percent; (4) 25 percent. 5. ______

Receptive Comprehension ______

6. The main purpose of this article is to (1) characterize Ogden; (2) present his ideas; (3) show how people react to him; (4) show where he gets his information. 6. ______
7. Ogden's chief concern was about our (1) shortsightedness; (2) future; (3) schools; (4) problems. 7. ______
8. Ogden seemed most impressed with (1) Japan; (2) France; (3) England; (4) Taiwan. 8. ______
9. What would you infer Ogden considered of most importance? (1) industry; (2) technology; (3) communication; (4) education and training. 9. ______
10. You'd call Ogden's attitude primarily (1) scientific; (2) reflective; (3) pessimistic; (4) radical. 10. ______

(10 points for each correct answer)

Reflective Comprehension ______
TOTAL READING COMPREHENSION SCORE ______

VOCABULARY CHECK QUESTIONS

			without context I	with context II
1.	**huff**	(1) hurry; (2) bluff; (3) stew; (4) fear; (5) shell.	1. ______	______
2.	**tabs**	(1) costs; (2) track of; (3) schedules; (4) failures; (5) scores.	2. ______	______
3.	**purveyor**	(1) leader; (2) writer; (3) fact-finder; (4) supplier; (5) ruler.	3. ______	______
4.	**gamut**	(1) rating; (2) orders; (3) range; (4) street urchin; (5) risk.	4. ______	______
5.	**insatiable**	(1) insane; (2) immediate; (3) complete; (4) limitless; (5) satisfied.	5. ______	______

(10 points for each correct answer)

Word Comprehension without *contextual help (I)* ______
Word Comprehension with *contextual help (II)* ______
TOTAL WORD COMPREHENSION SCORE ______

EXERCISES

DEALING WITH VOCABULARY CHECK QUESTIONS BY NOTING CONTEXT

What do you read? Words, of course! And if you don't know what a word means, comprehension suffers. With that in mind, take a closer look at why the vocabulary check questions are structured as they are.

Assume that you have finished one of the five-item tests, putting the numbers indicating your answers in the column headed *without context.* For example, look at the five words in the test on the preceding page: *huff, tabs, purveyor, gamut,* and *insatiable.* Ask yourself if those words are all in your active vocabulary—are indeed words that you use rather frequently and without effort. If someone asked you what those words meant, could you define them? Could you rather easily put each into a sentence? If you can do all those things, you show yourself at home with them.

Try your hand at composing a sentence for each one now.

huff: ____

____

tabs: ____

____

purveyor: ____

____

gamut: ____

____

insatiable: ____

____

If you are perfectly at home with a word, you don't need context to help. Just imagine the same answers in the second column as in the first; then check the answer key. See how well you know yourself—and the words! Score 100 and you know both yourself and the word without the need of context.

If, on the other hand, you don't feel that comfortable with one or two of the words, work through the following pattern. For example, suppose you are not sure about the meaning of *huff.* You think of that phrase "I'll huff and I'll puff. . ." and decide that *huff* may mean "to blow." But that's not one of the choices. Well, perhaps "hurry" is the right answer. You are not sure but you enter a "1" in the space that follows. Whenever you are not sure, that's when you look at the context. So—scan the article for the word *huff.* (Because the five words are always in the order of appearance, *huff* comes first. If you see *tabs*, you'll know that you have missed *huff* and should look back.) Here is what you will see: ". . . there have been those, he says proudly, who've thrown chairs and cups of coffee and walked out in a huff." This context tells you that *huff* is a noun and, as you look back at the choices, that it probably means "stew." They may be in a hurry, but the context points up the more important fact that they are upset and angry—in a stew—not in a bluff, in a fear, or in a shell. Enter a "3" for that item in the second column headed *with context.* When you check your answers, you will then know for sure (1) whether you knew the word without contextual help and (2) whether you are skilled enough in using context to get the right meaning for column II.

In addition to bringing you important insights and awarenesses, this pattern develops added skill in using context as well as added skill in scanning—both important facets of reading skill. When you check context in that way, you should then know exactly how the word is used. The dictionary entry for *huff* actually has seven different definitions: three as a transitive verb, three as an intransitive verb, and one as a noun—"a condition of smoldering anger or resentment." If you are in a stew about something, the dictionary says that you are in a state of vexation, perhaps ready to throw something!

When a word has several definitions, the dictionary cannot tell you exactly which definition applies; context does that. So—depend more and more on context for help in arriving at accurate meanings.

Try another example. Take *tabs*. Your dictionary probably has three different entries for *tabs*—with eight or nine different definitions, plus listings of some colloquialisms. Again, what is the context? "In an age in which Ogden claims knowledge is doubling every 20 months, he has kept tabs on the flow for the past 10 years." Which choice fits that context best? Has Ogden kept "costs," "track of," "schedules," "failures," or "scores" on the flow? If you're using contextual clues well, you'll have the right answer: "kept track of."

Or take *purveyor*. Does it mean "leader," "writer," "fact-finder," "supplier," or "ruler"? Again, if you are uncertain, look at context. Ogden "looks more like a retired professor than a purveyor of futuristic facts." Develop the ability to get meaning from context and you hardly need the dictionary. Ogden is obviously a "supplier" of facts.

To summarize, follow the pattern suggested. Before checking results, check to see if there are any words in the test you are uncertain about. Check the context for those words. Put down answers in the second column headed *with context* before checking your answers. Work toward having a perfect score in the second column. When you score yourself 10 for each one right, score the number right in both columns—100 being a perfect score.

Now for the final step. In a sense, nothing belongs to you until you put it to use—not your language, your mind, or your abilities. So to make any word yours, you need to *use* it! After speaking or writing it at least three times, it should start coming to the tip of your tongue or pen almost without effort—just when you need it.

Give the words a workout. Never get in a huff. Keep close tabs on how your vocabulary is improving. You will find both context and dictionary valuable purveyors of essential information. Your vocabulary scores my run the whole gamut from 0 to 100, but don't let that diminish your enthusiasm. If your appetite for improvement is insatiable, you will soon see phenomenal progress.

NAME ______________ DATE ______________ READING RATE ______________ WPM

COMPREHENSION CHECK QUESTIONS

1. The earthquake occurred (1) in the afternoon; (2) in the evening; (3) at night; (4) in the morning. 1. _______
2. Adams attended an exposition in (1) London; (2) Rome; (3) Paris; (4) Brussels. 2. _______
3. The author mentions (1) Edison; (2) Newton; (3) Galileo; (4) Roentgen. 3. _______
4. What date was said to mark the change from rapid to radical change? (1) 1880; (2) 1900; (3) 1920; (4) 1950. 4. _______
5. The amount of technical information doubles every how many years? (1) ten; (2) twenty; (3) thirty; (4) forty. 5. _______

Receptive Comprehension _______

6. The main idea of the article is to (1) reveal the importance of change; (2) help us understand and guide the forces of change; (3) point up the acceleration of change; (4) explain the function of time spanners. 6. _______
7. The Shafter cow incident was intended primarily to show what about change? (1) its suddenness; (2) its importance; (3) its severity; (4) its unexpectedness. 7. _______
8. The article is organized basically (1) from past to present; (2) from the ordinary to the unusual; (3) from basic to less basic; (4) from cause to effect. 8. _______
9. Adams was most concerned about (1) change; (2) time; (3) thought; (4) force. 9. _______
10. The author's outlook is best described as (1) optimistic; (2) pessimistic; (3) uncertain; (4) casual. 10. _______

(10 points for each correct answer)

Reflective Comprehension _______
TOTAL READING COMPREHENSION SCORE _______

VOCABULARY CHECK QUESTIONS

			without context I	with context II
1.	**ken**	(1) area; (2) thought; (3) knowledge; (4) intent; (5) love.	1. _______	_______
2.	**quest**	(1) end; (2) pursuit; (3) doubt; (4) twist; (5) question.	2. _______	_______
3.	**irruption**	(1) fall; (2) trick; (3) blow; (4) breakdown; (5) bursting into.	3. _______	_______
4.	**arbitrary**	(1) military; (2) dated; (3) disputed; (4) fixed; (5) curved.	4. _______	_______
5.	**amenable**	(1) responsive; (2) immoral; (3) entertaining; (4) combined; (5) repairable.	5. _______	_______

(10 points for each correct answer)

Word Comprehension without *contextual help (I)* _______
Word Comprehension with *contextual help (II)* _______
TOTAL WORD COMPREHENSION SCORE _______

Exercises

Noting Organizational Clues

With reading as with driving, looking ahead is imperative. With a dense fog obscuring your view, you must of necessity creep along or risk running off the road. The same is true with reading. You must cultivate the habit of noting any and all clues that suggest the direction the writer is taking.

Read the first words of the opening paragraph of *The Dynamics of Change*—"At exactly 5:13 A.M. . . . ." Ask yourself what those words suggest about the remainder of the paragraph. Mention of a specific time suggests a chronological ordering of events. Notice the first word of the second sentence—"Suddenly, ..."

Taste the satisfaction of having looked ahead with accuracy to the second sentence—even before reading it. That kind of foreshadowing means better comprehension and more rapid reading, for you are less likely to get off the track because of the clear way ahead.

At exactly 5:13 A.M., the 18th of April, 1906, a cow was standing somewhere between the main barn and the milking shed on the old Shafter Ranch in California, minding her own business. Suddenly, the earth shook, the skies trembled, and when it was all over, there was nothing showing of the cow above ground but a bit of her tail sticking up.

Try the second paragraph in the same way. Read the first few words—"For the student of change . . . ." Again ask yourself what those words suggest about direction. In the first place, the word *change* stands out, reminding you that that word summarizes the first paragraph nicely. It also suggests that change will be further developed in the second paragraph, perhaps in a way analogous to that of the first.

As you read on, you note that the cow is called a "symbol of our times." Again, ask yourself what is foreshadowed by that statement. You will expect some explanation to follow. When you come to the words "like the Shafter cow," you see confirmation of your expectations. Furthermore, you're told exactly what to expect in the remainder of the article—what's going to be talked about now.

To take further steps in establishing habits of using words to point the road ahead, move on to the end of the article.

For the student of change, the Shafter cow is a sort of symbol of our times. She stood quietly enough, thinking such gentle thoughts as cows are likely to have, while huge forces outside her ken built up all around her and—within a minute—discharged it all at once in a great movement that changed the configuration of the earth, and destroyed a city, and swallowed her up. And that's what we are going to talk about now; how, if we do not learn to understand and guide the great forces of change at work on our world today, we may find ourselves like the Shafter cow, swallowed up by vast upheavals in our way of life—quite early some morning.

Take the sentence "Society has many built-in time spanners that help link the present generation with the past." What would you expect to follow in the remaining part of the paragraph? Write down your expectations in the space below; then check back to the article to see how accurately you were foreshadowing what was said.

____

____

Do the same with the next paragraph. Here is the opening sentence: "No such time spanners enhance our sense of the future." What do you think follows that sentence on down the road?

____

____

Establish this way of reading as your normal habit. Let it keep you on track.

NAME ______________________ DATE ______________ READING RATE ______________ WPM

Comprehension Check Questions

1. Voyager One's mission was to (1) Venus; (2) Saturn; (3) Mars; (4) Jupiter. 1. _______
2. How many world's languages were mentioned? (1) 55; (2) 700; (3) 1,870; (4) 2,700. 2. _______
3. German, when compared with French, is estimated to have (1) a smaller vocabulary; (2) about the same size vocabulary; (3) a larger vocabulary; (4) no estimate given. 3. _______
4. Mention was made of (1) Silicon Valley; (2) Russia; (3) Shanghai; (4) all the preceding places. 4. _______
5. English was said to be a second language in (1) Holland; (2) India; (3) France; (4) Spain. 5. _______

Receptive Comprehension _______

6. This article mainly shows what about the English language? (1) its widespread use; (2) its history; (3) its origins with Shakespeare; (4) its growth as a second language. 6. _______
7. The reference to Caesar was to point up (1) the beginnings of English; (2) how fast English spread; (3) how much Latin contributed; (4) the military uses of English. 7. _______
8. Which best describes this selection? (1) practical; (2) stimulating; (3) inspirational; (4) witty. 8. _______
9. The primary purpose is to (1) persuade; (2) clarify; (3) inform; (4) entertain. 9. _______
10. The main idea is developed largely by (1) facts and figures; (2) quoting authorities; (3) logical reasoning; (4) anecdotes. 10. _______

(10 points for each correct answer)

Reflective Comprehension _______
TOTAL READING COMPREHENSION SCORE _______

Vocabulary Check Questions

			without context I	with context II
1.	**ecumenical**	(1) wholesome; (2) universal; (3) solid; (4) critical; (5) enlarged.	1. _______	_______
2.	**sway**	(1) turn; (2) push; (3) force; (4) swerve; (5) hang.	2. _______	_______
3.	**emergence**	(1) superiority; (2) grouping; (3) prominence; (4) appearance; (5) generality.	3. _______	_______
4.	**legacy**	(1) inheritance; (2) allowance; (3) advice; (4) arrangement; (5) legality.	4. _______	_______
5.	**flux**	(1) flavor; (2) change; (3) control; (4) stop; (5) polish.	5. _______	_______

(10 points for each correct answer)

Word Comprehension without *contextual help (I)* _______
Word Comprehension with *contextual help (II)* _______
TOTAL WORD COMPREHENSION SCORE _______

Exercises

Spotting the Central Idea

The good reader is one who is able to see past all the details and grasp the central or topic idea of a paragraph. Try this with some of the paragraphs in this selection. In each paragraph look for the one sentence that most clearly catches the essence of the paragraph—the topic sentence.

1. In the paragraph beginning "The rise of English. . . ," the topic sentence is sentence # _____.
2. In the paragraph beginning "Four hundred years later. . . ," the topic sentence is sentence # _____.
3. In the paragraph beginning "The statistics of English. . . ," the topic sentence is sentence # _____.
4. In the paragraph beginning "English has a few rivals. . . ," the topic sentence is sentence # _____.

Good writers will usually express a topic idea in the first or, less often, last sentence. In the paragraphs cited above, all the topic sentences were first.

The topic sentence gives you an appropriate mindset for getting what follows. When you start the paragraph "Four hundred years later, the contrast is extraordinary," you know that what follows will contrast with what the previous paragraph has just discussed. When you read "The statistics of English are extraordinary," you can expect extraordinary facts and figures to follow. What a help topic sentences can be! Use them to keep yourself on track.

Levels in the Cognitive Domain

The last five questions making up *reflective comprehension* attempt to move into this domain—the domain of intellectual development. Ideally, comprehension check questions should touch on all levels of cognition so as to provide maximum stimulus for a reader's intellectual development. Only recently have levels of cognition been rather clearly delineated. Seven levels deserve particular attention, as follows:

1. Memory (remembering what was expressly said)
2. Translation (putting what was said into other words or form)
3. Interpretation (noting unstated relationships)
4. Application (applying a principle recognized)
5. Analysis (breaking a subject down into its parts for examination)
6. Synthesis (fusing parts into a whole)
7. Evaluation (formulating a standard and using it to judge the worth of something)

Reading to Remember

The first cognitive level is memory—what you depend on to answer even the *receptive comprehension* questions accurately. Good reading should include good remembering. Use associations to connect things you want to remember with things you already know. For example, is it *indispensable* or *indispensible*? Use associations. Just remember that an *able* man is indeed indispens*able*. Let that association remember the right spelling for you. And is it *attendance* or *atendence*? If you're not sure, remember that a good time to start dancing is at ten—*at-ten-dance.*

List below five words that you tend to misspell; then make up some association or mnemonic for each, to help you remember the correct form.

	Word	**Association or Mnemonic**
1.	______________	______________________________
2.	______________	______________________________
3.	______________	______________________________
4.	______________	______________________________
5.	______________	______________________________

NAME ______________________ DATE ______________ READING RATE ______________ WPM

Comprehension Check Questions

1. One tool specifically mentioned was (1) a screwdriver; (2) a thermometer; (3) an auger; (4) a can opener. 1. _______
2. The author speaks of (1) a physician; (2) a dentist; (3) an aviator; (4) a mechanic. 2. _______
3. Our present numerical system came originally from (1) India; (2) Greece; (3) Rome; (4) England. 3. _______
4. Language is viewed here as a (1) communication tool; (2) magic tool; (3) brain tool; (4) social tool. 4. _______
5. What is *not* discussed? (1) increasing your vocabulary; (2) studying diacritical marks; (3) studying etymology; (4) comparing languages. 5. _______

Receptive Comprehension _______

6. This selection is intended primarily to explain (1) the function of language; (2) how to use language more effectively; (3) the dependence of tool and user; (4) the limitation of language. 6. _______
7. The opening paragraphs about a certain tool were intended to point up the tool's (1) range of uses; (2) limitations; (3) relationship to the user; (4) all the preceding. 7. _______
8. The reference to the exact third of a meter was to show (1) that tools have limitations; (2) the advantages of the metric system; (3) how tools increase brain power; (4) that skilled users improve tool efficiency. 8. _______
9. Learning a new language was mentioned to show how (1) we tend to think in English; (2) a foreign vocabulary is mastered; (3) a tool increases thinking power; (4) tool and user form a complex unit. 9. _______
10. The style of this article is best described as (1) concise; (2) amusing; (3) elevated; (4) conversational. 10. _______

(10 points for each correct answer)

Reflective Comprehension _______

TOTAL READING COMPREHENSION SCORE _______

Vocabulary Check Questions

		without context I	with context II
1. **cope**	(1) confine; (2) work together; (3) cook; (4) contend; (5) accompany.	1. _______	_______
2. **cumbersome**	(1) cumulative; (2) curative; (3) antiquated; (4) gaunt; (5) clumsy.	2. _______	_______
3. **shackles**	(1) shanties; (2) rags; (3) shambles; (4) restraints; (5) goals.	3. _______	_______
4. **competence**	(1) ability; (2) complacency; (3) compulsion; (4) obedience; (5) compliment.	4. _______	_______
5. **advocate**	(1) confess; (2) favor; (3) advise; (4) oppose; (5) speak.	5. _______	_______

(10 points for each correct answer)

Word Comprehension without *contextual help (I)* _______

Word Comprehension with *contextual help (II)* _______

TOTAL WORD COMPREHENSION SCORE _______

EXERCISES

READING SENTENCES AND PARAGRAPHS

As a reader, one of your problems is recalling details—the type of problem tested in the first five comprehension check questions for all the articles in this text. Usually, details are supporting evidence leading to a conclusion or generalization. That means that as you read you should not only note details but also see what they add up to.

Take these details: With a hammer you (1) drive nails; (2) pull nails; (3) split a board; (4) break stones; (5) bang someone on the head; (6) and so forth.

What do those details add up to? What do you conclude? (1) that many things can be done with a hammer? (2) that many things cannot be done with a hammer?

Now take another set of details: With a hammer you cannot (1) saw a piece of word; (2) drive a screw; (3) bore a hole.

What do those details add up to? (1) that many things can be done with a hammer? (2) that many things cannot be done with a hammer?

Fit both sets of details into one paragraph and what central idea do you have? (1) that many things can be done with a hammer? (2) that many things cannot be done with a hammer? (3) that many things can and cannot be done with a hammer?

Now turn back to the article and reread the first paragraph to review the common relationship between details and generalizations.

PARALLEL CONSTRUCTION

As a reader you will usually find that ideas of similar weight are in constructions of a similar kind. As an example, try reading the following sentence where this principle is violated:

> The automobile gives us the seven-league boots of fairy tales; wings come to us from the airplane; if we want the muscular strength of a Titan, it can be obtained from the hydraulic press.

Now look at the same sentence as it originally appeared, constructed so as to put parallel ideas into parallel form:

> The automobile gives us the seven-league boots of fairy tales, the airplane gives us wings, the hydraulic press gives us the muscular strength of a Titan.

See how helpful parallel form is, to both reader and writer! Improve the parallelism of the following sentence:

You cannot saw a piece of wood; driving a screw is impossible; or to bore a hole cannot be done.

Revision: ______________________________

____

____

When you have finished, compare your version with the original in the first paragraph on page 11.

ALERTNESS TO PARALLELISM

Alertness to parallelism pays off nicely, helping you see relationships more easily. As a further example, turn back to the article to look for four consecutive paragraphs where the author uses parallelism in the first few words. See if you can identify those paragraphs, entering the first two words in each paragraph in the spaces below:

A. ____________________ C. ____________________

B. ____________________ D. ____________________

Each paragraph begins with a question. In the first paragraph the answer is *no*. The parallel form suggests what about the answer to the questions in the next three paragraphs? Sharpen your awareness of parallel form. It helps.

NAME ______________________ DATE ______________ READING RATE ______________ WPM

Comprehension Check Questions

1. The day of the story is (1) cool; (2) warm; (3) cloudy; (4) windy. 1. _______
2. Specific mention was made of the (1) banker; (2) blacksmith; (3) baker; (4) pastor. 2. _______
3. The teacher was wearing a handsome (1) blue coat; (2) velvet jacket; (3) black coat; (4) uniform. 3. _______
4. Little Frantz (1) is scolded by the teacher; (2) has to recite; (3) doesn't have to recite; (4) is too late to recite. 4. _______
5. How many years had Monsieur Hamel taught there? (1) 45; (2) 40; (3) 34; (4) 28. 5. _______

Receptive Comprehension _______

6. This selection mainly shows the (1) feelings about language loss; (2) importance of education; (3) strong Prussian-French conflict; (4) the teacher's nationalistic feeling. 6. _______
7. What best describes Monsieur Hamel's feelings? (1) despair; (2) kindness; (3) love of country; (4) anger. 7. _______
8. M. Hamel places chief blame for not learning French on the (1) parents; (2) people of Alsace; (3) pupils; (4) school system. 8. _______
9. You would infer that the old villagers were introduced primarily to point up their (1) love of country; (2) respect for the teacher; (3) fear of the Prussians; (4) love of learning. 9. _______
10. Keeping the class to the end showed, above all, M. Hamel's (1) strong interest in education; (2) sense of duty; (3) personal courage; (4) patriotism. 10. _______

(10 points for each correct answer)

Reflective Comprehension _______
TOTAL READING COMPREHENSION SCORE _______

Vocabulary Check Questions

		without context I	with context II
1. **placard**	(1) poster; (2) brochure; (3) score; (4) folder; (5) location.	1. _______	_______
2. **entitled**	(1) named; (2) favored; (3) prepared; (4) allowed; (5) traced.	2. _______	_______
3. **reproaches**	(1) gathers; (2) blame; (3) steals; (4) help; (5) returns.	3. _______	_______
4. **servitude**	(1) attitude; (2) change; (3) bondage; (4) self-service; (5) age.	4. _______	_______
5. **festooned**	(1) fastened; (2) sounded; (3) turned; (4) decorated; (5) colored.	5. _______	_______

(10 points for each correct answer)

Word Comprehension without *contextual help (I)* _______
Word Comprehension with *contextual help (II)* _______
TOTAL WORD COMPREHENSION SCORE _______

Exercises

Reading Narration Versus Reading Exposition

You can label almost all of your textbook reading as exposition—the setting forth of facts and ideas to explain things in all the various subject-matter areas. Narration, on the other hand, is the telling of a story or happening, as in "The Last Class." To sharpen the distinction between the two kinds of communication, look at the following examples.

Suppose you are writing exposition, not narration. You would probably say, "This story begins in the morning"— a plain six-word statement of fact. If you were telling a story, you would probably say, "I was late for school that morning." That first word introduces a major character; the remaining six words let you know that he or she is supposed to go to school, and that it is morning. That comparison points up one of the chief differences between exposition and narration. Narration focuses on persons—persons doing something, feeling something, and thinking or saying something. Exposition provides the facts but tends to overlook the feelings. When you read between the words of that short narrative sentence, you can sense a feeling of worry about being late.

Take another example. In writing exposition you might say, "This story takes place in a little French-speaking village in Alsace, conquered by the Prussians." When you write a narrative, you will probably use vivid details that, little by little, add up to the same thing. The storyteller mentions "wandering about the fields," "the blackbirds whistling on the edge of the wood," and "the Prussians going through their drill." Such details begin to suggest a little, rural village. As you note "little board" and "Monsieur Hamel's little yard," the picture grows sharper and clearer.

You can begin to see how reading narration differs from reading exposition. You can see you should concentrate on *why* characters act as they do—on visualizing the unfolding action—and on savoring the vivid sensory details. Picture the sights—"Monsieur Hamel walking back and forth with the terrible iron ruler under his arm"—and the sounds—"the teacher's stout ruler beating on the desk." Put yourself right in the middle of the action to read narration with feeling.

Following the pattern of the examples you just read, pick still another example to show the difference between exposition and narration. Put the narrative phrase or sentence under the heading narration, then compose an expository rephrasing of the same idea.

Narration	**Exposition**
______________________________	______________________________
______________________________	______________________________
______________________________	______________________________
______________________________	______________________________
______________________________	______________________________

Using Your Time Effectively

For one entire week, Monday through Sunday, keep an accurate, detailed record of how you spend your time. If it is to be accurate, you will have to keep your record during the day, not at the end of the day by memory. Otherwise you will miss recording or noting how long you talked with a friend after class or how long it took you to eat or to get from home to school. Then, and only then, are you in a position to know how effectively you are using your time and what changes can be made to real advantage.

At the end of the week, a total of 168 hours, summarize your findings, using such headings as the following:

Sleep	Meals	Class and laboratory	Study	Outside work	Personal care	Travel	Leisure	Social	Waste time	Total
____	____	____	____	____	____	____	____	____	____	168

If you have never kept an accurate, detailed record of this kind, you have much to learn about yourself. The next step, of course, is to plan with care exactly how to make more effective use of time to ensure having sufficient time for all major activities.

Now try working out a personal study schedule so as to develop the work and study habits that will serve you to best advantage. Remember, the student who looks and plans ahead is the one who gets ahead.

NAME ______________________ DATE ______________ READING RATE ______________ WPM

Comprehension Check Questions

1. Specific reference was made to a (1) baby book; (2) crib; (3) teddy bear; (4) diaper. 1. ____
2. The father mentions his (1) grandfather; (2) uncle; (3) brother; (4) own father. 2. ____
3. What sound finally startled the baby? (1) a door slamming; (2) a truck backfiring; (3) a phone ring; (4) a thunder clap. 3. ____
4. The author has studied this subject for how many years? (1) ten; (2) fifteen; (3) twenty; (4) twenty-five. 4. ____
5. To learn to be an optimist, the author advocates (1) learning new cognitive skills; (2) taking his course; (3) listening to special tapes; (4) following an established program. 5. ____

Receptive Comprehension ____

6. This selection primarily shows the (1) results of pessimism; (2) advantages of optimism; (3) characteristics of both outlooks; (4) way to change outlook. 6. ____
7. This is organized on what basis? (1) cause to effect; (2) the ordinary to the unusual; (3) example to discussion; (4) the past to the present. 7. ____
8. In style this is best described as (1) conversational; (2) elegant; (3) simple; (4) lively. 8. ____
9. The author is addressing his remarks primarily to (1) men; (2) women; (3) adults in general; (4) older people. 9. ____
10. You would infer that the best way of determining what you are is by (1) self-analysis; (2) asking others; (3) seeing a psychiatrist; (4) being tested. 10. ____

(10 points for each correct answer)

Reflective Comprehension ____
TOTAL READING COMPREHENSION SCORE ____

Vocabulary Check Questions

			without context I	with context II
1.	**ruminating**	(1) observing; (2) rumbling; (3) thinking; (4) summarizing; (5) learning.	1. ____	____
2.	**marital**	(1) warlike; (2) unending; (3) effective; (4) matrimonial; (5) troublesome.	2. ____	____
3.	**squabble**	(1) squeal; (2) quarrel; (3) squish; (4) wiggle; (5) squall.	3. ____	____
4.	**surmountable**	(1) changeable; (2) conquerable; (3) high; (4) level; (5) calm.	4. ____	____
5.	**debilitating**	(1) expensive; (2) weakening; (3) decent; (4) strengthening; (5) complicating.	5. ____	____

(10 points for each correct answer)

Word Comprehension without *contextual help (I)* ____
Word Comprehension with *contextual help (II)* ____
TOTAL WORD COMPREHENSION SCORE ____

Exercises

Developing Skill in Interpretation

Interpretation is one of the important cognitive levels, focusing on how effectively you deal with *unstated relationships*. As an alert reader, you will want to develop maximum skill in anticipating what will either be stated or implied.

Take this sentence from an article on nonverbal communication: "Anyone who owns a cat, a dog, or a baby is well aware that certain meanings can be clearly expressed without the use of words." After such a generalization, what would you anticipate next? Can you make a supposition?

The next sentence actually begins: "The cat sits up politely for a morsel of turkey, the _____?" What specific word do you anticipate next? Hopefully, as you looked back at the series, "a cat, a dog, or a baby," you were led to anticipate the word *dog*. If you did, congratulate yourself. You anticipated well. The next word is *dog*.

Suppose we go a step further. Which of the following choices would best fit your anticipation? The dog (1) sleeps on the floor; (2) sniffs the air; (3) scratches on the door. If you selected the third choice, you are again anticipating well, for that was the phrase used.

For further practice, try a technique often used to test reading efficiency. See how accurately you can supply the exact missing words in the following passage. Every fifth word of the original is omitted. By anticipating and reasoning, fill in all the blanks. Then check back to the selection to see how accurate you were. If you get 18 right out of the 21, you have an excellent score. If you are a good reader, you do not have to read every word; your mind will furnish the right word much of the time. Check up on yourself.

"The optimists and the ____________________: I have been studying ____________________ for the past twenty-five ____________________. The defining characteristic of ____________________ is that they tend ____________________ believe bad events will ____________________ a long time, will ____________________ everything they do, and ____________________ their own fault. The ____________________, who are confronted with ____________________ same hard knocks of ____________________ world, think about misfortune ____________________ the opposite way. They ____________________ to believe defeat is ____________________ a temporary setback, that ____________________ causes are confined to ____________________ one case. The optimists ____________________ defeat is not their ____________________: Circumstances, bad luck, or ____________________ people brought it about. ____________________ people are unfazed by ____________________. Confronted by a bad ____________________, they perceive it as ____________________ challenge and try harder.

NAME ____________________ DATE ______________ READING RATE ______________ WPM

COMPREHENSION CHECK QUESTIONS

1. Most of us don't use more than what percent of our ability to remember? (1) 10; (2) 20; (3) 30; (4) 40. 1. ______
2. One essential for better memory is (1) training; (2) desire; (3) practice; (4) discipline. 2. ______
3. How many basic laws were discussed? (1) only one; (2) two; (3) three; (4) four. 3. ______
4. Specific mention was made of (1) Plato; (2) Virgil; (3) Crito; (4) Aristotle. 4. ______
5. The author discusses how to (1) memorize poetry; (2) study; (3) take notes; (4) listen better. 5. ______

Receptive Comprehension ______

6. This article is mainly about (1) prerequisites for remembering; (2) how to improve memory; (3) the Laws of Association; (4) the need to love people. 6. ______
7. Mention of commercials was made to point up the value of (1) repetition; (2) humor; (3) the personal; (4) cleverness of expression. 7. ______
8. To improve memory, it's most important to (1) associate; (2) visualize; (3) repeat; (4) understand. 8. ______
9. This article is chiefly to (1) entertain; (2) describe; (3) explain; (4) inspire. 9. ______
10. The line from Alexander Pope was to emphasize the importance of (1) visualizing; (2) caring; (3) concentrating; (4) associating. 10. ______

(10 points for each correct answer)

Reflective Comprehension ______

TOTAL READING COMPREHENSION SCORE ______

VOCABULARY CHECK QUESTIONS

		without context I	with context II
1. **native**	(1) inborn; (2) national; (3) general; (4) rude; (5) foreign.	1. ______	______
2. **inherent**	(1) pure; (2) essential; (3) harmless; (4) sticky; (5) indirect.	2. ______	______
3. **cited**	(1) mentioned; (2) built; (3) strengthened; (4) played; (5) read.	3. ______	______
4. **retention**	(1) thought; (2) memory; (3) plan; (4) holder; (5) reach.	4. ______	______
5. **contiguity**	(1) contagion; (2) emergency; (3) nearness; (4) series; (5) sameness.	5. ______	______

(10 points for each correct answer)

Word Comprehension without *contextual help (I)* ______

Word Comprehension with *contextual help (II)* ______

TOTAL WORD COMPREHENSION SCORE ______

Exercises

Reading Paragraphs

A close inspection of a well-planned paragraph will suggest how important it is to read for ideas, not words. Often from a fourth to a half of the words in a paragraph are unessential modifiers and connectives or words needed to fit the ideas into conventional English sentence patterns.

Reading the skeleton versions below should suggest how mind and eye should work together to focus on the essentials and suggest the place of stylistic connectives and modifiers. After reading the versions over several times, try filling in some of the gaps, and then check back with the original paragraph.

Version A (Skeleton topic idea and forward step—7 percent of total paragraph)

Lack of self-confidence ....one of ....great problems ....

in most cases such .... is unnecessary.

Version B (Skeleton topic idea, supporting development, and forward step—43 percent of total paragraph)

Lack of self-confidence ....one of..........great problems ....survey ....six hundred students.................................. ....asked to state.........most difficult .... problem. Seventy-five percent listed lack....confidence ....same...................... true...........population generally. Everywhere.............. people......................afraid,.......shrink ....life, ... suffer.......deep............inadequacy......insecurity, ... doubt..............own powers. .... mistrust.....ability........meet responsibilities or.....grasp opportunities. ....beset by...................... ....fear.........something.......not .... right. ....not believe.. be what they want .... , ...so ....make ....content with ....less than ....capable. Thousands................go................ through life................................, defeated .... afraid. ....in most cases such..........................is unnecessary.

Drawing Inferences from Main or Topic Ideas

After a cursory reading of an article, you are apt to feel that your answers to the questions are just guesses. To demonstrate the difference between guesses based on pure chance and inferences, a class of thirty was asked to choose a number between 0 and 100. Since there was little reason to select either a high or low number, the class average was roughly midpoint—an average of 46.

The class was then asked to infer from their own experience what percentage of a sample of six hundred college students listed lack of self-confidence as one of their major problems. Here the class average was 56 percent, still roughly toward the midpoint mark.

To point up the role of the topic sentence in affecting the accuracy of an inference, the topic sentence of the paragraph in the versions printed above was read aloud to the class. The students were then asked to give the percentage figure. Here the class average was 72—only three points away from the actual figure given later in the paragraph, which was 75 percent.

In short, there is an observable difference in results among using (1) pure chance, (2) personal experience and background, and (3) a specific topic sentence. Inferences drawn from general ideas should not be confused with pure chance reactions. If a rapid reading of a selection does give you the main ideas, intelligent use of that information should lead to quite accurate information about details that you did not actually read.

NAME ______________ DATE ______________ READING RATE ______________ WPM

COMPREHENSION CHECK QUESTIONS

1. The article mentions a (1) chair; (2) door; (3) cup; (4) telephone. 1. _______
2. Who created the vacuum cleaner? (1) H. C. Booth; (2) N. B. Holt; (3) D. F. Bremer; (4) C. D. Wright. 2. _______
3. Creativity as a concept was not mentioned until what century? (1) 16th; (2) 17th; (3) 18th; (4) 19th. 3. _______
4. Specific mention was made of (1) Newton; (2) Hero; (3) Columbus; (4) all the preceding. 4. _______
5. Creativity was called a state of (1) chance; (2) mind; (3) exploration; (4) desire. 5. _______

Receptive Comprehension _______

6. This selection is mainly to do what with creativity? (1) define it; (2) explain its origin; (3) point up its role in life; (4) explain how to develop it. 6. _______
7. You would infer that creativity (1) is inborn; (2) is learned through experience; (3) results from schooling; (4) varies widely between individuals. 7. _______
8. This is best described as (1) practical; (2) general; (3) positive; (4) visionary. 8. _______
9. By implication, concerning creativity, everyone should (1) appreciate its value; (2) learn its origins; (3) define it; (4) accept personal limitations. 9. _______
10. Mention of mollusks and plants was intended to illustrate (1) discovery; (2) invention; (3) natural growth of the new; (4) uncreative change. 10. _______

(10 points for each correct answer)

Reflective Comprehension _______

TOTAL READING COMPREHENSION SCORE _______

VOCABULARY CHECK QUESTIONS

		without context I	with context II
1. **environment**	(1) surroundings; (2) plains; (3) suburbs; (4) classifications; (5) encampments.	1. _______	_______
2. **symbols**	(1) rules; (2) collections; (3) feelings; (4) representations; (5) conferences.	2. _______	_______
3. **innate**	(1) intentional; (2) indirect; (3) inborn; (4) brave; (5) familiar.	3. _______	_______
4. **endowed**	(1) approved; (2) provided; (3) intended; (4) strengthened; (5) helped.	4. _______	_______
5. **pervades**	(1) convinces; (2) spreads through; (3) vacates; (4) runs back; (5) prepares.	5. _______	_______

(10 points for each correct answer)

Word Comprehension without *contextual help (I)* _______

Word Comprehension with *contextual help (II)* _______

TOTAL WORD COMPREHENSION SCORE _______

Exercises

Creativity in Learning

Did you ever notice how anything new tends to catch your interest? The usual and ordinary we may pass without a second glance, but if a totally new-looking car comes into view, we will probably stare at it until it is out of sight. The same is true with learning. A new way of learning something—or practicing something—always brings heightened interest.

For example, a totally new way of looking at a paragraph should spark greater interest. One of the exercises for Selection 6, for example, was a new structuring designed to get you to provide the missing words in a paragraph. That new pattern sharpened your ability to read with true understanding—sufficiently well, even, to supply the exact missing words. That requires a special grasp of what is being said. Try it again with the paragraph that follows. You have 22 blanks to fill. If you get 16 exactly right, congratulations!

We don't know, of __________, just where you happen __________ be at this moment, __________ chances are that you __________ in a manufactured environment; __________ office, your home, a __________ room, library, or public __________ where you have time __________ read. Glance about and __________ will see that almost __________ surrounding you has been __________ and designed by someone __________; some person at some __________ engaged in a creative __________, and the sum total __________ those acts makes up __________ world you live in. __________ applies not only to __________ physical environment, but your __________ one as well—your __________ is filled almost entirely __________ symbols originally formed by __________ persons.

Creative Step for Getting the Main Idea

Have you ever tried getting the essence—the main idea—of each paragraph you read? Is that a new way of looking at a paragraph? If it is, it should be both interesting and helpful.

Take the paragraph that you just worked with. Try to express in as few words as possible the main idea of that 111-word paragraph. You might write the following 14-word sentence: "Your world and mind are filled with things and symbols formed by creative persons." To boil down 111 words to 14 requires you to think more about meaning than does your normal way of reading paragraphs. When you read an article that way, you will find it much easier to fit the main ideas of each paragraph into the big, main idea of the selection.

Try the same thing with two more paragraphs. Going back to the original article, read each paragraph indicated below; then write a concise rephrasing of the central idea. Turn back and read the second paragraph, beginning: "Consider what these. . . . " Then do the same with paragraph 3.

Paragraph	**Main idea phrasing**
Paragraph 2	__________
	__________
	__________
Paragraph 3	__________
	__________
	__________

Keep thinking of creative ways to improve your learning habits. It pays!

NAME ____________ DATE ____________ READING RATE ____________ WPM

COMPREHENSION CHECK QUESTIONS

1. Franklin sometimes sat up all night reading (1) *Pilgrims's Progress;* (2) Plutarch's *Lives*; (3) *Paradise Lost;* (4) *Gulliver's Travels.* 1. ______
2. Darwin's father sent him to the University of Glasgow to study (1) medicine; (2) music; (3) for the ministry; (4) for government service. 2. ______
3. Mozart attempted to strike harmonious intervals on the clavier at the age of (1) three; (2) four; (3) five; (4) six. 3. ______
4. One of the following was *not* mentioned: (1) Napoleon; (2) Henslow; (3) Goethe; (4) Shakespeare. 4. ______
5. "Men of genius," when compared with ordinary men, are (1) quite different; (2) more imaginative; (3) essentially the same; (4) more temperamental. 5. ______

Receptive Comprehension ______

6. The purpose of this selection is to suggest the (1) importance of hard, sustained effort; (2) role of deep and ardent curiosity; (3) significance of flashes of inspiration; (4) special insights of men of genius. 6. ______
7. The author implies that Franklin learned to write chiefly because he (1) was urged to write; (2) read so widely; (3) practiced so hard; (4) wanted to so much. 7. ______
8. By implication, good speaking probably results from (1) intelligent practice; (2) strong desire; (3) hard work; (4) wide reading. 8. ______
9. In selecting reading for an anthology, the author would probably favor most strongly getting the reactions of (1) the teachers using the book; (2) the students using the book; (3) well-known writers and critics; (4) literary figures and reviewers. 9. ______
10. The author implies that in selecting reading material the most important consideration would be (1) difficulty; (2) literary merit; (3) timeliness; (4) personal appeal. 10. ______

(10 points for each correct answer)

Reflective Comprehension ______

TOTAL READING COMPREHENSION SCORE ______

VOCABULARY CHECK QUESTIONS

			without context I	with context II
1.	**scant**	(1) limited; (2) rapid; (3) frightening; (4) colorful; (5) designed.	1. ______	______
2.	**fervor**	(1) search; (2) intensity; (3) charm; (4) fete; (5) sickness.	2. ______	______
3.	**verdant**	(1) colorful; (2) populated; (3) golden; (4) verbal; (5) green.	3. ______	______
4.	**propensity**	(1) liking; (2) scheme; (3) propellent; (4) hatred; (5) expression.	4. ______	______
5.	**sundry**	(1) bright; (2) various; (3) costly; (4) warm; (5) sullen.	5. ______	______

(10 points for each correct answer)

Word Comprehension without *contextual help (I)* ______

Word Comprehension with *contextual help (II)* ______

TOTAL WORD COMPREHENSION SCORE ______

EXERCISES

DEALING WITH SYNTHESIS AND ANALYSIS

The good reader is one who is familiar with a variety of ways of organizing material. In the same way, a good driver is one who is familiar with a wide variety of highway signs and markers and can travel with a minimum of error. Synthesis and analysis are patterns of organization that should be well known.

Suppose we look more closely at each. Synthesis is essentially a fitting together of parts or ideas to form a whole—a generalization or thesis. For example, when you add the prefix *in-* to the prefix *de-* to the root *pend* to the suffix *-ence,* you get the word *independence*, formed from a synthesis of language elements. Analysis is just the opposite. You start with a whole and break it down into its parts so as to understand it better. With *independence*, that would mean breaking the word down into the two prefixes, root, and suffix forming the word.

Now think back to the article on interest. Notice how the author turns to three careers, synthesizing from each the parts that can be put together to form a single generalization or thesis. Look back to see exactly what words he uses as road markers to call attention to a new thought division. Write the first six words of each paragraph that marks the beginning of his treatment of another individual. Use the following spaces.

1. ____________________

2. ____________________

3. ____________________

To pull together the threefold pattern, the elements to be synthesized, the author uses what might be called a summary statement serving as a transition leading on to his generalization. The paragraph that serves this important function begins with what fourteen words? Enter them below.

____

____

What generalization comes from the synthesis of these three careers—the truth to be distilled as a matter of major concern? Enter the statement of that truth below.

____

____

The remaining paragraphs lead on to a somewhat modified final truth, growing out of the additional development. State that final truth below, underlining the portion added to the initial generalization synthesized from the three careers.

____

____

____

EXAMINING YOUR READING INTERESTS

Analyze your own reading interests below, listing two conclusions—one focused on a major strength, one on a major weakness.

A. ____________________

____

B. ____________________

____

NAME ______________________ DATE ______________ READING RATE ______________ WPM

COMPREHENSION CHECK QUESTIONS

1. To kill the dragons Gawaine used a (1) sword; (2) lance; (3) battle-ax; (4) spear. 1. ______
2. When Gawaine is first told he is to kill dragons, he asks for (1) an enchanted cap; (2) a magic word; (3) more training; (4) some other job. 2. ______
3. After killing a dragon, Gawaine would always bring back (1) the claws; (2) a lock of hair; (3) a tooth; (4) the ears. 3. ______
4. Gawaine said he thought some of the dragons were (1) 50 feet long; (2) 100 feet long; (3) 200 feet long; (4) 500 feet long. 4. ______
5. The dragon that finally killed Gawaine was (1) a small one; (2) a fair-sized one; (3) a large one; (4) of unknown size. 5. ______

Receptive Comprehension ______

6. This story illustrates the importance of (1) training; (2) courage; (3) attitude; (4) magic. 6. ______
7. Gawaine's record of fifty killings was primarily attributable to (1) his skill; (2) his assurance; (3) his training; (4) none of those factors. 7. ______
8. You would infer that the Headmaster regarded Gawaine (1) highly; (2) with some aversion; (3) as likable but a mediocre student; (4) as a capable but lazy student. 8. ______
9. The humor of this article is best described as (1) mildly satiric; (2) rather obvious; (3) farcical; (4) stilted. 9. ______
10. You would infer from this that to read well one should be (1) well educated; (2) interested in books; (3) confident; (4) experienced. 10. ______

(10 points for each correct answer)

Reflective Comprehension ______
TOTAL READING COMPREHENSION SCORE ______

VOCABULARY CHECK QUESTIONS

			without context I	with context II
1.	**restive**	(1) subdued; (2) limited; (3) nervous; (4) respected; (5) happy.	1. ______	______
2.	**versatile**	(1) upright; (2) dizzy; (3) visible; (4) competent; (5) vested.	2. ______	______
3.	**impetuously**	(1) rudely; (2) furiously; (3) impassively; (4) imperfectly; (5) fairly.	3. ______	______
4.	**indulgently**	(1) slowly; (2) ravishingly; (3) with lenience; (4) with a smile; (5) honestly.	4. ______	______
5.	**debauch**	(1) outlet; (2) rubbish; (3) collapse; (4) dissipation; (5) evening.	5. ______	______

(10 points for each correct answer)

Word Comprehension without *contextual help (I)* ______
Word Comprehension with *contextual help (II)* ______
TOTAL WORD COMPREHENSION SCORE ______

Exercises

Interpreting What You Read

The difference between what is stated and what is unstated focuses on the difference between receptive questions—those among the first five—and reflective questions—those among the last five. To see that difference more clearly, take a typical question on "The Fifty-first Dragon." Find in that article the actual statement answering the following question: "The dragon that finally killed Gawaine was (1) a small one; (2) a fair-sized one; (3) a large one; (4) of unknown size."

Enter the exact stated words from the article that answer the question:

____

In answering such questions the reader must read and remember a stated fact.

Now take a typical question from among the last five, which demand interpretation. Here it is often a matter of drawing inferences or conclusions based on certain relevant evidence. To understand the problem, examine the article closely for evidence bearing on each of the four choices. Enter the exact words under the appropriate choice to see what evidence supports each possibility.

Here is the question. Space is given with each choice for entering relevant evidence.

"You would infer that the Headmaster regarded Gawaine (1) highly; (2) with some aversion; (3) as likable but a mediocre student; (4) as a capable but lazy student."

1. highly ____

____

2. with some aversion____

____

3. as likable but a mediocre student ____

____

4. as a capable but lazy student____

Try still another question from the last five. This time, imagine that you are arguing with someone, not only about which is the right answer but about why you think the other answers are wrong. List under each of the four choices the specific evidence you would use in making your point. Here is the question.

"Gawaine's record of fifty killings was primarily attributable to (1) his skill; (2) his assurance; (3) his training; (4) none of those factors."

1. his skill ____

____

2. his assurance____

____

3. his training ____

____

4. none of those factors ____

____

NAME ______________________ DATE ______________ READING RATE ______________ WPM

COMPREHENSION CHECK QUESTIONS

1. When Ali started home after his University experience, he came on (1) a jackass; (2) foot; (3) a spirited Arabian; (4) a camel. 1. _______
2. How many years did Ali study at the University of El-Azhar? (1) two; (2) four; (3) six; (4) eight. 2. _______
3. At his first stop in the village, Ali found the Khatib preaching about the (1) prophetic powers of Mohammed; (2) miraculous deeds of Mohammed; (3) nature of God as revealed by Mohammed; (4) punishment of sinners and unbelievers as described by Mohammed. 3. _______
4. What indignity was *not* suffered by Ali at the hands of the villagers? (1) stoning; (2) imprisonment; (3) beating; (4) destruction of his diploma. 4. _______
5. When Ali came to the village of the Khatib a second time, (1) he was dressed in silks and satins; (2) he was dressed in the coarse raiment of a scholar; (3) he was dressed in the garb of a foreigner; (4) no mention was made of his dress. 5. _______

Receptive Comprehension _______

6. The purpose of this selection is to show the need for (1) worldly wisdom; (2) book learning; (3) tact and cleverness; (4) a well-rounded development. 6. _______
7. The selection was intended primarily to (1) entertain; (2) persuade; (3) describe; (4) explain. 7. _______
8. When Ali and the Khatib first met, (1) Ali was apparently in the right in their argument; (2) the Khatib was apparently in the right; (3) both were mistaken; (4) both were equally well informed about Mohammed. 8. _______
9. You would infer from Ali's first experience with the Khatib that in an argument the deciding factor is most likely to be (1) the truth; (2) tact; (3) authority; (4) personality. 9. _______
10. You would judge from this that the best way of convincing someone is to (1) cite direct evidence; (2) contradict the opposite viewpoint; (3) appeal to authority; (4) present your case indirectly without seeming to disagree. 10. _______

(10 points for each correct answer)

Reflective Comprehension _______

TOTAL READING COMPREHENSION SCORE _______

VOCABULARY CHECK QUESTIONS

			without context I	with context II
1.	**aphorisms**	(1) insects; (2) drugs; (3) peaks; (4) visitors; (5) sayings.	1. _______	_______
2.	**raiment**	(1) beams; (2) surface; (3) curve; (4) parapet; (5) garments.	2. _______	_______
3.	**credulous**	(1) easily convinced; (2) critical; (3) shy; (4) apt; (5) worthy of praise.	3. _______	_______
4.	**boon**	(1) log; (2) sound; (3) structure; (4) favor; (5) fate.	4. _______	_______
5.	**meticulously**	(1) hurriedly; (2) decisively; (3) very carefully; (4) actually; (5) quite gayly.	5. _______	_______

(10 points for each correct answer)

Word Comprehension without *contextual help (I)* _______

Word Comprehension with *contextual help (II)* _______

TOTAL WORD COMPREHENSION SCORE _______

EXERCISES

READING FOR IMAGERY

One of the important differences between reading exposition and narration is in savoring the mental pictures typical of narration. These demand a special response by the reader to the sense impressions provided—a vicarious enjoyment of things seen, heard, tasted, felt, or smelled.

As a means of sharpening your awareness of such sense impressions, make your own list of from three to ten specific sensory images in each of the following five categories. For example, "black coffee" is primarily a sight impression, but if you are reading imaginatively it should also be listed under *taste* or *smell.*

Sights	Tastes	Smells	Feels	Sounds
________	________	________	________	________
________	________	________	________	________
________	________	________	________	________
________	________	________	________	________
________	________	________	________	________
________	________	________	________	________
________	________	________	________	________
________	________	________	________	________
________	________	________	________	________
________	________	________	________	________

Look back over each of the words or phrases you listed; then concentrate your full attention on each, imagining as vividly as possible what is described. How well did you imagine the taste of "black coffee"? Did you think of it as deliciously hot, pleasantly warm as it ran down your throat? Did you imagine its aroma? Did you visualize the steam slowly rising from the cup? In short, did you imaginatively bring together the whole range of sensory impressions found in "black coffee"?

DEVELOPING AN IDEA

Actually, as a reader, when you get the main idea, you strip away the author's development of a thesis or point to get the kernel. To understand the process better, look at it from the writer's point of view. Starting with a main idea, the writer then goes on to develop it fully.

See how this works with a single sentence. Contrast the sentence "Ali then took a hair from the Khatib's beard" with the original passage describing that act. How does an author develop parts of a narrative and bring them to life?

GETTING THE MAIN IDEA

This is a story told to illustrate a general principle. Write the thesis or central idea developed, using the author's phrasing.

"To be truly educated, one should ____

____

____

NAME ______________________ DATE ______________ READING RATE ______________ WPM

COMPREHENSION CHECK QUESTIONS

1. You were told to act like a 12th-century (1) scribe; (2) monastic; (3) artisan; (4) apprentice. 1. _______
2. One couple hired (1) an efficiency expert; (2) a relative; (3) a secretary; (4) a "wife." 2. _______
3. How many listed items are considered reasonable? (1) twenty; (2) fifteen; (3) ten; (4) five. 3. _______
4. One man used what color of paper for his lists? (1) yellow; (2) pink; (3) buff; (4) orange. 4. _______
5. One expert named was (1) Mary Grieve; (2) Larry Baker; (3) Lucille Nichols; (4) William Cadman. 5. _______

Receptive Comprehension _______

6. This article is mainly about (1) sources of help for getting organized; (2) managing time better; (3) how to get organized; (4) eliminating unproductive activities. 6. _______
7. Mention of Great-grandma was to show that the basic principles of good organization (1) are laughable; (2) are old; (3) need revision; (4) are outdated. 7. _______
8. The Judy Lipton illustration was to get you to (1) make lists; (2) learn to delegate; (3) eliminate unproductive activities; (4) call in an expert. 8. _______
9. Which word best describes this article? (1) practical; (2) stimulating; (3) theoretical; (4) entertaining. 9. _______
10. Points are developed largely by (1) citing figures; (2) logical reasoning; (3) concrete illustrations; (4) personal opinion. 10. _______

(10 points for each correct answer)

Reflective Comprehension _______

TOTAL READING COMPREHENSION SCORE _______

VOCABULARY CHECK QUESTIONS

			without context I	with context II
1.	**tactics**	(1) traces; (2) problems; (3) methods; (4) hopes; (5) trends.	1. _______	_______
2.	**hew**	(1) help; (2) stick; (3) save; (4) depart; (5) smell.	2. _______	_______
3.	**delegate**	(1) delay; (2) please; (3) detract; (4) convince; (5) entrust.	3. _______	_______
4.	**deem**	(1) dread; (2) think; (3) desire; (4) appear; (5) order.	4. _______	_______
5.	**feasibility**	(1) amiability; (2) regulation; (3) feature; (4) action; (5) practicability.	5. _______	_______

(10 points for each correct answer)

Word Comprehension without *contextual help (I)* _______

Word Comprehension with *contextual help (II)* _______

TOTAL WORD COMPREHENSION SCORE _______

EXERCISES

READING PARAGRAPHS

Increased awareness of paragraph structure is an important step toward intelligent adjustment of rate to material. Just as a driver who sees a clear, straight stretch of highway ahead can accelerate without fear of consequences, so the reader who makes effective use of a topic sentence can shift into high for the remainder of the paragraph. A topic sentence is, in a sense, a highway marker to facilitate our attempts to follow the writer's thoughts.

Analyze the following five paragraphs to determine (a) whether the topic idea is expressed or implied, (b) if expressed, what it suggests by way of development. If the topic idea is implied, skip (b) and (c).

EXAMPLE: Paragraph beginning "First, you. . . ." **(Skim through the selection until you find the paragraph, then go ahead with the analysis.)**

(a) Expressed __✓__ or implied _____

(b) The topic sentence is the 1st in the paragraph.

(c) It suggests that the rest of the paragraph will deal more specifically with how to unjam your schedule.

Paragraph beginning "Then there are the tasks. . . ."

(a) Expressed _____ or implied _____

(b) The topic sentence is the _____ in the paragraph.

(c) It suggests that the rest of the paragraph____

____

Paragraph beginning "Lists work especially well. . . ."

(a) Expressed _____ or implied _____

(b) The topic sentence is the _____ in the paragraph.

(c) It suggests that the rest of the paragraph____

____

Paragraph beginning "Twenty years ago, ..."

(a) Expressed _____ or implied _____

(b) The topic sentence is the _____ in the paragraph.

(c) It suggests that the rest of the paragraph____

____

Paragraph beginning "Suppose you are a chemist. . . ."

(a) Expressed _____ or implied _____

(b) The topic sentence is the _____ in the paragraph.

(c) It suggests that the rest of the paragraph____

____

Paragraph beginning "A number of books. . . ."

(a) Expressed _____ or implied _____

(b) The topic sentence is the _____ in the paragraph.

(c) It suggests that the rest of the paragraph____

____

Compare your results with those of other students; discuss any differences in an attempt to resolve them.

NAME ______________________ DATE ______________ READING RATE ______________ WPM

Comprehension Check Questions

1. In the U.S., how many are literate? (1) two-thirds; (2) three-fourths; (3) four-fifths; (4) nine-tenths. 1. ______

2. Mention was made of (1) preparing résumés; (2) filling out job forms; (3) job interviewing; (4) writing application letters. 2. ______

3. Reference was made to (1) Spain; (2) Russia; (3) France; (4) Germany. 3. ______

4. NAEP refers to (1) a government agency; (2) an act of Congress; (3) a national measurement instrument; (4) a national commission. 4. ______

5. Who are alarmed at the growing illiteracy? (1) American business leaders; (2) Congress; (3) school administrators; (4) teachers. 5. ______

Receptive Comprehension ______

6. The purpose of this article is mainly to do what about cultural literacy? (1) define it; (2) discuss falling scores; (3) point up its key importance; (4) show student unawareness of it. 6. ______

7. For us, what best describes the situation with cultural literacy? (1) of uncertain concern; (2) of growing concern; (3) of lessening concern; (4) of major concern. 7. ______

8. The Harvard Square research illustration was to show the (1) way strangers are judged; (2) difficulty of giving clear directions; (3) importance of external clues; (4) importance of shared information. 8. ______

9. To prove his point, the author relies primarily on quoting (1) reading authorities; (2) business leaders; (3) test results; (4) news magazines. 9. ______

10. The son's reference to *The Alamo* was to show what about his students? (1) their ignorance; (2) their overconfidence; (3) their lack of common knowledge; (4) their accumulation of new information. 10. ______

(10 points for each correct answer)

Reflective Comprehension ______

TOTAL READING COMPREHENSION SCORE ______

Vocabulary Check Questions

			without context I	with context II
1.	**paramount**	(1) chief; (2) enlarged; (3) rising; (4) parallel; (5) dividing.	1. ______	______
2.	**foster**	(1) debate; (2) join; (3) resist; (4) promote; (5) discover.	2. ______	______
3.	**mandated**	(1) covered; (2) marked; (3) ordered; (4) attracted; (5) divided.	3. ______	______
4.	**juxtapose**	(1) discover; (2) put beside; (3) put back; (4) judge; (5) prepare.	4. ______	______
5.	**ephemeral**	(1) lasting; (2) short-lived; (3) effective; (4) timely; (5) satisfying.	5. ______	______

(10 points for each correct answer)

Word Comprehension without *contextual help (I)* ______

Word Comprehension with *contextual help (II)* ______

TOTAL WORD COMPREHENSION SCORE ______

Exercises

Seeing Cultural Literacy at Work

Eleanor Rosch conducted some experiments to discover exactly how we see and react to things. Looking out of a window, you may see branches and leaves. What do you say you see? Most people will say "trees"—not "leaves and branches." Such middle-level categories, according to Rosch, make up "the basic furniture of our conceptual world."

Try one of her experiments. Put five specific names under each of the general categories below, ranking the names from the most to the least typical.

Fruit	**Furniture**	**Bird**
__________	__________	__________
__________	__________	__________
__________	__________	__________
__________	__________	__________
__________	__________	__________

Now compare your listings with her research findings given below. Her findings were quite consistent from person to person.

Fruit	**Furniture**	**Bird**
apple	chair	robin
plum	dresser	swallow
cherry	davenport	eagle
watermelon	footstool	crow
fig	lamp	pheasant

Such research suggests that when you read the word *bird* you think of a robinlike creature. With that in mind, Rosch checked further, asking subjects to compose sentences using the word *bird.*

Here are some typical ones:

> I heard a bird twittering outside my window.
> Three birds sat on a branch of a tree.
> A bird flew down and began eating.

Now try substituting specific birds for the word *bird* in those sentences. Replace *bird* with *robin* and the sentences still make sense. Replace *bird* with *eagle* or *pheasant* and they don't. Who has heard an eagle twitter—or a pheasant? In short, she discovered that our shared mental pictures color our reading and understanding of words. Cultural literacy depends on such shared knowledge.

Putting Cultural Literacy to Work

Hirsch's father, who was in the commodity business, often wrote letters that alluded to Shakespeare. Timing of sales and purchases was all-important. He would sometimes write or say, "There is a tide," without further elaboration. Without shared knowledge those words are meaningless. Both had to know this passage from Shakespeare's *Julius Caesar*:

> There is a tide in the affairs of men,
> Which, taken at the flood, leads on to fortune;
> Omitted, all the voyage of their life
> Is bound in shallows and in miseries.

On such a full sea are we now afloat;
And we must take the current when it serves,
Or lose our ventures.

Those four words actually say, "Buy (or sell) now and make a fortune, but if you fail to act right away, you may regret it the rest of your life." Four words, not twenty-five, say the same thing—provided that there is shared literate background knowledge. In the back of *Cultural Literacy* Hirsch lists the essential knowledge that we should possess in order to communicate well. To see how well you know the essentials, complete the following bits drawn from his list.

Sample: "Well, you know what absence makes!" Absence makes the heart grow fonder.

1. Well, you know all's fair . . . ____________________
2. All's well that . . . ____________________
3. All that glitters . . . ____________________
4. Ask not what your country can do for you. Ask . . . ____________________
5. Better late . . . ____________________
6. The best things in life . . . ____________________
7. Better safe than . . . ____________________
8. Birds of a feather . . . ____________________
9. Don't cross the bridge till . . . ____________________
10. You can't teach an old dog . . . ____________________

With shared information, part of the quotation communicates the whole, as with "There is a tide."

Answers: 1. in love and war; 2. ends well; 3. is not gold; 4. what you can do for your country; 5. than never; 6. are free; 7. sorry; 8. flock together; 9. you come to it; 10. new tricks.

NAME ______________________ DATE ______________ READING RATE ______________ WPM

COMPREHENSION CHECK QUESTIONS

1. According to the Duke of Wellington, habit is (1) stronger than nature; (2) ten times nature; (3) nature personified; (4) our hidden nature. 1. _______

2. The critical age period for forming intellectual habits was said to be (1) between twenty and thirty; (2) below twenty; (3) the first ten years; (4) the first six years. 2. _______

3. The writer quotes (1) Goethe; (2) Shakespeare; (3) the Bible; (4) Alexander Pope. 3. _______

4. The author says there is no more contemptible type of character than the (1) agitator; (2) drifter; (3) dreamer; (4) exploiter. 4. _______

5. The article refers specifically to (1) Robinson Crusoe; (2) Rip Van Winkle; (3) Shylock; (4) Samson. 5. _______

Receptive Comprehension _______

6. The primary purpose of this selection is to (1) suggest the key role of habit in education; (2) prove that habit is our best friend; (3) explain the difficulties of habit formation; (4) contrast habit with thought. 6. _______

7. The story about the discharged veteran and the practical joker was to show (1) the thoroughness of military training; (2) how absent-minded the veteran was; (3) our natural tendency to obey; (4) the strength of habit. 7. _______

8. Apparently the best way to break the smoking habit would be to (1) stop abruptly; (2) taper off gradually; (3) first cut down to only two cigarettes a day; (4) stay away from other smokers. 8. _______

9. You would conclude that a tendency to act comes primarily from (1) motivation; (2) reasoning; (3) willing; (4) doing. 9. _______

10. You would infer that the author would particularly favor (1) meeting things as they come; (2) avoiding too rigid a schedule; (3) relaxing during the weekends; (4) following a weekly schedule. 10. _______

(10 points for each correct answer)

Reflective Comprehension _______

TOTAL READING COMPREHENSION SCORE _______

VOCABULARY CHECK QUESTIONS

			without context I	with context II
1.	**ordinance**	(1) statement; (2) reputation; (3) movement; (4) established custom; (5) new publication.	1. _______	_______
2.	**inanition**	(1) ridicule; (2) anger; (3) worry; (4) growth; (5) exhaustion.	2. _______	_______
3.	**sovereign**	(1) greatest; (2) fixed; (3) habitual; (4) costly; (5) memorable.	3. _______	_______
4.	**aspire**	(1) cause; (2) breathe; (3) hope; (4) agree; (5) motivate.	4. _______	_______
5.	**gratuitous**	(1) useful; (2) meaningful; (3) casual; (4) unnecessary; (5) grateful.	5. _______	_______

(10 points for each correct answer)

Word Comprehension without *contextual help (I)* _______

Word Comprehension with *contextual help (II)* _______

TOTAL WORD COMPREHENSION SCORE _______

EXERCISES

READING PARAGRAPHS

Each paragraph should have a single central idea. If it is expressed in a sentence, the sentence is called a topic sentence and may come at the beginning, middle, or end of the paragraph. But at times the main idea is not expressed but only implied.

Analyze the specified paragraphs from the article on habit. If the paragraph contains a topic sentence, write it in the space provided below. If the main idea is implied, try to compose an appropriate topic sentence for the paragraph, writing it in the space provided below.

Paragraph 1

Reread the first paragraph in the article. Check the appropriate choice.
Is the topic idea expressed _____ or implied? _____
If the topic idea is expressed, enter the exact words that express it:

If the topic idea is implied, express it in a sentence that you devise and write here:

It seems to be expressed in the phrase, "habit is ten times nature." The words "degree to which this is true" lead on to the example of the soldier who, by years of discipline and the ingraining of habit, is fashioned "completely over again."
Now take the next paragraph and analyze it in similar fashion.

Paragraph 2

Is the topic idea expressed _____ or implied? _____
If the topic idea is expressed, enter the exact words that express it:

If the topic idea is implied, express it in a sentence that you devise and write here:

Paragraph 3

Is the topic idea expressed _____ or implied? _____
Notice how much of the paragraph deals with "domestic beasts." How much deals with "men"? How much with wild animals?
If the topic idea is expressed, enter the exact words that express it:

If the topic idea is implied, express it in a sentence that you devise and write here:

Paragraph 4

Is the topic idea expressed _____ or implied? _____
What is the function of the single word *it*, which is used to begin the six sentences immediately following the first sentence? Does this help you in your analysis?
If the topic idea is expressed, enter the exact words that express it:

If the topic idea is implied, express it in a sentence that you devise and write here:

NAME ____________________ DATE ____________ READING RATE ____________ WPM

COMPREHENSION CHECK QUESTIONS

1. People who have only one or two topics of conversation illustrate (1) dead-level abstraction; (2) content rigidity; (3) formal rigidity; (4) underverbalization. 1. ______
2. Wendell Johnson is called a (1) grammarian; (2) psychiatrist; (3) sociologist; (4) semanticist. 2. ______
3. *Science and Sanity* was written by (1) Johnson; (2) Heatter; (3) Hayakawa; (4) Korzybski. 3. ______
4. The author talked about learning to (1) swim; (2) dive; (3) tread water; (4) float. 4. ______
5. Johnson is concerned with the specific problem of (1) amnesia; (2) pronunciation; (3) stuttering; (4) inflections. 5. ______

Receptive Comprehension ______

6. The chief purpose of the article is to (1) stress the importance of vocabulary; (2) discuss Johnson's research; (3) review Johnson's book; (4) provide a general introduction to semantics. 6. ______
7. The general thesis developed is that a person's language habits (1) are determined by heredity; (2) are less important than his feelings and actions; (3) influence his life; (4) grow out of his life experience. 7. ______
8. The opening descriptions of kinds of people was largely intended to point up (1) verbal peculiarities; (2) language habits; (3) common problems; (4) classification categories. 8. ______
9. Discussion of the word *success* was to show the importance of (1) a life goal; (2) a comfortable income; (3) formulating word meanings; (4) achieving a given goal. 9. ______
10. The reference to a can of sardines and the nail-clippers was to show (1) the reality of the world of not-words; (2) the importance of the right words; (3) the need for verbal tools; (4) the importance of outside help. 10. ______

(10 points for each correct answer)

Reflective Comprehension ______
TOTAL READING COMPREHENSION SCORE ______

VOCABULARY CHECK QUESTIONS

			without context I	with context II
1. clichés	(1) clippings; (2) statements; (3) clues; (4) books; (5) platitudes.	1.	______	______
2. affected	(1) loving; (2) natural; (3) ambiguous; (4) influenced; (5) helpful.	2.	______	______
3. aberrations	(1) savages; (2) sores; (3) deviations; (4) skills; (5) oaths.	3.	______	______
4. pervasive	(1) cranky; (2) agitated; (3) penetrating; (4) relevant; (5) oppressive.	4.	______	______
5. epigram	(1) parasite; (2) plague; (3) gourmet; (4) folk song; (5) witty saying.	5.	______	______

(10 points for each correct answer)

Word Comprehension without *contextual help (I)* ______
Word Comprehension with *contextual help (II)* ______
TOTAL WORD COMPREHENSION SCORE ______

Exercises

Parallelism to Mark Organization

At times a writer will use parallelism to fuse several paragraphs into a larger unit. In this selection, for example, how many paragraphs make up what would be called the introduction? ____________________

How does each paragraph begin? ____________________

____

What two-word phrase accents the pulling together of the previous paragraphs and serves as a transition into the main part of the article? ____________________

Noting Words That Link

Read the paragraph on the left below. Then study the linking words indicated on the right.

In short, what are the language habits of the people around you—and also, what are your own? For many of *these people* are in messes, always quarreling, or always overexcited, or always suffering from feelings of inadequacy, or always being victimized by their own prejudices. *They* are people in quandaries. Is there any connection between *their quandaries* and their language habits? Are *they*, as Wendell Johnson says, merely the froth on the beer or an important ingredient of the beer itself?

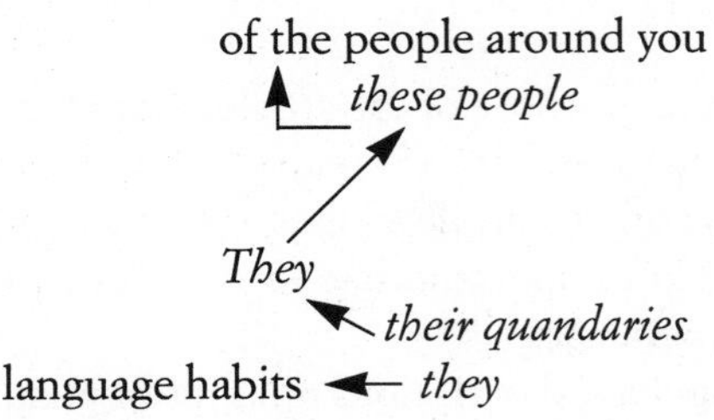

Notice how frequently pronouns with antecedents in the previous sentence provide the essential link between sentences. To reinforce the connection, repetition is also used, as with *people* and *quandaries*.

Using Words That Link

The following sentences make up one paragraph but are jumbled so that they lack proper order. First, underline all words that link sentences with sentences. Next, through attention to those linking words, reorder the sentences to make a readable, coherent paragraph. Check back to the original passage (paragraph 16, p. 38), when you have finished, to see if there is agreement.

In spite of good positions or comfortable incomes, such persons manage to keep themselves miserable, because the goal they set up for themselves is so vaguely defined that *they can't ever tell whether they have reached it or not.* An example of this primitivism is the kind of person who, unconsciously believing that, because there is such a word as "success," there is such a thing, keeps trying to attain it—without ever having attempted to formulate what he means by "success." (If the reader asks at this point, "But what is success?" he needs Johnson's book very badly.) Hence a lifelong uneasiness, with hypertension or gastric ulcers to boot.

NAME ______________________ DATE ______________ READING RATE ______________ WPM

COMPREHENSION CHECK QUESTIONS

1. Toffler also wrote (1) *The Coming Revolution;* (2) *In Transition*; (3) *The Third Wave*; (4) *Power Poor.* 1. _______

2. Toffler predicts that power will shift to those best at (1) speed reading; (2) controlling information; (3) information judo; (4) computer excellence. 2. _______

3. The selection refers to (1) professors; (2) *Spycatcher*; (3) Tiananmen Square; (4) all the preceding. 3. _______

4. How many million PCs were said to be in home use? (1) 22; (2) 18; (3) 14; (4) 12. 4. _______

5. Manufacturing will shift to countries with (1) brainiest factories; (2) cheap labor; (3) most raw materials; (4) top computer experts. 5. _______

Receptive Comprehension _______

6. The purpose of this article is chiefly to do what with Toffler's book? (1) review it; (2) promote it; (3) summarize it; (4) criticize it. 6. _______

7. Chief emphasis is on the (1) how; (2) what; (3) who; (4) why. 7. _______

8. This is best classified as (1) narration; (2) persuasion; (3) description; (4) exposition. 8. _______

9. The reference to *Spycatcher* was to show the (1) difference between Britain and the United States; (2) scope of international problems; (3) need for more knowledge control; (4) the loss of knowledge monopoly. 9. _______

10. Toffler's *Powershift* should especially encourage the (1) terrorists; (2) educators; (3) have-nots; (4) CIOs. 10. _______

(10 points for each correct answer)

Reflective Comprehension _______

TOTAL READING COMPREHENSION SCORE _______

VOCABULARY CHECK QUESTIONS

			without context I	with context II
1.	**hubris**	(1) humility; (2) polish; (3) glory; (4) arrogance; (5) applause.	1. _______	_______
2.	**delectable**	(1) determined; (2) sweet; (3) limited; (4) sad; (5) delightful.	2. _______	_______
3.	**equivocators**	(1) liars; (2) agents; (3) counselors; (4) equals; (5) drivers.	3. _______	_______
4.	**ubiquitous**	(1) stubborn; (2) tireless; (3) present everywhere; (4) uniform; (5) unpleasant.	4. _______	_______
5.	**dispassionate**	(1) calm; (2) emotional; (3) biased; (4) fair; (5) disturbed.	5. _______	_______

(10 points for each correct answer)

Word Comprehension without *contextual help (I)* _______

Word Comprehension with *contextual help (II)* _______

TOTAL WORD COMPREHENSION SCORE _______

EXERCISES

NOTING TRANSITIONAL AND CONNECTIVE DEVICES

A good driver has to be alert to all road signs and road conditions. In the same way, an efficient reader must be alert to any words or phrases that help to ease the path set by the writer. When skilled readers read, "Now Toffler is back, with *Powershift*," they have reason to think that previous mention has been made of Toffler—probably a mention of an earlier book or two, since he's back with a new one.

Various words in any selection tend to serve as guideposts–signs of where the writer is going or where he has been. Some such words or phrases suggest cause, result, comparison, repetition, and the like. Enhance your alertness to such aids by classifying the following words and phrases taken from this selection. Use the following classifications:

1. Addition
2. Example
3. Repetition
4. Comparison
5. Contrast
6. Emphasis
7. Cause-effect

Example: "as was said . . ." 3

a. "He predicts . . ." _______

b. "as well as . . ." _______

c. "facts of life are two:" _______

d. "for example . . ." _______

e. "but . . ." _______

f. "if he . . ." _______

g. "Toffler also thinks . . ." _______

h. "while some like . . ." _______

i. "most nightmarish example . . ." _______

j. "Add economic distress . . ." _______

k. "In addition . . ." _______

Answers: a. 1 or 2; b. 1; c. 1; d. 2; e. 4 or 5; f. 7; g. 1; h. 5; i. 2; j. 1; k. 1.

NAME ______________ DATE ______________ READING RATE ______________ WPM

COMPREHENSION CHECK QUESTIONS

1. In what year did Gore propose his information superhighways? (1) 1979; (2) 1983; (3) 1986; (4) 1989. 1. _____
2. Gore mentioned (1) Sputnik; (2) the Library of Congress; (3) General Motors; (4) the Space Museum. 2. _____
3. Gore asks what happens when an advanced computer costing $20 million today sells for (1) $10 million; (2) $5 million; (3) $500,000; (4) 250,000. 3. _____
4. What was spoken of as one of the most important scientific engineering achievements of the last 25 years? (1) digital television; (2) electronic mail; (3) the transistor; (4) fiber-optic communication. 4. _____
5. Gore mentions (1) General Omar Bradley; (2) Douglas MacArthur; (3) Richard Nixon; (4) Eisenhower. 5. _____

Receptive Comprehension _____

6. This article mainly shows what about information superhighways? (1) its beginnings; (2) its need; (3) its growth; (4) its difficulties. 6. _____
7. This is primarily to (1) persuade; (2) inform; (3) entertain; (4) inspire. 7. _____
8. The reference to starving children was used to point up (1) government problems; (2) the need for change; (3) agricultural problems; (4) the need to curb waste. 8. _____
9. "To steer by the stars" means to (1) have courage; (2) plan carefully; (3) have vision; (4) focus on immediate concerns. 9. _____
10. Concerning information superhighways, Gore's attitude toward government is best described as (1) accepting; (2) positive; (3) critical; (4) understanding. 10. _____

(10 points for each correct answer)

Reflective Comprehension _____

TOTAL READING COMPREHENSION SCORE _____

VOCABULARY CHECK QUESTIONS

			without context I	with context II
1.	**reluctant**	(1) reliable; (2) unwilling; (3) lazy; (4) applicable; (5) rigid.	1. _____	_____
2.	**endorse**	(1) support; (2) decide; (3) enter; (4) end; (5) force.	2. _____	_____
3.	**decipher**	(1) determine; (2) compose; (3) add up; (4) deliver; (5) explain.	3. _____	_____
4.	**synergy**	(1) sentence; (2) energy; (3) substitute; (4) relationship; (5) cooperation.	4. _____	_____
5.	**prototypes**	(1) files; (2) printings; (3) promotions; (4) properties; (5) models.	5. _____	_____

(10 points for each correct answer)

Word Comprehension without *contextual help (I)* _____

Word Comprehension with *contextual help (II)* _____

TOTAL WORD COMPREHENSION SCORE _____

Exercises

Reading Punctuation

What do you read? Words! Yes, but you also read the punctuation marks that help you make sense out of the words. For example, try reading the following words in a meaningful way:

> Bill where Jim had had had had had had had had had had had the approval of the language experts.

Without the help of punctuation that sentence is probably meaningless. Try reading the same sentence, this time *with* punctuation:

> Bill, where Jim had had "had had," had had "had"; "had had" had had the approval of the language experts.

Punctuation does indeed make for easier, more meaningful reading.

Try the following matching exercise to sharpen your awareness of some of the most common meanings of punctuation marks. Enter the most appropriate word or words from the right in the space after each mark of punctuation on the left.

Matching Exercise

1. ? ____________	a. namely
2. ! ____________	b. stop
3. " " ____________	c. startling, isn't it
4. , ____________	d. and
5. : ____________	e. said
6. . ____________	f. stop-and-go
7. ; ____________	g. who, what, when, where, how
8. — ____________	h. an aside
9. ( ) ____________	i. interruption

Try punctuating the following sentences to improve readability; then check back to the article to see how closely your punctuation agrees with the original:

> The United States could benefit greatly in research in education in economic development and in scores of other areas by efficiently processing and dealing with information that is available but unused.

> Remember that electronic mail didn't exist until ARPANET the U S Department of Defense's Advanced Research Projects Agency network 20 years ago and today electronic mail is a billion dollar a year business and growing very rapidly.

> When one is in the middle of a technological revolution one has two choices to follow yesterday's map or quickly chart a new course and grab the opportunities that we find.

Answers: 1. g; 2. c; 3. e; 4. d; 5. a; 6. b; 7. f; 8. i; 9. h.

NAME ______________________ DATE ______________ READING RATE ______________ WPM

COMPREHENSION CHECK QUESTIONS

1.	This selection begins by showing a child wandering through a (1) clothing store; (2) supermarket; (3) hardware store; (4) department store.	1. _______
2.	The author boxed with (1) Firpo; (2) Louis; (3) Dempsey; (4) Levinsky.	2. _______
3.	The author discusses in some detail (1) basketball; (2) bowling; (3) tennis; (4) wrestling.	3. _______
4.	The author speaks particularly about (1) fielding a long hit; (2) playing first base; (3) pitching to a crack hitter; (4) catching a curve-ball.	4. _______
5.	On the race track the author went (1) 90 miles per hour; (2) 107 mph; (3) 126 mph; (4) 180 mph.	5. _______
	Receptive Comprehension	_______
6.	The central idea of this selection is to establish (1) the difficulty of understanding the skills required of sportsmen; (2) the importance of firsthand experience and observation; (3) the difference between spectators and participants; (4) the way to develop skill in reporting.	6. _______
7.	Levinsky's statements ("It don't feel like nuttin' " and "in a transom") were intended to suggest that (1) experience is most important; (2) the gift of expression is most important; (3) the same experience affects people differently; (4) experience and expression are equally important.	7. _______
8.	This selection is organized chiefly around (1) specific sports; (2) types of sports; (3) personal experiences in chronological order; (4) the two headings—participants and spectators.	8. _______
9.	With respect to the gap between reading about something and actually doing it, you would infer that good reporting (1) eliminates it; (2) has no effect on it; (3) increases it; (4) decreases it.	9. _______
10.	The author apparently thinks of the average spectator with feelings of (1) irritation; (2) respect; (3) indifference; (4) amusement.	10. _______

(10 points for each correct answer)

Reflective Comprehension _______

TOTAL READING COMPREHENSION SCORE _______

VOCABULARY CHECK QUESTIONS

		without context I	with context II
1. admonished	(1) urged; (2) admired; (3) limited; (4) reproved; (5) selected.	1. _______	_______
2. ascertain	(1) arise; (2) join; (3) learn; (4) create; (5) look up.	2. _______	_______
3. donned	(1) put on; (2) started; (3) took off; (4) sat down; (5) sounded.	3. _______	_______
4. vacuously	(1) engagingly; (2) stupidly; (3) freely; (4) lightly; (5) hopelessly.	4. _______	_______
5. truculent	(1) mechanical; (2) truthful; (3) trusting; (4) strong; (5) fierce.	5. _______	_______

(10 points for each correct answer)

Word Comprehension without *contextual help (I)* _______

Word Comprehension with *contextual help (II)* _______

TOTAL WORD COMPREHENSION SCORE _______

Exercises

Checking Paragraph Coherence

One important characteristic of a well-written paragraph is its coherence—the closeness with which the sentences are related. One test of coherence is to jumble the sentences around so that they are completely out of order, then to see if you can put them together again by relying on the many devices a writer uses to relate one sentence to another and show a gradual progression of thought.

To develop added insight into paragraph structure, coherence, and writing, try rearranging the following sentences into the most coherent order. In each of the paragraphs there is one sentence that does not belong. First, decide which sentence is out of place and eliminate it; then rearrange the remaining sentences in the most coherent order. Finally, check your arrangement with the original paragraph.

A.
1. I was always a child who touched things and I have always had a tremendous curiosity with regard to sensation.
2. The average person says: "Here, let me see that," and holds out his hand.
3. Mother is convinced that the child only does it to annoy or because it is a child, and usually hasn't the vaguest inkling of the fact that Junior is "touching" because he is a little blotter soaking up information and knowledge, and "feel" is an important adjunct to seeing.
4. A child wandering through a department store with its mother, is admonished over and over again not to touch things.
5. Adults are exactly the same, in a measure, as you may ascertain when some new gadget or article is produced for inspection.
6. What he means is that he wants to get it into his hands and feel it so as to become better acquainted.
7. He doesn't mean "see," because he is already seeing it.

The sentence that violates paragraph unity is #_____

The remaining six sentences should be in this order: #_____, #_____, #_____, #_____, #_____, #_____.

B.
1. My burning curiosity got the better of prudence and a certain reluctance to expose myself to physical pain.
2. It seems that I had gone to an expert for tuition.
3. I had been assigned to my first training-camp coverage, Dempsey's at Saratoga Springs, where he was preparing for his famous fight with Luis Firpo.
4. I asked Dempsey to permit me to box a round with him.
5. For days I watched him sag a spar boy with what seemed to be no more than a light cuff on the neck, or pat his face with what looked like no more than a caressing stroke of his arm, and the fellow would come all apart at the seams and collapse in a useless heap, grinning vacuously or twitching strangely.
6. I had never boxed before, but I was in good physical shape, having just completed a four-year stretch as a galley slave in the Columbia eight-oared shell.

The sentence that violates paragraph unity is #_____.

The remaining five sentences should be in this order: #_____, #_____, #_____, #_____, #_____.

C.
1. It is all a man can do to get up after being stunned by a blow, much less fight back.
2. From that afternoon on, also, dated my antipathy for the spectator at prizefights who yells: "Come on, you bum, get up and fight! Oh, you big quitter! Yah yellow, yah yellow!"
3. And how a man is able to muster any further interest in a combat after being floored with a blow to the pit of the stomach will always remain to me a miracle of what the human animal is capable of under stress.
4. I have never regretted these researches.
5. Yellow, eh?
6. But they do it.

The sentence that violates paragraph unity is #_____.

The remaining five sentences should be in this order: #_____, #_____, #_____, #_____, #_____.

NAME ______________________ DATE ______________ READING RATE ______________ WPM

Comprehension Check Questions

1. Brent's father came from (1) Russia; (2) Hungary; (3) Austria; (4) France. 1. ______
2. Brent's father was a (1) tea drinker; (2) card player; (3) pipe smoker; (4) baseball fan. 2. ______
3. His father's favorite author was (1) Scott; (2) Dostoevsky; (3) Tolstoy; (4) Melville. 3. ______
4. The author's teacher in senior high was (1) Jesse Feldman; (2) Stan Cohen; (3) Homan; (4) Rosenberg. 4. ______
5. Melville wrote that he started life at what age? (1) 13; (2) 18; (3) 21; (4) 25. 5. ______

Receptive Comprehension ______

6. This article primarily points up (1) the importance of reading; (2) the right time to start reading; (3) the influence of Brent's father; (4) the tragedy of loneliness. 6. ______
7. Which word best describes this selection? (1) lively; (2) dramatic; (3) personal; (4) literary. 7. ______
8. Basically this is organized (1) in a problem-solution fashion; (2) in a cause-effect pattern; (3) logically; (4) chronologically. 8. ______
9. Most emphasis is placed on reading as it contributes to (1) financial success; (2) relief of boredom; (3) understanding the world; (4) knowing yourself. 9. ______
10. The author's attitude toward himself is best described as (1) casual; (2) tolerant; (3) reflective; (4) proud. 10. ______

(10 points for each correct answer)

Reflective Comprehension ______

TOTAL READING COMPREHENSION SCORE ______

Vocabulary Check Questions

			without context I	with context II
1.	**imbued**	(1) built; (2) boasted; (3) filled; (4) teased; (5) imbalanced.	1. ______	______
2.	**advent**	(1) opening; (2) promotion; (3) admittance; (4) experience; (5) coming.	2. ______	______
3.	**ingenuity**	(1) graciousness; (2) smartness; (3) reality; (4) cleverness; (5) similarity.	3. ______	______
4.	**deprecatory**	(1) definite; (2) apologetic; (3) uncertain; (4) casual; (5) deepening.	4. ______	______
5.	**lards**	(1) embellishes; (2) destroys; (3) covers; (4) limits; (5) smooths.	5. ______	______

(10 points for each correct answer)

Word Comprehension without *contextual help (I)* ______

Word Comprehension with *contextual help (II)* ______

TOTAL WORD COMPREHENSION SCORE ______

EXPLORING FACTORS AFFECTING COMPREHENSION

After reading the short selection, "Treat Causes, Not Symptoms" (pp. 308–309), look at yourself more closely. Try to determine your major problems, then move toward solving them. Standardized test scores are particularly helpful if they are available. But this text is laid out to provide fairly complete evidence for helping you diagnose and assess most problems.

Under each of the following headings, record any concrete evidence available. Then, on the basis of your evaluation, look at the suggestions for dealing with the problem.

Vocabulary. Is this a major problem? To see, get some of the evidence down, as follows:

A. Enter the number you did correctly on the 20-item vocabulary test, p. 201. _______
   Enter the salary-expectation figure from p. 442. _______
B. When you have completed any ten of the five-item Vocabulary Check Questions (a total of fifty items), enter the number you did correctly out of the fifty. _______
C. Turn to p. 195 and cover the column of words to the right of the column heading PREFIX. Try to supply the common meaning for each of the twenty prefixes listed. Check your answers by uncovering the column. Enter the number you did correctly out of the twenty. _______
D. Take your comprehension scores on the first ten selections read, average them, and enter the *average* score here. An average below 70 percent suggests vocabulary deficiency. _______

   Now, looking over the evidence you have accumulated for rating your vocabulary, check one of the following three choices:
   No problem _______
   Minor problem _______
   Major problem _______

Now what can you do to improve? Here are some suggestions. Check each when you have completed it.

1. Read the short selection "Context—Key to Meaning," p. 438, noting and applying relevant portions.
2. Read with particular emphasis the ten selections in Section VI on vocabulary for pertinent suggestions.
3. Complete the five-item Vocabulary Check Questions for each selection. Discover all unknown words and work them into your active vocabulary. Build added skill with context by using the first column *(without context),* then scanning the article to see how each word is used in context, putting a second set of answers in the column headed *with context*.
4. Read the article "A Master-Word Approach to Vocabulary," pp. 194–196, and follow all suggestions given.
5. Do the vocabulary improvement Exercises, pp. 414–443.

Interest. Is this a major problem? Again, check by getting some of the evidence down.

A. Look at the personal interest rating scale mentioned on p. 499. Use this scale with the first twenty selections you read, then average your ratings. If your average is above 2, interest should be no problem. If it is below 3, it looks like a major problem.
B. Check the relationship between your interest rating and comprehension. Does interest seem to make a consistent difference? Data from some 200 students using selections from an earlier edition of *Efficient Reading* should permit you to make meaningful comparisons. Notice that as articles are more difficult, interest tends to drop. If the drop is more pronounced with you, build stronger interests.

READING EASE GROUPING	AVERAGE INTEREST RATING	YOUR INTEREST RATING (AVERAGE)
Easy	2.109	______
Fairly Easy	2.299	______
Standard	2.346	______
Fairly Difficult	2.359	______
Difficult	2.381	______
Very Difficult	2.454	______

Looking back over this evidence, how would you rate interest? No problem ______ Minor problem ______ Major problem ______

Now what can you do to improve interest level? Here are some specific suggestions. Check each when completed.

1. Read "The Importance of Being Interested" (Sel. 9, p. 20). ______
2. Apply the suggestions in the selections on pages 312 and 316. ______
3. Keep rating each selection read for interest, averaging each set of ten to see if there is improvement. ______

Difficulty. Is this a major problem? Look at the evidence.

A. Using the Flesch Reading Ease Score beginning on p. 481, figure your average comprehension for the first twenty selections read.
B. Compare your average with those from some 200 students who used an earlier edition of *Efficient Reading.*

READING EASE GROUPING	AVERAGE COMPREHENSION	YOUR AVERAGE COMPREHENSION
Fairly Easy	68.5	______
Standard	67.5	______
Fairly Difficult	65.2	______
Difficult	67.4	______

The relationship between ease and comprehension is not perfectly consistent, suggesting that other factors may be more important than difficulty. If, however, for you the relationship is consistent and the differences in comprehension are more pronounced, you know difficulty is a problem. Rate yourself as before: No problem ______ Minor problem ______ Major problem ______

Now what can you do to deal with difficult material effectively?

Read Selection 13, p. 31, and "Organization—Your Reading Satellite," pp. 340–341.

Explorations of *rate*, as suggested on p. 286, of *background*, of *concentration*, and *mechanical difficulties*—such as vocalizing, regressing, and perceiving—lend themselves to similar analysis.

NAME ______________ DATE ______________ READING RATE ______________ WPM

COMPREHENSION CHECK QUESTIONS

1. The improvement of reading should serve (1) one function; (2) two functions; (3) three functions; (4) four functions. 1. _______

2. The article includes a quotation from (1) Darwin; (2) Milton; (3) Carlyle; (4) Shakespeare. 2. _______

3. In reading 100 words, college students regress an average of (1) 5 times; (2) 10 times; (3) 15 times; (4) 20 times. 3. _______

4. College students were said to be (1) omnivorous readers; (2) educated readers; (3) word-by-word readers; (4) fast readers. 4. _______

5. What one word was said to sum up our age best? (1) speed; (2) change; (3) nuclear; (4) frustrating. 5. _______

Receptive Comprehension _______

6. The chief focus of the article is on (1) habits that slow down reading; (2) making more reading time; (3) faster-than-comfortable reading; (4) methods for improving reading skill. 6. _______

7. The eye movement data was discussed primarily to show (1) how poorly college students read; (2) how time consuming regressions are; (3) what differences exist between ninth graders and college students; (4) how little one's habits change. 7. _______

8. The author implies that what contributes most toward managing higher reading speeds is (1) theory; (2) direction; (3) background; (4) experience. 8. _______

9. You would infer that present conditions demand (1) less reading; (2) a different kind of reading; (3) more careful reading; (4) more reading. 9. _______

10. In discussing the three reading brakes the author focuses largely on (1) defining the concepts; (2) noting cause-effect relationships; (3) underlining individual differences; (4) suggesting techniques for their elimination. 10. _______

(10 points for each correct answer)

Reflective Comprehension _______

TOTAL READING COMPREHENSION SCORE _______

VOCABULARY CHECK QUESTIONS

		without context I	with context II
1. perspective	(1) outlook; (2) statement; (3) inspection; (4) conclusion; (5) suspicion.	1. _______	_______
2. plays havoc	(1) fights; (2) aids; (3) ruins; (4) shelters; (5) acquires.	2. _______	_______
3. regress	(1) look back; (2) read again; (3) resume; (4) progress; (5) fixate.	3. _______	_______
4. persist	(1) remain; (2) cease; (3) convince; (4) distort; (5) pursue.	4. _______	_______
5. unprecedented	(1) factual; (2) unpleasant; (3) illogical; (4) disrespectable; (5) extraordinary.	5. _______	_______

(10 points for each correct answer)

Word Comprehension without *contextual help (I)* _______

Word Comprehension with *contextual help (II)* _______

TOTAL WORD COMPREHENSION SCORE _______

EXPLORING YOUR RATE-COMPREHENSION RELATIONSHIP

One of your first and most important moves in improving your reading is to explore the relationship between reading rate and comprehension. Such an exploration will let you know how important a factor rate is and, by implication, how important such matters as vocabulary, concentration, interest, and background are.

Beginning at about 100 words per minute, read ten selections of comparable difficulty (see Index According to Order of Difficulty, p. 481). Try to read each one about 60 wpm faster than you read the previous one. Then check your comprehension on each selection, plotting your results on the graph below. Keep increasing rate until comprehension drops to the 40 percent level or below, even if you have to call your activity skimming instead of reading. The resulting graph will provide evidence for a more intelligent approach to your reading improvement efforts. Specifically, it should answer the following three questions:

1. Is it true that the slower you read, the better you comprehend?
2. What is your present optimum speed for comprehension?
3. What is your present best practice speed?

Generally speaking, the faster you read, within limits, the better you comprehend. Is this so with you? If it is, what are the limits? For most students, optimum comprehension comes at speeds somewhat above their slowest rates. A rapid drop-off as rate is increased indicates that rate is indeed of primary importance as a factor. A gradual drop-off or rather lengthy plateau area suggests that other factors are probably more important.

Further analysis of your graph record will suggest what those factors may be. For example, if comprehension never rises above a 60 or 70 percent level, despite wide variations in rate, you have reason to consider vocabulary as a possible limiting factor. If you do not drop below the 40 percent level, you have reason to conclude that you have an excellent general background and are able to pick up additional information even at extremely high rates. If your record is quite erratic, this suggests that differences in difficulty, background, or interest are more important than differences in rate, and should be explored further.

When you have completed your exploration, you should have definite answers to all three questions.

1. Was your best comprehension score achieved at your slowest rate?
2. At what specific rate or rates did you get your best comprehension, whether 70, 80, 90, or 100 percent?
3. Finally, what is your present best practice speed? Your answer to this question depends on your answer to the preceding one. Your best present practice speed must be faster than the speed at which you now get best comprehension. After all, you don't want to waste precious time practicing what you already do well. No—you want to develop the skill to get that same comprehension but at speeds from 300 to 600 wpm faster than present speeds. To do that with maximum effectiveness, use the procedure described in "Swing Three Bats" (pp. 304–305).

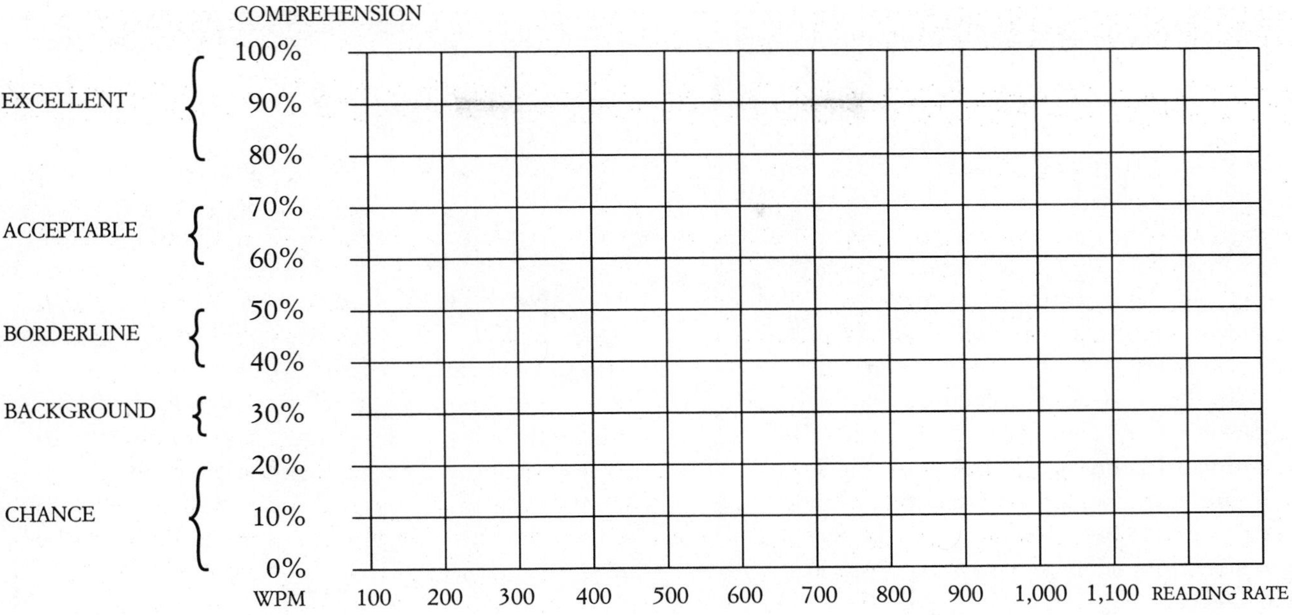

When graphing your results, identify your first reading with numeral 1. Then connect the dot for each subsequent reading with the preceding one by a line, to indicate the order in which it was read. Results for a group of 100 students, following these directions with ten readings, show the following average changes: 197, 293, 359, 305, 306, 350, 411, 406, 432 and 467 wpm. Can you achieve a better than average range? Try a slower beginning rate as well as a faster final rate than indicated in the averages given above.

NAME ______ DATE ______ READING RATE ______ WPM

Comprehension Check Questions

1. These super-speeds were said to put you where the (1) action is; (2) essence is; (3) substance is; (4) detail is. 1. ______
2. In the time normally taken to read one article in the usual fashion, you should be able to survey (1) 3 to 5; (2) 6 to 10; (3) 15 to 18; (4) 20 to 30. 2. ______
3. The bulk of our reading was spoken of as (1) expository; (2) persuasive; (3) descriptive; (4) narrative. 3. ______
4. For one example, specific mention was made of the word, (1) *rubles;* (2) *afghan;* (3) *steppes;* (4) *communes.* 4. ______
5. One intensive training session on scanning was said to get a class up to an average scanning speed of about (1) 4,000 wpm; (2) 9,000 wpm; (3) 14,000 wpm; (4) 22,000 wpm. 5. ______

Receptive Comprehension ______

6. This article mainly concerns (1) speed reading; (2) overviewing techniques; (3) special reading techniques; (4) the type of item to skip. 6. ______
7. By inference, the word *reading* is best defined as understanding (1) the details; (2) the main ideas; (3) the meaning from print; (4) every word. 7. ______
8. You would infer that these approaches should (1) be modified to suit the material being read; (2) be followed exactly; (3) all be used together; (4) be substituted for regular reading activities. 8. ______
9. The teeter-totter analogy was intended primarily to suggest (1) the need to balance slow and fast reading; (2) a way to counteract slow reading; (3) a way to improve comprehension; (4) the need to balance attention to details and main ideas. 9. ______
10. The visual example (TIE) was used to indicate the importance of (1) background; (2) experience; (3) perspective; (4) mind-set. 10. ______

(10 points for each correct answer)

Reflective Comprehension ______

TOTAL READING COMPREHENSION SCORE ______

Vocabulary Check Questions

			without context I	with context II
1.	**paradox**	(1) self-sufficiency; (2) self-contradiction; (3) inactivity; (4) possessiveness; (5) a model.	1. ______	______
2.	**foreshadowing**	(1) darkening; (2) presaging; (3) hindering; (4) preferring; (5) following.	2. ______	______
3.	**expository**	(1) analytical; (2) poetic; (3) theoretical; (4) substantial; (5) explanatory.	3. ______	______
4.	**reiterates**	(1) repeats; (2) rejects; (3) compensates; (4) describes; (5) states.	4. ______	______
5.	**fulcrum**	(1) weight; (2) plank; (3) supply; (4) support; (5) movement.	5. ______	______

(10 points for each correct answer)

Word Comprehension without *contextual help (I)* ______

Word Comprehension with *contextual help (II)* ______

TOTAL WORD COMPREHENSION SCORE ______

EXERCISES

INTRODUCING SQ3R

Formulas help you do all kinds of things better, including reading. For example, take the SQ3R formula. You will find it particularly useful. Try it! Here's how it works.

The first step is to survey the book, article, or chapter in hand. How do you survey? Rather than repeat here what was said in Selection 21, "Super-Speeds for the Knowledge Explosion," turn to that selection now and read—or reread—the four paragraphs under the heading *Surveying*, page 57.

Add to those survey directions another clarifying tactic. Ask yourself why you are reading this. What's your purpose? Is it for entertainment—leisure reading? Is it to satisfy a particular interest? Is it to provide needed information for some project you have in mind? Is it because you want to be well informed about some subject? Is it because of course requirements—required reading? Only when you put purpose clearly into the picture can you establish the mind-set that brings maximum results from your survey.

If you are driving, say, from St. Paul to Phoenix, you automatically bring purpose into the picture. Is it to be a leisurely trip or a hurried trip? Your planning and map reading will be governed by that purpose. It's the same with reading. Purpose should govern reading just as it should govern trip planning. So, make determining your purpose a part of your survey.

Next in the formula comes Q, which stands for *Question*. Raise questions that you want answered by your reading. This move whets your interest in what is to be read and adds immediate personal incentive. That means heightened interest, the perfect preliminary for reading.

Now for the *3R* part of the formula. The first *R* is *Read*. You have already established a purpose that will now govern how you read. You have raised questions that will sharpen your focus on matters of special importance. Your reading now becomes much more effective because of those preliminary steps.

The second *R* stands for *Review*. This is particularly important in study-type reading of textbooks and reference material. This step serves to fix important details more firmly in mind—a very important memory aid. To check the usefulness of this step in the formula, one of my classes took a short test over a selection that was read in class. A week later, the class was divided into two groups; one half was given one minute to review certain details from that selection read earlier, the other half did not have that review opportunity. Two weeks later the whole class was given the same short test over the article. When I compared their scores, the half that reviewed for only one minute scored 67 percent better on the retest than the half that had not reviewed. The review step is obviously important!

The last *R* stands for *Recite*. If you have to answer certain questions, recite your answers as you will have to later—in discussion or on paper, as in a test. Then check by referring back to the selection to ensure accuracy. This provides the final assurance that you know what you want to know.

In summary, increase your effectiveness in dealing with all study-type reading by applying *SQ3R*. The more frequently you apply it, the better your results will be. Make it habitual. It pays off handsomely.

APPLYING SQ3R

Several specialized formulas are designed to help you get more from your reading. You may want to concentrate on one, or you may prefer to have several in your repertoire. Try applying *SQ3R*, using it with Selection 22, "Reading for Meaning," to see exactly how it works.

Survey:	(1) Determine your purpose in reading this selection.
	(2) <u>Survey</u> the selection.
Q (Question):	Raise several questions you want answered by reading the selection.
3R:	(1) <u>Read</u> the selection.
	(2) <u>Review</u> the selection
	(3) <u>Recite</u> important details.

When you have finished, think back over the process. Appraise your feelings about comprehension when using the formula versus your feelings when not using it. You should notice a definite increase in confidence with the formula.

NAME ______________________ DATE ______________ READING RATE ______________ WPM

COMPREHENSION CHECK QUESTIONS

1. Comprehension is likened to (1) a coin; (2) an ocean; (3) a sheet of paper; (4) a face. 1. _______
2. What specific time is mentioned? (1) 8 o'clock; (2) 9 o'clock; (3) 10 o'clock; (4) 11 o'clock. 2. _______
3. Details are likened to (1) the forest; (2) raindrops; (3) the trees; (4) particles of sand. 3. _______
4. A leap from the known into the unknown is said to be (1) an inference; (2) a hint; (3) a guess; (4) a hope. 4. _______
5. Writers tend to put important points (1) first; (2) last; (3) first and last; (4) in the middle. 5. _______

Receptive Comprehension _______

6. This reading is mainly about (1) deciding what things are important; (2) understanding what complete comprehension means; (3) making the detail-meaning relationship clear; (4) getting the main idea. 6. _______
7. The bit about reading a love letter is to show (1) the importance of getting the essentials; (2) the importance of noting word meanings; (3) how inferences are made; (4) when complete comprehension occurs. 7. _______
8. The discussion of "It's . . . o'clock" is intended to point up (1) the confusion of communication; (2) the difficulty of getting meaning; (3) the two aspects of communication; (4) the importance of getting what's said. 8. _______
9. Apparently the most important thing is to (1) read between the lines; (2) draw proper inferences; (3) draw logical conclusions; (4) get the main idea. 9. _______
10. Judging from the number of questions in this test dealing with facts and meaning (1) getting details is more important; (2) getting meaning is more important; (3) both are important; (4) both are equally important. 10. _______

(10 points for each correct answer)

Reflective Comprehension _______

TOTAL READING COMPREHENSION SCORE _______

VOCABULARY CHECK QUESTIONS

			without context I	with context II
1.	**inseparable**	(1) distinct; (2) hopeless; (3) insupportable; (4) internal; (5) indivisable.	1. _______	_______
2.	**ambiguity**	(1) helplessness; (2) uncertainty; (3) ambition; (4) failure; (5) facility.	2. _______	_______
3.	**insinuation**	(1) sly hint; (2) smoothness; (3) influence; (4) instability; (5) insight.	3. _______	_______
4.	**accusation**	(1) addition; (2) feeling; (3) advice; (4) charge; (5) remark.	4. _______	_______
5.	**subtle**	(1) substantial; (2) gracious; (3) elusive; (4) definite; (5) much needed.	5. _______	_______

(10 points for each correct answer)

Word Comprehension without *contextual help (I)* _______

Word Comprehension with *contextual help (II)* _______

TOTAL WORD COMPREHENSION SCORE _______

EXERCISES

PERCEPTUAL DEVELOPMENT

College and adult readers without special training habitually perceive words one at a time. Obviously one way to improve reading rate is to train yourself to take in two or more words at a quick look.

By using a 3 × 5 card and a daily paper, you can develop added perceptual span and accuracy. Just cover a headline in a column of print with the 3 × 5 card. Then jerk the card rapidly down and back to expose for a few seconds the first line of the headline. Repeat if necessary to get the complete line. Do the same thing with the next line and so on through the first paragraph of the news story.

For additional perceptual training, practice on the three-division and two-division lines below. Use the 3 × 5 card to cover the print, leaving only the black dot visible. Jerk the card quickly down and back to expose the phrase below for a second. Try to read the entire phrase at one quick look. Ordinarily practice of this kind is provided by a tachistoscope. The procedure just described, however, is a close approximation and should show comparable results.

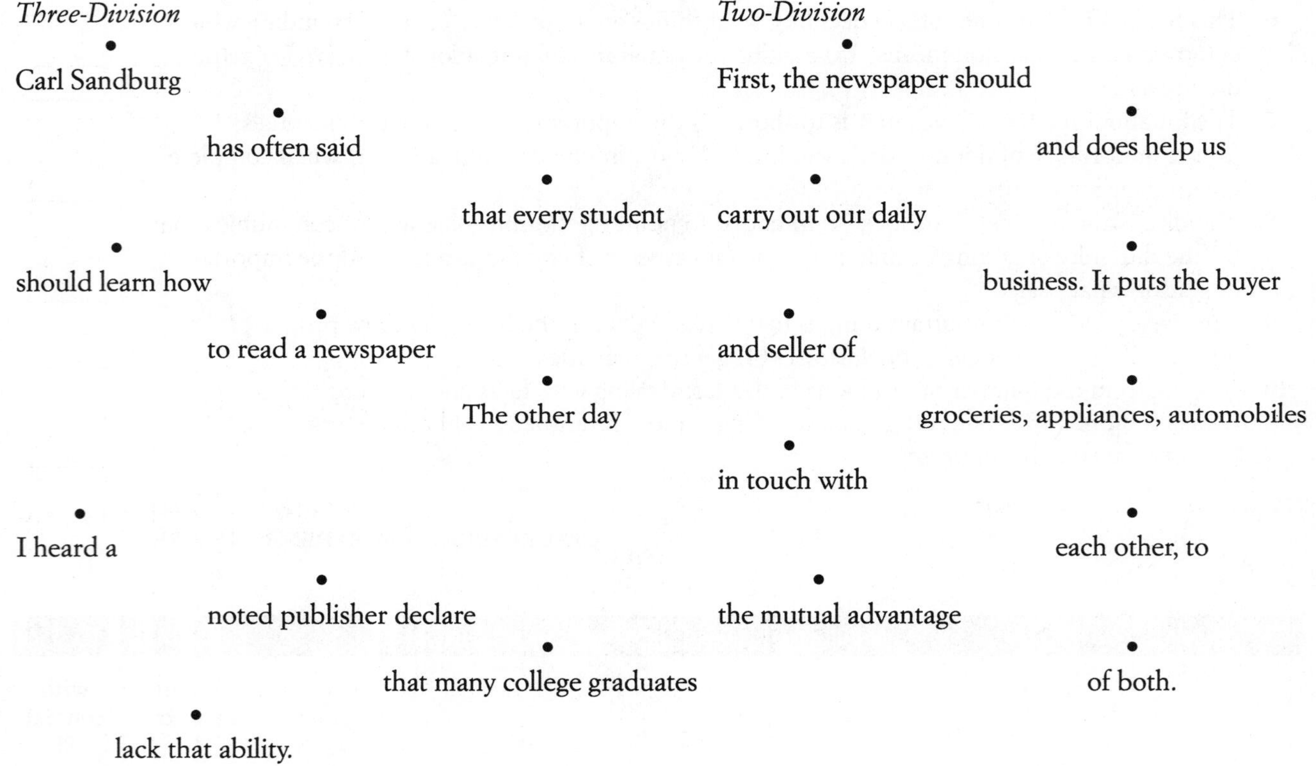

LEANING ON KEY DETAILS TO FORMULATE MAIN IDEAS

Daily newspapers provide ideal exercise material for developing added skill in getting main ideas. Just cover the headline for any story, read the story—at least the first paragraph—and then write a headline that captures the essence in just four to six words. As an aid, think in terms of six key questions: Who? What? Why? When? Where? and How? Once you have answered those questions about the news story, ask yourself one more question. Of those six, which one or two seem most important? In this way, you can decide which main idea or ideas deserve to dominate the headline.

Try this with the following brief paragraph of a news story:

> Farmers in central Minnesota reported serious crop damage yesterday as a result of an early morning frost combined with an unseasonably cold weekend.

Answer the six questions by looking back at that paragraph; then star the two you consider most important.

Who? ______________________________

What? ______________________________

When? ______________________________

When? ______________________________

Where? ______________________________

How? ______________________________

Finally, which of the following do you think actually appeared as headline for that story?

1. CENTRAL MINNESOTA FARMERS SUFFER FROM BAD FROST
2. CROP DAMAGE CAUSED BY EARLY FROST
3. SERIOUS CROP DAMAGE FOLLOWS EARLY FROST
4. FROST CAUSES CROP DAMAGE FOR FARMERS

Answer: Headline 3 was actually used.

NAME ______________ DATE ______________ READING RATE ______________ WPM

COMPREHENSION CHECK QUESTIONS

1. The patient referred specifically to (1) the parables; (2) Revelation; (3) the Gospels; (4) the Golden Rule. 1. _______
2. The psychiatrist mentions (1) Carl Gustav Jung; (2) Freud; (3) Adler; (4) William James. 2. _______
3. One of the fears we're born with was said to be fear of (1) furry objects; (2) loud noise; (3) falling; (4) large black objects. 3. _______
4. Mention was made of the wife of (1) an enlisted man; (2) a pilot; (3) a gunner; (4) a reserve officer. 4. _______
5. The psychiatrist refers to (1) Samson; (2) Jonah; (3) Job; (4) Luke. 5. _______

Receptive Comprehension _______

6. The central idea is to read the Bible (1) for moral guidance; (2) to love your neighbor; (3) for helpful psychiatric insights; (4) to eliminate worry. 6. _______
7. You would infer from the opening question, "Do you—a psychiatrist—read the Bible?" that the patient was primarily expressing (1) curiosity; (2) pleasure; (3) approval; (4) surprise. 7. _______
8. With regard to the Bible, greatest emphasis is put on (1) how to study it; (2) who should study it; (3) what verses to study; (4) when to study it. 8. _______
9. The author would probably agree most fully that people need (1) security; (2) truth; (3) love; (4) joy. 9. _______
10. Apparently, the author feels that the matter of most concern should be (1) love and hate; (2) conscious and subconscious; (3) guilt and innocence; (4) good and evil. 10. _______

(10 points for each correct answer)

Reflective Comprehension _______
TOTAL READING COMPREHENSION SCORE _______

VOCABULARY CHECK QUESTIONS

			without context I	with context II
1.	**acute**	(1) severe; (2) clever; (3) active; (4) slow; (5) weighty.	1. _______	_______
2.	**insomnia**	(1) sleeplessness; (2) tiredness; (3) insight; (4) failure; (5) alertness.	2. _______	_______
3.	**wanes**	(1) stops; (2) grows; (3) works; (4) decreases; (5) warms.	3. _______	_______
4.	**camouflage**	(1) change; (2) disguise; (3) cover; (4) scared; (5) explode.	4. _______	_______
5.	**elemental**	(1) charitable; (2) lofty; (3) serious; (4) qualified; (5) fundamental.	5. _______	_______

(10 points for each correct answer)

Word Comprehension without *contextual help (I)* _______
Word Comprehension with *contextual help (II)* _______
TOTAL WORD COMPREHENSION SCORE _______

EXERCISES

WORD GROUPING

Can you read this?

THESE LINES ARE JUST AN EYE-CATCHING WAY
CHANGING THAT REALIZE TO YOU HELPING OF
YOUR PERCEPTUAL HABITS MAY SEEM DIFFICULT,
SOON VERY WILL INSIGHT AND PRACTICE BUT
BRING MASTERY OF THE CHANGES. READ THESE
WAY NEW THE IN—NOW AGAIN ONCE LINES FEW
SEE HOW QUICKLY YOU LEARN TO CHANGE?

Practice moving your eye down the middle of the column as you read.

Prove for yourself
why reading by phrases
aids comprehension
and is better than
word-for-word reading.
Notice what happens
when you read
one
word
at
a
time
or take time to
divide a word
into
syl-
-la-
-bles
as you read.

"Some books
are to be tasted,
others to be swallowed,
and some few
to be chewed
and digested;
that is, some books
are to be read
only in parts,
others to be read
but not curiously,
and some few
to be read wholly
and with diligence
and attention . . .
Reading maketh a full man,
conference a ready man,
and writing
an exact man." Bacon

Now try reading some square span.

Your eyes don't see	in narrow horizontal lines	but see an area	on all sides of the place	where they are focused.	Andrews, a student editor	at Southern Methodist University,	devised Square Span,
a way of modifying	the printed page	to fit man's natural	eye habits much better	than the ordinary arrangement	of printed words.	Tests show that	a majority of readers
could read it	with greater speed than	they could read	conventional printed matter.	At least it offers	an exercise in the grouping	of words that should	serve to discourage word-for-word tendencies.
Try a few more lines	just for additional	practice in grouping words	and in developing a rhythmic	eye movement across the page.	Adapting your reading speed	to the material	is the main thing
in reading.	It is as foolish	to speed through a	poem by Keats as it is	to slow to a snail's pace	in reading material obviously designed	to be read in a hurry.	
Experimental flashes with the tachistoscope	reveal that it is possible	to see five or six words	strung out in this manner	when flashed on a screen			
at 1/100 of a second.	Are you developing	suitable word-grouping habits?					

NAME ______________________ DATE ______________ READING RATE ______________ WPM

COMPREHENSION CHECK QUESTIONS

1. The author specifically speaks of feeding the mind (1) candy bars; (2) bonbons; (3) chocolate pudding; (4) sugar-plums. 1. _______

2. The article mentions eating at one sitting two or three (1) loaves of bread; (2) heads of lettuce; (3) cauliflowers; (4) beefsteaks. 2. _______

3. Specific reference is made to what kind of mind? (1) lean; (2) elegant; (3) fat; (4) mechanical. 3. _______

4. In the selection, mention was made of (1) Emerson's *Essays*; (2) Shakespeare's *King Lear;* (3) Gray's *Elegy;* (4) Pope's *Dunciad.* 4. _______

5. A specific rule was given for determining whether someone was (1) wise or foolish; (2) young or old; (3) educated or uneducated; (4) rich or poor. 5. _______

Receptive Comprehension _______

6. This article is mainly about (1) reading a properly balanced fare; (2) selecting a varied reading fare; (3) thinking over what you have read; (4) spacing reading activities properly. 6. _______

7. The opening paragraphs were primarily to make us think about (1) the care lavished on our bodies; (2) the care we give to our mind; (3) how forgetful we are; (4) how important both body and mind are. 7. _______

8. The illustration of the thirsty haymaker was intended to remind us of the importance of (1) sufficient reading; (2) a wide variety of reading; (3) not reading too many kinds at once; (4) not reading too many of one kind of book. 8. _______

9. In essence, by "ticketing," the author means (1) buying; (2) using; (3) reading extensively; (4) labeling. 9. _______

10. His example of a "mental bun" suggested a way to test a person's (1) depth of reading interests; (2) mental health; (3) ability to concentrate; (4) taste for culture. 10. _______

(10 points for each correct answer)

Reflective Comprehension _______

TOTAL READING COMPREHENSION SCORE _______

VOCABULARY CHECK QUESTIONS

			without context I	with context II
1.	**ensue**	(1) enter; (2) take action; (3) follow; (4) charge; (5) report.	1. _______	_______
2.	**conundrums**	(1) visits; (2) faults; (3) props; (4) riddles; (5) bats.	2. _______	_______
3.	**mastication**	(1) slicing; (2) chewing; (3) overcoming; (4) swallowing; (5) ruling.	3. _______	_______
4.	**impetus**	(1) search; (2) solution; (3) force; (4) method; (5) move.	4. _______	_______
5.	**crucial**	(1) short; (2) favorable; (3) fair; (4) decisive; (5) sudden.	5. _______	_______

(10 points for each correct answer)

Word Comprehension without *contextual help (I)* _______

Word Comprehension with *contextual help (II)* _______

TOTAL WORD COMPREHENSION SCORE _______

Exercises

Developing Specialized Reading Skills

Scanning: To function effectively, a mechanic needs many different tools— he doesn't use a file to loosen a bolt or a wrench to tighten a screw. Similarly, to read and study effectively you need many different techniques, not just one.

Scanning is the technique to use when you want to find one small bit of information within a relatively large body of printed material. It fits the proverbial needle-in-the-haystack situation. It can and should be the fastest of the specialized reading speeds. The survey provides a quick, high-level view, skimming provides a lower-level view to bring more details into sight, and scanning zooms you in for a close, sharp view of only one detail.

With practice, you should scan accurately at from 10,000 to 15,000 wpm. Students in the Efficient Reading classes at the University of Minnesota scan initially, on the average, at about 1,500 wpm. After practice the class average moves up to about 15,000 wpm.

This text is designed to help you make enviable progress toward that top-level performance. Your first move is to check both the speed and accuracy with which you now can scan. Use the following table to get your approximate rate. You can use it as it is with articles of approximately 2,000 words in length, such as Selections 31, 39, and 50. Then, dividing the figure in the time column by 2, you can also use it with selections of approximately 1,000 words in length, such as Selections 3, 22, and 25.

Scan Time	Wpm Rate	Scan Time	Wpm Rate	Scan Time	Wpm Rate	Scan Time	Wpm Rate
10 sec.	12,000 wpm	30 sec.	4,000 wpm	60 sec.	2,000 wpm	100 sec.	1,200 wpm
15 sec.	8,000 wpm	40 sec.	3,000 wpm	80 sec.	1,500 wpm	120 sec.	1,000 wpm
20 sec.	6,000 wpm	50 sec.	2,400 wpm	90 sec.	1,333 wpm	140 sec.	855 wpm

Scan-checking to improve vocabulary: The five-item vocabulary tests for each selection are designed to help you make better use of context in arriving at word meanings. Getting word meaning from context is a rather specialized skill of the utmost importance. Use scanning to develop that skill. Take each five-item vocabulary test, putting your answers in the first column, headed *without context.* Then scan the selection rapidly, underlining each of the five words when you find them. Examine the context for clues to word meaning, changing any answers by entering revised answers in the second column, headed *with context.* If you make effective use of context, the answers in that second column should be perfect. If vocabulary is not a major problem, scan for only one word in each five-item test—the most difficult or unfamiliar of the five. This will help you to become a more rapid and accurate scanner as well as to improve word mastery.

Scan-checking to improve receptive or reflective comprehension: If a certain type of math problem tends to give you difficulty, you need to work through problems of that type very carefully, rethinking each one until it is clear. This rethinking is equally useful in improving comprehension.

Here's how it works. Read a selection and finish the test as usual. Before checking the answers with the key in the back, select one or two questions—those you feel least sure about—reread each, then scan through the selection as rapidly as possible until you find the exact place where the question is answered. In short, you check the accuracy, not by consulting the key but by returning to the article itself.

When you are dealing with one of the reflective-type questions, scanning is not quite so simple. With them you will seldom be able to find any one statement that answers the question. Here you need to scan for all bits of relevant evidence. Then, by weighing one bit with another, you can finally arrive at a tenable conclusion as to the best answer. Such rethinking of difficult questions should eliminate or lessen present difficulties in handling similar questions, thus improving comprehension. For example, you may notice that the term *exposition* poses difficulties that will be cleared up as you notice the problem and check meaning.

Here are some sample general statements for use with any and all of the selections:

1. Take any comprehension check question, reread it, and then scan rapidly to find the exact spot where the question is answered.
2. Take the most difficult reflective-type question. Reread it, then scan the entire selection for all relevant information. Weigh the evidence for and against each of the four choices before deciding which is best. You may want to imagine that you are in a debate, forced to prove to an unwilling believer that your answer is indeed the best.

NAME ______________________ DATE ______________ READING RATE ______________ WPM

Comprehension Check Questions

1. At first, the author calls the day, (1) perfect; (2) bright; (3) gloomy; (4) windy. 1. ______
2. One bench had the name (1) Leo Tolstoy; (2) Coleridge; (3) Shakespeare; (4) Victor Hugo. 2. ______
3. How many benches were there? (1) 14; (2) 17; (3) 19; (4) 22. 3. ______
4. The library frieze contained the names of (1) inventors; (2) musicians; (3) scientists; (4) all the preceding. 4. ______
5. The author's favorite commodity is (1) fresh knowledge; (2) literature; (3) how-to books; (4) biographies. 5. ______

Receptive Comprehension ______

6. The main idea was to do what about the library? (1) show its cultural role; (2) point up its availability; (3) stress its educational value; (4) praise it. 6. ______
7. This selection is organized mainly (1) on a general-to-specific order; (2) on a problem-solution plan; (3) on a time sequence; (4) on a point-by-point basis. 7. ______
8. You would infer the author is probably (1) still college age; (2) still youthful; (3) middle-aged; (4) old. 8. ______
9. Apparently writers must, above all else, have (1) a love of reading; (2) a college degree; (3) a nearby library; (4) taken several writing courses. 9. ______
10. To develop ideas the author depends largely on (1) pertinent details; (2) personal experience; (3) expert opinion; (4) examples. 10. ______

(10 points for each correct answer)

Reflective Comprehension ______
TOTAL READING COMPREHENSION SCORE ______

Vocabulary Check Questions

			without context I	with context II
1.	**bemused**	(1) stared; (2) preoccupied; (3) inspired; (4) contained; (5) decided.	1. ______	______
2.	**balustrade**	(1) post; (2) banner; (3) tripod; (4) decoration; (5) railing.	2. ______	______
3.	**encountered**	(1) met; (2) added; (3) arranged; (4) solved; (5) returned.	3. ______	______
4.	**bemoaned**	(1) cried; (2) explored; (3) regretted; (4) spoke; (5) failed.	4. ______	______
5.	**viable**	(1) various; (2) meaningful; (3) sober; (4) worthy; (5) vague.	5. ______	______

(10 points for each correct answer)

Word Comprehension without *contextual help (I)* ______
Word Comprehension with *contextual help (II)* ______
TOTAL WORD COMPREHENSION SCORE ______

THE GOAL? ADAPTABILITY

James I. Brown

What's a good car? One that's speedy? Easy to handle? Well designed? What about low initial cost, economy of operation, roominess, low maintenance, or riding ease? Perhaps you'll agree that no *one* factor provides a completely satisfying answer.

What's a good reader? Here, too, no one factor is enough. Speed isn't everything; neither is comprehension. More important than either one is the *ability to adapt*—to adapt rate to purpose and to a wide variety of reading materials. Adaptability, then, is the true mark of a good reader.

How do you measure adaptability? How better than by actually putting yourself into different reading situations to see how well you adapt? For example, using three articles of comparable difficulty, check your performance when reading normally, thoroughly, and rapidly:

1. To discover your normal leisure reading habits, read an article neither faster nor slower than you ordinarily do when you have some leisure and want to settle down comfortably with a magazine. Don't try to comprehend more or less than usual in that situation. When you have finished and taken the test, determine your reading rate and comprehension.
2. Next, see how well you adapt yourself to the problem of getting meaning. In reading the next article, your purpose is to get as much comprehension as possible in a single reading. Keep track of reading time, but remember that it's comprehension you're after.
3. With the last article, your purpose is to cover ground rapidly. Read it at your top rate. Although speed is your primary concern, check comprehension to see what price you ordinarily pay for haste.

These three sets of rate and comprehension scores provide a useful composite index of adaptability, a three-dimensional picture of yourself as a reader. Careful analysis of these scores should reveal information of importance in directing future practice efforts and achieving maximum results. As Kettering once said: "A problem well-stated is a program half-solved." In reading, that might well be paraphrased: "A problem *well-identified* is a problem half-solved."

For example, what about the range of reading rates at your command? Subtract your slowest rate from your top rate for that figure. Is it 200 wpm or more? If so, you're among the top 20 percent of adults *before* training in reading. If that figure is 50 wpm or less, you'll want to overcome your tendencies toward one-speed reading.

When reading at top speed, a rate under 300 wpm probably means vocalizing and regressing.

Did you get comprehension when that was your purpose? And did you get details as well as main ideas and inferences? Was comprehension consistently good or did it vary considerably? Consistently good comprehension without considerable range in rate may indicate an unwillingness to recognize the importance of both depth and breadth as you read, an overlooking of Bacon's dictum: "Some books are to be tasted, others to be swallowed, and some few to be chewed and digested."

Such an analysis touches significant facets of this thing called *adaptability*, so important in defining a good reader.

(500 words)

COMPREHENSION CHECK QUESTIONS

1. The good reader is likened to a good (1) car; (2) motor; (3) driver; (4) model. 1. _______

2. You were told to use articles of comparable (1) column width; (2) difficulty; (3) length; (4) subject matter. 2. _______

3. Mention was made of (1) Byron; (2) Ford; (3) Lamb; (4) Kettering. 3. _______

4. Reference was made to (1) stuttering; (2) word-for-word reading; (3) the tachistoscope; (4) one-speed reading. 4. _______

5. A speed range of 200 wpm or more was said to put you among the top (1) 60 percent; (2) 40 percent; (3) 20 percent; (4) 5 percent. 5. _______

6. The primary purpose of this selection is to (1) define what is meant by a good reader; (2) define adaptability; (3) explain how to measure adaptability; (4) explain how to identify vocalizing difficulties. 6. _______

7. The emphasis in this selection is on (1) wisdom is power; (2) knowing thyself; (3) reading maketh a full man; (4) the reading man is the thinking man. 7. _______

8. The threefold check is intended to (1) eliminate reading difficulties; (2) identify reading difficulties; (3) test reading improvement; (4) determine reading potential. 8. _______

9. A vocabulary deficiency would be suggested by (1) consistently low comprehension; (2) consistently slow rate; (3) a drop in comprehension as rate is increased; (4) an increase in comprehension as rate is decreased. 9. _______

10. Difficulty with concentration would be suggested if (1) rapid reading brought better comprehension; (2) rapid reading did not affect comprehension; (3) normal rate brought better comprehension; (4) comprehension remained fairly constant. 10. _______

SCORE _______

Answers: 1. 1; 2. 2; 3. 4; 4. 4; 5. 3; 6. 1; 7. 2; 8. 2; 9. 1; 10. 1.

NAME ______________________ DATE ______________ READING RATE ______________ WPM

COMPREHENSION CHECK QUESTIONS

1. The verger's old gowns were (1) discarded; (2) hung in his closet; (3) kept in his wardrobe drawers; (4) kept in the basement. 1. _______
2. The new vicar was (1) like the old one; (2) more energetic; (3) more aristocratic; (4) more fashionable. 2. _______
3. The verger had served St. Peter's for how many years? (1) 12; (2) 16; (3) 19; (4) 22. 3. _______
4. The verger's wife (1) handled their finances; (2) read to him; (3) wrote his letters; (4) told him all the news. 4. _______
5. Foreman ended up with how many shops? (1) three; (2) six; (3) eight; (4) ten. 5. _______

Receptive Comprehension _______

6. This story focuses primarily on (1) personality conflicts; (2) the value of reading; (3) how to capitalize on an overlooked need; (4) how to achieve success. 6. _______
7. What word best describes the verger? (1) stubborn; (2) tactful; (3) clever; (4) enterprising. 7. _______
8. The verger's attitude toward the new vicar was mainly (1) suspicious; (2) cordial; (3) tolerant; (4) disapproving. 8. _______
9. The verger's inability to read brought dismissal largely because of a fear of (1) discovery; (2) some resulting accident; (3) appearances; (4) the resulting ignorance. 9. _______
10. His shopkeeping decision came primarily out of his (1) dismissal; (2) wanting a cigarette; (3) wish not to return to domestic service; (4) wish to be his own master. 10. _______

(10 points for each correct answer)

Reflective Comprehension _______

TOTAL READING COMPREHENSION SCORE _______

VOCABULARY CHECK QUESTIONS

		without context I	with context II
1. **complacence**	(1) stillness; (2) compliment; (3) charge; (4) self-satisfaction; (5) complication.	1. _______	_______
2. **discreet**	(1) talkative; (2) disturbing; (3) successful; (4) understandable; (5) careful.	2. _______	_______
3. **benignity**	(1) dignity; (2) casualness; (3) kindliness; (4) benefit; (5) coolness.	3. _______	_______
4. **sallow**	(1) colorless; (2) dark; (3) narrow; (4) observant; (5) tender.	4. _______	_______
5. **demean**	(1) save; (2) defend; (3) hurt; (4) lower; (5) discover.	5. _______	_______

(10 points for each correct answer)

Word Comprehension without *contextual help (I)* _______

Word Comprehension with *contextual help (II)* _______

TOTAL WORD COMPREHENSION SCORE _______

SWING THREE BATS

James I. Brown

Suppose you are a 200-word-a-minute reader. Realizing the distinct advantage of increased reading efficiency, you immediately set to work. Your goal? Double your present rate with the same or better comprehension.

Now, how do you go about reaching that goal? Well, how do you learn to play golf—or the piano? For one thing, by practicing. Paderewski once said: "I practice faithfully every day. If I miss one day, I notice it. If I miss two days, the critics notice it. And if I miss three, my audience notices it."

But that is hardly specific enough to be helpful. Take Henry Smith, freshman. Henry was one of those 200-word-a-minute readers, struggling to keep up in an assignment-filled world. His English teacher, sensing his problem, encouraged him to work on improving his reading. After three weeks of determined "practice," Henry reported disconsolately back to his teacher—*no real progress.*

Records of his practice session showed that only once—his second session—had he tried reading faster than 300 words a minute. But comprehension fell to a low of 30 percent, so for the remaining sessions he dropped back to his usual rate. To be sure, as he continued to practice, his comprehension rose from an initial 80 to 90 percent. But Henry's real need was for improvement in rate, and three weeks of fairly conscientious practice had not brought results.

But what had he been practicing? Suppose a hunt-and-peck typist wanted to improve her typing efficiency. Would she expect to master the touch system by practicing hunt-and-peck methods? And Henry—could he expect to master rapid reading by practicing slow reading?

Again, how to develop reading efficiency? What is best—a gradual increase in rate of about twenty-five words a minute every week or an immediate jump to double your present rate?

At first thought, a gradual increase might seem best. Yet that approach tends to reinforce old habits more than establish new ones. It may never provide the momentum needed for overcoming the inertia of long-established habits. Furthermore, since nothing succeeds like success, this method may result in loss of interest and discouragement. Jumping immediately to double your present rate has the advantage of a clean break with old habits. But failure to adjust immediately to this difficult new level often means frustration and discouragement.

There is still a third possibility, one which student records suggest is best. It is a zigzag pattern, embodying a rather sharp break from old habits with moves that reduce the accompanying frustration. Watch a batter swing three bats, throw two down, then step up and knock a homer. That one bat feels much lighter and easier to handle after swinging three. Try the same psychology in reading. Jump from your customary 200-word-a-minute rate to 300 words a minute before dropping back to 250. If 250 is your top speed, it will always seem uncomfortably fast. If 300 is top speed, 250 will soon seem much slower and easier reading.

Swing three bats!

(500 words)

Comprehension Check Questions

1. Critics noticed a difference when Paderewski missed practicing for (1) one day; (2) two days; (3) three days; (4) four days. 1. _______

2. Henry was encouraged to work on reading by (1) an English teacher; (2) a psychology teacher; (3) a counselor; (4) a high school teacher. 2. _______

3. Henry's initial comprehension was (1) 80 percent; (2) 60 percent; (3) 40 percent; (4) not specifically mentioned. 3. _______

4. Jumping immediately to double one's present rate was said to have the advantage of (1) eliminating needless frustration; (2) giving one a feeling of immediate success; (3) making a clean break with old habits; (4) heightening interest. 4. _______

5. Before reporting back, Henry practiced (1) two weeks; (2) three weeks; (3) four weeks; (4) five weeks. 5. _______

6. The chief purpose of this selection is to (1) suggest how improvement may best be made; (2) establish the importance of practice; (3) discuss the reasons for failure and discouragement; (4) stress the importance of rate. 6. _______

7. The Paderewski story was used to (1) stress the importance of swinging three bats; (2) emphasize the importance of practice; (3) explain Henry's failure; (4) stress the importance of daily effort. 7. _______

8. The analogy to the hunt-and-peck typist was intended to suggest that (1) Henry had been practicing the wrong things; (2) Henry had not been working long enough to see results; (3) reading is like typing; (4) mechanical aids are particularly helpful. 8. _______

9. You would infer from this selection that reading efficiency depends largely on (1) a series of intensive practice sessions; (2) strong motivation and interest; (3) intelligence; (4) a specified practice procedure. 9. _______

10. As used in this selection, "swing three bats" means (1) work energetically; (2) coordinate your efforts; (3) look on practice as a game; (4) work beyond the desired level. 10. _______

SCORE _______

Answers: 1. 2; 2. 1; 3. 1; 4. 3; 5. 2; 6. 1; 7. 4; 8. 1; 9. 4; 10. 4.

NAME ____________________ DATE ____________ READING RATE ____________ WPM

COMPREHENSION CHECK QUESTIONS

1. At the top of the pyramid is (1) a star; (2) an eye; (3) a date; (4) a sun. 1. _______
2. It was specifically said that in a democracy everybody is capable of (1) discovering truth; (2) making true judgments; (3) getting true knowledge; (4) learning the right. 2. _______
3. *Novus Ordo Seclorum* means "A new order of (1) mankind"; (2) living"; (3) thinking"; (4) the world." 3. _______
4. Specific reference was made to (1) the *Arabian Nights;* (2) Aladdin; (3) Jove; (4) Plato. 4. _______
5. The tetrakys is a (1) rectangle; (2) triangle; (3) circle; (4) seal. 5. _______

Receptive Comprehension _______

6. The central idea relates our great seal to (1) myths; (2) the deists; (3) Solomon's Seal; (4) the number thirteen. 6. _______
7. The thesis idea is developed primarily by (1) quoting authorities; (2) logical reasoning; (3) cause-effect reasoning; (4) specific examples. 7. _______
8. This selection is chiefly (1) description; (2) exposition; (3) persuasion; (4) narration. 8. _______
9. In the beginning chief emphasis for our government was placed on (1) religion; (2) power; (3) reasoning; (4) diplomacy. 9. _______
10. Most importantly, you would infer, people should identify with their (1) planet; (2) country; (3) community; (4) family. 10. _______

(10 points for each correct answer)

Reflective Comprehension _______

TOTAL READING COMPREHENSION SCORE _______

VOCABULARY CHECK QUESTIONS

			without context I	with context II
1.	**temporal**	(1) rash; (2) timely; (3) worldly; (4) calm; (5) safe.	1. _______	_______
2.	**fallibilities**	(1) errors; (2) failures; (3) problems; (4) lies; (5) dreams.	2. _______	_______
3.	**coincidental**	(1) logical; (2) agreeable; (3) restful; (4) accidental; (5) grateful.	3. _______	_______
4.	**counterpart**	(1) signal; (2) duplicate; (3) portion; (4) flat surface; (5) coupon.	4. _______	_______
5.	**manifests**	(1) practices; (2) freshens; (3) dates; (4) orders; (5) shows.	5. _______	_______

(10 points for each correct answer)

Word Comprehension without *contextual help (I)* _______

Word Comprehension with *contextual help (II)* _______

TOTAL WORD COMPREHENSION SCORE _______

TREAT CAUSES, NOT SYMPTOMS

James I. Brown

When you step into a doctor's office with a splitting headache, you expect more than an aspirin. That headache is usually a symptom of something that needs attention—something that is causing discomfort. A doctor, if he is to be genuinely helpful, must treat causes, not symptoms.

It helps to look at reading from this same vantage point. Suppose a student comprehends poorly and goes to a clinician for help. It will take more than the admonition, "Try to comprehend better" to bring results.

Poor comprehension is really a symptom—a symptom of what? That's the question which must be answered. Unfortunately the answer is likely to be complex, not simple. Many causes, not one, have to be examined.

For example, if a student reads that "Elizabeth is taciturn," he may not comprehend the statement because of a vocabulary deficiency. That's one important cause to check.

Sometimes a student may read a whole page or chapter and get very little. Why? Frankly because he was bored—had no real interest in it. Lack of interest, then, is another cause of poor comprehension.

Difficulty is still another factor accounting for low comprehension. The Flesch Reading Ease Score provides one method of determining difficulty, rating reading matter on a scale from 0 to 100 or from very easy to very difficult. Both word length and sentence length are used to determine difficulty.

A well-trained mechanic can often just listen to motor sounds and diagnose engine difficulties. He has had sufficient background and experience to do what one lacking that background would find impossible. In reading, also, low comprehension may be caused by inadequate background in a subject matter area.

And of course your reading rate affects comprehension. Reading either too rapidly or too slowly may affect comprehension adversely. For most students there is usually a "just-right" speed which provides maximum comprehension.

Lack of concentration is still another reason for low comprehension. Some readers have never developed proper techniques for dealing successfully with distractions, have never disciplined themselves to give concentrated attention to anything for any length of time. In this day of commercials, station breaks, and coffee breaks, we may be losing the ability to concentrate for extended periods of time.

This does not exhaust the list of causes, although those certainly deserve major attention. Other factors need to be kept in mind—temperature, noise, and movement, for example. Then there are the mechanics of reading—fixation patterns, regression patterns, vocalizings, word-for-word habits.

What does this add up to? Look closely and carefully at each of these possible causes. Try to decide which factor or combination of factors probably explains your low comprehension. Fortunately, without exception, you can do something about each of them. So set up a program for dealing with the causes underlying your symptoms. Then and only then can you begin to see good results.

(500 words)

Comprehension Check Questions

1. The article specifically mentions (1) a dentist; (2) a doctor; (3) an intern; (4) a receptionist. 1. _______
2. Poor comprehension is spoken of as (1) a symptom; (2) a disease; (3) a cause; (4) an accident. 2. _______
3. The Reading Ease Score mentioned was developed by (1) Flesch; (2) Fischer; (3) Flexner; (4) Garrison. 3. _______
4. The article mentions (1) a well-trained mechanic; (2) an experienced teacher; (3) a pilot; (4) a trouble-shooter. 4. _______
5. The article mentions (1) wage hikes; (2) coffee breaks; (3) bonus gifts; (4) hypos. 5. _______
6. The central idea is to get you to (1) discover symptoms; (2) deal with causes; (3) improve comprehension; (4) check vocabulary deficiency. 6. _______
7. The allusion to station breaks was primarily to suggest (1) the importance of variety; (2) their effect on habits of concentration; (3) their encouragement of vocalization; (4) the importance of visual aids. 7. _______
8. A student who comprehends poorly (1) is reading too rapidly; (2) is not really interested; (3) is not concentrating; (4) may be doing none of these things. 8. _______
9. If your reading speed is not increasing, you should apparently try to (1) find out how to increase it; (2) use a new method; (3) discover why not; (4) work harder. 9. _______
10. Apparently, the most helpful move to ensure progress is (1) careful self-analysis; (2) extensive practice; (3) a higher goal; (4) more work on vocabulary. 10. _______

SCORE _______

Answers: 1. 2; 2. 1; 3. 1; 4. 1; 5. 2; 6. 2; 7. 2; 8. 4; 9. 3; 10. 1.

NAME ______________________ DATE ______________ READING RATE ______________ WPM

COMPREHENSION CHECK QUESTIONS

1. Specific mention was made of (1) "The Sound of Music"; (2) "Oklahoma"; (3) "The Music Man"; (4) "My Fair Lady." 1. _______
2. In his office Mr. Stern had (1) an oversized desk; (2) a big bar; (3) some colorful filing cabinets; (4) a FAX machine. 2. _______
3. The author alluded to (1) Truman; (2) de Gaulle; (3) Hitler; (4) Charley Chaplin. 3. _______
4. Turned-in toes indicate (1) assurance; (2) lack of self-confidence; (3) growing uneasiness; (4) open-mindedness. 4. _______
5. You are asked to observe yourself when you are (1) frightened; (2) angry; (3) embarrassed; (4) tired. 5. _______

Receptive Comprehension _______

6. The main idea is to (1) describe body language; (2) explain how to use it; (3) show its value in business; (4) advise what basic signals to look for. 6. _______
7. The opening episode was chiefly to (1) arouse interest; (2) introduce the main character; (3) suggest how body change brings feeling change; (4) explain the role of body language in business. 7. _______
8. The Stern episode was primarily to show what about body language? (1) its subtlety; (2) its dominance; (3) how to counter it; (4) how to understand it. 8. _______
9. Apparently when body and speech disagree, you should rely primarily on (1) what you hear; (2) what you see; (3) a proper combination of the two; (4) other related factors. 9. _______
10. This selection is best described as (1) inspirational; (2) theoretical; (3) practical; (4) realistic. 10. _______

(10 points for each correct answer)

Reflective Comprehension _______
TOTAL READING COMPREHENSION SCORE _______

VOCABULARY CHECK QUESTIONS

			without context I	with context II
1.	**drab**	(1) drastic; (2) dull; (3) rainy; (4) bright; (5) faint.	1. _______	_______
2.	**immaculately**	(1) perfectly; (2) hastily; (3) soberly; (4) colorfully; (5) poorly.	2. _______	_______
3.	**flubbed**	(1) began; (2) beat; (3) ended; (4) rubbed; (5) bungled.	3. _______	_______
4.	**immobile**	(1) changing; (2) motionless; (3) resting; (4) soundless; (5) standing.	4. _______	_______
5.	**supersede**	(1) hold up; (2) formulate; (3) avoid; (4) replace; (5) suspend.	5. _______	_______

(10 points for each correct answer)

Word Comprehension without *contextual help (I)* _______
Word Comprehension with *contextual help (II)* _______
TOTAL WORD COMPREHENSION SCORE _______

CAPITALIZE ON INTEREST

James I. Brown

What is interest? Witty defines it as a "disposition or tendency which impels an individual to seek out certain goals . . . ." Another authority calls it "a learned motive which drives an individual to act . . . ."

Impels, drives—those are the key words. Wrapped up in them you will discover the vital nature of interest. The best car ever made needs gasoline before it takes you anywhere. In the same way, the best mind needs a strong interest before it leads to outstanding achievement. Interest led Napoleon to become a military leader of world renown. Interest led Charles Darwin to discover the principles he described in the *Origin of Species*. Interest led Glenn Cunningham to overcome a major physical handicap and become a record-breaking mile runner. Just as gunpowder speeds a bullet toward its mark, so interest can speed you toward whatever goal you have in mind.

Take your reading. A comprehensive survey by Shaw of over 400 colleges and universities disclosed that an estimated 64 to 95 percent of all college freshmen are handicapped by reading deficiencies. This suggests that no matter how well you read, you still probably read more slowly and ineffectively than you should—probably just became you are not interested enough in reading. You prefer TV, hunting, dancing or any of the other countless ways of spending time.

If this is so, what can you do about it? Specifically, how can you heighten your reading pleasure?

First, notice that people tend to like best those things which they do fairly well. If you are the worst bridge player ever, you will hardly look forward with interest to an evening of bridge—an evening of showing off your ineptitude.

That is equally true with reading—the better you read, the more you enjoy it. If you read slowly and painfully, you miss much of the fun. Your first step, then, is to develop added facility as a reader. This, in turn, means reading more than usual. It is almost that simple—to read better, you must read more.

At this point you may say, "But I don't want to read, let alone read more." Obviously, this is the time to make interest your ally—your driving force. What are your present strongest interests? Build on them for maximum help.

For example, if hunting is at the top of your list, start reading full-length books on that subject. Try *Hunter* or *Between the Elephant's Eyes*. You will be pleasantly surprised at how that interest in hunting will lead you through enough books to make you a more interested reader in general. Then gradually expand your interest in hunting to include such books as Maxwell's *Ring of Bright Water,* which stars two lively otters.

Each book read makes you a more proficient reader, makes the next one that much easier to read, and adds measurably to your general interest in reading.

So start now. Read a book every two or three weeks—one of your own choice, growing naturally out of your own present interests.

(500 words)

Comprehension Check Questions

1. The article mentioned (1) Strang; (2) Leedy; (3) Clark; (4) Witty. 1. ______

2. Reference was made to (1) *Man and Superman;* (2) *Origin of Species;* (3) *Voyage of the Beagle;* (4) *Story of Mankind.* 2. ______

3. Mention is made of (1) polo; (2) bridge; (3) rummy; (4) poker. 3. ______

4. You are told to build on your (1) favorite sport; (2) strongest interest; (3) educational background; (4) best subject matter area. 4. ______

5. Reference was made to (1) an arrow; (2) a dart; (3) an atomic bomb; (4) a bullet. 5. ______

6. This passage is mainly to (1) define interest; (2) discuss the importance of interest; (3) reveal a helpful connection between interest and reading; (4) urge the reading of more books. 6. ______

7. The author would apparently favor (1) more textbook reading; (2) having students select their own reading; (3) having the teacher assign an interesting novel; (4) providing a book list to choose from. 7. ______

8. You would infer that the most important aspect of interest is its (1) power; (2) variability; (3) universality; (4) individuality. 8. ______

9. The article implies that reading ability comes largely through (1) selected reading; (2) magazine reading; (3) careful reading; (4) varied reading. 9. ______

10. The article suggests that college courses in Efficient Reading should be for (1) poor readers; (2) average readers; (3) most students; (4) above-average students. 10. ______

SCORE ______

Answers: 1. 4; 2. 2; 3. 2; 4. 2; 5. 4; 6. 3; 7. 2; 8. 1; 9. 1; 10. 3.

NAME ______________________ DATE ______________ READING RATE ______________ WPM

Comprehension Check Questions

1. It was said that (1) there is a single proven study method; (2) what works well with some students doesn't for others; (3) you need a different method for every subject matter area; (4) a how-to-study book is indispensable. 1. ______
2. If you get behind, you are advised to (1) get notes covering the missed material from another student; (2) skip to the material currently being covered; (3) skim over missed material; (4) catch up. 2. ______
3. At your first reading you are told to (1) underline main points; (2) circle unknown words; (3) make marginal notes; (4) use color-coded checks. 3. ______
4. When beginning a test, (1) outline each question before writing; (2) start right in on question 1; (3) start on the most difficult question; (4) read the test through completely first. 4. ______
5. How many rules are discussed at some length? (1) one; (2) two; (3) three; (4) four. 5. ______

Receptive Comprehension ______

6. The main idea is to (1) keep you from falling behind; (2) get you to mark your books; (3) help you do better on tests; (4) help you do better in school. 6. ______
7. Strongest emphasis is placed on (1) where to study; (2) proper management of study; (3) needed study aids and supplies; (4) the best time to study. 7. ______
8. The chief purpose of this selection was apparently to (1) guide; (2) clarify; (3) persuade; (4) evaluate. 8. ______
9. You would infer from this selection that the writers (1) were too unrealistic; (2) knew students well; (3) were too idealistic; (4) did not understand student problems. 9. ______
10. The tone of the selection is best described as (1) formal; (2) humorous; (3) straightforward; (4) imaginative. 10. ______

(10 points for each correct answer)

Reflective Comprehension ______

TOTAL READING COMPREHENSION SCORE ______

Vocabulary Check Questions

		without context I	with context II
1. **virtuous**	(1) brave; (2) truthful; (3) youthful; (4) righteous; (5) extraordinary.	1. ______	______
2. **incentive**	(1) encouragement; (2) reluctance; (3) distraction; (4) fine; (5) happening.	2. ______	______
3. **deface**	(1) overlook; (2) mar; (3) dry up; (4) drop; (5) find.	3. ______	______
4. **caricatures**	(1) pen drawings; (2) critical statements; (3) models; (4) falsified images; (5) ludicrous likenesses.	4. ______	______
5. **pseudo-students**	(1) sham students; (2) star students; (3) former students; (4) self-made students; (5) graduate students.	5. ______	______

(10 points for each correct answer)

Word Comprehension without *contextual help (I)* ______

Word Comprehension with *contextual help (II)* ______

TOTAL WORD COMPREHENSION SCORE ______

BUILDING SPECIFIC INTERESTS

James I. Brown

Frank complained that he could not remember chemical symbols or formulas. Still he could reel off detailed information about big-league baseball for hours. How come? The secret, of course, was his strong interest in baseball.

Obviously, if you can build a fairly strong interest in any subject matter field, your mastery of it is greatly facilitated. Churchill divided people into two categories—"those whose work is work and whose pleasure is pleasure, and secondly, those whose work and pleasure are one." Interest makes the difference. Why not take full advantage of this in dealing with difficult subjects?

Suppose, for example, that you are taking chemistry but find it dull and uninteresting. This probably means you will avoid studying it and will be likely to do poorly or fail—unless you can develop an interest.

Try these positive suggestions to stimulate added interest in any subject.

First, cultivate the acquaintance of genuinely interested students. After a chemistry lecture, listen for a student who is talking with some enthusiasm and interest about a point raised in class. Fall into step with him or her. Suggest a cup of coffee. You'll be pleasantly surprised how soon some of that enthusiasm will rub off on you. Take the student who drew a bird-watcher for a roommate. At first he smiled to hear all the talk about birds. Two months later, however, he had bought binoculars and bird books and was himself going on early morning trips to identify birds. Fortunately, interest is contagious.

Second, read popular books on the subject. A man with no interest in art read Stone's book, *Lust for Life,* a biography of Vincent Van Gogh. When he finished he amazed his wife by suggesting a visit to an art museum. Stefansson, the arctic explorer, traced his life-long interest in exploring to the reading of one book. Henri Fabre, famous French entomologist, is another whose life was changed by a book. Take the book *Crucibles: The Story of Chemistry,* by Jaffe. Read about the chemist Lavoisier, who lost his head on the guillotine. "It took but a moment to cut off that head, although a hundred years perhaps will be required to produce another like it." So said a contemporary. Such personal glimpses should take you back to your textbook with new zest and interest.

Third, spend extra time on dull, difficult subjects. The more you know about something, the more interested you become. If you know nothing about football you're not likely to be as interested as one who has watched many games and knows both players and rules.

Fourth, watch for educational TV shows or movies in the area of your low interest. The movie "Tom Jones" has stimulated many to read the book. In the same way, a movie about Pasteur can stimulate added interest in chemistry.

Now, get busy! Develop interest in specific subjects. More than anything else, this can change your outlook, can turn study from work to pleasure, can turn a potential *D* into a *B*.

(500 words)

Comprehension Check Questions

1. Frank was said to be interested in (1) baseball; (2) tennis; (3) football; (4) the Olympics. 1. _______

2. Which of the following was quoted? (1) Kennedy; (2) Stevenson; (3) Churchill; (4) Roosevelt. 2. _______

3. Reference was made to (1) a physicist; (2) a biologist; (3) an entymologist; (4) a sculptor. 3. _______

4. You were told to (1) listen to CD's; (2) collect stamps; (3) travel; (4) watch TV. 4. _______

5. How many specific suggestions were given? (1) none; (2) two; (3) three; (4) four. 5. _______

6. This dealt chiefly with (1) why interest should be cultivated; (2) how to develop interests; (3) the why and how of developing interests; (4) what specific interest should be developed. 6. _______

7. The quotation about "work and pleasure" was intended to point up (1) individual differences; (2) how interesting work really is; (3) the importance of interest; (4) how work stimulates interest. 7. _______

8. To develop interest in nuclear physics, which of the following books would be most helpful? (1) *College Physics;* (2) *Nuclear Physics;* (3) *The Atomic Structure of the Universe;* (4) *Our Friend the Atom.* 8. _______

9. Other things being equal, you would assume from this that the best grades are made by students who (1) are most interested; (2) study hardest; (3) are most intelligent; (4) have developed the most effective study habits. 9. _______

10. You would expect the writer to favor (1) a special hour for review; (2) two hours of preparation for every class hour; (3) provision for more leisure time; (4) less preparation time for interesting subjects. 10. _______

SCORE _______

Answers: 1. 1; 2. 3; 3. 3; 4. 4; 5. 4; 6. 3; 7. 3; 8. 4; 9. 1; 10. 4.

NAME ______________________ DATE ______________ READING RATE ______________ WPM

Comprehension Check Questions

1. One writer suggested we read Gibbon's *Decline and Fall* (1) in a day; (2) over a cup of instant coffee; (3) during breakfast; (4) at ten thousand words a minute. 1. _______

2. The average adult was said to read at about (1) 125 wpm; (2) 200 wpm; (3) 250 wpm; (4) 300 wpm. 2. _______

3. The author calls slow readers (1) good readers; (2) studious readers; (3) sloppy readers; (4) childish readers. 3. _______

4. The author refers specifically to (1) Voltaire; (2) Shakespeare; (3) Shelley; (4) Keats. 4. _______

5. To read the *Decline and Fall* at an average rate was said to take (1) 98 hours; (2) 83 hours; (3) 71 hours; (4) 64 hours. 5. _______

Receptive Comprehension _______

6. With respect to how fast to read, this discussion is mainly (1) a comparison of extreme views; (2) an evaluation of the advantages; (3) a realistic look at the whole question; (4) a defense of the middle ground or average position. 6. _______

7. The author's chief concern is with (1) speed; (2) overall reading ability; (3) comprehension; (4) flexibility. 7. _______

8. The author is best described as (1) an extremist; (2) a theorist; (3) a pragmatist; (4) a conservative. 8. _______

9. The author most strongly favors (1) fast reading; (2) average reading speeds; (3) reading at speeds the material deserves; (4) using a variety of reading techniques. 9. _______

10. The writer believes that good reading is (1) natural; (2) God-given; (3) the result of learning; (4) a matter of intellect. 10. _______

(10 points for each correct answer)

Reflective Comprehension _______

TOTAL READING COMPREHENSION SCORE _______

Vocabulary Check Questions

		without context I	with context II
1. blasphemy	(1) seriousness; (2) loudness; (3) irreverence; (4) aimlessness; (5) rejection.	1. _______	_______
2. blitheness	(1) nonsense; (2) sadness; (3) openness; (4) cheerfulness; (5) quietness.	2. _______	_______
3. reputable	(1) restrained; (2) haphazard; (3) limited; (4) unpublished; (5) respectable.	3. _______	_______
4. ethereal	(1) airy; (2) perfumed; (3) childlike; (4) proper; (5) continual.	4. _______	_______
5. mundane	(1) moderate; (2) monetary; (3) generous; (4) heavenly; (5) practical.	5. _______	_______

(10 points for each correct answer)

Word Comprehension without *contextual help (I)* _______

Word Comprehension with *contextual help (II)* _______

TOTAL WORD COMPREHENSION SCORE _______

READ TRIPLE-THREAT BOOKS

James I. Brown

If you are not feeling well, you visit a doctor. He prescribes the proper regime—diet, exercise, or medication—to make you feel better.

But what about reading? Here too the proper regime helps. And a steady diet of textbooks is *not it*. Textbook reading tends to undermine good reading habits by encouraging such things as excessive regressions, a slower rate, and word-by-word reading. Even now your reading habits are probably suffering from the ill effects of such a diet.

With every course you take, you must keep three things, not one, in mind—the mastery of the course materials, the further improvement of reading ability, and the development of essential vocabulary. Yet all too often your efforts in one direction may nullify those in another.

To be sure, there are books such as this one for improving reading efficiency, others for building a better vocabulary, plus all the usual ubiquitous textbooks. But what student has time for extra books? Most students have trouble enough keeping up with the required texts.

That's why triple-threat books make the ideal prescription. You read one, not three, yet are helped three ways. As you know, a triple-threat football player is, in a sense, three men rolled into one—one who can run, pass, and kick. Triple-threat books are equally versatile, helping you improve reading speed and comprehension, expand and sharpen vocabulary, and develop background appropriate for mastery of a given subject.

To discover such books, keep these criteria in mind. First, it must be genuinely interesting. Next, it must be easy to read—requiring a minimum of effort. Now you can see how essential these books are in providing needed balance for your reading diet.

What you do is decide what subject needs your special attention. Then you look in the card catalog for titles under that heading, selecting the one with the most interest-rousing title. Examine a sample page to note the proportion of unfamiliar words. If you see more than twelve, try another. You want only a sprinkling of strange words per page for best results in vocabulary development. For example, "Eschew polysyllabic verbal symbols" is not a very useful context for revealing the meaning of *eschew*. You should find the following more helpful: "Eschew big words and long, involved sentences. Only by avoiding these things can you write simple, understandable English."

If the books meets all these requirements—is interesting, easy to read, and contains only a sprinkling of strange words—it is indeed the student's best friend, that ideal three-in-one combination, rightly called a triple-threat book. Put it to work immediately to build needed course background, develop reading flexibility and power, and contribute significantly to vocabulary.

Read a few every quarter. They will do wonders. And, as a hoped-for extra dividend, remember what Fabre, the French entomologist wrote: "There are for each of us, according to his turn of mind, certain books that open up horizons hitherto undreamed of and mark an epoch in our mental life."

(500 words)

Comprehension Check Questions

1. Textbook reading was said to do what to your good reading habits? (1) undermine them; (2) improve them; (3) consolidate them; (4) have no effect on them. 1. _______
2. One thing to keep in mind when selecting a triple-threat book is (1) print size; (2) interest; (3) novelty; (4) length. 2. _______
3. You were told to try another book if you found how many unfamiliar words per page? (1) fewer than 6; (2) fewer than 9; (3) more than 12; (4) more than 20. 3. _______
4. Specific mention was made of (1) the card catalog; (2) Rousseau; (3) *The Reader's Guide;* (4) paperback books. 4. _______
5. Your reading habits are probably suffering from what? (1) lack of proper reading instruction; (2) disuse; (3) too much light reading; (4) a steady diet of textbooks. 5. _______
6. This passage is mainly about (1) balancing your reading diet; (2) selecting triple-threat books; (3) the nature and advantages of triple-threat books; (4) the importance of the right context. 6. _______
7. You would infer from the context given that the word *eschew* probably means (1) use; (2) taste; (3) avoid; (4) discover. 7. _______
8. The purpose of this selection is to get you (1) to understand; (2) to consider; (3) to evaluate; (4) to act. 8. _______
9. The opening reference to a doctor was used to point up the importance of (1) expert advice; (2) the proper regime; (3) careful diagnosis; (4) physical well-being. 9. _______
10. You would assume that the selection of a triple-threat book is best done by (1) a librarian; (2) an English teacher; (3) the individual concerned; (4) the reading teacher. 10. _______

SCORE _______

Answers: 1. 1; 2. 2; 3. 3; 4. 1; 5. 4; 6. 3; 7. 3; 8. 4; 9. 2; 10. 3.

NAME ______________________ DATE ______________ READING RATE ______________ WPM

Comprehension Check Questions

1. Allen plays the (1) guitar; (2) banjo; (3) harmonica; (4) ukulele. 1. ______
2. Allen started school at (1) Tennessee U.; (2) Carroll College; (3) Bethel College; (4) Vanderbilt U. 2. ______
3. His mother abandoned him when he was (1) 2; (2) 4; (3) 6; (4) 8. 3. ______
4. Who taught Allen to read? (1) Aunt Bevie Jones; (2) Uncle Eddie; (3) Aunt Ida; (4) a teacher for the homebound. 4. ______
5. Allen once taught (1) philosophy; (2) humanities; (3) English; (4) poetry. 5. ______

Receptive Comprehension ______

6. This article mainly shows how (1) isolated Allen was; (2) reading comforted him; (3) much reading speeded getting his degree; (4) reading transformed his life. 6. ______
7. What apparently sparked his great interest in literature? (1) the Bible; (2) Shakespeare; (3) Homer; (4) Milton. 7. ______
8. You would infer Allen's major problem was (1) finding a job; (2) finding his place in the modern world; (3) setting realistic life goals; (4) expressing his painful family experiences. 8. ______
9. Which word best describes this article? (1) entertaining; (2) inspirational; (3) lively; (4) practical. 9. ______
10. The author's attitude toward Allen can best be described as (1) puzzled; (2) amused; (3) tolerant; (4) sympathetic. 10. ______

(10 points for each correct answer)

Reflective Comprehension ______

TOTAL READING COMPREHENSION SCORE ______

Vocabulary Check Questions

			without context I	with context II
1.	**enigmatic**	(1) baffling; (2) energetic; (3) obvious; (4) gracious; (5) enlightening.	1. ______	______
2.	**unkempt**	(1) unclear; (2) neat; (3) untidy; (4) poor; (5) unhappy.	2. ______	______
3.	**aura**	(1) hope; (2) desire; (3) cloud; (4) air; (5) grade.	3. ______	______
4.	**sheer**	(1) false; (2) pure; (3) sole; (4) happy; (5) shameful.	4. ______	______
5.	**reconcile**	(1) repeat; (2) stay behind; (3) rearrange; (4) condense; (5) bring together.	5. ______	______

(10 points for each correct answer)

Word Comprehension without *contextual help (I)* ______

Word Comprehension with *contextual help (II)* ______

TOTAL WORD COMPREHENSION SCORE ______

A New Look at an Old Method

James I. Brown

Step into almost any efficient reading class. What do you find? What is perhaps the oldest, most widely used, yet newest approach in evidence? The answer? *Pacing*!

Most visual aids now in use, for example, are essentially pacing devices. Take the various sets of films for improving reading. They are but ways of getting you through print at projected speeds. Or take the various mechanical accelerators, using a shade, wire, bar, or band of light. Again, they are but machines to pace you through print. As you can see, almost every teacher of reading probably relies on some kind of pacing—films, accelerators, or stop watch.

The newest modification of this old approach comes in a highly commercialized course costing $495. Pacing is the heart of the course. The innovation is transforming the student's ubiquitous hand into a pacer and eliminating the need for machines or films.

Now why is pacing so common? Well, it works. I will never forget one student in my adult Efficient Reading class. At our first session when checking normal reading rate by having the class read a short selection, this young man plodded along at 80 wpm. The class waited patiently for him to finish, their average rate being 254, and the range, except for him, between 201 and 362 wpm.

After class I suggested he cancel the course. He looked at me in desperation. "I need this more than anyone," he said. I agreed but added that it was hardly fair to the others to have to wait for him. He begged to stay, saying, "You won't have to wait. Pay no attention to me. I'll just get what I can." Well, I finally consented.

After seven weeks I noted an amazing change. The class had progressed nicely from 253 to 481 wpm, but he had shot from 80 to 460 wpm. I stopped him after class to ask what he was doing. He had wired his electric clock to the radio so that every time the sweep second hand passed twelve, the radio came on briefly. This let him know a minute had passed.

Fifteen minutes every night, *without fail,* he would read the *Reader's Digest*—approximately 500 words per page. At first he tried to read one column a minute. After a few weeks when he could manage that, he tried a whole page. This daily pacing had brought spectacular results. As he said, "You can't learn to read fast by practicing at slow rates."

Some students use a tape recorder to give themselves pacing signals. Others use book markers and oven timers to get themselves through a set number of pages. Still others enlist the help of a roommate, friend, or spouse.

So—ensure outstanding results from your own efforts through pacing. It can shut out distractions, heighten concentration, and provide invaluable experience at speeds faster than your usual. At first comprehension may suffer somewhat, but gradually, through practice, you will find yourself developing confidence and skill. Eventually your gains will become consolidated.

(500 words)

Comprehension Check Questions

1. The article mentions (1) overhead projectors; (2) accelerators; (3) eye-movement cameras; (4) graphs. 1. _______
2. One reading course costs (1) $195; (2) $295; (3) $395; (4) $495. 2. _______
3. The slow reader was asked to (1) cancel the course; (2) take another course; (3) take the course later; (4) get extra tutoring. 3. _______
4. Every night he paced himself for (1) 10 minutes; (2) 15 minutes; (3) 20 minutes; (4) 30 minutes. 4. _______
5. Pacing was said to (1) improve comprehension; (2) stimulate interest; (3) build background; (4) heighten concentration. 5. _______
6. The main idea is (1) to explain pacing; (2) to discuss various kinds of pacing; (3) to encourage the use of pacing; (4) to show how widely pacing is used. 6. _______
7. You would infer from this passage that films for speeding reading (1) are useless; (2) are only partially helpful; (3) need to be redesigned; (4) are quite helpful. 7. _______
8. What is apparently the chief reason for advocating the use of pacing? (1) its widespread use; (2) its use of interesting visual devices; (3) its effectiveness; (4) its novelty. 8. _______
9. The story of the slow reader was primarily intended to illustrate (1) the serious problems some students have; (2) the kind of results to expect; (3) a way to make a pacer; (4) the need for daily use. 9. _______
10. The major advantage of the hand as a pacer is apparently (1) its great flexibility; (2) its ever-present availability; (3) its elimination of costly machines; (4) its outstanding effectiveness. 10. _______

SCORE _______

Answers: 1. 2; 2. 4; 3. 1; 4. 2; 5. 4; 6. 3; 7. 4; 8. 3; 9. 2; 10. 2.

NAME ______________________ DATE ______________ READING RATE ______________ WPM

Comprehension Check Questions

1. The author mentions (1) Bennett; (2) Maugham; (3) Stevenson; (4) Hardy. 1. _______
2. In reading, we're specifically told to (1) play a waiting game; (2) change character; (3) shift gears; (4) dream dreams. 2. _______
3. How many conditions for adult reading are discussed? (1) one; (2) two; (3) three; (4) four. 3. _______
4. Marya is a character in (1) *War and Peace;* (2) *Dover Beach;* (3) *Anna Karenina;* (4) *Fathers and Sons.* 4. _______
5. The author refers to (1) *Gone with the Wind;* (2) *Old McDonald's Farm;* (3) *Robinson Crusoe;* (4) *Growth of the Soil.* 5. _______

Receptive Comprehension _______

6. This article is mainly about (1) why we read; (2) conditions for adult reading; (3) recognizing the author's existence; (4) why we read and what is involved. 6. _______
7. The conditions for adult reading are arranged in order (1) from least to most important; (2) from the simple to the complex; (3) from the ordinary to the unusual; (4) from early to late in development. 7. _______
8. You might call this style (1) factual; (2) lively; (3) poetic; (4) impersonal. 8. _______
9. Least attention is given to (1) mastering basic reading skills; (2) the work of reading; (3) developing awareness of author; (4) living through reading. 9. _______
10. Uppermost in the author's mind is the fact that reading is extremely (1) difficult; (2) satisfying; (3) complicated; (4) practical. 10. _______

(10 points for each correct answer)

Reflective Comprehension _______

TOTAL READING COMPREHENSION SCORE _______

Vocabulary Check Questions

			without context I	with context II
1.	**equanimity**	(1) fate; (2) equality; (3) calmness; (4) justice; (5) vagueness.	1. _______	_______
2.	**corollary**	(1) crown; (2) what follows; (3) petal; (4) heart attack; (5) wreath.	2. _______	_______
3.	**fraught**	(1) heavy; (2) free; (3) fresh; (4) filled; (5) friendly.	3. _______	_______
4.	**blasé**	(1) tired; (2) fat; (3) bored; (4) cheerful; (5) blasted.	4. _______	_______
5.	**amalgamates**	(1) improves; (2) molds; (3) melts; (4) joins; (5) establishes.	5. _______	_______

(10 points for each correct answer)

Word Comprehension without *contextual help (I)* _______

Word Comprehension with *contextual help (II)* _______

TOTAL WORD COMPREHENSION SCORE _______

USE THE SSQ FORMULA

James I. Brown

Before a new pitcher heads for the mound, he takes time to warm up. Before you begin reading, you too should do some warming up—some preparing

When you sit down to study, those first few minutes are not too productive. Interest and **concentration cannot be switched on** and **off,** as a light switch. **Unrelated thoughts** have to be **pushed out** gradually, as you begin a new activity. Can you **shorten this** warm-up process? **Yes**—by the following formula.

Survey: This first step gives you the best possible overview in the shortest possible time. To survey an article or chapter, **read** the **title,** the **first paragraph,** all **headings, italicized words,** and the **last paragraph**. You should then have the **bare essentials.**

To illustrate, note the underlined parts here. They are **what** you would **read in** your **survey. If** you can **read** the entire 500-word **selection in two minutes,** it will take only **twelve seconds to survey** it. Or take a **longer chapter** from an anthropology text. **Surveying** the 7,650-word chapter means reading only 350 words—**over twenty-one times faster** than normal reading. This diving in headfirst—this sudden immersion—**forces** almost immediate **concentration.**

Skim: Skimming builds up an even stronger foundation. For this, **read** the **title** and **first paragraph,** as in the survey. **Then** read the **first sentence** and **key words in** all the **following paragraphs, plus** any **headings, heavy-type** or **italicized words.** When you reach the **last paragraph, read it** completely. As you see, this means rereading all parts covered in the survey, but taking an important next step. **This** selective **reading** of from 20 to 40 percent of the material, **takes** only **about** a **fifth to** a **third** your **usual** reading **time. Note** the **parts** in **heavier type** on this page. It **marks what** you would **cover in skimming.** Instead of two minutes, it should take only fifty-two seconds.

Questions: Generally, a faster-than-comfortable reading speed means better-than-usual concentration. One **student,** however, slipped into an **unfortunate habit,** while trying to develop added concentration. He **tried** so hard to **finish** a certain number of pages **in** a **limited time** that he was **not actually reading**—just **going through** the **motions. To break himself** of this habit, he used this third step—**raising questions.**

More than anything else, a question is likely to drive unwanted thoughts out of mind. This tends to **shorten** the needed **warming-up** period. **Raise questions** both after surveying and after skimming the material. For example, take the reader who reads the title and consciously asks—"What does SSQ stand for?" He will obviously **read with** much **more purpose** than one who has not evidenced such curiosity. Naturally, **when** you **survey** and **skim, much** is **missed.** In a sense, however, this **tends** to **encourage** more **questions** than in normal reading, making this dynamic third step an almost automatic consequence of the first two.

So—use these prereading steps. Survey the material. Skim it rapidly. Then raise questions—ideal preparation for the reading to follow.

(500 words)

Comprehension Check Questions

1. The article mentions (1) a catcher; (2) a curve ball; (3) a fly; (4) a pitcher. 1. ______

2. The first few minutes of study were said to be (1) crucial; (2) important; (3) unimportant; (4) unproductive. 2. ______

3. Surveying this article was said to take (1) six seconds; (2) twelve seconds; (3) twenty seconds; (4) thirty-six seconds. 3. ______

4. Skimming is spoken of as (1) speed reading; (2) a useful substitute for reading; (3) useful only with textbook material; (4) selective reading. 4. ______

5. One student was said to (1) read too fast; (2) concentrate poorly; (3) go through the motions of reading; (4) spend too much time in skimming. 5. ______

6. This selection focuses mainly on (1) explaining the formula; (2) describing its origin; (3) encouraging its use; (4) pointing up its advantages. 6. ______

7. Major attention is placed on (1) the actual reading; (2) the selection of appropriate approaches; (3) the proper sequence of steps; (4) preparation for reading. 7. ______

8. The mention of the troubled student was to point up primarily the (1) need for a warm-up period; (2) danger in too much reading speed; (3) importance of concentration; (4) usefulness of questions. 8. ______

9. In the allusion "diving in headfirst," the water is analogous to (1) meaning; (2) print; (3) the act of reading; (4) preparation for reading. 9. ______

10. You would infer that the reference to SSQ in the title was primarily to (1) aid memory; (2) summarize; (3) arouse interest; (4) save space. 10. ______

SCORE ______

Answers: 1. 4; 2. 4; 3. 2; 4. 4; 5. 3; 6. 3; 7. 4; 8. 4; 9. 2; 10. 3.

NAME ______________________ DATE ______________ READING RATE ______________ WPM

Comprehension Check Questions

1. Most students encountered were said to exhibit (1) simple reading disability; (2) emotional response to reading; (3) complex difficulties; (4) somewhat below average development. 1. _______
2. Ms. H. was said to spend what percent of her working time on reading tasks? (1) one-tenth; (2) one-third; (3) one-half; (4) three-quarters. 2. _______
3. The increases described in the case of Ms. H. would save her (1) one day per week; (2) one week per month; (3) one day per month; (4) one hour per day. 3. _______
4. Benefits that Ms. H. was said to realize were stated in terms of (1) time saved; (2) time and money saved; (3) time, money, and personal development; (4) none of the above. 4. _______
5. In setting up a course of training the article recommends (1) a specific source of information; (2) a specific commercial agency; (3) a duplication of the Minnesota course; (4) professional assistance. 5. _______

Receptive Comprehension _______

6. The ultimate purpose of this article is (1) to publicize the Minnesota Efficient Reading Course; (2) to reveal the personal benefits possible through improved reading efficiency; (3) to prove that reading can be a "time stretcher"; (4) to encourage the installation of reading training programs by pointing out their value. 6. _______
7. This article is directed to the (1) professional individual; (2) teacher; (3) student; (4) executive. 7. _______
8. The author considers reading as (1) a skill generally mastered in the fourth grade; (2) a process that is refined only by education; (3) a simple skill; (4) a developmental process. 8. _______
9. Emphasized *least* in the training described was (1) guided practice; (2) visual training; (3) motivation; (4) psychology of reading. 9. _______
10. From this article you would infer that courses in efficient reading are at the present time (1) not readily available; (2) few, but increasing in number; (3) widespread and becoming more so; (4) limited to university campuses. 10. _______

(10 points for each correct answer)

Reflective Comprehension _______

TOTAL READING COMPREHENSION SCORE _______

Vocabulary Check Questions

			without context I	with context II
1.	**tycoon**	(1) tropical storm; (2) animal; (3) machine; (4) magnate; (5) factory.	1. _______	_______
2.	**esoteric**	(1) secret; (2) useful; (3) speedy; (4) legal; (5) complicated.	2. _______	_______
3.	**optimum**	(1) visible; (2) hopeful; (3) opposite; (4) best; (5) rich.	3. _______	_______
4.	**hypothetical**	(1) critical; (2) supposed; (3) sick; (4) actual; (5) hysterical.	4. _______	_______
5.	**opportune**	(1) assumed; (2) fitting; (3) depressing; (4) approaching; (5) belated.	5. _______	_______

(10 points for each correct answer)

Word Comprehension without *contextual help (I)* _______

Word Comprehension with *contextual help (II)* _______

TOTAL WORD COMPREHENSION SCORE _______

PROBING PARAGRAPH PATTERNS

James I. Brown

And so, to summarize, be sure to remember those three structurally oriented kinds of paragraphs just discussed.

Did that opening sentence confuse you? If it did, you will realize how important it is to be able to fit a paragraph into a proper framework of reference. Obviously, you—the reader—must be sensitive to the various kinds. An introductory paragraph, for example, should not be read in the same way as a transitional or concluding paragraph—the three kinds that provide key information about structure and emphasis.

The introductory paragraph normally has two functions—to arouse interest and suggest direction and content. It is as if the writer were to shine a flashlight in your face to attract attention–then turn the beam down the path to give you a quick glimpse of what is to be explored. As a reader, you must take full advantage of any and all directional cues so as to move without hesitation in the direction indicated by the writer.

And watch for transitional paragraphs. If read properly, they let you follow the writer with sure steps as he makes an abrupt change in his train of thought.

Finally, when you arrive at a concluding paragraph, slow down and take note. You may find a summary that brings together the very essence of what was said. Or, if the selection is short, you may have the main idea reiterated or put into a broader setting.

But this classification is incomplete. We need still another grouping to cover all varieties.

By far the greater number of paragraphs come under what might be called the expository type, particularly in textbook reading. They are the paragraphs that explain and develop ideas. Some such paragraphs contain one or more examples for clarification of a point. Some contain a mass of relevant details. Some may be built around a comparison or contrast. Black looks blacker when placed beside white. We see it better because of that juxtaposition. Analogy—a special kind of comparison—is another pattern to be noted. Life is like a river—with a beginning, a course, and an ending. Repetition or restatement is still another variety.

Each of these subvarieties can be dealt with more effectively if the reader has developed a sharpened awareness of them all. Often reading only a word or so will let him fit the paragraph into a frame of reference that lets him read it with much greater ease and understanding.

Finally, in addition to expository paragraphs, there are narrative, descriptive, and persuasive types. Narrative paragraphs usually give us action and people. Descriptive paragraphs give us a sensory view of life—let us feel, hear, see, smell, or taste it. And persuasive paragraphs are designed to get us to do something or believe something, thus going a step beyond plain explanation.

This quick look at two different categories of paragraph classification should help you read them with added effectiveness. The more familiar you are with common paragraph building-block patterns, the better you can deal with them.

(500 words)

Comprehension Check Questions

1. The first classification mentioned covered what were called (1) narrative paragraphs; (2) transitional paragraphs; (3) complex paragraphs; (4) structured paragraphs. 1. _______

2. Specific mention was made of (1) a candle; (2) a flashlight; (3) an X-ray; (4) a spotlight. 2. _______

3. When you read a concluding paragraph you are told to (1) slow down; (2) underline portions; (3) make notes; (4) guess what is coming. 3. _______

4. There is specific reference to (1) writing book reports; (2) reading *War and Peace;* (3) reading novels; (4) textbook reading. 4. _______

5. Narrative paragraphs were said to be characterized by (1) vivid details; (2) action; (3) sensory impressions; (4) a definite setting. 5. _______

6. In purpose, this passage is mainly to help you (1) read paragraphs more effectively; (2) become a better reader; (3) classify paragraphs more accurately; (4) recognize the importance of expository paragraphs. 6. _______

7. You would infer that the opening one-sentence paragraph was intended primarily (1) to introduce the subject; (2) to indicate content; (3) to confuse; (4) to awaken interest. 7. _______

8. You would infer that transitional paragraphs are most analogous to which highway sign? (1) Slow; (2) Curve; (3) Hill; (4) Cross Road. 8. _______

9. Most emphasis was placed on what kind of paragraph? (1) introductory; (2) expository; (3) narrative; (4) factual. 9. _______

10. Which of the following types of paragraphs is most likely to contain the word *because*? (1) persuasive; (2) expository; (3) concluding; (4) transitional. 10. _______

SCORE _______

Answers: 1. 2; 2. 2; 3. 1; 4. 4; 5. 2; 6. 1; 7. 4; 8. 2; 9. 2; 10. 1.

NAME ____________ DATE ____________ READING RATE ____________ WPM

Comprehension Check Questions

1. The number of functional illiterates was estimated at more than (1) 10 million; (2) 17 million; (3) 21 million; (4) 27 million. 1. ______
2. Specific mention was made of (1) the Fortune 500; (2) General Motors; (3) Nancy Reagan; (4) the United Nations. 2. ______
3. Haley got a slice of a redwood tree on what birthday? (1) fourth; (2) fifth; (3) sixth; (4) seventh. 3. ______
4. Rivera was born in (1) Puerto Rico; (2) Knoxville; (3) New Orleans; (4) Syracuse, N. Y. 4. ______
5. Rivera's first reading lesson started with (1) "See the bird"; (2) "This is a bird"; (3) "The bird is red"; (4) "See the red bird." 5. ______

Receptive Comprehension ______

6. The main idea is to point up (1) the value of literacy; (2) what organizations are available to overcome illiteracy; (3) the value of a tutorial program; (4) the link between literacy and store management. 6. ______
7. This selection is mainly to (1) inform; (2) entertain; (3) criticize; (4) convince. 7. ______
8. The account of Haley's birthday was introduced primarily to (1) underline the importance of reading; (2) explain his interest in history; (3) show what inspired him to read; (4) point up the important role of parental encouragement. 8. ______
9. You would infer the prime responsibility for Rivera's illiteracy lies with (1) him; (2) his parents; (3) the schools; (4) the community. 9. ______
10. What finally moved Rivera to intensify his efforts to read? (1) his wife; (2) a better job; (3) his baby; (4) Haley. 10. ______

(10 points for each correct answer)

Reflective Comprehension ______

TOTAL READING COMPREHENSION SCORE ______

Vocabulary Check Questions

			without context I	with context II
1. **gerbils**	(1) gems; (2) pills; (3) game birds; (4) flowers; (5) small rodents.	1.	______	______
2. **enticements**	(1) plays; (2) favors; (3) lures; (4) inscriptions; (5) understandings.	2.	______	______
3. **evoke**	(1) call forth; (2) approach; (3) vacate; (4) imagine; (5) disturb.	3.	______	______
4. **afflicted**	(1) joined; (2) suffering; (3) met; (4) declaring; (5) fined.	4.	______	______
5. **conveyed**	(1) changed; (2) accompanied; (3) called; (4) communicated; (5) marked.	5.	______	______

(10 points for each correct answer)

Word Comprehension without *contextual help (I)* ______

Word Comprehension with *contextual help (II)* ______

TOTAL WORD COMPREHENSION SCORE ______

MAKE PURPOSE PREVAIL

James I. Brown

A good hunter doesn't rush into the woods, shooting aimlessly and muttering, "Maybe I'll hit something!" No—if he's hunting pheasants, that purpose dominates all his preparations, determining where, when, how and with what he hunts.

So it is with reading. If purpose is not crystal clear, the results will suffer. One freshman asked another, "What's the assignment about?" "About forty pages," was the reply. Hardly reflects a well-defined purpose, does it?

One way of looking at purpose is to think of reasons for reading. You might put reading for information first, with reading for understanding a close second—a move into depth. Your purpose? To go beyond facts into relationships that give them meaning, just as Sherlock Holmes noted clues, then built case-solving hypotheses. For a third purpose, there is entertainment, and for a fourth, stimulation. Just as a catalyst sparks a chemical reaction, so wide reading sparks new ideas. And, finally, you may read for inspiration. For generations, the Bible has inspired both nations and individuals.

But you must move from the general to the specific, to capitalize fully on purpose. For a specific purpose, turn to Lambuth's *Golden Book on Writing:* "Good writing may be acquired only by wide and intelligent reading. And in no other way whatsoever." Reading to become a better writer, to pass a psych quiz, to learn more about the stars or about yourself are all more specific purposes. Now you can see why it is said—"Tell me what you read and I'll tell you what you are."

Still another way of looking at purpose is in terms of the SPD Formula. In a sense, purpose in reading can only be determined after knowing something about the material to be read. The *S* stands for *S*urveying the material, the *P* for *P*rereading it—reading the first paragraph, topic sentences of following paragraphs, and final paragraph. This brings us to *D*—*D*ecide. Only after the first two steps can you with intelligence decide to do one of four things—skip, skim, read, or study the material. This deserves thoughtful consideration.

What are the major advantages of accenting purpose? Well, it aids concentration, for one thing. Obviously, if you know the target, you can hit it more easily. Secondly, it aids memory. For example, experimental evidence shows that raising questions before reading—a way of sharpening purpose—improves both immediate and delayed recall, more so than reading plus rereading.

Finally, Darwin's *Journal* adds eloquent testimony. After losing his taste for poetry and music, he wrote, pathetically—"If I had to live my life again, I would have made a rule to read some poetry and listen to some music at least once every week; for perhaps that part of my brain now atrophied would thus have been kept alive through use. The loss of those tastes is a loss of happiness . . . ."

To be sure, no one can live his life again. We can all, however, profit from the experience of others. As readers, we can always remember this: *Keep purpose uppermost.*

(500 words)

Comprehension Check Questions

1. Specific reference is made to hunting (1) ducks; (2) pheasants; (3) deer; (4) bears. 1. ______

2. How many specific reasons for reading were mentioned? (1) none; (2) two; (3) three; (4) five. 2. ______

3. It was said that good writing may be acquired only by (1) practice; (2) special instruction; (3) reading; (4) heredity. 3. ______

4. Mention was made of (1) taking true-false tests; (2) raising questions before reading; (3) stating purpose in writing; (4) looking for a statement of purpose. 4. ______

5. A passage is quoted from the writing of (1) Malthus; (2) Darwin; (3) Solomon; (4) Emerson. 5. ______

6. The main idea is to get you to (1) look for a purpose; (2) emphasize purpose in reading; (3) apply the SPD Formula; (4) plan your life around purpose. 6. ______

7. The about-forty-pages anecdote points up primarily the (1) way to establish purpose; (2) way most students think; (3) need for a teacher-set purpose; (4) need for a purpose. 7. ______

8. You would assume from this article that Sherlock Holmes is famous largely because of (1) his nose for information; (2) his ability to go behind the facts; (3) the way he has inspired present-day detectives; (4) his influence on current mysteries. 8. ______

9. The reasons for reading were discussed in (1) the order of diminishing importance; (2) the order of frequency of appearance; (3) a general to specific order; (4) a specific to general order. 9. ______

10. The SPD Formula is based primarily on the assumption that to pass judgment on something demands (1) a well-developed critical faculty; (2) some knowledge of it; (3) good intelligence; (4) a strong degree of interest. 10. ______

SCORE ______

Answers: 1. 2; 2. 4; 3. 1; 4. 2; 5. 2; 6. 2; 7. 4; 8. 2; 9. 3; 10. 2.

NAME ______________________ DATE ______________ READING RATE ______________ WPM

COMPREHENSION CHECK QUESTIONS

1. In the past, the formula for success was (1) useful contacts; (2) intelligence; (3) good background; (4) hard work. 1. ______
2. The average high school graduate should know how many words from the short vocabulary quiz provided? (1) eight; (2) five; (3) two; (4) none. 2. ______
3. On the vocabulary test, the most recent high school graduates (1) showed a wide range of ability; (2) scored about average; (3) scored higher than the others; (4) had the lowest scores of all. 3. ______
4. The author speaks of teaching (1) political science; (2) freshman English; (3) literature; (4) economics. 4. ______
5. How much time each day should be spent in reading? At least (1) four hours; (2) two hours; (3) one hour; (4) forty-five minutes. 5. ______

Receptive Comprehension ______

6. The value of reading receiving most attention in this selection is the (1) practical; (2) recreational; (3) cultural; (4) intellectual. 6. ______
7. Vocabulary is stressed largely because words are (1) basic to all communication; (2) tools of thought; (3) useful socially; (4) helpful in getting good grades. 7. ______
8. The first consideration in encouraging one to read more is to provide (1) suitable instruction; (2) interesting reading; (3) additional incentives; (4) more "good" books. 8. ______
9. The survey of reading habits was mentioned largely to illustrate (1) the good taste of some students; (2) how reading interests change; (3) the value of pocket books; (4) the reason for decline in reading. 9. ______
10. To get children to read, parents should rely mostly on (1) direct advice; (2) example; (3) magazines; (4) book lists. 10. ______

(10 points for each correct answer)

Reflective Comprehension ______

TOTAL READING COMPREHENSION SCORE ______

VOCABULARY CHECK QUESTIONS

		without context I	with context II
1. **reassessed**	(1) agreed; (2) repriced; (3) evaluated again; (4) reassigned; (5) stated again.	1. ______	______
2. **extolled**	(1) extracted; (2) praised; (3) spoke out; (4) rang; (5) released.	2. ______	______
3. **verbal**	(1) spoken; (2) written; (3) factual; (4) related to words; (5) active.	3. ______	______
4. **correlation**	(1) correspondence; (2) confirmation; (3) correction; (4) figure; (5) average.	4. ______	______
5. **induce**	(1) order; (2) refer; (3) try; (4) persuade; (5) lessen.	5. ______	______

(10 points for each correct answer)

Word Comprehension without *contextual help (I)* ______

Word Comprehension with *contextual help (II)* ______

TOTAL WORD COMPREHENSION SCORE ______

ORGANIZATION—YOUR READING SATELLITE

James I. Brown

NAPL. What does that mean? You don't know? No wonder—those letters need to be organized before they make PLAN. Now you see the important role of organization.

Organizing and reading must go hand-in-hand, if reading is to be truly effective. It helps to remember that reading is the reverse of writing; the writer sends, the reader receives. Fortunately, most writers try to organize their remarks carefully enough to ensure clear, accurate communication. The reader, by trying to discover the writer's plan, gets as close as possible to his original meaning. Comprehension is thereby increased.

How is organization revealed? As a reader, you should become more sensitive to three kinds of special devices—typographical, rhetorical, and verbal. To make certain parts stand out, a writer may resort to CAPITAL LETTERS, **boldface type,** or *italics*. Or he may turn to such rhetorical devices as repetition, parallelism, or balance. Repeating a key word or phrase helps the reader fit what is said into a more orderly pattern. When Lincoln spoke of government "of the people, by the people, and for the people," he used parallelism to accent the three-fold pattern he wanted to emphasize. And Patrick Henry's "give me liberty or give me death," used balance to heighten the two-fold nature of that choice. Finally, verbal devices help the reader mark transitions, note methods of development, and discover outline form. The word *another*, for example, suggests a transition. *Consequently* suggests a development based on cause-and-effect relationships. And such words as *first* or *finally* are most useful indicators of outline form. All these devices, like road signs, help the reader keep on the track.

The other way is through noting paragraph structure. Major thought units are marked off by paragraphs. Each paragraph has a topic sentence, expressed or implied, plus supporting details. In outlining any article, rely heavily on paragraphing to make the plan clear.

What does organization contribute? When you have developed real skill in noting organization, the benefits fall into two categories—a sharpened awareness of certain key factors as well as improved ability in two areas.

A sharpened awareness of the thesis or main idea is one important benefit. Getting the main idea of this 500-word selection, for example, is greatly simplified by reducing the 500 words to a manageable skeleton—or outline. Organization also brings added awareness of the interrelationships between parts. Subordinate parts are seen as exactly that, their relationship to major divisions being more obvious.

Finally, organization improves both understanding and remembering. Knowledge and understanding are, in a sense, different. It is possible to know the facts but not understand what they mean. Organization helps here. And it contributes added retention. It is much easier to remember details if you have an outline as a frame of reference. It is easier, for example, to remember CAPITALS, **boldface type,** and *italics*, when they are grouped under the heading *Typographical devices*.

So, make organization a concomitant to reading. It can turn NEMAGIN into MEANING, the obscure into the obvious.

(500 words)

Comprehension Check Questions

1. You were told to keep organizing and reading (1) as separate activities; (2) as consecutive steps; (3) hand-in-hand; (4) apart. 1. _______
2. Reading is spoken of as (1) the reverse of writing; (2) the spark for comprehension; (3) easier than writing; (4) the road to outlining. 2. _______
3. Reference was made to (1) Franklin; (2) Washington; (3) Monroe; (4) Lincoln. 3. _______
4. The special devices discussed were likened to (1) keys; (2) road signs; (3) timetables; (4) road maps. 4. _______
5. Parallelism is classed as a (1) typographical device; (2) verbal device; (3) rhetorical device; (4) paragraph device. 5. _______
6. This passage is mainly about (1) how organization is revealed; (2) what organization contributes to reading; (3) outlining techniques; (4) the role of organization in reading. 6. _______
7. The opening reference to NAPL (PLAN) was intended to show (1) how to organize; (2) the simplicity of good organization; (3) the importance of organization; (4) how slight changes make big differences. 7. _______
8. Two of the main divisions are marked off by (1) boldface type; (2) headings; (3) italics; (4) capital letters. 8. _______
9. The phrase "make organization a concomitant to reading" apparently means to make it (1) a supplement; (2) an aid; (3) an end; (4) an accompaniment. 9. _______
10. Most attention is given to (1) how to organize; (2) what purpose organization has; (3) when to organize; (4) what organization is. 10. _______

SCORE _______

Answers: 1. 3; 2. 1; 3. 4; 4. 2; 5. 3; 6. 4; 7. 3; 8. 3; 9. 4; 10. 2.

NAME ______________________ DATE ______________ READING RATE ______________ WPM

COMPREHENSION CHECK QUESTIONS

1. The author mentions (1) Syria; (2) Israel; (3) France; (4) Egypt. 1. _______

2. Durrell termed a phone call what form of communication? (1) non; (2) speed; (3) second-rate; (4) instant. 2. _______

3. You are advised to start your letter with (1) best wishes; (2) questions to be answered; (3) the here and now; (4) reference to the last letter received. 3. _______

4. The writer talked about her (1) father; (2) mother; (3) uncle; (4) sister. 4. _______

5. Specific reference was made to (1) pen pals; (2) Hallmark; (3) Western Union; (4) AT&T. 5. _______

Receptive Comprehension _______

6. This article is chiefly to (1) encourage you to write letters; (2) tell you how to write a letter; (3) explain why fewer letters are being written; (4) show why celebrities write letters. 6. _______

7. The bit about National Letter-Writing Week was intended to show that personal letters (1) are important; (2) need to be encouraged; (3) are diminishing; (4) compete with junk mail. 7. _______

8. The paragraph about Auntie Bessie was chiefly to who what about letters? (1) their welcome reception; (2) their key role in relationships; (3) their slowness in coming; (4) their pleasure in being prepared. 8. _______

9. The material is organized largely (1) on a point-by-point basis; (2) in a cause-effect sequence; (3) from simple to complex; (4) from general to specific. 9. _______

10. Points are developed largely by (1) logical reasoning; (2) contrast; (3) analogy; (4) specific examples. 10. _______

(10 points for each correct answer)

Reflective Comprehension _______

TOTAL READING COMPREHENSION SCORE _______

VOCABULARY CHECK QUESTIONS

		without context I	with context II
1. daunted	(1) dismayed; (2) determined; (3) performed; (4) shown; (5) dared.	1. _______	_______
2. au courant	(1) public sale; (2) courage; (3) race; (4) reality; (5) up-to-date.	2. _______	_______
3. colloquy	(1) conspiracy; (2) fellow worker; (3) conversation; (4) search; (5) combination.	3. _______	_______
4. raconteur	(1) noise; (2) framework; (3) scheme; (4) story-teller; (5) conclusion.	4. _______	_______
5. touted	(1) displayed; (2) promoted; (3) traded; (4) sounded; (5) discovered.	5. _______	_______

(10 points for each correct answer)

Word Comprehension without *contextual help (I)* _______

Word Comprehension with *contextual help (II)* _______

TOTAL WORD COMPREHENSION SCORE _______

Exercises

Capitals, Italics, and Other Punctuation

To check your handling of such marks, use the following passage. Circle every letter that should be capitalized, underline every word that should be italicized, and insert all punctuation marks where they are needed. When you have finished, turn back to Selection 36 and compare your version with the original (paragraph 4 and the next-to-last paragraph).

> perhaps letter writing scares some people they may worry about going on record in an unretractable form and not trusting the recipient to protect the privacy of the relationship others are daunted by the mechanics of putting together a proper handmade communication still others suffer letter writers block immediately after writing dear auntie flo
>
> is the age of correspondence really over george o connell wrote in the new york times that his aunt maude proclaims ma bell and even cousin hallmark have displaced the postman she longs for caring and literate letters to hold a family together

Consult your handbook to resolve any differences between the two versions. In preparing a bibliography and making footnotes, you will want to know when to use italics and quotation marks. The sooner you straighten out such matters, the more professional your reports will appear.

Active Versus Passive Verbs

Use active verbs whenever possible. In the following sentences, change the italicized verbs from passive to active voice, making whatever other changes are necessary to complete the sentences. Check back with the article to compare your version with the original. Notice the relative effectiveness of the two voices.

1. "Supper *was had*. A watermelon *was finished* by me. My shoes *were taken* off."

___

___

2. The power of a letter *was learned* by me when I was eight . . . .

___

3. It *was proclaimed* by Aunt Maude . . .

___

4. It *was felt* by our mailman . . .

___

Directions: Think of someone you'd like to write a letter to (or receive one from) and try your hand at writing a few opening sentences, following the suggestions given in the article.

___

___

___

___

___

NAME ______________________ DATE ______________ READING RATE ______________ WPM

COMPREHENSION CHECK QUESTIONS

1. When class began, the teacher (1) had the wrong notes; (2) lost the class roll; (3) dropped his notebook; (4) lost his chalk. 1. _______
2. Specific mention is made of (1) Stanford; (2) M.I.T.; (3) Harvard; (4) U.C.L.A. 2. _______
3. When studying for an essay exam, you were advised to (1) memorize your notes; (2) recite answers orally; (3) highlight key points; (4) work with one or two people in the class. 3. _______
4. The author could whip off 20 pages of a term paper (1) in two or three nights; (2) in a week; (3) in ten nights; (4) in two weeks. 4. _______
5. The author was currently taking a graduate-level course in (1) English; (2) grammar; (3) writing; (4) literature. 5. _______

Receptive Comprehension _______

6. This selection is mainly to tell you how to (1) deal with multiple-choice questions; (2) write term papers; (3) manage college effectively; (4) read instructors. 6. _______
7. The introduction stresses the author's (1) advice-giving qualifications; (2) professional attitude; (3) humanness; (4) absent-mindedness. 7. _______
8. The points are developed largely by (1) citing authorities; (2) logical reasoning; (3) facts; (4) illustrations. 8. _______
9. The writing style is best described as (1) lively; (2) direct; (3) simple; (4) concise. 9. _______
10. The major purpose is to (1) entertain; (2) inform; (3) persuade; (4) advise. 10. _______

(10 points for each correct answer)

Reflective Comprehension _______

TOTAL READING COMPREHENSION SCORE _______

VOCABULARY CHECK QUESTIONS

			without context I	with context II
1.	**quixotic**	(1) lively; (2) difficult; (3) helpful; (4) impractical; (5) extreme.	1. _______	_______
2.	**coherent**	(1) cluttered; (2) intelligible; (3) clever; (4) basic; (5) summarized.	2. _______	_______
3.	**maxims**	(1) options; (2) similarities; (3) rules; (4) successes; (5) marks.	3. _______	_______
4.	**idiosyncratic**	(1) ignorant; (2) destructive; (3) sympathetic; (4) high-toned; (5) whimsical.	4. _______	_______
5.	**fetishes**	(1) irrationalities; (2) tendencies; (3) failures; (4) handouts; (5) traces.	5. _______	_______

(10 points for each correct answer)

Word Comprehension without *contextual help (I)* _______

Word Comprehension with *contextual help (II)* _______

TOTAL WORD COMPREHENSION SCORE _______

BE A PERFECT SPELLER IN 30 MINUTES

Norman Lewis

Can you become a perfect speller? Yes—if you are willing to memorize a few intriguing rules and give your memory a stimulating jolt. I have demonstrated again and again in my adult classes at the City College of New York that anyone who possesses normal intelligence and has had an average education should have no trouble in becoming a perfect speller in 30 minutes or even less!

What makes the task so easy and rapid?

1. Investigations have proved that 95 percent of our spelling mistakes occur in just 100 words. Not only do we all seem to misspell the same words, but we usually misspell them in just about the same way.
2. Correct spelling depends entirely on memory, and the most effective way I know of to train your memory is by means of association—or by *mnemonics* (pronounced *nemonics*).

If you are a poor speller, the chances are that you've developed a complex because you misspell some or all of the 100 words with which this article deals. When you have mastered this list by means of association and memory, 95 percent of your spelling difficulties will vanish.

So let's start with the 25 troublesome words listed below. In addition to the correct spelling of each of the words, you will find the simple mnemonic that will enable you to fix that correct spelling indelibly in your memory.

all right: Two words, no matter what it means. Keep in mind that it's the opposite of *all wrong*.

repetition: The first four letters are the same as those in *repeat*.

irritable, inimitable: Think of allied forms *irritate* and *imitate*.

recommend: *Commend,* which is easy to spell, plus the prefix *re-*.

ridiculous: Think of the allied form *ridicule,* which is usually spelled correctly, thus avoiding *rediculous*.

despair: Again think of another form—*desperate*—and so avoid *dispair*.

stationery: The word that means paper; notice the *er* in *pap***er**.

stationary: This means standing, so notice the *a* in *st***a***nd*.

superintendent: The superintendent in an apartment house collects the **re***nt*—thus you avoid *superintendant*.

coolly: You can spell *cool*—simply add the adverbial ending *-ly*.

separate, comparative: Look for a rat in both words.

supersede: The only word in the language ending in *-sede*.

succeed, proceed, exceed: The only three words in the language ending in *-ceed*. In the order given here the initial letters form the first 3 letters in **spe***ll*.

cede, recede, precede, etc: All other words with a final syllable sounding similar end in *-cede*.

procedure: One of the double *e*'s in *proc***ee***d* moves to the end in *proc***e***dur***e**.

absence: Think of the allied form *absent,* and you will not be tempted to misspell it *abscence*.

conscience: *Science,* plus the prefix *con-*.

anoint: Think of *an ointment,* hence no double *n*.

ecstasy: To *sy* (sigh) with *ecsta***sy**.

analyze, paralyze: The only two non-technical words in the language ending in *-yze*.

Whether or not you have faith in your ability as a speller you will need only 30 seconds to overcome your difficulties with each of the 25 words in the list, or 12 1/2 minutes all told. And as you probably misspell only some of the words, not the entire 25, you should be able to eliminate your errors in even less time. Just try spending 30 seconds, now, on each of the words you're doubtful about—then put your new-found learning to the test by filling in the missing letters in the same list of words that follows. To your delight, you'll find that it's not at all difficult to make a perfect score. Try it and see for yourself.

A_RIGHT
REP_TITION
IRRIT_BLE
INIMIT_BLE
RE_O_MEND
R_DICULOUS
D_SPAIR
STATION_RY (paper)
STATION_RY (standing)
SUPERINTEND_NT
COO_Y
SEP_RATE
COMPAR_TIVE
SUPER_ _ _ _
SUC_ _ _ _
PROC_ _ _ _
EXC_ _ _ _
PREC_ _ _
PROC_DURE
AB_ENCE
CON_ _ _NCE
A_OINT
ECSTA_Y
ANAL_ _E
PARAL_ _E

(continued on page 350)

NAME ______________________ DATE ______________ READING RATE ______________ WPM

COMPREHENSION CHECK QUESTIONS

1. The teacher's name was (1) Stamm; (2) Steele; (3) Stone; (4) Smith. 1. _______
2. Mention is made of reading a poem by (1) Keats; (2) Shelley; (3) Burns; (4) Byron. 2. _______
3. The teacher stirred their imagination by asking them how they would like to live in (1) England during the reign of Elizabeth; (2) Italy during the Renaissance; (3) Greece at the height of its glory; (4) France at the time of the French Revolution. 3. _______
4. For the good-bye party the boys prepared a (1) eulogy; (2) gift; (3) parody; (4) play. 4. _______
5. The class met in Room (1) 308; (2) 318; (3) 288; (4) 280. 5. _______

Receptive Comprehension _______

6. The purpose of this article is to (1) tell about an unusual character; (2) describe how he taught English; (3) suggest the importance of wide reading; (4) help us feel an appreciation for this character. 6. _______
7. The teacher's comment on the phrase "tender age" was (1) one of approval; (2) not given; (3) one suggesting lazy writing; (4) one suggesting a specific revision. 7. _______
8. His attempts to get students to see if they could improve on a poem were intended to lead to (1) a better understanding of the poem; (2) a better appreciation of literature; (3) an improvement in writing and speaking; (4) improvement of discussion techniques. 8. _______
9. His most important piece of advice was to (1) study; (2) work; (3) browse; (4) read. 9. _______
10. The article implies that we should read things of (1) personal interest; (2) recognized merit; (3) current interest; (4) literary worth. 10. _______

(10 points for each correct answer)

Reflective Comprehension _______
TOTAL READING COMPREHENSION SCORE _______

VOCABULARY CHECK QUESTIONS

			without context I	with context II
1.	**condescension**	(1) condemnation; (2) grief; (3) control; (4) insulation; (5) air of superiority.	1. _______	_______
2.	**melee**	(1) combining; (2) confused mass; (3) melting; (4) maturing; (5) orderly plan.	2. _______	_______
3.	**abhorred**	(1) clung to; (2) hated; (3) wandered; (4) gave up; (5) assumed.	3. _______	_______
4.	**bestow**	(1) give; (2) assign; (3) beset; (4) beg; (5) elevate.	4. _______	_______
5.	**concocted**	(1) finished; (2) exploded; (3) devised; (4) seasoned; (5) drank.	5. _______	_______

(10 points for each correct answer)

Word Comprehension without *contextual help (I)* _______
Word Comprehension with *contextual help (II)* _______
TOTAL WORD COMPREHENSION SCORE _______

BE A PERFECT SPELLER IN 30 MINUTES *(continued from page 347)*

Mere repetitious drill, however, will not teach you to spell correctly. If you drive a car or sew or do any familiar manual work, you know how your hands carry on automatically while your mind is far away. So if you hope to learn how to spell by filling pages with a word, about all you'll get for your trouble will be writer's cramp.

The only way to learn to spell the words that now plague you is to devise a mnemonic for each one.

If you are never sure whether it's *indispensible* or *indispensable,* you can spell it a thousand or a million times—and the next time you have occasion to write it you'll still wonder whether to end with *ible* or *able*. But if you say to yourself just once that *able* men are generally indispens*able,* you've conquered another spelling demon.

In the test below are another 25 words from the list of 100, each presented in both the correct form and in the popular misspelling. Go through the list quickly, checking what you consider the proper choices. In this way you will discover which of the 25 would stump you in a spelling test. Then devise a personal mnemonic for each word you failed to get right, writing your result in the margin of the page.

Don't be alarmed if some of your mnemonics turn out to be silly—the sillier they are, the easier to recall them in an emergency. One of my pupils, who could never remember how many *l's* to put into tranquillity (or is it *tranquility?*), came up with this: "In the old days life was more tranquil, and people wrote with *quills* instead of fountain pens. Hence—*tranquillity!*" That is the preferred form, though either is correct.

Another pupil, a girl, who always chewed her nails over *irresistible* before deciding whether to end it with *ible* or *able*, suddenly realized that a certain brand of lipstick was called "Irresistible," the point being that the only vowel in *lipstick* is *i*—hence, *ible!* Silly, mnemonics, aren't they? But they work. Now tackle the test and see how clever—or silly—you can be.

DO THESE WORDS STUMP YOU?

The following list shows the correct and incorrect spellings of 25 words commonly misspelled. Check a or b, whichever you think is correct. Then look at the answers to see how well you did.

1. (a) *supprise* (b) *surprise*
2. (a) *inoculate* (b) *innoculate*
3. (a) *definitely* (b) *definately*
4. (a) *priviledge* (b) *privilege*
5. (a) *incidently* (b) *incidentally*
6. (a) *predictible* (b) *predictable*
7. (a) *embarassment* (b) *embarrassment*
8. (a) *descriminate* (b) *discriminate*
9. (a) *description* (b) *discription*
10. (a) *pronounciation* (b) *pronunciation*
11. (a) *occurence* (b) *occurrence*
12. (a) *developement* (b) *development*
13. (a) *arguement* (b) *argument*
14. (a) *assistant* (b) *asisstant*
15. (a) *grammer* (b) *grammar*
16. (a) *parallel* (b) *paralell*
17. (a) *drunkeness* (b) *drunkenness*
18. (a) *suddeness* (b) *suddenness*
19. (a) *dissipate* (b) *disippate*
20. (a) *weird* (b) *wierd*
21. (a) *baloon* (b) *balloon*
22. (a) *noticeable* (b) *noticable*
23. (a) *truely* (b) *truly*
24. (a) *vicious* (b) *viscious*
25. (a) *insistent* (b) *insistant*

By now you're well on the way to developing a definite superiority complex about your spelling. Remember: you want to spell correctly so that in correspondence you will not give your reader the impression your education has been sadly neglected. The conquest of the 100 words most commonly misspelled is not guaranteed to make you top man in a spelling bee, but it's certain to improve your writing and do a lot to bolster your ego.

So far you have worked with 50 of the 100 spelling demons. The remainder of the list appears below. Test yourself, and discover which words are your Waterloo. Study each one you miss, observe how it's put together, then devise whatever association pattern will fix the correct form in your mind.

Once you've mastered this list, you are a good speller. And—if you've truly applied yourself—your goal has been achieved in 30 minutes or less!

How Good Are You Now?

Here are fifty words that also frequently stump the expert speller. See how quickly you can master them by finding a simple association for each.

misspelling	*vacillate*	*possesses*
conscious	*oscillate*	*professor*
indispensable	*forty*	*category*
disappear	*dilettante*	*rhythmical*
disappoint	*changeable*	*vacuum*
corroborate	*accessible*	*benefited*

sacrilegious	*accommodate*	*committee*
persistent	*license*	*grievous*
exhilaration	*panicky*	*judgment*
newsstand	*seize*	*plebeian*
desirable	*leisure*	*tariff*
irresistible	*receive*	*sheriff*
tranquillity	*achieve*	*connoisseur*
dilemma	*holiday*	*necessary*
perseverance	*existence*	*sergeant*
until	*pursue*	*irrelevant*
tyrannize	*pastime*	

Answers: 1. b; 2. a; 3. a; 4. b; 5. b; 6. b; 7. b; 8. b; 9. a; 10. b; 11. b; 12. b; 13. b; 14. a; 15. b; 16. a; 17. b; 18. b; 19. a; 20. a; 21. b; 22. a; 23. b; 24. a; 25. a.

NAME ______________________ DATE ______________ READING RATE ______________ WPM

COMPREHENSION CHECK QUESTIONS

1. The author talks about a (1) one-mile run; (2) two-mile run; (3) three-mile run; (4) four-mile run. 1. _______
2. Mention is made of the (1) Boston Marathon; (2) Clam Beach Run; (3) New York Marathon; (4) Olympic Marathon. 2. _______
3. The writer specifically mentions typing (1) "Chapter One"; (2) "The End"; (3) "Synopsis"; (4) "Story Outline." 3. _______
4. The writer's movie screen is located (1) on her desk; (2) inside her forehead; (3) on the ceiling; (4) on the back of her hand. 4. _______
5. Where was the woman in the imagined story? (1) on a raft; (2) on a sandy beach; (3) in a gorge; (4) at the edge of a cliff. 5. _______

Receptive Comprehension _______

6. The purpose of this article is to (1) tell you to start with "the"; (2) explain how to use your movie screen; (3) suggest how to begin writing; (4) show similarities between writing and running. 6. _______
7. Apparently the author is primarily a writer of (1) novels; (2) short stories; (3) magazines articles; (4) newspaper features. 7. _______
8. What was the point of the example of her friend with a contract for a juvenile mystery? The difficulty (1) of outlining; (2) of visualizing; (3) of starting; (4) of getting an acceptance. 8. _______
9. The reference to being surprised at meeting someone you'd heard of was to (1) suggest where to start a story; (2) point up the need to observe; (3) show how ideas grow; (4) prove the existence of a movie screen. 9. _______
10. Chief emphasis is on the (1) what; (2) when; (3) how; (4) why. 10. _______

(10 points for each correct answer) *Reflective Comprehension* _______
TOTAL READING COMPREHENSION SCORE _______

VOCABULARY CHECK QUESTIONS

			without context I	with context II
1.	**sedentary**	(1) local; (2) segmented; (3) hard; (4) isolated; (5) sitting.	1. _______	_______
2.	**massive**	(1) bulky; (2) towering; (3) compacted; (4) dull; (5) metallic.	2. _______	_______
3.	**harrowingly**	(1) sharply; (2) distressingly; (3) rather; (4) smoothly; (5) aimlessly.	3. _______	_______
4.	**excruciatingly**	(1) often; (2) excitingly; (3) excessively; (4) hardly; (5) extremely.	4. _______	_______
5.	**albeit**	(1) despite; (2) beforehand; (3) in place of; (4) because; (5) although.	5. _______	_______

(10 points for each correct answer)

Word Comprehension without *contextual help (I)* _______
Word Comprehension with *contextual help (II)* _______
TOTAL WORD COMPREHENSION SCORE _______

EXERCISES

FINDING WORDS FOR WHAT YOU OBSERVE

Observing may be thought of as a third channel of learning, one closely related to the signs and symbols present in our environment. We learn by reading, listening, and looking. If we sharpen our powers of observation and develop the vocabulary to express with sureness what we have observed, we are that much better equipped to write and speak with effectiveness as well as to read and listen appreciatively.

1. The first suggestion is to *be specific.* Which of the following two sentences is more interesting to you?

> "We know of people being on a structure and observing the presence of vehicles that go over the structure for a space of time."

> "We hear of inquirers standing on London Bridge and counting the number of motor-buses, foot-passengers, lorries, and white horses that pass over the bridge in an hour."

Do you agree that the second, more specific account is better? If so, use the sharp, clear details, not the blurred generalization. Perhaps you are not interested in dating a "good-looking girl," but if you are told she has ash-blonde hair, deep blue eyes, long curly eyelashes, and full, cherry-red lips, (or, perhaps, glistening, jet-black hair, olive skin, and black eyes) you may well change your mind. *Be specific.*

Think of all the synonyms you can, then select the one that makes the sharpest picture. Instead of having someone "move" down the street, think of synonyms of *move*—travel, disappear, walk, stride, trudge, etc. Then select the word that creates the picture you have in mind.

2. The second suggestion is to record all the specific details possible in any simple scene. Aim at getting down 100 specific sensory impressions. The following headings will keep you from overlooking anything:*

SIGHT Form or Outline (as *towering smokestacks*):

__________ __________ __________

__________ __________ __________

__________ __________ __________

Motion or Position (as *flitting sparrows*):

__________ __________ __________

__________ __________ __________

__________ __________ __________

Shade or Color (as *glowing red sky*):

__________ __________ __________

__________ __________ __________

__________ __________ __________

*This is the form suggested by F. S. Appel in his book, *Write What You Mean.*

SOUND (as *screech of car brakes*):

SMELL (as of *hot rubber*):

TOUCH (as of *cooling breeze*):

TASTE (as of *sour lemon*):

3. The last suggestion is to select those details from the large listing that create the dominant impression of the scene on the observer and weave them together into a coherent paragraph that will make the desired impression on the reader.

NAME ______________________ DATE ______________ READING RATE ______________ WPM

Comprehension Check Questions

1. You're told to do what about NCD? (1) use it; (2) avoid it; (3) begin with it; (4) conclude with it. 1. _______

2. You're told to (1) make an outline; (2) read extensively; (3) develop good interviewing techniques; (4) type even your first rough draft. 2. _______

3. There is specific mention of (1) Pascal; (2) Pope; (3) Shakespeare; (4) Virgil. 3. _______

4. The article refers to (1) a BMW; (2) a Cadillac; (3) a Rolls Royce; (4) a Mercedes. 4. _______

5. Specific reference is made to (1) *The Writer's Handbook;* (2) *The Elements of Style;* (3) *On Writing Well;* (4) *Better English.* 5. _______

Receptive Comprehension _______

6. This selection is primarily to (1) inspire; (2) persuade; (3) explain; (4) describe. 6. _______

7. The analogy to a baseball pitcher warming up was to get writers to (1) open with warm-up material; (2) throw away warm-up material; (3) reduce warm-up time; (4) enliven warm-up material. 7. _______

8. Introductions should be (1) interest-rousing; (2) avoided; (3) suspense-building; (4) humorous. 8. _______

9. Of the following phrasings, which would the author prefer? (1) be brief; (2) it pays to be brief; (3) conciseness is preferred; (4) you should never use unnecessary words. 9. _______

10. Most emphasis is placed on (1) getting to the point; (2) organizing well; (3) practice; (4) keeping moving. 10. _______

(10 points for each correct answer)

Reflective Comprehension _______

TOTAL READING COMPREHENSION SCORE _______

Vocabulary Check Questions

		without context I	with context II
1. digress	(1) ramble; (2) summarize; (3) decide; (4) scatter; (5) emphasize.	1. _______	_______
2. exposition	(1) exposure; (2) exponent; (3) position; (4) description; (5) explanation.	2. _______	_______
3. configuration	(1) list; (2) number; (3) limit; (4) form; (5) decision.	3. _______	_______
4. succinct	(1) solid; (2) tight; (3) long; (4) aimless; (5) brief.	4. _______	_______
5. implicit	(1) rash; (2) favorable; (3) defective; (4) suggested; (5) inserted.	5. _______	_______

(10 points for each correct answer)

Word Comprehension without *contextual help (I)* _______

Word Comprehension with *contextual help (II)* _______

TOTAL WORD COMPREHENSION SCORE _______

EXERCISES

OUTLINING YOUR THOUGHTS

One of the ten tips in this article reads, "Get your story in order." Of course that probably means making an outline. To prepare yourself for that task, turn to the short selection entitled "Organization—Your Reading Satellite," on pages 340–341. Read it carefully, underlining all words and phrases that suggest the specific plan used. Then reconstruct in the blank outline form below what you think is the outline the writer used for that selection. Work carefully, for you want to learn as much as possible about outline form and procedure. Look back to the selection as often as you wish. When you have finished, compare your outline with the exact outline used by the writer of that selection. The original outline is on page 368.

OUTLINE FOR "ORGANIZATION—YOUR READING SATELLITE"

I. ____________________

II. ____________________

III. ____________________

A. ____________________

1. ____________________

a. ____________________

b. ____________________

c. ____________________

2. ____________________

a. ____________________

b. ____________________

c. ____________________

3. ____________________

a. ____________________

b. ____________________

c. ____________________

B. ____________________

1. ____________________

2. ____________________

IV. ____________________

A. ____________________

1. ____________________

2. ____________________

B. ____________________

1. ____________________

2. ____________________

V. ____________________

NAME ______________________ DATE ______________ READING RATE ______________ WPM

Comprehension Check Questions

1. The author put what first? (1) her writing; (2) her husband and children; (3) both writing and family equally; (4) point not specifically mentioned. 1. ______
2. One of her books was rejected because it began with a (1) rape; (2) suicide; (3) death; (4) murder. 2. ______
3. Which of her books was under serious consideration? (1) *The Lost Innocent;* (2) *A Winter's Love;* (3) *Meet the Austins;* (4) *A Wrinkle in Time.* 3. ______
4. On what birthday did she hear of the book's rejection? (1) thirtieth; (2) fortieth; (3) fiftieth; (4) not specifically mentioned. 4. ______
5. She felt she could not write if she lost her ability to (1) set a goal; (2) plan her time; (3) visualize imaginatively; (4) laugh. 5. ______

Receptive Comprehension ______

6. The main focus is on (1) problems with publishers; (2) the demands of homemaking; (3) the need to write; (4) the weight of failure. 6. ______
7. This piece is organized largely on a (1) point-by-point basis; (2) chronological plan; (3) cause-effect pattern; (4) simple-to-complex pattern. 7. ______
8. This selection is primarily to (1) entertain; (2) describe; (3) encourage; (4) explain. 8. ______
9. The author's attitude toward herself is best described as (1) modest; (2) critical; (3) disapproving; (4) accepting. 9. ______
10. You would infer that the author's eventual success came primarily from her (1) persistence; (2) desire; (3) background; (4) work habits. 10. ______

(10 points for each correct answer)

Reflective Comprehension ______

TOTAL READING COMPREHENSION SCORE ______

Vocabulary Check Questions

		without context I	with context II
1. **siblings**	(1) brothers or sisters; (2) grandparents; (3) twins; (4) cousins; (5) nephews.	1. ______	______
2. **amour-propre**	(1) self-help; (2) fascination; (3) antagonism; (4) deliberation; (5) self-esteem.	2. ______	______
3. **icons**	(1) truths; (2) proverbs; (3) images; (4) lamps; (5) gaps.	3. ______	______
4. **overtly**	(1) strongly; (2) openly; (3) busily; (4) glowingly; (5) virtuously.	4. ______	______
5. **renunciation**	(1) declaration; (2) compensation; (3) announcement; (4) giving up; (5) giving back.	5. ______	______

(10 points for each correct answer)

Word Comprehension without *contextual help (I)* ______

Word Comprehension with *contextual help (II)* ______

TOTAL WORD COMPREHENSION SCORE ______

SPELLING

Are common spelling errors putting you at a continual disadvantage? The following words taken from an exhaustive study by Polluck ("Spelling Report," *College English,* November, 1954) should provide an excellent check of your spelling ability. With the help of 599 college teachers of English in fifty-two colleges and universities, 31,375 misspellings were tabulated. The following words and word groups were misspelled 100 or more times.

Get someone to dictate the following words and sentences to you as you try your hand at spelling these troublemakers. If you miss 10 or more, you have reason to turn to the spelling section of your handbook or to the Pollock study for additional help. If you miss 20 or more, you will probably want the more detailed guidance of a book on improving your spelling.

receive
receiving

exist
existence
existent

occur
occurred
occurring
occurrence

definite
definitely
definition
define

separate
separation

believe
belief

occasion

lose
losing

write
writing
writer

description
describe

benefit
benefited
beneficial

precede

referring

success
succeed
succession

privilege

environment

perform
performance

similar

professor
profession

necessary
unnecessary

Those *two* were *too* tired *to* go along *too*.

They're getting *their* books to put *there*.

It's wagging *its* tail.

The problem of staff *personnel* is a very *personal* problem.

Then I walked farther *than* he did.

The school *principal* gave the *principal* speech on the subject, *Principles* of Education.

My choice is to *choose* the same thing that I *chose* before.

Improving Your Spelling

Make your own list of personal spelling troublemakers. Start with the words you missed from the Pollock listing but keep adding to it as your papers are marked and as you continue to deal with new words. Review the list periodically.

Words I Misspell

______________	______________	______________	______________
______________	______________	______________	______________
______________	______________	______________	______________
______________	______________	______________	______________
______________	______________	______________	______________
______________	______________	______________	______________
______________	______________	______________	______________
______________	______________	______________	______________
______________	______________	______________	______________
______________	______________	______________	______________
______________	______________	______________	______________
______________	______________	______________	______________

NAME ______________________ DATE ______________ READING RATE ______________ WPM

COMPREHENSION CHECK QUESTIONS

1. According to the selection, the purpose of a resumé is to get you (1) properly organized; (2) ready to compete effectively; (3) a job; (4) job interviews. 1. _______
2. You're told to (1) be a bit vague about what job you want; (2) summarize your job-related abilities; (3) use a specific job title; (4) stress willingness to learn. 2. _______
3. Be sure to (1) say references will be provided upon request; (2) list at least five references; (3) make no mention of references; (4) list both character and work references. 3. _______
4. Your work experience is spoken of as what part of your resumé? (1) core; (2) climax; (3) center; (4) heart. 4. _______
5. One employment manager says he rejects what percentage of the resumés purely because of appearance? (1) 10%; (2) 15%; (3) 20%; (4) 25%. 5. _______

Receptive Comprehension _______

6. This article is mainly about what aspect of a resumé? (1) how you should write it; (2) what help you can get from books and professional writers; (3) why you should prepare it; (4) what you should do with it when it's completed. 6. _______
7. Most emphasis should be on (1) neatness; (2) your education; (3) what you've done; (4) your attitude. 7. _______
8. The points are developed primarily by (1) citing authorities; (2) repetition; (3) use of analogies; (4) use of details. 8. _______
9. You would infer that the resumé format (1) varies widely; (2) is firmly fixed; (3) still leaves room for originality; (4) is dictated by job requirements. 9. _______
10. You would call this style (1) involved; (2) dramatic; (3) informal; (4) lively. 10. _______

(10 points for each correct answer)

Reflective Comprehension _______

TOTAL READING COMPREHENSION SCORE _______

VOCABULARY CHECK QUESTIONS

			without context I	with context II
1.	**innovations**	(1) starts; (2) remarks; (3) notions; (4) novelties; (5) rules.	1. _______	_______
2.	**format**	(1) custom; (2) strength; (3) make-up; (4) formula; (5) content.	2. _______	_______
3.	**affiliations**	(1) profiles; (2) problems; (3) feelings; (4) connections; (5) orders.	3. _______	_______
4.	**curtailed**	(1) lengthened; (2) raised; (3) rounded; (4) cleaned; (5) shortened.	4. _______	_______
5.	**stilted**	(1) original; (2) stiffly formal; (3) stuffed; (4) highly dramatic; (5) suppressed.	5. _______	_______

(10 points for each correct answer)

Word Comprehension without *contextual help (I)* _______

Word Comprehension with *contextual help (II)* _______

TOTAL WORD COMPREHENSION SCORE _______

EXERCISES

TRANSLATING FROM I-CENTERED TO YOU-CENTERED ENGLISH

For both resumés and letters of application you need a strong you-centered approach. Look at the following actual letter of application received by Miller Cafeteria; it is one of the worst in their files. You can probably learn more from examining it critically than from studying a well-written example.

Read it over. Then circle all the first-person pronouns. Next, try to rewrite the letter so as to establish a strong you-centered point of view. That means eliminating as many of the first-person references as possible or at least balancing any remaining *I's* with *you's*. Notice what a difference this makes.

Miller Cafeteria
Minneapolis, Minnesota

Dear Sir:

I am asking for a job that would give me experience in my field of Institutional Management. I could get the best experience possible in your cafeteria, due to its size and excellent management. Are there any vacancies for me at this time?

A position where I could start at the bottom and work up would be the most satisfactory to me. I would like all the opportunities available. My health is excellent, and I am single; therefore I could devote much of my time to the work given me.

May I come to your office next Tuesday morning at nine o'clock for an interview? If I have no reply, I shall come to your office at that time. Thanking you in advance, I am

Yours very truly,

TRANSLATING FROM TECHNICAL TO CONVERSATIONAL ENGLISH

In discussing resumés, the inevitable advice is, "Use correct, straightforward English—active verbs, short and simple words." Practice the use of such language by translating difficult material into standard English. Psychologists emphasize that rephrasing the words of a textbook or lecture into your own nontechnical language is an excellent way to aid learning. Try it as part of your regular study routine.

In the space below, enter a difficult yet fairly short passage from one of your textbooks. Then translate the passage into simple English:

Text version: ______________________

Your version: ______________________

NAME ______________________ DATE ______________ READING RATE ______________ WPM

COMPREHENSION CHECK QUESTIONS

1. Vonnegut mentions (1) free-lance writers; (2) newspaper reporters; (3) editors; (4) script writers. 1. _______

2. Vonnegut suggests writing (1) a love letter; (2) a term paper; (3) a letter to the editor; (4) a movie review. 2. _______

3. Vonnegut grew up in (1) Chicago; (2) New York; (3) Detroit; (4) Indianapolis. 3. _______

4. There was an allusion to (1) Churchill; (2) Monet; (3) Picasso; (4) Mark Antony. 4. _______

5. The author spoke highly of (1) Robert Browning; (2) E. B. White; (3) Macmillan; (4) Wordsworth. 5. _______

Receptive Comprehension _______

6. The main idea is to get you to write (1) simply; (2) briefly; (3) effectively; (4) originally. 6. _______

7. Mention of Shakespeare and Joyce was to stress the importance of (1) clarity; (2) brevity; (3) simplicity; (4) originality. 7. _______

8. The article is organized (1) on a step-by-step procedure; (2) on a point-by-point basis; (3) on a simple-to-complex pattern; (4) on a cause-to-effect basis. 8. _______

9. The primary purpose is to (1) explain; (2) make clear; (3) convince; (4) describe. 9. _______

10. You would infer that the most important concern is to write about something you (1) think is novel; (2) find interesting; (3) know about; (4) care about. 10. _______

(10 points for each correct answer)

Reflective Comprehension _______

TOTAL READING COMPREHENSION SCORE _______

VOCABULARY CHECK QUESTIONS

		without context I	with context II
1. egomaniac	(1) overly conceited person; (2) selfish person; (3) insane person; (4) selfless person; (5) overly ambitious person.	1. _______	_______
2. chowderhead	(1) ignoramus; (2) good-for-nothing; (3) overeater; (4) thinker; (5) softy.	2. _______	_______
3. profound	(1) profitable; (2) farfetched; (3) satisfying; (4) productive; (5) learned.	3. _______	_______
4. piquant	(1) familiar; (2) tearful; (3) exciting; (4) quaint; (5) light.	4. _______	_______
5. vehemently	(1) cautiously; (2) passionately; (3) clearly; (4) freely; (5) thoughtfully.	5. _______	_______

(10 points for each correct answer)

Word Comprehension without *contextual help (I)* _______

Word Comprehension with *contextual help (II)* _______

TOTAL WORD COMPREHENSION SCORE _______

EXERCISES

SENTENCE VARIETY

The following sentences all follow a deadly, unvarying subject-verb pattern. By rearranging the words in each sentence and making a few slight changes in wording, revise the following passage to get desirable variety of sentence pattern and form. Compare with the original below when you finish.

> Most educated people are, from time to time, called upon to act as writers. They might not think of themselves as such. They dash off a personal note. They dictate a memo. They are writers. They are practicing a difficult and demanding craft. They are facing its inborn challenge: to find the right words and put them in the right order. The thoughts they represent can then be understood.

CONNECTING IDEAS

No writer wants his reader to slip out of his article between sentences or paragraphs. Sentences must be closely connected so that the reader will pass easily from one to the next without losing continuity.

The skillful writer or speaker will see to it that at least one word in each sentence connects back to the preceding sentence or points ahead to the next one. Four common categories of words are used for this purpose:

1. Connecting words and phrases such as *and, in contrast, but,* and *however*, which help the reader follow the thought.
2. Pronouns that refer back to a word in the preceding sentence.
3. Repetition of words or ideas.
4. Parallel structure—to connect sentences and ideas.

In the following paragraph, circle all words and phrases that serve a connective function. Classify each according to the four categories listed above.

Paragraph	*Classification*
In the working world, bad writing is not only bad manners, it is bad business. The victim of an incomprehensible letter will at best be annoyed and at worst decide that people who can't say what they mean aren't worth doing business with. Write a sloppy letter, and it might rebound on you when the recipient calls for clarification. Where one carefully worded letter would have sufficed, you might have to write two or more.	

Original paragraph: From time to time most educated people are called upon to act as writers. They might not think of themselves as such as they dash off a personal note or dictate a memo, but that is what they are. They are practising a difficult and demanding craft, and facing its inborn challenge. This is to find the right words and to put them in the right order so that the thoughts they represent can be understood.

NAME ____________ DATE ____________ READING RATE ____________ WPM

COMPREHENSION CHECK QUESTIONS

1. Which book did Franklin have? (1) *Robinson Crusoe;* (2) *Gulliver's Travels;* (3) *Pilgrim's Progress;* (4) *Swiss Family Robinson.* 1. ______
2. His father's library contained mostly (1) religious books; (2) literary works; (3) novels; (4) practical volumes. 2. ______
3. Who was said to have discouraged Franklin from his verse-making? (1) his brother; (2) his friend; (3) his readers; (4) his father. 3. ______
4. Franklin attempted to imitate the prose found in (1) Plutarch's *Lives;* (2) Defoe's *Essays;* (3) Stevenson's *Essays;* (4) the *Spectator.* 4. ______
5. In comparing his version with the original, Franklin said he discovered (1) punctuation difficulties; (2) a vocabulary deficiency; (3) spelling problems; (4) sentence problems. 5. ______

Receptive Comprehension ______

6. This selection is chiefly to (1) explain Franklin's love of books; (2) tell why he decided to write prose, not poetry; (3) explain why he wanted to learn to write; (4) tell about the procedure he adapted to improve his writing. 6. ______
7. You would conclude that the chief reason for Franklin's turning away from writing poetry was (1) its difficulty; (2) its poor reception; (3) its poor financial return; (4) its lack of prestige. 7. ______
8. As a self-critic, Franklin was apparently (1) fairly accurate; (2) overly critical; (3) fairly generous; (4) quite unrealistic. 8. ______
9. The part about John Collins, another bookish boy, was mainly to indicate (1) how Franklin got interested in writing; (2) why one should avoid argumentation; (3) the value of arguing; (4) the influence of reading certain books. 9. ______
10. The primary purpose of the article is to (1) teach; (2) describe; (3) moralize; (4) evaluate. 10. ______

(10 points for each correct answer)

Reflective Comprehension ______

TOTAL READING COMPREHENSION SCORE ______

VOCABULARY CHECK QUESTIONS

			without context I	with context II
1.	**ingenious**	(1) naive; (2) frank; (3) mechanical; (4) trusting; (5) clever.	1. ______	______
2.	**confuting**	(1) predicting; (2) storing; (3) denying; (4) joining; (5) confounding.	2. ______	______
3.	**disputatious**	(1) argumentative; (2) displeasing; (3) productive; (4) stingy; (5) concerned.	3. ______	______
4.	**enmities**	(1) preliminaries; (2) foes; (3) laxatives; (4) antagonisms; (5) encouragements.	4. ______	______
5.	**amended**	(1) complained; (2) charged; (3) corrected; (4) added; (5) suggested.	5. ______	______

(10 points for each correct answer)

Word Comprehension without *contextual help (I)* ______

Word Comprehension with *contextual help (II)* ______

TOTAL WORD COMPREHENSION SCORE ______

EXERCISES

SUBJECTS FOR WRITING

Select from the following subjects five on which you have a strong opinion. Then write a sentence about each in which you express that opinion, either positively or negatively. (*Example:* All people who use hard drugs should be imprisoned for a minimum of five years.)

Drugs
Welfare programs
Pornography
Mercy killing
Sex education in the public schools
Smoking
Violence on television
Freeways
Abortion
Homosexuality

Now write a paragraph on each of the five subjects you chose in which you defend the *opposite* opinion from the one expressed in your sentence. Try to clear your mind of all prejudices and to present the case convincingly and objectively.

REPRODUCING THE AUTHOR'S ORIGINAL OUTLINE

Consider the effectiveness of the prose in the following brief passage from Frederick Jackson Turner's *The Frontier in American History:*

> American democracy was born of no theorist's dream. It was not carried in the *Susan Constant* to Virginia, nor in the *Mayflower* to Plymouth. It came stark and strong and full of life out of the American forest, and it gained new strength each time it touched a new frontier.

Now jot down in as few words as possible the basic idea in each sentence. (*Example:* Democracy not of theoretical origin.) Put your notes aside for a few days. When you return to them, try writing the passage in complete sentences without looking at the original. Compare your version to Turner's. In what ways is your version weaker than, or superior to his?

Follow the same procedure with any other piece of writing you admire.

AUTHOR'S ORIGINAL OUTLINE FOR "ORGANIZATION—YOUR READING SATELLITE"

I. The role of organization
II. Reading is the reverse of writing
III. How is organization revealed?
    A. Through special devices
        1. Typographical devices
            a. Capitals
            b. Bold-face type
            c. Italics
        2. Rhetorical devices
            a. Repetition
            b. Parallelism
            c. Balance
        3. Verbal devices
            a. To mark transitions
            b. To mark methods of development
            c. To mark outline form
    B. Through paragraph structure
        1. Topic sentences
        2. Supporting details
IV. What does organization contribute?
    A. Sharpened awareness
        1. Of main idea or thesis
        2. Of interrelationships
    B. Improved ability
        1. To understand
        2. To remember
V. Summary of purpose or role of organization

(Compare with your own version on page 358.)

NAME ______________________ DATE ______________ READING RATE ______________ WPM

COMPREHENSION CHECK QUESTIONS

1. Joan Didion says she stole her title from (1) Isaac Asimov; (2) George Orwell; (3) P. D. James; (4) Jean M. Auel. 1. ______
2. To graduate she needed a course in (1) Wordsworth; (2) Shakespeare; (3) John Donne; (4) Milton. 2. ______
3. She mentions (1) schizophrenia; (2) agoraphobia; (3) mental telepathy; (4) depression. 3. ______
4. One of her books was titled (1) *A Book of Common Prayer;* (2) *The Eternal Airport;* (3) *Play It Soft;* (4) *Bienvenue.* 4. ______
5. One character ordered (1) gin and tonic; (2) hot chocolate; (3) tea; (4) coffee. 5. ______

Receptive Comprehension ______

6. The main focus is on (1) getting ideas; (2) composing good sentences; (3) the act of writing; (4) getting vivid pictures to write about. 6. ______
7. What does Didion seem best at? (1) getting ideas; (2) seeing the big picture; (3) noting sensory impressions; (4) noting symbolism. 7. ______
8. Her style is best described as (1) highly imaginative; (2) lively; (3) original; (4) informal. 8. ______
9. What most influences her sentence forms? (1) grammar; (2) the picture; (3) the characters; (4) clarity. 9. ______
10. According to Didion, what is the chief reason to write? (1) because you want to; (2) because you have to; (3) to find yourself; (4) to stimulate the creative act.. 10. ______

(10 points for each correct answer)

Reflective Comprehension ______

TOTAL READING COMPREHENSION SCORE ______

VOCABULARY CHECK QUESTIONS

			without context I	with context II
1.	**ellipses**	(1) remedies; (2) omissions; (3) ledges; (4) glimpses; (5) elements.	1. ______	______
2.	**evasions**	(1) means; (2) ends; (3) grants; (4) procedures; (5) avoidances.	2. ______	______
3.	**veered**	(1) rushed; (2) stopped; (3) accepted; (4) fell; (5) shifted.	3. ______	______
4.	**inexorably**	(1) instantly; (2) surely; (3) inevitably; (4) finally; (5) inexcusably.	4. ______	______
5.	**peripheral**	(1) exterior; (2) central; (3) substantial; (4) perfect; (5) new.	5. ______	______

(10 points for each correct answer)

Word Comprehension without *contextual help (I)* ______

Word Comprehension with *contextual help (II)* ______

TOTAL WORD COMPREHENSION SCORE ______

EXERCISES

MANAGING DEGREES OF INFORMALITY

One important difference between formal and informal writing is the personal element. Term papers and reports are generally written in an impersonal style without any personal pronouns. Popular articles, on the other hand, are done in a personal style, since reader interest is an important consideration. For example, in formal writing, "experiments are performed," "the mixture is weighed," and "students are directed." In informal writing, "He performed the experiment," "I weighted the mixture," and "She directed the students."

A student should develop skill in both formal and informal expression, using an impersonal or personal style when the situation demands. Translate the following passage into informal English by making it more personal. Use the first-person point of view. When you have finished the translation, check the original passage (paragraph 4) and compare the two versions.

> In short it was an attempt to think. It was a failure. Attention was turned back inexorably to the specific, to the tangible, to what was generally considered by everyone known then and for that matter known since as the peripheral. The Hegelian dialectic was contemplated and contemplation was turned instead on a flowering pear tree outside the window and on the particular way the petals fell on the floor. Reading linguistic theory was attempted and it was wondered instead if the lights were on in the bevatron up the hill. When it was said that it was wondered if the lights were on in the bevatron, it might be immediately suspected if ideas were being dealt with at all that the bevatron was being registered as a political symbol.

____

____

____

____

____

____

____

____

____

____

NAME ______________________ DATE ______________ READING RATE ______________ WPM

Comprehension Check Questions

1. Carnegie says that he learned his secret of easy public speaking (1) from a book; (2) in college; (3) in a public speaking course; (4) from experience. 1. _______

2. Gay Kellogg was from (1) New Jersey; (2) New York; (3) New Concord; (4) New Haven. 2. _______

3. The article contains (1) three rules; (2) five rules; (3) seven rules; (4) ten rules. 3. _______

4. The late Ida Tarbell was spoken of as a distinguished (1) novelist; (2) biographer; (3) journalist; (4) lecturer. 4. _______

5. The struggling young composer whom Gershwin met was working for (1) \$35 a week; (2) \$45 a week; (3) \$55 a week; (4) \$65 a week. 5. _______

Receptive Comprehension _______

6. The purpose of this article is to (1) make us more effective speakers; (2) suggest how to organized and deliver an effective speech; (3) reveal the secret of effective public speaking; (4) explain where to find appropriate speech subjects. 6. _______

7. The story about Ida Tarbell was used to illustrate the importance of (1) using illustrations; (2) rehearsing a speech; (3) knowing more about a subject than you need; (4) being yourself instead of imitating someone else. 7. _______

8. The story about Gay Kellogg was used to illustrate the importance of (1) writing out the speech; (2) speaking from experience; (3) being yourself; (4) using illustrations. 8. _______

9. The author implies that the difference between written and spoken English is (1) negligible; (2) important; (3) largely in subject matter; (4) largely in slanting for a specific audience. 9. _______

10. The article suggests that if you are frightened when you make a speech, (1) you are naturally shy; (2) you have not had enough speaking experience; (3) you have not prepared carefully enough; (4) you have not chosen a subject of real interest to yourself. 10. _______

(10 points for each correct answer)

Reflective Comprehension _______

TOTAL READING COMPREHENSION SCORE _______

Vocabulary Check Questions

			without context I	with context II
1.	**craved**	(1) wished; (2) unbalanced; (3) moved slowly; (4) desired intensely; (5) drugged.	1. _______	_______
2.	**taut**	(1) tense; (2) ridiculed; (3) awkward; (4) very tall; (5) active.	2. _______	_______
3.	**elicited**	(1) explained; (2) escaped; (3) eliminated; (4) hurried; (5) drew forth.	3. _______	_______
4.	**irresistibly**	(1) regularly; (2) not compatible; (3) compellingly; (4) irrelevantly; (5) indecisively.	4. _______	_______
5.	**sage**	(1) useful; (2) wise; (3) tangy; (4) bitter; (5) crafty.	5. _______	_______

(10 points for each correct answer)

Word Comprehension without *contextual help (I)* _______

Word Comprehension with *contextual help (II)* _______

TOTAL WORD COMPREHENSION SCORE _______

Exercises

Remembering What You Hear or Read

This selection listed seven rules to help in preparing a speech. What are they? How many can you remember without looking back at the selection? List all you can think of in the spaces below.

1. ______________________________
2. ______________________________
3. ______________________________
4. ______________________________
5. ______________________________
6. ______________________________
7. ______________________________

Unless you are one in a million, you did not list all seven with perfect accuracy. As a reader, what can you do to remember what you hear or read more effectively? For one thing, you can devise a learning or remembering aid. For example, when daylight savings time starts in the spring, which way do you set your watch—ahead or back? Most people start a long process of reasoning that will eventually provide an answer. Others will use a mnemonic device or memory aid. Just think "Spring ahead, fall back" and you will have little more trouble with remembering.

Can you name the five Great Lakes? If you have trouble thinking of them, try another type of mnemonic device. Just think of the word HOMES. It will help you remember Huron, Ontario, Michigan, Erie, and Superior.

Take still another type of mnemonic device, one used often by doctors and medical students. How do they remember the twelve cranial nerves? A sentence helps; the key is the first letter in each word. Here is the sentence: "On old Olympus' towering top, a fat-assed German viewed a hop." How else could one remember "olfactory, optic, oculomotor, trochlear, trigeminal, abducens, facial, acoustic, glossopharyngeal, vagus, accessory, hypoglossal!"

Now, going back to the seven rules, try to work out-some mnemonic device. Can you select a single letter to remind you of each—letters that would combine to make one seven-letter word or two shorter words? Write the word or words here and explain:

If that doesn't work out easily, try a seven-word sentence. Each word (or the first letter of each word) help you recall one of the seven points or rules. Write the sentence here:

Actually your efforts to manufacture a mnemonic device will do wonders in helping you remember, whether you come up with a device or not. Compare notes with other students to see what they devised.

Substituting Narration for Exposition

You may explain something by relying almost entirely on rather pure expository techniques, or you may lean very heavily on narration to make your explanation both interesting and clear. Take some of the following topic ideas and explain them orally or in writing by using a narrative form:

1. Use illustrations to make your ideas interesting and clear.
2. Narration and exposition are different in several important respects.
3. Efficient reading is extremely important for the student (or business executive, or professional).
4. Your voice is your fortune.
5. Background is important.

NAME ______________________ DATE ______________ READING RATE ______________ WPM

Comprehension Check Questions

1. To figure the number of spoken words, a rate of how many words a minute is used? (1) 100 wpm; (2) 115 wpm; (3) 135 wpm; (4) 150 wpm. 1. _______
2. It is said that the urge to talk (1) is stronger in women; (2) is stronger in men; (3) is about equally strong in both men and women; (4) varies more with age than with sex. 2. _______
3. Basically we were said to talk for (1) one reason only; (2) two reasons; (3) three reasons; (4) four reasons. 3. _______
4. One illustration centered on a (1) broken window; (2) stalled car; (3) sunburnt back; (4) cup of coffee. 4. _______
5. The author says (1) man is a political animal; (2) speak low when you speak love; (3) true self-love and social action are the same; (4) no man is an island. 5. _______

Receptive Comprehension _______

6. The article deals mainly with (1) our speed of speech; (2) how much we speak; (3) speech as interaction; (4) why we speak. 6. _______
7. In the last part of the article the attention is focused primarily on (1) individual needs; (2) business needs; (3) social needs; (4) advertising needs. 7. _______
8. The reference to a caveman was to develop the idea of (1) inter-thinking; (2) ethics; (3) persuasion; (4) words as tools. 8. _______
9. You would call this article primarily (1) informative; (2) persuasive; (3) descriptive; (4) narrative. 9. _______
10. You would infer that in dictatorships speech (1) is of uncertain importance; (2) is equally important; (3) is more important; (4) is less important. 10. _______

(10 points for each correct answer)

Reflective Comprehension _______

TOTAL READING COMPREHENSION SCORE _______

Vocabulary Check Questions

			without context I	with context II
1.	**probe**	(1) push; (2) solve; (3) conduct; (4) question; (5) explore.	1. _______	_______
2.	**facets**	(1) causes; (2) groups; (3) aspects; (4) truths; (5) skills.	2. _______	_______
3.	**inanities**	(1) foolish remarks; (2) beginnings; (3) inactions; (4) clever sayings; (5) utterances.	3. _______	_______
4.	**enlivened**	(1) taught; (2) stimulated; (3) increased; (4) enjoyed; (5) dignified.	4. _______	_______
5.	**merge**	(1) blend; (2) manage; (3) change; (4) send; (5) break.	5. _______	_______

(10 points for each correct answer)

Word Comprehension without *contextual help (I)* _______

Word Comprehension with *contextual help (II)* _______

TOTAL WORD COMPREHENSION SCORE _______

EXERCISES

NOTING THE WRITER'S PLAN

The skilled reader is one who is able to see the writer's organization as he reads an article. Develop added skill by using the outline pattern below. Select the two or three words that most clearly mark the various divisions and subdivisions found in this article.

I. ______________________________

   A. To______________________

   B. To______________________

   C. To______________________

II. ______________________________

   A. To______________________

   B. To______________________

GENERATING ADDED INTEREST

Interest is a key factor in comprehension. Lack of interest in any subject means a sharp drop in comprehension. An important way to cultivate and broaden interest is to turn conversation into that subject-matter area. To see how this works, make an informal survey of the next five or six individuals you talk with. Get answers to these four questions, so that you can make a general summary of your findings. Ask them:

1. How many words a day they think they speak.
2. What they think their speaking rate is in words per minute.
3. Who talks most—men or women.
4. What they consider to be the chief role of speech.

Bring your data together into a brief report, for either oral or written presentation. Notice how this activity tended to heighten your interest in speech. Remember that the same procedure can build interest in other areas as well.

NAME ______________________ DATE ______________ READING RATE ______________ WPM

COMPREHENSION CHECK QUESTIONS

1. At first Twain used (1) 3 × 5 cards; (2) a full page of notes; (3) typed abbreviations; (4) calling-card-size notes. 1. _______

2. For a typical evening's lecture, Twain would memorize how many key sentence beginnings? (1) eleven; (2) eight; (3) five; (4) three. 2. _______

3. The article mentions (1) Reno; (2) Salt Lake; (3) Santa Fe; (4) Carson City. 3. _______

4. The nervous doctor lived in (1) Dubuque; (2) San Francisco; (3) Des Moines; (4) Moline. 4. _______

5. You're told to include figures in the pictures (1) as captions; (2) coming out of people's mouths; (3) resting on a person's hand; (4) alongside the picture. 5. _______

Receptive Comprehension _______

6. This article is mainly about (1) making an outline; (2) identifying the central points; (3) speaking naturally; (4) keeping sequence in mind. 6. _______

7. It is primarily (1) narration; (2) exposition; (3) description; (4) persuasion. 7. _______

8. The organization is essentially (1) cause-effect; (2) problem-solution; (3) simple-to-complex; (4) by analysis. 8. _______

9. What is the tone of this essay? (1) enthusiastic; (2) realistic; (3) critical; (4) serious. 9. _______

10. The purpose of the opening bit about "strategy" is chiefly to (1) pose the problem; (2) provide humor; (3) introduce the subject; (4) arouse interest. 10. _______

(10 points for each correct answer)

Reflective Comprehension _______

TOTAL READING COMPREHENSION SCORE _______

VOCABULARY CHECK QUESTIONS

		without context I	with context II
1. dilemma	(1) ruin; (2) limit; (3) decision; (4) predicament; (5) choice.	1. _______	_______
2. spontaneous	(1) self-acting; (2) sponsored; (3) planned; (4) showy; (5) stimulating.	2. _______	_______
3. alleged	(1) calmed; (2) walked; (3) supported; (4) declared; (5) reduced.	3. _______	_______
4. pathetic	(1) pitiful; (2) paternal; (3) diseased; (4) sudden; (5) pastoral.	4. _______	_______
5. lurking	(1) startling; (2) harmful; (3) lying in wait; (4) glaring sternly; (5) luring.	5. _______	_______

(10 points for each correct answer)

Word Comprehension without *contextual help (I)* _______

Word Comprehension with *contextual help (II)* _______

TOTAL WORD COMPREHENSION SCORE _______

Exercises

Substituting Narration for Persuasion or Exposition

Macaulay called narration "the mighty engine of argument." The next time you need to explain something or persuade someone of something, try using an anecdote or story to make your point.

It is possible, for example, to explain that Coleridge was famous as a talker by mentioning that his London landlord offered him free quarters if he would stay on and talk, or by mentioning details of his success as a lecturer. The same point could also be made by a story. Coleridge once found Lamb hastening along a busy street and, drawing him into a doorway by a button, closed his eyes as was his habit, and started talking. Lamb, who was in a great hurry, cut off the button and left him. Hours later, so the story goes, Lamb found him in the same spot, holding the button and talking. True or not, the story serves well to remind us that Coleridge was a talker.

Taking any of the following ideas (or others that may be suggested), make a point through use of a story you either know or invent for the purpose:

Vocabulary bring success.	Your voice is your fortune.
Haste makes waste.	Knowledge is power.
Practice makes perfect.	Reading pays off.

Preparing a Story Speech

Using the suggestions in this selection as a basis of criticism, prepare a story that would be appropriate whenever you happen to be called upon unexpectedly to "say a few words." Be prepared to tell it before the class at any time for their critical evaluation. Be sure to provide a transition from situation to story and another transition that will get you gracefully back into your seat. Here is a sample. Find or make up another to serve the same purpose.

> Friends, the last time anyone called upon me to make a speech, a man stopped afterward, gravely shook hands, then said, "Whoever told you you could speak?"
>
> I replied a bit sharply, "I'll have you know I've spent $8,000 in speech lessons."
>
> He thought for a minute, then said, "I'd like you to meet my brother."
>
> "Why? Is he a speech teacher?"
>
> "No. He's a lawyer. He'll get your money back for you."
>
> I think you can see now why I make no more speeches.

That gets you gracefully back to your seat, no matter what the situation—and makes you appear to be in command of yourself. Now find another.

If you have a hard time creating such a story, go to the library to find a book of stories or anecdotes. List the titles of two such books below.

1. ______________________________

2. ______________________________

Review one book for the class, telling the funniest story you found. Notice how the stories are grouped and what aids are provided for finding an appropriate one for a given situation.

NAME ______________________ DATE ______________ READING RATE ______________ WPM

Comprehension Check Questions

1. There is specific mention of (1) trick question; (2) crisis questions; (3) a red flag; (4) a shoot-from-the-hip answers. 1. _______
2. The man applying for the comptroller job said his greatest weakness was (1) lack of strong interest; (2) dislike of computers; (3) hatred of detail; (4) lack of educational training. 2. _______
3. The author once recommended someone (1) confined to a wheelchair; (2) with a wooden leg; (3) with one arm; (4) who stuttered. 3. _______
4. The article discusses (1) pensions; (2) fringe benefits; (3) moving expenses; (4) health plans. 4. _______
5. One of the 11 questions focuses on (1) voice; (2) weight; (3) smoking; (4) age. 5. _______

Receptive Comprehension _______

6. The main focus is on (1) preparation; (2) company background; (3) personality; (4) relaxation. 6. _______
7. For this advice, the author relies chiefly on (1) his own personal experience; (2) business clients; (3) candidate feedback; (4) all the preceding sources about equally. 7. _______
8. The author's approach is best described as (1) positive; (2) objective; (3) casual; (4) vague. 8. _______
9. The coverage is (1) general; (2) abstract; (3) comprehensive; (4) limited. 9. _______
10. The primary intent is to (1) warn; (2) convince; (3) inform; (4) illustrate. 10. _______

(10 points for each correct answer)

Reflective Comprehension _______

TOTAL READING COMPREHENSION SCORE _______

Vocabulary Check Questions

		without context I	with context II
1. **empathy**	(1) superiority in rank; (2) lack; (3) force; (4) sharing of feelings; (5) gain.	1. _______	_______
2. **candor**	(1) sweetness; (2) frankness; (3) thrift; (4) song; (5) container.	2. _______	_______
3. **trepidation**	(1) tribute; (2) transom; (3) weakness; (4) concern; (5) fright.	3. _______	_______
4. **dissertation**	(1) lengthy discourse; (2) distribution; (3) agreement; (4) change; (5) distraction.	4. _______	_______
5. **pending**	(1) referring; (2) taking part in; (3) awaiting; (4) writing; (5) dividing into parts.	5. _______	_______

(10 points for each correct answer)

Word Comprehension without *contextual help (I)* _______

Word Comprehension with *contextual help (II)* _______

TOTAL WORD COMPREHENSION SCORE _______

Exercises

Checking Your Voice

Make copies of the appropriate rating scale provided below. Have several people who know you well rate you on all six points—points specifically mentioned in the article.

For Men

	Quite pronounced	More than average	Average	Less than average	Not noticeable
1. Mumbling	______	______	______	______	______
2. Rasping	______	______	______	______	______
3. Sullenness	______	______	______	______	______
4. Tonal monotony	______	______	______	______	______
5. Overloud	______	______	______	______	______
6. Stilted accent	______	______	______	______	______

For Women

	Quite pronounced	More than average	Average	Less than average	Not noticeable
1. Whining	______	______	______	______	______
2. Shrillness	______	______	______	______	______
3. Nasal tones	______	______	______	______	______
4. Raucous and strident	______	______	______	______	______
5. Baby talk	______	______	______	______	______
6. Affected accents	______	______	______	______	______

Self-Analysis

Read aloud the first seven or eight paragraphs of this selection, using a cassette recorder to record your voice. Play it back several times, and make a personal evaluation of yourself. Ask others in your family to do the same, noting both good and bad characteristics. Then plan a program of improvement.

Surveying Objectionable Habits

You may wish to check further on those speech habits or defects that most irritate listeners. To do so, make an informal survey of students or faculty to see what they consider the six most objectionable speech characteristics. Is there agreement with those specifically mentioned above?

NAME ______________________ DATE ______________ READING RATE ______________ WPM

COMPREHENSION CHECK QUESTIONS

1. The opening episode took place in (1) 1950; (2) 1954; (3) 1956; (4) 1958. 1. ______
2. How long was Berman's dramatic appearance? (1) one minute; (2) two minutes; (3) four minutes; (4) time not mentioned. 2. ______
3. Berman appealed to the noncoms by saying he wanted to (1) win his case; (2) save the Marine Corps; (3) save the sergeant; (4) save the noncoms. 3. ______
4. One rule is called the (1) Iron Fist Rule; (2) All Out Rule; (3) Last Resort Rule; (4) Last Chance Rule. 4. ______
5. How many rules are given? (1) five; (2) six; (3) seven; (4) eight. 5. ______

Receptive Comprehension ______

6. The main idea is to show the importance of (1) a dramatic approach; (2) taking risks; (3) knowing when to stop; (4) following the lessons of experience. 6. ______
7. Major emphasis is on (1) who; (2) why; (3) how; (4) when. 7. ______
8. The everyday matter of a son asking Dad for the car was introduced to (1) illustrate how the rules work; (2) show the importance of worthy emotional reasons; (3) show how not to ask; (4) illustrate common parental prejudices. 8. ______
9. The rules came largely from (1) the author's experience; (2) Zuke Berman's actions; (3) the opinions of experts; (4) experimental findings. 9. ______
10. What word best describes this article? (1) factual; (2) stimulating; (3) inspirational; (4) practical. 10. ______

(10 points for each correct answer)

Reflective Comprehension ______
TOTAL READING COMPREHENSION SCORE ______

VOCABULARY CHECK QUESTIONS

			without context I	with context II
1.	**palpable**	(1) aroused; (2) evident; (3) gone; (4) painful; (5) shared.	1. ______	______
2.	**embodiment**	(1) preparation; (2) ending; (3) suggestion; (4) encouragement; (5) manifestation.	2. ______	______
3.	**alleviate**	(1) sustain; (2) raise; (3) lessen; (4) verbalize; (5) introduce.	3. ______	______
4.	**deferential**	(1) distant; (2) submissive; (3) aware; (4) aggressive; (5) influential.	4. ______	______
5.	**belabor**	(1) dwell upon; (2) prepare; (3) explain; (4) persuade; (5) begin.	5. ______	______

(10 points for each correct answer)

Word Comprehension without *contextual help (I)* ______
Word Comprehension with *contextual help (II)* ______
TOTAL WORD COMPREHENSION SCORE ______

HOW TO PRONOUNCE A WORD

Norman Lewis

No matter how carefully you try to conceal certain facts about yourself, your pronunciation gives you away. Only under the most unusual circumstances could an error cost you your job, your friends or your social standing, as some speech missionaries absurdly proclaim. But under ordinary circumstances an expert can draw from your pronunciation a number of interesting conclusions about your geographical background, your education, your cultural environment, and your personality.

For instance, if you say something approaching *ahl* for all or *pak* for park, you are advertising that you grew up in or around Boston. If you call the city *Shi-kaw-go*, you are probably a native of the city, while if you say *Shi-kah-go*, you are more likely from the East.

Greezy for greasy may indicate that you have Southern or Western speech habits; a sharp *r* in *park* will similarly identify you with the Western part of the country, and the complete omission of the *r* in the same word will indicate your background as the Eastern seaboard. Explode your *t's (wett, hurtt)* or click your *ng's (singg ga songg, Longg gIsland)* and you almost reveal the street on which you live in the Bronx; or pronounce the three words *Mary, marry, merry*, and you name the section of the country in which you formed your linguistic habits—the West if you say these words almost identically, the East if the words are distinctly different in sound.

Your pronunciation of certain other words, for example *either, aunt, athletic, film, grimace, comparable*, and *verbatim*, will reveal to the experienced ear more secrets than you may realize. By taking a few simple tests, we can arrive at a fairly accurate analysis of the impression your speech habits give to the world.

DO YOU USE ILLITERATE FORMS?

Check in each case, in the test below, the form of the word which you habitually and naturally use. As this is not a test of knowledge but of speech patterns, you should be guided solely by what you believe you say, not by what you think is correct.

In the test, the first choice in each case is the illiterate form, the second choice the accepted or educated pronunciation. If you checked form *(b)* right down the line, or did not wander from this straight path more than a couple of times, you may feel assured your speech bears no stigma of illiteracy. If, however, you made several unfortunate choices, consider this a danger signal. As a further check on pronunciation habits, ask yourself whether you are guilty of saying *axed* for asked, *myoo-ni-SIP-'l* for municipal, *lyeberry* for library, *fasset* for faucet, *rassle* for wrestle, *drownd-ded* for drowned, or *lenth* and *strenth* for length and strength.

1.	*aviator*	(a) AVV-ee-ay-ter	(b) AY-vee-ay-ter
2.	*bronchial*	(a) BRON-ikle	(b) BRON-kee-al
3.	*radiator*	(a) RADD-ee-ay-ter	(b) RAY-dee-ay-ter
4.	*vanilla*	(a) vi-NELL-a	(b) va-NILL-a
5.	*modern*	(a) MOD-ren or MAR-den	(b) MOD-urn
6.	*February*	(a) FEB-yoo-ar-y	(b) FEB-roo-ar-y
7.	*mischievous*	(a) mis-CHEE-vee-us	(b) MISS-chi-vus
8.	*attacked*	(a) at-TACK-ted	(b) at-TACKT
9.	*athletic*	(a) ath-a-LET-ic	(b) ath-LET-ic
10.	*elm, film*	(a) ellum, fillum	(b) elm, film
11.	*genuine*	(a) JEN-yoo-wyne	(b) JEN-yoo-in
12.	*zoology*	(a) zoo-OL-o-gy	(b) zoe-OL-o-gy
13.	*comparable*	(a) com-PAR-able	(b) COM-par-able
14.	*bouquet*	(a) boe-KAY	(b) boo-KAY
15.	*human*	(a) YOO-man	(b) HYOO-man
16.	*robust*	(a) ROE-bust	(b) ro-BUST
17.	*garage*	(a) ga-RAHDJ	(b) ga-RAHZH
18.	*clandestine*	(a) CLAN-de-styne	(b) clan-DESS-tin
19.	*preferable*	(a) pre-FER-able	(b) PREF-er-able
20.	*plebeian*	(a) PLEE-bee-an	(b) ple-BEE-an

(continue on page 382)

NAME ____________ DATE ____________ READING RATE ____________ WPM

COMPREHENSION CHECK QUESTIONS

1. A typical after-dinner audience is said to number (1) 25; (2) 35; (3) 45; (4) 55. 1. ______

2. Conwell's "Acres of Diamonds" speech was largely (1) personal opinion; (2) stories; (3) facts; (4) technical information. 2. ______

3. The simple outline mentioned starts with (1) a preface; (2) a preview; (3) an "icebreaker"; (4) a salutation. 3. ______

4. The "haymaker" belongs in (1) the conclusion; (2) the body; (3) the introduction; (4) any relevant part of the speech. 4. ______

5. Specific mention was made of (1) Toscanini; (2) Fiedler; (3) Peter Nero; (4) John Williams. 5. ______

Receptive Comprehension ______

6. Chief focus is on the (1) when; (2) where; (3) why; (4) how. 6. ______

7. The prime purpose is to (1) entertain; (2) motivate; (3) inspire; (4) instruct. 7. ______

8. The selection is organized (1) on a problem-solution basis; (2) on a cause-effect basis; (3) on a point-by-point basis; (4) on a general-to-specific basis. 8. ______

9. The author develops his ideas largely through (1) illustrative examples; (2) experimental findings; (3) comparisons; (4) repetition. 9. ______

10. From the discussion of "conversationality" you would infer what to deserve most attention? (1) voice quality; (2) body action; (3) eye contact; (4) facial expression. 10. ______

(10 points for each correct answer)

Reflective Comprehension ______

TOTAL READING COMPREHENSION SCORE ______

VOCABULARY CHECK QUESTIONS

			without context I	with context II
1.	**extensively**	(1) gradually; (2) exclusively; (3) clearly; (4) closely; (5) broadly.	1. ______	______
2.	**relevance**	(1) fitness; (2) loudness; (3) clarity; (4) honesty; (5) plainness.	2. ______	______
3.	**mediocre**	(1) unclear; (2) strong; (3) inferior; (4) favorable; (5) lengthy.	3. ______	______
4.	**enumerate**	(1) criticize; (2) name; (3) enter; (4) suggest; (5) prepare.	4. ______	______
5.	**faux pas**	(1) report; (2) blunder; (3) lie; (4) exclamation; (5) favor.	5. ______	______

(10 points for each correct answer)

Word Comprehension without *contextual help (I)* ______

Word Comprehension with *contextual help (II)* ______

TOTAL WORD COMPREHENSION SCORE ______

EXERCISES

HOW TO PRONOUNCE A WORD *(continued from p. 380)*

DO YOU AVOID AFFECTED SPEECH?

Check, as before, the forms you habitually use in the test below.

1.	*again*	(a) a-GAYNE	(b) a-GEN
2.	*either*	(a) EYE-ther	(b) EE-ther
3.	*vase*	(a) vahz	(b) vayze or vayse
4.	*tomato*	(a) to-MAH-to	(b) to-MAY-to
5.	*chauffeur*	(a) SHO-fer	(b) sho-FURR
6.	*aunt*	(a) ahnt	(b) ant
7.	*secretary*	(a) SEC-re-tree	(b) SEC-re-terry
8.	*rather*	(a) rah-ther	(b) ra-ther (rhyme with *gather*)
9.	*program*	(a) pro-grum	(b) pro-gramm
10.	*ask*	(a) ahsk	(b) ask

Except for certain sections of New England and parts of the South, the second alternative offered in the above test is in every case the popular, current and standard form. Therefore, the greater the number of (b) pronunciations you checked, the more natural and unaffected will listeners consider your speech.

If you generally mix in social, business or geographical groups in which *ahnt, tomahto* and *eyether* are accepted pronunciations, you are relatively safe in using some or all of the (a) forms in the test. Nevertheless, you should bear in mind that these are not the pronunciations common to the majority of Americans and that you may occasionally run the risk of being thought "snooty" or supercilious by your more earthy listeners.

The third and last analysis, which appears below, is just for fun, and will serve to prove that we cannot become too fussy about "correct" pronunciation. These are "catch" words; that is, you are expected to get most of them wrong. They are, with one exception, bookish words rarely used in everyday speech—thus there is no reason why you should be familiar with the dictionary pronunciations.

Most people taking this test will make seven or more errors. If you get more than three right, you may credit yourself with unusual language gifts. If you manage to come anywhere near a perfect score, you are absolutely phenomenal. To see how well you did, check with the inverted answers below the test itself.

In your own pronunciation, you are following the wisest course if you avoid uneducated forms and silly affectations. As an aid to improving pronunciation, you can consult the dictionary, study the simple rules of speech, observe and adopt the good pronunciation habits used by literate people.

The time you spend in improving your pronunciation will pay generous dividends. Actions, we are often told, speak louder than words. But the world bases its first impression of you on what you say—and *how* you say it.

1. *finis* (the end) (a) FIN-iss, (b) fee-NEE, (c) FYE-niss
2. *eighth* (the number) (a) ayt-th, (b) ayth
3. *secretive* (concealing) (a) SEEK-re-tive, (b) se-KREE-tive
4. *cerebrum* (portion of the brain) (a) SER-e-brum, (b) se-REE-brum
5. *dour* (stern, forbidding) (a) rhyme with poor, (b) rhyme with sour
6. *congeries* (a heap) (a) CON-je-reez, (b) con-JEER-ee-eez
7. *ignominy* (disgrace) (a) IG-no-mi-ny, (b) ig-NOM-i-ny
8. *gramercy*! (a Shakespearian exclamation) (a) GRAM-er-see, (b) gra-MUR-see
9. *vagary* (whim) (a) VAG-a-ree, (b) VAY-ga-ree, (c) va-GARE-ee
10. *quay* (a wharf) (a) kway, (b) kay, (c) key

Remember—pronunciations change—dictionaries vary!

Answers: 1. a; 2. a; 3. a; 4. a; 5. a; 6. b; 7. a; 8. b; 9. b; 10. c.

NAME ______________________ DATE ______________ READING RATE ______________ WPM

COMPREHENSION CHECK QUESTIONS

1. Miss Markham was said to be a (1) school principal; (2) relative; (3) counselor; (4) school teacher. 1. _______
2. Cissa is the name of the author's (1) cat; (2) daughter; (3) neighbor; (4) friend. 2. _______
3. The author has a son named (1) Larry; (2) Russell; (3) John; (4) Lynn. 3. _______
4. Mention is made of (1) Moses; (2) Solomon; (3) Noah; (4) Cleopatra. 4. _______
5. One conversation reported had to do with (1) Hamlet; (2) Shylock; (3) Portia; (4) Ophelia. 5. _______

Receptive Comprehension _______

6. This selection is mainly about (1) listening; (2) being sincere; (3) keeping an open mind; (4) communication. 6. _______
7. The chief purpose of this article is to (1) entertain; (2) teach; (3) stimulate; (4) describe. 7. _______
8. The author makes most extensive use of (1) exposition; (2) narration; (3) persuasion; (4) description. 8. _______
9. The part of the article about Dr. Peale was intended to illustrate (1) the importance of valuing opinion; (2) the importance of registering no disapproval; (3) how to phrase questions; (4) how to combine telling and asking. 9. _______
10. *Most* importance is attached to (1) really caring; (2) keeping quiet; (3) asking leading questions; (4) asking questions. 10. _______

(10 points for each correct answer)

Reflective Comprehension _______
TOTAL READING COMPREHENSION SCORE _______

VOCABULARY CHECK QUESTIONS

			without context I	with context II
1.	**mull**	(1) cheat; (2) ponder; (3) pronounce; (4) read; (5) make.	1. _______	_______
2.	**zany**	(1) wicked; (2) outlandish; (3) colorful; (4) windy; (5) cold.	2. _______	_______
3.	**ineptness**	(1) awkwardness; (2) strangeness; (3) wildness; (4) vagueness; (5) willingness.	3. _______	_______
4.	**incisive**	(1) questioning; (2) harsh; (3) rude; (4) dumb; (5) penetrating.	4. _______	_______
5.	**provocative**	(1) chief; (2) brief; (3) stimulating; (4) proverbial; (5) near.	5. _______	_______

(10 points for each correct answer)

Word Comprehension without *contextual help (I)* _______
Word Comprehension with *contextual help (II)* _______
TOTAL WORD COMPREHENSION SCORE _______

Exercises

Asking the Right Question

Some questions seem to close more doors than they open, whereas others lead to a real dialogue. How good are you at the art of asking questions? Test yourself on this list of general questions by putting + beside the good ones, and – beside the poor ones. (Answers are at the bottom of the page.)

_____ 1. What did you do today?
_____ 2. Would you explain that to me?
_____ 3. How was the party?
_____ 4. How did you feel about that?
_____ 5. Is something the matter?
_____ 6. What would you have done?
_____ 7. Do you love me?
_____ 8. Why did you say that?
_____ 9. Oh, really?
_____ 10. For instance?
_____ 11. Did you enjoy yourself?
_____ 12. And then what happened?
_____ 13. Is that so?
_____ 14. What do you like best?
_____ 15. Did you have a good day at the office?
_____ 16. Which book did you like best?

Noting Conversation Stimulators

Listen carefully to some conversations and jot down the specific questions that seem to spark the most lively discussion. Try the same kind of analysis in a class or group discussion, observing which questions serve best as stimuli to talk. Remember some of the most interesting conversations you have ever had. What questions seemed to evoke an easy flow of communication?

Answers: The odd-numbered questions (1, 3, 5, etc.) are poor because they are conversation-stoppers usually answered by one or two words. The even-numbered questions are good ones because they call for thought-provoking answers that can send the conversational stone rolling downhill, initiating other topics for discussion. If you put + by more than three odd-numbered questions, it may be time to revitalize your sense of curiosity.

NAME ______________ DATE ______________ READING RATE ______________ WPM

Comprehension Check Questions

1. The author specifically alludes to the conversation of (1) baseball enthusiasts; (2) artists; (3) families; (4) movie fans. 1. ______
2. The author lists (1) five rules; (2) eight rules; (3) ten rules; (4) twelve rules. 2. ______
3. The author belonged to (1) a conversation club; (2) a bridge club; (3) a dinner club; (4) an artist colony. 3. ______
4. Mention is made of (1) Eugene Field; (2) Ellis Parker Butler; (3) Edna St. Vincent Millay; (4) Alexander Pope. 4. ______
5. When the author read something aloud to get criticisms, he said he was helped most by (1) individual comments; (2) answers to specific questions; (3) watching listeners' eyes or fingers; (4) noticing when they laughed. 5. ______

Receptive Comprehension ______

6. The purpose of this selection is to (1) help us become better conversationalists; (2) tell us what to avoid when we converse; (3) give us some necessary rules to guide our conversation; (4) suggest appropriate subjects for conversation. 6. ______
7. Apparently the secret of talking well is (1) reading widely; (2) thinking well; (3) listening intently; (4) talking distinctly. 7. ______
8. When a good conversationalist hears someone tell about running into another car, he will (1) narrate some similar story from his own experience; (2) ask about some of the details; (3) shift the conversation to less subjective matters; (4) make no comment until a more appropriate subject is introduced. 8. ______
9. The Japanese tea ceremony is used to illustrate the rule: (1) don't monopolize the conversation; (2) don't make dogmatic statements of opinion; (3) show an active interest in what is said; (4) avoid all purely subjective talk. 9. ______
10. The story about the guests who tried not to say anything destructive in tone for a day illustrated the need for (1) a Pollyanna attitude; (2) a limited amount of destructive talk; (3) eliminating unnecessary critical remarks; (4) looking on both the pleasant and unpleasant sides of life. 10. ______

(10 points for each correct answer)

Reflective Comprehension ______

TOTAL READING COMPREHENSION SCORE ______

Vocabulary Check Questions

			without context I	with context II
1.	**dilate**	(1) hint; 2) expand; (3) refer; (4) close; (5) suffer.	1. ______	______
2.	**interpolate**	(1) pronounce; (2) insert; (3) converse; (4) meet; (5) tempt.	2. ______	______
3.	**desist**	(1) lose hope; (2) intend; (3) begin; (4) wish; (5) cease.	3. ______	______
4.	**diversion**	(1) appeal; (2) digression; (3) start; (4) form; (5) remark.	4. ______	______
5.	**self-effacement**	(1) pride; (2) confidence; (3) righteousness; (4) modesty; (5) egotism.	5. ______	______

(10 points for each correct answer)

Word Comprehension without *contextual help (I)* ______
Word Comprehension with *contextual help (II)* ______
TOTAL WORD COMPREHENSION SCORE ______

EXERCISES

ORGANIZING IDEAS

Thinking and reading are inseparable. As a writer you must organize your ideas coherently or your reader is in trouble. On the other hand, as an alert reader you must constantly check for yourself the relationships and interrelationships as you read, so that you may evaluate and understand more accurately.

To encourage more thoughtful, active reading, here are some jumbled paragraphs for you to reorder and rethink. Try arranging the following groups of sentences into the most coherent paragraph unit. In each paragraph there is one sentence from an adjoining paragraph, which is somewhat out of place. First, decide which numbered sentence does not belong, entering its number in the blank indicated. Then rearrange the remaining sentences in their most coherent order. Finally, check the accuracy of your thinking by referring to the original paragraph in Selection 53 (A: Rule 2; B: Rule 4; C: Rule 10).

A. 1. You roared with laughter, but after a while you grew restless and yearned for a more quiet, comfortable talk with plenty of give-and-take.
2. Don't monopolize the conversation.
3. Flat contradiction is another conversation-stopper.
4. One of my friends long ago was a laughing, attractive person, who told stories well, with a mixture of highbrow terms and slang that was most amusing.
5. You couldn't help remembering what old John Dryden said about those "who think too little, and who talk too much."
6. But his stories were too long and too many.

The sentence that violates paragraph unity is ______.
The remaining five sentences should be arranged in this order: ______ ______ ______ ______ ______

B. 1. But to interpolate views of your own is not only discourteous, but leaves what the speaker has to say unfinished when he perhaps hasn't yet made his point.
2. Don't abruptly change the subject.
3. It should have rhythm and tempo to be gracious and truly social.
4. Don't interrupt.
5. Conversation is like an ordered dinner where each is served in turn.
6. Of course, when you toss a few grace notes into the talk such as, "How wonderful!" or "You mean she didn't know?" it doesn't throw the train of conversation off the track.

The sentence that violates paragraph unity is ______.
The remaining five sentences should be arranged in this order: ______ ______ ______ ______ ______

C. 1. Did you ever attempt to live for a single day without saying anything destructive in tone?
2. If you said you didn't like bananas, another dollar; and so on.
3. Avoid destructive talk.
4. Evil, of course, must be condemned and opposed.
5. At a house party, long ago, I was one of half a dozen guests who agreed to try it.
6. If one of us went to the window and said, "It looks like rain," there would be a whoop of glee, and a fine of one dollar.

The sentence that violates paragraph unity is ______.
The remaining five sentences should be arranged in this order: ______ ______ ______ ______ ______

NAME ______________________ DATE ______________ READING RATE ______________ WPM

COMPREHENSION CHECK QUESTIONS

1. The title of Conwell's lecture was (1) *America's Penniless Millionaire;* (2) *Acres of Diamonds;* (3) *The Story of Ali Hafed;* (4) *Opportunity Knocks But Once.* 1. ______
2. Conwell lived his early life (1) on a farm; (2) in a city; (3) in a small town; (4) in New Haven. 2. ______
3. In the Civil War Conwell was (1) an orderly; (2) a lieutenant; (3) a captain; (4) a major. 3. ______
4. Conwell was directly instrumental in the building of (1) a new church; (2) two new churches; (3) three new churches; (4) four new churches. 4. ______
5. Conwell delivered his famous lecture about (1) 1,000 times; (2) 2,000 times; (3) 4,000 times; (4) 6,000 times. 5. ______

Receptive Comprehension ______

6. The purpose of this article is to (1) explain the importance of cultivating your own back yard; (2) tell us about a famous speech; (3) tell us about Conwell; (4) suggest the importance of reading. 6. ______
7. The story of John Ring is used to demonstrate Conwell's ability to (1) command; (2) lay hold of symbols and fit them into his life; (3) keep an extravagant vow; (4) understand human nature and motives. 7. ______
8. Conwell apparently considered the most important communication skill to be (1) writing; (2) speaking; (3) listening; (4) reading. 8. ______
9. Conwell would probably agree that a man's success depends primarily on (1) the contacts he makes; (2) his environment; (3) being at the right place at the right time; (4) making the most of his opportunities. 9. ______
10. You would infer that the most effective exposition is (1) narrative; (2) descriptive; (3) humorous; (4) witty. 10. ______

(10 points for each correct answer)

Reflective Comprehension ______

TOTAL READING COMPREHENSION SCORE ______

VOCABULARY CHECK QUESTIONS

			without context I	**with context II**
1.	**diversity**	(1) category; (2) deity; (3) pleasure; (4) variety; (5) popularity.	1. ______	______
2.	**guises**	(1) plants; (2) guides; (3) secrets; (4) aspects; (5) creeds.	2. ______	______
3.	**intuitive**	(1) inborn; (2) intrusive; (3) useless; (4) fickle; (5) unwilling.	3. ______	______
4.	**tenaciously**	(1) temptingly; (2) temporarily; (3) moderately; (4) persistently; (5) quietly.	4. ______	______
5.	**stipulated**	(1) dotted; (2) paid; (3) drew; (4) estimated; (5) specified.	5. ______	______

(10 points for each correct answer)

Word Comprehension without *contextual help (I)* ______

Word Comprehension with *contextual help (II)* ______

TOTAL WORD COMPREHENSION SCORE ______

Exercises

Noting Subtle Degrees of Emphasis

Many different shades of emphasis are reflected in the way that ideas are coordinated or subordinated in a sentence. An idea may be given added importance by being put into an independent clause, where it can stand alone as a complete statement or sentence. It can be given slightly less importance by being put into a dependent clause, which cannot stand alone. If it deserves even less emphasis, the verb can be removed and the idea expressed in phrase form, either prepositional or verbal. Finally, if the idea deserves minimal emphasis, it can sometimes be boiled down to a single word.

Take this sentence: "A man was digging a ditch, and he had a big nose." This contains two independent clauses connected with an *and.* In essence this suggests that the writer considered the two ideas of equal importance, putting them both into independent clauses. If the action is to get slightly more emphasis, the second clause could be made a dependent clause as follows: "The man who had a big nose was digging a ditch." For even less emphasis, see how the sentence reads when the dependent clause is made a phrase: "The man with a big nose was digging a ditch." Finally, it is possible to move from a phrase to a single word, the sentence now reading: "The big-nosed man was digging a ditch." In this rather subtle way a writer may communicate degrees of emphasis on ideas he is expressing — emphasis that you, the reader, should be aware of.

To develop that awareness more fully, try expressing shades of emphasis in the following sentence, using the patterns suggested in the model.

> "*Conwell's speech was fascinating* and *it could have made him a millionaire.*"

Put the idea expressed in the first independent clause into a dependent clause.

____

Now subordinate it further, making it a phrase of some kind.

____

As a last move, boil the idea in the first clause into a single word.

____

Getting Proper Emphasis Through Subordination

Revise the following sentences as directed, noting how proper subordination improves each one. When you have finished, check back to the original in Selection 54.

A. Subordinate by changing the italicized portion from an independent clause to a dependent clause, making any other changes necessary:

   Example: *He was making tens of thousands,* **and he would rarely have more than a hundred ready dollars of his own. Though he was making tens of thousands, he would . . . .**
   (The dependent clause emphasizes the causal relationship present.)

   1. There is an event of his military service, and *it demonstrates his facility for laying hold of symbols* . . . .
   2. *The Civil War broke*, and it was as if he had anticipated the opportunity to become "the recruiting orator of the Berkshires."

B. Subordinate by changing the italicized portion from an independent clause to a verbal phrase, making any other changes necessary:
   1. He chips a corner, *and he finds an eye of blue-white fire* looking at him . . . .
   2. It stands, very possibly, in our own boots, *and it wears our own socks.*

C. Subordinate by changing the italicized portion from a clause to a phrase of some kind, making any other changes necessary:
   1. *It was the appointed day*, and he borrowed tools and came out.
   2. *Eighteen months passed*, and he had been ordained their minister . . . .

NAME ______________________ DATE ______________ READING RATE ______________ WPM

COMPREHENSION CHECK QUESTIONS

1. Some of the experiments were conducted at (1) Yale; (2) Cornell; (3) Chicago; (4) Harvard. 1. _______
2. One of the experimental speakers was (1) a salesman; (2) an accountant; (3) a taxi driver; (4) a musician. 2. _______
3. Guessing age was done accurately (1) when speakers were over 40; (2) when speakers were under 40; (3) over the entire age range; (4) only by totally blind listeners. 3. _______
4. As compared with radio, putting speakers behind a curtain (1) made no difference in accuracy; (2) actually resulted in a loss of accuracy; (3) added about 7 percent more accuracy; (4) added about 14 percent more accuracy. 4. _______
5. Monotone is closely related to (1) maladjustment; (2) age; (3) physical health; (4) body build. 5. _______

Receptive Comprehension _______

6. The purpose of this selection is (1) to suggest how best to train your voice; (2) to show how accurately age can be judged from voice; (3) to indicate what your voice reveals about you; (4) to indicate how closely all experimental findings in this area agree. 6. _______
7. The selection is organized primarily around (1) the various experimental studies; (2) the various characteristics studied; (3) a chronological sequence; (4) an evidence-to-conclusion basis. 7. _______
8. Evidence was cited to show that (1) personality improvement led to voice improvement; (2) voice improvement led to personality improvement; (3) personality change did not affect voice; (4) voice change did not affect personality. 8. _______
9. In this selection the points are developed chiefly through use of (1) anecdotes; (2) detail; (3) analogies; (4) repetition. 9. _______
10. This article is aimed primarily at (1) psychologists; (2) college students; (3) adults; (4) women. 10. _______

(10 points for each correct answer)

Reflective Comprehension _______
TOTAL READING COMPREHENSION SCORE _______

VOCABULARY CHECK QUESTIONS

			without context I	with context II
1. **incredibly**	(1) helpfully; (2) unbelievably; (3) lastingly; (4) moderately; (5) slowly.	1.	_______	_______
2. **invariably**	(1) inconstantly; (2) always; (3) invincibly; (4) usually; (5) softly.	2.	_______	_______
3. **reliance**	(1) force; (2) dependence; (3) rest; (4) aid; (5) fact.	3.	_______	_______
4. **corroborated**	(1) consumed; (2) folded; (3) debased; (4) abated; (5) confirmed.	4.	_______	_______
5. **nuances**	(1) new developments; (2) standards; (3) delicate variations; (4) annoyances; (5) loud voices.	5.	_______	_______

(10 points for each correct answer)

Word Comprehension without *contextual help I)* _______
Word Comprehension with *contextual help (II)* _______
TOTAL WORD COMPREHENSION SCORE _______

EXERCISES

GETTING VARIETY BY USING BOTH LOOSE AND PERIODIC SENTENCES

A periodic sentence is one in which the meaning is not completed until the end or nearly the end. A loose sentence is one that continues after a complete statement is made. Loose sentences are more conversational; periodic sentences more formal.

Change the following sentences from loose to periodic or from periodic to loose, noticing the difference in effect. Compare your versions with the originals in Selection 55, noting any differences.

Example: (Periodic) "If you want to write a really popular song, one that will fall naturally from the lips of millions, be sure that somewhere in your chorus you assault the English language in no uncertain terms."

(Loose) Be sure you assault the English language in no uncertain terms somewhere in your chorus, if you want to write a really popular song, one that will fall naturally from the lips of millions.

1. (Loose) The estimates tended to be less accurate, however, in judging the ages of the persons who were over 45.

   (Periodic) ____________________

   ____

2. (Periodic) Voices having been broadcast over a public address system, the body build of the speakers was to be identified by the students.

   (Loose) ____________________

   ____

3. (Loose) His other senses seem to become more sensitive and acute, including hearing, when a person loses his sight, because he places greater reliance upon them.

   (Periodic) ____________________

   ____

4. (Loose) Harvard University scientists conducted a similar test in the United States, impressed by the findings of the Vienna study.

   (Periodic) ____________________

   ____

GETTING VARIETY BY INTERRUPTING THE NORMAL SENTENCE PATTERN OF SUBJECT-VERB-OBJECT

Revise the following sentences by placing part of the sentence so as to interrupt the normal pattern. Compare your versions with the original sentences in Selection 55.

1. The Psychological Institute of the University of Vienna conducted a fascinating experiment to test these findings.

   ____

   ____

2. The investigators believe this finding indicates that a slight degree of distortion was produced when the voices were transmitted over the radio.

   ____

   ____

3. Take the person who speaks in a dull monotone, for example.

   ____

NAME ______________ DATE ______________ READING RATE ______________ WPM

Comprehension Check Questions

1. To cut down on talking, the husband suggested (1) chewing gum vigorously and constantly; (2) taping their lips; (3) using a word-rationing system; (4) taking turns talking with visitors. 1. _______
2. Specific mention was made of their (1) color TV; (2) open fire; (3) sunny patio; (4) stereo. 2. _______
3. Dan Blake told a long story about the (1) deer he shot; (2) accident he had; (3) train trip he took; (4) big bass he caught. 3. _______
4. The agreed signal for the other to stop talking was to (1) touch the lips; (2) pull an ear; (3) touch the forehead; (4) clear the throat. 4. _______
5. The doctor diagnosed the husband as having (1) eye trouble; (2) sinus trouble; (3) hearing problems; (4) allergy problems. 5. _______

Receptive Comprehension _______

6. The chief purpose of this selection is to (1) entertain; (2) instruct; (3) explain; (4) stimulate. 6. _______
7. Which of the following statements is closest to the idea developed in this selection? (1) good listening makes good friends; (2) listen well to learn well; (3) good listening pays; (4) he who listens well, eats well. 7. _______
8. Which of the two seemed to take the leadership in the couple's decision? (1) the husband, primarily; (2) both equally; (3) the wife, primarily; (4) first one, then the other. 8. _______
9. This selection would be most accurately classified as (1) exposition; (2) persuasion; (3) narration; (4) description. 9. _______
10. In style, you would call this selection (1) informal; (2) verbose; (3) humorous; (4) intimate. 10. _______

(10 points for each correct answer)

Reflective Comprehension _______

TOTAL READING COMPREHENSION SCORE _______

Vocabulary Check Questions

			without context I	with context II
1.	**phlegmatic**	(1) small; (2) unemotional; (3) lively; (4) flattering; (5) slow.	1. _______	_______
2.	**chagrined**	(1) amused; (2) transformed; (3) pleased; (4) thanked; (5) humiliated.	2. _______	_______
3.	**repercussion**	(1) blow; (2) sound; (3) repair; (4) rebounding; (5) censure.	3. _______	_______
4.	**fiasco**	(1) authorization; (2) betrothed person; (3) complete failure; (4) conclusion; (5) award.	4. _______	_______
5.	**moratorium**	(1) deferment; (2) burial; (3) bad situation; (4) payment; (5) inclination.	5. _______	_______

(10 points for each correct answer)

Word Comprehension without *contextual help (I)* _______

Word Comprehension with *contextual help (II)* _______

TOTAL WORD COMPREHENSION SCORE _______

Exercises

Checking up on Yourself as a Listener

Try an experiment to see how you rate as a listener. Begin by taking the following twelve-item spelling quiz to see how many of the words you know how to spell accurately. To each of the following twelve words, add an *-ing*, spelling the resulting combination on the line following the word, in the column headed *Initial Spelling*.

Words	Initial Spelling (before listening)	Final Spelling (after listening)
1. din + ing	____________	____________
2. shine + ing	____________	____________
3. begin + ing	____________	____________
4. quiz + ing	____________	____________
5. unfurl + ing	____________	____________
6. occur + ing	____________	____________
7. label + ing	____________	____________
8. man + ing	____________	____________
9. droop + ing	____________	____________
10. equip + ing	____________	____________
11. profit + ing	____________	____________
12. defer + ing	____________	____________

When you have finished, do not check your answers. Instead, hand this text to someone else, asking him to read aloud the Final Consonant Rule below, while you listen carefully. Ask him to read it slowly twice, to make sure you understand the rule. After listening, spell the same twelve words in the column headed *Final Spelling*, trying to apply the rule perfectly. If you understood and applied the rule, you should have a perfect score in the last column. This becomes, in a sense, a measure of your listening ability. Here is the rule that is to be read aloud to you twice as you listen: FINAL CONSONANT RULE: For words ending in a single final consonant, preceded by a single vowel, and with the last syllable accented, double the final consonant when you add a suffix beginning with a vowel. (Repeat the rule.)

Now check both columns with the answers at the bottom of the page to see how many you got right. What do your findings mean? Your scores for the two trials will put you into one of three categories:

1. When 92 university students followed the same procedure, 23 were either slightly confused after listening to the rule or thoroughly confused, scoring from 1 to 6 points *lower* after listening to the rule. One student, for example, who scored 11 right the first time, spelled only 5 right the second.
2. Then 19 of the 92 did not change at all after hearing the rule. One student scored 7 right the first time and 7 right after listening to the rule. This suggests a strong mind-set that interfered with learning through listening.
3. Finally, the remaining 50 improved from 1 to 5 points after listening to the rule. One student improved from 7 to 12, a perfect score after listening to the rule.

Coming back to your own results, if you improved by 1 point, you have a somewhat better listening ability than found in the 92 students tested. If you improved to a perfect 12 in the second column, even if you moved up only from 11 to 12, you improved as much as possible. If you scored any less than 12 right in the last column, ask yourself why. One student, in answering that question, wrote that he "didn't know what a consonant was." Word meaning was apparently part of his problem. Do you have a clear, accurate concept of what a syllable is? a suffix? a vowel? an accent? Any one of those may be a potential stumbling block.

Answers: 1. dinning; 2. shining; 3. beginning; 4. quizzing; 5. unfurling; 6. occurring; 7. labeling; 8. manning; 9. drooping; 10. equipping; 11. profiting; 12. deferring.

NAME ______________________ DATE ______________ READING RATE ______________ WPM

COMPREHENSION CHECK QUESTIONS

1. One conversation mentioned is overheard in the airport at (1) San Francisco; (2) Seattle; (3) Chicago; (4) Phoenix. 1. _______
2. What catastrophe is *not* mentioned? (1) Pearl Harbor; (2) sinking of the *Titanic;* (3) MGM Grand fire; (4) Johnstown flood. 2. _______
3. The divorce figure for each year is said to be (1) 250,000; (2) 500,000; (3) one million; (4) two million. 3. _______
4. What percent of our waking time is spent in communicating? (1) 55%; (2) 60%; (3) 70%; (4) 80%. 4. _______
5. Of the twenty most critical managerial competencies, listening actually ranks (1) at the very top; (2) next to the top; (3) third; (4) fourth. 5. _______

Receptive Comprehension _______

6. This selection is mainly about (1) the importance of listening; (2) the teaching of listening; (3) the effects of bad listening; (4) the need for listening in management. 6. _______
7. The opening three incidents are related primarily to (1) arouse interest; (2) show that men are the poorest listeners; (3) suggest the prevalence of bad listening habits; (4) reveal the costly effects of poor listening. 7. _______
8. You would infer that the intended reading audience is (1) teachers; (2) the general public; (3) business personnel; (4) training directors. 8. _______
9. Points are developed largely by (1) description; (2) details; (3) comparison; (4) research findings. 9. _______
10. The style is essentially (1) lively; (2) inspirational; (3) conversational; (4) factual. 10. _______

(10 points for each correct answer)

Reflective Comprehension _______

TOTAL READING COMPREHENSION SCORE _______

VOCABULARY CHECK QUESTIONS

			without context I	with context II
1.	**quantitative**	(1) factual; (2) quarrelsome; (3) capable of measurement; (4) bulky; (5) explicit.	1. _______	_______
2.	**audits**	(1) sums; (2) drills; (3) examinations; (4) arrangements; (5) sounds.	2. _______	_______
3.	**reciprocate**	(1) receive; (2) summarize; (3) correct; (4) interchange; (5) prove.	3. _______	_______
4.	**miscontrue**	(1) build poorly; (2) suspect; (3) lie; (4) misunderstand; (5) miscalculate.	4. _______	_______
5.	**tortuous**	(1) winding; (2) painful; (3) slow; (4) hot; (5) arid.	5. _______	_______

(10 points for each correct answer)

Word Comprehension without *contextual help (I)* _______

Word Comprehension with *contextual help (II)* _______

TOTAL WORD COMPREHENSION SCORE _______

EXERCISES

CHECKING YOUR LISTENING HABITS

Dr. Ralph G. Nichols, pioneer in the field of listening, has devised a special Listening Index for use in analyzing your bad listening habits. Check up on yourself—but be honest!

HOW WELL DO YOU LISTEN?

How often do you indulge in ten almost universal bad listening habits? Check yourself carefully on each one, tallying your score as follows:

For every "Almost always" checked, give yourself a score of	2
For every "Usually" checked, give yourself a score of	4
For every "Sometimes" checked, give yourself a score of	6
For every "Seldom" checked, give yourself a score of	8
For every "Almost never" checked, give yourself a score of	10

HABIT	FREQUENCY					SCORE
	Almost Always	Usually	Some-times	Seldom	Almost Never	
1. Judging the subject uninteresting	____	____	____	____	____	____
2. Criticizing the speaker's delivery	____	____	____	____	____	____
3. Getting *over*stimulated by some point within the speech	____	____	____	____	____	____
4. Listening only for facts	____	____	____	____	____	____
5. Trying to outline everything	____	____	____	____	____	____
6. Faking attention to the speaker	____	____	____	____	____	____
7. Tolerating or creating distractions	____	____	____	____	____	____
8. Avoiding listening to difficult expository material	____	____	____	____	____	____
9. Letting emotion-laden words arouse personal antagonism	____	____	____	____	____	____
10. Wasting the advantage of thought speed	____	____	____	____	____	____
					TOTAL	______

TOTAL SCORE INTERPRETATION:
BELOW 70—YOU NEED TRAINING.
FROM 70 TO 90—YOU LISTEN WELL.
ABOVE 90—YOU ARE EXTRAORDINARY GOOD.

NAME ______________________ DATE ______________ READING RATE ______________ WPM

COMPREHENSION CHECK QUESTIONS

1. White collar workers are said to devote what percent of their working time to listening? (1) no figure given; (2) 40; (3) 25; (4) 12. 1. ______

2. One company mentioned as providing training in listening is (1) IBM; (2) Ford Motor Co.; (3) Remington-Rand; (4) Monsanto Chemical. 2. ______

3. The worst listeners thought that note-taking was synonymous with (1) summarizing; (2) noting main ideas; (3) noting facts; (4) outlining. 3. ______

4. One of the ten suggestions was to (1) get the facts; (2) sit toward the front; (3) exercise your mind; (4) involve your emotions. 4. ______

5. We are told that we live in a (1) "mechanized age"; (2) "noisy age"; (3) "jet age"; (4) "wordy age". 5. ______

Receptive Comprehension ______

6. The focus is mainly on (1) how to listen better; (2) reasons for poor listening; (3) the importance of listening; (4) the value of listening training. 6. ______

7. This selection is addressed primarily to (1) business people; (2) students; (3) women; (4) adults in general. 7. ______

8. By inference, an interesting speech should particularly stress the (1) novel; (2) unique; (3) useful; (4) colorful. 8. ______

9. The most important suggestion is apparently to (1) keep your mind open; (2) be flexible; (3) capitalize on thought speed; (4) hold your fire. 9. ______

10. The list of "red flag" words was to develop the point that you should (1) resist distractions; (2) judge content, not delivery; (3) keep your mind open; (4) find areas of interest. 10. ______

(10 points for each correct answer)

Reflective Comprehension ______

TOTAL READING COMPREHENSION SCORE ______

VOCABULARY CHECK QUESTIONS

			without context I	with context II
1.	**component**	(1) constant; (2) comrade; (3) complex; (4) part; (5) constituent.	1. ______	______
2.	**tap**	(1) see; (2) trade; (3) give; (4) extract; (5) buy.	2. ______	______
3.	**inept**	(1) awkward; (2) crude; (3) erratic; (4) motionless; (5) infallible.	3. ______	______
4.	**recapitulation**	(1) summary; (2) statement; (3) analogy; (4) energy; (5) inflection.	4. ______	______
5.	**transpires**	(1) raises; (2) happens; (3) sees through; (4) changes; (5) snares.	5. ______	______

(10 points for each correct answer)

Word Comprehension without *contextual help (I)* ______

Word Comprehension with *contextual help (II)* ______

TOTAL WORD COMPREHENSION SCORE ______

Exercises

Rating Yourself as a Listener

Here are ten questions based on Dr. Nichols's research in the area of listening–questions that will serve nicely as an informal rating device. Check up on yourself. Answer each question with a *yes* or *no*.

1. Science says you think four times faster than a person usually talks to you. Do you use this excess time to turn your thoughts elsewhere while you are keeping general track of a conversation? 1. ______
2. Do you listen primarily for facts, rather than ideas, when someone is speaking? 2. ______
3. Do certain words, phrases, or ideas so prejudice you against the speaker that you cannot listen objectively to what is being said? 3. ______
4. When you are puzzled or annoyed by what someone says, do you try to get the question straightened out immediately—either in your own mind or by interrupting the speaker? 4. ______
5. If you feel it would take too much time and effort to understand something, do you go out of your way to avoid hearing about it? 5. ______
6. Do you deliberately turn your thoughts to other subjects when you believe a speaker will have nothing particularly interesting to say? 6. ______
7. Can you tell by a person's appearance and delivery that he won't have anything worthwhile to say? 7. ______
8. When somebody is talking to you, do you try to make him think you're paying attention when you're not? 8. ______
9. When you're listening to someone, are you easily distracted by outside sights and sounds? 9. ______
10. If you want to remember what someone is saying, do you think it a good idea to write it down as he goes along? 10. ______

Answers: If you answer *no* to all these questions, then you are that rare individual—the perfect listener. Every *yes* answer means that you are guilty of a specific bad listening habit.

Now you should know what habits, if any, you need to change to make yourself a better listener, a move that will mean improved understanding, closer friendships, and increased general efficiency.

Comparing Listening and Reading Time

Some years ago Paul T. Rankin made a survey of the time spent in communicating. Selecting 68 adults, he asked them to keep a careful record, every fifteen minutes, of the amount of time spent in talking, reading, writing, and listening. Data collected over a two-month period led to the discovery that 70 percent of his subjects' waking day was spent in verbal communication. Of that communication time, listening made up 45 percent, reading 16 percent. But that was back in 1929.

What is true today with you? Make a survey of the time you spend in listening and reading during an average day. Compare your findings with those reported by Dr. Rankin.

NAME ______________________ DATE ______________ READING RATE ______________ WPM

Comprehension Check Questions

1. The author says that most of us do not (1) hear as we should; (2) listen; (3) listen to friends; (4) listen to strangers. 1. _______
2. He quotes (1) Coleridge; (2) Shelley; (3) Keats; (4) Wordsworth. 2. _______
3. Listening is spoken of as (1) a very active business; (2) an automatic reaction; (3) varying with age; (4) varying with sex. 3. _______
4. The author specifically speaks of listening with our (1) imagination; (2) insights; (3) experience; (4) heart. 4. _______
5. He mentions opening a book and listening to (1) Socrates; (2) Aristotle; (3) Plato; (4) Hippocrates. 5. _______

Receptive Comprehension _______

6. This discussion is focused mainly on (1) how one should listen; (2) how similar listening and reading are; (3) how to become an active listener; (4) how listening enriches human experience. 6. _______
7. The two-line bit of poetry is used to remind us that (1) we can't help listening; (2) listening is mental and emotional; (3) listening is a physical thing; (4) listening is a matter of choice. 7. _______
8. You would assume you know a person is listening (1) from his silence; (2) from his vocal response; (3) from his internal changes; (4) from his muscular responses. 8. _______
9. The word "listen," as used in this selection, means essentially (1) reading as well as listening; (2) listening only; (3) hearing; (4) experience. 9. _______
10. Most emphasis is placed on the idea that individuals (1) do not listen; (2) simulate attention too often; (3) have major difficulties in listening; (4) are prisoners of their own experience. 10. _______

(10 points for each correct answer)

Reflective Comprehension _______

TOTAL READING COMPREHENSION SCORE _______

Vocabulary Check Questions

		without context I	with context II
1. **comatose**	(1) unconscious; (2) punctuated; (3) slow; (4) free-flowing; (5) hostile.	1. _______	_______
2. **biased**	(1) based; (2) stitched; (3) individualized; (4) prejudiced; (5) injured.	2. _______	_______
3. **inevitably**	(1) usually; (2) finally; (3) certainly; (4) completely; (5) elusively.	3. _______	_______
4. **code**	(1) creed; (2) supplement; (3) ending; (4) judgment; (5) system.	4. _______	_______
5. **inhibition**	(1) not hospitable; (2) commencement; (3) combination; (4) insert; (5) restriction.	5. _______	_______

(10 points for each correct answer)

Word Comprehension without *contextual help (I)* _______

Word Comprehension with *contextual help (II)* _______

TOTAL WORD COMPREHENSION SCORE _______

EXERCISES

CHECKING YOUR LISTENING ATTITUDE

Effective listening depends partly on attitude, partly on actions. Here is another special Listening Index devised by Dr. Nichols to help you evaluate your listening habits and develop improved insights. As you rate your attitudes and actions, think in terms of the more common face-to-face listening situations. Circle your frequency score for each item.

ARE YOU A GOOD LISTENER?

	Almost Always	Usually	Occa-sionally	Seldom	Almost Never
Attitudes					
1. Do you like to listen to other people talk?	5	4	3	2	1
2. Do you encourage other people to talk?	5	4	3	2	1
3. Do you listen even if you do not like the person who is talking?	5	4	3	2	1
4. Do you listen equally well whether the person talking is man or woman, young or old?	5	4	3	2	1
5. Do you listen equally well to friend, acquaintance, stranger?	5	4	3	2	1
Actions					
6. Do you put what you have been doing out of sight and out of mind?	5	4	3	2	1
7. Do you look at the person who is speaking?	5	4	3	2	1
8. Do you ignore the distractions about you?	5	4	3	2	1
9. Do you smile, nod your head, and otherwise encourage him to talk?	5	4	3	2	1
10. Do you think about what he is saying?	5	4	3	2	1
11. Do you try to figure out what he means?	5	4	3	2	1
12. Do you try to figure out why he is saying it?	5	4	3	2	1
13. Do you let him finish what he is trying to say?	5	4	3	2	1
14. If he hesitates, do you encourage him to go on?	5	4	3	2	1
15. Do you restate what he has said and ask him if you got it right?	5	4	3	2	1
16. Do you withhold judgment about his idea until he has finished?	5	4	3	2	1
17. Do you listen regardless of his manner of speaking and choice of words?	5	4	3	2	1
18. Do you listen even though you anticipate what he is going to say?	5	4	3	2	1
19. Do you question him in order to get him to explain his ideas more fully?	5	4	3	2	1
20. Do you ask him what unfamiliar words mean as he uses them?	5	4	3	2	1
				TOTAL	______

TOTAL SCORE INTERPRETATION:

IF YOUR SCORE IS 75 OR BETTER, YOU ARE A GOOD LISTENER.

IF YOUR SCORE IS 50–75, YOU ARE AN AVERAGE LISTENER.

IF YOUR SCORE IS BELOW 50, YOU ARE A POOR LISTENER.

NAME ______ DATE ______ READING RATE ______ WPM

COMPREHENSION CHECK QUESTIONS

1. Americans are spoken of as (1) passive listeners; (2) better than average listeners; (3) average listeners; (4) not very good listeners. 1. ______
2. In "listening clinics" (1) tape recordings are used; (2) motion pictures are used; (3) someone reads aloud; (4) several people discuss some problem. 2. ______
3. Specific mention is made of (1) Colonel Grayson; (2) Major Estes; (3) Charles Hasbargen; (4) Dulles. 3. ______
4. One of the suggestions was made in the form of a (1) radio exercise; (2) classroom discussion device; (3) party game; (4) tape recording check. 4. ______
5. The writer mentions (1) critical listening; (2) appreciative listening; (3) music listening; (4) creative listening. 5. ______

Receptive Comprehension ______

6. The purpose of this selection is to tell us (1) how Americans listen; (2) how to listen critically; (3) how to listen better; (4) how difficult listening actually is. 6. ______
7. This article is directed primarily toward (1) the adult reader; (2) the business executive; (3) representatives of labor; (4) educators. 7. ______
8. The author develops his points largely through (1) specific examples; (2) contrast and comparison; (3) straight exposition; (4) details. 8. ______
9. The portion about foreman Bill and his supervisor was intended to show (1) how voice inflection creates misunderstandings; (2) the difference between listening and telling; (3) how important clear directions are; (4) the need for watching facial expressions. 9. ______
10. You would infer from this selection that the major reason for poor listening is (1) hearing difficulties; (2) inadequate vocabulary; (3) emotional involvement; (4) pronunciation difficulties. 10. ______

(10 points for each correct answer)

Reflective Comprehension ______
TOTAL READING COMPREHENSION SCORE ______

VOCABULARY CHECK QUESTIONS

			without context I	with context II
1.	**ostensibly**	(1) forcibly; (2) apparently; (3) secretly; (4) happily; (5) sadly.	1. ______	______
2.	**competent**	(1) capable; (2) well-paid; (3) agreeable; (4) gathered; (5) compliment.	2. ______	______
3.	**acrimonious**	(1) greedy; (2) active; (3) agreeable; (4) bitter; (5) snail-like.	3. ______	______
4.	**slant**	(1) show bias; (2) rearrange; (3) slip; (4) turn; (5) run out.	4. ______	______
5.	**larded**	(1) eaten; (2) baked; (3) melted; (4) garnished; (5) shortened.	5. ______	______

(10 points for each correct answer)

Word Comprehension without *contextual help (I)* ______
Word Comprehension with *contextual help (II)* ______
TOTAL WORD COMPREHENSION SCORE ______

Exercises

Listening and Grades

What is the most important thing that education can do for you? This was one of the questions raised in a recent nationwide survey of the goals of education, as reported in the magazine *Phi Delta Kappan*. Results showed that the very first goal in order of importance, as indicated by those surveyed, was to "develop skills in reading, writing, speaking, and listening." The goal second in importance was to "develop pride in work and a feeling of self-worth."

Obviously reaching the second goal depends in large part on how well the first goal is achieved. The better you read, write, speak, and listen, the stronger your feelings of positive self-worth, security, and self-assurance. It is with these goals in mind that all the exercises in this text are designed expressly: to hasten your achievement in these areas of primary importance.

Actually the two assimilative skills of reading and listening can and should work most closely together, attention to one providing significant insights of importance to the other. Your academic success is dependent in large part on how skilled you are in assimilating by eye and ear.

The Commission on the English Curriculum points to the fact that "pupils from pre-school through college learn more frequently by listening than by any other means." Three separate studies made at Stephens College indicate that listening is more important than reading for success in 38 to 42 percent of the college courses taken by freshmen.

Additional evidence of the significance of listening comes from research based on the first standardized test of listening ability, the *Brown-Carlsen Listening Comprehension Test*. Research findings based on that test indicate that for a group of university sophomores grade-point averages are related somewhat more closely to listening ability than to reading ability.

Evidence such as this suggests how important it is to know both what kind of reader and what kind of listener you are as you face problems of effective assimilation of information at the college and adult levels. Use this text for that purpose, in case you do not have standardized test scores providing specific percentile figures.

Use six selections—three that you read, three that are read aloud to you. For each, take the comprehension test and begin to note any differences between the reading and listening channels. A total of the three scores in each area, although not so reliable as standardized test scores, will still provide relevant evidence.

Reading Comprehension Scores	**Listening Comprehension Scores**
Selection ______________	Selection ______________
Selection ______________	Selection ______________
Selection ______________	Selection ______________
TOTAL SCORE: ___________	**TOTAL SCORE:**___________

Are you about equally good as reader and listener? Are you a better listener than reader or a better reader than listener? The sooner you begin to find out, the sooner you can make desired adjustments.

As a further aid, look more closely at the figures. Are the differences in performances caused by differences in difficulty, length, or interest? For example, when 44 students were given two short selections, one to be read silently, the other to be listened to, the average comprehension was slightly better in the reading situation. The average was 66 percent in reading, 58 percent in listening. Yet among the 44 tested, one scored 80 percent in reading and only 20 percent in listening. On the same two selections, another student scored 50 percent in reading and 100 percent in listening.

NAME ______________________ DATE ______________ READING RATE ______________ WPM

COMPREHENSION CHECK QUESTIONS

1. How old was the "Wild Boy" when he was captured? (1) 10; (2) 11; (3) 12; (4) 13. 1. _______

2. Listening is said to take up how much of our waking time? (1) 50 percent; (2) 60 percent; (3) 70 percent; (4) 80 percent. 2. _______

3. Listening is the most efficient learning channel up to what grade? (1) fifth; (2) sixth; (3) seventh; (4) eighth. 3. _______

4. Mention is made of (1) Poe; (2) Twain; (3) Will Rogers; (4) Walt Whitman. 4. _______

5. Who wrote the four-line poem quoted at the end? (1) Toffler; (2) Fallows; (3) Thompson; (4) Wilt. 5. _______

Receptive Comprehension _______

6. This article makes what main point about listening? (1) its language-learning role; (2) its grade school role; (3) its college role; (4) its life role. 6. _______

7. The piece is primarily organized (1) from past to present; (2) from the simple to the complex; (3) on a time sequence; (4) on a cause-effect pattern. 7. _______

8. The chief purpose is to (1) persuade; (2) describe; (3) entertain; (4) explain. 8. _______

9. You would infer that listening is (1) of growing importance; (2) of lessening importance; (3) properly emphasized in school; (4) closely related to hearing. 9. _______

10. Chief emphasis is placed on the need for (1) special research; (2) listening textbooks; (3) attention to presently available research; (4) answers to specific questions. 10. _______

(10 points for each correct answer)

Reflective Comprehension _______

TOTAL READING COMPREHENSION SCORE _______

VOCABULARY CHECK QUESTIONS

			without context I	with context II
1.	**enhanced**	(1) embraced; (2) improved; (3) hoped; (4) entered; (5) helped.	1. _______	_______
2.	**atrophy**	(1) shrink; (2) win; (3) fix; (4) aid; (5) conquer.	2. _______	_______
3.	**implications**	(1) suggestions; (2) packets; (3) orders; (4) procedures; (5) explanations.	3. _______	_______
4.	**bombard**	(1) disappoint; (2) wound; (3) retard; (4) blast; (5) hold.	4. _______	_______
5.	**apropos**	(1) out-of-date; (2) dignified; (3) positive; (4) solid; (5) fitting.	5. _______	_______

(10 points for each correct answer)

Word Comprehension without *contextual help (I)* _______

Word Comprehension with *contextual help (II)* _______

TOTAL WORD COMPREHENSION SCORE _______

Exercises

Listening Versus Reading

In the spaces below list the important advantages and disadvantages of learning through listening and learning through reading.

A. Advantages

Learning through listening	Learning through reading
1. ______	1. ______
2. ______	2. ______
3. ______	3. ______
4. ______	4. ______
5. ______	5. ______
6. ______	6. ______

B. Disadvantages

Learning through listening	Learning through reading
1. ______	1. ______
2. ______	2. ______
3. ______	3. ______
4. ______	4. ______
5. ______	5. ______
6. ______	6. ______

Noting Obstacle-Words

While serving with Air University, Norman Stageberg prepared an article, "Obstacle-Words in Group Discussion," for the *Journal of Communication.* This article discussed seven kinds of words that tend to cause delay and confusion in speaking-listening situations.

Here is one of important kinds of obstacle-words he discusses:

> *Relative words.* Relative words are words whose meanings are vague and fluctuating, and depend on what the word is related to or compared with. Take, for example, the adjectives *tall* and *short.* Is a six-story building tall or short? If it is located in a town of 4,000 and related to the one- and two-story buildings of the community, it will probably be called tall. If however, the same building is located in a metropolis of 5,000,000 and is related to the surrounding skyscrapers, it will be considered short. Likewise, all opposite relative adjectives, e.g., *fast* and *slow, heavy* and *light, hot* and *cold,* can be used to describe exactly the same thing. Our indispensable *good* is a relative adjective. When it is stamped in purple on beef in "U. S. grade good," it means the second best of four grades. But in some mail-order catalogues, when applied to articles for sale, it means the lowest of three grades, the others being *better* and *best.* Here, then, *good* means poorest.

List four relative words you find in Selection 61. Does the author attempt to add other information or details that make them less relative?

Relative words	Other details to clarify?
1. ______	______
2. ______	______
3. ______	______
4. ______	______

NAME ______________________ DATE ______________ READING RATE ______________ WPM

Comprehension Check Questions

1. Where did the two-car collision occur? (1) New York; (2) Chicago; (3) Detroit; (4) city not named. 1. _______

2. You were asked to picture what? (1) a roomful of shouting people; (2) two angry people shouting; (3) a noisy schoolroom; (4) a noisy town meeting. 2. _______

3. The author specifically mentions (1) stop, look, and listen; (2) hearing with your eyes; (3) I-I/me-me; (4) all the above. 3. _______

4. One episode concerns (1) a schoolteacher; (2) an elderly woman; (3) a barber; (4) a receptionist. 4. _______

5. How many rules are given? (1) five; (2) six; (3) seven; (4) eight. 5. _______

Receptive Comprehension _______

6. The main focus is on the importance of (1) listening with the inner ear; (2) assuming nothing; (3) using listening to be heard; (4) saying what you mean. 6. _______

7. The example of the professionals discussing long-range plans illustrates what rule? (1) assume nothing; (2) say what you mean; (3) listen to the concerns of others; (4) listen with an inner ear. 7. _______

8. This selection is best described as (1) lively; (2) factual; (3) practical; (4) dramatic. 8. _______

9. Points are developed primarily by (1) examples; (2) logical reasoning; (3) quoting authorities; (4) making comparisons. 9. _______

10. The rules are arranged from (1) least to most important; (2) listening to speaking; (3) speaking to listening; (4) the simple to the complex. 10. _______

(10 points for each correct answer) *Reflective Comprehension* _______

TOTAL READING COMPREHENSION SCORE _______

Vocabulary Check Questions

		without context I	with context II
1. inestimable	(1) ineffectual; (2) disgraceful; (3) capable; (4) immeasurable; (5) hopeless.	1. _______	_______
2. arrogantly	(1) haughtily; (2) graciously; (3) wisely; (4) quickly; (5) airily.	2. _______	_______
3. valid	(1) costly; (2) different; (3) vain; (4) brave; (5) sound.	3. _______	_______
4. maliciously	(1) cautiously; (2) carefully; (3) spitefully; (4) sadly; (5) poorly.	4. _______	_______
5. cardinal	(1) desirable; (2) chief; (3) capable; (4) carefree; (5) normal.	5. _______	_______

(10 points for each correct answer) *Word Comprehension* without *contextual help (I)* _______

Word Comprehension with *contextual help (II)* _______

TOTAL WORD COMPREHENSION SCORE _______

Exercises

Improving Listening Skill

One way of testing any idea is by trying it. Charles E. Irvin mentions some activities that have proved successful in the well-developed listening-training program at Michigan State College. Try them yourself and decide which are most effective for you.

A. To make yourself "listening conscious," construct a *Code of Listening Manners.*

"Do's and Don'ts" of Acceptable Listening Deportment

1. __________
2. __________
3. __________
4. __________
5. __________
6. __________

B. Prepare an Inventory of your strengths and weaknesses in the listening activity.

Strengths	Weaknesses
1. __________	1. __________
2. __________	2. __________
3. __________	3. __________
4. __________	4. __________
5. __________	5. __________
6. __________	6. __________

C. List distracting factors present in your classroom—anything that tends to take your mind off listening. Discussion of such distractions often leads to the elimination of some and adjustments to others.

List of Distractions

1. __________
2. __________
3. __________
4. __________
5. __________
6. __________

D. Ask several people to write down the central idea in a talk. Compare and discuss any differences in the perceived main topic.

E. Ask a speaker to prepare a short talk in which he makes at least three main points, each of which is supported by a different kind of evidence. Ask the listeners to draw a line down the center of their note sheet. As they listen they are to write down the main points on one side of the line, the development details on the other. Compare notes with the speaker afterward to see if there is agreement.

NAME ______________________ DATE ______________ READING RATE ______________ WPM

COMPREHENSION CHECK QUESTIONS

1. When talking with someone, you are told to look at that person's (1) eyes; (2) hairline; (3) neckline; (4) all the preceding features. 1. ______
2. *A* stands for (1) **A**sk questions; (2) **A**void interrupting; (3) **A**ctive participation; (4) **A**void changing the subject. 2. ______
3. The author classifies questions into (1) no types; (2) two types; (3) four types; (4) five types. 3. ______
4. The author specifically mentions (1) Senator Dole; (2) Charles Dickens; (3) Rudyard Kipling; (4) Plato. 4. ______
5. Some people are said to get angry about (1) certain words; (2) lack of attention; (3) shifty eye contact; (4) being questioned. 5. ______

Receptive Comprehension ______

6. The main idea is to teach you how to (1) ask questions artfully; (2) understand what is said; (3) practice better listening; (4) learn better listening. 6. ______
7. In style this is best described as (1) lively; (2) formal; (3) informal; (4) journalistic. 7. ______
8. Emphasis is on the (1) who; (2) how; (3) when; (4) why. 8. ______
9. The Mike Douglas bit is primarily to show (1) Herman's salesmanship; (2) Mike's questioning ability; (3) Herman's listening ability; (4) Herman's use of questions. 9. ______
10. This piece is chiefly to (1) explain; (2) amuse; (3) make clear; (4) provide help. 10. ______

(10 points for each correct answer)

Reflective Comprehension ______

TOTAL READING COMPREHENSION SCORE ______

VOCABULARY CHECK QUESTIONS

			without context I	with context II
1.	**intent**	(1) direction; (2) hindrance; (3) purpose; (4) cover; (5) question.	1. ______	______
2.	**concise**	(1) complicated; (2) definite; (3) smooth; (4) natural; (5) brief.	2. ______	______
3.	**rapport**	(1) agreement; (2) entrance; (3) supply; (4) statement; (5) reaction.	3. ______	______
4.	**curb**	(1) cure; (2) connect; (3) gather; (4) restrain; (5) fold.	4. ______	______
5.	**prone**	(1) pretended; (2) disposed; (3) stop; (4) failed; (5) proof.	5. ______	______

(10 points for each correct answer)

Word Comprehension without *contextual help (I)* ______

Word Comprehension with *contextual help (II)* ______

TOTAL WORD COMPREHENSION SCORE ______

Exercises

Using the Radio to Improve Your Listening

To develop improved concentration, accuracy, and skill in listening, put your radio to work. In the morning, listen carefully to a fifteen-minute newscast, noting each story with a one- to five-word identifying phrase. When the broadcast is over, count the number of stories covered, turn your notes over, and see how many you can remember. Put a check after each story remembered. Record the newscast date and the number of stories you remembered in the first two columns below.

	Newscast	Stories remembered	Details remembered
1.			
2.			
3.			
4.			
5.			
6.			
7.			
8.			
9.			
10.			
11.			
12.			
13.			
14.			
15.			

With practice you should develop the ability to listen with enough skill to remember each story covered. The next step is to fill in the third column, headed *Details remembered.* See how many specific facts you can add for each story. When you have done this for two or three weeks, you will see improvement in both the second and third columns.

This practice lends itself well to class or group activity and works even better if the newscast is recorded and can be played back on a tape recorder or cassette. The entire group can listen, not even keeping a tally. After the newscast, the leader or teacher can give them the total number of stories covered, asking them to list the stories and to add as much factual information as possible.

The group can compare notes, try to resolve any differences in factual statements or opinions, and then listen again to the newscast. Such an exercise should also develop added awareness of details met in reading.

NAME ______________________ DATE ______________ READING RATE ______________ WPM

Comprehension Check Questions

1. Mention is made of a sports fan interested in (1) football; (2) hockey; (3) baseball; (4) tennis. 1. ______
2. How many processes of reasoning are described? (1) only one; (2) two; (3) three; (4) four. 2. ______
3. The authors say that you persuade by the way you (1) groom yourself; (2) dress; (3) stand; (4) gesture. 3. ______
4. The authors specifically mention (1) World War I; (2) World War II; (3) the CIA; (4) the KGB. 4. ______
5. You are expressly told to do what with an original belief or attitude? (1) trace its origin; (2) identify who contributed to it; (3) identify what contributed to it; (4) rate its strength on a scale from one to ten. 5. ______

Receptive Comprehension ______

6. This article is mainly to help you do what better? (1) recognize persuaders' strategies; (2) listen evaluatively; (3) identify propaganda techniques; (4) develop desired objectivity. 6. ______
7. You would infer that the receptive questions in this text are closest to Adler's (1) understanding step; (2) judgment step; (3) two steps equally; (4) no logical connection. 7. ______
8. This selection is best classified as (1) persuasion; (2) description; (3) exposition; (4) narration. 8. ______
9. You would conclude that effective evaluation depends primarily on (1) intelligence; (2) interest; (3) information; (4) logic. 9. ______
10. Apparently you should listen evaluatively to what kind of messages? (1) all kinds; (2) descriptive; (3) explanatory; (4) persuasive. 10. ______

(10 points for each correct answer)

Reflective Comprehension ______
TOTAL READING COMPREHENSION SCORE ______

Vocabulary Check Questions

			without context I	with context II
1.	**evaluate**	(1) judge; (2) escape; (3) create; (4) remove; (5) make equal.	1. ______	______
2.	**premises**	(1) promises; (2) advances; (3) folders; (4) prizes; (5) assertions.	2. ______	______
3.	**modulated**	(1) marked; (2) adjusted; (3) damaged; (4) supported; (5) criticized.	3. ______	______
4.	**monitor**	(1) manipulate; (2) molest; (3) check; (4) pacify; (5) rotate.	4. ______	______
5.	**converse**	(1) accompanying; (2) conventional; (3) identical; (4) opposite; (5) vertical.	5. ______	______

(10 points for each correct answer)

Word Comprehension without *contextual help (I)* ______
Word Comprehension with *contextual help (II)* ______
TOTAL WORD COMPREHENSION SCORE ______

Exercises

Sharpening Awareness of Common Propaganda Devices

Look for two or three examples of each of the devices listed below as you watch TV commercials, listen to the radio, or read newspapers and magazines. Record what you find in the space provided.

1. *Name calling:* Speakers or writers sometimes try to persuade by attaching names to certain individuals or groups. For example, a candidate may call his opponent a "big spender," using that name to try to persuade people to vote against the candidate.

2. *Glittering generalities:* Somewhat similar to name calling, this technique resorts to labels flooded with emotion such as "motherhood," "friend of the people," or "patriotic duty." After all, who wants to be considered unpatriotic or against motherhood?

3. *Plain folks:* We usually feel more comfortable with someone who looks, acts, and talks like us. Some speakers try to take advantage of that by talking like workers when talking to workers and dressing so as not to isolate themselves from those they are addressing. They want to look and act just like their audience—ordinary folk.

4. *Transfer:* This strategy involves transferring a positive reaction from something or someone liked to the speakers themselves. As a speaker, if you select a clergyman to introduce you, you hope the normal positive feelings toward clergy will transfer over to you. You arrange to have an American flag beside you on the platform, trusting that your listeners, feelings toward the flag will rub off on you.

5. *Testimonial:* When a football star advertises shaving cream, the speaker hopes that the admiration and respect given to the star will sell the product or increase the stature of the speaker.

6. *Card stacking:* By this device the speaker mentions all the arguments in favor of the question to be advanced, hoping that arguments against the question will be overlooked. Or the speaker may stack the cards in the other direction, mentioning only reasons to oppose the move.

7. *Bandwagon:* When you hear someone say "Everyone does it," your tendency is probably to think that must be right. The speaker's hope is that you too will want to get on the bandwagon. Figures on those using a certain medication or buying a certain product often use the bandwagon device.

Mini-check of Listening Versus Reading

For a quick comparison of your performance in the two assimilative areas of learning—listening and reading—take any of the 500-word exercise selections from this text (see the listing, pp. 237–238). Read one, take the comprehension test, and record your score. Then have someone read aloud to you another similar short selection, also reading the ten questions once only as you listen and answer them. Compare your two comprehension scores. If your performance in listening is much below your performance in reading, give additional thought and attention to the readings in this section on listening and work at developing added skill.

LISTENING COMPREHENSION SCORE: _______

READING COMPREHENSION SCORE: _______

NAME ______________________ DATE ______________ READING RATE ______________ WPM

Comprehension Check Questions

1. We listen empathically largely for what reasons? (1) intrinsic; (2) extrinsic; (3) personal profit; (4) educational. 1. _______
2. What do the authors call empathic listening? (1) the heart; (2) the up-side; (3) the nadir; (4) the pinnacle. 2. _______
3. Who originated empathic listening? (1) Carl Rogers; (2) Karl Menninger; (3) Jung; (4) Freud. 3. _______
4. When listening empathically, you are told to (1) give advice; (2) praise the speaker; (3) remain silent; (4) talk about similar experiences. 4. _______
5. Ellen's friend was named (1) Bill; (2) Fred; (3) Tim; (4) Carl. 5. _______

Receptive Comprehension _______

6. The focus is mainly on doing what about empathic listening? (1) defining it; (2) explaining how it differs from other listening; (3) telling us how to improve it; (4) revealing the empathy-seeking speaker's goals. 6. _______
7. An empathy-seeking speaker mainly wants to (1) get therapy; (2) get advice; (3) express feelings; (4) arouse sympathy. 7. _______
8. Empathic listening demands above all that the listener (1) comprehends the message; (2) understands the feelings; (3) communicates those understandings back to the speaker; (4) all the above. 8. _______
9. In empathic listening, who or what must take center stage? (1) the speaker; (2) the listener; (3) the message; (4) the situation. 9. _______
10. The headache-doctor-patient episode primarily points up the importance of (1) self-discovery; (2) proper diagnosis; (3) silence; (4) a caring response. 10. _______

(10 points for each correct answer)

Reflective Comprehension _______

TOTAL READING COMPREHENSION SCORE _______

Vocabulary Check Questions

		without context I	with context II
1. **intrinsic**	(1) fearless; (2) unimportant; (3) safe; (4) inborn; (5) casual.	1. _______	_______
2. **potent**	(1) vague; (2) intentional; (3) sinister; (4) tragic; (5) powerful.	2. _______	_______
3. **distraught**	(1) distributed; (2) separated; (3) confused; (4) choked; (5) teased.	3. _______	_______
4. **deterrent**	(1) end; (2) obstacle; (3) flood; (4) cleaner; (5) debris.	4. _______	_______
5. **diffuse**	(1) spread; (2) hold back; (3) stop; (4) put out; (5) wait.	5. _______	_______

(10 points for each correct answer)

Word Comprehension without *contextual help (I)* _______

Word Comprehension with *contextual help (II)* _______

TOTAL WORD COMPREHENSION SCORE _______

EXERCISES

YOUR DECODING SKILLS

Communication is essentially a partnership arrangement—between speaker and listener, between writer and reader.

For example, suppose you are listening to an uninspired speaker drone monotonously through a lecture, eyes fixed on his well-worn notes. You remember a definition of the lecture system—"a system whereby information passes from the notes of the teacher to the notes of the student without affecting the minds of either." This starts your mind off on an interesting tangent for the rest of the hour. Result? A complete breakdown of communication!

Bring that word *partnership* back into the picture. In a successful partnership, the less one partner does, the more the other must do if the result is to be the same. The listener, if sufficiently alert, may supply essential background material that the speaker neglects to mention. He may also generate interest in what is being said even though the speaker makes no attempts in that direction. In short, through his own skill as listener, he may compensate significantly for speaker shortcomings.

A study reported in the *Quarterly Journal of Speech* involved the classroom presentation of a lecture before two equally matched groups of students, to one group by a poor speaker, to the other by an outstanding speaker. Results showed that alert, well-motivated listeners got practically as much from the poorly delivered presentation as from the other, tangible evidence that you can compensate significantly.

The skillful reader can do likewise. "Tis the good reader that makes the good book," is Emerson's way of pointing up the key role of the reader. Adler, in his book, *How to Read a Book,* writes of one situation where everyone willingly carries full responsibility:

> When they are in love and are reading a love letter, they read for all they are worth. They read every word three ways: they read between the lines and in the margins; they read the whole in terms of the parts, and each part in terms of the whole; they grow sensitive to context and ambiguity, to insinuation and implication; they perceive the color of words, the odor of phrases, and the weight of sentences. They may even take the punctuation into account. Then, if never before or after, they read.

The intelligent student may infer from this that well-directed efforts to improve his reading and listening efficiency should give him a real academic advantage.

As one university dean expresses it, "Success in college will depend on the student's ability in silent reading, more than on any other agency, and on the discriminating use of that ability." According to a study completed at Yale, students who received training in reading earned significantly higher final grade averages than did untrained students of equal predicted grade status and slightly higher initial reading status. That difference brought the trained students better grades—better by about 15 percentile ranks. Listening shows a similar relationship.

Enough said. Start immediately to sharpen both your reading and listening skills.

(500 words)

COMPREHENSION CHECK QUESTIONS

1. The writer mentions (1) lecture notes; (2) class quizzes; (3) labs; (4) educational movies. 1. _______

2. A good listener was said to be able to (1) predict what is coming; (2) generate interest in the speaker; (3) develop increased hearing acuity; (4) develop added word power. 2. _______

3. The selection mentions the (1) *Quarterly Journal of Speech;* (2) *English Journal;* (3) *Speech Quarterly;* (4) *Theatre Arts.* 3. _______

4. Mention is made of the reading of a (1) diary; (2) joke book; (3) letter; (4) theme. 4. _______

5. One study mentioned was done at (1) Yale; (2) Harvard; (3) Vassar; (4) Monmouth. 5. _______

6. This is mainly about (1) how to improve your reading ability; (2) the skills relating to academic success; (3) the importance of listening; (4) the chief role of communication. 6. _______

7. The definition of the lecture system was intended to show the need for (1) taking good notes; (2) visual aids; (3) alert listening; (4) discussion techniques. 7. _______

8. The study involving two speakers, one outstanding, the other poor, was used to show the value of (1) effective delivery; (2) strong interest; (3) concentration; (4) good listening. 8. _______

9. The quoted passage from Adler's book was intended to point up (1) how difficult the reading process is; (2) the meaning of reading; (3) the need to rely on context; (4) the importance of personal relationships. 9. _______

10. Which of the following statements is most closely in accord with this selection? (1) hard work means success in college; (2) concentrate on skills, not subject matter; (3) the smartest students get the best grades; (4) listening skills bring higher grades than comparable reading skills. 10. _______

SCORE _______

Answers: 1. 1; 2. 2; 3. 1; 4. 3; 5. 1; 6. 2; 7. 3; 8. 4; 9. 2; 10. 2.

NAME ______________________ DATE ______________ READING RATE ______________ WPM

COMPREHENSION CHECK QUESTIONS

1.	Vocabulary books are said to (1) sell well; (2) sell poorly; (3) be easy reading; (4) be difficult reading.	1. _______
2.	The test accompanying this article was devised by (1) William Morris; (2) John Strachey; (3) Norman Lewis; (4) Wilfred Funk.	2. _______
3.	A widely accepted figure for the number of words in the English language is (1) 1,250,000; (2) 1,000,000; (3) 750,000; (4) 500,000.	3. _______
4.	In building a vocabulary, crossword puzzles are said to be (1) extremely helpful; (2) moderately helpful; (3) useless; (4) of uncertain value.	4. _______
5.	The writer specifically mentions (1) Mark Twain; (2) Washington Irving; (3) Emerson; (4) Galsworthy.	5. _______
	Receptive Comprehension	_______
6.	The purpose of this selection is to help the reader (1) understand the power of words; (2) measure and increase his vocabulary; (3) enjoy reading the classics; (4) calculate how many words he should know.	6. _______
7.	Word-building books are criticized for (1) their difficulty; (2) their artificiality; (3) their organization; (4) their length.	7. _______
8.	Crossword puzzles are criticized for (1) their repetition of certain words; (2) their oversimplification of definitions; (3) their concern with freak words; (4) no specified reason.	8. _______
9.	You would infer from this selection that the important thing to do is to read (1) certain books; (2) any books; (3) technical books; (4) the dictionary.	9. _______
10.	The chief reason for interest in words is (1) increased salary; (2) admiration for the fluent speaker; (3) the urge for self-improvement; (4) not discussed.	10. _______

(10 points for each correct answer)

Reflective Comprehension	_______
TOTAL READING COMPREHENSION SCORE	_______

VOCABULARY CHECK QUESTIONS

			without context I	with context II
1.	**prowess**	(1) favor; (2) priority; (3) difficulty; (4) skill; (5) slowness.	1. _______	_______
2.	**prestige**	(1) wealth; (2) privacy; (3) closeness; (4) education; (5) distinction.	2. _______	_______
3.	**correlation**	(1) conflict; (2) likeness; (3) newness; (4) training; (5) argument.	3. _______	_______
4.	**absorption**	(1) payment; (2) assimilation; (3) picture; (4) abuse; (5) relaxation.	4. _______	_______
5.	**formidable**	(1) difficult; (2) shapely; (3) angry; (4) calm; (5) sincere.	5. _______	_______

(10 points for each correct answer)

Word Comprehension without *contextual help (I)*	_______
Word Comprehension with *contextual help (II)*	_______
TOTAL WORD COMPREHENSION SCORE	_______

ANSWER KEY TO SELF-SCORING VOCABULARY TEST

Check your answers for the vocabulary test on pp. 182–184 against the key below.

Section I

1. u	6. k	11. e	16. o	21. y
2. d	7. p	12. j	17. r	22. b
3. c	8. g	13. s	18. a	23. i
4. m	9. x	14. l	19. n	24. t
5. q	10. w	15. f	20. v	25. h

Section II

1. b	6. r	11. g	16. u	21. c
2. m	7. n	12. d	17. x	22. v
3. p	8. f	13. a	18. q	23. w
4. l	9. o	14. s	19. j	24. h
5. y	10. i	15. t	20. k	25. e

Section III

1. d	6. b	11. c	16. a	21. b	26. a	31. b	36. d	41. b	46. c
2. c	7. b	12. d	17. c	22. b	27. b	32. a	37. b	42. a	47. a
3. b	8. c	13. d	18. b	23. a	28. d	33. d	38. a	43. c	48. b
4. d	9. d	14. d	19. d	24. b	29. a	34. c	39. d	44. a	49. d
5. a	10. a	15. d	20. c	25. b	30. d	35. c	40. b	45. d	50. a

HOW TO SCORE YOURSELF

To score Sections I and II: Find the number of *correct* answers and multiply by 800. Thus if you had 30 *correct* answers, your score would be 24,000.

To score Section III: Count the number of *mistakes* you made and multiply by 533. Subtract the total from 20,000. Thus if you had 20 *mistakes,* you should deduct 10,660 from 20,000, which would give you a score of 9,340.

Add the scores of all three sections to find the *approximate* number of words in your recognition vocabulary. In the example, this would be 24,000 plus 9,340, or 33,340 words—an excellent score for most people.

This test does not consider the number of proper names that may be in your vocabulary. This part of vocabulary varies so greatly from person to person that no attempt to evaluate it is practicable.

Most of us use, besides our general vocabulary, a jargon of our trade or profession, which may run from fifty to a thousand or more words in the case of law or medicine. It is thus safe to say that a professional man's vocabulary will be substantially larger than this test may indicate.

On this test a rating of 15,000 words is excellent for a high school student. An adult high school graduate should score 25,000. A college graduate should score well above 30,000, and a person who uses words regularly in his work—an author or newspaperman—should rate above 40,000.

PAGING MRS. MALAPROP

These sentences contain some vocabulary slips. Cross out the wrong word and substitute the intended one.

1. During the battle the soldier was wounded in a venerable spot. ____________
2. Because of their part in the escapade, they were dispelled from school. ____________
3. The deviation of a word is given in an unabridged dictionary. ____________
4. The entire crew of the ill-fated ship was taken into custardy. ____________
5. They tried in vain to distinguish the raging conflagration. ____________

USING THE RIGHT WORD

In the following sentences, select the word that should be used. Answers are below.

1. This medicine should have a good (affect, effect).
2. The writer did not mean to (imply, infer) that.
3. With complete satisfaction, the worker (lay, laid) down the hammer.
4. The students (deprecated, depreciated) their efforts.
5. The press and radio seem (complementary, complimentary) rather than competitive.

Answers: 1. vulnerable; 2. expelled; 3. derivation; 4. custody; 5. extinguish; 1. effect; 2. imply; 3. laid; 4. deprecated; 5. complementary.

NAME ______________________ DATE ______________ READING RATE ______________ WPM

COMPREHENSION CHECK QUESTIONS

1. Words, taken separately, are likened to (1) building stones; (2) bricks; (3) windows; (4) arrows. 1. _______
2. The article refers to (1) an orator; (2) a politician; (3) an actress; (4) a minister. 2. _______
3. The article compares (1) the pen and the sword; (2) the thinker and the dreamer; (3) newsmen and newsmakers; (4) spoken and written words. 3. _______
4. Words are said to have (1) glamour; (2) independent ability; (3) egotism; (4) picturesque origins. 4. _______
5. Mention is made of (1) Washington; (2) Lincoln; (3) Mark Twain; (4) Plato. 5. _______

Receptive Comprehension _______

6. This is mostly about how words (1) improve on our ideas; (2) absorb and convey feeling; (3) reflect personal feelings; (4) must be selected with care. 6. _______
7. The sentence "The boy is fat" is used to illustrate how (1) easily words communicate ideas; (2) well words express feelings; (3) readily words can be made into sentences; (4) important the human element is. 7. _______
8. Apparently the best advice to the would-be writer is to (1) expand your vocabulary; (2) study great literature; (3) take a course in writing; (4) care about your subject. 8. _______
9. Most emphasis is on the (1) when; (2) how; (3) who; (4) where. 9. _______
10. The tone of the essay is (1) humorous; (2) colloquial; (3) lively; (4) matter-of-fact. 10. _______

(10 points for each correct answer)

Reflective Comprehension _______

TOTAL READING COMPREHENSION SCORE _______

VOCABULARY CHECK QUESTIONS

			without context I	with context II
1.	**convey**	(1) guide; (2) carry; (3) drive; (4) change; (5) collect.	1. _______	_______
2.	**symbols**	(1) feelings; (2) groups; (3) syllables; (4) representations; (5) instruments.	2. _______	_______
3.	**respond**	(1) regard; (2) decorate; (3) react; (4) continue; (5) breathe.	3. _______	_______
4.	**duly**	(1) properly; (2) keenly; (3) gloomily; (4) lastly; (5) simply.	4. _______	_______
5.	**competent**	(1) profitable; (2) intricate; (3) contestant; (4) poetic; (5) able.	5. _______	_______

(10 points for each correct answer)

Word Comprehension without *contextual help (I)* _______

Word Comprehension with *contextual help (II)* _______

TOTAL WORD COMPREHENSION SCORE _______

EXERCISES

SENSING THE POWER OF WORDS

Some years ago *The New York Times* carried an editorial headed "Vocabulary and Marks," which began by asking if there was any magic formula for getting high marks in college. The president of Stevens Institute was quoted as saying that those students who worked on vocabulary their freshman year "were thereby enabled to do relatively better work in all their sophomore courses than their fellow classmates did. Those who improved most in vocabulary averaged three or four places nearer the top of their class during their sophomore year than during their freshman year. Conversely, those who did not improve at all in vocabulary averaged 7.5. places nearer the bottom of their class during the sophomore year." Apparently a new word a day keeps the low grades away!

Those results suggested the need to check the relationship between frequency of dictionary use and success in a single class, such as in a University of Minnesota Efficient Reading class. Since all students in such classes take a standardized reading test at the beginning and end of the course, any differences could be noted exactly. On the last day of class students were asked how frequently they had used their dictionary during the quarter. Those who said they had used a dictionary once a week or less improved on the pre- and post-test standardized score 11 percent. By comparison, those who said they had used a dictionary once a day or more improved 26 percent or 136 percent more than those who used a dictionary less frequently. In a reading improvement course, a new word a day keeps the low grades away also. Academically speaking, a student's best friend looks like the dictionary. Keep it handy. Use it frequently. It will pay off well. Don't underestimate the power of words.

WORDS THAT SMILE AND SNARL

Our words usually reflect our attitudes. If a boy meets a thin girl and is favorably impressed, he is likely to use the word *slender* to describe her. If he is not impressed, the word *skinny* may slip out. They both mean the same thing; yet one has a favorable, the other an unfavorable, connotation. Yes, you can say she's a vision, but not she's a sight.

Observations	Favorable	Unfavorable
EXAMPLE: She is thin.	**slender**	**skinny**
1. He is *fat*.	______	______
2. He *asked for* a favor.	______	______
3. He made a *long speech*.	______	______
4. She *spends money carefully*.	______	______
5. Her hat was *different*.	______	______

WORDS THAT WALK AND LIVE

Some words in common use today are actually mythological characters still living on in our language. Use your dictionary to discover the character behind each of the following words and the characterizing detail that gives the word its meaning.

Words	Characters	Characterizing Details
EXAMPLE: herculean	**Hercules**	**strength (to do the difficult)**
1. tantalize	______	______
2. procrustean	______	______
3. panic	______	______
4. venereal	______	______
5. odyssey	______	______

Many words can be used as more than one part of speech. In the following exercise, compose sentences for each part of speech indicated by the label. You may want help from your dictionary for this, distinctions of this kind being quite important.

Words	Sentences
EXAMPLE: like (as adj.)	**You must pay a like sum to the other party.**
1. *round* (as adj.)	______________________
2. *round* (as noun)	______________________
3. *round* (as v.t.)	______________________
4. *round* (as prep.)	______________________

NAME ______________________ DATE ______________ READING RATE ______________ WPM

Comprehension Check Questions

1. The author prefers to think in terms of what dictionary? (1) *Funk and Wagnalls*; (2) *Webster's New International*; (3) *Thorndike-Barnhart*; (4) *Webster's New World*. 1. _______
2. The article lists some words brought into our vocabulary by (1) playing the piano; (2) stargazing; (3) gardening; (4) sailing. 2. _______
3. Specific mention is made of the root (1) *auto*; (2) *nym*; (3) *lex*; (4) *floris*. 3. _______
4. The devil in "between the devil and the deep blue sea" is (1) a reference to a myth; (2) Satan; (3) a cliff overhanging the water; (4) a part of a boat. 4. _______
5. One of the rare words mentioned is (1) *alb*; (2) *podagra*; (3) *manubrium*; (4) *volute*. 5. _______

Receptive Comprehension _______

6. The main idea is to (1) help you improve your vocabulary; (2) stimulate interest in vocabulary development; (3) show how vocabulary grows; (4) describe four stages of vocabulary development. 6. _______
7. Most emphasis is on (1) firsthand experience; (2) daily effort; (3) frequent use; (4) attention to key roots and prefixes. 7. _______
8. Particular stress is on (1) reading aloud; (2) getting fun out of words; (3) correct pronunciation; (4) reading more. 8. _______
9. Mention of *nasturtium* and *nightmare* is to get us to (1) be more precise in definition; (2) develop interest in word origins; (3) pronounce words carefully; (4) notice spelling difficulties. 9. _______
10. Most of the main points are developed by (1) analogies; (2) stories; (3) specific details; (4) generalities. 10. _______

(10 points for each correct answer)

Reflective Comprehension _______

TOTAL READING COMPREHENSION SCORE _______

Vocabulary Check Questions

			without context I	with context II
1.	**obsolete**	(1) colloquial; (2) stubborn; (3) worn out; (4) evident; (5) out of date.	1. _______	_______
2.	**recalcitrant**	(1) unruly; (2) hard; (3) reciprocal; (4) reassuring; (5) calculation.	2. _______	_______
3.	**lethargic**	(1) healthy; (2) lively; (3) dull; (4) deadly; (5) elevated.	3. _______	_______
4.	**lissome**	(1) lazy; (2) lisping; (3) irregular; (4) nimble; (5) messy.	4. _______	_______
5.	**alb**	(1) bird; (2) robe; (3) excuse; (4) holder; (5) powder.	5. _______	_______

(10 points for each correct answer)

Word Comprehension without *contextual help (I)* _______

Word Comprehension with *contextual help (II)* _______

TOTAL WORD COMPREHENSION SCORE _______

EXERCISES

THE LDE FORMULA

Can you get meanings for strange words or word parts without your dictionary? Certainly! It's just a matter of harnessing brain power to word power and applying the LDE Formula. Here's how it works.

Take the strange Latin word *omnis*, which gives us the prefix *omni-*. What does it mean? You don't know? You've never taken Latin? When dealing with words, never say, "I don't know." That shuts the door to important vocabulary growth. You probably do know, but just don't know that you do. Think again. What's an omnidirectional radio receiver? One that receives sound waves from all directions, you say. Now if you know that, you really know what *omni-* means. It means "all."

That kind of reasoning lies behind the LDE Formula. Your first step when meeting a strange prefix, root, or suffix is to LIST several words containing that element. With *omni-*, let's say you listed *omnidirectional* and *omnipotent*. Maybe that's all you thought of. Or perhaps you also listed *omnipresent* and *omniscient*. You don't necessarily need that many. Sometimes one word is enough, although usually the more the better. That's step one of the formula: LIST.

The second step? DEFINE each word you listed. Let's say you define *omnidirectional* as "in all directions," *omnipotent* as "all-powerful," *omnipresent* as "always present," and *omniscient* as "all-knowing." That's step two: DEFINE.

The third and last step is to EXTRACT the common denominator or meaning. What do the *omni-* words have in common? The meaning "all"! The formula made you aware of that meaning. From now on when you see a word beginning *omni-*, look for that meaning. An omnivorous reader has to be a reader of "all" kinds of things.

That's how the three-step LDE Formula works. It's not only three-step, it's also three-way—to be used with all three kinds of word parts: prefixes, roots, and suffixes. Furthermore, if one word part can be a shortcut to the meanings of over a thousand words, this formula deserves the label *super-shortcut*, for it works with all elements. You'll be more than pleased with the way it speeds your vocabulary growth, not one word at a time but up to a thousand.

That doesn't mean you'll always arrive at the right meaning, but you should always be closer. Even if the formula works only 70 percent of the time, that gives you a 70 percent advantage over those who don't apply it—an advantage well worth having.

APPLYING THE LDE FORMULA

To get better acquainted with the LDE Formula, work through the following exercise. It will pay off nicely.

What does the prefix *syn-* mean? First, list some *syn* words. Suppose you list *synchronize*, *synonym*, and *synthesize*. Now define each. To synchronize two watches is to bring them together in time. Synonyms are words that belong together in meaning. And to synthesize is to bring separate parts together into a whole. Finally, extract the common meaning. You see that *syn-* probably means "together."

Now try the formula with another prefix: *hyper-*. What does it mean? Again, make a list—perhaps *hyperactive*, *hypertension*, and *hypersensitive*. Define each. Hyperactive means "more active than normal." *Hypertension* means "abnormally high tension"; and *hypersensitive*, "excessively sensitive." Extract the common meaning and you have "more" or "above normal" as meanings of *hyper-*.

Now try the formula with some roots. What does *gress* (from Latin *gradi*) mean? First, make a list. Since you may not think of any words beginning with *gress*, try adding some prefixes. Let's say you list *progress*, *regress*, and *digress*. If you progress, you "move forward." If you regress, you "move back"; and if you digress, you "move away" from the subject or point you're making. Extract the common denominator and you get "move" as the meaning of *gress*. Actually *gress* means "step," but if you got "move" or "go," that's close enough.

Try another: the Latin root *tractus*. What does it mean? Take off the ending to get closer to the English form, in this case *tract*. Suppose you list *tractor*, *attract*, and *contract*. Define them, filling in the blanks below.

A tractor is a vehicle for __________ loads.
To attract is to __________ attention to.
A contract is an agreement __________ up between two or more parties.

The Latin word *tractus* apparently means "to draw."

Finally, try the formula on a suffix. What does *-ic* mean? Let's say you list *metallic* and *angelic*. You define them: *metallic* is "like metal" and *angelic* is "like an angel." Extracting the common meaning, *-ic*, apparently means "like."

Never say that you don't know what any and all such elements mean. Just put the LDE Formula to work and discover the meanings.

NAME ______________________ DATE ______________ READING RATE ______________ WPM

COMPREHENSION CHECK QUESTIONS

1. The writer's first job was as (1) refuse-collection person; (2) copyboy; (3) receptionist; (4) paper delivery person. 1. _______

2. Mention is made of a restaurant located in (1) San Francisco; (2) Los Angeles; (3) Berkeley; (4) Long Beach. 2. _______

3. The writer mentions (1) Jack the Ripper; (2) Boston Strangler; (3) the Manson killings; (4) Bluebeard. 3. _______

4. In reference to a male person, specific mention was made of (1) smelly sweat socks; (2) a dingy sweatshirt; (3) grimy shirt collars; (4) baggy sweat pants. 4. _______

5. This writer is presently writing a book about (1) cattlemen; (2) Southwest history; (3) Arizona; (4) the rodeo. 5. _______

Receptive Comprehension _______

6. This selection is mainly focused on doing what about the desexing problem? (1) pointing up its presence; (2) suggesting a solution; (3) suggesting its insolubility; (4) pointing up its ridiculous effects. 6. _______

7. Points are developed largely through use of (1) contrast and comparison; (2) specific examples; (3) description; (4) analogies. 7. _______

8. The tone of this article is best described as (1) matter-of-fact; (2) dramatic; (3) humorous; (4) cynical. 8. _______

9. The primary purpose is to (1) make clear; (2) warn; (3) amuse; (4) explain. 9. _______

10. Transpersons were mentioned apparently (1) as further complications; (2) as supporters of the new trend; (3) as supporters of a return to gender; (4) as genderless persons. 10. _______

(10 points for each correct answer)

Reflective Comprehension _______

TOTAL READING COMPREHENSION SCORE _______

VOCABULARY CHECK QUESTIONS

			without context I	with context II
1.	**gentility**	(1) pleasantness; (2) generosity; (3) genius; (4) refinement; (5) kindness.	1. _______	_______
2.	**generic**	(1) vague; (2) popular; (3) generous; (4) courteous; (5) universal.	2. _______	_______
3.	**replete**	(1) renewed; (2) well-filled; (3) replicate; (4) plain; (5) pleasing.	3. _______	_______
4.	**suffuses**	(1) satisfies; (2) suffers; (3) chokes; (4) overspreads; (5) substitutes.	4. _______	_______
5.	**ludicrous**	(1) sad; (2) fortunate; (3) absurd; (4) profitable; (5) clear.	5. _______	_______

(10 points for each correct answer)

Word Comprehension without *contextual help (I)* _______

Word Comprehension with *contextual help (II)* _______

TOTAL WORD COMPREHENSION SCORE _______

DICTIONARY— THE READER'S BEST FRIEND

How often do you use your dictionary? Your answer to that important question should tell you how much improvement in reading to expect. At the end of a reading improvement course, students were asked a number of questions, one relating to their use of the dictionary. Those who said they used it "once a week or less" improved only 11 percentile ranks in reading. Those in the same class who answered, "once a day or more" improved over *twice* as much—26 percentile ranks.

As you can see, the dictionary is a real help—*if you use it frequently and accurately*.

The word *accurately* needs particular emphasis. A freshman class was asked to look up the word *gargoyle* in the dictionary to discover its proper plural form. The class was almost evenly divided. Forty-one per cent said the dictionary gave *gargoyle* for both singular and plural. Fifty-nine per cent said the dictionary gave only *gargoyles* as proper. Yet the dictionaries all agreed. Only the readers disagreed—far too many unable to read the dictionary accurately.

The dictionary is difficult reading largely because of its brevity and its many special conventions, so easily overlooked. For example, in one desk dictionary a comma between two different spellings does far more than just separate them, as normal convention would suggest. That comma has this special meaning: "spellings proper in British use are regularly set off by a comma from the American spellings." That's a lot to say with one small comma, but that is what a reader of dictionaries has to be aware of.

In wondering where to divide the word *transit* at the end of a line, suppose you consult the dictionary. The entry is divided in this way—*trans it*, but in parenthesis right after that entry it is divided *tran sit*. Does this mean it can be divided at either point or is one correct and the other not? Again, you will find individuals reading the dictionary yet coming away with totally different impressions, some becoming informed, others misinformed because of failure to read with accuracy.

Or suppose you decide to see exactly what that common word *nice* means. Here is what one dictionary says: "1. foolish, stupid." Does this mean we are all misusing that word? How are the definitions arranged in your dictionary—in chronological order, in order of frequency, in order of importance? Obviously, this is something you must know in order to read your dictionary accurately.

And can you find such things as the height of Mount Everest, the date Socrates drank the fatal hemlock, and the length of the Mississippi River in your desk dictionary? Are fictitious characters listed—such as Lochinvar, Shylock, or Frankenstein?

If you cannot answer all those questions easily and accurately, turn to that section in the front of your dictionary called the "Explanatory Notes," "Guide," or "Plan," and study it with the utmost care. Then, and only then, can you use the dictionary with the sureness and maturity that this invaluable reference aid deserves.

(500 words)

Comprehension Check Questions

1. Students who used the dictionary most improved how many percentile ranks? (1) 11; (2) 15; (3) 21; (4) 26. 1. _______

2. After consulting the dictionary about the plural of *gargoyle*, (1) the students all agreed; (2) a few had trouble; (3) the class was almost evenly divided; (4) dictionaries were found to disagree. 2. _______

3. One reason given to explain the difficulty of reading a dictionary was (1) its complexity; (2) its size; (3) its brevity; (4) the large number of words included. 3. _______

4. There was specific discussion of (1) pronunciation; (2) derivation; (3) spelling; (4) word division. 4. _______

5. There was mention of (1) Mount Etna; (2) Lochinvar; (3) Shakespeare; (4) Amazon River. 5. _______

6. This is mainly intended to show what about the dictionary? (1) its importance; (2) the difficulties in reading it; (3) its wealth of interesting information; (4) the variety of information. 6. _______

7. The discussion of *nice* is intended to get you to think about (1) differences between dictionaries; (2) the different meanings a word may have; (3) the way context changes meaning; (4) the way definitions are arranged. 7. _______

8. This selection is intended to get you to (1) do something; (2) believe something; (3) understand something; (4) enjoy something. 8. _______

9. The discussion on *transit* was to show (1) the importance of proper word division; (2) the acceptable variations in usage; (3) how usage is changing; (4) the difficulties of getting accurate information 9. _______

10. This topic is developed largely through (1) examples; (2) definitions; (3) figures; (4) analysis. 10. _______

SCORE _______

Answers: 1. 4; 2. 3; 3. 3; 4. 4; 5. 2; 6. 2; 7. 4; 8. 1; 9. 4; 10. 1.

NAME ______________________ DATE ______________ READING RATE ______________ WPM

Comprehension Check Questions

1. Bimbi is spoken of as (1) a safe blower; (2) an old-time burglar; (3) a second-story man; (4) a dope pusher. 1. ______

2. The author says he didn't know a verb from a (1) noun; (2) book; (3) hole in the ground; (4) house. 2. ______

3. The author felt that he should try to improve his (1) speech; (2) arithmetic; (3) grammar; (4) penmanship. 3. ______

4. How many words does he think he wrote while in prison? (1) two million; (2) a million; (3) half a million; (4) amount not specified. 4. ______

5. Lights out came at what time? (1) nine P.M.; (2) ten P.M.; (3) eleven P.M.; (4) no exact time given. 5. ______

Receptive Comprehension ______

6. The main focus is on how (1) Bimbi inspired Malcolm X; (2) Malcolm X developed his reading abilities and interests; (3) Malcolm X developed his vocabulary; (4) strongly Malcolm X was motivated. 6. ______

7. Malcolm X apparently felt that Bimbi was respected, largely for what reason? (1) age; (2) experience; (3) words; (4) personality. 7. ______

8. What subject of discussion attracted Malcolm X most strongly to Bimbi? (1) the science of human behavior; (2) Thoreau; (3) religion; (4) historical events and figures. 8. ______

9. Copying the dictionary seemed to please Malcolm X primarily because he (1) could remember the words easily; (2) improved his handwriting greatly; (3) learned words he didn't know existed; (4) found he could use them frequently. 9. ______

10. Of the following words, which best characterizes Malcolm X? (1) tough; (2) clever; (3) persistent; (4) sociable. 10. ______

(10 points for each correct answer)

Reflective Comprehension ______

TOTAL READING COMPREHENSION SCORE ______

Vocabulary Check Questions

			without context I	with context II
1.	**quota**	(1) query; (2) figure; (3) proportional share; (4) large quantity; (5) pursuit.	1. ______	______
2.	**expounded**	(1) crushed; (2) explained; (3) investigated; (4) transported; (5) tried.	2. ______	______
3.	**emulate**	(1) hire; (2) sooth; (3) antagonize; (4) hinder; (5) imitate.	3. ______	______
4.	**riffling**	(1) occurring frequently; (2) shooting; (3) opening; (4) leafing rapidly; (5) guessing	4. ______	______
5.	**dormant**	(1) sleeping; (2) uniformed; (3) worn; (4) carefully planned; (5) sympathetic.	5. ______	______

(10 points for each correct answer)

Word Comprehension without *contextual help (I)* ______

Word Comprehension with *contextual help (II)* ______

TOTAL WORD COMPREHENSION SCORE ______

Exercises

Learning and Using Suffixes

Do you use four or five words to express an idea when one would do it more effectively? If so, put suffixes to work. For example, "capable of being read" boils down neatly into the word *readable* when you utilize the right suffix. Use the twenty suffixes listed below to complete the words in the right-hand column.

Suffixes:

-able	**-er**	**-ile**	**-ly**	**-tion**
-al	**-esque**	**-ish**	**-ock**	**-trix**
-ate	**-ess-**	**-ive**	**-ory**	**-ule**
-dom	**-ful**	**-less**	**-ose**	**-ulent**

1. A small hill or mound is a hill__________
2. The state of being wise is called wis__________.
3. Of or pertaining to an infant is infant__________.
4. Full of or characterized by fraud is fraud__________.
5. One who is young is youth__________.
6. A woman aviator is an avia__________.
7. Something capable of being retracted is retract__________.
8. If someone works without tiring, he is tire__________.
9. A situation that lends itself to remedy is remedi__________.
10. One who helps is a help__________.
11. Something in the manner or style of a picture is called pictur__________.
12. To cause something to become antique is to antiqu__________.
13. A female lion is a lion__________.
14. Something pertaining to a book is book__________.
15. A minute globe is a glob__________.
16. Having the nature of a commendation means commendat__________.
17. To act toward instigating something is to instiga __________ it.
18. A scheme full of grandeur is grandi__________.
19. Action tending toward a conclusion is conclus__________.
20. An object moved in the direction of heaven moves in a heaven __________ direction.

Answers: 1. hillock; 2. wisdom; 3. infantile; 4. fraudulent; 5. youthful; 6. aviatrix; 7. retractable; 8. tireless; 9. remedial; 10. helper; 11. picturesque; 12. antiquate; 13. lioness; 14. bookish; 15. globule; 16. commendatory; 17. instigate; 18. grandiose; 19. conclusive; 20. heavenly or heavenward.

NAME ______________________ DATE ______________ READING RATE ______________ WPM

COMPREHENSION CHECK QUESTIONS

1. This account took place in (1) London; (2) Manhattan; (3) Chicago; (4) Los Angeles. 1. _______
2. In the restaurant, the Old Man drank (1) beer; (2) whiskey; (3) tea; (4) ale. 2. _______
3. In his office the Old Man had a photograph of (1) Jung; (2) Adler; (3) Coue; (4) Freud. 3. _______
4. The journal the Old Man pulled out toward the end was written by (1) Jonathan; (2) Jonathan's wife; (3) Jonathan's sister; (4) Jonathan's fiancée. 4. _______
5. Shortly after this conversation the Old Man (1) retired; (2) died; (3) moved; (4) became an invalid. 5. _______

Receptive Comprehension _______

6. This article primarily shows (1) the importance of vocabulary; (2) how words can affect life; (3) how psychiatrists think and work; (4) how life affects choice of words. 6. _______
7. The purpose is primarily (1) persuasion; (2) exposition; (3) narration; (4) description. 7. _______
8. You would assume that the young man probably (1) had arranged the meeting to get help with his problem; (2) had wanted to hide his problems from the Old Man; (3) had talked about them largely at the Old Man's urging; (4) had often gotten into difficulties. 8. _______
9. The most important difference between the two phrases is in (1) the timing of their application; (2) the attention given to the mistakes; (3) the direction they tend to point; (4) the center-of-stage position. 9. _______
10. The story about Jonathan was used to remind us to (1) profit from mistakes; (2) weigh all factors before judging; (3) act before it is too late; (4) work hard at the business of living. 10. _______

(10 points for each correct answer)

Reflective Comprehension _______
TOTAL READING COMPREHENSION SCORE _______

VOCABULARY CHECK QUESTIONS

			without context I	with context II
1.	**gnome**	(1) column; (2) puzzle; (3) antelope; (4) spur; (5) dwarf.	1. _______	_______
2.	**berated**	(1) rebuked; (2) deprived; (3) left; (4) begged; (5) judged.	2. _______	_______
3.	**perverse**	(1) abundant; (2) uncertain; (3) contrary; (4) lucid; (5) impudent.	3. _______	_______
4.	**ruefully**	(1) pleasantly; (2) roughly; (3) unruly; (4) mournfully; (5) ruddy colored.	4. _______	_______
5.	**retrieve**	(1) carry; (2) recover; (3) reduce; (4) retain; (5) retrace.	5. _______	_______

(10 points for each correct answer)

Word Comprehension without *contextual help (I)* _______
Word Comprehension with *contextual help (II)* _______
TOTAL WORD COMPREHENSION SCORE _______

EXERCISES

THOUGHT-STRUCTURING FOR MASTERY OF NEW PREFIX, ROOT, AND SUFFIX ELEMENTS

Use this technique to determine the meanings of word elements without going to the dictionary. Suppose, for example, that you do not know the meaning of the prefix *pre-*. You can, of course, consult the dictionary, but it is far better to establish a way of thinking to achieve the same results. Here is the pattern to establish. Start thinking of some common words containing that prefix, define each, then see what meaning is common to all. For example, you might think of *preview*, *prepare*, and *precede*, meaning "to view before," "to make ready before," and "to go before." Obviously the meaning common to all probably belongs to the prefix common to all.

To develop added skill with this approach, do the following exercises with prefix, root, and suffix elements.

1. If *commingle* means to mingle _____ and *compress* means to press or squeeze _____, the prefix *com-* probably means _____.
2. If *descend* means to come _____ and *depress* means to press _____, the prefix *de-* probably means _____.
3. If *depart* means to go _____ and *deprive* means to take _____, the prefix *de-* probably also means _____.
4. If *obstruct* means to work _____ something and *object* means to protest _____ something, the prefix *ob-* probably means _____.
5. If *hyperactive* means _____ active and *hypercritical* means _____ly critical, the prefix *hyper-* probably means _____.
6. If *portable* means able to be carried and *transport* to carry across, the root *portare* probably means _____.
7. If *attract* means to draw to and *extract* to draw out, the root *trahere* probably means _____.
8. If *tangible* means something that can be touched and *tangent* means touching, the root *tangere* probably means _____.
9. If *statuesque* means like a statue and *picturesque* means like a picture, the suffix *-es*que probably means _____.
10. If a *kitchenette* is a little kitchen and a *statuette* a little statue, the suffix *-ette* probably means _____.

DISCOVERING VARIANT FORMS

Some prefixes have several variant forms. If you are to put your prefix knowledge to full use, you must know all these forms well. That means, for example, recognizing *com-* in *collaborate* as well as in *compare*. Using your dictionary, find as many variant forms as possible for each of the following prefixes, the most changeable to be found.

Prefixes	**Variant Forms**
1. *ab-*	______________________
2. *ad-*	______________________
3. *in-*	______________________
4. *com-*	______________________
5. *sub-*	______________________
6. *ob-*	______________________
7. *syn-*	______________________
8. *trans-*	______________________
9. *ex-*	______________________
10. *dis-*	______________________

NAME ______________________ DATE ______________ READING RATE ______________ WPM

COMPREHENSION CHECK QUESTIONS

1. This selection lists (1) ten master words; (2) twelve master words; (3) fourteen master words; (4) sixteen master words. 1. _______
2. The Latin verb *plicare* means to (1) play; (2) fold; (3) place; (4) tease. 2. _______
3. In our language, words derived from the Latin and Greek make up approximately (1) 20 percent; (2) 40 percent; (3) 60 percent; (4) 80 percent. 3. _______
4. The relationship between the derivation and common definitions of a word is (1) identical; (2) remote; (3) varied; (4) close. 4. _______
5. One of the following words is *not* discussed: (1) predilection; (2) explication; (3) cooperation; (4) prevarication. 5. _______

Receptive Comprehension _______

6. The purpose of this selection is to (1) encourage vocabulary building; (2) suggest the importance of Latin and Greek elements in our language; (3) describe a technique for improving one's vocabulary; (4) suggest how knowledge of certain classical elements makes spelling easier. 6. _______
7. You would infer that *prescience* means (1) modern; (2) foreknowledge; (3) quietness; (4) intelligence. 7. _______
8. Our common word *affect* probably contains an assimilated form of the prefix (1) *a-*; (2) *abs-*; (3) *ad-*; (4) *af-*. 8. _______
9. If you wished to build a vocabulary quickly, several words at a time, probably the most useful part of a dictionary entry would be the (1) definitions; (2) derivation; (3) synonyms; (4) examples of the word in context. 9. _______
10. The phrase "vocabulary is a concomitant to success" probably means that vocabulary (1) results from success; (2) leads to success; (3) is unrelated to success; (4) goes along with success. 10. _______

(10 points for each correct answer)

Reflective Comprehension _______
TOTAL READING COMPREHENSION SCORE _______

VOCABULARY CHECK QUESTIONS

		without context I	with context II
1. **invaluable**	(1) cheap; (2) ordinary; (3) fairly valuable; (4) very valuable; (5) useless.	1. _______	_______
2. **converting**	(1) reflecting; (2) carrying; (3) conversing; (4) meeting; (5) transforming.	2. _______	_______
3. **partiality**	(1) bias; (2) portion; (3) speck; (4) follower; (5) partner.	3. _______	_______
4. **intricacies**	(1) plans; (2) origins; (3) complexities; (4) peculiarities; (5) pledges.	4. _______	_______
5. **touchstone**	(1) criticism; (2) hope; (3) diet; (4) criterion; (5) failure.	5. _______	_______

(10 points for each correct answer)

Word Comprehension without *contextual help (I)* _______
Word Comprehension with *contextual help (II)* _______
TOTAL WORD COMPREHENSION SCORE _______

EXERCISES

USING THE MASTER-WORD APPROACH

What does it mean to *know* the twenty prefixes and fourteen roots in the masterword approach? Actually it means mastery of four kinds or levels of knowing: memorization; (2) identification; (3) application; and (4) generalization.

MEMORIZATION

The first step or level of knowing is relatively easy. It means learning the common meaning or meanings of each prefix and root element listed in the table on page 195. Memorizing those meanings will not take long. Just cover the answers in the Common Meaning columns, check to see how many meanings you know, then memorize the others perfectly. To review, turn to the table, cover the meaning column in order to supply the meanings yourself, and uncover the answers for an immediate check.

Since things learned by rote tend to be easily forgotten, work out a mnemonic aid to link each element meaningfully with its common meaning. Take the prefix *epi-*. What does it mean, commonly? Help yourself remember its meaning by thinking of a familiar word containing that prefix—a word where the meaning "upon" is so obvious that you no longer have to memorize. The association remembers for you. For example, you know perfectly well what an *epitaph* is. It's the inscription carved "upon" a tombstone. Take another example. You know what your epidermis is. It's the outermost layer of your skin—the "upon" layer, so to speak. Such words serve as mnemonic aids to link the prefix *epi* with the meaning "upon," thus helping you remember.

Now devise a mnemonic add for each prefix and root element in the table to insure a mastery of the first step in knowing—knowledge of common meanings.

IDENTIFICATION

It is not enough, however, to know the prefix or root meaning. You must also be able to identify the presence of an element as it appears in a word—otherwise knowing its meaning is useless. Most of the time the elements are rather easily spotted, but sometimes there are real difficulties. To see the problem more clearly, try the following quiz, dealing with one of the most difficult prefixes of all to identify.

Look at the following words, checking only the ones which you can identify as containing the prefix *ad-*:

________	1. accuse	________	6. acquire	________	11. aspire
________	2. afferent	________	7. arrive	________	12. astringent
________	3. agglutinate	________	8. associate	________	13. agnate
________	4. allude	________	9. attract	________	14. adynamia
________	5. annex	________	10. ascend		

How well did you identify the prefix in question 14—the prefix *ad-*? You should have checked all but the last one. All but the last contain a form of the prefix *ad-*. To be sure, this is perhaps the most difficult of all prefixes to identify. It is a reminder of the importance of knowing at the second level and of using the dictionary as a help in mastering this second step.

Look at the following dictionary entry for the prefix *ad-*. It should prepare you for the variant forms in the quiz.

> **ad**-. Indicates motion toward; for example, **adsorb**. [Latin, from *ad,* to, toward, at. See **ad**- in Appendix. In borrowed Latin compounds ad- indicates: 1. Motion toward, as in **advent**. 2. Proximity, as in **adjacent**. 3. Addition, increase, as in **accrue**. 4. Relationship, dependence, as in **adjunct**. 5. Intensified action, as in **accelerate**. Before *c, f, g, l, n, q, r, s,* and *t, ad-* is assimilated to *ac-, af-, ag-, al-, an-, acq-, ar-, as-,* and *at-*; before *sc, sp, st,* and *gn,* it is reduced to *a-*.]

Roots also show wide variations in form. Since it is important to relate prefix and root closely to the words containing those elements, suppose for the next exercise that you start with the variant forms of a root and come up with certain words containing those forms. In the preceding exercise you started with words and were to note those containing the prefix.

Take the root *facere*, meaning "to make or do." English words derived from that source are likely to have one of the following five forms: *fac, fic, fea, fec,* and *fas*. In the following exercise, for each of the phrase definitions supply a single word containing one of the five forms and fitting the definition. For example, what would you call "a building where things are made"? You would call it a *factory*. The word, derived from *facere*, does contain one of the five forms, the form *fac*. And it does fit the definition. Go ahead with the exercise.

Definitions	**Words**	**Definitions**	**Words**
1. not easily done	____________	6. evil doer	____________
2. made by hand or machinery	____________	7. blemish or fault	____________
3. a notable act or deed	____________	8. something without flaw	____________
4. to make it easy to do	____________	9. conquer or overcome	____________
5. tender attachment	____________	10. accepted style of doing	____________

(Exercise continued on page 434)

Answers: 1. difficult; 2. manufacture or fashion; 3. feat; 4. facilitate; 5. affection; 6. malefactor; 7. imperfection or defect; 8. perfect; 9. defeat; 10. fashion or fashionable.

NAME ______________________ DATE ______________ READING RATE ______________ WPM

COMPREHENSION CHECK QUESTIONS

1. Mama is called what kind of a creature? (1) warm; (2) vocal; (3) giant; (4) busy. 1. _______
2. Word-sentence language is specifically spoken of as a (1) tool; (2) miracle; (3) giant learning step; (4) strange accident. 2. _______
3. When an infant knows change, what is said to begin? (1) intelligence; (2) life-in-motion; (3) abstract thought; (4) world-knowledge. 3. _______
4. The author mentions (1) Peterson; (2) Butler; (3) Bloomfield; (4) Wright. 4. _______
5. When beginning school, children are estimated to have a vocabulary of about (1) 8,000 words; (2) 16,000 words; (3) 21,000 words; (4) 24,000 words. 5. _______

Receptive Comprehension _______

6. This selection is mainly to trace the early development of (1) speech sounds; (2) word formation; (3) abstract thought; (4) language growth. 6. _______
7. This selection is organized primarily on what plan? (1) chronological; (2) simple to complex; (3) general to specific; (4) point-by-point. 7. _______
8. The points are developed mainly by (1) opinions of authorities; (2) experimental data; (3) personal observations; (4) comparisons. 8. _______
9. This piece seems chiefly intended to (1) entertain; (2) arouse readers to action; (3) inform; (4) tell how to solve a problem. 9. _______
10. You would infer that the author's attitude toward TV is best described as (1) positive; (2) negative; (3) uncertain; (4) critical. 10. _______

(10 points for each correct answer)

Reflective Comprehension _______
TOTAL READING COMPREHENSION SCORE _______

VOCABULARY CHECK QUESTIONS

			without context I	with context II
1.	**labial**	(1) liquid; (2) lip-formed; (3) raw; (4) formal; (5) common.	1. _______	_______
2.	**counters**	(1) gains; (2) shelves; (3) skills; (4) pedestals; (5) indicators.	2. _______	_______
3.	**sophisticated**	(1) worldly-wise; (2) creditable; (3) reasonable; (4) sociable; (5) powerful.	3. _______	_______
4.	**insulated**	(1) fashioned; (2) isolated; (3) intended; (4) shocked; (5) elevated.	4. _______	_______
5.	**prologue**	(1) promise; (2) prohibition; (3) gain; (4) preliminary; (5) ending.	5. _______	_______

(10 points for each correct answer)

Word Comprehension without *contextual help (I)* _______
Word Comprehension with *contextual help (II)* _______
TOTAL WORD COMPREHENSION SCORE _______

EXERCISES

USING THE MASTER-WORD APPROACH *(continued from p. 431)*

APPLICATION

To a mathematician such words as *abscissa, exponential,* and *asymptote* are common. To a botanist, *mitosis meiosis,* and *stomata* are equally so. But to a student just beginning to study higher mathematics or botany, such technical words are probably meaningless. One student during his first week in college came across the words *ebracteate* and *exospore* in a botany text and *extravasate* in geology; he heard a medical doctor use the word *exostosis*. Then in his general reading he came across the others listed below. How many of them do you now? Try the following quiz to see. Enter the answers in the column headed I.

			I	II
1.	**ebracteate**	(1) with bracts; (2) without bracts; (3) rounded bracts; (4) pointed bracts; (5) stiff bracts.	1. ______	______
2.	**exospore**	(1) core; (2) source; (3) middle layer; (4) outer spore layer; (5) stem.	2. ______	______
3.	**extravasate**	(1) melt; (2) shrink; (3) solidify; (4) crack; (5) erupt.	3. ______	______
4.	**exostosis**	(1) outgrowth; (2) leg bone; (3) paralysis; (4) joint; (5) scab.	4. ______	______
5.	**ebullition**	(1) bruise; (2) boiling out; (3) seeping in; (4) repair; (5) warmth.	5. ______	______
6.	**elicit**	(1) draw forth; (2) make illegal; (3) hide; (4) prove; (5) close.	4. ______	______
7.	**expunge**	(1) dive in; (2) soak; (3) erase; (4) swim; (5) save.	5. ______	______
8.	**effete**	(1) worn out; (2) strong; (3) difficult; (4) shut in; (5) wealthy.	8. ______	______
9.	**exhume**	(1) moisten; (2) work; (3) put in; (4) pay for; (5) dig out.	9. ______	______
10.	**evulsion**	(1) hatred; (2) rotation; (3) lotion; (4) extraction; (5) description.	10. ______	______
		TOTAL SCORES:		______

Before checking your answers, think back to what you did. Did you notice, for example, that all ten words began with an *e*—five of them with an *ex*-? Do you know what the prefix *ex*- commonly means? In short, did you apply some knowledge of prefixes as you took the test? If you did, your score should reflect that fact.

Now retake the same test, using column II for your answers. Consciously apply one additional bit of information—that all ten words contain a prefix meaning "out." Lean heavily on that prefix meaning as you retake the test. Check both sets of answers with the key at the bottom of the page.

You can see more clearly how this approach works. Once you know what a prefix or root means and can identify it accurately in a word, you are ready for the pay-off step—application. A group of 78 adults tried the test without being encouraged to lean on prefix meaning. They were then told, as you were, that each word contained a prefix meaning "out." That knowledge improved their average score 36 percent.

A perfect score in the second column means that you applied your knowledge well. With the adults, while improvement was general, some scored only 70 or 80 the second time through. Since even a desk-size dictionary contains over a thousand words with a prefix meaning "out," the dramatic usefulness of this shortcut seems apparent.

Answers: 1. 2; 2. 4; 3. 5; 4. 1; 5. 2; 6. 1; 7. 3; 8. 1; 9. 5; 10. 4.

GENERALIZATION

Even when you develop enviable ability with the first three steps, be sure not to overlook the fourth and last step—generalization. For example, by studying only twenty prefixes you can still learn things about all the other prefixes—if you know how.

Take the prefix *ad-*. See what happens when it combines with *lude* to make *allude*. Can you now generalize about another prefix—the prefix *com-*? If *com-* were to be added to *lude*, would the resulting word be *comlude*, *colude*, or *collude*? How accurately can you generalize?

Take still another kind of generalization. In a sense, you know the meaning of most prefixes—but you don't know that you know. For example, you may say you don't know exactly what the prefix *re-* means. Try some generalizing with this pattern. If to *reread* is "to read again" and *reheat* is "to heat again," you have reason to conclude that a common meaning of *re-* is "again." Generalizing on the basis of that sample, you now have a formula for discovering the meaning of any prefix or root.

Take the prefix *omni-*. What does it mean? Think of some words with *omni-*, such as *omnipresent*, *omnipotent*, or *omnivorous*. Use the formula to generalize. If *omnipresent* means "present in all places" and *omnipotent* means "all-powerful," apparently one meaning of *omni-* is "all." Finding the meaning common to any given prefix is like finding a common denominator in a math problem. Some generalizations are, of course, more complex and difficult than others. But as you develop improved insights, you develop the skill to handle much more difficult problems, just as in mathematics.

NAME ______________________ DATE ______________ READING RATE ______________ WPM

COMPREHENSION CHECK QUESTIONS

1. The author likens words to (1) arrows; (2) money; (3) diamonds; (4) magnets. 1. ______
2. Successful people usually (1) have large vocabularies; (2) read widely and well; (3) have a large library; (4) speak fluently and well. 2. ______
3. The writer discusses (1) no specific type of vocabulary; (2) two types of vocabulary; (3) three types of vocabulary; (4) four types of vocabulary. 3. ______
4. The author suggests (1) vocabulary flash cards; (2) a specific vocabulary-building book; (3) a vocabulary notebook; (4) use of a tape recorder. 4. ______
5. When you come across a new word in your reading, you are told to (1) put a check in the margin and read on; (2) stop and consult the dictionary; (3) analyze it into prefix, root, and suffix; (4) write it down immediately. 5. ______

Receptive Comprehension ______

6. This selection is concerned chiefly with (1) how to improve your vocabulary; (2) defining what is meant by vocabulary; (3) establishing importance of vocabulary; (4) suggesting when a vocabulary can best be developed. 6. ______
7. Vocabulary exercises like those in this book are closely related to the suggestion in this selection to (1) write a sentence using the word; (2) review the words studied; (3) pronounce the words accurately; (4) get meanings from context. 7. ______
8. You would infer that this selection is probably taken from a complete text on (1) reading; (2) vocabulary-building; (3) composition; (4) communication. 8. ______
9. This selection is chiefly (1) narration; (2) description; (3) persuasion; (4) exposition. 9. ______
10. The specific suggestions for improving vocabulary at the end are listed in order of (1) importance; (2) difficulty; (3) effectiveness; (4) time. 10. ______

(10 points for each correct answer)

Reflective Comprehension ______

TOTAL READING COMPREHENSION SCORE ______

VOCABULARY CHECK QUESTIONS

			without context I	with context II
1.	**consider**	(1) select; (2) judge; (3) decide; (4) provide; (5) ponder.	1. ______	______
2.	**medium**	(1) source; (2) means; (3) process; (4) act; (5) ritual.	2. ______	______
3.	**assume**	(1) believe; (2) agree; (3) suppose; (4) trust; (5) say.	3. ______	______
4.	**block**	(1) reduce; (2) obstruct; (3) delay; (4) force; (5) eliminate.	4. ______	______
5.	**maintain**	(1) balance; (2) postpone; (3) increase; (4) sustain; (5) rely.	5. ______	______

(10 points for each correct answer)

Word Comprehension without *contextual help (I)* ______

Word Comprehension with *contextual help (II)* ______

TOTAL WORD COMPREHENSION SCORE ______

CONTEXT—KEY TO MEANING

James I. Brown

When you come to an unknown word in your reading, what should you do? Eighty-four percent of the students in one college class answered—"look it up in the dictionary."

Take a closer look at that answer. Suppose you see the word *extenuate*. You consult the dictionary and find what? Not *the* meaning of *extenuate* but *four* meanings! Furthermore, the dictionary can never tell you exactly which meaning is intended.

Or take the common word *fast*. What does it mean? You answer—"quickly or rapidly," and you're quite right. But you're equally right if you say "firmly fastened." As a matter of fact, the one word *fast* is really not one word but 21, all rolled into one. It has twelve meanings as an adjective, five as an adverb, two as a verb, and two as a noun. And that's talking in terms of the relatively small collegiate-size dictionary.

So—what does *fast* mean? You have to say *it all depends*—depends on the context, on the way the author used the word. To be sure, a dictionary should list all the different meanings. Even when a word is used in a new sense, that new meaning should eventually get into the dictionary, if it is used enough to become established. But unless the word has only one definition, we must always rely on context, not the dictionary, for its exact meaning. When you remember that the 500 most commonly used words have a total of 14,070 separate meanings, an average of 28 per word—you can see why context must come first.

Furthermore, individuals vary widely in their ability to use contextual clues to arrive at accurate word meanings. In one class, for example, students took a difficult vocabulary test—first without any context to help, then a second time with sentence contexts for each word. Two students made identical scores of 30 the first time through. On the second time through one moved up to 40 but the other jumped up to 90. He had developed uncanny skill in getting word meanings through context. Obviously, that is a skill which deserves top priority. Research by Holmes accents its importance. He discovered that *vocabulary in context* contributed more to reading power than any other first-order factor isolated—37 percent.

One sure way of developing that skill is to keep away from your dictionary until you have inferred a meaning from context alone. Then, and only then, should you turn to the dictionary for confirmation. If you go to the dictionary first you, by that move, discourage the development of the very skills and insights you need. Furthermore you'll find your interest is whetted by putting context first. You become more eager and alert to check your inference.

So—from now on—when you spot a strange word, look first at the context, formulate a tentative definition, *then* check it with the dictionary. You'll remember those new words much longer with that treatment. You'll also ensure better comprehension.

(500 words)

COMPREHENSION CHECK QUESTIONS

1. Specific mention is made of (1) a high school class; (2) a college class; (3) a TV class; (4) an English class. 1. _______
2. *Fast* has how many different meanings? (1) 5; (2) 12; (3) 16; (4) 21. 2. _______
3. The author specifically mentions (1) a collegiate-sized dictionary; (2) the *Oxford English Dictionary*; (3) Webster's dictionary; (4) a dictionary of slang. 3. _______
4. In the use of contextual clues, individuals were said to (1) be about the same; (2) vary widely; (3) vary with I.Q.; (4) improve with age. 4. _______
5. When first meeting a strange word, you are told to (1) look it up; (2) note any familiar prefix or root; (3) infer its meaning from context; (4) skip it and come back to study it later. 5. _______
6. This selection is chiefly about (1) the relationship between context and meaning; (2) multiple word meanings; (3) kinds of context; (4) developing skill with context. 6. _______
7. Primary emphasis is on (1) when context should be used; (2) how context should be used; (3) why context deserves priority; (4) what context includes. 7. _______
8. The discussion of *extenuate* and *fast* illustrated (1) two different points; (2) somewhat the same point; (3) different kinds of dictionary entries; (4) how dictionaries differ. 8. _______
9. You would infer from this that going to the dictionary first is most like (1) diving into deep water; (2) beginning a race; (3) using a crutch; (4) climbing a mountain. 9. _______
10. You were most strongly cautioned against (1) consulting the dictionary first; (2) guessing at word meanings; (3) neglecting common words; (4) relying solely on context. 10. _______

SCORE _______

Answers: 1. 2; 2. 4; 3. 1; 4. 2; 5. 3; 6. 1; 7. 3; 8. 2; 9. 3; 10. 1.

NAME ______________________ DATE ______________ READING RATE ______________ WPM

Comprehension Check Questions

1. This selection was written by someone in the field of (1) testing; (2) English; (3) industry; (4) teaching. 1. _______
2. The Human Engineering Laboratory was founded by (1) Martin Johnson; (2) Thomas O'Brien; (3) Lynn Sabini; (4) Johnson O'Connor. 2. _______
3. Each year the Laboratory is said to administer how many vocabulary tests? (1) 10,000; (2) 20,000; (3) 30,000; (4) no figure given. 3. _______
4. A vocabulary test was given to the president of (1) an oil company; (2) a mail-order company; (3) a coal-mining company; (4) a milling company. 4. _______
5. We are cautioned against (1) crossword puzzles; (2) misusing words; (3) poor dictionary habits; (4) using slang. 5. _______

Receptive Comprehension _______

6. This selection is primarily to show (1) how vocabulary and success are related; (2) how to improve your vocabulary; (3) how to measure your word power; (4) how important the dictionary is. 6. _______
7. Dizzy Dean's comment is used to point up the need for (1) something beyond vocabulary; (2) a good vocabulary; (3) proper opportunities; (4) intelligence. 7. _______
8. You would infer that the best estimate of a man's vocabulary would come from a (1) look at his I.Q.; (2) look at his wife's vocabulary score; (3) check on his years of informal education; (4) check on his reading habits. 8. _______
9. Which should come *first?* (1) finding a good job; (2) building a good vocabulary; (3) developing a good personality; (4) reading widely. 9. _______
10. The style of this selection is (1) forceful; (2) conversational; (3) witty; (4) formal. 10. _______

(10 points for each correct answer)

Reflective Comprehension _______

TOTAL READING COMPREHENSION SCORE _______

Vocabulary Check Questions

			without context I	with context II
1.	**potential**	(1) intelligence; (2) power; (3) drive; (4) latent ability; (5) training.	1. _______	_______
2.	**initiative**	(1) punishment; (2) restraint; (3) brain power; (4) heritage; (5) enterprise.	2. _______	_______
3.	**malapropism**	(1) word misuse; (2) sickness; (3) mistake; (4) support; (5) awkwardness.	3. _______	_______
4.	**avid**	(1) careless; (2) old; (3) eager; (4) advanced; (5) clumsy.	4. _______	_______
5.	**incentive**	(1) desire; (2) gift; (3) position; (4) salary; (5) bonus.	5. _______	_______

(10 points for each correct answer)

Word Comprehension without *contextual help (I)* _______

Word Comprehension with *contextual help (II)* _______

TOTAL WORD COMPREHENSION SCORE _______

ANSWERS TO THE 20-WORD QUIZ ON PAGE 201

Check your answers, then find your age group in the columns below, and you'll learn your probable peak future income. Don't be discouraged if you didn't score well—read the article for tips on how you can improve your vocabulary and your income potential.

1. *churchmen*
2. *slatted vents*
3. *oval*
4. *dreadful*
5. *wealth*
6. *perfection*
7. *hateful*
8. *limited*
9. *accent*
10. *marriage*
11. *shading*
12. *wood nymph*
13. *store*
14. *hermit*
15. *ridged*
16. *forked*
17. *tuberculosis*
18. *majority*
19. *interpret*
20. *widow*

Figure your top income by looking up the number of correct words under your age heading. Then adjust for inflation by adding 50 percent to all figures given below.

Age 30 and Up

Score	
20-19	$36,500 and up
18-17	$24,300-$36,500
16-15	$16,200-$24,300
14-13	$12,200-$16,200
12-11	$ 8,500-$12,200
10-7	$ 6,500-$ 8,500
Below 7	Under $6,500

Age 21-29

Score	
20-17	$36,500 and up
16-15	$24,300-$36,500
14-13	$16,200-$24,300
12-11	$12,200-$16,200
10-5	$ 6,500-$12,200
Below 5	Under $6,500

Age 17-20

Score	
20-15	$36,500 and up
14-13	$24,300-$36,500
12-11	$16,200-$24,300
10-9	$12,200-$16,200
8-7	$ 8,500-$12,200
6-3	$ 6,500-$ 8,500
Below 3	Under $6,500

Age 13-16

Score	
20-12	$36,500 and up
11-10	$24,300-$36,500
9-8	$16,200-$24,300
7-6	$12,200-$16,200
5-4	$ 8,500-$12,200
3-2	$ 6,500-$ 8,500
Below 2	Under $6,500

Age 9-12

Score	
20-10	$36,500 and up
9-8	$24,300-$36,500
7-6	$16,200-$24,300
5-4	$12,200-$16,200
3-2	$ 8,500-$12,200
1	$ 6,500-$ 8,500
0	Under $ 6,500

VOCABULARY IMPROVEMENT THROUGH CONTEXTUAL CLUES

Wide reading is said to be an invaluable aid to vocabulary development. This is particularly true if you sharpen your awareness of contextual clues by noting the following three common situations, so helpful in dealing with new and strange words:

1. Words used in pairs, either similar or opposite pairs.
2. Words surrounded by illustrative details that suggest meaning.
3. Words followed or preceded by "remote synonyms" that make meaning clear.

For example, suppose you don't know what the word *octogenarian* means. If you find it in the following context of opposite pairs, meaning will be clarified: "Man or woman, millionaire or pauper, octogenarian or infant—all are affected by this new regulation." Or if you don't know the meaning of *lexicographers*, the meaningful details in the following context should help: "Lexicographers worked through the file marked 'new words' in an attempt to determine which words to include in the new desk dictionary." Such details strongly suggest that lexicographers are dictionary makers. As a last example, lean on a remote synonym to get the meaning of *lave*: "You must lave the area four times daily. The only way you can hope to alleviate the pain is by such regular bathing with warm water."

In the textbooks that you are studying, find two clearly defined illustrations of each of these three situations. Enter them below.

1. Illustrations of word pairs:

   a. ______________________________

   b. ______________________________

2. Illustrations of meaningful details:

   a. ______________________________

   b. ______________________________

3. Illustrations of "remote synonyms":

   a. ______________________________

   b. ______________________________

NAME ______________________ DATE ______________ READING RATE ______________ WPM

COMPREHENSION CHECK QUESTIONS

1. The average person believes which is most important? (1) happiness; (2) money; (3) power; (4) family. 1. ______
2. "The imposter phenomenon" means some successful people feel they are (1) deserving; (2) undeserving; (3) honest; (4) unaccomplished. 2. ______
3. The author believes our souls are hungry for (1) comfort; (2) fame; (3) meaning; (4) peace. 3. ______
4. Kushner seems convinced most people will not be satisfied with (1) wealth; (2) notoriety; (3) success; (4) independence. 4. ______
5. Most people fear that their lives will (1) end too soon; (2) be boring; (3) be incomplete; (4) not have mattered. 5. ______

Receptive Comprehension ______

6. The purpose of this selection is to (1) define happiness; (2) define success; (3) question life's significance; (4) question people's motives. 6. ______
7. The author suggests that many apparently successful people are (1) eluding happiness; (2) unhappy; (3) satisfied; (4) driven by impulse. 7. ______
8. Oscar Wilde believed people are often unhappy when they (1) realize their dreams; (2) fail to dream; (3) avoid success; (4) focus on others. 8. ______
9. The content of this selection would be suitable for a (1) newspaper feature; (2) political speech; (3) self-help text; (4) biology class lecture. 9. ______
10. The man whose friend had just died worried that his life would be (1) empty; (2) too busy; (3) compromised; (4) for naught. 10. ______

(10 points for each correct answer)

Reflective Comprehension ______

TOTAL READING COMPREHENSION SCORE ______

VOCABULARY CHECK QUESTIONS

			without context I	with context II
1.	**unmask**	(1) obscure; (2) masquerade; (3) crush; (4) impose; (5) expose.	1. ______	______
2.	**agitated**	(1) tranquilized; (2) excited; (3) soothed; (4) collected; (5) tortured.	2. ______	______
3.	**expending**	(1) undergoing; (2) researching; (3) enhancing; (4) advancing; (5) consuming.	3. ______	______
4.	**obviously**	(1) acutely; (2) unobtrusively; (3) evidently; (4) consistently; (5) inadvertently.	4. ______	______
5.	**perpetual**	(1) transitory; (2) precautions; (3) continuous; (4) reflective; (5) pernicious.	5. ______	______

(10 points for each correct answer)

Word Comprehension without *contextual help (I)* ______

Word Comprehension with *contextual help (II)* ______

TOTAL WORD COMPREHENSION SCORE ______

EXERCISES

HISPANIC AMERICANS

1 *Mexican Americans.* The biggest segment of Hispanic Americans has come from Mexico. Indeed, the immigration of Mexicans in the twentieth century is one of history's great population movements. In 1985 there were approximately 8,750,000 Americans of Mexican origin.

2 The first Mexican Americans were not immigrants, of course, but the descendants of Spanish families living on the land conquered from Mexico. Those dwelling in California called themselves *Californios*: in New Mexico the labels *Nuevo Mexicanos* and *Hispanos* were used. Today some Mexican Americans who have been born and raised in the United States prefer to call themselves *Chicanos*.

3 Large numbers of Mexicans began to cross the United States border at the beginning of the twentieth century, mostly in search of agricultural jobs. Later, when World War I pulled American workers into the army and factories, the jobs left behind offered Mexicans fresh opportunity.

4 In addition to low wages, inadequate housing, and seasonal unemployment, Mexican Americans—in the cities no less than on the farms—faced prejudice and discrimination. They gathered in *barrios*, or communities, which sprang up in El Paso, Los Angeles, Denver, Seattle, Minneapolis, Chicago, and elsewhere.

5 In recent decades, Mexican Americans have been organizing in order to exert political strength. In Los Angeles in 1949 they formed the Community Service Organization with the goal of electing a Mexican American to the city council. After succeeding, the group went on to challenge discrimination in housing, jobs, and schools.

6 In Texas, the Political Association of Spanish-Speaking Organizations (PASSO) was established in 1960. Working with other groups, it voted in a whole slate of city candidates in Crystal City, Texas. In 1981 Henry Cisneros, who holds a doctor of public administration degree, became mayor of San Antonio, Texas.

7 In rural areas. Mexican farm workers benefited from the leadership of Cesar Chavez, a Chicano whose parents, once well-to-do, had lost their money in the Great Depression. In 1965, inspired by the black civil rights movement, he organized migrant farm workers into the United Farm Workers. After a struggle, it won agreements in 1970 with several large producers. Chavez did not rely on strikes alone. He encouraged people throughout the country to boycott produce from growers whose workers were on strike.

FINDING THE MAIN IDEA—GUESSWORK OR SKILL?

To comprehend a paragraph or a longer piece—say, an essay or article—you must be able to (1) identify the main idea of each paragraph, if stated, or compose one if it is implied; (2) see the relationship between the details and the main idea; and (3) if you are reading a multiparagraph selection, see the relationship between the main idea of each paragraph and the overall main idea of the piece—the thesis—whether it is stated or implied.

The main idea is the most general sentence, expressed or suggested, which all other sentences support. Main ideas in paragraphs may be at the beginning, middle, or end but are most often found early in the text. However, the main idea in a longer piece, called the thesis, is usually found toward the end of the introduction and is supported by the main ideas and details of the paragraphs that follow.

To determine the main idea of a paragraph, first ask yourself, Who or what is this about? The answer to that question yields the topic. Read paragraph 1 above once again. Who or what is the paragraph about?

Topic, paragraph 1: *Hispanic Americans* ____________________

Now ask yourself, What point(s) is the author making about Hispanic Americans in this paragraph? Does a single sentence state the main idea, or do several sentences suggest it? If you picked the first sentence of the paragraph as the main idea statement, you are correct: *The biggest segment of Hispanic Americans has come from Mexico.*

Now try your hand at determining the main idea of paragraph 4.

Who or what is the paragraph about? ______________________________

If you answered *Mexican Americans*, you are correct.

What point(s) is the author making about the topic? Does a single sentence expresses the main idea of the paragraph? If you answered *yes* and chose the first sentence, you are right. However, not all of the words in the sentence are necessary to express the main idea. The first part of the sentence, "In addition to low wages, inadequate housing, and seasonal unemployment" and the middle section, "in the cities no less than on the farms," give important information about the topic, *Mexican Americans,* but are not parts of the main point the author is making about the topic. What is left of the sentence; *Mexican Americans faced prejudice and discrimination,* is the main idea.

To determine the main idea or thesis of the entire selection, repeat the steps in determining the main idea of paragraphs. However, this time ask yourself, Who or what is the entire piece about, and what overall point(s) is the author making about the topic? Usually, this information is presented or suggested in the introduction. However, when the thesis is not directly stated, as is the case in this selection, an effective way to compose an overall main idea or thesis is to "add up" the main ideas of all paragraphs, then form a statement that is general enough for each of those main ideas to support. The result of this process yields the thesis of the selection.

Now, compose a statement that is the thesis of this entire selection.

Topic of the selection: ______________________________

Main idea or thesis: ______________________________

____

Check you answers below.

If you follow the procedure outlined above, you will increase your comprehension ability and be able to recall more of what you read.

Answers: Topic of the selection: *Mexican Americans.* Main idea or thesis: *Many Mexican Americans have faced hardships in America; however, they are beginning to reap the benefits of their economic and political power struggles.*

NAME ____________ DATE ____________ READING RATE ____________ WPM

COMPREHENSION CHECK QUESTIONS

1. What were the men digging? (1) a well; (2) a foundation; (3) a trench; (4) a hole. 1. _______
2. There is a reference to (1) Hercules; (2) Adam and Eve; (3) Robinson Crusoe; (4) *Swiss Family Robinson.* 2. _______
3. The author says the arts of the hand (1) are built on leisure; (2) are having a rebirth; (3) have disappeared; (4) are noticeably affected by economic conditions. 3. _______
4. The citizens of Utopia worked in what kind of canning factory? (1) asparagus; (2) tomato; (3) bean; (4) pea. 4. _______
5. Which of the following modes of travel was *not* mentioned? (1) dog-cart; (2) train; (3) mule; (4) car. 5. _______

Receptive Comprehension _______

6. This selection is mainly to suggest (1) how machines save work; (2) the problem posed by machines; (3) how machines provide leisure; (4) the proper use of machines. 6. _______
7. The author believes that work is (1) worthwhile; (2) to be avoided at all costs; (3) unnecessary; (4) the author's attitude is unclear. 7. _______
8. You would infer that as a hobby the author would consider carpentering (1) impractical; (2) satisfying; (3) work; (4) creative. 8. _______
9. The purpose of this article is primarily to (1) predict; (2) inform; (3) convince; (4) entertain. 9. _______
10. The style is best described as (1) lively; (2) chatty; (3) elevated; (4) direct. 10. _______

(10 points for each correct answer)

Reflective Comprehension _______

TOTAL READING COMPREHENSION SCORE _______

VOCABULARY CHECK QUESTIONS

			without context I	with context II
1.	**drudgery**	(1) slowness; (2) force; (3) tiresome work; (4) idleness; (5) quaint humor.	1. _______	_______
2.	**antithesis**	(1) opposite; (2) aged; (3) hatred; (4) antiquity; (5) chant.	2. _______	_______
3.	**hedonists**	(1) rulers; (2) drug addicts; (3) unbelievers; (4) health-seekers; (5) pleasure-seekers.	3. _______	_______
4.	**interregnum**	(1) question; (2) power; (3) interference; (4) pause; (5) glory.	4. _______	_______
5.	**cumbrous**	(1) comfortable; (2) cumulative; (3) careful; (4) primitive; (5) unwieldy.	5. _______	_______

(10 points for each correct answer)

Word Comprehension without *contextual help (I)* _______

Word Comprehension with *contextual help (II)* _______

TOTAL WORD COMPREHENSION SCORE _______

KWANZAA: AN AFRICAN-AMERICAN ORIGINAL

Many cultures have contributed to the evolution of the December holiday season. It began with winter solstice rites—the Roman Saturnalia, the Teutonic Yule, the Druid celebrations. Hanukkah celebrates the Maccabees' defeat of the Syrians in 164 B.C.E. Then there is Christmas, a major religious holiday and a commercial bonanza.

The newest addition to the lot is Kwanzaa, a colorful African-American celebration of family, community, and culture.

The word Kwanzaa comes from a phrase that means "first fruits" of the harvest in Swahili. The seven-day festival, which begins on December 26 and ends on New Year's Day, has been steadily growing in popularity since it originated in 1966.

"This is a holiday based on traditions surrounding the first fruits; it adopts practices prevalent throughout Africa," says Kwanzaa creator Maulana Karenga, Ph.D., chair of the Department of Black Studies at California State University, Long Beach. "First-fruit celebrations are a bringing together of a living human harvest, a time for renewing and strengthening the bonds between people. Kwanzaa teaches respect for the family, for the community and our traditions. Its values are one of our contributions to the best of human culture."

The heart and soul of Kwanzaa are the *Nguzo Saba* (seven principles)—guidelines for year-round living: *Umoja* (unity), *Kujichagulia* (self-determination), *Ujima* (collective work and responsibility), *Ujamaa* (cooperative economics), *Nia* (purpose), *Kuumba* (creativity), and *Imani* (faith). Each day of the festival is dedicated to one of those principles.

Every evening of Kwanzaa the family gathers to discuss the principle for the day. A candle is lit and placed in the seven-branch *kinara* (candleholder) to symbolize giving light and life to the seven principles and to the ancient African concept of raising up light to lessen both spiritual and intellectual darkness. Small gifts—preferably handcrafted—are exchanged.

There is a seriousness of purpose, a sense of belonging not just to a family, but to a culture with rich ancient traditions. "Kwanzaa's most important lessons are for children because it gets them away from the commercial aspects of the season and helps them emphasize the spiritual," says Cerise Richardson, a Long Beach, California, poet, dancer, and single parent of a four-year-old. "During Kwanzaa I sit down with my son, Nathaniel, explain each principle and let him know that it is not just for one day, but is to be incorporated into his entire life."

According to Karenga, Kwanzaa is now celebrated by some 15 million people in the U.S., Africa, Canada, the Caribbean, and parts of Europe. Although it contains many spiritual elements, it is not a religious but a cultural holiday that is observed by people of all faiths.

"I like Kwanzaa because it involves the children and celebrates our ancestors," say Angela Kinamore, poetry editor of *Essence* magazine in New York and mother of three. "I've been celebrating it for three years and I intended to continue; I think it's important to instill those principles in our children at an early age."

The observance's noncommercial aspect has made an impression on many people, including Kenyette Adrine-Robinson, writer-in-residence at Kent State University's Department of Pan-African Studies and mother of 14-year-old Jua. "I have been celebrating Kwanzaa since 1971," she says. "Christmas just feeds the merchants, so I go with the holiday of African-American origin. Most of the people I know celebrate it."

While most Kwanzaa activities are family affairs, on December 31 family and friends join with other members of the community for the *karamu* (feast). This final event is particularly festive. The karamu site is decorated in the rich red, black, and green that has come to symbolize Africa, adults and children wear colorful African garments, and all present contribute dishes to the karamu table.

It is a time for good fellowship, a time for learning, a time for sharing.

Comprehension Check Questions

1. Of the ones listed, which is the newest December celebration? (1) Hanukkah; (2) Christmas; (3) Saturnalia; (4) Kwanzaa; (5) Teutonic Yule. 1. ______
2. *Karamu* means (1) principles; (2) scholars; (3) karma; (4) feast; (5) symbol. 2. ______
3. Kwanzaa is which kind of holiday? (1) religious; (2) educational; (3) cultural; (4) political; (5) international. 3. ______
4. Kwanzaa's creator was (1) Cerise Richardson; (2) Manulana Karenga; (3) Kenyette Adrine-Robinson; (4) Angela Kinamore; (5) Ken Wibecan. 4. ______
5. The primary reason people gather at Kwanzaa is to (1) rededicate themselves to *Nguzo Saba;* (2) teach children about the "first fruits"; (3) have a great feast; (4) denounce Christmas; (5) to exchange gifts. 5. ______
6. Lighting candles each day illustrates that celebrants (1) are religious; (2) acknowledge the twelve days of Christmas; (3) denounce the eight days of Hanukkah; (4) are committed to the seven principles of Kwanzaa; (5) denounce modern conveniences. 6. ______
7. Most who celebrate Kwanzaa believe (1) commercialism has overshadowed the purpose of Christmas; (2) people in all countries should celebrate Kwanzaa; (3) red, black, and green symbolize reverence to God; (4) gifts should be given only to *Nia;* (5) Kwanzaa will become more popular than Christmas. 7. ______
8. Most important to Kwanzaa is (1) community; (2) God; (3) family; (4) adults; (5) children. 8. ______

SCORE ______

Answers: 1. 4; 2. 4; 3. 3; 4. 2; 5. 2; 6. 4; 7. 1; 8. 3.

NAME ________________ DATE ________________ READING RATE ________________ WPM

Comprehension Check Questions

1. The unenviable Mrs. Jones is (1) in her mid-thirties; (2) in her mid-forties; (3) in her late twenties; (4) of unmentioned age. 1. _______

2. Herb Smith is a (1) psychiatrist; (2) minister; (3) social worker; (4) medical doctor. 2. _______

3. One specific bit of advice is to pay more attention to (1) people; (2) books; (3) appearance; (4) political and social issues. 3. _______

4. Mention is made of a (1) large ant; (2) butterfly; (3) robin; (4) furry caterpillar. 4. _______

5. Norman Vincent Peale speaks of his own advice as (1) pious; (2) innovative; (3) practical; (4) religious. 5. _______

Receptive Comprehension _______

6. This selection is mainly about how to (1) avoid monotony; (2) live fully; (3) find love; (4) discover goodness. 6. _______

7. The phrase "horizontal living" apparently means (1) routine living; (2) intense living; (3) sustained and satisfying living; (4) intellectual living. 7. _______

8. The point of the story about Martha is to suggest the need to (1) give emotions full rein; (2) take our mind off ourselves; (3) develop a problem-solving attitude; (4) look at life more realistically. 8. _______

9. Writing a letter without an *I, me,* or *mine* is intended primarily to help (1) fight self-centeredness; (2) fight deadening routine; (3) set and meet challenges; (4) develop a different writing style. 9. _______

10. The magnifying glass episode is intended to show the need to (1) generate interest in living; (2) find beauty; (3) escape monotony; (4) get close to nature. 10. _______

(10 points for each correct answer)

Reflective Comprehension _______

TOTAL READING COMPREHENSION SCORE _______

Vocabulary Check Questions

			without context I	with context II
1.	**futility**	(1) stuffiness; (2) success; (3) prospect; (4) enthusiasm; (5) uselessness.	1. _______	_______
2.	**valid**	(1) venturesome; (2) accurate; (3) sound; (4) relaxing; (5) varied.	2. _______	_______
3.	**mutely**	(1) silently; (2) markedly; (3) uniformly; (4) strongly; (5) stealthily.	3. _______	_______
4.	**imperative**	(1) improper; (2) urgent; (3) hopeless; (4) unnecessary; (5) constructive.	4. _______	_______
5.	**uncomprehensible**	(1) obscure; (2) without feeling; (3) compressed; (4) extended; (5) feeble.	5. _______	_______

(10 points for each correct answer)

Word Comprehension without *contextual help (I)* _______

Word Comprehension with *contextual help (II)* _______

TOTAL WORD COMPREHENSION SCORE _______

DISPOSING OF THE NUCLEAR AGE

By the largest calculation, there are over 3,000 warheads headed for early retirement, containing about 25 tons of enriched uranium and 10 tons of plutonium—both radioactive and both difficult to dispose of. Moreover, the Department of Energy's Pantex bomb-assembly facility near Amarillo, Texas, which was expecting to build some 3,500 warheads over the next few years, suddenly has to reverse gears and begin dismantling weapons. Says Thomas Cochran, a nuclear-arms expert with the Natural Resources Defense Council: "It's doable, but if weapons production continues, it will strain the system."

Technically speaking, the process of decommissioning nukes is not very complicated—and in fact some 40,000 of the 60,000 weapons built since 1945 have already been retired, mostly because of obsolescence. After deactivation of their electronic triggers, the warheads are loaded back into their original, customized packing crates and, if overseas, flown back to the U. S. Under heavy guard, they are then shipped to Pantex by truck or train, along routes that are constantly changed and always kept secret. The most sensitive part of disassembly comes not in handling the uranium and highly toxic plutonium, which are shielded in metal, but in dealing with the conventional explosives needed to trigger a nuclear chain reaction. Disassembly therefore takes place in underground bunkers known as "Gravel Gerties," whose roofs are mounded with gravel to contain any accidental blasts.

Once disassembly is complete, the real question arises. What to do with the leftover radioactive material from the bombs? When nuclear weapons were a growth industry, their parts could be recycled into new nukes. Now, however, the most readily reusable weapons ingredient is tritium, a radioactive gas used in some warheads to increase the power of the nuclear reaction. Tritium decays rapidly, so existing bombs must be periodically replenished. This tritium windfall may even keep the Department of Energy from reactivating the accident-prone Savannah River plant near Aiken, S. C., where the gas is manufactured.

But aside from some uranium that will be recycled for use in nuclear-powered submarines, most of the fuel will have to be stored or dumped as waste. Unfortunately, the nation does not have a reliable, long-term plan for disposing of this deadly material. Most will probably be stockpiled at weapons plants, but there is a danger of loss, theft, and environmental damage from mishandling.

A far bigger problem, from an environmental standpoint, is what to do with the tens of thousands of tons of hot waste left over from 46 years of weapons production—everything from gloves to ball bearings. This material will remain radioactive for millenniums. The U.S. has only one facility designed to store this production waste, but the opening of the Waste Isolation Pilot Plant, 655 m. (2,150 ft.) underground in massive salt domes near Carlsbad, N. Mex., has been stymied by political wrangling and safety concerns. Last week the Department of Energy attempted to sidestep congressional deliberations on the matter and ship the first load of waste to the plant. It was halted after New Mexico filed a federal lawsuit, and the *doe* agreed to postpone the shipment. For the time being, 1 million bbl. of the deadly stuff continue to sit in temporary storage, as they have for decades.

Comprehension Check Questions

1. There are over how many warheads headed for early retirement? (1) 2,000; (2) 3,000; (3) 3,500; (4) 40,000 (5) 60,000. 1. _______
2. Since 1945, many nuclear weapons have been decommissioned primarily because of (1) high costs; (2) reduced need; (3) competition; (4) obsolescence; (5) public opinion. 2. _______
3. Which part of disassembling a bomb is most sensitive? (1) handling the uranium; (2) handling the plutonium; (3) handling the explosives; (4) loading the bomb; (5) transporting the bomb. 3. _______
4. The most readily reusable part of a dismantled bomb is the (1) uranium; (2) triggers; (3) casement; (4) explosives; (5) tritium. 4. _______
5. The selection focuses on the problems of (1) building nuclear weapons; (2) disposing of nuclear arms; (3) securing bombs; (4) assessing the warheads inventory; (5) nuclear-weapons recycling. 5. _______
6. One could infer that because the Cold War is over, the United State will (1) produce the same number of warheads; (2) destroy all of its nuclear weapons; (3) recycle hot waste; (4) disarm many of its nukes; (5) store all nuclear weapons in salt domes. 6. _______
7. No facility exists to (1) store hazardous waste; (2) safely dispose of all nuclear waste currently on hand; (3) deactivate electronic triggers; (4) process reusable nuclear weapons ingredients; (5) retrieve tritium, a radioactive gas. 7. _______
8. The article suggests U.S. military leaders believe (1) nuclear weapons have become ineffective; (2) there are no threats to U.S. security; (3) the nuclear age is over; (4) nuclear weapons are too costly to produce; (5) nuclear waste is not a serious problem. 8. _______

SCORE _______

Answers: 1. 2; 2. 4; 3. 3; 4. 5; 5. 2; 6. 4; 7. 2; 8. 3.

NAME ____________________ DATE ____________ READING RATE ____________ WPM

Comprehension Check Questions

1. In the last ten years the total annual number of divorces is said to have (1) leveled off; (2) dropped slightly; (3) risen steeply; (4) doubled. 1. ______

2. Second marriages tend to have (1) a longer life span than the first; (2) the same life span; (3) an unpredictable life span; (4) a shorter life span. 2. ______

3. Today what percentage of the low-birth-weight babies are born to mothers in their teens? (1) 25; (2) 20; (3) 15; (4) not given. 3. ______

4. It is said that divorce hangs over a young wife (1) when she first becomes pregnant; (2) as soon as she's married; (3) even before the ceremony; (4) the minute she stops working. 4. ______

5. It is said that a good marriage takes (1) money; (2) similar backgrounds; (3) hard work; (4) parental help. 5. ______

Receptive Comprehension ______

6. The main idea is to (1) indicate the problem; (2) suggest ways of dealing with the problem; (3) encourage more parental guidance; (4) persuade people to postpone getting married. 6. ______

7. What best describes the attitude taken here toward new-style alternates to marriage? (1) noncritical; (2) critical; (3) evasive; (4) encouraging. 7. ______

8. What factor appears most likely to lead to divorce? (1) lack of education; (2) early marriage; (3) health; (4) children. 8. ______

9. In tone this selection is (1) sarcastic; (2) straightforward; (3) somewhat flowery; (4) colloquial. 9. ______

10. By implication, it would seem most important for young couples to (1) read for new insights and ideas; (2) spend more time apart; (3) watch TV together more; (4) plan things to do with each other. 10. ______

(10 points for each correct answer)

Reflective Comprehension ______

TOTAL READING COMPREHENSION SCORE ______

Vocabulary Check Questions

			without context I	with context II
1.	**peers**	(1) superiors; (2) inferiors; (3) parents; (4) equals; (5) strangers.	1. ______	______
2.	**fending**	(1) using; (2) complaining; (3) concluding; (4) destroying; (5) managing.	2. ______	______
3.	**interloper**	(1) runner; (2) eloquent plea; (3) foreigner; (4) intruder; (5) foreman.	3. ______	______
4.	**ambivalence**	(1) conflicting feeling; (2) dexterity; (3) pleasantness; (4) slow gait; (5) slumber.	4. ______	______
5.	**limbo**	(1) leg; (2) indeterminate state; (3) distress signal; (4) dialect; (5) distaste.	5. ______	______

(10 points for each correct answer)

Word Comprehension without *contextual help (I)* ______

Word Comprehension with *contextual help (II)* ______

TOTAL WORD COMPREHENSION SCORE ______

EXERCISES

LEAVES

Being specialized for capturing sunlight for photosynthesis, most leaves are thin and flat. Although this structure may be typical, it is certainly not universal. Leaves are the most variable organ of plants. This variability represents adaptations to environmental conditions. . . .

Leaves of desert plants are often modified into protective spines. Since spines are relatively small, they reduce the surface area from which water can evaporate. In cactuses, little photosynthesis occurs in the spines; most photosynthesis takes place in the stems.

An uncommon modification of leaves occurs in insectivorous plants such as the pitcher plant. In insectivorous plants leaves often function as animals traps. These plans usually grow in soil that is relatively poor in nitrogen and phosphorus. The insects contain a large amount of these nutrients, and the plant receives essential macronutrients when it digests them.

Leaves can be round, straplike, needlelike, or heart shaped, and their edges range from smooth to serrate. Regardless of their external structure, all leaves are made up of ground, dermal, and vascular tissues. Secondary tissues rarely occur in leaves.

COMPREHENSION CHECK QUESTIONS

1. Which of the following is necessary for photosynthesis? (1) moisture; (2) sunlight; (3) darkness; (4) stillness; (5) chlorine. 1. _______

2. The parts of plants that are most dissimilar are (1) stems; (2) buds; (3) roots; (4) nodes; (5) leaves. 2. _______

3. The spines of desert plants are (1) small; (2) large; (3) ribbed; (4) striated; (5) thick. 3. _______

4. The pitcher plant is a hazard to (1) all other plants; (2) only desert plants; (3) insects; (4) humans; (5) the environment. 4. _______

5. Variability in a plant's leaf structure is the result of (1) adaptation to the environment; (2) grafting; (3) the aging process; (4) photosynthesis; (5) its density. 5. _______

6. The amount of moisture that evaporates from desert plants is determined by (1) leaf color; (2) stem thickness; (3) root size; (4) spine size; (5) leaf density. 6. _______

7. The primary purpose of this passage is to (1) give advice; (2) describe all the parts of the plant; (3) help with gardening; (4) inform; (5) persuade. 7. _______

8. You would judge that this selection most likely comes from (1) an editorial on the environment; (2) a landscaping design book; (3) a naturalist's biography; (4) a seed catalog; (5) a high school biology textbooks. 8. _______

SCORE _______

Answers: 1. 2 (93); 2. 5 (78); 3. 1 (90); 4. 3 (87); 5. 1 (72); 6. 4 (48); 7. 4 (78); 8. 5 (57). This selection was used in the preliminary forms of the *Nelson-Denny Reading Test* but not in the final forms. The numbers in parentheses indicate the difficulty level of the questions. The lower the number, the harder the question. Compare your performance to those of students who participated in the norming sample

NAME ______________________ DATE ______________ READING RATE ______________ WPM

Comprehension Check Questions

1. The author confesses that during graduate school he felt (1) fortunate; (2) exploited; (3) embarrassed; (4) proud. 1. ____

2. Rodriguez's early education was (1) poor; (2) average; (3) slightly above average; (4) excellent. 2. ____

3. The author studied for a Ph. D. at (1) Columbia; (2) Berkeley; (3) Stanford; (4) Yale. 3. ____

4. Rodriguez's office mate claimed Affirmative Action fosters (1) quota systems; (2) equal treatment; (3) racial integration; (4) cultural diversity. 4. ____

5. In Rodriguez's letters of application, he disclaimed being (1) Mexican-American; (2) exceptionally bright; (3) disadvantaged; (4) a teaching assistant. 5. ____

Receptive Comprehension ____

6. The main idea is that Affirmative Action is (1) generally fair; (2) generally unfair; (3) fair to none; (4) fair only to some. 6. ____

7. The author believes the most seriously disadvantaged (1) ignore Affirmative Action; (2) benefit from Affirmative Action; (3) do not benefit from Affirmative Action; (4) challenge Affirmative Action. 7. ____

8. Rodriguez believes his employment offers were (1) unimpressive; (2) fairly awarded; (3) unfairly awarded; (4) hoaxes. 8. ____

9. The author did not accept the offers he received because he felt (1) unworthy; (2) underprepared; (3) overprepared; (4) overpaid. 9. ____

10. Rodriguez implies he was chosen for jobs because of his (1) professors; (2) grades; (3) alma mater; (4) ethnicity. 10. ____

(10 points for each correct answer)

Reflective Comprehension ____

TOTAL READING COMPREHENSION SCORE ____

Vocabulary Check Questions

		without context I	with context II
1. complied	(1) conformed; (2) traded; (3) gathered; (4) crushed; (5) withered.	1. ____	____
2. dossier	(1) amount; (2) part; (3) back; (4) file; (5) point.	2. ____	____
3. rasped	(1) coughed; (2) panted; (3) scraped; (4) rolled; (5) slid.	3. ____	____
4. inevitable	(1) evil; (2) uneventful; (3) destructive; (4) unavoidable; (5) apparent.	4. ____	____
5. drones	(1) screams; (2) tracks; (3) speeds; (4) hums; (5) throbs.	5. ____	____

(10 points for each correct answer)

Word Comprehension without *contextual help (I)* ____

Word Comprehension with *contextual help (II)* ____

TOTAL WORD COMPREHENSION SCORE ____

Exercises

Marie Curie

When Marie Curie discovered a new radioactive element in 1898, she named it polonium in honor of Poland, her native land. At that time, there was no country called Poland. It had been divided and swallowed up by Austria, Prussia, and Russia. By choosing the name polonium, Marie Curie was reminding the world that Poles wanted a country of their own.

Marie Curie was born in the city of Warsaw in 1867. When she was 18, she took a job as a governess to help pay her older sister's way through medical school in Paris. Six years later Marie herself went to Paris to study science. There she met and married Pierre Curie.

Together Marie and Pierre Curie began the research on radioactivity for which they shared the Nobel Prize in physics in 1903. After Pierre died in a traffic accident in 1906, Marie Curie continued their work. In 1911 she won the Nobel Prize in chemistry for isolating pure radium. No one had ever won two Nobel Prizes before.

Over the following years, Marie Curie worked to establish centers for the study of radioactivity. She trained a new generation of physicists and chemists, many of whom made significant discoveries. In 1934 she died of leukemia brought on by years of working unprotected with radioactive material.

Comprehension Check Questions

1. Marie Curie was the first person to (1) win two Nobel Prizes; (2) win a Nobel Prize in physics; (3) win a Nobel Prize in chemistry; (4) research plutonium; (5) research leukemia. 1. _______

2. Marie Curie's sister studied (1) music; (2) polonium; (3) medicine; (4) physics; (5) chemistry. 2. _______

3. Marie Curie's husband (1) defected to Paris; (2) worked in Warsaw; (3) discovered radium; (4) won a Nobel Prize in chemistry; (5) was her associate. 3. _______

4. According to the passage, the Curies researched (1) polonium; (2) radioactivity; (3) chemistry; (4) leukemia; (5) medicine. 4. _______

5. Marie Curie discovered polonium (1) at the beginning of the 1800s; (2) at the beginning of the 1900s; (3) after her husband's death; (4) while living in Paris; (5) while living in Poland. 5. _______

6. Before becoming a scientist, Marie Curie worked as a (1) teacher; (2) secretary; (3) medical assistant; (4) nurse; (5) clerk. 6. _______

7. The focus of this selection is on Curie's (1) allegiance to Poland; (2) personal life; (3) contributions to science; (4) understanding of physics; (5) understanding of chemistry. 7. _______

8. The organization of this selection is (1) from least important to most important; (2) from most difficult to least difficult; (3) spatial; (4) chronological; (5) general to specific. 8. _______

SCORE _______

Answers: 1. 1 (84); 2. 3 (92); 3. 5 (76); 4. 2 (90); 5. 4 (15); 6. 1 (23); 7. 3 (76); 8. 4 (44). This selection was used in the preliminary forms of the *Nelson-Denny Reading Test* but not in the final forms. The numbers in parentheses indicate the difficulty level of the questions. The lower the number, the harder the question. Compare your performance to those of students who participated in the norming sample

NAME ______________________ DATE ______________ READING RATE ______________ WPM

COMPREHENSION CHECK QUESTIONS

1. This essay starts with a reference to (1) Portsmouth; (2) the Bill of Rights; (3) The Code Napoleon; (4) Plymouth. 1. _______
2. The Arab child was spoken of as a lost (1) Mozart; (2) Chopin; (3) Beethoven; (4) Caruso. 2. _______
3. How many misunderstandings are discussed? (1) one; (2) two; (3) three; (4) four. 3. _______
4. In place of the hickory stick, we are said to have (1) the psychiatrist; (2) the counselor; (3) personality tests; (4) nothing. 4. _______
5. Toynbee said that all progress comes from (1) insight; (2) discipline; (3) challenge; (4) values. 5. _______

Receptive Comprehension _______

6. The main focus of the article is on the freedom to (1) determine our own goals; (2) think as we please; (3) realize our full potential; (4) set our own values. 6. _______
7. This discussion is organized primarily on a (1) problem-solution pattern; (2) cause-effect pattern; (3) question-answer pattern; (4) time-sequence pattern. 7. _______
8. The purpose of this article is to get us to (1) understand; (2) act; (3) believe; (4) evaluate. 8. _______
9. Judging from this article, any work on efficient reading should above all (1) be practical; (2) have set standards of achievement; (3) cover the widest possible number of techniques; (4) be demanding. 9. _______
10. The ending is best described as (1) a challenge; (2) a prediction; (3) a supplication; (4) a summary. 10. _______

(10 points for each correct answer)

Reflective Comprehension _______
TOTAL READING COMPREHENSION SCORE _______

VOCABULARY CHECK QUESTIONS

			without context I	with context II
1.	**nought**	(1) now; (2) newness; (3) nothing; (4) originality; (5) circular.	1. _______	_______
2.	**unprecedented**	(1) unsurpassed; (2) uncertain; (3) inexact; (4) customary; (5) pressured.	2. _______	_______
3.	**tenets**	(1) doctrines; (2) renters; (3) occupants; (4) lawyers; (5) structures.	3. _______	_______
4.	**ultimates**	(1) origins; (2) claims; (3) actions; (4) choices; (5) fundamentals.	4. _______	_______
5.	**discerned**	(1) disappeared; (2) perceived; (3) scowled; (4) heard; (5) soothed.	5. _______	_______

(10 points for each correct answer)

Word Comprehension without *contextual help (I)* _______
Word Comprehension with *contextual help (II)* _______
TOTAL WORD COMPREHENSION SCORE _______

EXERCISES

THE AMERICAN POLITICAL SYSTEM

People who are governed by a political system place **demands** on it regarding a variety of issues. For example, some people may want to escalate or withdraw from a war; they may want the government to control or not to control prices and wages. The greater the demands, the greater the stress on the system because more resources must be used to satisfy them. The level of support given by the people to the political system may range from very high to very low, depending upon how satisfied they are with the system's performance. A high level of support reduces stress, and a low level increases it. If the stress becomes too great, the political system may collapse. If a system suffers great stress and still survives, it ranks high in stability; if it collapses, it may be transformed into another type of system.

The American political system has survived a bloody civil war, two world wars and five other major military conflicts; it has survived a major depression and several recessions in the twentieth century; and it has survived major scandals in the White House in the administrations of Ulysses Grant, Warren Harding, and Richard Nixon. The American system ranks high in stability.

COMPREHENSION CHECK QUESTIONS

1. One issue specifically identified is (1) war; (2) taxes; (3) housing; (4) foreign aid; (5) pollution. 1. ______
2. A major scandal occurred during the administration of President (1) Ulysses Grant; (2) Grover Cleveland; (3) William McKinley; (4) Woodrow Wilson; (5) Herbert Hoover. 2. ______
3. In this selection there is mention of (1) support levels; (2) a depression; (3) major military conflicts; (4) a recession; (5) all of the above. 3. ______
4. The American political system was specifically said to rank high in (1) strength; (2) stability; (3) continuity; (4) permanence; (5) durability. 4. ______
5. Apparently, increased stress on a political system would tend to (1) increase support; (2) lessen demand; (3) increase support and lessen demand; (4) lessen support and increase demand; (5) lessen both support and demand. 5. ______
6. Concerning the functioning of a political system, the first paragraph focuses mainly on the question (1) Who developed it? (2) When was it formed? (3) Why was it organized? (4) How does it function? (5) What does it consist of? 6. ______
7. The last paragraph emphasizes the American political system's (1) stress and strain; (2) survival; (3) degree of support; (4) pattern over time; (5) changing demands. 7. ______
8. The attitude taken toward the American political system is primarily (1) pessimistic; (2) matter-of-fact; (3) optimistic; (4) objective; (5) subjective. 8. ______

SCORE ______

Answers: 1. 1 (73); 2. 1 (87); 3. 5 (68); 4. 2 (69); 5. 4 (39); 6. 4 (57); 7. 2 (56); 8. 3 (27). This selection was used in the preliminary forms of the *Nelson-Denny Reading Test* but not in the final forms. The numbers in parentheses indicate the difficulty level of the questions. The lower the number, the harder the question. Compare your performance to those of students who participated in the norming sample.

NAME ______________________ DATE ______________ READING RATE ______________ WPM

Comprehension Check Questions

1. For what percent of people is time and energy expenditure said to be out of step with life goals? (1) 45; (2) 60; (3) 75; (4) 90. 1. _______
2. One of the seven questions is specifically on (1) production of income; (2) environmental needs and life style; (3) sense of responsibility; (4) physical fitness as related to mental fitness. 2. _______
3. Who is quoted? (1) Kennedy; (2) Pogo; (3) Peanuts; (4) Hitler. 3. _______
4. At what age is parallel play said to be typical? (1) age 1; (2) age 2; (3) age 2 or 3; (4) age 3 or 4. 4. _______
5. Reference is made to (1) Hollywood; (2) Utopia; (3) Great Britain; (4) San Francisco. 5. _______

Receptive Comprehension _______

6. This selection is chiefly about how to (1) discover our problems; (2) solve our problems; (3) check up on our mental health; (4) strengthen our relationships with others. 6. _______
7. The aphorism "physician, heal thyself" is used to develop the idea that self-examination (1) is difficult; (2) is common; (3) should be done by physicians; (4) is actually impossible to do. 7. _______
8. The seven areas are ordered essentially on what basis? (1) from the global to the individual; (2) according to a developing time sequence; (3) from the particular to the general; (4) from most to least importance. 8. _______
9. By implication, an avocation is considered primarily as a way of (1) avoiding problems; (2) gaining emotional fulfillment; (3) finding needed relaxation; (4) developing stronger self-reliance. 9. _______
10. In style you would call this article (1) conversational; (2) lively; (3) dignified; (4) dreary. 10. _______

(10 points for each correct answer)

Reflective Comprehension _______

TOTAL READING COMPREHENSION SCORE _______

Vocabulary Check Questions

			without context I	with context II
1.	**autonomy**	(1) technical perfection; (2) independence; (3) motor-driven; (4) composite; (5) welfare state.	1. _______	_______
2.	**castigate**	(1) punish; (2) discard; (3) evolve; (4) tear down; (5) smooth over.	2. _______	_______
3.	**pre-empt**	(1) suggest; (2) spare; (3) turn over; (4) get beforehand; (5) force into submission.	3. _______	_______
4.	**germane**	(1) relevant; (2) cultivated; (3) original; (4) infected; (5) weakened.	4. _______	_______
5.	**hallmark**	(1) shipping label; (2) entryway; (3) engraving tool; (4) symbol of excellence; (5) gift.	5. _______	_______

(10 points for each correct answer)

Word Comprehension without *contextual help (I)* _______

Word Comprehension with *contextual help (II)* _______

TOTAL WORD COMPREHENSION SCORE _______

EXERCISES

RICHARD WRIGHT, 1908–1960

Richard Wright was the earliest of twentieth-century authors to examine the social, economic, and moral conditions of the urban black ghetto. He was born on a plantation near Natchez, Mississippi, but grew up in Memphis, Tennessee. When Wright was quite young, his mother, who was ill, placed her children first in an orphanage and then in the care of various relatives. At the age of nineteen, shortly before the advent of the Great Depression, Wright and one of his aunts made their way to Chicago. They were soon joined there by Wright's mother and brother, and survival became the family's constant worry.

Wright published his first collection of short stories in 1938 but became well known with the publication in 1940 of his first novel, *Native Son*. *Native Son* is significant in American literature for bringing unprecedented attention to African-American literature and African-American writers. *Black Boy,* the story of Wright's experiences growing up in the south, appeared in 1945. This autobiographical work brought him the highest literary acclaim. After World War II, Wright moved with is family to Paris, where he lived until his death. He continued to write about the plight of the African-American, and his work has served as an example and encouragement to many black writers. The critic Irving Howe attributed Wright's success to his having "kept faith with the experience of the boy who had fought his way out of the depths to speak for those who remained behind."

In addition to *Native Son* and *Black Boy,* which are among his finest contributions to American literature, Wright produced many other volumes, including *The God That Failed* (1950) and *Eight Men* (published posthumously in 1961). In 1977 *American Hunger,* the second part of Wright's autobiography, was published. Written in the 1940's, it continues the story begun in *Black Boy,* which ends with Wright's leaving the South. *American Hunger* begins with his arrival in Chicago in 1927.

Comprehension Check Questions

1. Wright lived most of his teen years in (1) Natchez, Mississippi; (2) Memphis, Tennessee; (3) Chicago; (4) Paris; (5) an orphanage. 1. _______

2. According to the author, *Black Boy* is (1) Wright's most celebrated work; (2) Wright's last novel; (3) the story of an African male; (4) the story of Wright's early years; (5) the story of the African-American male. 2. _______

3. Wright wrote primarily about (1) the Great Depression; (2) urban African-Americans; (3) rural African-Americans; (4) his family; (5) his life in an orphanage. 3. _______

4. Wright's examination of life in the urban ghetto was (1) unprecedented; (2) superficial; (3) unpublished; (4) fantasy; (5) cursory. 4. _______

5. One could infer that moving to Chicago (1) made Wright's life easy; (2) was a risk for Wright and his family; (3) stifled Wright's creativity; (4) estranged Wright from his family; (5) provided Wright peace of mind. 5. _______

6. Richard Wright believed (1) there is no way out of poverty; (2) education is the only way out of poverty; (3) people should know about the lifestyles of urban African-Americans; (4) rural African-Americans should not move to American cities; (5) Paris is not a good place for African-Americans to live. 6. _______

7. One could conclude that Wright's work is largely (1) unimpressive; (2) unemotional; (3) inspirational; (4) autobiographical; (5) humorous. 7. _______

8. The best inference is that Wright's early life was (1) privileged; (2) stable; (3) unprecedented; (4) arduous; (5) felicitous. 8. _______

SCORE _______

Answers: 1. 2 (85); 2. 4 (81); 3. 2 (74); 4. 1 (69); 5. 2 (68); 6. 3 (36); 7. 4 (78); 8. 4 (49). This selection was used in the preliminary forms of the *Nelson-Denny Reading Test* but not in the final forms. The numbers in parentheses indicate the difficulty level of the questions. The lower the number, the harder the question. Compare your performance to those of students who participated in the norming sample.

NAME ______________ DATE ______________ READING RATE ______________ WPM

Comprehension Check Questions

1. Scientists began carefully assessing the abilities of newborns about how many years ago? (1) 5; (2) 15; (3) 20; (4) 25. 1. _______

2. Fifty years ago, a leading investigator of child development was (1) Dr. Elliot Blass; (2) Dr. Arnold Gesell; (3) Dr. Barry Lester; (4) Dr. Anthony DeCasper. 2. _______

3. Babies communicate needs and respond to others (1) from birth; (2) at 1 month; (3) at 2 months; (4) around 3 months. 3. _______

4. When mothers sent contradictory messages to their infants, the babies were (1) amused; (2) astounded; (3) diffused; (4) disturbed. 4. _______

5. Many minute-old infants turned their heads to see a (1) blank square; (2) mobile; (3) human-like drawing; (4) light. 5. _______

Receptive Comprehension _______

6. This is mainly about (1) how babies control their environments; (2) how adults control babies' environments; (3) what newborns know; (4) how much babies can learn. 6. _______

7. Human infants are born with an innate need to (1) be left alone; (2) socialize; (3) cry indiscriminately; (4) be quiet. 7. _______

8. Tronick found that a six-week-old infant's reaction to his behavior was (1) unrelated; (2) sporadic; (3) deliberate; (4) random. 8. _______

9. Newborns' senses are (1) completely developed; (2) sufficiently developed; (3) undeveloped; (4) interdependent. 9. _______

10. One can assume that until about three months, babies are physically unready to (1) visualize; (2) communicate; (3) adapt; (4) vocalize. 10. _______

(10 points for each correct answer)

Reflective Comprehension _______

TOTAL READING COMPREHENSION SCORE _______

Vocabulary Check Questions

			without context I	with context II
1.	**tabula rasa**	(1) flesh; (2) blank mind; (3) clay; (4) dough; (5) flower.	1. _______	_______
2.	**neonates**	(1) lights; (2) rocks; (3) signs; (4) newborns; (5) plans.	2. _______	_______
3.	**devised**	(1) invented; (2) invested; (3) advised; (4) divested; (5) faced.	3. _______	_______
4.	**evolutionary**	(1) unfolding; (2) obstructing; (3) religious; (4) controversial; (5) voluntary.	4. _______	_______
5.	**purses**	(1) pokes; (2) puckers; (3) opens; (4) closes; (5) fills.	5. _______	_______

(10 points for each correct answer)

Word Comprehension without *contextual help (I)* _______

Word Comprehension with *contextual help (II)* _______

TOTAL WORD COMPREHENSION SCORE _______

EXERCISES

VATICAN CITY

For centuries, Roman Catholic popes have dwelt in a complex of palaces and churches known as the Vatican. Surrounded by medieval and Renaissance walls, the Vatican stands on the west bank of Rome's famed Tiber River. The heart of the Vatican is St. Peter's Church, first built during the Roman Empire and rebuilt in the 1500s.

Before Italy was united, the Vatican was just one of many Italian territories ruled by the Pope. These lands were known as the Papal States. Like other parts of Italy, the Papal States were caught up in the drive for national unity during the 1850's and 1860's. Early Italian nationalists hoped that the Pope would help them unite Italy. Pope Pius IX turned against nationalism, however, and insisted on keeping his political power over the Papal States.

By 1870 most of the Papal States had become part of Italy, but the Pope still held Rome. On September 20, 1870, Italian troops marched on the city. A few hours of artillery fire ended centuries of papal rule. Pope Pius IX withdrew to the Vatican.

Vatican City became an independent state within Rome and was recognized as such by Italy in 1929. The Pope remains the head of its government. With an area of just 108.7 acres, Vatican City is the smallest independent state in the world.

COMPREHENSION CHECK QUESTIONS

1. Vatican city is a (1) barren, walled mountain community; (2) group of simple unadorned buildings; (3) group of churches and palaces; (4) small religious resort; (5) small group of churches. 1. _______

2. St. Peter's Church was first built during the (1) Renaissance; (2) Roman Empire; (3) 1500s; (4) 1850s; (5) 1860s. 2. _______

3. During the 1850s and 1860s, Italian nationalists (1) were in the Vatican; (2) were at war with Europe; (3) were political enemies of Italy; (4) wanted to unite Italy; (5) wanted to unite church and state. 3. _______

4. Pope Pius IX was (1) a political enemy of Italy; (2) a proponent of national unity; (3) opposed to national unity; (4) the last resident of the Vatican; (5) the victim of Vatican nationalists. 4. _______

5. When Italy was made up of many territories, the Pope ruled (1) much of Italy; (2) only Rome; (3) only the Vatican; (4) none of the Papal States; (5) Rome and Vatican City. 5. _______

6. Pope Pius IX was the first Pope to (1) rule Europe; (2) rule Vatican City; (3) have political power over Catholics; (4) command Italian troops; (5) unite Italy. 6. _______

7. The Pope relinquished his control of Rome because he (1) no longer needed Roman support; (2) moved to another Italian territory; (3) refused to denounce nationalism; (4) lacked the power to thwart military advances; (5) acknowledged Rome's secession from Italy. 7. _______

8. The best title for this selection is (1) Papal States; (2) The History of Italy; (3) The History of Vatican City; (4) Early Italian Territories; (5) Vatican City. 8. _______

SCORE _______

Answers: 1. 3 (70); 2. 2 (65); 3. 3 (85); 4. 4 (66); 5. 1 (37); 6. 2 (55); 7. 4 (49); 8. 3 (58). This selection was used in the preliminary forms of the *Nelson-Denny Reading Test* but not in the final forms. The numbers in parentheses indicate the difficulty level of the questions. The lower the number, the harder the question. Compare your performance to those of students who participated in the norming sample.

NAME ______________ DATE ______________ READING RATE ______________ WPM

Comprehension Check Questions

1. The organizing principle that underlies how one thinks is a (1) dyad; (2) pyramid; (3) microcosm; (4) paradigm. 1. ______

2. Three-part paradigms are common in societies shaped by (1) matriarchy and religious divisions; (2) patriarchy and racial divisions; (3) abstractions; (4) revolutions. 2. ______

3. Becoming a part of nature rather than trying to conquer it is an example of which kind of paradigm? (1) binary; (2) cyclical; (3) hierarchical; (4) linear. 3. ______

4. In long-term hierarchies, the people at the bottom feel (1) hopeful; (2) resentful; (3) accepted; (4) critical. 4. ______

5. Kohn's research indicates people perform better when they (1) cooperate; (2) compete; (3) contest; (4) concede. 5. ______

Receptive Comprehension ______

6. The purpose of this selection is to (1) define organizing principles; (2) question ingrained thinking patterns; (3) examine the communication revolution; (4) rekindle interest in pantheistic paradigms. 6. ______

7. Steinem favors which of the paradigms? (1) linear; (2) hierarchical; (3) binary; (4) cyclical. 7. ______

8. The author believes a linear paradigm (1) redirects us; (2) redeems us; (3) restricts us; (4) refocuses us. 8. ______

9. Circularity requires (1) self-doubt; (2) keen competition; (3) self-fulfillment; (4) immediate gratification. 9. ______

10. A nonlinear, nonbinary, nonhierarchical paradigm fosters a culture that is (1) competitive; (2) tolerant; (3) passive; (4) aggressive. 10. ______

(10 points for each correct answer)

Reflective Comprehension ______

TOTAL READING COMPREHENSION SCORE ______

Vocabulary Check Questions

		without context I	with context II
1. immutable	(1) alterable; (2) inalterable; (3) silent; (4) stationary; (5) speechless.	1. ______	______
2. paradigm	(1) design; (2) anomaly; (3) pattern; (4) projection; (5) example.	2. ______	______
3. microcosm	(1) epitome of the world; (2) epitome of oneself; (3) small sample; (4) exact copy; (5) enlarged copy.	3. ______	______
4. degradation	(1) delineation; (2) evaluation; (3) degeneration; (4) obliteration; (5) existence.	4. ______	______
5. annihilation	(1) habitation; (2) abolition; (3) hostility; (4) criticism; (5) prejudice.	5. ______	______

(10 points for each correct answer)

Word Comprehension without *contextual help (I)* ______

Word Comprehension with *contextual help (II)* ______

TOTAL WORD COMPREHENSION SCORE ______

Exercises

Astronomer

Astronomy is a branch of physics that holds a strong fascination for many people. Current research in astronomy covers a variety of areas: the origin and characteristics of the solar system, the birth and evolution of stars, galaxies and their motions, the origin of the universe, and many more. Astronomy is different from other sciences in that astronomers cannot experiment with the objects they study. Practically all of our contact with the universe comes indirectly, through light and other forms of radiation. Moon rocks and meteorites are the only objects from outside the earth an astronomer can actually touch.

The work of astronomers has two aspects: theory and observation. Most astronomers do both types of work, but some are involved primarily in one or the other. Theoretical work in astronomy is developing mathematical equations to compute models. Mathematical models of stars and the ways in which they evolve are examples of this type of work. Observational work is observing stars or other objects, and analyzing and explaining the results.

Astronomy is a difficult field of study. Astronomers typically have a bachelor's degree in physics or mathematics, and hold a Ph. D. in astronomy. Opportunities for individuals with only a bachelor's degree are extremely limited. There are also some jobs available at the technician's level for people with two years' training.

Comprehension Check Questions

1. Light is a form of (1) gas; (2) convection; (3) radiation; (4) electric current; (5) astronomy. 1. _______

2. In astronomy, developing mathematical equations to compute models is (1) theoretical work; (2) field work; (3) laboratory work; (4) a simple task; (5) a low priority. 2. _______

3. The explanation of how stars evolve is said to be (1) factual; (2) a hoax; (3) theoretical; (4) irrelevant; (5) irrational. 3. _______

4. An astronomy technician needs (1) one year of college; (2) two years' training; (3) two years of college; (4) a bachelor's degree; (5) a Ph.D. in astronomy. 4. _______

5. The author suggests that astronomers are primarily interested in (1) objective data; (2) subjective data; (3) objective and subjective data; (4) historical data; (5) aesthetics. 5. _______

6. The author implies that astronomy is (1) appealing and unique; (2) time-consuming and exhausting; (3) time-consuming and impractical; (4) fascinating to a select group of people; (5) fascinating to astronomers only. 6. _______

7. With what is the passage primarily concerned? (1) the preparation of astronomers; (2) the training of technicians; (3) the solar system; (4) galaxies and their motions; (5) a branch of physics called astronomy. 7. _______

8. One could infer that astronomers primarily focus on (1) what was; (2) what should be; (3) why; (4) how and why; (5) how and when. 8. _______

SCORE _______

Answers: 1. 3 (69); 2. 1 (78); 3. 3 (69); 4. 2 (38); 5. 3 (55); 6. 1 (33); 7. 5 (57); 8. 4 (54). This selection was used in the preliminary forms of the *Nelson-Denny Reading Test* but not in the final forms. The numbers in parentheses indicate the difficulty level of the questions. The lower the number, the harder the question. Compare your performance to those of students who participated in the norming sample.

NAME ______________________ DATE ______________ READING RATE ______________ WPM

COMPREHENSION CHECK QUESTIONS

1. Since 1980, part-time employment has grown (1) 6%; (2) 20%; (3) 21%; (4) 30%. 1. _______

2. Not suited to part-time scheduling are jobs that require (1) little supervision; (2) expensive equipment; (3) extensive travel; (4) extensive client contact. 2. _______

3. The best opportunities for part-time scheduling are in jobs that are (1) team-structured; (2) project-oriented; (3) service-oriented; (4) deadline-dependent. 3. _______

4. A 1978 law requires federal agencies to (1) reduce the number of part-time jobs; (2) regularly rotate part-time workers; (3) prorate part-time salaries; (4) increase employee benefits. 4. _______

5. Many of the best part-time opportunities are offered by (1) large companies; (2) governmental agencies; (3) foreign employers; (4) nonprofit organizations. 5. _______

Receptive Comprehension _______

6. The main idea is that finding good part-time employment (1) is difficult; (2) is uncomplicated; (3) requires an employment agency; (4) requires diligence. 6. _______

7. A company that advertises a new gym or parental leave policies is likely to have (1) many senior-level employees; (2) few part-time job opportunities; (3) nontraditional scheduling; (4) a traditional office environment. 7. _______

8. Successful flexible scheduling may (1) revolutionize the economy; (2) cause management chaos; (3) decrease efficiency; (4) revolutionize the workplace. 8. _______

9. Main ideas in this selection are developed primarily through (1) analogies; (2) example; (3) description; (4) narration. 9. _______

10. One would expect part-time employment opportunities to (1) escalate; (2) stabilize; (3) diminish; (4) defuse. 10. _______

(10 points for each correct answer)

Reflective Comprehension _______

TOTAL READING COMPREHENSION SCORE _______

VOCABULARY CHECK QUESTIONS

		without context I	with context II
1. pilot	(1) sample; (2) guess; (3) wager; (4) plot; (5) plan.	1. _______	_______
2. prorate	(1) pinpoint; (2) claim; (3) rank; (4) search; (5) equalize.	2. _______	_______
3. scrutinizing	(1) cleaning; (2) examining; (3) discarding; (4) shuffling; (5) negotiating.	3. _______	_______
4. accommodating	(1) calculating; (2) attending; (3) obliging; (4) accompanying; (5) separating.	4. _______	_______
5. options	(1) scenes; (2) choices; (3) careers; (4) eyes; (5) enemies.	5. _______	_______

(10 points for each correct answer)

Word Comprehension without *contextual help (I)* _______

Word Comprehension with *contextual help (II)* _______

TOTAL WORD COMPREHENSION SCORE _______

Exercises

Waters of the Land

The earth has been recycling its water for about three billion years. The distribution changes, but the total supply remains constant.

When it rains, people get involved in the water cycle. Rivers and lakes are our main source of fresh water for drinking, cleaning, and irrigation. Before the invention of the steam engine, waterways were the major routes for the exchange of people, goods, and ideas. For many of us, fresh water also provides recreation and natural beauty.

In some river valleys, such as the Nile in the past, people have depended on flooding to enrich the soil each year. But in many regions floods are natural disasters. Spring floods are caused by melting snow and seasonal rains over great river basins.

Throughout much of history, the dependence of people on water has led them into great efforts to control the waters of the land. Some of these attempts have not turned out well because all of the consequences could not be predicted.

When rain falls, some of it flows over the surface of the earth into streams, some evaporates, and some seeps into the ground. . . . You do not see the invisible water vapor moving from the land back into the atmosphere. And ordinarily people are unaware of the reservoir of water beneath the earth's surface. But the storage and flow of water beneath the surface is one of the primary concerns of earth scientists.

Comprehension Check Questions

1. What are the main sources of fresh water? (1) creeks and ponds; (2) oceans and rivers; (3) gulfs and rivers; (4) lakes and creeks; (5) lakes and rivers. 1. _______

2. Before the steam engine was invented, waterways were (1) clogged with row boats; (2) narrow and winding; (3) poorly maintained; (4) the primary routes for human transportation; (5) important sites of war battles. 2. _______

3. Which is a major cause of springs floods? (1) tributaries; (2) isolated thunderstorms; (3) soil erosion; (4) wind erosion; (5) melting snow. 3. _______

4. Water management results have (1) never been tried; (2) been unreliable; (3) pleased earth scientists; (4) eliminated spring flooding; (5) increased spring flooding. 4. _______

5. When it rains, the earth's water supply (1) is unaltered; (2) is evenly distributed; (3) becomes contaminated; (4) becomes diluted; (5) evaporates. 5. _______

6. The evaporation of rain water (1) decreases the world's water reserve; (2) causes winter to be a dry season; (3) causes heavy snows; (4) decreases the amount of water on the earth's surface; (5) occurs only in the spring. 6. _______

7. One could conclude that the reservoir of underground water is (1) contaminated; (2) an invaluable resource; (3) readily available; (4) in abundant supply; (5) not affected by rain. 7. _______

8. Water is, to some degree, responsible for this planet's (1) natural beauty; (2) position in the solar system; (3) ecological imbalances; (4) atmospheric pressure; (5) water pollution. 8. _______

SCORE _______

Answers: 1. 5 (87); 2. 4 (86); 3. 5 (83); 4. 2 (43); 5. 1 (16); 6. 4 (57); 7. 2 (28); 8. 1 (36). This selection was used in the preliminary forms of the *Nelson-Denny Reading Test* but not in the final forms. The numbers in parentheses indicate the difficulty level of the questions. The lower the number, the harder the question. Compare your performance to those of students who participated in the norming sample.

NAME ______________________ DATE ______________ READING RATE ______________ WPM

COMPREHENSION CHECK QUESTIONS

1. Self-segregation is often the result of (1) cultural amnesia; (2) active discrimination; (3) political correctness; (4) homogeneity. 1. ______

2. Segmentation is referred to as (1) discrimination; (2) pluralism; (3) Balkanization; (4) assimilation. 2. ______

3. Self-segregation on college campuses is (1) new; (2) continuing; (3) ending; (4) diminishing. 3. ______

4. Which was mentioned as a historically self-segregated campus unit? (1) fraternities; (2) faculty; (3) cafeterias; (4) libraries. 4. ______

5. In the early years of campus integration, those who self-segregated most often were (1) African-Americans; (2) whites; (3) Asians; (4) Hispanics. 5. ______

Receptive Comprehension ______

6. This selection is mainly about (1) where segmentation occurs; (2) why self-segregation occurs; (3) who practices segmentation; (4) how colleges cope with segmentation. 6. ______

7. Critics of segmentation are (1) broad-minded; (2) condescending; (3) unyielding; (4) myopic. 7. ______

8. Berkeley research suggests synergistic relationships develop when groups interact (1) daily; (2) only academically; (3) as equals; (4) only socially. 8. ______

9. Some students believe segmentation is a necessary defense against (1) campus stress; (2) separatism; (3) pluralism; (4) ethnic isolationism. 9. ______

10. To accommodate cultural diversity, Euro-centric curricula on college campuses are likely to be (1) strengthened; (2) de-emphasized; (3) defended; (4) initiated. 10. ______

(10 points for each correct answer)

Reflective Comprehension ______

TOTAL READING COMPREHENSION SCORE ______

VOCABULARY CHECK QUESTIONS

			without context I	with context II
1. segmented	(1) separated; (2) meshed; (3) united; (4) identified; (5) preferred.	1.	______	______
2. reversion	(1) turning away; (2) turning back; (3) secession; (4) space; (5) position.	2.	______	______
3. prestigious	(1) commanding; (2) presumptuous; (3) honored; (4) defamed; (5) tendentious.	3.	______	______
4. hegemony	(1) subservience; (2) well mixed; (3) harmony; (4) generosity; (5) influence.	4.	______	______
5. ramifications	(1) parts; (2) causes; (3) effects; (4) reckless actions; (5) random choices.	5.	______	______

(10 points for each correct answer)

Word Comprehension without *contextual help (I)* ______

Word Comprehension with *contextual help (II)* ______

TOTAL WORD COMPREHENSION SCORE ______

EXERCISES

HAGIA SOPHIA

When riots swept through Constantinople in 532 and nearly drove Justinian from his throne, much of the city was destroyed by fire. Among the churches that burned was Hagia Sophia, built in the time of Constantine. Justinian resolved to rebuild this church and make it the most splendid in the world.

Many cathedrals in Europe took more than a generation to build. The new Hagia Sophia, however, took only five years (532-537). The work went quickly because the emperor poured money into the project—enough to hire as many as 10,000 laborers.

From the outside, Hagia Sophia was impressive. A cluster of arched roofs rose up to the mighty central dome, which stood 180 feet above the city. By sheer height and mass, the cathedral dominated Constantinople. Yet its true beauty could be seen only from the inside. The huge dome, built with tons of marble and concrete, looked almost weightless from within the church. It seemed to float on a halo of sunlight from the circle of windows around its base. One historian wrote that the dome looked as if it were "suspended by a golden chain from heaven."

The columns and walls gleamed with many-colored marble and polished stone. Glittering mosaics reflected the light of a thousand lamps and candles. The scent of incense filled the air. Overwhelmed by all this beauty, some visiting nobles from Russia were sure they saw angels hovering in the lofty dome.

COMPREHENSION CHECK QUESTIONS

1. One result of the riots of Constantinople was (1) a population exodus; (2) a population influx; (3) raids; (4) fires; (5) wars. 1. _______

2. According to the selection, upon entering Hagia Sophia, one would notice (1) soldiers; (2) armed guards; (3) a grand chandelier; (4) visiting nobles from Russia; (5) the aroma of incense. 2. _______

3. Which part of Hagia Sophia's structure seemed to some observers to be suspended? (1) the steeples; (2) the walls; (3) its dome; (4) its windows; (5) its ceiling. 3. _______

4. Hagia Sophia's dome (1) was weightless; (2) weighed tons; (3) was transparent; (4) contained hundreds of windows; (5) was suspended by a gold chain. 4. _______

5. Hagia Sophia was the result of (1) community effort; (2) political decree; (3) spiritual awakening; (4) an emperor's dream; (5) an emperor's revenge. 5. _______

6. The passage suggests that during the riots of 532, (1) Justinian went into exile; (2) Justinian commanded large armies; (3) Justinian was killed in a fire; (4) Justinian's sovereignty was threatened; (5) Justinian's armies were defeated. 6. _______

7. Which of the following influenced the building of Hagia Sophia? (1) politics; (2) war; (3) money; (4) human error; (5) natural disaster. 7. _______

8. Justinian was which of the following when Hagia Sophia was built? (1) the emperor's advisor; (2) the emperor's architect; (3) the builder; (4) Constantinople's ruler; (5) a military general. 8. _______

SCORE _______

Answers: 1. 4 (92); 2. 5 (58); 3. 3 (83); 4. 2 (49); 5. 4 (62); 6. 4 (57); 7. 3 (53); 8. 4 (67). This selection was used in the preliminary forms of the *Nelson-Denny Reading Test* but not in the final forms. The numbers in parentheses indicate the difficulty level of the questions. The lower the number, the harder the question. Compare your performance to those of students who participated in the norming sample.

NAME ____________ DATE ____________ READING RATE ____________ WPM

COMPREHENSION CHECK QUESTIONS

1. The sixfold job classification came from a professor from (1) Harvard; (2) Yale; (3) Columbia; (4) Johns Hopkins. 1. ______
2. People attracted to realistic jobs are described as usually (1) talkative; (2) practical; (3) ambitious; (4) sociable. 2. ______
3. The job of bookkeeper is classified as (1) a social job; (2) a realistic job; (3) a conventional job; (4) an investigative job. 3. ______
4. Those attracted to artistic jobs are described as (1) dependable; (2) assertive; (3) social; (4) emotional. 4. ______
5. Sales jobs come under the heading of (1) artistic jobs; (2) conventional jobs; (3) jobs of leadership; (4) social jobs. 5. ______

Receptive Comprehension ______

6. This selection is written chiefly to help readers (1) know the satisfactions of certain types of jobs; (2) know the key characteristics of success; (3) choose a career; (4) know what interest patterns to note. 6. ______
7. The primary purpose is to (1) persuade; (2) teach; (3) clarify; (4) entertain. 7. ______
8. The style is best described as (1) colloquial; (2) straightforward; (3) dramatic; (4) inspirational. 8. ______
9. Points are developed largely by (1) details from personal research findings; (2) the author's firsthand experience; (3) logical reasoning; (4) case histories. 9. ______
10. Chief emphasis is on describing (1) job satisfactions; (2) educational backgrounds; (3) job characteristics; (4) personal attributes. 10. ______

(10 points for each correct answer)

Reflective Comprehension ______

TOTAL READING COMPREHENSION SCORE ______

VOCABULARY CHECK QUESTIONS

		without context I	with context II
1. **robust**	(1) even-tempered; (2) tall; (3) full-bosomed; (4) vigorous; (5) ungainly.	1. ______	______
2. **tangible**	(1) actual; (2) twofold; (3) jumbled; (4) worn; (5) finished.	2. ______	______
3. **ambiguity**	(1) distinctiveness; (2) aimlessness; (3) inexactness; (4) helplessness; (5) continuity.	3. ______	______
4. **analytical**	(1) preparatory; (2) rearranged; (3) planned; (4) anatomical; (5) separating.	4. ______	______
5. **introspective**	(1) reckless; (2) looking within; (3) thoughtful; (4) not essential; (5) active.	5. ______	______

(10 points for each correct answer)

Word Comprehension without *contextual help (I)* ______

Word Comprehension with *contextual help (II)* ______

TOTAL WORD COMPREHENSION SCORE ______

EXERCISES

SELF-SCORING CAREER COMPATIBILITY TEST

Your personality—the characteristics that define you as an individual—provide a clue to the type of career for which you are best suited.

How would you describe yourself? This little quiz is designed to let you become your own career counselor and see yourself as you really are.

To take this test, write 2 in the blank beside the words below that could usually be considered descriptive of you; write 1 beside words that are sometimes applicable (or if you are not sure). Leave blanks beside the words the definitely *do not apply* to you.

1. Adventuresome _____F
2. Ambitious _____F
3. Analytical _____C
4. Argumentative _____F
5. Athletic _____A
6. Attention-seeking _____E
7. Calm _____B
8. Challenged by ambiguous situations _____C
9. Cheerful _____E
10. Competitive _____F
11. Complicated _____D
12. Confident of your own intellectual abilities _____C
13. Conforming _____A
14. Conscientious _____B
15. Cooperative _____E
16. Creative-minded _____C
17. Curious _____C
18. Dependable _____B
19. Disciplined _____B
20. Discussion-oriented _____E
21. Disinterested in physical activity _____B
22. Disorderly (not "organized") _____D
23. Domineering _____F
24. Efficient _____B
25. Emotional _____D
26. Energetic _____F
27. Enjoy puzzles _____C
28. Enthusiastic _____F
29. Flirtatious _____F
30. Frank _____A
31. Friendly _____E
32. Function best when activities are planned _____B
33. Helpful _____E
34. Idealistic _____D
35. Impractical _____D
36. Impulsive _____D
37. Independent _____C
38. Inhibited _____B
39. Introspective _____D
40. Intuitive _____D
41. Lacking in persuasive skills _____C
42. Materialistic _____A
43. Mechanically adept _____A
44. Nonconforming _____D
45. Obedient _____B
46. Optimistic _____F
47. Orderly _____B
48. Oriented toward the arts _____D
49. Original in thinking _____C
50. Persistent _____A
51. Persuasive _____F
52. Popular _____E
53. Practical _____A
54. Prefer a subordinate role _____B
55. Prefer working with people rather than machines _____E
56. Problem- or task-oriented _____C
57. Reserved _____C
58. Risk-taking _____D
59. Rugged, strong _____A
60. Scientifically inclined _____C
61. Self-confident _____F
62. Sensitive to surroundings _____D
63. Shy _____A
64. Socially oriented _____E
65. Sports-minded _____A
66. Stable in outlook and performance _____A
67. Tactful _____E
68. Teaching-oriented _____E
69. Thrifty _____A
70. Understanding with people _____E
71. Verbally skilled _____F
72. Work well without public recognition _____B

Scoring

Each item has a letter key (after the scoring space) that will be used to calculate your scores. Go back through the quiz and tally your score for each letter. For example, if you entered 2 for numbers 5, 13, 30, 42, 43, 50, 53, 59, 63, 65, 66, 69, you would write the figure 24 for your A total below. Then follow the same procedure for B, C, D, E, and F.

A	B	C	D	E	F
Total________	Total______	Total______	Total______	Total_________	Total________

Analyses

Each letter indicates a job category as follows:

A = Realistic Jobs   D = Artistic Jobs
B = Conventional Jobs   E = Social Jobs
C = Investigative Jobs   F = Jobs of Leadership

The analyses in Selection 87 will tell you more about each category.

You will probably find one category in which your score is considerably higher than the rest. This is the field in which you are likely to find the most satisfaction and success.

However, there may be more than one category in which you have a relatively high score. Some jobs fall directly into one category—"auto mechanic," for example, falls directly into the Realistic category (A), and "secretary" falls directly into the Conventional category (B). Other jobs fall in between—"art teacher," for example, falls about halfway between Artistic and Social, and "sales manager" falls about halfway between Jobs of Leadership (F) and Conventional Jobs (B).

Careful reading of the category in which you score highest will help you learn more about yourself.

APPENDIX

Index
According to Order of Difficulty

Selection		Flesch Reading Ease Score
72	A Master-Word Approach to Vocabulary	64
31	The Most Precious Gift	64
42	Write a Resumé That Gets the Job	64
7	How to Remember: Some Basic Principles	63
29	Reading for A's	63
73	Warming Up to Words	63
30	How Fast Should a Person Read?	62
43	How to Write with Style	62
10	The Fifty-first Dragon	61
52	Ask, Don't Tell	61
61	Listening Is a 10-Part Skill	61
44	On Learning How to Write	61
45	Why I Write	61
Fairly Difficult		
32	Why Do We Read?	59
62	"After This Manner, Therefore, Listen"	59
1	Future Shock's Doc	58
11	The Educated Man	58
12	Getting Organized	58
79	Too Many Divorces, Too Soon	58
74	Vocabulary First-Aid	57
2	The Dynamics of Change	56
14	Habit: Make It Your Friend, Not Your Enemy	55
33	Do You Need a Time Stretcher?	55
53	Conversation Is More Than Talk	55
80	None of This Is Fair	54
3	An English Speaking World	53
63	What Has Listening Done for Us?	53
81	The Fifth Freedom	53
34	Why Reading Matters	52
82	Seven Keys to the Puzzle of Coping with Life	52
83	Presumed Innocents	52
13	Cultural Literacy—What Is It?	51
15	Your Words Make You What You Are	51
Difficult		
75	Do You Know How Words Can Make You Rich?	49
16	Around the World in 80 Nanoseconds	48
35	You Can't Get Ahead Today Unless You Read	48
84	The Great Paradigm Shift	46
64	Four Strategies for Improving Evaluative Listening	45
65	Empathic Listening	43
18	The Feel	38
54	America's Penniless Millionaire	38
17	Information Superhighways	37
85	Tactics That Win Good Part-Time Jobs	34
55	Your Voice Gives You Away	33
87	Which Career Is the Right One for You?	32
86	Understanding Self-Segregation on Campus	31

E = Easy **St = Standard** **Dif = Difficult**
FE = Fairly Easy **FD = Fairly Difficult**

Selection	Flesch Score
Starting to Read (Sel. 19)	83—Easy
Super-Speeds for the Knowledge Explosion (Sel. 21)	64—St
Tactics That Win Good Part-Time Jobs (Sel. 85)	34—Dif
Ten Tips to Help You Write Better (Sel. 40)	72—FE
Test Your Vocabulary (Sel. 66)	71—FE
Too Many Divorces, Too Soon (Sel. 79)	58—FD
The Bible's Timeless—and Timely—Insights (Sel. 23)	73—FE
The Dynamics of Change (Sel. 2)	56—FD
The Educated Man (Sel. 11)	58—FD
The 11 Toughest Job Interview Questions . . . and How to Answer Them (Sel. 49)	67—St
The Feel (Sel. 18)	38—Dif
The Fifth Freedom (Sel. 81)	53—FD
The Fifty-first Dragon (Sel. 10)	61—St
"The" First Word (Sel. 39)	77—FE
The Great Paradigm Shift (Sel. 84)	46—Dif
The Hustle (Sel. 37)	78—FE
The Importance of Being Interested (Sel. 9)	64—St
The Last Class (Sel. 5)	78—FE
The Most Precious Gift (Sel. 31)	64—St
The Most Unforgettable Character I've Met (Sel. 38)	77—FE
The Road to Success in Writing (Sel. 41)	72—FE
The 30,000 Words a Day We Talk (Sel. 47)	78—FE
The Verger (Sel. 26)	76—FE
Two Ways of Looking at Life (Sel. 6)	77—FE
Two Words to Avoid, Two to Remember (Sel. 71)	68—St
Understanding Self-Segregation on Campus (Sel. 86)	31—Dif
Vocabulary First-Aid (Sel. 74)	57—FD
Warming Up to Words (Sel. 73)	63—St
Was There Something I Was Supposed to Do with My Life? (Sel. 76)	77—FE
We Quit Talking—and Now the Cupboard Is Bare (Sel. 56)	75—FE
What Has Listening Done for Us? (Sel. 63)	53—FD
Which Career Is the Right One for You? (Sel. 87)	32—Dif
Why Do We Read? (Sel. 32)	59—FD
Why I Write (Sel. 45)	61—St
Why Reading Matters (Sel. 34)	52—FD
Words That Laugh and Cry (Sel. 67)	71—FE
Write a Résumé That Gets the Job (Sel. 42)	64—St
You Are the Next Speaker (Sel. 51)	65—St
You CAN Be Persuasive (Sel. 50)	66—St
You Can't Get Ahead Today Unless You Read (Sel. 35)	48—Dif
Your Words Make You What You Are (Sel. 15)	51—FD
Your Voice Gives You Away (Sel. 55)	33—Dif

Pacing Aid Sheets

(For Pacing at 500, 750, 1,000, 1,500, or 2,000 wpm)

The figures below will serve as a substitute for individual reading accelerator machines. Through use of these figures an individual or entire class can be paced through any selection in this text at speeds of 500, 750, 1,000, 1,500, or 2,000 words per minute, thus expediting the development of superior reading, scanning, and skimming skills.

At the signal "Begin," the individuals or class are to begin reading at what they feel is the indicated rate. When they should be finishing the first column, reading at that rate, say, "Next." If they have not quite finished, they are to skip the remaining portion of the column and start reading the next column somewhat faster. In that way as they are paced through a selection, they are able to adjust their rate as closely as possible to the paced rate.

Following the selection numbers and pages in the left-hand column, you will notice two sets of figures, one for each column of print for the selection. They indicate the time in minutes and seconds for reading the column at the speed given in the heading (e.g. @ 500, @ 750, etc.). For Selection #1, for example, the figures 0/36 and, for the second column, 1/13, mean that the first column should be finished in exactly zero minutes and 36 seconds and the second column in one minute and 13 seconds, or 37 seconds of additional time, since the time figures are cumulative. These figures would apply for pacing at 500 wpm. For pacing at 750 wpm, the signal "Next" would come after 24 seconds and, for the next column after 48 seconds.

For pacing at 2,000 wpm, divide each reading-time figure in the column headed @ 1,000 by two. (Similarly, for 3,000 wpm, divide the figure in the column headed @ 1,500 by two.)

Selection and Page	1st Column				2nd Column			
	@ 500	@ 750	@ 1000	@ 1500	@ 500	@ 750	@ 1000	@ 1500
#1	0/36	0/24	0/18	0/12	1/13	0/48	0/36	0/24
p.6	2/0	1/20	1/0	0/40	2/46	1/50	1/23	0/55
#2	0/41	0/28	0/20	0/14	1/22	0/54	0/41	0/27
p. 8	2/16	1/30	1/8	0/45	3/10	2/7	1/35	1/4
p. 9	3/20	2/13	1/40	1/7	3/23	2/16	1/42	1/8
#3	0/27	0/18	0/13	0/9	0/48	0/32	0/24	0/16
p. 10	1/30	1/0	0/45	0/30	2/0	1/21	1/0	0/40
#4	0/36	0/24	0/18	0/12	1/11	0/47	0/35	0/24
p. 12	1/48	1/12	0/54	0/36	2/22	1/35	1/11	0/47
#5	0/35	0/23	0/18	0/12	1/12	0/48	0/36	0/24
p. 14	2/10	1/26	1/5	0/43	3/11	2/7	1/36	1/4
p. 15	3/24	2/16	1/42	1/8	3/30	2/20	1/45	1/10
#6	0/21	0/14	0/11	0/7	0/43	0/28	0/21	0/14
p.16	1/31	1/0	0/45	0/30	2/14	1/29	1/7	0/45
#7	0/32	0/22	0/16	0/11	1/5	0/43	0/33	0/22
p.18	1/40	1/7	0/50	0/34	2/12	1/28	1/6	0/44
#8	0/40	0/27	0/20	0/13	1/18	0/52	0/39	0/26
p. 20	1/46	1/10	0/53	0/35	2/8	1/26	1/4	0/43
#9	0/8	0/6	0/4	0/3	0/16	0/10	0/8	0/5
p. 21	1/8	0/45	0/34	0/23	2/2	1/21	1/1	0/41
p. 22	2/56	1/57	1/28	0/59	3/48	2/32	1/54	1/16
p. 23	4/11	2/47	2/6	1/24	4/29	3/0	2/15	1/30

Selection and Page	1st Column				2nd Column			
	@ 500	@ 750	@ 1000	@ 1500	@ 500	@ 750	@ 1000	@ 1500
#10	0/15	0/10	0/7	0/5	0/24	0/16	0/12	0/8
p. 24	1/18	0/52	0/39	0/26	2/7	1/25	1/4	0/42
p. 25	3/4	2/2	1/32	1/1	3/59	2/39	1/59	1/20
p. 26	4/49	3/13	2/25	1/36	5/40	3/46	2/50	1/53
p. 27	5/54	3/56	2/57	1/58	6/2	4/2	3/1	2/1
#11	0/22	0/14	0/11	0/7	0/42	0/28	0/21	0/14
p. 28	1/38	1/5	0/49	0/33	2/31	1/41	1/16	0/50
p. 29	2/38	1/45	1/19	0/53				
#12	0/25	0/17	0/13	0/8	0/52	0/34	0/26	0/17
p. 30	1/47	1/11	0/53	0/36	2/37	1/44	1/18	0/52
p. 31	2/38	1/46	1/19	0/53				
#13	0/32	0/22	0/16	0/11	1/3	0/42	0/31	0/21
p. 32	1/55	1/17	0/58	0/38	2/48	1/52	1/24	0/56
p. 33	3/22	2/15	1/41	1/7	3/51	2/34	1/56	1/17
#14	0/38	0/25	0/19	0/13	1/19	0/52	0/39	0/26
p. 35	2/18	1/32	1/9	0/46	3/16	2/10	1/38	1/5
p. 36	3/56	2/37	1/58	1/19	4/30	3/0	2/15	1/30
#15	0/31	0/21	0/16	0/10	1/7	0/45	0/33	0/22
p. 38	1/58	1/18	0/59	0/39	2/51	1/18	1/25	0/39
p. 39	3/35	2/44	1/47	1/22	4/14	2/49	2/7	1/25
#16	0/37	0/25	0/19	0/12	1/12	0/48	0/36	0/24
p. 41	2/0	1/20	1/0	0/40	2/52	1/54	1/26	0/57
p. 42	3/0	2/0	1/30	1/0	3/2	2/1	1/31	1/1
#17	0/24	0/16	0/12	0/8	0/52	0/34	0/26	0/17
p. 43	1/41	1/7	0/51	0/34	2/27	1/38	1/14	0/49
p. 44	2/52	1/54	1/26	0/57	3/13	2/8	1/36	1/4
#18	0/13	0/9	0/6	0/4	0/26	0/17	0/13	0/9
p. 45	1/26	0/57	0/43	0/29	2/28	1/39	1/14	0/49
p. 46	3/27	2/18	1/43	1/9	4/28	2/59	2/14	1/29
p. 47	5/27	3/38	2/44	1/49	6/29	4/19	3/15	2/10
p. 48	7/29	4/59	3/44	2/30	8/26	5/38	4/13	2/48
p. 49	8/45	5/50	4/22	2/55	8/56	5/57	4/28	2/59
#19	0/41	0/27	0/20	0/14	1/12	0/51	0/36	0/25
p. 54	2/4	1/23	1/2	0/41	2/45	1/50	1/13	0/55
#20	0/35	0/23	0/18	0/12	1/7	0/45	0/34	0/22
p. 56	1/43	1/9	0/52	0/34	2/12	1/28	1/6	0/44
#21	0/33	0/22	0/16	0/11	1/4	0/43	0/32	0/21
p. 58	1/52	1/15	0/56	0/37	2/32	1/42	1/16	0/51
p. 59	2/41	1/47	1/20	0/54	2/44	1/49	1/22	0/55
#22	0/24	0/16	0/12	0/8	0/47	0/31	0/23	0/16
p. 60	1/24	0/56	0/42	0/28	1/59	1/20	1/0	0/40
#23	0/36	0/24	0/18	0/12	1/10	0/47	0/35	0/23
p. 62	2/0	1/20	1/0	0/40	2/54	1/56	1/27	0/58
p. 63	2/59	1/59	1/29	1/0				

Selection and Page	1st Column				2nd Column			
	@ 500	@ 750	@ 1000	@ 1500	@ 500	@ 750	@ 1000	@ 1500
#24	0/34	0/23	0/17	0/11	1/5	0/43	0/33	0/22
p. 64	2/4	1/22	1/2	0/41	3/2	2/1	1/31	1/1
p. 65	3/24	2/16	1/42	1/8	3/43	2/29	1/52	1/14
#25	0/15	0/10	0/7	0/5	0/31	0/21	0/15	0/10
p. 66	1/18	0/52	0/39	0/26	2/3	1/22	1/2	0/41
#26	0/29	0/19	0/14	0/10	1/16	0/51	0/38	0/25
p. 68	2/8	1/25	1/4	0/43	3/3	2/2	1/32	1/1
p. 69	4/4	2/43	2/2	1/21	5/0	3/20	2/30	1/40
p. 70	5/22	3/34	2/41	1/47	5/38	3/45	2/49	1/53
#27	0/13	0/8	0/6	0/4	0/28	0/18	0/14	0/9
p. 71	1/23	0/55	0/41	0/28	2/18	1/32	1/9	0/46
p. 72	2/52	1/55	1/26	0/57	3/28	2/19	1/44	1/9
#28	0/38	0/25	0/19	0/13	1/14	0/49	0/37	0/25
p. 74	2/7	1/25	1/4	0/42	2/53	1/55	1/26	0/58
p. 75	3/37	2/25	1/48	1/12	4/20	2/53	2/10	1/27
#29	0/42	0/28	0/21	0/14	1/26	0/57	0/43	0/29
p. 77	2/21	1/34	1/11	0/47	3/15	2/10	1/37	1/5
p. 78	3/47	2/31	1/53	1/16	4/10	2/47	2/5	1/23
#30	0/5	0/3	0/2	0/1	0/9	0/6	0/5	0/3
p. 79	0/59	0/40	0/30	0/20	1/53	1/15	0/56	0/38
p. 80	2/43	1/49	1/22	0/54	3/28	2/19	1/44	1/9
#31	0/40	0/27	0/20	0/13	1/18	0/52	0/39	0/26
p. 82	2/14	1/29	1/7	0/45	3/8	2/5	1/34	1/3
p. 83	3/40	2/27	1/50	1/13	4/6	2/44	2/3	1/22
#32	0/39	0/26	0/20	0/13	1/20	0/53	0/40	0/27
p. 85	1/59	1/20	1/0	0/40	2/32	1/41	1/16	0/51
#33	0/38	0/25	0/19	0/13	1/13	0/48	0/36	0/24
p. 87	2/0	1/20	1/0	0/40	2/54	1/54	1/27	0/52
p. 88	3/24	2/16	1/42	1/8	3/51	2/34	1/56	1/17
#34	0/34	0/23	0/17	0/11	1/7	0/45	0/34	0/22
p. 90	1/56	1/17	0/58	0/39	2/50	1/53	1/25	0/57
p. 91	3/16	2/11	1/38	1/5	3/36	2/24	1/48	1/12
#35	0/13	0/9	0/7	0/4	0/27	0/18	0/13	0/9
p. 92	1/9	0/46	0/34	0/23	2/3	1/22	1/2	0/41
p. 93	2/57	1/58	1/29	0/59	3/46	1/31	1/53	1/15
#36	0/38	0/25	0/19	0/13	1/17	0/51	0/38	0/26
p. 98	1/59	1/19	0/59	0/40	2/32	1/41	1/16	0/51
#37	0/37	0/25	0/19	0/12	1/9	0/46	0/35	0/23
p. 100	1/58	1/19	0/59	0/39	2/52	1/54	1/26	0/57
p. 101	3/48	2/32	1/54	1/16	4/46	3/10	2/23	1/35
p. 102	4/59	3/19	2/30	1/40	5/5	3/23	2/32	1/42
#38	0/26	0/17	0/13	0/9	0/51	0/34	0/26	0/17
p. 103	1/45	1/10	0/53	0/35	2/36	1/44	1/18	0/52

Selection and Page	1st Column				2nd Column			
	@ 500	@ 750	@ 1000	@ 1500	@ 500	@ 750	@ 1000	@ 1500
#39	0/46	0/31	0/23	0/15	1/27	0/58	0/44	0/29
p. 105	2/24	1/36	1/12	0/48	3/19	2/13	1/39	1/6
p. 106	3/41	2/27	1/51	1/14	3/54	2/36	1/57	1/18
#40	0/17	0/11	0/8	0/6	0/35	0/23	0/17	0/12
p. 107	1/24	0/56	0/42	0/28	2/12	1/28	1/6	0/44
p. 108	2/44	1/49	1/22	0/55	3/13	2/9	1/36	1/4
#41	0/43	0/29	0/22	0/14	1/25	0/57	0/43	0/28
p. 110	1/57	1/18	0/59	0/39	2/23	1/35	1/11	0/48
#42	0/8	0/5	0/4	0/3	0/16	0/11	0/8	0/5
p. 111	1/5	0/44	0/33	0/22	1/52	1/14	0/56	0/37
p. 112	2/43	1/49	1/21	0/54	3/31	2/21	1/45	1/10
#43	0/36	0/24	0/18	0/12	1/14	0/49	0/37	0/25
p. 114	1/57	1/18	0/59	0/39	2/32	1/41	1/16	0/51
#44	0/43	0/28	0/21	0/14	1/27	0/58	0/43	0/29
p. 116	1/41	1/7	0/51	0/34	1/50	1/13	0/55	0/37
#45	0/22	0/15	0/11	0/7	0/51	0/34	0/25	0/17
p. 117	1/52	1/15	0/56	0/37	2/51	1/56	1/26	0/57
p. 118	3/54	2/36	1/57	1/18	4/56	3/17	2/28	1/39
p. 119	5/5	3/24	2/33	1/42	5/11	3/27	2/35	1/44
#46	0/40	0/27	0/20	0/13	1/17	0/51	0/38	0/26
p. 124	2/10	1/26	1/5	0/43	3/3	3/2	1/31	1/1
p. 125	3/54	2/38	1/57	1/18	4/37	3/4	2/18	1/32
#47	0/43	0/29	0/22	0/14	1/27	0/58	0/44	0/29
p. 127	2/19	1/33	1/10	0/46	3/7	2/5	1/34	1/2
#48	0/36	0/24	0/18	0/12	1/13	0/48	0/36	0/24
p. 129	1/42	1/8	0/51	0/34	2/6	1/24	1/3	0/42
#49	0/5	0/3	0/3	0/2	1/11	0/7	0/6	0/4
p. 130	1/5	0/43	0/33	0/22	1/54	1/16	0/57	0/38
p. 131	2/39	1/46	1/20	0/53	3/21	2/14	1/40	1/7
#50	0/38	0/26	0/19	0/13	1/19	0/53	0/40	0/26
p. 133	2/16	1/30	1/8	0/45	3/12	2/8	1/36	1/4
p. 134	3/37	2/25	1/49	1/12	3/59	2/39	1/59	1/20
#51	0/9	0/6	0/5	0/3	0/20	0/14	0/10	0/7
p. 135	1/10	0/47	0/35	0/23	1/47	1/11	0/53	0/36
p. 136	2/38	1/46	1/19	0/53	3/12	2/8	1/36	1/4
p. 137	3/56	2/37	1/58	1/19	4/50	3/13	2/25	1/37
p. 138	5/20	3/34	2/40	1/47	5/43	3/49	2/51	1/54
#52	0/36	0/24	0/18	0/12	1/15	0/50	0/37	0/25
p. 140	2/6	1/24	1/3	0/42	3/0	2/0	1/30	1/0
p. 141	3/57	2/38	1/58	1/19	4/37	3/4	2/18	1/32
p. 142	4/44	3/9	2/22	1/35	4/47	3/12	2/24	1/36
#53	0/25	0/17	0/13	0/8	0/53	0/36	0/27	0/18
p. 143	1/47	1/11	0/54	0/36	2/39	1/46	1/19	0/53
p. 144	3/19	2/13	1/40	1/6	3/49	2/33	1/55	1/16

Selection and Page	1st Column				2nd Column			
	@ 500	@ 750	@ 1000	@ 1500	@ 500	@ 750	@ 1000	@ 1500
#54	0/39	0/26	0/20	0/13	1/19	0/53	0/40	0/26
p. 146	2/13	1/28	1/6	0/44	3/4	2/3	1/32	1/1
p. 147	3/57	2/38	1/59	1/19	4/52	3/14	2/26	1/37
p. 148	5/0	3/20	2/30	1/40	5/4	3/22	2/32	1/41
#55	0/26	0/17	0/13	0/9	0/51	0/34	0/26	0/17
p. 149	1/39	1/6	0/49	0/33	2/28	1/39	1/14	0/49
p. 150	2/54	1/56	1/27	0/58	3/19	2/13	1/29	1/6
#56	0/37	0/25	0/19	0/12	1/17	0/51	0/38	0/26
p. 154	1/39	1/6	1/49	0/33	1/53	1/16	0/57	0/38
#57	0/17	0/11	0/9	0/6	0/36	0/24	0/18	0/12
p. 155	1/27	0/58	0/44	0/29	2/15	1/30	1/8	0/45
p. 156	2/30	1/40	1/15	0/50	2/35	1/44	1/18	0/52
#58	0/19	0/13	0/10	0/6	0/38	0/25	0/19	0/13
p. 157	1/27	0/58	0/44	0/29	2/17	1/31	1/8	0/46
p. 158	3/4	2/3	1/32	1/1	3/49	2/33	1/55	1/16
p. 159	4/28	2/59	2/14	1/39	4/59	3/20	2/30	1/40
#59	0/37	0/25	0/19	0/12	1/14	0/49	0/37	0/25
p. 161	2/6	1/24	1/3	0/42	2/52	1/55	1/26	0/57
#60	0/36	0/24	0/18	0/12	1/12	0/48	0/36	0/24
p. 163	1/56	1/18	0/58	0/39	2/33	1/42	1/17	0/51
#61	0/35	0/23	0/18	0/12	1/9	0/46	0/34	0/23
p. 165	1/57	1/18	0/58	0/39	2/47	1/51	1/24	0/55
p. 166	3/40	2/27	1/50	1/12	4/26	2/57	2/13	1/29
p. 167	4/28	2/59	2/14	1/30				
#62	0/30	0/20	0/15	0/10	1/3	0/42	0/32	0/21
p. 168	1/56	1/17	0/58	0/39	2/46	1/51	1/23	0/55
p. 169	2/56	1/57	1/28	0/59	3/1	2/1	1/30	1/0
#63	0/25	0/16	0/12	0/8	0/50	0/33	0/25	0/17
p. 170	1/44	1/10	0/52	0/35	2/37	1/44	1/18	0/52
p. 171	3/28	2/19	1/44	1/9	4/19	2/53	2/10	1/26
p. 172	5/5	3/23	2/32	1/42	5/50	3/53	2/55	1/57
#64	0/36	0/24	0/18	0/12	1/11	0/48	0/36	0/24
p. 174	1/57	1/18	0/59	0/39	2/41	1/47	1/20	0/54
p. 175	2/44	1/49	1/22	0/55				
#65	0/27	0/18	0/14	0/9	0/55	0/37	0/28	0/19
p. 176	1/43	1/9	0/52	0/34	2/31	1/40	1/15	0/50
p. 177	3/23	2/15	1/42	1/8	4/16	2/51	2/8	1/25
p. 178	4/24	2/56	1/12	1/28	4/28	2/58	2/14	1/29
#66	0/39	0/26	0/20	0/13	1/18	0/52	0/39	0/26
p. 182	1/37	1/5	0/49	0/32	1/46	1/11	0/53	0/35
#67	0/43	0/29	0/22	0/14	1/28	0/59	0/44	0/29
p. 186	1/36	1/4	0/48	0/32				

Selection and Page	1st Column				2nd Column			
	@ 500	@ 750	@ 1000	@ 1500	@ 500	@ 750	@ 1000	@ 1500
#68	0/28	0/19	0/14	0/9	1/58	0/39	0/29	0/19
p. 187	1/51	1/14	0/57	0/37	2/47	1/51	1/23	0/56
p. 188	3/2	2/2	1/31	1/1	3/13	2/9	1/36	1/4
#69	0/21	0/14	0/10	0/7	0/41	0/28	0/21	0/14
p. 189	1/32	1/2	0/46	0/31	2/15	1/30	1/8	0/45
#70	0/42	0/28	0/21	0/14	1/25	0/57	0/42	0/28
p. 191	2/22	1/35	1/11	0/47	3/23	2/16	1/42	1/8
p. 192	3/26	2/17	1/43	1/9				
#71	0/33	0/22	0/16	0/11	1/5	0/43	0/32	0/22
p. 193	2/1	1/21	1/0	0/40	2/56	1/57	1/28	0/59
p. 194	3/6	2/4	1/33	1/2	3/11	2/8	1/36	1/4
#72	0/24	0/16	0/12	0/8	0/47	0/31	0/24	0/16
p. 195	1/8	0/45	0/34	0/23	1/30	1/0	0/45	0/30
p. 196	1/53	1/15	0/57	0/38	2/12	1/28	1/6	0/44
#73	0/17	0/11	0/8	0/6	0/35	0/23	0/17	0/12
p. 197	1/34	1/3	0/47	0/31	2/35	1/43	1/17	0/52
p. 198	2/39	1/46	1/20	0/53				
#74	0/33	0/22	0/16	0/11	1/5	0/43	0/32	0/22
p. 199	1/51	1/14	0/56	0/37	2/41	1/48	1/21	0/54
p. 200	2/46	1/51	1/23	0/55				
#75	0/28	0/19	0/14	0/9	0/57	0/38	0/28	0/19
p. 201	1/20	0/53	0/40	0/27	1/35	1/3	0/47	0/32
#76	0/44	0/31	0/22	0/15	1/32	1/1	0/46	0/31
p. 206	2/32	1/41	1/16	0/51	3/38	2/26	1/49	1/13
p. 207	3/47	2/31	1/54	1/16	3/49	2/33	1/55	1/16
#77	0/46	0/31	0/23	0/16	1/24	0/57	0/42	0/28
208	2/16	1/30	1/8	0/45	3/0	2/1	1/30	1/0
#78	0/40	0/26	0/20	0/13	1/16	0/51	0/38	0/25
p. 210	2/14	1/30	1/7	0/45	3/9	2/6	1/34	1/3
p. 211	4/9	2/46	2/4	1/23	5/5	3/23	2/33	1/42
p. 212	5/16	3/31	2/38	1/45	5/20	3/34	2/40	1/42
#79	0/34	0/22	0/17	0/11	1/3	0/42	0/31	0/21
p. 213	1/58	1/19	0/59	0/39	2/55	1/57	1/28	0/58
p. 214	3/52	2/34	1/56	1/17	4/42	3/8	2/21	1/34
#80	0/37	0/24	0/18	0/12	1/18	0/52	0/39	0/26
p. 216	2/16	1/31	1/8	0/45	3/15	2/10	1/38	1/5
p. 217	3/29	2/19	1/44	1/10	3/36	2/24	1/48	1/12
#81	0/39	0/26	0/20	0/13	1/10	0/47	0/35	0/23
p. 218	1/42	1/8	0/51	0/34	2/12	1/28	1/6	1/44
#82	0/6	0/4	0/3	0/2	0/10	0/7	0/5	0/4
p. 219	1/12	0/48	0/36	0/24	2/6	1/24	1/3	0/42
p. 220	2/56	1/57	1/28	0/58	3/50	2/32	1/54	1/16
p. 221	4/44	3/9	2/22	1/34	5/38	3/45	2/49	1/53
p. 222	5/54	3/56	2/57	1/58	6/1	4/0	3/0	2/0

Selection and Page	1st Column				2nd Column			
	@ 500	**@ 750**	**@ 1000**	**@ 1500**	**@ 500**	**@ 750**	**@ 1000**	**@ 1500**
#83	0/21	0/14	0/11	0/7	0/43	0/29	0/22	0/14
p. 223	1/34	1/3	0/47	0/31	2/29	1/39	1/14	0/49
p. 224	3/5	2/3	1/32	1/2	3/35	2/24	1/47	1/12
#84	0/39	0/26	0/20	0/13	1/34	1/3	0/47	0/31
p. 226	2/8	1/25	1/4	1/42	2/37	1/44	1/19	0/52
#85	0/38	0/25	0/19	0/13	1/21	0/54	0/41	0/27
p. 228	2/28	1/38	1/14	0/49	3/12	2/8	1/36	1/4
p. 229	3/42	2/28	1/51	1/14	3/10	2/42	2/2	2/21
#86	0/4	0/3	0/2	0/1	0/4	0/3	0/2	0/1
p. 230	0/55	0/37	0/27	0/18	1/47	1/12	0/54	0/36
p. 231	2/40	1/47	1/20	0/53	3/26	2/17	1/43	1/9
p. 232	3/35	2/23	1/47	1/12	3/40	2/27	1/50	1/13
#87	0/21	0/14	0/11	0/7	0/51	0/34	0/25	0/17
p. 233	1/36	1/4	0/48	0/32	2/24	1/36	1/12	0/48
p. 234	3/3	2/2	1/32	1/1	3/33	2/22	1/46	1/11

Answers

Selection Number

Comprehension Check Questions

	1	2	3	4	5	6	7	8	9	10	11	12	13	14	15	16	17	18	19	20	21	22	23	24	25	26	27	28	29
1.	1	4	4	2	2	1	1	1	2	3	1	2	1	2	2	3	1	4	1	3	2	2	4	4	1	3	2	4	2
2.	4	3	4	1	2	1	2	1	1	1	4	4	2	1	4	2	2	3	3	3	4	3	2	1	3	2	3	1	4
3.	3	4	3	1	1	2	3	3	1	4	2	3	1	1	4	4	4	3	3	3	1	3	3	3	4	2	4	3	2
4.	3	4	4	3	2	4	4	4	4	4	2	1	3	3	4	2	4	4	1	3	1	1	4	3	4	3	1	2	4
5.	1	1	2	2	2	1	2	2	2	1	1	2	1	2	3	1	1	3	4	2	3	3	3	2	1	4	2	2	3
6.	2	2	1	1	1	2	3	3	2	3	4	3	3	1	3	1	2	2	1	2	3	2	3	1	4	3	1	2	4
7.	2	2	2	4	3	3	3	1	4	2	2	2	4	4	3	2	1	2	3	2	3	4	4	1	3	4	4	1	2
8.	1	1	2	1	2	1	1	3	2	2	1	3	4	1	2	4	2	1	4	4	1	3	3	3	2	4	2	2	1
9.	3	4	3	4	1	3	3	1	2	1	2	1	3	4	3	4	3	4	4	4	2	2	2	4	1	3	3	2	2
10.	4	1	1	4	3	4	4	4	4	3	4	3	3	4	1	3	3	1	3	2	4	4	2	2	1	1	1	3	3

Vocabulary Check Questions

	1	2	3	4	5	6	7	8	9	10	11	12	13	14	15	16	17	18	19	20	21	22	23	24	25	26	27	28	29
1.	3	3	2	4	1	3	1	1	1	3	5	3	1	4	5	4	2	4	3	1	2	5	1	3	2	4	3	2	4
2.	2	2	3	5	4	4	2	4	2	4	5	2	4	5	4	5	1	3	5	3	2	2	1	4	5	5	1	1	1
3.	4	5	4	4	2	2	1	3	5	2	1	5	3	1	3	1	5	1	4	1	5	1	4	2	1	3	4	5	2
4.	3	4	1	1	3	2	2	2	1	4	4	2	2	3	3	3	5	2	2	1	1	4	2	3	3	1	2	2	5
5.	4	1	2	2	4	2	3	2	2	4	3	5	2	4	5	4	5	5	1	5	4	3	5	4	2	4	5	4	1

Selection Number

Comprehension Check Questions

	30	31	32	33	34	35	36	37	38	39	40	41	42	43	44	45	46	47	48	49	50	51	52	53	54	55	56	57	58
1.	2	2	2	1	4	4	4	1	3	4	2	3	4	2	3	2	4	4	2	3	3	2	1	1	2	4	2	2	2
2.	3	4	3	2	1	3	1	4	1	1	1	3	2	1	1	4	1	3	1	3	1	2	2	3	1	3	2	4	2
3.	3	3	4	1	1	4	3	4	4	2	1	1	1	4	4	1	3	3	4	1	2	3	2	1	3	2	4	3	4
4.	2	1	1	3	3	2	2	1	3	2	4	2	4	3	4	1	2	2	1	1	3	1	2	2	2	3	3	4	3
5.	2	3	4	4	2	2	2	3	2	3	2	4	2	2	2	3	1	4	2	4	3	1	1	3	4	1	2	1	2
6.	3	4	4	4	1	1	1	3	4	3	3	3	1	3	4	4	1	4	4	1	4	4	4	1	3	3	1	1	1
7.	2	2	1	4	4	2	3	1	3	1	2	2	3	3	3	3	3	3	2	4	3	4	2	2	2	1	1	4	1
8.	3	2	3	4	2	2	2	3	2	3	2	4	4	2	1	3	2	3	2	1	2	3	2	2	4	1	3	3	3
9.	3	1	1	4	3	2	1	2	3	4	1	4	3	1	2	1	2	1	1	3	2	1	1	2	4	2	3	2	3
10.	3	3	2	3	3	2	4	4	1	3	3	2	3	4	2	2	4	4	1	3	4	3	1	3	1	3	3	4	3

Vocabulary Check Questions

	30	31	32	33	34	35	36	37	38	39	40	41	42	43	44	45	46	47	48	49	50	51	52	53	54	55	56	57	58
1.	3	1	3	4	5	3	1	4	5	5	1	1	4	1	5	2	4	5	4	4	2	5	2	2	4	2	2	3	5
2.	4	3	2	1	3	2	5	2	2	1	5	5	3	1	5	5	1	3	1	2	5	1	2	2	4	2	5	3	4
3.	5	4	4	4	1	4	3	3	2	2	4	3	4	5	1	5	5	1	4	5	3	3	1	5	1	2	4	4	1
4.	1	2	3	2	2	1	4	5	1	5	5	2	5	3	4	3	3	2	1	1	2	2	5	2	4	5	3	4	1
5.	5	5	4	2	4	4	2	1	3	5	4	4	2	2	3	1	2	1	3	3	1	2	3	4	5	3	1	1	2

Selection Number

Comprehension Check Questions

	59	60	61	62	63	64	65	66	67	68	69	70	71	72	73	74	75	76	77	78	79	80	81	82	83	84	85	86	87
1.	2	4	3	4	4	3	2	1	2	3	2	2	2	3	3	2	1	4	3	1	3	3	4	4	4	4	3	2	4
2.	4	3	3	1	1	2	4	1	1	4	1	4	4	2	1	1	4	2	3	1	4	4	1	3	2	2	4	3	2
3.	1	2	2	4	2	2	1	3	4	2	3	4	4	3	2	2	3	3	3	1	1	2	3	2	2	2	2	2	3
4.	4	3	1	2	3	1	3	3	2	4	1	2	2	3	3	3	3	3	2	4	1	1	1	3	4	2	3	1	4
5.	1	1	3	3	1	4	3	2	2	1	4	2	2	4	4	1	2	4	1	3	3	3	3	1	3	1	4	2	3
6.	4	3	4	3	4	2	3	2	2	1	4	2	2	3	4	1	1	3	2	2	2	2	3	3	3	2	4	2	3
7.	2	1	3	2	3	1	3	2	1	1	2	3	3	2	1	4	1	2	3	1	1	3	1	1	2	4	3	4	3
8.	3	1	1	3	2	3	4	3	4	2	3	3	3	3	3	1	2	1	1	2	2	3	2	1	3	3	4	3	2
9.	1	2	1	1	4	3	1	1	2	2	3	3	3	2	3	4	4	3	3	2	2	1	4	2	2	3	2	1	1
10.	4	3	4	2	4	4	3	3	3	3	1	3	3	4	1	4	2	4	4	1	1	4	1	3	4	2	1	2	4

Vocabulary Check Questions

	59	60	61	62	63	64	65	66	67	68	69	70	71	72	73	74	75	76	77	78	79	80	81	82	83	84	85	86	87
1.	1	2	2	4	3	1	4	4	2	5	4	3	5	4	2	5	4	5	3	5	4	1	3	2	2	2	1	1	4
2.	4	1	1	1	5	5	5	5	4	1	5	2	1	5	5	2	5	2	1	3	5	4	1	1	4	3	5	2	1
3.	3	4	1	5	1	2	3	2	3	3	2	5	3	1	1	3	1	5	5	1	4	3	1	4	1	1	2	3	3
4.	5	1	4	3	4	3	2	2	1	4	4	4	4	3	2	2	3	3	4	2	1	3	5	1	1	3	3	5	5
5.	5	4	5	2	2	4	1	1	5	2	3	1	2	4	4	4	1	3	5	1	2	4	2	4	2	2	2	3	2

Conversion Table: Seconds to Words per Minute

The general procedure for getting word-per-minute (wpm) rate is to divide the number of words by the reading time in seconds and then multiply that quotient by sixty. This conversion table provides a convenient shortcut to that procedure for most reading times.

To use the table, find the figure in the left-hand column that is closest to your reading time. Then look along that line to the column headed by the number of the selection read to get your wpm rate.

For reading times between one and two minutes (60 to 120 seconds), double your reading time before looking in the table. Then double the number in the table to get your rate.

For reading times over 420 seconds, divide your reading time by half before looking in the table. Then divide the number in the table by half to get your rate.

Time in Seconds (and Minutes)	Selection Number 1	2	3	4	5	6	7	8	9	10	11	12	13	14	15	16	17	18	19
60(1)	1380	1680	1010	1180	1750	1120	1100	1070	2250	3000	1320	1320	1930	2245	2108	1520	1610	4470	1380
120(2)	690	840	505	590	875	560	550	535	1125	1500	660	660	965	1123	1054	760	805	2235	690
130	636	775	466	545	808	517	508	494	1038	1384	609	609	891	1036	973	702	743	2063	636
140	592	720	433	506	750	480	472	446	963	1284	566	566	827	962	903	651	690	1916	592
150	552	672	404	472	700	448	440	428	900	1200	528	528	772	898	840	608	644	1788	552
160	518	630	378	443	656	420	413	401	843	1125	495	495	724	842	790	570	604	1676	518
170	486	593	357	417	618	395	388	378	794	1059	466	466	681	792	744	536	568	1578	486
180(3)	460	560	337	393	583	373	367	357	750	1000	440	440	643	748	703	507	537	1490	460
190	436	531	319	373	553	354	348	338	710	947	417	417	609	709	665	480	508	1412	436
200	414	504	303	354	525	336	330	321	675	900	396	396	579	674	632	456	483	1341	414
210	396	480	289	338	500	320	314	306	642	856	377	377	551	641	602	434	460	1277	396
220	376	458	276	322	477	306	300	292	612	818	360	360	526	612	575	414	439	1219	376
230	360	438	264	308	457	292	287	279	587	782	344	344	503	586	550	396	420	1166	360
240(4)	345	420	253	295	438	280	275	267	563	750	330	330	483	562	527	380	403	1118	345
250	332	403	243	283	420	269	264	257	540	720	317	317	463	539	506	365	386	1073	332
260	318	388	233	273	404	259	254	247	519	692	305	305	446	518	486	351	372	1032	318
270	306	373	225	262	389	249	244	238	500	667	294	294	429	499	468	338	358	993	306
280	296	360	217	253	375	240	238	229	482	642	283	283	414	481	451	326	345	958	296
290	286	348	209	244	362	232	228	221	465	620	273	273	399	464	436	314	333	925	286
300(5)	276	336	202	236	350	224	220	213	450	600	264	264	386	449	422	304	322	894	276
310	266	325	195	228	339	217	213	207	435	580	256	256	374	435	408	294	311	865	266
320	258	315	189	222	328	210	207	201	422	563	248	248	362	421	395	285	302	838	258
330	250	305	184	215	318	204	199	195	409	545	240	240	351	408	383	276	293	813	250
340	244	296	179	209	309	198	194	189	397	530	233	233	341	396	372	268	284	789	244
350	236	288	174	202	300	192	189	183	386	514	226	226	331	385	361	261	276	766	236
360(6)	230	280	169	197	292	187	184	178	375	500	220	220	322	374	351	253	269	745	230
370	224	272	164	191	284	182	178	174	365	486	214	214	313	364	341	246	261	725	224
380	218	265	160	187	276	177	174	169	355	474	208	208	305	354	332	240	254	706	218
390	212	258	156	182	269	172	169	165	346	462	203	203	297	345	325	234	247	688	212
400	207	252	152	177	264	168	165	161	338	450	198	198	290	337	316	228	242	671	207
410	202	246	148	173	256	164	161	157	329	439	193	193	282	329	308	222	235	654	202
420(7)	197	240	144	169	250	160	157	153	321	429	186	186	276	321	301	217	230	639	197

Time in Seconds (and Minutes)	Selection Number																						
	20	21	22	23	24	25	26	27	28	29	30	31	32	33	34	35	36	37	38	39	40	41	42
60(1)	1100	1370	1000	1490	1866	1030	2820	1740	2170	2090	1734	2050	1270	1930	1800	1880	1270	2540	1300	1950	1610	1190	1760
120(2)	550	685	500	745	935	515	1410	870	1085	1045	867	1025	635	965	900	940	635	1270	650	975	805	595	880
130	508	632	461	687	861	475	1302	803	1001	964	800	946	588	891	831	868	586	1172	600	900	743	549	812
140	472	587	428	639	799	441	1209	746	930	896	743	879	546	827	771	806	544	1089	557	836	690	510	754
150	440	548	400	596	746	412	1128	697	868	836	694	820	510	772	720	752	508	1016	520	780	644	476	703
160	413	514	375	559	699	386	1058	653	814	783	650	769	478	724	675	705	476	953	488	731	604	446	660
170	388	484	353	526	659	363	995	615	766	737	612	724	450	681	635	664	448	896	459	688	568	420	621
180(3)	367	457	333	497	622	343	940	580	723	697	578	683	425	643	600	627	423	847	433	650	537	396	587
190	348	433	316	471	589	325	891	550	685	660	548	647	403	609	568	593	401	802	410	616	508	376	556
200	330	411	300	447	560	309	846	522	651	627	520	615	383	579	540	564	381	763	389	585	483	357	528
210	314	392	286	426	533	294	806	497	620	597	495	586	364	551	514	537	363	732	369	557	460	340	503
220	300	374	273	406	509	281	769	474	592	570	472	559	347	526	491	513	348	693	353	532	439	324	480
230	287	358	261	389	485	268	736	453	566	545	452	535	332	503	470	490	331	663	337	509	420	310	459
240(4)	275	343	250	373	467	258	705	435	543	523	434	513	319	483	450	470	318	635	325	488	403	297	440
250	264	330	240	358	448	247	677	417	521	492	416	492	306	463	432	451	305	609	312	468	386	285	422
260	254	317	231	344	441	238	651	401	501	482	400	473	294	445	415	434	293	586	300	450	372	274	406
270	244	305	222	331	415	229	627	386	482	464	385	456	283	429	400	418	282	564	288	433	358	264	391
280	238	294	214	319	400	220	604	372	465	448	371	439	273	414	386	403	272	544	279	418	345	255	377
290	228	283	207	308	386	213	583	360	449	439	359	424	263	399	372	389	263	525	269	403	333	246	364
300(5)	220	274	200	298	373	206	564	348	434	418	347	410	255	386	360	376	254	508	260	390	322	238	352
310	213	265	193	288	359	199	546	337	420	404	336	397	247	374	348	364	246	492	251	377	311	230	341
320	207	257	188	279	350	193	529	326	407	392	325	385	239	363	338	353	238	476	243	366	302	223	330
330	200	249	182	271	339	187	513	316	395	380	315	373	232	351	327	342	231	462	238	355	293	216	320
340	194	242	176	263	329	181	498	307	383	369	306	363	225	341	318	332	224	448	229	344	284	210	311
350	189	235	171	255	319	176	483	298	372	358	297	353	219	331	309	322	218	436	222	334	276	204	302
360 (6)	184	228	167	248	311	172	470	290	362	348	289	342	212	322	300	314	212	423	217	325	269	198	294
370	178	222	162	242	302	167	457	282	352	339	281	333	207	313	292	306	206	411	212	316	261	193	285
380	174	216	158	235	294	163	445	274	343	330	273	324	202	305	282	297	201	401	206	308	254	188	278
390	169	210	154	229	287	158	434	267	334	321	266	316	196	297	277	290	195	391	199	300	247	183	271
400	165	205	150	224	280	155	423	261	326	313	260	308	192	290	270	282	191	381	195	293	242	179	264
410	161	200	146	218	273	151	413	253	318	306	253	300	187	282	263	275	186	372	191	285	235	174	258
420(7)	157	196	143	213	267	147	403	248	310	299	248	293	182	276	275	269	181	363	186	279	230	170	251

Time in Seconds (and Minutes))	Selection Number 43	44	45	46	47	48	49	50	51	52	53	54	55	56	57	58	59	60	61	62	63	64	65
60(1)	1270	920	2590	2310	1560	1050	1670	1990	2860	2394	1910	2530	1660	950	2910	1510	1275	1290	2490	1434	2240	1370	2230
120(2)	635	460	1295	1155	780	525	835	995	1430	1197	955	1265	830	475	1455	755	638	645	1245	717	1120	685	1115
130	586	425	1195	1066	720	484	770	918	1320	1105	882	1168	766	438	1343	697	588	595	1150	662	1034	632	1029
140	544	394	1110	990	669	450	716	853	1226	1026	819	1084	711	407	1247	647	546	553	1071	615	960	587	956
150	508	370	1036	924	624	420	669	796	1144	958	764	1012	664	380	1164	604	510	516	996	574	896	548	892
160	476	345	971	866	585	394	627	746	1073	898	716	948	623	356	1091	566	479	484	934	538	840	514	836
170	448	325	914	815	551	371	589	702	1009	845	674	893	586	335	1027	533	450	455	879	506	791	484	787
180(3)	423	307	863	770	520	350	556	663	953	798	637	843	553	317	970	503	425	430	830	478	747	457	743
190	401	291	817	729	493	332	527	628	903	756	603	798	524	300	919	477	403	407	786	453	707	433	704
200	381	276	777	693	468	315	501	597	858	718	573	759	498	285	873	453	383	387	747	430	672	411	669
210	362	263	740	660	446	300	477	569	817	684	546	722	474	271	832	431	364	369	711	410	640	391	637
220	345	251	705	630	425	285	456	543	780	653	521	690	453	259	794	412	348	351	680	391	610	373	608
230	330	240	675	603	407	274	436	519	746	625	498	660	433	248	756	394	332	326	650	374	585	357	582
240(4)	318	230	648	578	390	263	417	498	715	599	478	633	415	238	728	377	319	323	623	359	560	343	558
250	305	221	622	554	374	252	400	478	686	575	458	607	398	228	698	362	307	309	598	344	538	329	535
260	293	212	598	533	360	242	385	459	660	552	441	584	383	219	672	348	294	298	575	331	517	316	515
270	282	204	576	513	347	233	371	442	636	532	424	562	369	211	647	336	284	287	553	319	498	304	496
280	272	197	555	495	334	225	359	427	613	513	409	542	356	204	624	324	273	277	536	307	480	294	478
290	262	190	537	478	323	217	346	412	592	495	395	523	343	197	602	312	264	266	515	297	463	283	461
300(5)	254	184	518	462	312	210	332	398	572	479	382	506	332	190	582	302	255	258	498	287	448	274	446
310	246	178	500	447	302	203	322	385	554	463	370	490	322	184	563	292	247	249	480	278	433	265	432
320	238	173	486	433	293	197	312	373	536	449	358	474	312	178	546	283	239	242	467	269	420	257	418
330	231	167	471	420	284	191	302	362	520	435	347	460	302	173	529	275	232	234	453	261	407	249	405
340	224	162	457	408	275	186	293	351	505	422	337	447	293	168	514	266	225	228	440	253	395	242	392
350	218	158	444	396	267	180	284	341	490	410	327	434	284	163	499	259	219	221	427	246	384	235	382
360(6)	212	153	432	385	260	175	278	332	477	399	318	422	277	158	485	252	213	215	415	239	373	229	372
370	207	149	422	375	253	170	269	323	464	388	310	410	269	154	472	245	207	209	404	233	363	223	362
380	202	145	409	365	246	166	262	314	452	378	302	399	262	150	459	238	201	204	393	226	354	216	352
390	196	142	399	355	240	161	255	306	440	368	294	389	255	146	448	232	196	198	383	221	345	210	343
400	192	138	389	347	234	158	249	299	429	359	287	379	249	143	437	227	191	193	374	215	336	206	335
410	186	135	379	338	228	154	243	291	419	350	280	370	243	139	426	221	187	189	364	210	327	200	326
420(7)	181	131	370	330	223	150	238	284	409	342	273	361	237	136	416	216	182	184	356	205	320	196	319

Time in Seconds (and Minutes)	Selection Number 66	67	68	69	70	71	72	73	74	75	76	77	78	79	80	81	82	83	84	85	86	87
60(1)	890	800	1600	1125	1720	1596	1090	1330	1380	790	1810	1380	2654	2225	1790	934	3010	1790	1310	2520	1900	1750
120(2)	445	400	800	563	860	798	545	665	690	395	905	690	1327	1113	895	467	1505	895	655	1260	950	875
130	410	369	738	519	794	737	503	614	636	365	835	636	1225	1026	826	431	1389	826	605	1163	877	808
140	380	343	686	482	737	684	467	570	592	339	776	592	1137	953	767	400	1290	767	561	1080	814	751
150	356	320	640	450	688	638	436	532	552	316	724	552	1062	890	716	374	1204	716	524	1008	760	701
160	331	300	600	422	645	599	409	498	518	296	679	518	995	834	671	350	1129	671	491	945	713	658
170	311	283	566	397	607	563	385	469	486	279	639	486	937	785	632	330	1062	632	462	889	671	619
180(3)	297	267	533	375	573	532	363	443	460	263	603	460	855	742	597	311	1003	597	437	840	633	583
190	281	253	506	355	543	504	344	420	436	249	572	436	828	703	565	295	951	565	414	796	600	552
200	267	240	480	337	516	479	327	399	414	237	543	414	796	668	537	280	903	537	393	756	570	525
210	253	228	456	321	491	456	312	379	396	226	517	396	758	636	511	267	860	511	374	720	543	501
220	242	214	436	307	469	435	297	362	376	215	494	376	724	607	488	255	821	488	357	687	518	478
230	230	209	418	293	449	416	284	346	360	206	472	360	692	580	467	244	785	467	342	657	496	457
240(4)	222	200	400	281	430	399	273	332	346	198	452	346	664	556	447	234	753	447	327	630	475	438
250	214	192	384	270	413	383	262	319	332	190	434	332	637	534	430	224	722	430	314	605	456	421
260	206	185	369	259	397	368	252	307	318	182	418	318	612	513	413	216	695	413	302	582	438	405
270	188	178	356	250	382	355	242	295	306	176	402	306	590	495	398	208	669	398	291	560	422	390
280	191	172	343	241	368	342	234	285	296	169	388	296	569	477	384	200	645	384	281	540	407	376
290	184	166	331	233	356	330	226	275	286	163	375	286	549	460	370	193	623	370	271	521	393	363
300(5)	178	160	320	225	344	319	218	266	276	158	362	276	531	445	358	187	602	358	262	504	380	350
310	174	155	310	218	333	309	211	257	266	153	350	266	514	431	346	181	583	346	254	488	368	339
320	166	150	300	211	323	299	205	249	258	148	339	258	498	417	336	175	564	336	246	473	356	329
330	162	146	291	204	313	290	198	242	250	144	329	250	483	405	325	170	547	325	238	458	345	318
340	156	142	283	198	303	282	193	235	244	139	319	244	468	393	316	165	531	316	231	445	335	309
350	152	137	274	193	295	274	187	228	236	135	310	236	455	381	307	160	516	307	225	432	326	300
360(6)	148	133	267	187	287	266	182	221	230	132	302	230	442	371	298	156	502	298	218	420	317	292
370	144	130	260	182	279	259	177	216	224	128	294	224	430	361	290	151	488	290	212	409	308	289
380	140	127	253	177	272	252	172	210	218	125	286	218	419	351	283	147	475	282	207	398	300	276
390	136	123	246	173	264	246	168	205	212	122	278	212	408	342	275	144	463	275	202	388	292	270
400	133	120	240	169	258	239	164	199	207	119	272	207	398	334	269	140	452	269	197	378	285	263
410	130	117	234	164	252	234	160	195	202	116	265	202	388	326	262	137	440	262	192	369	278	256
420(7)	127	114	229	161	246	228	156	190	197	113	259	197	379	318	256	133	430	256	187	360	271	250

Progress Record

Students and teachers alike will find a Progress Record invaluable. Such a record helps spot specific reading strengths and weaknesses, points up growth and improvement, and heightens the personal satisfaction found in achievement.

Some students may wish to use only the columns for word-per-minute rate and Total Comprehension. Others may wish to keep a much more complete record. Space is provided for the following kinds of information:

1. Date
2. Selection Number
3. Difficulty. As a measure of difficulty, enter the *Flesch Reading Ease Score* and *Classification* from the Index on pages 481–482.
4. Interest Rating. Enter your personal Interest Reading for the selection. Enter a *1* if you think it is "very interesting," a *2* if "somewhat interesting," a *3* if "of average interest," a *4* if "somewhat uninteresting," and a *5* if "very uninteresting." The effect of interest on rate and comprehension is often a necessary aid to interpreting and understanding results.
5. WPM Rate. Enter your word-per-minute reading rate for the selection.
6. Total Comp. Enter the Total Comprehension Score here—10 points for each correct answer.
7. R. E. Index. It is often desirable to have a single figure to indicate Reading Efficiency, an index that reflects both rate and comprehension factors. A Reading Efficiency Index may be obtained by multiplying wpm rate by comprehension and dividing by 100. For example, if you read a selection at 320 wpm with 60 percent comprehension, your Reading Efficiency Index would be 192.

$$\frac{320 \times 60}{100} = 192$$

8. Percentage of Improvement. Improvement is sometimes best understood in terms of percentage gain. To determine the percent of improvement, subtract your initial Reading Efficiency Index from the last Reading Efficiency Index. The difference will be the number of points gained. Add two zeros to the number of points gained and divide that amount by the initial Reading Efficiency Index. The result will be your percent of improvement.

   For example, suppose you have a Reading Efficiency Index (REI) of 192, as in the example above. In your next reading, you read somewhat slower—300 wpm—but score higher in comprehension—80%. In short, you've lost reading speed but gained comprehension. Have you actually improved? Calculate your new REI:

$$300 \text{ wpm} \times 80 \div 100 = 240$$

   Subtract 192 from 240, a gain of 48 REI. Now add 2 zeros and divide by your initial REI:

$$48 + 00 = 4800 \div 192 = 25\% \text{ improvement}$$

   Usually, of course, you will go back to your very first reading to measure gains.
9. Vocabulary. If you do the vocabulary check questions, both without and with the help of context, score them by giving yourself 10 points for each correct answer. If you just check vocabulary without context, give yourself 20 points for each correct answer and enter your scores.

The Progress Record grouping of ten entry lines for ten selections is done to facilitate the averaging of any of the scores.

Progress Record

Date	Selection Number	Diffi-culty	Interest Rating	WPM Rate	Total Comp.	R.E. Index	Percent of Improvement	Vocab-ulary
1.								
2.								
3.								
4.								
5.								
6.								
7.								
8.								
9.								
10.								
AVERAGE								
1.								
2.								
3.								
4.								
5.								
6.								
7.								
8.								
9.								
10.								
AVERAGE								
1.								
2.								
3.								
4.								
5.								
6.								
7.								
8.								
9.								
10.								
AVERAGE								